DICTIONARY
OF FOREIGN PHRASES
AND
ABBREVIATIONS

DICTIONARY
OF
FOREIGN PHRASES
AND
ABBREVIATIONS

THIRD EDITION

Translated and Compiled by

KEVIN GUINAGH

Formerly Head, Department of Languages, Eastern Illinois University

THE H. W. WILSON COMPANY

NEW YORK

Dictionary of Foreign Phrases and Abbreviations
Copyright © 1965, 1972, 1983
By KEVIN GUINAGH

First Edition 1965
Second Edition 1972
Third Edition 1983

Printed in the United States of America

Library of Congress Cataloging in Publication Data
Guinagh, Kevin, 1897-
Dictionary of foreign phrases and abbreviations.
1. English language—Foreign words and phrases—
Dictionaries. I. Title.
PE1670.G8 1983   422'.4'03   82-8486
ISBN 0-8242-0675-4   AACR2

To Marie, tireless aid

CONTENTS

EDITOR'S NOTE TO THE THIRD EDITION

The third edition, made possible by the generous reception of the second, has given me the opportunity to increase by more than 500 the number of phrases and abbreviations, to add the sources of numerous expressions, to omit a few and expand others, and to correct some errors, both mine and the printer's. I am grateful to correspondents, reviewers, friends, and teachers for helpful suggestions, and to Bruce R. Carrick, Editor of General Publications, for his assistance.

KEVIN GUINAGH

Temple Terrace, Florida
October 1982

NOTE ON PRONUNCIATION

For readers who have shown an interest in knowing how to pronounce the phrases and abbreviations an attempt has been made in the third edition to set down the sound of the entries in simplified untechnical style.

In the case of the modern languages these transcriptions are approximations of the correct pronunciation of a native speaker. It is not always possible to find an accurate symbol to illustrate a foreign sound: some French sounds, for example, do not occur in English.

Following is a list of the symbols used to represent the foreign sound by the use of examples in English words.

SYMBOL	SOUND	EXAMPLE
a	a	cat
ah	a	father
ay	a	fate
ee	ee	heed
eh	e	set, care
g	g	go
I	i	nice
ih	i	bit
oh	o	vote
ö	i	fir
oo	u	rude
uh	u	put
oi	oi	boil
ow	ow	now
ch	ch	church
j	j	jet
kh	ch	loch
sh	sh	she
y	y	yet
zh	z	azure

The sound of the German u with an umlaut (ü), the French u, and the Greek upsilon (u) is represented by the symbol ü. All three are produced by pronouncing *ee* with lips rounded as if to pronounce *oo*.

N indicates a nasal sound. Nasal vowels and nasal combinations with *n* or *m* have no identical sound in English, though often transposed as *ng*. These sounds represented by N are produced by letting the breath pass through the mouth and nasal passages at the same time. This sound occurs in French and Portuguese.

The doubling of a consonant indicates that the preceding vowel is short. A double *s* is a warning that the sound of *z* should be avoided.

The accent is written after the syllable to which it refers. In French the accent has been omitted because there is, as a rule, no accent but rather a stress generally falling on the last syllable of a word or phrase. However, the syllable on which the stress falls may vary with rhythm or sense grouping.

Spanish and Portuguese entries are transposed in the American pronunciation.

THE PRONUNCIATION OF LATIN

The number of Latin entries in this compilation exceeds that of any other language. This can be explained by the fact that many professions, including the arts, law, medicine, literature, and religion have adopted Latin phrases that have a definite, readily understood meaning in these areas. This vocabulary has been accumulating for centuries, and although interest in the study of Latin has declined in our schools, its phrases, axioms, and proverbs remain current.

Recording the pronunciation of Latin creates a problem because of the different systems that are used. Indeed, nationality is often revealed by a speaker's Latin accent. Some speakers, lawyers especially, pronounce Latin as if it were English. Those who have read James Hilton's *Goodbye Mr. Chips* will recall that Chips was censured by the new head of his school for teaching students the "wrong" pronunciation of Latin instead of using the newer pronunciation accpeted by scholars as the ancient Roman method of speaking the language.

In this Roman system a careful distinction is made between long and short vowels. The distinction between the long *a* (as in *father*) and the short *a* (as in *idea*) is for our purpose so slight that it has not been stressed. The same may be said of the long *o* in *vote* and the short *o* in *obey*. *V* is given the sound of *w*, *ae* that of *i* in *nice*, and recorded as a capital *I*.

The Continental pronunciation, which had general acceptance in the United States before the Roman pronunciation became popular in the public schools, is still widely used. In this system little attention is given to whether the sounds of *a* and *o* are long or short. *Ae* is sounded as the *a* in fate and *v* as in English. There are other differences that are noted in the transcriptions.

A fourth system of pronouncing Latin is the Italian, which is quite distinct from the others. Entries that are church-related follow this method. The short vowels have the same sound as the long but are less prolonged. Other differences are of more interest to the editor than a reader inquiring after the pronunciation of a particular phrase.

These four systems may be illustrated by Julius Caesar's laconic war report, "I came, I saw, I conquered," *Veni, vidi, vici (q.v.)*. To each of these Caesar's name is added to show some differences in the four systems.

English: vee'-nI vI'-dI vI'-sI (see'-suhr)
Roman: way'-nee wee'-dee wee'-kee (kI'-sahr)
Continental: vay'-nee vee'-dee vee'-see (tsay'-sahr)
Italian: vay'-nee vee'-dee vee'-chee (chay'-sahr)

In transposing the pronunciation for the different Latin phrases the traditional or prevalent usage has generally been followed. Where there is any doubt, the Roman pronunciation is given, as always in the case of quotations from ancient Latin authors.

Temple Terrace, Florida
October 1982

Kevin Guinagh

PREFACE

This work has been compiled to aid those who wish to know the meaning of foreign expressions in what they hear or read. The word *phrase* as used in the title is to be understood in the recognized and not uncommon meaning of a pithy, quotable expression, such as a proverb, motto, or maxim. It is not necessarily to be taken in its narrow grammatical use, as, for instance, a preposition followed by an object, though there are many items that could be classified in this way. The entries range from hoary legal principles inherited from the Romans to the wisdom of the common man, *die Weisheit der Gasse (q.v.)*, from terms of philosophy to business expressions.

People unacquainted with foreign expressions popular in English are often inclined to think that those who scatter such phrases in their writing or conversation are pedantic. There is no doubt that this practice can be overdone, and that at times it may be in bad taste. However, to those who are acquainted with a subject being discussed, the use of such terms is often a short cut to making a meaning clear. In numerous areas, such as law, business, philosophy, medicine, and music, certain foreign phrases have a fixed meaning that is immediately understood by those who are familiar with the subject. Similarly, to people with literary interests certain expressions may brighten a conversation by their aptness or sum up a concept that might otherwise require several sentences for a clear explanation. No matter how theoretically sound attacks by English purists may be, people will continue to employ such phrases, possibly even with greater frequency now that the study of foreign languages is receiving increased emphasis in American education.

The different languages have not been listed separately for the reason that the general reader unacquainted with a foreign expression may not know in what section he should look. In each case the abbreviation for the language is given immediately after the expression. The following abbreviations are used: *Fr*—French; *Ger*—German; *Gk*—Greek; *Heb*—Hebrew; *Ir*—Irish; *It*—Italian; *L*—Latin; *Port*—Portuguese; *Rus*—Russian; *Sp*—Spanish. The language from which most entries have been drawn is Latin. Of the modern languages French predominates, with Italian a distant second.

Quotations in a foreign tongue are often rearranged or adapted from the original. For that reason, if a phrase is not found where the reader searches for it, it may be helpful to look about to find the correct wording. Misquotation is especially frequent in Latin, where the word order is not as uniform as it is in English. Thus one may hear *Errare est humanum, Errare humanum est, Humanum errare est,* or *Humanum est errare.*

When one is certain of the language in which the expression is written but not of the word order or spelling, he may more quickly ascertain both wording and spelling by consulting the list of phrases arranged by languages at the end of the book. In Latin quotations the letter *j* is used instead of the consonant *i*.

Items longer than a couplet have been omitted since they can hardly be classed as phrases; at the other end of the scale, single words, with a few exceptions, are not included since these are proper material for foreign language dictionaries. Latin and Greek nomenclature used in the biological sciences is not included since this is technical information available in manuals on these subjects.

The translation that follows the identification of the language in which the entry is written is at times literal, though generally it is free. If the entry is a proverb, the corresponding proverb in English may be given. The translation may be followed by a few explanatory words if the meaning of the phrase is not self-evident or if its historical context is of special interest. There may also be a cross reference to a parallel expression found elsewhere in the book.

At the end of many entries the source is given. This consists of the author's name, the work in which the phrase is found, the particular book (if the work is divided into books), the chapter, and the verse or beginning line in the case of poetry. Sometimes a writer is given credit as the author of a quotation even though it is likely that the expression was current long before he lived. For example, many proverbs are found in Cervantes' *Don Quixote.* He is regarded as the author, but no doubt the phrase was old when he wrote it. It may be one of those *Geflügelte Worte (q.v.)* that pass from one language to another. Take the proverb "One swallow does not make a summer." This is heard so frequently that one would be pardoned for thinking that it is original with one of our own writers. However, in Cervantes we read, *Una golondrina sola no hace verano (q.v.).* The same idea is found in German, *Eine Schwalbe macht keinen Sommer (q.v.).* In Italian it runs, *Una rondine no fa primavera (q.v.).* A much earlier version is found in Aristotle, *Mia gar chelidon ear ou poiei (q.v.),* which was probably an old saw even in his day. In short, a given source does not necessarily indicate the origin of an expression. Often the author who incorporated it in his work receives the credit. The fact that he has adopted the proverb lends it the authority of his genius.

Such a compilation as this is bound to reflect in some measure the tastes and interests of the compiler. Much material, however, must be included because of frequent usage. The problem, then, is one of selection from among thousands of phrases that might be included. For some time I collected expressions that I had heard or remembered. I first went through the sixth American edition (1831) of the once popular *Dictionary of Select and Popular Quotations* published by J. Grigg, Philadelphia, without author statement. The search continued through many English classics, Roget's *Thesaurus*, Brewer's *Dictionary of Phrase and Fable, Authors' and Printers' Dictionary* by Collins, Hoyt's *Encyclopedia of Practical Quotations*, Shankle's *Current Abbreviations*, Mawson's *Dictionary of Foreign Terms*, the unabridged dictionaries, and numerous other works. *The Dictionary of Foreign Phrases and Classical Quotations* by H. P. Jones, Bartlett's *Familiar Quotations*, and the *Oxford Dictionary of Quotations* have frequently been consulted with profit. *Classical and Foreign Quotations* by W. Francis H. King and *Geflügelte Worte und Zitatenschatz* by Georg Büchmann have identified the sources of a number of phrases.

Quotations from Pascal's *Pensées* follow Brunschvicg's text used in *Collection Gallia* published without date by J. M. Dent & Sons, London, those from La Rochefoucauld follow the editing of *La Rochefoucauld: Maximes,* F. C. Green, Cambridge at the University Press, 1946.

The quotations from Publilius Syrus are given different numbers by different editors, who arrange in a loose alphabetical order the material they accept as genuine. For that reason no number is cited.

Though the number of entries in such compilations can always be increased, it is hoped that no omission of a frequently used expression or abbreviation will be noted.

I am grateful to Guy R. Lyle, Director of the Emory University Libraries, for suggesting this compilation, and to John Jamieson, Editor of General Publications of the H. W. Wilson Company, for his valuable assistance.

KEVIN GUINAGH

Mayagüez, Puerto Rico, and Temple Terrace, Florida
November 1964-October 1982

vowels have the same sound as the long but are less prolonged. Other differences are of more interest to the editor than a reader inquiring after the pronunciation of a particular phrase.

These four systems may be illustrated by Julius Caesar's laconic war report, "I came, I saw, I conquered," *Veni, vidi, vici (q.v.)*. To each of these Caesar's name is added to show some differences in the four systems.

> English: vee'-nI vI'-dI vI'-sI (see'-suhr)
> Roman: way'-nee wee'-dee wee'-kee (kI'-sahr)
> Continental: vay'-nee vee'-dee vee'-see (tsay'-sahr)
> Italian: vay'-nee vee'-dee vee'-chee (chay'-sahr)

In transposing the pronunciation for the different Latin phrases the traditional or prevalent usage has generally been followed. Where there is any doubt, the Roman pronunciation is given, as always in the case of quotations from ancient Latin authors.

Temple Terrace, Florida
October 1982

KEVIN GUINAGH

ABBREVIATIONS USED IN THIS WORK

cf	compare	*LL*	Late Latin
f	feminine	*m*	masculine
Fr	French	*NL*	New Latin
Ger	German	*OF*	Old French
Gk	Greek	*pl*	plural
Heb	Hebrew	*Port*	Portuguese
Ir	Irish	*q.v.*	which see
It	Italian	*Rus*	Russian
L	Latin	*Sp*	Spanish

A

A. A. Auswärtiges Amt [ows-vehr′-tikh-gus ahmpt] *Ger*—Foreign Office.

A. A. C. *See* Anno ante Christum.

a. a. O. am angeführten Orte [ahm ahn-guh-für′-tun or′-tuh] *Ger*—In the place cited.

A. A. S. S. Americanae Antiquarianae Societatis Socius [ah-meh-rih-kah′-nI ahn-tih-kwah-rih-ah′-nI so-kih-eh-tah′-tiss so′-kih-uhs] *L*—Fellow of the American Antiquarian Society.

A. B. Artium Baccalaureus [ahr′-tih-uhm bahk-kah-low′-reh-uhs] *L*—Bachelor of Arts.

Ab abusu ad usum non valet consequentia [ahb ah-boo′-soo ahd oo′-suhm nohn vah′-let kohn-say-kwen′-tsih-ah] *L*—The abuse of a thing is no argument against its proper use. A legal maxim.

À barbe de fou, on apprend à raire [ah bahrb duh foo ohn-nah-prahN tah rair] *Fr*—One learns to shave on the chin of a fool. *See also* Alla barba dei pazzi . . .

À bas [ah bah] *Fr*—Down with, as in *À bas le traître*, Down with the traitor.

Ab asino lanam [ahb ah′-sih-noh lah′-nahm] *L*—Wool from an ass. You can't get blood from a stone.

À bâtons rompus [ah bah-tohN rohN-pü] *Fr*—By fits and starts; without method.

À beau jeu, beau retour [ah boh zhuh boh ruh-toor] *Fr*—One good turn deserves another. It is also used in the opposite sense: A bad turn must expect a bad return.

À beau mentir qui vient de loin [ah boh mahN-teer kee vyaN duh lwaN] *Fr*—Those who come from afar can lie with impunity.

A beneplacito [ah bay-nay-plah′-chee-toh] *It*—At will; at one's pleasure.

Abends wird der Faule fleissig [ah′-benz virt dehr fow′-luh flIs′-sik] *Ger*—The lazy man becomes industrious in the evening. The implication is that he has loafed all day.

Abeunt studia in mores [ah′-beh-uhnt stuh′-dih-ah in moh′-rays] *L*—Zeal develops into habit. Ovid, *Heroides*, 15; 83.

ab ex. ab extra [ahb ex′-trah] *L*—From the outside.

Ab extrinseco [ahb ex-trihn′-seh-koh] *L*—From the outside.

abgk. abgekürzt [ahp-guh-kürtst′] *Ger*—Abbreviated.

Ab hoc et ab hac et ab illa [ahb hohk et ahb hahk et ahb il′-lah] *L*—By this man and this woman and that woman. The talk of gossips; such and such a person did or said this or that.

A. B. I. Associazione Bibliotecari Italiani [ah-soh-chee-ah-tsee-oh′-nay bee-blee-oh-tay-kah′-ree ee-tah-lee-ah′-nee] *It*—Association of Italian Librarians.

À bientôt [ah byaN-toh] *Fr*—See you soon; so long!

Abiit ad majores [ah′-bih-it ahd mah-yoh′-rays] *L*—He has gone to his forefathers; he is dead.

Abiit ad plures [ah′-bih-it ahd ploo′-rays] *L*—He has gone to the majority; he is dead. Petronius, *Satyricon*, 42; 5.

Abiit, excessit, evasit, erupit [ah′-bih-it ex-kes′-sit ay-wah′-sit ay-roo′-pit] *L*—He [Catiline] has gone, he has left, he has fled, he has rushed forth. Cicero, *2 Against Catiline*, 1.

1

Ab imo pectore [ahb ee'-moh pek'-toh-reh] *L*—From the bottom of the heart.

Ab incunabulis [ahb in-koo-nah'-buh-lees] *L*—Literally, from the cradle. Used in connection with early printed books, especially those published before the end of the 15th century. Such books are called *incunabula* (literally, swaddling clothes).

Ab init. ab initio [ahb in-ih'-tih-oh] *L*—From the beginning.

Ab initio temporis [ahb in-ih'-tih-oh tem'-po-riss] *L*—From the beginning of time.

Ab intestato [ahb in-tes-tah'-toh] *L*—From or by a person dying intestate, i.e., without a valid will.

Ab intra [ahb in'-trah] *L*—From within.

Ab invito [ahb in-vee'-toh] *L*—By an unwilling person.

Ab irato [ahb ee-rah'-toh] *L*—From or by an angry man. Implying that what was said or done was not necessarily intended.

À bis ou (et) à blanc [ah bee oo (ay) ah blahN] *Fr*—By fits and starts.

Abnormis sapiens crassaque Minerva [ahb-nor'-mis sah'-pih-ayns krahs'-sah-kweh mih-nehr'-wah] *L*—Literally, an unusual, wise man of rough genius. A homespun philosopher. Horace, *Satires*, 2; 2, 3.

À bon appétit il ne faut point de sauce [ah bohn ah-pay-tee eel nuh foh pwaN duh sohss] *Fr*—A good appetite needs no sauce.

À bon chat, bon rat [ah bohN shah bohN rah] *Fr*—For a good cat, a good rat. The parties are well matched; tit for tat.

À bon cheval point d'éperon [ah bohN shuh-vahl pwaN day-peh-rohN] *Fr*—Do not spur the willing horse.

À bon chien il ne vient jamais un bon os [ah bohN shyaN eel nuh vyaN zhah-mehz uhN bohn ohs] *Fr*—A good dog does not always get a good bone. Merit is not always recognized.

À bon commencement bonne fin [ah bohN kuh-mahNs-mahN buhn faN] *Fr*—A good beginning leads to a good end.

À bon compte [ah bohN kohNt] *Fr*—At a bargain price.

Abondance de bien(s) ne nuit pas [ah-bohN-dahNss duh byaN nuh nwee pah] *Fr*—Literally, an abundance of good things does no harm. It never hurts to be well off.

À bon droit [ah bohN drwah] *Fr*—With good reason; rightly.

À bon marché [ah bohN mahr-shay] *Fr*—At a bargain price.

À bon vin point d'enseigne [ah bohN vaN pwaN dahN-seh-nyuh] *Fr*—Literally, a good wine needs no sign. A good product needs no advertising. *See also* A buon vino . . . , and Vino vendibili . . .

Ab origine [ahb oh-ree'-gih-neh] *L*—From the origin.

A bove majore discit arare minor [ah boh'-weh mah-yoh'-reh dis'-kit ah-rah'-reh mih'-nor] *L*—A young ox learns to plow from an older one; the young learn from their elders.

Ab ovo [ahb oh'-woh] *L*—Literally, from the egg; from the beginning. Horace observes that epic poets do not begin their narratives at the hero's birth, but *in medias res* (*q.v.*). *Art of Poetry*, 147.

Ab ovo usque ad mala [ahb oh'-woh oos'-kwe ahd mah'-lah] *L*—From the egg to the apples, i.e., from the beginning to the end of a Roman banquet; from soup to nuts. Horace, *Satires*, 1; 3, 6.

À bras ouverts [ah brah-zoo-vehr] *Fr*—With open arms.

Abscissio infiniti [ahp-skis'-sih-oh een-fee-nee'-tee] *L*—The cutting off of the infinite. In logic, the process of rejecting unworkable hypotheses until the correct conclusion is reached.

Absence d'esprit [ahp-sahNss des-pree] *Fr*—Absent-mindedness.

Absens haeres non erit [ahp'-sens hay'-rays nohn eh'-rit] *L*—The man who is absent will not be an heir. Out of sight, out of mind.

Absent le chat, les souris dansent [ahp-sahN luh shah lay soo-ree dahNss] *Fr*— When the cat's away, the mice will play.

Absente reo [ahp-sen'-teh reh'-oh] *L*— The defendant being absent.

abs. feb. absente febre [ahp-sen'-teh feh'-bre] *L*—While fever is absent. A medical direction.

Absit invidia [ahp'-sit in-wee'-dih-ah] *L*— Let there be no envy.

Absit omen [ahp'-sit oh'-men] *L*—May there be no ill omen. Omens were prophetic of good or ill and were interpreted by soothsayers, supposed to be skilled in observing signs sent by heaven. When a speaker referred to some evil, he might follow it with this prayer that no harm would follow his mentioning disaster or misfortune. Today, in a similar situation, people may rap on wood, as if this act could ward off evil.

Absque argento omnia vana [ahps'-kweh ahr-gen'-toh om'-nih-ah wah'-nah] *L*— Without money all efforts are in vain.

Absque ulla conditione [ahps'-kweh oo'-lah kohn-dih-tih-oh'-neh] *L*—Without any condition.

abs. re. *See* Absente reo.

Absurdum quippe est ut alios regat qui seipsum regere nescit [ahp-suhr'-duhm kwip'-peh est uht ah'-lih-ohs reh'-gaht kwee say-ip'-suhm reh'-geh-reh nehs'-kit] *L*—It is certainly absurd that a man who cannot rule himself should rule others. A medieval legal axiom.

A buen entendedor, pocas palabras [ah bwchn ehn-tehn-deh-dohr' poh'-kahs pah-lah'-brahs] *Sp*—To a good understanding, a few words will suffice.

Ab uno disce omnes [ahb oo'-noh dis'-keh om'-nays] *L*—From one learn all. Aeneas' complete statement reads: Listen now to the trick of the Greeks, and from one crime judge all the Greeks. A maxim for the injudicious. Vergil, *Aeneid*, 2; 65.

A buon vino non bisogna frasca [ah boo-ohn' vee'-noh nohn bee-sohn'-yah frahs'-kah] *It—See* À bon vin .., and Vino vendibili ...

Ab urbe condita [ahb uhr'-beh kohn'-dih-tah] *L*—From the founding of the city. The traditional date for the founding of Rome is 753 B.C.

Abusus non tollit usum [ah-boo'-suhs nohn tol'-lit oo'-suhm] *L*—Abuse does not take away use. *See also* Ab abusu ad usum ...

A. C. année courante [ah-nay koo-rahNt] *Fr* —The current year.

a. c. ante cibum [ahn'-teh sih'-buhm] *L*— Before food. A direction indicating that medicine should be taken before meals.

a. c. argent comptant [ahr-zhahN kohN-tahN] *Fr*—Spot cash; ready money. A commercial term.

a. C. avanti Cristo [ah-vahn'-tee krees'-toh] *It*—Before Christ; B.C. (*q.v.*).

A caballo [ah kah-bah'-yoh] *Sp*—On horseback.

A cader va chi troppo alto sale [ah kah-dehr' vah kee trop'-poh ahl'-toh sah'-lay] *It*—He is set for a fall who climbs too high.

A cane scottato l'acqua fredda pare calda [ah kah'-nay skot-tah'-toh lah'-kwah fred'-dah pah'-ray kahl'-dah] *It*—To the scalded dog cold water seems hot; the burnt child shuns the fire.

A capite ad calcem [ah kah'-pih-teh ahd kahl'-kem] *L*—From head to toe; completely.

A cappella [ah kahp-pel'-lah] *It*—In chapel style. A term referring to liturgical vocal music, usually unaccompanied.

A cara o cruz [ah kah'-rah oh krooss] *Sp*— Face or cross (on a coin); heads or tails.

A caridade começa por casa [ah kah-ree-dah'-dee koN-meh'-suh por kah'-zuh] *Port* —Charity begins at home.

A casar y a ir a guerra no se aconseja [ah kah-sar' ee ah eer ah gayr'-rah noh say ah-kon-say'-hah] *Sp*—One never advises a person to marry or go to war.

A cavallo donato non si guarda in bocca [ah kah-vahl'-loh doh-nah'-toh nonn see gwahr'-dah een bok'-kah] *It*—Don't look a gift horse in the mouth. *See also* A cavallo regalado . . .

A cavallo regalado noh hay que mirarle el diente [ah kah-bah'-yoh ray-gah-lah'-doh no ah'-ee kay mee-rahr'-lay el dyehn'-tay] *Sp*—*See* A cavallo donato . . .

Accedas ad curiam [ahk-kay'-dahs ahd koo'-ree-ahm] *L*—You may appeal the case.

Accelerando [ahch-chay-lay-rahn'-doh] *It* —Musical direction to play with increasing speed.

Accessit [ahk-kes'-sit] *L*—He came near; e.g., he nearly won first honors in an academic contest.

Accordez vos flûtes [ah-kohr-day voh flüt] *Fr*—Tune your flutes; settle the matter among yourselves.

Accusare nemo se debet [ahk-koo-sah'-reh nay'-moh say day'-bet] *L*—No one is obliged to incriminate himself. A legal maxim.

Acerbarum facetiarum apud praepotentes in longum memoria est [ah-kehr-bah'-ruhm fah-kay-tih-ah'-ruhm ah'-puhd prI-po-ten'-tays in lon'-guhm meh-moh'-rih-ah est] *L*—The mighty remember a cutting witticism for a long time. Tacitus, *Annals*, 5; 2.

Acetum Italum [ah-kay'-tuhm ee'-tah-luhm] *L*—*See* Sal Atticum.

À chacun son fardeau pèse [ah sha-kuhN sohN fahr-doh pehz] *Fr*—Everyone has his own burden to bear.

À chaque fou plaît sa marotte [ah shak foo pleh sah mah-ruht] *Fr*—Every fool is delighted with his own hobby.

À chaque oiseau son nid est beau [ah shak wah-zoh sohn nee eh boh] *Fr*—Every bird thinks its nest beautiful; be it ever so humble, there's no place like home. *See also* Ad ogni uccello . . .

À chaque saint sa chandelle (cierge) [ah shak saN sa shahN-dell (see-ehrzh)] *Fr*—To each saint his candle; honor to whom honor is due.

À cheval [ah shuh-vahl] *Fr*—On horseback.

A chi consiglia non duole il capo [ah kee kon-seel'-yah nonn doo-oh'-lay eel kah'-poh] *It*—The man with ready advice does not have the headache; advice is cheaper than help.

A chi dici il tuo segreto, doni la tua libertà [ah kee dee'-chee eel too'-oh say-gray'-toh doh'-nee lah too'-ah lee-behr-tah'] *It*—You give your liberty to the one to whom you tell your secret.

A chi fa male, mai mancano scuse [ah kee fah mah'-lay mah'-ee mahn'-kah-noh skoo'-say] *It*—The wrongdoer never lacks excuses.

A chi ha testa, non manca cappello [ah kee ah tess'-tah nonn mahn'-kah kah-pell'-loh] *It*—A man with a head will not be without a hat.

A chi vuole, non mancano modi [ah kee voo-oh'-lay nonn mahn'-kah-noh moh'-dee] *It*—Where there's a will, there's a way.

A. C. I. assuré contre l'incendie [ah-sür-ray kohN-tr laN-sahN-dee] *Fr*—Insured against fire.

À coeur ouvert [ah kuhr oo-vehr] *Fr*—With open heart; candidly.

À compte [ah kohNt] *Fr*—On account; in part payment.

À confesseurs, médecins, avocats, la vérité ne cèle de ton cas [ah kohN-feh-suhr mayd-saN ah-voh-kah lah vay-ree-tay nuh sel duh tohN kah] *Fr*—Do not conceal the truth of your situation from your confessor, your doctor, or your lawyer. *See also* Al confessor, medico . . .

À contre coeur [ah kohN-tr kuhr] *Fr*—Reluctantly, unwillingly.

À corps perdu [ah kor pehr-dü] *Fr*—Headlong; desperately; post haste.

À coups de bâton [ah koo duh bah-tohN] *Fr*—With blows from a stick.

À coup sûr [ah koo sür] *Fr*—With a sure aim.

À couvert [ah koo-vehr] *Fr*—Under cover.

4

A cruce salus [ah kroo'-keh sah'-loos] *L*—Salvation comes from the cross.

Acta est fabula [ahk'-tah est fah'-buh-lah] *L*—The play is over (words used at the end of a play in ancient Rome). The supposed last words of the emperor Augustus. *See also* La farce est jouée.

Acte d'accusation [ahkt dah-kü-zah-syohN] *Fr*—An indictment.

Acte gratuit [ahkt grah-twee] *Fr*—An unwarranted, needless act.

Actum ne agas [ahk'-tuhm nay ah'-gahs] *L*—Don't do what has already been done. Terence, *Phormio*, 2; 3, 72.

Actus Dei nemini facit injuriam [ahk'-tuhs deh'-ee nay'-mih-nee fah'-kit in-yoo'-ree-ahm] *L*—An act of God does wrong to no man. An individual cannot be held responsible for damage beyond his control, caused by lightning, tornado, earthquake, or other natural phenomena.

Actus me invito factus, non est meus actus [ahk'-tuhs may in-wee'-toh fahk'-tuhs nohn est meh'-uhs ahk'-tuhs] *L*—An act I perform unwillingly is not my act.

Actus non facit reum nisi mens est rea [ahk'-tuhs nohn fah'-kit reh'-uhm nih'-sih mayns est reh'-ah] *L*—The act does not make a criminal unless the intention is criminal. Legal maxim.

Actus purus [ahk'-tuhs poo'-ruhs] *L*—Pure act; St. Thomas Aquinas' concept of God, indicating that the deity is not composed of matter and form.

A cuenta [ah kwehn'-tah] *Sp*—A payment on account.

A cushla agus asthore machree [ah koosh'-luh ah'-guhs as-thor' mah-kree'] *Ir*—O pulse and treasure of my heart.

A. D. anno Domini [ah'-noh do'-mih-nee] *L*—In the year of our Lord. Indicates the number of years from the birth of Christ. In the 6th century, Dionysius Exiguus initiated the system of expressing dates by referring events to the birth of Christ. According to his calculations, Christ was born in 754 A.U.C. (*q.v.*). However, it is generally agreed that Christ was born at least four years before the date set by Dionysius. A.D. is much more frequently used than its equivalent, A.H.S. (*q.v.*).

a. D. ausser Dienst [owss'-uhr deenst] *Ger*—Retired.

Adagio ma non troppo [ah-dah'-joh mah nonn trop'-poh] *It*—Slowly but not too slowly.

Ad amussim [ahd ah-muhs'-sim] *L*—Literally, according to a mason's or a carpenter's rule or line; exactly.

ad an. ad annum [ahd ahn'-nuhm] *L*—Up to the year.

Ad arbitrium [ahd ahr-bih'-trih-uhm] *L*—At will.

Ad astra per aspera [ahd ahs'-trah pehr ah'speh-rah] *L*—To the stars through difficulties. Motto of Kansas: To the stars through bolts and bars.

Ad captandam benevolentiam [ahd kahp-tahn'-dahm beh-neh-woh-len'-tih-ahm] *L*—To win good will. The aim of the orator.

Ad captandum vulgus [ahd kahp-tahn'-duhm wul'-guhs] *L*—To impress the crowd.

Ad cautelam [ahd kow-tay'-lahm] *L*—For caution's sake.

add. addatur [ahd-dah'-tuhr] *L*—Let there be added. Used in pharmacy.

Adde parvum parvo, magnus acervus erit [ahd'-deh pahr'-wuhm pahr'-woh mahg'-nuhs ah-kehr'-wuhs eh'-rit] *L*—Add little to little and you will have a great heap. Adapted from Ovid, *Amores*, 1; 8, 90.

ad 2 vic. ad duas vices [ahd duh'-ahs vee'-says] *L*—For two doses. A medical direction.

Adel sitzt im Gemüte, nicht im Geblüte [ah'-del zittst im guh-mü'-tuh nikht im guh-blü'tuh] *Ger*—Nobility lies in the heart, not in birth.

À demi [ah duh-mee] *Fr*—By halves.

A Deo et Rege [ah deh'-oh et ray'-geh] *L*—From God and the King.

5

À dessein [ah-day-saN] *Fr*—By design; intentionally.

Adeste, Fideles [ah-des'-teh fih-day'-lays] *L*—Come, all ye faithful. The music for this Christian hymn was composed by John Reading (1677-1764).

À deux [ah duh] *Fr*—For two only.

ad ex. ad extremum [ahd ex-tray'-muhm] *L*—To the very end.

ad fin. ad finem [ahd fee'-nem] *L*—To the end.

A. D. G. B. Allgemeiner Deutscher Gewerkschaftsbund [ahl-guh-mI'-nuhr doit'-shur guh-vehrk'-shahfts-buhnt] *Ger*—German Trade Union Congress.

Adgnosco veteris vestigia flammae [ahd-gnos'-koh weh'-teh-ris wehs-tee'-gih-a flahm'-mI] *L*—I feel the traces of the old flame of love. Through the trickery of Venus the heart of the widowed Dido was distraught for love of Aeneas. Vergil, *Aeneid*, 4; 23.

Ad gustum [ahd guhs'-tuhm] *L*—To one's taste.

ad h. l. *or* **a. h. l.** ad hunc locum [ahd huhnk loh'-kuhm] *L*—To this place.

Ad hoc [ahd hok] *L*—Created or designed for a particular purpose.

Ad hominem. *L—See* Argumentum ad hominem.

Adhuc neminem cognovi poetam qui sibi non optimus videretur [ahd'-hook nay'-mih-nehm kog-noh'-wee po-ay'-tahm kwee sih'-bih nohn op'-tih-muhs wih-day-ray'-tuhr] *L*—I have yet to meet a poet who did not think himself excellent. Cicero, *Tusculan Disputations*, 5; 22.

A die datus [ah dih'-ay dah'-tuhs] *L*—Dated from a certain day.

Adieu, canaux, canards, canaille! [ah-dyuh kah-noh kah-nahr ka-nah-yuh] *Fr*—Farewell, canals, ducks, and rabble! Voltaire's farewell to Holland.

Adieu la voiture, adieu la boutique [ah-dyuh lah vwah-tür ah-dyuh lah boo-teek]

Fr—Good-bye to the carriage, good-bye to the shop. The affair is all over.

Ad impossibile nemo tenetur [ahd im-pos-sih'-bih-leh nay'-moh teh-nay'-tuhr] *L*—Nobody is held to the impossible.

ad inf. ad infinitum [ahd in-fee-nee'-tuhm] *L*—Indefinitely into the future; endlessly.

ad init. ad initium [ahd in-ih'-tih-uhm] *L*—To or at the beginning.

ad int. ad interim [ahd in'-teh-rim] *L*—Temporarily; in the meantime.

Ad internecionem [ahd in-tehr-neh-kih-oh'-nehm] *L*—To extermination.

À discrétion [ah dees-kray-syohN] *Fr*—At one's discretion.

Ad judicium [ahd yoo-dih'-kih-uhm] *L*—An appeal to common sense.

Ad Kalendas Graecas [ahd kah-len'-dahs grI'-kahs] *L*—On the Greek Calends. In the Roman calendar the Calends meant the first day of the month. Since the Greeks did not have this term, the expression was used by the Romans to designate an event that would never occur. Suetonius, *Lives of the Twelve Caesars, Augustus*, 87.

Adler brüten keine Tauben [ahd'-lehr brü'-tun kI'-nuh tow'-bun] *Ger*—Eagles do not hatch out doves; brave men do not breed cowards.

ad lib. ad libitum [ahd lih'-bih-tuhm] *L*—At will; as one wishes. It is used in music where the composer leaves interpretation to the performer, or where passages may be omitted or varied. In the theater the phrase has given rise to the term *ad-libbing*, meaning improvisation.

Ad limina Apostolorum [ahd lee'-mih-nah ah-pos-toh-loh'-ruhm] *L*—A term used to designate a pilgrimage to the basilicas of St. Peter and of St. Paul in Rome.

Ad litem [ahd lee'-tem] *L*—For the lawsuit; for litigation. Thus a guardian may be appointed *ad litem* to act for an incompetent person.

Ad literam [ahd lee'-teh-rahm] *L*—Literally.

Ad locum [ahd lo'-kum] *L*—At the place indicated.

Ad majorem Dei gloriam [ahd mah-yoh'-rem deh'-ee gloh'-rih-ahm] *L*—To the greater glory of God. The motto of the Jesuits.

Ad manum [ahd mah'-nuhm] *L*—At hand.

Ad multos annos [ahd muhl'-tohs ahn'-nohs] *L*—For many years.

Ad nauseam. *L*—*See* Usque ad nauseam.

Ad oculos [ahd o'-kuh-lohs] *L*—Before one's eyes.

Ad ogni uccello suo nido è bello [ahd ohn'-yee ut-chel'-loh soo'-oh nee'-doh ay bel'-loh] *It*—To every bird his own nest is beautiful. *See also* À chaque oiseau . . .

Ad patres [ahd pah'-trays] *L*—Gathered to his fathers; among the dead.

Ad perpetuam rei memoriam [ahd per-peh'-tuh-ahm reh'-ee meh-moh'-rih-ahm] *L* —In perpetual memory of the event.

Ad rem [ahd rehm] *L*—Speaking to the point, to the matter in hand.

À droite [ah drwaht] *Fr*—To the right. A direction for the traveler.

adr. tél. adresse télégraphique [ah-dress tay-lay-gra-feek] *Fr*—Telegraphic address.

Adscriptus glebae *or* **glaebae** [ahd-skrip'-tuhs glay'-bay] *L*—A person bound to the soil; a serf.

adst. feb. adstante febre [ahd-stahn'-teh feh'-bre] *L*—While fever is present. A medical direction.

Adsum [ahd'-suhm] *L*—I am present. Spoken by students at roll call.

Ad summum [ahd suhm'-muhm] *L*—To the utmost.

Ad un colpo non cade a terra l'albero [ahd oon kol'-poh nonn kah'-day ah tehr'-rah lahl'-bay-roh] *It*—*See* Al primo colpo . . .

Ad unguem [ahd uhn'-gwehm] *L*—To a nicety; accurately. Horace, *Satires*, 1; 5, 32.

Ad unum omnes [ahd oo'-nuhm om'-nays] *L*—To the last man.

Ad usum [ahd oo'-suhm] *L*—According to custom.

Ad utrumque paratus [ahd uh-truhm'-kweh pah-rah'-tuhs] *L*—Prepared for either eventuality.

ad val. ad valorem [ahd vah-loh'-rem] *L*—According to the value; a tax or duty based on value.

Adversis etenim frangi non esse virorum [ahd-wehr'-sees eh'-teh-nim frahn'-gee nohn es'-seh wih-roh'-ruhm] *L*—Real men are not vanquished by adversity. Silius Italicus, *Punica*, 10; 618.

Ad vitam aut culpam [ahd vee'-tahm owt kuhl'-pahm] *L*—For life or until removed for some fault. A phrase used to indicate length of tenure in an office.

Advocatus diaboli [ahd-voh-kah'-tuhs dih-ah'-boh-lee] *L*—The devil's advocate. An official appointed by the papal court to make objections to the canonization of a virtuous person.

Advocatus juventutis [ahd-woh-kah'-tuhs yuh-wen-too'-tiss] *L*—The advocate of youth. An expression patterned after Advocatus diaboli (*q.v.*).

A. E. F. Afrique Équatoriale Française [ah-freek ay-kwah-toh-ree-ahl frahN-sez] *Fr*—French Equatorial Africa.

Aegrescit medendo [I-gress'-kit meh-den'-doh] *L*—He grows sick from the treatment; the remedy is worse than the disease. Vergil, *Aeneid*, 12, 46.

Aegrotat daemon, monachus tunc esse volebat:/Daemon convaluit, daemon ut ante fuit [I-groh'-taht dI'-mohn moh'-nah-kuhs toonk es-seh woh-lay'-baht/dI'-mohn kohn-wah'-luh it dI'-mohn uht ahn'-teh fuh'-it] *L*—The devil was sick, the devil a monk would be:/The devil was well, the devil a monk was he. The source of this popular quotation is unknown. It has been stated that it occurs in Rabelais, 4; 24, but this was added by a translator in further explanation of Passato il pericolo . . . (*q.v.*).

Aegroto dum anima est, spes esse dicitur [I-groh'-toh duhm ah'-nee mah est spays es'-seh dee'-kih-tuhr] *L*—As long as he is alive, the sick man has hope. Cicero, *To Atticus*, 9; 10.

Aei gar eu piptousin hoi Dios kyboi [ah-ay' gahr oy pip'-too-sin hoy dee-os' kü'-boy] *Gk*—Literally, the dice of Zeus always fall right. Emerson in *Compensation* gives the translation: "The dice of the gods are always loaded."

Aemulatio aemulationem parit [I-muh-lah'-tih-o I-muh-lah-tih-o'-nem pah'-rit] *L*—Emulation (both in a virtuous and vicious sense) begets emulation.

Aemulatio vicini [ay-muh-lah'-tsi-oh vee-see'-nee] *L*—Malice of a neighbor. A legal term.

Aequam memento rebus in arduis servare mentem [I'-kwahm meh-men'-toh ray'-buhs in ahr'-duh-ees sehr-wah'-reh men'-tem] *L*—Remember to keep calm in time of trouble. Horace, *Odes*, 2; 3, 1.

Aequo animo [I'-kwoh ah'-nee-moh] *L* —With a calm mind.

Aerarium sanctius [I-rah'-ree-uhm sahnk'-tih-uhs] *L*—A special treasury reserved for emergencies.

Aere perennius. *See* Exegi monumentum . . .

Aes in praesenti [Is in prI-sen'-tee] *L*—Ready cash.

Aes triplex [Is trih'-plex] *L*—Triple bronze, characterizing the courage in the heart of man. Title of an essay by Robert Louis Stevenson. Horace, *Odes*, 1; 3, 9.

aet. aetas [I'-tahs] *L*—Age.

Aetas parentum, peior avis, tulit/ nos nequiores, mox daturos/ progeniem vitiosiorem [I'-tahs pah-ren'-tuhm peh'-yor ah'-wees tuh'-lit nohs nay-kwih-oh'-rays mox dah-too'-rohs proh-geh'-nih-em wih-tih-oh-sih-oh'-rem] *L*—Our parents, worse than our grandparents, have produced us, more depraved still, and we shall soon give birth to offspring even more corrupt. Horace, *Odes*, 3; 6, 46-8.

Aetatis suae [I-tah'-tis suh'-I] *L*—Of his or her age.

8

Aeternum servans sub pectore vulnus [I-ter'-nuhm ser'-wahns suhb pek'-to-reh wuhl'-nuhs] *L*—Forever nursing an offense in one's heart. Originally, a reference to Juno's undying hatred for the Trojans. Vergil, *Aeneid*, 1; 36.

A falta de hombres buenos, le hacen a mi padre alcalde [ah fahl'-tah day om'-brays bweh'-nos lay ah'-sen ah mee pah'-dray ahl-kahl'-day] *Sp*—Because good men were scarce, they made my father mayor.

Affaire d'amour [ah-fehr dah-moor] *Fr*—A love affair.

Affaire d'honneur [ah-fehr duh-nuhr] *Fr* —An affair of honor, involving a duel with deadly weapons.

Affaire du coeur [ah-fehr dü kuhr] *Fr*—A love affair.

Affirmanti incumbit probatio [ahf-fihr-mahn'-tee in-kuhm'-bit pro-bah'-tih-oh] *L*—The burden of proof rests with the accuser. A legal maxim.

Afflavit Deus et dissipantur [ahf-flah'-wit deh-uhs et dihs-see-pahn'-tuhr] *L*—God sent a tempest and they were scattered. An inscription on a medal struck by Queen Elizabeth I after the defeat of the Spanish Armada in 1588.

À fond [ah fohN] *Fr*—Thoroughly.

À forfait [ah for-feh] *Fr*—By contract.

A fortiori [ah for-tih-o'-ree] *L*—For a stronger reason; all the more so.

À fripon fripon et demi [ah free-pohN free-pohN-nay duh-mee] *Fr*—Set a thief to catch a thief.

A. G. Aktiengesellschaft [ahk'-tee-en-guh-zell'-shahft] *Ger*—Joint stock company.

Agapa ton plesion [ah-gah'-pah tohn play-see'-ohn] *Gk*—Love thy neighbor. *Thales.*

À gauche [ah gohsh] *Fr*—To the left. A direction for a traveler.

À genoux! [ah zhuh-noo] *Fr*—Down on your knees!

Agenti incumbit probatio [ah-jen'-tee

in-kuhm′-bit pro-bah′-tsih-oh] *L*—The burden of proof rests on the accuser. A legal maxim.

Agent provocateur [ah-zhaN pruh-vo-kah-tuhr] *Fr*—An undercover police or government agent who gains the confidence of suspected criminals or members of an opposing group and encourages them to commit crimes in which they are apprehended.

Age quod agis [ah′-geh kwuhd ah′-gis] *L*—Do what you are doing.

Ager publicus [ah′-gehr poo′-blih-kuhs] *L*—Public domain.

Aggregatio mentium [ahg-greh-gah′-tih-oh men′-tih-uhm] *L*—A meeting of minds.

agit. vas. agitato vase [ah-jee-tah′-toh vah′-seh] *L*—Shake well before using. A medical direction.

Agnus Dei [ahg′-nuhs deh′-ee] *L*—The lamb of God (words uttered by John the Baptist when he saw Christ coming toward him). *Vulgate, John,* 1; 29, 36.

À grands frais [ah grahN freh] *Fr*—At great expense.

A. H. anno Hebraico [ahn′-noh hay-brah′-ih-koh] *L*—In the Hebrew year. This is calculated by adding 3,760 to the current year of the Christian era.

A. H. anno hegirae [ahn′-noh hay-gee′-ray] *L*—In the year of the hegira (year of the Moslem calendar, dating from the flight of Mohammed from Mecca in 622 A.D.).

À haute voix [ah oht vwah] *Fr*—In a loud voice.

A. H. S. anno humanae salutis [ahn′-noh hoo-mah′-nI sah loo′ tiss] *L*—In the year of man's redemption. Equivalent to A. D. (*q.v.*)

À huis clos [ah wee kloh] *Fr*—Behind closed doors.

Aide-de-camp [ehd duh kahN] *Fr*—A military assistant to a general or other high army officer.

Aide mémoire [ehd may-mwahr] *Fr*—An aid to memory; words or notes to assist

the memory. In diplomacy, a summary in writing of points to be checked in a possible agreement.

Aide-toi, le ciel t'aidera [ehd twah luh syell teh-drah] *Fr*—Heaven will help you if you help yourself; God helps those who help themselves. La Fontaine, *Fables,* 6; 18.

A idos de mi casa, y qué queréis con mi mujer, no hay responder [ah ee′-dos day mee kah′-sah ee kay keh-ray′-iss kon mee moo-hehr noh ah′-ee rays-pon-dehr′] *Sp*—There is no answer for "Leave my house," and "What do you want with my wife?" Cervantes, *Don Quixote,* 2; 43.

Ai mali estremi, estremi rimedi [ah′-ee mah′-lee ess-tray′-mee ess-tray′-mee ree-may′-dee] *It*—For extreme evils, extreme remedies.

Aîné (m), aînée (f) [eh-nay eh-nay] *Fr*—Senior.

Ainsi de suite [aN-see duh sweet] *Fr*—And so forth.

Ainsi soit-il. [aN-see swah-teel] *Fr*—So be it; amen.

Aio te, Aeacida, Romanos vincere posse [ah′-yoh tay I-ah′-kih-dah roh-mah′-nohs win′-keh-reh pos′-seh] *L*—I say, Aeacides, that you can defeat the Romans *or* I say, Aeacides, that the Romans can defeat you. An ambiguous reply from the Delphic oracle given Pyrrhus of Epirus, according to tradition. Ennius.

Aiutati che Dio t'aiuta [ah-yoo′-tah-tee kay dee′-oh tah-yoo′-tah] *It*—God helps those who help themselves.

Akademiya Nauk [ah-kah-deh′-myah nah-ook′] *Rus*—Academy of Sciences.

A. L. anno lucis [ahn′-noh loo′-kiss] *L*—In the year of light. This is computed by adding 4,000 years to A. D. (*q.v.*) Used by Freemasonry.

a. l. après livraison [ah-preh lee-vreh-zoN] *Fr*—After delivery of goods.

a. l. avant la lettre [ah-vahN lah leh-tr] *Fr*—Before lettering; proof of an engraving before any inscription has been added.

À la [ah lah] *Fr*—In the style or fashion of.

À la belle étoile [ah lah bell ay-twahl] *Fr*—In the open air; under the stars.

À la bonne heure [ah lah buhn uhr] *Fr*—Splendid! well done! right!

À la bourgeoise [ah lah boor-zhwahz] *Fr*—In simple, common, middle-class style.

À l'abri [ah lah-bree] *Fr*—Under cover; sheltered.

À la campagne [ah lah kahN-pan-yuh] *Fr*—In the country.

À la carte [ah lah kahrt] *Fr*—According to the menu on which the price of each item of food or drink is listed.

À la dérobée [ah lah day-ruh-bay] *Fr*—Furtively, secretly.

À la diable [ah lah dyah-bl] *Fr*—In a disorderly fashion; highly spiced.

À la française [ah lah frahN-sehz] *Fr*—In the French style or manner.

À la grecque [ah lah grek] *Fr*—In the Greek style or manner.

À la lanterne [ah lah lahN-tehrn] *Fr*—To the lamppost. The cry of the Paris mob during the Revolution when lampposts served as gallows.

À la lettre [ah lah leh-tr] *Fr*—To the letter; literally.

À la mode [ah lah mohd] *Fr*—According to the fashion.

À la mort [ah lah mohr] *Fr*—Unto death; forever.

À la napolitaine [ah lah nah-po-lee-tehn] *Fr*—Cooked in Neapolitan style.

À la page [ah lah pahzh] *Fr*—In style, up to date.

À la presse vont les fous [ah lah press vohN lay foo] *Fr*—Fools follow the crowd.

A la rústica. *See* En rústica.

À la sourdine [ah lah soor-deen] *Fr*—Played with a mute; by extension it means slyly, secretly, silently.

10

Alas sustineo [ah'-lahs suhs-tih'-neh-oh] *L*—I sustain the wings. The motto of ground communications in the Air Force.

A latere. *See* Legatus a latere.

Al bisogno si conosce un amico [ahl bee-zohn'-yo see koh-noh'-shay oon ah-mee'-koh] *It*—When in need you learn who your friends are. This is also found in the plural: *Al bisogno si conoscono gli amici.*

Albo lapide notatae [ahl'-boh lah'-pih-deh noh-tah'-tI] *L*—Literally, marked with a white stone; days recorded as lucky.

Al bugiardo non si crede la verità [ahl boo-jahr'-doh nonn see cray'-day lah veh-ree-tah'] *It*—A liar is not believed even when he tells the truth.

Alcinoo poma dare [ahl-kih'-no-oh poh'-mah dah'-reh] *L*—To give fruit to Alcinous, king of the Phaeacians. The island that he ruled was known for its fruits. To carry coals to Newcastle.

Al confessor, medico, ed avvocato, non si de' tener il vero celato [ahl kon-fess-sor' may'-dee-koh ed ahv-voh-kah'-toh nonn see day teh-nayr' eel veh'-roh chay-lah'-toh] *It*—One should not hold back the truth from one's confessor, doctor, or lawyer. *See also* Ao medico . . .

Al contado [ahl kohn-tah'-doh] *Sp*—For cash.

Al dente [ahl den'-tay] *It*—A culinary phrase used to describe pasta that is served while it still offers some resistance to the teeth and has not been overcooked.

Alea jacta est. *See* Jacta alea est.

À l'extérieur [ah lex-tay-ryuhr] *Fr*—On the outside.

Al fine [ahl fee'-nay] *It*—To the end. Musical term.

Al fresco [ahl fress'-koh] *It*—In open air; painting on fresh plaster.

À l'huile [ah lweel] *Fr*—In olive oil.

Aliena vitia in oculis habemus; a tergo nostra sunt [ah-lih-ay'-nah wih'-tih-ah in o'-kuh-lees hah-bay'-muhs ah tehr'-goh nos'-trah suhnt] *L*—Another's faults are before our eyes; our own are behind us. Seneca, *On Anger*, 2; 28, 6.

Alieni appetens, sui profusus [ah-lih-ay'-nee ahp'-peh-tayns suh'-ee pro-foo'-suhs] *L*—Covetous of the property of others, wasteful of his own. Sallust, *Catiline*, 5.

Alieni juris [ah-lih-ay'-nee yoo'-riss] *L*—Not possessing full legal power. Said of a person legally dependent upon another, as a slave or a minor.

À l'immortalité [ah leem-mohr-tah-lee-tay] *Fr*—To immortality. The motto of the Forty Immortals of the French Academy.

À l'impromptu [ah laN-prohNp-tü] *Fr*—On the spur of the moment.

À l'improviste [ah laN-pro-veest] *Fr*—Without a warning; unexpectedly.

Aliquando bonus dormitat Homerus [ah-lih-kwahn'-doh bo'-nuhs dor-mee'-taht hoh-may'-ruhs] *L*—See Indignor quandoque . . .

Aliquis in omnibus, nullus in singulis [ah'-lih-kwiss in om'-nih-buhs nool'-luhs in sing'-guh-leess] *L*—Jack of all trades but master of none.

Alis volat propriis [ah'-leess woh'-laht proh'-prih-eess] *L*—It flies with its own wings. Motto of the State of Oregon.

Alitur vitium vivitque tegendo [ah'-lih-tuhr wih'-tih-uhm wee-wit'-kweh teh-gen'-doh] *L*—A fault is nourished and lives by concealment. Vergil, *Georgics*, 3; 454.

Aliud corde premunt, aliud ore promunt [ah'-lih-uhd kor'-deh pray'-muhnt ah'-lih-uhd oh'-reh proh'-muhnt] *L*—They hide one thing in their hearts, but another comes from their mouths.

Alium silere quod voles, primus sile [ah'-lih-uhm sih-lay'-reh kwod woh'-lays pree'-muhs sih'-lay] *L*—If you want another to keep your secret, first keep it yourself. Seneca, *Hippolytus*, 876.

Al-ki [al'-kee] but local usage favors [al'-kI] *Chinookan*—By and by. The motto of the state of Washington, referring to the hope that by and by Seattle would equal New York City in size.

al. l. alia lectio [ah'-lih-ah lek'-tih-oh] *L*—Another reading; variant of a text.

Alla barba dei pazzi, il barbier impara a radere [ahl'-lah bahr'-bah day'-ee paht'-see eel bahr'-bee-ehr im-pah'-rah ah rah'-day-ray] *It*—The barber learns to shave on the chin of fools. *See also* À barbe de fou . . .

Alla cappella [ahl'-lah kahp-pell'-lah] *See* A cappella.

Allahu akbar [al-lah'-hoo uk'-bar] *Arabic* —God is most great.

Allá van leyes do quieren reyes [ah-yah' bahn lay'-yays doh kee-ay'-ren rray'-yays] *Sp*—The laws follow the will of kings. Alfonso VI, to determine whether the Gothic or the Roman missal should be used in his kingdom, threw both into the fire, intending to approve the one that survived the flames. When the Gothic did not burn, Alfonso threw it into the fire again and chose the Roman missal. The Spanish proverb grew out of this incident.

Alla vostra salute [ahl'-lah voss'-trah sah-loo'-tay] *It*—To your health.

Allegro moderato [ahl-lay'-groh moh-day-rah'-toh] *It*—Brisk in moderate tempo.

Alle Länder gute Menschen tragen [ahl'-luh len'-duhr goo'-tuh men'-shun trah'-guhn] *Ger*—All lands have good men. Lessing, *Nathan*, 2; 5, 1273.

Alle Menschen sind Lügner [ahl'-luh mehn'-shun zint lüg'-nuhr] *Ger*—All men are liars.

Aller Anfang ist schwer [ahl'-lehr ahn'-fahng ist shvehr] *Ger*—Every beginning is difficult. *See also* Arche hemisy pantos.

Aller guten Dinge sind drei [ahl'-lehr goo' tun ding'-uh zint drI] *Ger*—All good things go in threes.

Allez-vous-en! [ahl-lay voo-zahN] *Fr*—Go away!

Allmacht des Gedankens [ahl'-mahkht des guh-dahng'-kenz] *Ger*—The omnipotence of thought.

Allons, enfants de la patrie! [ahl-lohN zahN-fahN duh lah pah-tree] *Fr*—Come, children of the fatherland. The first words

11

of "La Marseillaise," the national anthem of France. Words and music by Claude-Joseph Rouget de Lisle (1760-1836).

All' ottava [ahl ot-tah'-vah] *It*—Notes to be played an octave higher than written.

Alma mater [ahl'-mah mah'-tehr] *L*—Foster mother; one's college or university.

Alma mater studiorum [ahl'-mah mah'-tehr stuh-dih-oh'-ruhm] *L*—Nourishing mother of studies. Linacre's appraisal of Italy's universities in the 15th century.

Alma Redemptoris Mater [ahl'-mah ray-demp-toh'-riss mah'-tehr] *L*—Dear Mother of the Redeemer. An antiphon sung at compline on certain Sundays. Mentioned by the Prioress in Chaucer's *The Canterbury Tales.*

Al nemico che fugge, fa un ponte d'oro [ahl nay-mee'-koh kay foo'-jay fah oon pon'-tay doh'-roh] *It*—Make a bridge of gold for a fleeing enemy, i.e., be happy when an enemy decides to retreat, and speed his flight.

À loisir [ah lwah-zeer] *Fr*—At leisure.

Al primo colpo, non cade l'albero [ahl pree'-moh kol'-poh nonn kah'-day lahl'-bay-roh] *It*—The tree does not fall at the first blow from an ax; heaven is not reached at a single bound. *See also* Der Baum fällt . . .

Alta vendetta d'alto silenzio è figlia [ahl'-tah ven-det'-tah dahl'-toh see-len'-tsee-oh eh feel'-yah] *It*—Deep vengeance is the child of deep silence.

alt. dieb. alternis diebus [ahl-tehr'-nees dih-ay'-buhs] *L*—Every other day. A medical direction.

Alter ego [ahl'-tehr eh'-goh] *L*—Another self; a bosom friend.

Alter idem [ahl'-tehr ee'-dem] *L*—Literally, another the same; a person or thing that is the image of another; second self. *See also* Alter ego.

Alter ipse amicus [ahl'-tehr ip'-seh ah-mee'-kuhs] *L*—A friend is a second self.

alt. hor. alternis horis [ahl-tehr'-nees hoh'-rees] *L*—Every other hour. A medical direction.

12

Altissima flumina minimo sono labuntur [ahl-tiss'-see-mah floo'-mih-nah mih'-nih-mo so'-no lah-buhn'-tuhr] *L*—The deeper the river the more quietly it flows; still rivers run deep. Adapted from Q. Curtius Rufus, *History of Alexander,* 7; 4, 13.

Alto rilievo [ahl'-toh ree-lee-ay'-voh] *It*—High relief. Sculptured figures that project half way or more from a wall.

a. M. am Main [ahm mIn] *Ger*—On the Main River.

A. M. *See* Anno mundi.

a. m. ante meridiem [ahn'-teh meh-ree'-dih-em] *L*—Before midday. Used to designate the hours between midnight and noon.

A. M. Artium Magister [ahr'-tih-uhm mah-gis'-tehr] *L*—Master of Arts.

À main armée [ah maN nahr-may] *Fr*—By force of arms.

amal. amiral [ah-mee-rahl] *Fr*—Admiral.

Ama l'amico tuo col vizio suo [ah'-mah lah-mee'-koh too'-oh kohl vee'-tsee-oh soo'-oh] *It*—Love your friend in spite of his faults.

Ama nesciri [ah'-mah ness-kee'-ree] *L*—Love of being unknown. The doctrine of self-effacement found in St. Bernard and Thomas à Kempis. *See also* Lathe biosas.

Amantes, amentes [ah-mahn'-tays ah-men'-tays] *L*—Lovers are mad. This is derived from Terence, *Andria,* 1; 3, 13: *Inceptio est amentium, haud amantium.* It [a proposed marriage] is the project of mad people, not of lovers.

Amantium irae amoris integratio est [ah-mahn'-tih-uhm ee'-rI ah-moh'-riss in-tay-grah'-tee-oh est] *L*—Lovers' quarrels renew love. Terence, *Andria,* 3; 3, 23.

Amare et sapere vix deo conceditur [ah-mah'-reh et sah'-peh-reh wiks deh'-oh kon-kay'-dih-tuhr] *L*—To be in love and wise at the same time is impossible, even for a god. Publilius Syrus.

Amar y saber no puede ser [ah-mahr' ee sah-behr' noh pway'-day sehr] *Sp*—It is impossible to love and be wise at the same time.

Ama si vis amari [ah'-mah see wees ah-mah'-ree] *L*—Love if you wish to be loved.

Amato non sarai, se a te solo penserai [ah-mah'-toh nonn sah-rah'-ee seh ah tay soh'-loh pen-say-rah'-ee] *It*—Nobody will love you if you think of nobody but yourself.

A maximis ad minima [ah mahx'-ih-mees ahd mih'-nih-mah] *L*—From the greatest to the smallest.

Ambigendi locus [ahm-bee-gen'-dee lo'-kuhs] *L*—Room for doubt.

Ambiguitas latens [ahm-bih-guh'-ih-tahs lah'-tayns] *L*—Latent ambiguity, as in a deed.

Ambiguitas patens [ahm-bih-guh'-ih-tahs pah'-tayns] *L*—Obvious ambiguity.

A. M. D. G. *See* Ad majorem Dei gloriam.

Âme damnée [ahm dah-nay] *Fr*—Literally, a damned soul; a tool, a drudge.

Âme de boue [ahm duh boo] *Fr*—A low, debased person.

Amende honorable [ah-mahNd uh-no-rah-bl] *Fr*—An acceptable apology.

A mensa et toro (*thoro* is incorrect usage) [ah mayn'-sah et toh'-roh] *L*—Literally, from table and bed; a legal separation granted a married couple.

Âme perdue [ahm pehr-dü] *Fr*—A lost soul.

À merveille [ah mehr-veh-yuh] *Fr*—Marvelously well done.

Amico d'ognuno, amico di nessuno [ah-mee'-koh dohn-yoo'-noh ah mee'-koh dee ness-soo'-noh] *It*—Everybody's friend, nobody's friend.

Amicus certus in re incerta cernitur [ah-mee'-kuhs kehr'-tuhs in ray in-kehr'-tah kehr'-nih-tuhr] *L*—A sincere friend is discovered in an uncertain issue; a friend in need is a friend indeed. Ennius, quoted by Cicero, *On Friendship*, 17.

Amicus curiae [ah-mee'-kuhs koo'-ree-ay] *L*—A friend of the court; a person ap-

pointed by a judge to assist by giving advice in the handling of a legal case.

Amicus humani generis [ah-mee'-kuhs hoo-mah'-nee geh'-neh'-riss] *L*—A friend of the human race.

Amicus Plato, sed magis amica veritas [ah-mee'-kuhs plah'-toh sed mah'-giss ah-mee'-kah way'-rih-tahs] *L*—Plato is dear to me but truth is dearer still. A refusal to abandon a conclusion in deference to a great name. Cervantes, *Don Quixote*, 2; 51. A variation of this saying reads: *Amicus Plato, amicus Socrates, sed major veritas*, Plato is my friend and so is Socrates, but the truth is greater still. Variations of this dictum are based on a passage in Plato's *Phaedo*, 40.

Amicus usque ad aras [ah-mee'-kuhs oos'-kweh ahd ah'-rahs] *L*—A friend as far as the altar. Friendship breaks down over matters of religious conviction.

Ami (amie) de coeur [ah-mee duh kuhr] *Fr*—Close, bosom friend.

Ami de cour [ah-mee duh koor] *Fr*—A friend of the court; a false friend.

Ami du peuple [ah-mee dü puh-pl] *Fr*—Friend of the people.

Amigo de todos y de ninguno, todo es uno [ah-mee'-goh day toh'-dos ee day neen-goo'-noh toh'-doh ess oo'-noh] *Sp*—Everybody's friend and nobody's friend, it's all the same.

Amittit merito proprium qui alienum appetit [ah-mit'-tit meh'-rih'-toh pro'-prih-uhm kwee ah-lih-ay'-nuhm ahp'-peh-tit] *L*—He deserves to lose property who covets another's. Phaedrus, *Fables*, 1; 4, 1.

A. M. M. Asociación Médica Mexicana [ah-so-syah-syohn' may'-dih-kah meh-hee-kah'-nah] *Sp*—Mexican Medical Association.

Amoenitates studiorum [ah-moi-nih-tah'-tays stuh-dih-oh'-ruhm] *L*—Refined literary pursuits. This is the source of the title of *Amenities of Literature* by Isaac Disraeli. Pliny the Elder, *Natural History*, preface, sec. 14.

À moitié [ah mwah-tyay] *Fr*—By halves.

À mon avis [ah mohN nah-vee] *Fr*—In my opinion.

13

Amor com amor se paga [uh-mohr' koN uh-mohr' see pah'-guh] *Port*—One pays for love with love.

Amor dei intellectualis [ah'-mor deh'-ee in-teh-lek-tuh-ah'-liss] *L*—Intellectual love of God.

Amor e carinho tudo vendem [uh-mohr' ee kuh-ree'-nyoo too'-doo vehN'-dehN] *Port*—Love and kindness sell everything.

Amore è cieco [ah-moh'-ray eh chee-ay'-koh] *It*—Love is blind.

Amor fati [ah'-mor fah'-tee] *L*—Willing acceptance of whatever fate decrees. According to Nietzsche, greatness lies not in merely accepting the ills of life but in loving them. *See also* Fiat voluntas tua.

Amor gignit amorem [ah'-mor gig'-nit ah-moh'-rem] *L*—Love begets love.

Amor nummi [ah'-mor nuhm'-mee] *L*—Love of money.

Amor omnibus idem [ah'-mor om'-nih-buhs ee'-dem] *L*—Love is the same for all living creatures. Vergil, *Georgics*, 3; 244.

Amor patriae [ah'-mor pah'-trih-I] *L*—Love for one's native country.

Amor tussisque non celantur [ah'-mor tuhs-siss'-kweh nohn kay-lahn'-tuhr] *L*—Love and a cough cannot be concealed.

Amor vincit omnia [ah'-mor win'-kit om'-nih-ah] *L*—Love conquers all.

Amour fait beaucoup mais l'argent fait tout [ah-moor feh boh-koo meh lahr-zhahN feh too] *Fr*—Love can do much but money can do everything.

Amour propre [ah-moor pro-pr] *Fr*—Self-respect, self-esteem, self-love, or conceit, depending on the context.

Amt ohne Geld macht Diebe [ahmt oh'-nuh gelt mahkt dee'-buh] *Ger*—Offices that carry no pay breed thieves.

A mucho hablar, mucho errar [ah moo'-choh ah-blahr' moo'-choh ay-rrahr'] *Sp*—Much talking, many mistakes.

A muertos y a idos, pocos amigos [ah mwayr'-tohs ee ah ee'-dohs poh'-kohs ah-mee'-gohs] *Sp*—The dead and the absent have few friends.

Am Werke erkennt man den Meister [ahm vehr'-kuh ehr-kehnt' mahn dayn mI-stuhr] *Ger*—One recognizes the master in his work.

Anagke oude theoi machontai [ah-nahn'-kay oo'-deh theh-oi' mah'-khohn-tI] *Gk*—The gods themselves do not try to fight necessity. Simonides of Ceos.

An armer Leute Bart lernt der Junge scheren [ahn ahr'-muhr loi'-tuh bahrt lehrnt dayr yoon'-guh shay'-run] *Ger*—The young barber learns to shave on poor people.

Anathema sit! [ah-nah'-teh-mah sit] *L*—Let him be accursed. An expression used by ecclesiastical authorities when condemning heretics. *Vulgate, Paul, I Corinthians*, 16; 22.

Anax andron [ahn'-ahx ahn-drohn'] *Gr*—Lord and master of men; applied to all heroes by Homer.

A. N. C. ante nativitatem Christi [ahn'-teh nah-tih-vih-tah'-tem kris'-tee] *L*—Before the birth of Christ. Equivalent to English B.C., before Christ.

Anch' io son' pittore [ahnk ee'-oh sohn peet-toh'-ray] *It*—I, too, am a painter. Attributed to Correggio on seeing Raphael's painting of Saint Cecilia. This is an exclamation of admiration on the part of Correggio, younger by twenty years than Raphael, for the work of a master. There is also in this expression a feeling of pride at being identified with such a profession.

Ancienne noblesse [ahN-syenn noh-bless] *Fr*—The aristocratic class in France prior to the Revolution of 1789.

Ancien régime [ahN-syaN ray-zheem] *Fr*—The former regime. Generally used when speaking of conditions in France prior to the French Revolution.

Ancilla theologiae [ahn-chil'-lah teh-oh-loh-jee'-ay] *L*—The handmaid of theology. Scholastic view of philosophy.

Andante [ahn-dahn'-tay] *It*—Direction that music be played slowly, steadily, and smoothly.

Andra moi ennepe, Mousa, polytropon [ahn'-drah moi en'-neh-peh moo'-sah po-

14

lü'-tro-pohn] *Gk*—Sing to me, O Muse, of the man who wandered afar. The opening words of the epic of the adventures of Odysseus. Homer, *Odyssey*.

Aner ho pheugon kai palin machesetai [ah-nayr' hoh foi'-gohn kI pah'-lin mah-keh'-seh-tI] *Gk*—He who fights and runs away,/May live to fight another day. Menander, *Monostichs*, 45.

Angeli, non Angli [ahn'-geh-lee nohn ahn'-glee] *L*—Angels, not Angles. A remark attributed to Gregory, later Pope Gregory the Great. While passing through the Roman forum he inquired about the nationality of certain handsome slaves. On being told they were Angles, he said, "They have the face of angels, and it is fitting that such be co-heirs of heaven with the angels." Bede, *Ecclesiastical History*, 2; 1.

Anguis in herba [ahn'-gwis in hehr'-bah] *L*—Snake in the grass; a disloyal friend. Vergil, *Eclogues*, 3; 93.

Animae dimidium meae [ah'-nih-mI dih-mih'-dih-uhm meh'-I] *L*—The half of my soul. A term of endearment applied by Horace to Vergil. Horace, *Odes*, 1; 3, 8.

Animal bipes implume [ah'-nih-mahl bih'-pays ihm-ploo'-meh] *L*—A two-footed animal without feathers. A translation of Plato's definition of man, successfully ridiculed by Diogenes when he brought a plucked cock into the school. *See also* Zoon dipoun apteroun. Plato, *Politics*, 266.

Anima naturaliter Christiana [ah'-nih-mah nah-too-rah'-lih-tehr kriss-tee-ah'-nah] *L*—A soul naturally Christian; a pagan who exemplifies Christian virtues.

Animis opibusque parati [ah'-nih-mees o-pih-buhs'-kweh pah-rah'-tee] *L*—Prepared in spirit and resources. A motto of South Carolina. *See also* Dum spiro spero.

Animo et fide [ah'-nih-moh et fee'-day] *L*—With courage and fidelity.

Animus furandi [ah'-nih-muhs foo-rahn'-dee] *L*—The intention to steal. A legal term.

Animus testandi [ah'-nih-muhs tess-tahn'-dee] *L*—The intention to make a last will.

anme anonyme [ah-no-neem] *Fr*—Anonymous. Used to indicate limited liability. *See also* Société anonyme.

An nescis longas regibus esse manus? [ahn ness'-kees lon'-gahs ray'-gih-buhs ess-seh mah'-noos] *L*—Don't you know that kings have long arms? The long arm of the law has become proverbial. Ovid, *Heroides*, 17; 166.

Anno aetatis suae [ahn'-noh I-tah'-tiss suh'-I] *L*—In the year of his age.

Anno ante Christum [ahn'-noh ahn'-teh kriss'-tuhm] *L*—In the year before Christ. Equivalent to B.C.

Anno Domini [ah'-noh do'-mih-nee] *L*—In the year of our Lord. Indicates the number of years from the birth of Christ. In the sixth century, Dionysius Exiguus initiated the system of expressing dates by referring events to the birth of Christ. According to his calculations, Christ was born in 754 A.U.C. (*q.v.*). It is generally agreed, however, that Christ was born at least four years earlier. A. D. is much more frequently used than its equivalent, A.H.S. (*q.v.*).

Anno humanae salutis [ahn'-noh hoo-mah'-nI sah-loo'-tis] *L*—In the year of man's redemption. Equivalent to A.D. (*q.v.*).

Anno mundi [ahn'-noh muhn'-dee] *L*—In the year of the world. According to the calculations of Bishop James Ussher (1581-1656), the world was created in 4004 B.C.

Anno urbis conditae. *See* Ab urbe condita.

Annuit coeptis [ahn'-nuh-it koip'-tees] *L*—He (God) has looked with favor upon our beginning. Words on the great seal of the United States adapted from a passage in Vergil, *Aeneid*, 9; 625, in which Ascanius prays to Jupiter for help in slaying an enemy. The words on the obverse of the seal, *Novus ordo seclorum*, mean "the new order of the ages," and are based on Vergil, *Eclogues*, 4; 5.

Annus luctus [ahn'-nuhs look'-toos] *L*—A year of mourning. Roman law forbade a widow to remarry within one year of her husband's death. The presumption was that any child born during this period was

15

the offspring of the deceased father. This Roman law was subsequently incorporated in the laws of other nations.

Annus magnus *or* **Platonicus** [ahn'-nuhs mahg'-nuhs *or* plah-toh'-nih-kuhs] *L*—The Great Year or the Platonic Year (a period of thousands of years ending when all the stars would be in the position that they occupied at the beginning of the world). One of these great years would include the four ages: gold, silver, bronze, and iron.

Annus mirabilis [ahn'-nuhs mee-rah'-bih-liss] *L*—A year of wonders. Generally refers to 1666 when London experienced a tragic fire and plague.

À nouvelles affaires, nouveaux conseils [ah noo-vel zah-fair noo-voh kohN-say] *Fr* —For new business, new plans.

Ante bellum [ahn'-teh bel'-luhm] *L*— Before the war; specifically, in the United States, before the Civil War.

Ante lucem [ahn'-teh loo'-kehm] *L*— Before daybreak.

Ante tubam trepidat [ahn'-teh tuh'-bahm treh'-pih-daht] *L*—He trembles before hearing the sound of the trumpet, i.e., before the battle begins.

Ante victoriam ne canas triumphum [ahn'-teh wik-toh'-rih-ahm nay kah'-nahs trih-uhm'-fuhm] *L*—Do not celebrate a triumph before victory; don't count your chickens before they are hatched.

Anthropos physei politikon zoon [ahn'-throh-poss fü'-seh poh-lih-tih-konn' zoh'-on] *Gr*—Man is by nature a political animal. Aristotle, *Politics*, 1; 2, 9.

Anulatus aut doctus aut fatuus [ah-nuh-lah'-tuhs out dok'-tuhs out fah'-tuh-uhs] *L*—The man who wears a ring is either learned or foolish.

A. O. F. Afrique Occidentale Française [ah-freek ok-see-dahN-tahl frahN-sez] *Fr*— French West Africa.

Ao medico, ao advogado, e ao abade falar verdade [ahoo meh'-dee-koo ahoo ahd-voo-gah'-doo ee ahoo ah-bah'-dee fuh-lar' ver-dah'-dee] *Port*—Tell the truth to your doctor, your lawyer, and your priest. *See also* Al confessor . . .

a.o. Prof. ausserordentlicher Professor [ows-suhr-or'-dunt-lee-khur pro-feh'-suhr] *Ger*—Extraordinary professor.

A. O. S. S. Americanae Orientalis Societatis Socius [ah-meh-rih-kahn'-I oh-rih-en-tah'-lis soh-kih-eh-tah'-tiss soh'-kih-uss] *L* —Fellow of the American Oriental Society.

À outrance [ah oo-trahNss] *Fr*—To the very end; to the utmost. *À l'outrance* is incorrect.

a. p. anni praesentis [ahn'-nee prI-sen'-tiss] *L*—In the present year.

A. P. À protester [ah proh-tess-tay] *Fr*—To be protested later on. A commercial term.

À pas de géant [ah pah duh zhay-ahN] *Fr*—With a giant's stride.

A paso de buey [ah pah'-soh day boo-ay'-ee] *Sp*—Literally, at the pace of an ox; at a snail's pace.

A. P. C. N. anno post Christum natum [ahn'-noh post kris'-tuhm nah'-tuhm] *L*— In the year of our Lord. A variant of A. D. (*q.v.*).

Apertura a destra [ah-pehr-too'-rah ah dess'-trah] *It*—An opening on the right for the conservatives in the government.

À perte de vue [ah pehrt duh vü] *Fr*—As far as the eye can see.

À peu de frais [ah puh duh freh] *Fr*—At little expense.

A piacere [ah pee-ah-chay'-ray] *It*—According to one's wish. *See also* Ad libitum.

À pied [ah pyay] *Fr*—On foot.

A plazo [ah plah'-soh] *Sp*—On credit.

ap(r). J.-C. après Jésus-Christ [ah-preh zhay-zü-kreest] *Fr*—After Christ; A. D. (*q.v.*).

À point [ah pwaN] *Fr*—Exactly, correctly, opportunely. *Cuit à point*—cooked to a turn.

Apologia pro vita sua [ah-poh-lo'-jee-ah pro vee'-tah suh'-ah] *L*—A defense (not an apology in the popular sense) of his life. The title of Cardinal John Henry Newman's spiritual autobiography (1864).

A posse ad esse [ah poss'-seh ahd ess'-seh] *L*—From possibility to reality.

A posteriori [ah pos-teh-rih-oh'-ree] *L*—In logic, a conclusion reached through experience rather than pure reason. Opposed to A priori (*q.v.*).

Apparatus belli [ahp-pah-rah'-tuss bel'-lee] *L*—The provisions or equipment for war. Cicero, *Academic Questions*, 2; 1.

Apparatus criticus [ahp-pah-rah'-tuss krih'-tih-kuss] *L*—Reference works useful in literary studies; a section in a classical author showing variant readings based on the different extant manuscripts of the text.

Apparent rari nantes in gurgite vasto [ahp-pah'-rent rah'-ree nahn'-tays in guhr'-gih-teh wahs'-toh] *L*—Here and there men are seen swimming in the vast abyss. Critics have used this to describe a literary work in which occasional bits of worthwhile material are scattered over a sea of words. Vergil, *Aeneid*, 1; 118.

Appartement meublé [ah-par-tuh-mahN muh-blay] *Fr*—Furnished apartment.

Appetito non vuol salsa [ahp-pay-tee'-toh nonn vwohl sahl'-sah] *It*—Hunger is the best sauce. *See also* À bon appétit . . .

Appetitus rationi oboediant [ahp-peh-tee'-tuhs rah-tee-oh'-nee oh-boy'-dee-ahnt] *L*—Let the appetites obey reason. Cicero, *Offices*, 1; 29, 102.

A. P. R. C. anno post Romam conditam [ahn'-noh post roh'-mahm kohn'-dih-tahm] *L*—In the year after the founding of Rome. The traditional date for the founding of Rome is 753 B. C. Equivalent to A. U. C. (*q.v.*).

A precio fijo [ah pray'-see-oh fee'-hoh] *Sp*—At a fixed price; no bargaining.

Après dommage chacun est sage [ah-preh doh-mahz sha-kuhn eh sahzh] *Fr*—Everybody is wise after the harm is done.

Après la mort, le médecin [ah-preh la mohr luh mayd-saN] *Fr*—Calling the doctor when the patient is dead; locking the stable door after the horse is stolen.

Après moi le déluge [ah-preh mwah luh day-lüzh] *Fr*—After me the deluge, attrib-uted to Louis XV, King of France, who spent lavishly and overtaxed the people. The saying, in the form *Après nous le déluge*, is sometimes attributed to Madame de Pompadour, the king's favorite.

A prima vista [ah pree'-mah vees'-tah] *It*—At first sight.

A primo ad ultimum [ah pree'-moh ahd uhl'-tih-muhm] *L*—From first to last.

A priori [ah pree-oh'-ree] *L*—In logic, a type of reasoning or conclusion derived from self-evident propositions rather than experience. Opposed to A posteriori (*q.v.*).

À propos [ah pruh-poh] *Fr*—Pertinent, seasonable; in regard to; with reference to.

À propos de [ah pruh-poh duh] *Fr*—With reference to, speaking of.

À propos de bottes [ah pruh-poh duh butt] *Fr*—Literally, as to the matter of boots; by the way; to change the subject.

À propos de rien [ah pruh-poh duh ryaN] *Fr*—À propos of nothing. Used to describe something that is off the subject.

aq. aqua [ah'-kwah] *L*—Water. This abbreviation is used with a number of adjectives: **astr.** astricta [ah-strik'-tah] frozen; **bull.** bulliens [bool'-lih-ayns] boiling; **com.** communis [kom-moo'-niss] common; **dest.** destillata [day-steel-lah'-tah] distilled; **ferv.** fervens [fehr'-vayns] hot; **mar.** marina [mah-ree'-nah] sea; **pluv.** pluvialis [ploo-vih-ah'-liss] rain; **pur.** pura [poo'-rah] pure; **tep.** tepida [teh'-pih-dah] tepid. Used in medical directions.

Aqua ardens [ah'-kwah ar'-dayns] *L*—Literally, burning water; the name the alchemists gave to alcohol.

Aqua fortis [ah'-kwah for'-tiss] *L*—Literally, strong water; nitric acid.

Aqua regia [ah'-kwah ray'-ghih-ah] *L*—Literally, royal water, a name given a mixture of nitric and hydrochloric acids capable of dissolving gold, the king of metals.

Aqua vitae [ah'-kwah wee'-tI] *L*—Brandy or any distilled liquor.

Aquila non captat muscas [ah'-kwih-lah nohn kap'-taht muhs'-kahs] *L*—An eagle does not hawk at flies; the mighty can afford to scorn the weak. Michael Apostolius.

Aquí se habla español [ah-kee' say ah'-blah ess-pah-nyohl'] *Sp*—Spanish is spoken here.

À quoi bon? [ah kwah bohN] *Fr*—What's the good of it?

À raconter ses maux souvent on les soulage [ah rah-kohN-tay say moh soo-vahN tohN lay soo-lahzh] *Fr*—We often lighten our troubles by talking about them. Corneille, *Polyeucte*, 1; 3.

Ara pacis [ah'-rah pah'-kiss] *L*—Altar of peace.

Arbiter bibendi [ahr'-bih-tehr bih-ben'-dee] *L*—The toastmaster.

Arbiter elegantiae (elegantiarum) [ahr'-bih-tehr ay-lay-gahn'-tih-I, ay-lay-gahn-tih-ah'-ruhm] *L*—The judge of elegance. Nero conferred this title on his favorite, Petronius, an authority on matters of taste and refined luxury. Tacitus, *Annals*, 16; 18.

Arbiter literarum [ahr'-bih-tehr lee-teh-rah'-ruhm] *L*—A judge or critic of literature.

Arbores serit diligens agricola, quarum adspiciet bacam ipse numquam [ahr'-bo-rays seh'-rit dee'-lih-ghens ah-grih'-ko-lah kwah'-ruhm ahd-spih'-kih-et bah'-kahm ip'-seh nuhm'-kwahm] *L*—The diligent farmer plants trees the fruit of which he will never see. Adapted from Cicero, *Tusculan Disputations*, 1; 14.

Arcades ambo [ahr'-kah-days ahm'-boh] *L*—Both Arcadians, i.e., gifted in pastoral song; friends of similar tastes and characteristics. The reference is to Corydon and Thyrsis, shepherds competing in a musical contest. Vergil, *Eclogues*, 7; 4.

Arcana imperii [ahr-kah'-nah im-peh'-rih-ee] *L*—State secrets.

Arcani disciplina [ahr-kah'-nee dis-kih-plee'-nah] *L*—Discipline of the secret. Policy of early Christians of not revealing their religion.

Arche hemisy pantos [ahr-khay' hay'-mih-sü pahn-tos'] *Gk*—The beginning is half of everything; well begun is half done. Pythagoras.

18

Ardentia verba [ahr-den'-tih-ah wehr'-bah] *L*—Glowing words; forceful language.

À reculons [ah ruh-kü-lohN] *Fr*—Backwards. Used of a backward movement, not necessarily physical.

Argent comptant [ahr-zhahN kohN-tahN] *Fr*—Spot cash; ready money. *See also* a. c.

Argumenti gratia [ahr-goo-men'-tee grah'-tih-ah] *L*—For the sake of argument.

Argumentum ad crumenam [ahr-goo-men'-tuhm ahd cruh-may'-nahm] *L*—An appeal to the purse; an argument based on monetary considerations.

Argumentum ad hominem [ahr-goo-men'-tuhm ahd ho'-mih-nem] *L*—An argument that appeals to the interests of the individual to whom it is directed. Such an argument may appeal to the prejudices of an opponent, to passion rather than reason. The same name is given to an argument in which one employs an opponent's words or actions. It has been said that an illustration of the *argumentum ad hominem* is found in the technique of the defense lawyer who, when at a loss for arguments, attacks the attorney for the plaintiff, but this is not the current usage of this phrase in the United States.

Argumentum ad ignorantiam [ahr-goo-men'-tuhm ahd ig-noh-rahn'-tih-ahm] *L*—An argument based on an adversary's ignorance of facts in a controversy.

Argumentum ad invidiam [ahr-goo-men'-tuhm ahd in-vih'-dih-ahm] *L*—An appeal to envy, jealousy, or ill will.

Argumentum ad judicium [ahr-goo-men'-tuhm ahd yoo-dih'-kih-uhm] *L*—An argument appealing to judgment.

Argumentum ad misericordiam [ahr-goo-men'-tuhm ahd mih-seh-rih-kor'-dih-ahm] *L*—An appeal to pity.

Argumentum ad populum [ahr-goo-men'-tuhm ahd po'-puh-luhm] *L*—An argument appealing to the interests of the populace.

Argumentum ad rem [ahr-goo-men'-tuhm ahd rem] *L*—An argument concerning the point under discussion.

Argumentum ad verecundiam [ahr-goo-men'-tuhm ahd weh-ray-kuhn'-dih-ahm] *L*—An appeal to an opponent's sense of decency.

Argumentum baculinum or **ad baculum** [ahr-goo-men'-tuhm bah-kuh-lee'-nuhm *or* ahd bah'-kuh-luhm] *L*—Argument with a cane; the appeal to force in a debate.

Ariston metron [ah'-ris-ton meh'-tron] *Gr*—The middle course is best; words attributed to Cleobulus, one of the seven wise men of Greece.

A rivederci (usually spelled **arrivederci**) [ah ree-vay-dayr'-chee] *It*—Until we meet again.

Arma virumque cano [ahr'-mah wih-ruhm'-kweh kah'-noh] *L*—I sing of arms and the man. Vergil, *Aeneid*, 1; 1.

Armut ist keine Schande [ahr'-moot ist kI'-nuh shahn'-duh] *Ger*—Poverty is no disgrace.

A Roma por todo [ah ro'-mah por toh'-doh] *Sp*—To Rome for everything.

Arrière-garde [ah-ryehr gard] *Fr*—Rear guard.

Arrière pensée [ah-ryehr pahN-say] *Fr*—A mental reservation. It does not mean an afterthought.

Arroz con pollo [ah-rros' kon poh'-yoh] *Sp*—Rice with chicken.

Ars artium omnium conservatrix [ahrs ahr'-tih-uhm om'-nih-uhm kohn-ser-wah'-trix] *L*—The art (of printing) that preserves all arts.

Ars (artis) est celare artem [ahrs—ahr'-tiss—est kay-lah'-reh ahr'-tem] *L*—Art lies in the concealment of art. An axiom among those artists who try to conceal the means by which they produce their effects. It is also a precept among painters who feel that art should reproduce nature.

Ars gratia artis [ahrs grah'-tih-ah ahr'-tiss] *L*—Art for art's sake. See *also* L'art pour l'art.

Ars longa, vita brevis [ahrs lon'-gah wee'-tah breh'-wiss] *L*—Art is long, and Time is fleeting, as translated by Longfellow in

"A Psalm of Life." See *also* Vita brevis, longa ars.

Ars omnibus communis [ahrs om'-nih-buhs kom-moo'-niss] *L*—Art belongs to everyone.

Ars Poetica [ahrs poh-ay'-tih-kah] *L*—The art of poetry. Title of a poem by the Roman poet Horace.

Ars prima regni est posse invidiam pati [ahrs pree'-mah rayg'-nee est poss'-seh in-wih'-dih-am pah'-tee] *L*—The first art of a ruler is to endure envy. Seneca, *Hercules Furens*, 353.

A. R. S. S. Antiquariorum Regiae Societatis Socius [ahn-tih-kwah-rih-oh'-ruhm ray'-gih-I so-kee-eh-tah'-tiss so'-kih-uss] *L*—Fellow of the Royal Society of Antiquaries.

Artes perditae [ahr'-tays pehr'-dih-tI] *L*—Lost arts.

Articolo di fondo [ahr-tee'-koh-loh dee fon'-doh] *It*—An editorial or leading article.

Artis sola domina necessitas [ahr'-tis soh'-lah do'-mih-nah neh-kes'-see-tahs] *L*—Necessity is the only master of art; said of architecture that must at times be ruled by practical requirements.

Artz, hilf dir selbst [ahrts hilf deer zelpst] *Ger*—See Medice, cura teipsum.

a/s aux soins de [oh swaN duh] *Fr*—In care of. Used on postal addresses.

Asbestos gelos [ahs'-bes-tos geh'-lohs] *Gk*—Unquenchable laughter; hence the proverbial Homeric laughter. Such laughter broke out among the gods when awkwardly limping Hephaestus acted as cupbearer to Zeus in place of the graceful Hebe or Ganymede. Homer, *Iliad*, 1; 599.

Asinus ad lyram [ah'-sih-nuhs ahd lih'-rahm] *L*—An ass at the lyre. Said of a person who has no appreciation of, or talent for art.

Asinus asino et sus sui pulcher [ah'-sih-nuhs ah'-sih-noh et soos suh'-ee pull'-kehr] *L*—An ass is beautiful to an ass and a pig to a pig.

A. S. L. V. assurance sur la vie [ah-sü-rahNs sür lah vee] *Fr*—Life insurance.

A. S. P. accepté sans protêt [ahk-sep-tay sahN proh-teh] *Fr*—Accepted without protest. A commercial term.

Aspice, viator [ah′-spih-keh wih-ah′-tohr] *L*—Behold, traveler. Inscription on Roman tombstones.

Astraea Redux [ah-stray′-ah ray′-dooks] *L*—Literally, Astraea returned. She was the goddess of justice, the last of the immortals to leave the earth. Dryden used this as a title for a poem celebrating the restoration of the monarchy after Cromwell's rule.

A-suilish mahuil agus machree! [ah-sul′-ish mah-weel′ ah′-gus mah-kree′] *Ir*—Light of my eyes and my heart.

A sus órdenes [ah soos or′-day-nays] *Sp*—At your service.

Asylum ignorantiae [ah-see′-luhm ig-noh-rahn′-tih-I] *L*—A refuge for ignorance.

À tâtons [ah tah-toN] *Fr*—Gropingly; warily.

Até amanhã [ah-teh′ ah-mahn′-yahN] *Port*—Until tomorrow.

Até logo [ah-teh′ lo′-goo] *Port*—Good-bye; till we meet again.

A tergo [ah tehr′-goh] *L*—From the rear.

Athanasius contra mundum [ah-tah-nah′-sih-uhs kohn′-trah muhn′-duhm] *L*—Athanasius against the world. Said of anybody who single-handedly battles heavy opposition. As bishop of Alexandria, he was a vigorous opponent of Arianism and endured exile five times for his support of Christian orthodoxy.

A. T. L. avant toute lettre [ah-vahN toot leh-tr] *Fr*—Before all the lettering. *See also* a. l. (avant la lettre).

A toda prisa [ah toh′-dah pree′-sah] *Sp*—At full speed.

À tort et à travers [ah tohr ay ah trah-vehr] *Fr*—At random; without rhyme or reason.

À tort ou à raison [ah tohr oo ah reh-zohN] *Fr*—Rightly or wrongly.

À tout prix [ah too pree] *Fr*—At any price; at any cost.

20

à. t. p. *See* À tout prix.

At spes non fracta [aht spays nohn frahk′-tah] *L*—But hope is not yet crushed.

A tuo beneplacito [ah too′-oh bay-nay-plah′-chee-toh] *It*—At your pleasure.

Au bout de son latin [oh boo duh sohN lah-taN] *Fr*—At the end of his Latin; at his wit's end; in desperation.

Au bout du compte [oh boo dü kohNt] *Fr*—Literally, at the end of the account; after all; on the whole.

A. U. C. *See* Ab urbe condita. The same abbreviation serves for anno urbis conditae [ah′-noh uhr′-bis kohn′-dih-tI].

Auch ein Haar hat seinen Schatten [owkh In hahr haht zI′-nun shaht′-un] *Ger*—See Etiam capillus unus . . .

Auch ich war in Arkadien geboren [owkh ihk vahr in ahr-kah′-dih-yun gu-boh′-run] *Ger*—I too have lived in Arcadia. *See also* Et in Arcadia ego.

Au contraire [oh kohN-trayr] *Fr*—On the contrary.

Au courant [oh koo-rahN] *Fr*—In the current of events; well-posted; up to date on current matters.

Aucun chemin de fleurs ne conduit à la gloire [oh-kuhN shuh-maN duh fluhr nuh kohN-dwee tah lah glwahr] *Fr*—The path to glory is not strewn with flowers. La Fontaine, *Fables*, 10; 14.

Audemus jura nostra defendere [ow-day′-muhs yoo′-rah nos′-trah day-fehn′-deh-reh] *L*—We dare defend our rights. Motto of Alabama.

Audendo magnus tegitur timor [ow-denn′-doh mahg′-nuhs teh′-gih-tuhr tih′-mor] *L*—Great fear is covered up by a display of daring. Lucan, *Pharsalia*, 4; 702.

Audentes deus ipse juvat [ow-denn′-tays deh′-uhs ip′-seh yuh′-wat] *L*—God helps the brave. Ovid, *Metamorphoses*, 10; 586.

Audentes fortuna juvat [ow-denn′-tays for-too′-nah yuh′-wat] *L*—Fortune is on the side of the brave. Vergil, *Aeneid*, 10; 284.

Aude sapere [ow′-day sah′-peh-reh] *L*—Dare to be wise.

Au désespoir [oh day-zehs-pwahr] *Fr*—In despair.

Audi alteram partem [ow'-dee ahl'-teh-rahm pahr'-tem] *L*—Hear the other side.

Au fait [oh feh] *Fr*—Skilled; masterly; well-informed.

Au fond [oh fohN] *Fr*—Basically; at bottom.

Auf Wiedersehen [owf vee'-duhr-zay-un] *Ger*—Until we meet again.

Au grand sérieux [oh grahN say-ryuh] *Fr*—In all seriousness.

Au gratin [oh grah-taN] *Fr*—Cooked with bread crumbs and grated cheese.

Aujourd'hui roi, demain rien [o-zhoor-dwee rwah duh-maN ryaN] *Fr*—Today a king, tomorrow nothing; a king today, tomorrow a clown.

Au jus [oh zhü] *Fr*—In the juice; served in its own gravy.

Au lecteur [oh lek-tuhr] *Fr*—To the reader.

a. u. n. absque ulla nota [ahps'-kweh ool'-lah noh'-tah] *L*—Without any marking.

Au naturel [oh nah-tü-rell] *Fr*—In the natural style or manner; in the nude.

Aunque la mona se vista de seda, mona se queda [ah'-uhn-kay lah moh'-nah say bis'-tah day say'-dah, moh'-nah say kay'-dah] *Sp*—A monkey dressed in silk is still a monkey.

Au pair [oh pehr] *Fr*—At par; said of a servant receiving room and board but no salary.

Au pied de la lettre [oh pyay duh lah leh-tr] *Fr*—Literally; exactly.

Au pis aller [oh pee-zah-lay] *Fr*—If the worst comes to the worst.

Au point [oh pwaN] *Fr*—In focus.

Aura epileptica [ow'-rah eh-pih-lep'-tih-kah] *L*—A chilling sensation before an attack of epilepsy.

Aura popularis [ow'-rah po-puh-lah'-rihs] *L*—The whim of the people.

Aurea mediocritas [ow'-reh-ah meh-dih-oh'-krih-tahs] *L*—The golden mean. This doctrine, popular among the ancient Greeks and Romans, holds that in all activity, e.g., in eating and drinking, gymnastics, and the pursuit of pleasure, the ideal is to avoid excess on the one hand and deficiency on the other. Horace, *Odes*, 2; 10, 5. *See also* In medio stat virtus; Meden agan; Medio tutissimus ibis; Ne quid nimis.

Aurea ne credas quaecunque nitescere cernis [ow'-reh-ah nay kray'-dahs kwI-kuhn'-kweh nih-tehs'-key-reh kehr'-niss] *L*—All that glitters is not gold.

Au reste [oh rest] *Fr*—Moreover; besides.

Au revoir [oh ruh-vwahr] *Fr*—Until we meet again.

Auribus teneo lupum [ow'-rih-buhs teh'-neh-oh luh'-puhm] *L*—I hold a wolf by the ears; you face danger if you hold on or let go. Terence, *Phormio*, 3; 2, 21.

Auri sacra fames [ow'-ree sah'-krah fah'-mays] *L*—The accursed greed for gold. The complete quotation reads: *Quid non mortalia cogis, auri sacra fames?* To what do you not drive the hearts of men, O cursed greed for gold? Vergil, *Aeneid*, 3; 57.

Aurora borealis [ow-roh'-rah bo-reh-ah'-liss] *L*—Literally, the northern dawn; popularly referred to as the northern lights.

Au royaume des aveugles les borgnes sont rois [oh rwah-yohm day-zah-vuh-gl lay bohr-nyuh sohN rwah] *Fr*—In the kingdom of the blind the man with one eye is king.

Aurum potabile [ow'-ruhm po-tah'-bih-leh] *L*—Drinkable gold. In ancient times it was thought that gold in solution was a panacea.

a. u. s. actum ut supra [ahk'-tuhm uht suh'-prah] *L*—Done as above.

Aus den Augen, aus dem Sinn [ows dayn ow'-ghun ows daym zinn] *Ger*—Out of sight, out of mind.

Aus der Hand in den Mund [ows dayr hahnt in dayn muhnt] *Ger*—Literally, from the hand into the mouth; a hand-to-mouth existence.

Aus Kindern werden Leute [ows kin'-durn ver'-dun loy'-tuh] *Ger*—Children grow up; the boy is father to the man.

Au secours! [oh suh-koor] *Fr*—To the rescue; help!

Au sérieux [oh say-ryuh] *Fr*—In a serious manner.

Au soleil [oh soh-lay] *Fr*—In the sunlight.

Aussitôt dit, aussitôt fait [oh-see-toh dee oh-see-toh feh] *Fr*—No sooner said than done.

Aut amat aut odit mulier, nihil est tertium [out ah'-maht out oh'-dit muh'-lee-ehr nih'-hil est tehr'-tih-uhm] *L*—A woman either loves or hates; there is no in-between. Publilius Syrus.

Autant d'hommes, autant d'avis [oh-tahN duhm oh-tahN dah-vee] *Fr*—So many men, so many opinions.

Aut Caesar aut nullus (aut nihil) [out kI'-sahr out nool'-luss, out nih'-hil] *L*—Either Caesar or nothing. Motto of the ambitious.

Aut disce, aut discede: manet sors tertia caedi [out dis'-keh out dis-kay'-deh mah'-net sors tehr'-tih-ah kI'-dee] *L*—Either learn or leave: a third lot remains, be flogged. Motto of early grammar school of Winchester College, England.

Aut doce aut disce aut discede [out do'-kay out dis'-keh out dis-kay'-deh] *L*—Teach, learn, or leave. Motto of St. Paul's Grammar School, London.

Auto-da-fé [ow'-toh dah feh] *Port*—Literally, an act of the faith. A religious demonstration in defense of the doctrines of the church. This was carried out with dramatic ceremonies at which the heretical views of the unrepentant were recited. The punishments decreed by the Inquisition, sometimes as barbarous as burning at the stake, were executed by the secular power.

Auto de fe [ow'-toh day fay] *Sp*—*See* Auto-da-fé.

Auto sacramental [ah'-oo-toh sah-krah-men-tahl'] *Sp*—A one-act religious play of the Middle Ages that dealt with an aspect of Church liturgy, especially the Eucharist.

Autos epha [ow-tos' eh'-fah] *Gk*—He himself said so. *See* Ipse dixit.

Autrefois acquit [oh-truh-fwah zah-kee] *Fr*—Previously acquitted of a charge.

Autres temps, autres moeurs [oh-tr tahN oh-tr muhrss] *Fr*—Other times, other customs.

Aut vincere aut mori [out win'-keh-reh out mo'-ree] *L*—Victory or death.

Au voleur! [oh vuh-luhr] *Fr*—Stop thief!

Aux aguets [oh zah-gheh] *Fr*—To be on the lookout; watchful.

Aux armes! [oh zarm] *Fr*—To arms!

Avant-coureur [ah-vahN koo-ruhr] *Fr*—A forerunner.

Avant-garde [ah-vahN gard] *Fr*—Advanced guard; pioneers. Leaders in new art forms not approved by conservatives are usually given this label.

Avant la lettre [ah-vahN lah leh-tr] *Fr*—Before the complete development.

Avant propos [ah-vahN pruh-poh] *Fr*—Preface.

Avant que de désirer fortement une chose, il faut examiner quel est le bonheur de celui qui la possède [ah-vahN kuh duh day-zee-ray fohrt-mahN ün shohz eel foh tehg-zah-mee-nay kehl eh luh buh-nuhr duh suh-lwee kee lah puh-sehd] *Fr*—Before desiring something passionately, one should inquire into the happiness of the man who possesses it. La Rochefoucauld, *Maxims*, 543.

Avant tout un bon dîner [ah-vahN too uhN bohN dee-nay] *Fr*—Before anything else, a good dinner. The reported first words of Napoleon on entering the Tuileries after escaping from Elba.

Avaritiam si tollere vultis, mater eius est tollenda, luxuries [ah-vah-rih'-tih-ahm see toll'-leh-reh wuhl'-tiss mah'-tehr eh'-yus est toll-len'-dah loox-uhr'-rih-ays] *L*—If you wish to do away with avarice, you must do away with its mother, luxury. Cicero, *On the Orator*, 2; 40, 171.

Avarus nisi cum moritur nil recte facit [ah-wah'-ruhs nih'-sih kuhm mo'-rih-tuhr neel rayk'-tay fah'-kit] *L*—The miser does nothing right except when he dies. Publilius Syrus.

Ave atque vale [ah'-way aht'-kweh wah'-lay] *L*—Hail and farewell. A Roman formula used at funerals when bidding farewell to the dead. The most notable use occurs in *Catullus*, 101; 10 where the poet writes of visiting the grave of his brother.

Ave Maria [ah'-vay mah-ree'-ah] *L*—Hail Mary. Greeting of the Angel Gabriel to the Virgin Mary.

A verbis ad verbera [ah wer'-bees ahd wehr'-beh-rah] *L*—From words to blows.

Avic machree [ah-vick' mah-kree'] *Ir*—Son of my heart.

A vinculo matrimonii [ah win'-kuh-loh mah-tri-moh'-nih-ee] *L*—From the bonds of marriage; a divorce.

av. J.-C. avant Jésus-Christ [ah-vahN zhay-zü kreest] *Fr*—Before Christ. Equivalent to English B.C., before Christ.

À volonté [ah vuh-lohN-tay] *Fr*—At will; at pleasure. *See also* Ad libitum.

A vostra salute [ah voss'-trah sah-loo'-tay] *It*—To your health.

À votre santé [ah vuh-tr sahN-tay] *Fr*—To your health.

À vue d'oeil [ah vü duh-yu] *Fr*—At a glance; clearly.

A vuelta de correo [ah vwel'-tah day ko-rray'-oh] *Sp*—By return mail.

A vuestra salud [ah vwes'-trah sah-lood'] *Sp*—A toast to your good health.

Avvocato del diavolo [ahv-voh-kah'-toh del dee-ah'-voh-loh] *It*—Devil's advocate. *See also* Advocatus diaboli.

¡Ay, bendito! [ah'-ee ben-dee'-toh] *Sp*—The poor fellow! the poor man! An expression of sorrow or pity. Much used in Puerto Rico.

Azeite, vinho e amigo, o mais antigo [ah-zay'-tee vee'-nyoo ee uh-mee'-goo oh mIz ahN-tee'-goo] *Port*—Oil, wine, and friends, the older the better.

B

B. A. *See* A. B.

bacc. en dr. baccalauréat en droit [bah-kah-loh-ray-ah ahN drwah] *Fr*—Baccalaureate in Law.

bacc. ès l. baccalauréat ès lettres [bah-kah-loh-ray-ah ess leh-tr] *Fr*—Baccalaureate in Literature. For the meaning of *ès*, *see* ès.

bacc. ès sc. baccalauréat ès sciences [bah-kah-loh-ray-ah ess syahNss] *Fr*—Baccalaureate in Science.

Bacio di bocca spesso cuor non tocca [bah'-choh dee boh'-kah spes'-soh kwohr nonn toh'-kah] *It*—A kiss on the lips often does not touch the heart.

B. A. I. Baccalaureus in Arte Ingeniaria [bah-kah-low'-reh-uhs in ahr'-teh in-geh-nih-ah'-ree-ah] *L*—Bachelor of Engineering.

Ballon d'essai [bah-lohN dehs-seh] *Fr*—A trial balloon released to determine the direction of the wind; a sounding out of public opinion, often in advance of announcement of official policy.

Banco regis [bang'-koh ray'-jis] *LL*—On the king's bench.

b. à p. billet à payer [bee-yeh ah peh-yay] *Fr*—Bill payable.

b. à r. billet à recevoir [bee-yeh ah ruh-suh-vwahr] *Fr*—Bill receivable.

Barba a barba [bahr'-bah ah bahr'-bah] *Sp*—Chin to chin; face to face.

Bar Mizvah (mitzvah, mitzwah) [bahr mits'-vah] *Heb*—Son of command; in Hebrew law a boy who has reached the age of responsibility (at the end of his thirteenth year); also the ceremony itself.

Bas bleu [bah bluh] *Fr*—Blue stocking. Often a slighting reference to an intellectual woman. The meetings of a London literary club of the eighteenth century were attended by a gentleman who wore blue stockings. His comments so pleased the women that the group came to be known as the Blue-Stocking Club.

Basis virtutum constantia [bah'-sihs wirh-too'-tuhm kohn-stahn'-tee-ah] *L*—The foundation of virtue is constancy.

Bas relief [bah ruh-lyef] *Fr*—Sculpture in which the subject does not stand out far from the background.

Basso buffo [bahs'-soh boof'-foh] *It*—A bass singer of comic opera roles.

Basso rilievo [bahs'-soh ree-lee-ay'-voh] *It*—*See* Bas relief.

Bataille rangée [bah-tI rahN-zhay] *Fr*—Pitched battle.

Bâtie en hommes [bah-tee ahN nuhm] *Fr*—Built of men. A phrase used to describe the medieval university.

Batti il ferro mentre è caldo [baht'-tee eel fehr'-roh men'-treh eh kahl'-doh] *It*—Strike the iron while it is hot. *See also* Bisogna battere . . .

B. Ch. D. Baccalaureus Chirurgiae Dentium [bak-kah-low'-reh-uhs kee-roor-gih'-I den'-tih-uhm] *L*—Bachelor of Dental Surgery.

b. d. s. bis die sumendum [biss dih'-ay soo-men'-duhm] *L*—To be taken twice a day. A medical direction.

B. E. brevet élémentaire [bruh-veh ay-lay-mahN-tehr] *Fr*—A certificate granted a primary school teacher passing French government examinations.

24

Beannacht libh [buhn-nacht' lib] *Ir*—Blessings be with you.

Beatae memoriae [beh-ah'-tI meh-moh'-rih-I] *L*—Of blessed memory.

Beata solitudo [beh-ah'-tah soh-lih-too'-doh] *L*—Blessed solitude.

Beata tranquillitas [beh-ah'-tah trahn-kwihl'-lih-tahs] *L*—Blessed serenity.

Beati pacifici [beh-ah'-tee pah-sih'-fih-see] *L*—Blessed are the peacemakers. One of the eight beatitudes. *Vulgate, Matthew,* 5; 9.

Beati possidentes [beh-ah'-tee pos-sih-den'-tays] *L*—Blessed are those who have. This phrase ironically suggests that there is for the worldly a ninth beatitude. In the *Vulgate* (*Matthew* 5) each of the beatitudes begins with the word *Beati,* meaning blessed.

Beati qui lugent [beh-ah'-tee kwee loo'-jent] *L*—Blessed are those who mourn. One of the beatitudes. *Vulgate, Matthew,* 5; 5.

Beatus ille qui procul negotiis [beh-ah'-tuhs ihl'-leh kwee proh'-kuhl neh-goh'-tih-ees] *L*—Happy the man who lives far away from the cares of business. The first line of a poem written in praise of the joys of living in the country. Horace, *Epodes* 2; 1.

Beaucoup de bruit, peu de fruit [boh-koo duh brwee puh duh frwee] *Fr*—Much talk, but little to show for it.

Beau garçon [boh garh-sohN] *Fr*—A handsome fellow; a dandy.

Beau geste [boh zhest] *Fr*—A generous or sympathetic gesture.

Beau idéal [boh ee-day-ahl] *Fr*—The model or ideal of perfection.

Beau monde [boh mohNd] *Fr*—The fashionable world.

Beau sabreur [boh sah-bruhr] *Fr*—Dashing cavalry officer.

Beauté du diable [boh-tay dü dyah-bl] *Fr*—Beauty of the devil; the bloom of youth.

Beauté insolente [boh-tay aN-soh-lahNt] *Fr*—Arrogant beauty or handsomeness.

Beaux arts [boh zahr] *Fr*—The fine arts.

Beaux esprits [boh zeh-spree] *Fr*—A brilliant coterie of wits.

Bei Nacht sind alle Katzen grau [bI nahkht zint ahl'-luh kaht'-tsun grow] *Ger*—At night all cats are gray; by night all witches are fair; the darkness covers blemishes.

Bel canto [bell kahn'-toh] *It*—Literally, beautiful song; a style of singing used in Italian and French 19th-century opera.

Bel esprit (*pl.* **beaux esprits**) [bel eh-spree, bohz eh-spree] *Fr*—A wit or genius.

Bella matribus detestata [bel'-lah mah'-trih-buhs day-tess-tah'-tah] *L*—War detested by mothers. Horace, *Odes*, 1; 1, 24.

Belle indifférence [bell aN-dee-fay-rahNss] *Fr*—An attitude on the part of neurotic persons in which they show indifference to their condition.

Bellende Hunde beissen nicht [bell'-en-duh huhn'-duh bIs'-sun nikht] *Ger*—Barking dogs don't bite.

Belles dames du temps jadis [bell dahm dü tahN zhah-dees] *Fr*—Beautiful women of the days gone by.

Belles lettres [bell leh-tr] *Fr*—Polite literature, the humanities. *See also* La letteratura amena.

Bellum ita suscipiatur ut nihil aliud nisi pax quaesita videatur [bel'-luhm ih'-tah suhs-kih-pih-ah'-tuhr uht nih'-hil ah'-lih-uhd nih'-sih pahx kwI-see'-tah wih'-deh-ah'-tuhr] *L*—Let war be undertaken so that nothing else is sought, it would seem, but peace. Cicero, *On Duties*, 1; 23, 79.

Bellum omnium contra omnes [bel'-lum om'-nee-um con'-trah om'-nays] *L*—Everyone warring against everyone. General lawlessness. Hobbes, *Leviathan*, ch. 18.

Beltion estin apax apothanein ê aei prosdokan [bel'-tee-on es-tin' ha'-pahx ah-po-than-nehn' ee ah-eh' pros-do-kahn'] *Gk*—Better to face death at once than live in expectation. Plutarch, *Caesar*, 57.

Benedicite Domino! [beh-neh-dee'-chee-teh doh'-mih-noh] *L*—Praise the Lord!

Beneficium accipere libertatem est vendere [beh-neh-fih'-kih-uhm ahk-kih'-peh-reh lee-behr-tah'-tem est wen'-deh-reh] *L*—To accept a favor is to sell one's freedom. Publilius Syrus.

Beneficium clericale [beh-neh-fih'-see-uhm klay-rih-kah'-leh] *L*—Benefit of clergy. During the Middle Ages clerics in England enjoyed exemption from trial by secular authorities.

Beneficium egenti bis dat, qui dat celeriter [beh-neh-fih'-kih-uhm eh-ghen'-tee biss daht kwee daht keh-leh'-rih-tehr] *L*—He gives twice who gives quickly to one in need of aid. Publilius Syrus.

Benemerentium praemium [beh-neh-meh-ren'-tih-uhm prI'-mih-uhm] *L*—A reward for the well-deserving.

Bene qui conjiciet, vatem hunc perhibebo optimum [beh'-neh kwee kohn-yih'-kih-et wah'-tem huhnk per-hih-bay'-boh op'-tih-muhm] *L*—I shall always maintain that the best guesser is the best prophet. Cicero, *On Divination*, 2; 5.

Bene qui latuit, bene vixit [beh'-neh kwee lah'-tuh-it beh'-neh weex'-it] *L*—He has lived a good life who has kept himself hidden. Descartes' motto. The expressed ideal of Francis Bacon, but a maxim he did not follow. Ovid, *Sorrows*, 3; 4, 25. *See also* Lathe biosas.

Berenicem statim ab urbe dimisit invitus invitam [beh-reh-nih'-kem stah'-tim ahb uhr'-beh dee-mee'-sit in-wee'-tuhs in-wee'-tahm] *L*—Unwillingly he at once sent from the city (of Rome) the unwilling Berenice. From this sentence Racine developed his play *Bérénice*. Suetonius, *Lives of Twelve Caesars, Titus*, 7; 2.

Berretta in mano non fece mai danno [ber-ret'-tah een mah'-noh nonn fay'-chay mah'-ee dahn'-noh] *It*—Cap in hand never did any man harm; one never loses anything by being polite.

B. ès A. Bachelier ès Arts [bahsh-ly-yay eh-zahr] *Fr*—Bachelor of Arts.

B. ès L. Bachelier ès Lettres [bahsh-ly-yay ess leh-tr] *Fr*—Bachelor of Letters.

B. ès S. Bachelier ès Sciences [bahsh-ly-yay ess syahNss] *Fr*—Bachelor of Science.

Besser spät als nie [bess'-suhr shpayt ahls nee] *Ger*—Better late than never.

Bête noire [bet nwahr] *Fr*—Black beast; a detested person. An object of aversion.

BGB. Bürgerliches Gesetzbuch [bür'-guhr-likh-uhs guh-zets'-bookh] *Ger*—Civil Code.

Biblia a-biblia [bih'-blih-ah ah-bih'-blih-ah] *Gk*—Books that are not books; nonbooks. This implies criticism of irrelevant materials brought together in one volume, simply to make a book.

Biblia pauperum [bih'-blih-ah pow'-peh-ruhm] *L*—Bible of the poor; pictures illustrating Bible stories for the illiterate.

Bibliophile de la vieille roche [bee-blee-oh-feel duh lah vyay rohsh] *Fr*—A book-collector of the old school whose interests ranged widely and who did not specialize in a narrow area.

Bibliothèque bleue [bib-lee-oh-teck bluh] *Fr*—Popular pamphlets with blue wrappers.

b. i. d. bis in die [biss in dih'-ay] *L*—Twice a day. A medical direction.

Bien entendu [byaN nahN-tahN-dü] *Fr*—Of course.

Bien predica quien bien vive [byehn' pray-dee'-kah kyehn' byehn' bee'-beh] *Sp*—The man who lives a good life gives the best sermons. Cervantes, *Don Quixote*, Part II, ch. 20. *See also* Chi ben vive...

Billet doux [bee-yeh doo] *Fr*—A love letter.

Bis dat qui cito dat [biss daht kwee kih'-toh daht] *L*—He gives twice who gives quickly. *See also* Beneficium egenti bis dat...

b. i. 7d bis in septem diebus [biss in sep'-tem dih-ay'-buhs] *L*—Twice a week.

Bisogna andare quando il diavolo è nella coda [bee-zohn'-yah ahn-dah'-reh kwahn'-doh eel dee-ah'-voh-loh eh nel'-lah koh'-dah] *It*—You have to move when the devil is at your heels.

Bisogna battere il ferro mentre è caldo [bee-zohn'-yah baht'-teh-reh eel fehr'-roh men'-treh eh kahl'-doh] *It*—Strike the iron while it is hot. *See also* Ferrum, dum in igni . . .

Bis peccare in bello non licet [biss pek-kah'-reh in bel'-loh nohn lih'-ket] *L*—There must be no second blunder in war.

Bis pueri senes [biss puh'-eh-ree seh'-nays] *L*—Old men are boys twice; the aged often become childish.

B. I. T. Bureau international du travail [bü-roh aN-tehr-nah-syoh-nahl dü trah-vI] *Fr*—International Labor Office.

Blagodaryu vas [blah-guh-dah'-rih-yoo vahs] *Rus*—Thank you.

Blitzkreig [blits'-kreek] *Ger*—Lightning war; Hitler's strategy of rapid conquest.

B. LL. Baccalaureus Legum [bahk-kah-low'-reh-uhs lay'-guhm] *L*—Bachelor of Laws.

Blut und Eisen *Ger—See* Eisen und Blut.

b. m. beatae memoriae [beh-ah'-tI meh-moh'-rih-I] *L*—Of blessed memory.

b. m. bene merenti [beh'-neh meh-ren'-tee] *L*—To the well-deserving one.

B'nai B'rith [bnay brith] *Heb*—Sons of the covenant. The name of a Jewish fraternal and service organization that has spread through the United States and Europe since it was founded in New York in 1843.

Boa noite [boh'-uh noy'-tee] *Port*—Good night.

Boa tarde [boh'-uh tahr'-dee] *Port*—Good afternoon; good evening.

Boca de mel, coração de fel [boh'-kuh dee mell, koo-ruh-sowN' dee fell] *Port*—A mouth full of honey and a heart full of gall; sweet lips and a bitter heart.

Bom dia [boN dee'-uh] *Port*—Good morning; good day.

Bona fide [boh'-nah fih'-day] *L*—In good faith.

Bona rerum secundarum optabilia, adversarum mirabilia [bo'-nah ray'-ruhm seh-kuhn-dah'-ruhm op-tah-bih'-lih-ah ahd-wehr-sah'-ruhm mee-rah-bih'-lih-ah] *L*—Francis Bacon, in his essay *Of Adversity*, translated and expanded a sentence in Seneca, *Letters to Lucilius* 66; 28: The good things which belong to prosperity are to be wished, but the good things that belong to adversity are to be admired.

Bona roba (from *buona roba*) [boh'-nah roh'-bah] *It*—Fine clothes. A name given a prostitute.

Bona vacantia [boh'-nah wah-kahn'-tih-ah] *L*—Goods of unknown ownership that escheat to the state.

Bon avocat, mauvais voisin [bohn-ah-voh-kah muh-veh vwah-zaN] *Fr*—A good lawyer is a bad neighbor.

Bon chien chasse de race [bohN shyaN shahss duh rahss] *Fr*—A good dog hunts naturally.

Bon goût [bohN goo] *Fr*—Good taste. Applied to both culinary and esthetic matters.

Bon gré, mal gré [bohN gray mahl gray] *Fr*—Whether one will or not; willy-nilly.

Boni mores [boh'-nee moh'-rayss] *L*—Good morals, which often develop into good manners.

Boni pastoris est tondere pecus, non deglubere [bo'-nee pahs-toh'-riss est tohn'-deh-reh peh'-kuhs nohn day-gluh'-beh-reh] *L*—It is the duty of a good shepherd to shear, not to skin his flock. Suetonius, *Tiberius*, 34.

Bonis avibus [bo'-nees ah'-wih-buhs] *L*—Under good auspices.

Bonis nocet quisquis pepercerit malis [bo'-nees noh'-ket kwiss-kwiss peh-pehr'-kerr-it mah'-lees] *L*—Whoever spares the wicked harms the good. Publilius Syrus.

Bonjour [bohN-zhoor] *Fr*—Good day; good morning.

Bon marché [bohN mahr-shay] *Fr*—A good buy, a bargain; cheap.

Bon mot [bohN moh] *Fr*—A witticism or clever expression.

Bonne amie [buhn ah-mee] *Fr*—Good friend; girl friend; lover.

Bonne année [buhn ah-nay] *Fr*—Happy New Year.

Bonne à tout faire [buhn ah too fehr] *Fr*—Maid of all work.

Bonne chance! [buhn shahNss] *Fr*—Good luck!

Bonne foi [buhn fwah] *Fr*—Good faith; honest purpose.

Bonne humeur [buhn ü-muhr] *Fr*—Good humor.

Bonne nuit [buhn nwee] *Fr*—Good night.

Bonne renommée vaut mieux que ceinture dorée [buhn ruh-nuhm-may voh myuh kuh saN-tür doh-ray] *Fr*—A good name is worth more than a golden belt; better a good name than riches.

Bonne santé [buhn sahN-tay] *Fr*—May you enjoy good health.

Bonnet rouge [bon-neh roozh] *Fr*—Red cap worn by French revolutionists.

Bons dias [boNz dee′-uhs] *Port*—Good morning.

Bon soir [bohN swahr] *Fr*—Good evening.

Bon ton [bohN tohN] *Fr*—Outstanding fashion.

Bonum commune [bo′-num kom-moo′-neh] *L*—The common good.

Bonum ex integra causa, malum ex quocumque defectu [bo′-num ex in′-teh-grah kow′-sah mah′-lumm ex kwoh-kuhm′-kweh day-fek′-too] *L*—An action is good when good in every respect; it is wrong when wrong in any respect.

Bon vivant [bohN vee-vahN] *Fr*—One to whom the good life is mostly pleasure in eating and drinking; a jolly good fellow.

Bon voyage! [bohN vwah-yahzh] *Fr*—Have a good trip!

Borgen macht Sorgen [bor′-gun mahkt zor′-gun] *Ger*—Borrowing makes for sorrowing.

Böse Beispiele verderben gute Sitten [bö′-zuh bI′-shpee-luh fehr-dehr′-bun goo′-tuh zitt′-tun] *Ger*—Bad examples corrupt good customs; evil communications corrupt good manners.

Bottes de sept lieues [butt duh set lyuh] *Fr*—Seven-league boots.

Bozhe moy [boh′-zhay moi] *Rus*—Literally, my God! For goodness sake!

B. P. Baccalaureus Pharmaciae [bahk-kah-low′-reh-uhs fahr-mah-kee′-I] *L*—Bachelor of Pharmacy.

B. Q. Bene quiescat [beh′-neh kwih-ays′-kaht] *L*—May he sleep well.

B. R. D. Bundesrepublik Deutschland [buhn′-dehs ray-poo-bleek′ doitsch′-lahnt.] *Ger*—Federal Republic of Germany; West Germany.

Brevet s. g. d. g. sans garantie du gouvernement [bruh-veh sahN gah-rahN-tee dü goo-vehr-nuh-mahN] *Fr*—A patent without government guarantee as to quality.

Brevi manu [breh′-wee mah′-noo] *L*—Literally, with a short hand; off-hand; immediately. In civil law, a term applied to a fictitious transfer.

Brevis esse laboro, obscurus fio [breh′-wiss ess′-seh lah-boh′-roh op-skoo′-ruhs fee′-oh] *L*—I strive to be brief, and I become obscure. Horace, *Art of Poetry*, 25.

Brutum fulmen (*pl.* **bruta fulmina**) [bruh′-tuhm fuhl′-men, *pl.* bruh′-tah fuhl′-mih-nah] *L*—Harmless thunderbolt; vain, senseless threat. Pliny, *Natural History*, 2; 43, 113.

B. S. brevet supérieur [breh-veh sü-pay-ryuhr] *Fr*—A certificate granted to an upper elementary school teacher passing French government examinations.

Buena fama hurto encubre [bweh′-nah fah′-mah uhr′-toh en-koo′-breh] *Sp*—A good reputation may be a mask for theft.

Buena ganga [bweh′-nah gahn′-gah] *Sp*—A good bargain.

Buenas noches [bweh′-nahs noh′-chays] *Sp*—Good night.

Buenas tardes [bweh′-nahs tahr′-days] *Sp*—Good afternoon.

¡Buena suerte! [bweh'-nah swehr'-teh] *Sp*—Good luck!

Buenos días [bweh'-nohs dee'-ahs] *Sp*—Good morning; good day.

Buey viejo surco derecho [boo-ay'-ee byeh'-hoh suhr'-koh day-ray'-choh] *Sp*—An old ox plows a straight furrow.

bull. bulliat [bool'-lih-aht] *L*—Let boil. A directive for pharmacists.

Buona mano [bwoh'-nah mah'-noh] *It*—A gratuity, a tip.

Buona notte [bwoh'-nah not'-teh] *It*—Good night.

Buon capo d'anno [bwohn kah'-poh dahn'-noh] *It*—Happy New Year.

Buon capo del anno! [bwohn kah'-poh del ahn'-noh] *It*—Happy New Year!

Buon giorno [bwohn jee-ohr'-noh] *It*—Good morning.

Buon Natale [bwohn nah-tah'-lay] *It*—Merry Christmas.

Buon principio, la mitad es hecha [bwohn preen-see'-pyoh lah mee-tahd' ess ay'-chah] *Sp*—Well begun is half done. *See also* Arche hemisy pantos.

Buon viaggio [bwohn vee-ah'-djoh] *It*—Have a good voyage, a good journey.

b. v. balneum vaporis [bahl'-neh-uhm vah-poh'-riss] *L*—Vapor bath.

B. V. Bene vixit [beh'-neh weex'-it] *L*—He lived a good life.

C

c. *See* ca.

C. A. Centroamérica [sen-troh-ah-may'-ree-kah] *Sp*—Central America.

ca. circa [seer'-kah] *L*—About; approximately.

c/a. cuenta abierta [kwen'-tah ah-bee-yehr'-tah] *Sp*—Open account.

Caballero andante [kah-bah-yeh'-ro ahn-dahn'-teh] *Sp*—Knight errant.

Cabinet d'aisance [kah-bee-neh deh-zahNs] *Fr*—Rest room; toilet.

Cacoethes carpendi [kah-koh-ay'-tehs kahr-pen'-dee] *L*—A passion for criticizing.

Cacoethes loquendi [kah-koh-ay'-tehs loh-kwen'-dee] *L*—An uncontrollable desire or mania for talking.

Cacoethes scribendi [kah-koh-ay'-tehs skree-ben'-dee] *L*—The writer's itch. Juvenal, 7; 52.

C.-à-d. *See* C'est-à-dire.

Cada cabello hace su sombra en el suelo [kah'-dah kah-bay'-yoh ah'-seh soo sohm'-brah en el sway'-loh] *Sp*—Every hair casts its own shadow on the ground. *See also* Etiam capillus unus . . .

Cada cabelo faz sua sombra na terra [kah'-duh kuh-bay'-loo fahz soo'-uh soN'-bruh nah teh'-ruh] *Port*—Every hair casts its shadow. *See also* Etiam capillus unus . . .

Cada maestro tiene su librito [kah'-dah mah-es'-troh tyeh'-nay soo lee-bree'-toh] *Sp*—Every teacher has his own little book, his own special methods.

Cada uno es hijo de sus obras [kah'-dah oo'-noh ess ee'-hoh day soos oh'-brahs] *Sp*—Every one is the product of his own works. Cervantes, *Don Quixote*, 1; 4.

30

Cada uno sabe donde le aprieta el zapato [kah'-dah oo'-noh sah'-bay dohn'-day lay ah-pree-ay'-tah el sah-pah'-toh] *Sp*—Every man knows where his shoe pinches. *See also* Chacun sait . . .

Cadit quaestio [kah'-dit kwIs'-tih-oh] *L*—The argument collapses; the argument is ended for want of proof.

Caelum, non animum mutant, qui trans mare currunt [kI'-luhm nohn ah'-nih-muhm moo'-tahnt kwee trahns mah'-reh kuhr'-ruhnt] *L*—They change the sky above but not their souls who rush overseas; you can't run away from yourself. Horace, *Epistles*, 1; 11, 27.

C. A. F. Coût, assurance, fret [koo ah-sü-rahNss freh] *Fr*—Cost, insurance, freight. In English, C. I. F.

Café au lait [kah-fay oh leh] *Fr*—Coffee with milk.

Cailín bán [kay-leen bahn] *Ir*—*See* Colleen bawn.

Ça-ira [sah ee-rah] *Fr*—It will go on. A popular song of the mob during the French Revolution. The burden of the song was that hanging aristocrats from lampposts would go on and on. *See also* À la lanterne.

Calceus major subvertet [kahl'-keh-uhs mah'-yohr suhb-wair'-tet] *L*—A shoe too large trips the wearer. Applied to enterprises or projects that fall apart because they become too large and unmanageable. Horace, *Epistles*, 1; 10, 42.

Callida junctura [kahl'-lih-dah yunk-too'-rah] *L*—Literally, an artistic joining; a clever literary reference in which an old familiar word is used in a novel setting. Horace, *Art of Poetry*, 47.

Calvo turpius est nihil comato [kahl'-woh tuhr'-pih'-uhs est nih'-hil koh-mah'-toh] *L*—There is nothing more dishonorable than a bald man with a wig. Martial, 10; 83, 11.

Camino de Santiago [kah-mee'-noh day sahn-tee-ah'-goh] *Sp*—The Milky Way, often referred to as la vía láctea (*q.v.*).

Camino real [kah-mee'-noh ray-ahl'] *Sp*— The royal highway.

Cane scottato ha paura dell'acqua fredda [kah'-neh skot-tah'-toh ah pah-oo'-rah del akh'-kwah fred'-dah] *It*—The scalded dog fears cold water; a burnt child dreads the fire.

Canimus surdis [kah'-nih-muhs suhr'-dees] *L*—We are singing to the deaf; we are preaching to deaf ears. A Roman proverb. It is used in the negative in Vergil, *Eclogues*, 10; 8.

Canis in praesepi [kah'-nis in prI-say'-pee] *L*—Dog in the manger. A reference found in several literary sources, notably *Aesop* 228. Applied to the attitude of those who, even though they cannot benefit by something themselves, prevent others from enjoying it.

Canis major [kah'-nis mah'-yohr] *L*—The larger dog, a constellation containing Sirius, the brightest star in the sky.

Canis minor [kah'-nis mih'-nohr] *L*—The lesser dog, a constellation.

Canis timidus vehementius latrat quam mordet [kah'-nis tih'-mih-duhs weh-heh-men'-tih-uhs lah'-traht kwahm mohr'-det] *L*—A cowardly dog barks more than it bites. Adapted from Q. Curtius Rufus, *Exploits of Alexander*, 7; 4, 13.

Cantab. Cantabrigiensis [kahn-tah-brih-gih-en'-sis] *L*—Pertaining to Cambridge, usually referring to Cambridge University.

Cantabit vacuus coram latrone viator [kahn-tah'-bit wah'-kuh-uhs koh'-rahm lah-troh'-neh wih-ah'-tohr] *L*—The traveler with empty pockets will sing in the presence of a robber. Juvenal, 10; 22.

Cantus planus [kahn'-tuhs plah'-nuhs] *L*—Plain song; Gregorian chant.

Cap-à-pie [kap-ah-pee] *See* De pied en cap.

Capa y espada [kah'-pah ee es-pah'-dah] *Sp*—Cape and sword. Type of comedy, by Lope de Vega and Calderón, among others, characterized by involved plots in which love and honor (*see* punto de honor) are the central themes.

Cape et épée [kahp ay ay-pay] *Fr*—Melodramatic, or cloak-and-dagger literature.

Capias [kah'-pih-ahs] *L*—Literally, you may take; a writ ordering an arrest.

Capias ad satisfaciendum [kah'-pih-ahs ahd sah-tiss-fah-kih-en'-duhm] *L*—You may seize to satisfy damages.

Caput gerat lupinum [kah'-put geh'-raht lu-pee'-nuhm] *L*—Literally, let his be a wolf's head. In Old English law this meant that a man could be hunted down as if he were a wolf.

Caput mortuum [kah'-put mor'-tuh-uhm] *L*—Literally, dead head; name alchemists gave to worthless material that remained after their experiments; by transfer, a worthless person.

Caput mundi [kah'-put muhn'-dee] *L*— The head, the center of the world; a reference to imperial Rome that carried over to the papacy in medieval times.

Cara sposa [kah'-rah spoh'-sah] *It*—Dear wife.

Caro sposo [kah'-roh spoh'-soh] *It*—Dear husband.

Carpe diem, quam minimum credula postero [kar'-peh dih'-em kwahm mih'-nih-muhm kray'-duh-lah pos'-teh-ro] *L*—Take advantage of today and place no trust in tomorrow. Horace, *Odes*, 1; 11, 8.

Carte blanche [kahrt blahNsh] *Fr*—A blank page with a signature affixed, permitting the holder to write particulars at will; unlimited authority; a blanket authorization.

Carte de visite [kahrt duh vee-zeet] *Fr*— Visiting card.

Carthago. *See* Delenda est Carthago.

Casa il figlio quando vuoi, e la figlia quando puoi [kah′-zah eel feel′-yoh kwahn′-doh voo-oh′-ee ay lah feel′-ya kwahn′-doh poo-oh′-ee] *It*—Marry your son when you wish, and your daughter when you can.

Cassis tutissima virtus [kahs′-sis too-tiss′-see-mah wir′-toos] *L*—Courage is the safest helmet.

Casta est, quam nemo rogavit [kahs′-tah est kwahm nay′-mo ro-gah′-wit] *L*—She is chaste whom nobody has asked. Ovid, *Amores*, 1; 8, 43.

Castella in Hispania [kahs-tel′-lah in hiss-pah′-nih-ah] *L*—Castles in Spain; castles in the air.

Castello che dà orecchio si vuol rendere [kahs-tel′-loh kay dah oh-rek′-kee-oh see voo-ohl′ ren′-day-ray] *It*—The castle that listens to proposals has a mind to surrender; the woman who listens is lost.

Castigat ridendo mores [kahs-tee′-gaht ree-den′-doh moh′-rays] *L*—He corrects morals by ridicule. Originally written as a tribute to a noted actor of comedy, this became the motto of the *Opéra Comique* of Paris. Jean de Santeul.

Castigo te non quod odio habeam, sed quod amem [kahs-tee′-go tay nohn kwod oh′-dih-o hah′-beh-ahm sed kwod ah′-mem] *L*—I chastise you not because I hate you but because I love you. An ancient preface to a flogging.

Casus belli [kah′-suhs bel′-lee] *L*—The occasion or pretext for war; the cause of war.

Casus conscientiae [kah′-suhs kohn-skih-en′-tih-I] *L*—A case of conscience.

Casus foederis [kah′-suhs foi′-deh-riss] *L*—A case falling within the stipulations of a treaty.

Casus fortuitus [kah′-suhs fohr-tuh′-ih-tuhs] *L*—A matter of chance.

Catalogue raisonné [kah-tah-lohg reh-zuh-nay] *Fr*—A catalogue of books or other articles in which each is described. A statement of value may also be added.

Causa finalis [kow′-sah fee-nah′-liss] *L*—Final cause; the purpose for which a thing is made.

Causa mortis [kow′-sa mor′-tis] *L*—The cause of death.

Cause célèbre [kohz say-leh-br] *Fr*—A celebrated legal trial exciting wide interest.

c. a. v. *or* **cur. adv. vult** curia advisari vult [koo′-rih-ah ahd-vih-sah′-ree vuhlt] *L*—The court wishes to take counsel.

Cavalier(e) errante [kah-vah-lee-air′ (ay) ehr-rahn′-tay] *It*—A knight errant.

Cavalier(e) servente [kah-vah-lee-air′ (ay) sehr-ven′-tay] *It*—A serving cavalier. A married woman's lover; a woman's escort.

Cave ab homine unius libri [kah′-vay ahb hoh′-mih-neh oo-nee′-uhs lih′-bree] *L*—Beware of the man of one book. *See also* Timeo virum unius libri.

Caveat emptor [kah′-veh-aht aymp′-tohr] *L*—Let the buyer beware. This is all that is usually quoted. The maxim continues, *Quia ignorare non debuit quod jus alienum emit*, meaning Because he should not be ignorant of the property that he is buying.

Caveat venditor [kah′-veh-aht ven-dee′-tor] *L*—Let the seller beware.

Cave canem. [kah′-vay kah′-nem] *L*—Beware of the dog. Petronius, *Satyricon*, 29.

Cavendo tutus [kah-wen′-doh too′-tuhs] *L*—Safe by reason of caution.

Cave quid dicis, quando et cui [kah′-way kwid dee′-kis kwan′-doh et kwee] *L*—Take care what you say, when, and to whom.

c. c. compte courant [kohNt koo-rahN] *Fr*—Current account.

c. c. courant continu [koo-rahN kohN-tee-nü] *Fr*—Direct electrical current; d.c. in English.

c/c *or* **c/cte.** cuenta corriente [kwen′-tah koh-rree-en′-teh] *Sp*—Current account; checking account in U.S. English.

C. de J. Compañia de Jesús [kom-pah-nyee′-ah day hay-sooss′] *Sp*—Company of Jesus; S.J. in English, initials for *Societatis Jesus*, of the Society of Jesus.

C. d. G. Compagnia di Gesù [kohm-pahn-yee'-ah dee jay-zoo'] *It*—Society of Jesus; S. J.

Céad míle fáilte! [kee'-ad mee'-lee fahl'-tee] *Ir*—A hundred thousand welcomes!

Cedant arma togae [kay'-dant ahr'-mah toh'-gI] *L*—Let arms yield to the toga; let the military yield to the civil power. Motto of Wyoming. Cicero, *On Duties*, 1; 22, 77.

Cela va sans dire [suh-lah vah sahN deer] *Fr*—That goes without saying.

Celsae graviore casu decidunt turres [kel'-sI grah-wih-oh'-rey kah'-soo day'-kih-duhnt tuhr'-rays] *L*—Lofty towers fall with a greater crash; the bigger they come, the harder they fall. Horace, *Odes*, 2; 10, 10f.

Celui qui a trouvé un bon gendre, a gagné un fils; mais celui qui en a rencontré un mauvais a perdu une fille [suh-lwee kee ah troo-vay uhN bohN zhahN-dr ah gah-nyay uhN fees meh suh-lwee kee ahN-nah rahN-kohN-tray uhN muh-veh ah pehr-dü ün fee] *Fr*—He who has found a good son-in-law has gained a son, but he who has acquired a bad one has lost a daughter.

Censor deputatus [ken'-sohr day-puh-tah'-tuhs] *L*—A censor charged with the task of examining a book to determine before publication if it contains anything contrary to faith or morals.

Cent jours [sahN zhoor] *Fr*—The hundred days; the period between Napoleon's second usurpation and the restoration of Louis XVIII.

Cepi corpus [kay'-pee kor'-puhs] *L*—Literally, I took the body. The endorsement of a sheriff upon a writ of arrest of a person.

Ce qui fait que les amants et les maîtresses ne s'ennuient point d'être ensemble, c'est qu'ils parlent toujours d'eux-mêmes [suh kee feh kuh lay zah-mahN ay lay meh-trehss nuh sahn-nwee pwaN deh-tr ahN-sahN-bl seh keel pahrl too-zhoor duh-mem] *Fr*—Lovers and mistresses keep from being bored when they are together because they always talk of themselves. La Rochefoucauld, *Maxims*, 312.

Ce qui n'est pas clair, n'est pas français [suh kee neh pah klair neh pah frahN-seh] *Fr*—If it is not clear, it is not French.

C. E. R. N. Centre européen des recherches nucléaires [sahN-tr uh-ruh-pay-aN day ruh-shehrsh nü-klay-air] *Fr*—European Center for Nuclear Research.

Certiorari [ker-tih-oh-rah'-ree] *L*—Literally, to be made more certain; a writ ordering a case transferred to a higher court.

C'est à dire [seh-tah deer] *Fr*—That is to say.

C'est ça [seh sah] *Fr*—That's it; that's right; that's the way it is.

C'est dommage [seh doh-mahzh] *Fr*—It's a pity.

C'est double plaisir de tromper le trompeur [seh doo-bl pleh-zeer duh trohN-pay luh trohN-puhr] *Fr*—It is a double pleasure to deceive a deceiver. La Fontaine, *Fables*, 2; 15.

C'est égal [seh tay-gahl] *Fr*—It's all the same.

C'est la guerre [seh lah ghehr] *Fr*—Blame it on the war.

C'est la profonde ignorance qui inspire le ton dogmatique [seh lah proh-fohNd ee-nyoh-rahNss kee aN-speer luh tohN duhg-mah-teek] *Fr*—A dogmatic tone is inspired by profound ignorance. La Bruyère, *Characters of Society*, 76 (1), p. 177 in Garapon's edition (1962).

C'est la vie [seh lah vee] *Fr*—That's life for you; that's the way life is.

C'est le dernier pas qui coûte [seh luh dehr-nyay pah kee koot] *Fr*—It is the last step that is difficult. Oliver Wendell Holmes would revise the proverb, Il n'y a que le premier pas qui coûte (*q.v.*).

C'est magnifique, mais ce n'est pas la guerre [seh mah-nyee-feek meh suh neh pah lah gehr] *Fr*—It is magnificent but it is not war. A comment of the French general Bosquet on the disastrous charge of the Light Brigade at Balaclava.

C'est presque toujours la faute de celui qui aime de ne pas connaître quand

on cesse de l'aimer [seh presk too-zhoor lah foht duh suh-lwee kee ehm duh nuh pah kuh-neh-tr kahN tohN sess duh leh-may] *Fr*—It is almost always the fault of the one who loves not to know when he is no longer loved. La Rochefoucauld, *Maxims*, 371.

C'est trop fort [seh troh fohr] *Fr*—That's really too bad.

Cestui que (qui) trust (*pl.* **Cestuis que trustent)** [sehs-twee kee trust, sehs-twiz kee trus-tent] *Anglo Fr*—One who has interest in property legally vested in a trustee.

Cestui que use [sehs-twee kee yooz] *Anglo-Fr*—A person having the use of property held by another.

Cestui que vie [sehs-twee kee vee] *Anglo Fr*—A person whose life determines the duration of an estate.

C'est une grande habilité que de savoir cacher son habilité [seh tün grahNd ah-bee-lee-tay khuh duh sah-vwahr kah-shay sohn ah-bee-lee-tay] *Fr*—It takes great skill to know how to conceal one's skill. La Rochefoucauld, *Maxims*, 245.

C'est une tempête dans un verre d'eau [seh-tün tahN-pet dahN-zuhN vehr doh] *Fr*—It is a tempest in a glass of water; a tempest in a teapot. Said of an insurrection in Geneva. Paul, Duke of Russia.

Cetera desunt [kay'-teh-rah day'-suhnt] *L*—The rest is missing. Found at the end of unfinished literary works or of ancient manuscripts, the endings of which have been lost.

Ceteris paribus [kay'-teh-rees pah'-ree-buhs] *L*—Other things being equal.

Ceterum censeo [kay'-teh-ruhm keyn'-seh-oh]. *See* Delenda est Carthago.

Ceux qui s'appliquent trop aux petites choses deviennent ordinairement incapables des grandes [suh kee sah-pleek troh oh pteet shohz duh-vyen ohr-dee-nehr-mahN aN-kah-pah-bl day grahNd] *Fr*—Those who busy themselves too much with petty things usually become incapable of great ones. La Rochefoucauld, *Maxims*, 41.

cf. confer [kon'-fer] *L*—Consult.

C. G. I. L. Confederazione generale italiana del lavoro [kon-fay-day-rah-tsee-oh'-neh jay-nay-rah'-leh ee-tah-lee-ah'-nah del lah-voh'-roh] *It*—Federation of Italian Trade Unions.

C. G. T. Confédération générale du travail [kohN-fay-day-rah-sy-ohN zhay-nay-rahl dü trah-vI] *Fr*—General Labor Confederation, the largest labor union in France.

Chacun à sa marotte [sha-kuhN-nah sah-mah-rot] *Fr*—Everyone follows his fancy; everyone has a bee in his bonnet.

Chacun à son goût [sha-kuhN-nah sohN goo] *Fr*—Every man to his taste; there is no disputing tastes.

Chacun pour soi, et Dieu pour tous [sha-kuhN poor swah ay dyuh poor toos] *Fr*—Everybody for himself, and God for everyone.

Chacun sait le mieux où le soulier le blesse [sha-kuhN say luh myuh oo luh soo-lyay luh bless] *Fr*—Each person knows best where his shoe hurts. *See also* Cada uno sabe . . .

Chacun selon ses facultés, à chacun selon ses besoins [sha-kuhN slohN say fah-kül-tay ah sha-kuhN slohN say buh-zwaN] *Fr*—Everyone should contribute according to his abilities and receive according to his needs. The ideal of a communistic society. Morelly, *Code de la Nature*, as quoted in Will Durant's *The Story of Civilization*, vol. 10, p. 81.

Chacun tire de son côté [sha-kuhN teer duh sohN koh-tay] *Fr*—Everybody pulls for his own side.

Chaire [khI'-reh] *Gk*—Welcome; hail; farewell. A greeting either at meeting or parting.

Chaise longue [shehz lohNg] *Fr*—Literally, a long chair; a chair with an extension for the legs.

Chambres meublées [shahN-br muh-blay] *Fr*—Furnished rooms.

Champs Elysées [shanN zay-lee-zay] *Fr*—Literally, Elysian Fields; a beautiful avenue in Paris.

Chanson de geste [shahN-soN duh zhest] *Fr*—In French literature an epic poem telling of the exploits of medieval knights. The most famous of these epics is *The Song of Roland.*

Chanson sans paroles [shahN-sohN sahN pah-rohl] *Fr*—Song without words.

Chansons de toile [shahN-sohN duh twahl] *Fr*—Songs sung by women as they spun. These medieval stories generally dealt with a maiden's love for a chevalier and the attendant frustrations.

Chant du cygne [shahN dü seen-yuh] *Fr*—Swan song; a final appearance or effort by an artist or public leader, often a farewell to the stage or public service. It is based on the legend that the swan, unmelodious in its life, sings beautifully just before its death.

Chapeau melon [shah-poh muh-lohN] *Fr*—A bowler hat, a derby.

Chapeau rouge de cardinal [shah-poh roozh duh kahr-dee-nahl] *Fr*—Cardinal's red hat, a symbol of the office.

Chapeaux bas! [shah-poh bah] *Fr*—Hats off!

Chapelle ardente [shah-pell ahr-dahNt] *Fr*—Literally, a burning chapel, so called because of the great number of candles burning about a body lying in state.

Chaque heure je vous aime de plus en plus [shahk uhr zhuh voo zehm duh plü zahN plü] *Fr*—Each hour I love you more and more. Popular inscription on a pendant, advertised as expressing a beautiful sentiment in romantic French.

Char-à-bancs [shah-rah-bahN] *Fr*—A long open vehicle with seats across the width, designed for sight-seeing.

Chargé d'affaires [shahr-zhay dah-fair] *Fr*—A temporary, duly accredited substitute for a high-ranking diplomat.

Chasseurs à cheval [shah-suhr ah shvahl] *Fr*—Light cavalry.

Châteaux en Espagne [shah-toh zahN-neh-spah-nyuh] *Fr*—Castles in Spain; castles in the air.

Chat échaudé craint l'eau froide [shah tay-shoh-day kraN loh frwahd] *Fr*—The scalded cat fears cold water.

Chef de cuisine [shef duh kwee-zeen] *Fr*—Head cook.

Chef d'oeuvre [sheh duh-vr] *Fr*—Masterpiece.

Chef-lieu [shehf lyuh] *Fr*—Chief town; principal residence.

Cheka (Two initial letters, che and ka, of the words *Chrezvy-chainaia Kommissiia*) [chrez-vuh-chah′-ee-nah-yah kah-mees′-syuh] *Rus*—Extraordinary Commission. Soviet secret police replaced by OGPU (*q.v.*) in 1922.

Che peccato! [kay pek-kah′-toh] *It*—What a pity!

Cherchez la femme [shehr-shay lah fahm] *Fr*—Look for the woman in the case. Alexandre Dumas, père.

Chercher midi à quatorze heures [shehr-shay mee-dee ah kah-torz uhr] *Fr*—Literally, to look for midday at 2 o'clock. To find difficulties where there are none.

Chère amie [shehr ah-mee] *Fr*—Literally, a dear friend (*f*); frequently, a mistress.

Cher maître [shehr meh-tr] *Fr*—Dear master.

Che sarà sarà [kay sah-rah′ sah-rah′] *It*—What will be, will be.

Cheval de bataille [shuh-vahl duh bah-tI] *Fr*—A war horse. Metaphorically applied to a subject or argument that is overused, or ridden to death.

Cheval-de-frise, *pl* **chevaux** [shuh-vahl, shuh-voh, duh freez] *Fr*—Literally, horse of Friesland. A portable barrier of pointed poles, sharp lengths of iron, or barbed wire, serving as defense against cavalry.

Chevalier d'industrie [shvah-lyay daN-düs-tree] *Fr*—A swindler; a man who lives by his wits.

Chez nous [shay noo] *Fr*—At our home.

Chi ama, crede [kee ah′-mah kray′-day] *It*—He who loves, trusts.

Chi ama me, ama il mio cane [kee ah'-mah may ah'-mah eel mee'-oh kah'-nay] *It* —Love me, love my dog.

Chi ascolta alla porta, ode il suo danno [kee ah-skohl'-tah ah-lah pohr'-tah oh'-day eel soo'-oh dahn'-noh] *It*—The man who eavesdrops hears nothing good about himself.

Chiave d'oro apre ogni porta [kee-ah'-vay doh'-roh ah'-pray on'-yee pohr'-tah] *It*—A key of gold opens any door.

Chi ben vive, ben predica [kee bayn vee'-vay bayn pray'-dee-kah] *It*—He gives a good sermon who lives a good life. *See also* Bien predica . . .

Chi compra il magistrato, forza è che venda la giustizia [kee kom'-prah eel mah-jees-trah'-toh fohr'-tsah eh kay venn'-dah lah joo-stee'-tsee-ah] *It*—He who buys public office is obligated to sell justice.

Chi dice i fatti suoi, mal tacerà quelli d'altrui [kee dee'-chay ee faht'-tee soo-oh'-ee mahl tah-chay-rah' kwell'-lee dahl-troo'-ee] *It*—The man who talks about his private affairs will hardly keep the business of others secret.

Chi dorme coi cani, si sveglia colle pulci [kee dohr'-may koh'-ee kah'-nee see zvay'-lyah kohl'-lay pool'-chee] *It*—The man who sleeps with dogs wakes up with fleas.

Chiesa libera in libero stato [kee-ay'-sah lee'-bay-rah een lee'-bay-roh stah'-toh] *It*—A free church in a free state. Camillo Benso di Cavour.

Chi fa il conto senza l'oste, gli convien farlo (lo fa) due volte [kee fah eel kohn'-toh sen'-tsah loh'-stay lyee kohn-vee-en' fahr'-loh, loh fah, doo'-ay vohl'-tay] *It*—Those who reckon without their host must reckon twice.

Chi ha denti, non ha pane; e chi ha pane, non ha denti [kee ah den'-tee nonn ah pah'-nay ay kee ah pah'-nay nonn ah den'-tee] *It*—The man who has teeth has no bread, and he who has bread has no teeth.

Chi la dura la vince [kee lah doo'-rah lah veen'-chay] *It*—The man who endures wins; patience overcomes any hardship.

36

Chi lo sa? [kee loh sah] *It*—Who knows?

Chimaera bombitans in vacuo [kee-mI'-rah bohm'-bih-tahns in wah'-kuh-oh] *L*— A monster buzzing in a vacuum. The chimaera was a mythological animal with a lion's head, a goat's body, and a dragon's tail; hence, a fanciful being. The phrase is used contemptuously of a system or project that is supported by oratory but is out of touch with the times.

Chi molte cose comincia, poche ne finisce [kee mohl'-tay koh'-say koh-meen'-chah poh'-kay nay fee-nees'-chay] *It*—The man who begins many things finishes few of them.

Chi niente sa, di niente dubita [kee nee-yenn'-tay sah dee nee-yenn'-tay doo'-bee-tah] *It*—He who knows nothing doubts nothing.

Chi non ama il vino, la donna, e il canto/Un pazzo egli sarà e mai un santo [kee nonn ah'-mah eel vee'-noh lah dohn'-nah ay eel kahn'-toh uhn pah'-tsoh ayl'-yee sah-rah' ay mah'-ee uhn sahn'-toh] *It*— He who does not love wine, woman, and song will be a fool but never a saint. For a German expression of this conviction, *see* Wer liebt nicht Weib, Wein und Gesang . . .

Chi non fa, non falla [kee nonn fah nonn fahl'-lah] *It*—The man who does nothing makes no mistakes.

Chi non ha danari in borsa, abbia miel in bocca [kee nonn ah dah-nah'-ree een bohr'-sah ahb'-bee-ah mee-ayl' een bok'-kah] *It*—The man who has no money in his purse needs honey in his mouth.

Chi non rompe l'uova, non fa la frittata [kee nonn rohm'-pay lwoh'-vah nonn fah lah free-tah'-tah] *It*—If you want an omelette, you must break some eggs. *See also* On ne saurait faire . . .

Chi non sa adulare, non sa regnare [kee nonn sah ah-doo-lah'-ray nonn sah rayn-yah'-ray] *It*—The man who does not know how to flatter, does not know how to rule.

Chi si scusa senz' esser accusato, fa chiaro il suo peccato [kee see skoo'-sah senz es'-sehr ahk-koo-sah'-toh fah kee-ah'-roh eel soo'-oh pek-kah'-toh] *It*—He who excuses himself before being accused confesses his fault.

Chi tace acconsente [kee tah'-chay ahk-kon-sen'-tay] *It*—Silence gives consent.

Chi tace confessa [kee tah'-chay kon-fess'-sah] *It*—The man who keeps silent confesses his guilt.

Chi t'ha offeso non ti perdona mai [kee tah of-fay'-zoh nonn tee pehr-doh'-nah mah'-ee] *It*—The man who has offended you will never forgive you.

Chi troppo abbraccia, poco stringe [kee trop'-poh ahb-braht'-chah poh'-koh streen'-jay] *It*—He who tries to seize too much lays hold of little.

Chi va al mulino, s'infarina [kee vah ahl moo-lee'-noh seen-fah-ree'-nah] *It*—If you go to the mill, you will be covered with flour.

Chi va piano, va sano e va lontano [kee vah pee-ah'-noh vah sah'-noh ay vah lon-tah'-noh] *It*—He who travels slowly, goes surely and far.

Chi vuol il lavoro mal fatto, paghi innanzi tratto [kee vwohl eel lah-voh'-roh mahl faht'-toh pah'-ghee een-nahn'-tsee traht'-toh] *It*—If you wish work badly done, pay in advance.

Chose jugée [shohz zhü-zhay] *Fr*—A matter already judged.

Christianos ad leonem! *sic* [kris-tih-ah'-nohs ahd leh-oh'-nem] *L*—To the lions with the Christians! The cry of the mob when any disaster occurred in the Roman Empire. Tertullian, *Apology*, 40.

Chronique scandaleuse [kruh-neek skahN-dah-luhz] *Fr*—A work revealing scandalous details; shocking gossip.

Cía companía [kom-pah-nee'-ah] *Sp*—Company.

Ci-devant [see-duh-vahN] *Fr*—Former; formerly. As a noun, it refers to an aristocrat stripped of his rank and prerogatives at the time of the French Revolution.

cie. compagnie [kohN-pah-nyee] *Fr*—Company.

C. I. F. Coste, seguro y flete [kos'-tay say-goo'-roh ee flay'-tay] *Sp*—Cost, insurance and freight.

C. I. G. Corpus Inscriptionum Graecarum [kor'-puhs in-skrip-tih-oh'-num grI-kah'-ruhm] *L*—A collection of Greek inscriptions.

Ci-gît [see-jee] *Fr*—Here lies. Beginning of the record written on a tombstone. Equivalent to Hic jacet.

C. I. L. Corpus Inscriptionum Latinarum [kor'-puhs in-skrip-tih-oh'-num lah-tee-nah'-rum] *L*—A collection of Latin inscriptions.

Cineri gloria sera venit [kih'-neh-ree gloh'-rih-ah say'-rah weh'-nit] *L*—Fame is tardy when it comes to a man's ashes. Martial, *Epigrams*, 1; 25, 8.

C. I. P. S. Conseil International de la Philosophie et des Sciences Humaines [kohN-say aN-tehr-nah-syoh-nahl duh lah fee-luh-zuh-fee ay day syahNss ü-mehn] *Fr*—International Council of Philosophy and Human Sciences.

cir. *See* ca.

Circuitus verborum [keer-kuh'-ih-tuhs wehr-boh'-ruhm] *L*—A circumlocution; a beating about the bush.

Circulus in probando [keer'-kuh-luhs in pro-bahn'-doh] *L*—Using a conclusion as a premise in an argument; a vicious circle. *See also* Circulus vitiosus.

Circulus vitiosus [keer'-kuh-luhs wih-tih-oh'-suhs] *L*—A vicious circle. *See also* Circulus in probando.

Citius venit periculum cum contemnitur [kih'-tih-uhs weh'-nit peh-ree'-kuh-luhm kuhm kohn-tehm'-nih-tuhr] *L*—Danger comes sooner when it is ignored.

Civilitas successit barbarum [kee-wee'-lih-tahs suhk-kes'-sit bahr'-bah-ruhm] *L*—Civilization has replaced the barbarian. Motto of Minnesota when it was a territory.

Civiliter mortuus [kee-wee'-lih-tehr mor'-tuh-uhs] *L*—Dead according to the civil laws of the state, i.e. deprived of legal rights.

Civis Romanus sum [kee'-wis roh-mah'-nuhs suhm] *L*—I am a Roman citizen. This boast lost its force when Caracalla granted citizenship to almost all his subjects. Cicero, *Against Verres*, 5; 57.

Civitas Dei [kee'-wih-tahs deh'-ee] *L*—The City of God, the title of a lengthy work by Saint Augustine of Hippo.

Civitas optimo jure [kee'-wih-tahs op'-tih-moh yoo'-reh] *L*—A community allied to ancient Rome and enjoying full rights.

Civitas sine suffragio [kee'-wih-tahs sih'-neh suhf-frah'-ghih-oh] *L*—A community allied to Rome without enjoying voting rights.

Civitates foederatae [kee-wih-tah'-tays foi-deh-rah'-tI] *L*—States allied by treaty to ancient Rome.

Civitates liberae et immunes [kee-wih-tah'-tays lee'-beh-rI et im-moo'-nays] *L*—Communities free and exempt from taxes in the ancient Roman state.

Civium in moribus rei publicae salus [kee'-wih-uhm in moh'-rih-buhs reh'-ee poo'-blih-kI sah'-loos] *L*—The safety of the republic rests on the morals of the citizens. Words on the University of Florida seal.

C. J. Can. Corpus Juris Canonici [kor'-puhs yoo'-riss kah-noh'-nee-chee] *L*—The body of canon law.

C. J. Civ. Corpus Juris Civilis [kor'-puhs yoo'-riss kee-wee'-liss] *L*—The body of civil law.

Clarum et venerabile nomen [klah'-ruhm et weh-neh-rah'-bih-leh noh'-men] *L*—A famous and venerable name. Words originally written about Pompey. Lucan, *Pharsalia*, 9; 199.

Clausula rebus sic stantibus [klow'-suh-lah ray'-buhs seek stahn'-tih-buhs] *L*—A conclusion that leaves matters as they stand.

Cloaca maxima [klo-ah'-kah mahx'-ih-mah] *L*—The largest sewer in ancient Rome.

c. n. s. cras nocte sumendus [krahs nok'-teh soo-men'-duhs] *L*—Medicine to be taken tomorrow night.

Coelestia canimus [koi-less'-tih-ah kah'-nih-muhs] *L*—We sing of heavenly themes.

Coeptis ingentibus adsis [koip'-tees in-gehn'-tih-buhs ahd'-sees] *L*—Aid these great beginnings. Vergil, *Aeneid*, 10; 461.

Cogito, ergo sum [koh'-ghi-toh ehr'-goh suhm] *L*—I think; hence I exist. Advanced by Descartes as *a priori* proof of existence. Descartes, *Discourse on Method*, 4.

Cognovit actionem [kog-noh'-wit ak-tih-oh'-nem] *L*—He has acknowledged the action; the defendant confesses that the plaintiff's cause of action is just.

Colleen bawn (English spelling of *Cailín bán*) *Ir*—A fair-haired girl, a sweetheart.

Coma Berenices [koh'-mah beh-reh-nee'-kayss] *L*—Literally, Berenice's hair. A cluster of stars. In mythology this queen's hair disappeared from an Egyptian temple and appeared in the heavens.

Comédie de moeurs [ko-may-dee duh muhrss] *Fr*—Comedy of manners.

Comes facundus in via pro vehiculo est [ko'-mess fah-kuhn'-duhs in wih'-ah proh weh-hih'-kuh-loh est] *L*—A pleasant, chatty companion on a trip is worth as much as the coach. Publilius Syrus.

Come sopra [koh'-may soh'-prah] *It*—As above.

Com fogo não se brinca [koN foh'-goo nowN see breeN'-kuh] *Port*—One does not play with fire.

Comitas inter gentes [ko'-mih-tahs in'-ter ghenn'-tays] *L*—Comity of nations; courtesy between nations.

Comitia centuriata [ko-mih'-tih-ah kehn-tuh-rih-ah'-tah] *L*—Assembly of the Roman people voting by centuries, of which there were 193 in the early Republic. The century originally numbered a hundred, but later it often numbered fewer voters.

Comme ci, comme ça [kum see kum sah] *Fr*—So-so.

Commedia dell' arte [kom-may'-dee-ah del ahr'-tay] *It*—Improvised theatrical comedy representing stock characters.

Comme deux gouttes d'eau [kum duh goot doh] *Fr*—As much alike as two drops of water; as like as two peas in a pod.

Comme il faut [kum eel foh] *Fr*—As it should be; proper.

Comment ça va? [kom-mahN sah vah] *Fr*—How are you? Popular usage may omit *Comment.*

Comment prétendons-nous qu'un autre garde notre secret, si nous ne pouvons le garder nous-mêmes? [kom-mahN pray-tahN-dohN noo kuhn oh-tr gahrd noh-tr suh-kreh see noo nuh poo-vohN luh gahr-day noo-mem] *Fr*—How can we require others to keep our secrets, if we cannot keep them ourselves? La Rochefoucauld, *Maxims,* 584.

Comme on fait son lit, on se couche [kum ohN feh sohN lee ohN suh koosh] *Fr*—You must lie on the bed you make.

Comme vous-y-allez! [kum voo zee ahl-lay] *Fr*—How you go at it!

Commis voyageur [kom-mee vwah-yah-zhuhr] *Fr*—Commercial traveler.

Communibus annis [kom-moo'-nih-buhs ahn'-nees] *L*—In average years.

Communi consensu [kom-moo'-nee kohn-sayn'-soo] *L*—By common consent.

Comoedia finita est [koh-moi'-dih-ah fee-nee'-tah est] *L*—The comedy is ended; reported last words of Beethoven.

Compagnon de voyage [kohN-pah-nyohN duh vwah-yazh] *Fr*—A traveling companion.

Compelle intrare [kohm-pell'-leh in-trah'-reh] *L*—Compel (them) to come in. From the parable of the wedding supper. *Vulgate, Luke,* 14; 23.

Compte rendu [kohNt rahN-dü] *Fr*—An account rendered; report of proceedings.

Con amore [kon ah-moh'-ray] *It*—With love.

Conatus sese praeservandi [koh-nah'-tuhs say'-say prI-sehr-wahn'-dee] *L*—The effort to preserve oneself; the will to live.

Concerto grosso [kon-chehr'-toh grohs'-soh] *It*—A musical composition for one or more solo instruments accompanied by an orchestra.

Concordia discors [kon-kohr'-dih-ah dis'-kohrs] *L*—Dissonant harmony; a cold war; an armed truce; a feigned friendship. Lucan, *Pharsalia,* 1; 98.

Con diligenza [kon dee-lee-jen'-zah] *It*—With diligence.

Conditio sine qua non [kon-dih'-tih-oh sih'-neh kwah nohn] *L*—An absolutely indispensable condition.

Con dolore [kon doh-loh-ray] *It*—mournfully.

Con furia [kon foo'-ree-ah] *It-Sp*—With fury; with mad haste.

Congé d'élire [kohN-zhay day-leer] *Fr*—Permission to elect a bishop granted to a chapter in the Anglican Church. This is generally a mere formality since the appointments are made by the Crown.

Congregatio de Propaganda Fide [kohn-gray-gah'-tsih-oh day proh-pah-gahn'-dah fee'-day] *L*—Congregation for Propagation of the Faith; a division of the Curia of the Roman Catholic Church.

Conjunctis viribus [kon-yoonk'-tees wee'-rih-buhs] *L*—With strength united.

Con molta passione [kon mohl'-tah pahs-see-oh'-nay] *It*—With much passion. A musical term.

Conscia mens recti famae mendacia risit [kohn'-skih-ah mayns rek'-tee fah'-mI men-dah'-kih-ah ree'-sit] *L*—The mind conscious of its innocence laughs (lit. laughed) at the lies of scandal-mongers. Ovid, *Fasti,* 4; 311.

Conseil de famille [kohN-say duh fah-mee] *Fr*—Family council.

Conseil d'état [kohN-say day-tah] *Fr*—Council of state.

Conseils aux visiteurs étrangers [kohN-say oh vee-zee-tuhr ay-trahN-zhay] *Fr*—Advice for foreign visitors.

Consejo a los visitantes extranjeros

39

[kon-say'-hoh ah lohs bee-see-tahn'-tays ex-trahn-hay'-rohs] *Sp*—Advice for foreign visitors.

Consensus facit legem [kohn-sen'-suhs fah'-kit lay'-ghem] *L*—Mutual consent makes the law. When two parties freely agree, the terms, if they do not violate the law, are no longer a matter of legal concern.

Consiglio europeo per le ricerche nucleari [kon-seel'-yoh ay-uh-roh-pay'-oh pehr lay ree-chehr'-kay noo-klay-ah'-ree] *It*—European Council for Nuclear Research.

Consilio melius vinces (vincas) quam iracundia [kohn-sih'-lee-oh meh'-lee-uhs win'-kays, win'-kahs, kwahm ee-rah-kuhn'-dih-ah] *L*—You win more easily by planning than by anger. Publilius Syrus.

Consilium abeundi [kohn-sih'-lih-uhm ah-bay-uhn'-dee] *L*—Advice to leave. A suggestion that a student cannot attain passing grades.

Consuetudo fit altera natura [kohn-suh-ay-too'-doh fit al'-teh-rah nah-too'-rah] *L*—Habit becomes second nature.

Consuetudo pro lege servatur [kohn-suh-ay-too'-doh pro lay'-gheh sehr-wah'-tuhr] *L*—Custom is to be held as a law, if no specific law exists. Legal maxim.

Consultum ultimum [kohn-suhl'-tuhm uhl'-tih-muhm] *L*—*See* Videant consules. . .

Consummatum est [kohn-suhm-mah'-tuhm est] *L*—It is finished. The last words spoken by Christ from the cross. *Vulgate, John,* 19; 30.

Con svantaggio grande si fa la guerra con chi non ha che perdere [kon zvahn-tahd'-joh grahn'-day see fah lah gwehr'-rah kon kee nonn ah kay pehr'-deh-ray] *It*—One fights at a great disadvantage with those who have nothing to lose. Guicciardini, *History of Italy.*

Conte de fées [kohNt duh fay] *Fr*—Fairy tale.

Conti chiari, amici cari [kon'-tee kee-ah'-ree ah-mee'-chee kah'-ree] *It*—Good accounts make good friends. For the French equivalent *see* Les bons comptes . . .

Conticuere omnes, intentique ora tenebant [kohn-tih-kuh-ay'-reh om'-nays in-ten'-tee-kweh oh-rah teh-nay'-bahnt] *L*—All grew silent and waited in eager expectation. Vergil, *Aeneid,* 2; 1.

Contra bonos mores [kohn'-trah boh'-nohs moh'-rays] *L*—Against good morals.

Contra fortuna no vale arte ninguna [kon'-trah for-too'-nah noh vah'-lay ahr'-tay neen-goo'-nah] *Sp*—There is no armor against fate.

Contra mundum [kohn'-trah muhn'-duhm] *L*—Against the whole world. Said of anybody who is willing to take on the whole world to bring about conditions in which he believes. Said of the younger Cato, who opposed Caesar, and also of Athanasius, who was exiled five times but kept fighting Arianism.

Cont. rem. Continuetur remedium [kohn-tih-nuh-ay'-tuhr reh-meh'-dih-uhm] *L*—Let the remedy be continued.

Copia verborum [koh'-pih-ah wehr-boh'-ruhm] *L*—Torrent of words; fluency.

Coq. in s. a. Coque in sufficiente aqua [koh'-kweh in suhf-fih-kih-en'-teh ah'-kwah] *L*—Boil in sufficient water.

Coram judice [koh'-rahm yoo'-dih-keh] *L*—Before the judge.

Coram nobis [koh'-rahm noh'-bees] *L*—In our presence.

Coram non judice [koh'-rahm nohn yoo'-dih-keh] *L*—Before a person not a judge and therefore one having no jurisdiction in the case.

Coram populo [koh'-rahm po'-puh-loh] *L*—Before the people; in public. Horace uses the expression in warning the dramatist not to stage murders or other horrors. Horace, *Art of Poetry,* 185.

Coram publico [koh'-rahm puhb'-lih-koh] *L*—Before the public.

Cordon bleu [kor-dohN bluh] *Fr*—Blue ribbon; decoration formerly worn by different orders of knights; a general decoration for distinction in one's field; now primarily an award for cooking.

Cordon sanitaire [kor-dohN sah-nee-tehr] *Fr*—Sanitary cordon; a line of officials charged with preventing the spread of contagion.

Cormach MacCarthy fortis me fieri facit, A.D. 1446 [Cormach MacCarthy fohr'-tis may fee'-eh-ree fah'-kit] *L*—The brave Cormach MacCarthy caused me to be made, 1446 A.D. The inscription on the Blarney Stone, at Blarney Castle, not far from Cobh, Ireland.

Cor ne edito [kor nay ay'-dih-toh] *L*—Do not eat your heart; better share your troubles with a friend. Pythagoras.

Corpo di Bacco! [kohr'-poh dee bahk'-koh] *It*—Body of Bacchus. A mild expletive such as Good heavens! *or* What the deuce!

Corps de ballet [kor duh bah-leh] *Fr*—Ballet company.

Corps de bâtiment [kor duh bah-tee-mahN] *Fr*—The main building.

Corps de logis [kor duh luh-zhee] *Fr*—The main portion of a building.

Corps diplomatique [kor dee-ploh-mah-teek] *Fr*—A body of officials representing the interests of a country overseas.

Corpus Christi [kor'-puhs kriss'-tee] *L*—Literally, the body of Christ; a festival celebrated in the Roman Catholic Church on the Thursday after Trinity Sunday. In some countries there are processions in the open air in which the priest carries the consecrated host. In the Middle Ages dramas were presented by the trade guilds on this feast.

Corpus delicti [kor'-puhs day-leek'-tee] *L*—The basic facts necessary to prove the existence of crime, such as catching a thief with stolen goods, or proof in a murder trial of the actual death of the victim. It does not mean the body of the victim.

Corpus Juris Canonici [kor'-puhs yoo'-riss kah-noh'-nee-chee] *L*—Code of canon law.

Corpus Juris Civilis [kor'-puhs yoo'-riss kee-wee'-lis] *L*—The body of civil law. The collection of Roman laws made under Justinian.

Corpus juris clausum [kor'-puhs yoo'-riss klow'-suhm] *L*—A collection of laws to which no new ones may be added.

Corrida de toros [koh-rree'-dah day toh'-rohs] *Sp*—A bull fight.

Corrigenda [kor-ree-ghen'-dah] *L*—A list of errors to be corrected, inserted in a book after it has been printed. Equivalent to errata (*q.v.*).

Corrumpunt bonos mores colloquia mala [kor-ruhm'-puhnt bo-nohs moh'-rays kohl-loh'-kwih-ah mah'-lah] *L*—Evil communications corrupt good manners. *Vulgate, Paul, I Corinthians,* 15; 30. This is a translation from Menander. *See* Phtheirousin ethe . . .

Corruptio optimi pessima [kor-ruhp'-tih-oh op'-tih-mee pess'-sih-mah] *L*—The corruption of the best man is the worst.

Corruptissima in republica plurimae leges [kor-ruhp-tiss'-see-mah in ray-puh'-blih-kah ploo'-rih-mI lay'-gays] *L*—The more corrupt the state, the more numerous the laws. Tacitus, *Annals,* 3; 27.

Corva sinistra [kor'-wah sih-niss'-trah] *L*—A crow on the left; an evil omen.

Cosa nostra [koh'-sah noss'-trah] *It*—Our affair; our business; the name of a secret underworld society, according to testimony presented before a U.S. Senate crime investigation committee in 1963.

Cosa rara [koh'-sah rah'-rah] *It-Sp*—A rare thing.

Così così [koh-see' koh-see'] *It*—So-so.

Così fan tutte [koh-see' fahn too'-tay] *It*—They are all like that. The title of an *opera buffa* by Mozart in which it is claimed that all women are fickle. The masculine form is *così fan tutti.*

Coup de bourse [koo duh bourss] *Fr*—A successful deal on the stock exchange.

Coup d'éclat [koo day-klah] *Fr*—A shattering blow; a brilliant stroke.

Coup de foudre [koo duh foo-dr] *Fr*—Flash of lightning; bolt from the blue.

Coup de grâce [koo duh grahss] *Fr*—A merciful shot intended to put a wounded man out of his misery (the classic example is that of the officer who puts a bullet into the head of a man still living in spite of shots from a firing squad); a finishing stroke.

Coup de main [koo duh maN] *Fr*—A sudden attack or undertaking; a bold stroke.

Coup de maître [koo duh meh-tr] *Fr*—A master stroke; a show of skill.

Coup d'épée [koo day-pay] *Fr*—A sword thrust.

Coup de pied de l'âne [koo duh pyay duh lahn] *Fr*—A kick from the hoof of an ass (a reference to the story in *Aesop 23* in which the ass kicked a sick lion). This implies kicking a man when he is down.

Coup de plume [koo duh plüm] *Fr*—A stroke of the pen; by extension this may be a satire or a fierce attack.

Coup de soleil [koo duh soh-lay] *Fr*—A sunstroke.

Coup d'essai [koo dehs-seh] *Fr*—A first attempt.

Coup d'état [koo day-tah] *Fr*—A sudden, unexpected overturning of the government of a state usually involving force or the threat of force.

Coup de tête [koo duh teht] *Fr*—Rash or impulsive act.

Coup de théâtre [koo duh tay-ah-tr] *Fr*—An unexpected, sensational act or turn of events.

Coup d'oeil [koo duh-yuh] *Fr*—A brief glance.

Courage sans peur [koo-rahzh sahN puhr] *Fr*—Courage without fear.

Cour des comptes [koor day kohNt] *Fr*—Audit office.

Cour du roi [koor dü rwah] *Fr*—King's Court or Council.

Coureur de bois [koo-ruhr duh bwah] *Fr*—A French trapper working in the Canadian woods who traded with Indians for furs.

42

Coûte que coûte [koot kuh koot] *Fr*—No matter the cost.

C. P. S. *See* Custos Privati Sigilli.

C. R. *See* Custos Rotulorum.

Crambe repetita [krahm'-bay reh-peh-tee'-tah] *L*—Warmed-over cabbage; a harping on the same theme. Juvenal 7; 154. *See also* Dis krambe . . .

Cras amet qui numquam amavit, quique amavit cras amet [krahs ah'-met kwee nuhm'-kwahm ah-mah'-wit kwee'-kweh ah-mah'-wit krahs ah'-met] *L*—Let those love now, who never loved before/ And those who always loved, now love the more. *The Vigil of Venus* translation of Thomas Parnell.

Crassa negligentia [krahs'-sah nay-gli-ghen'-tih-ah] *L*—Culpable negligence.

Credat qui vult [kray'-daht kwee wuhlt] *L*—Let whoever wishes believe.

Credebant hoc grande nefas et morte piandum,/Si juvenis vetulo non assurrexerat. [kray-day'-bahnt hok grahn'-deh neh'-fahss et mor'-teh pee-ahn'-duhm see yuh'-weh-niss weh'-tuh-loh nohn ahs-suhr-rayx'-eh-raht] *L*—They used to believe that it was great wickedness, one that should be expiated in death, if a youth did not rise in the presence of the aged. Juvenal, 13; 54.

Crede experto *L*—*See* Experto credite.

Crede ut intelligas [kray'-deh uht in-tel'-lih-gahs] *L*—Believe that you may understand.

Credo quia impossibile (absurdum) est [kray'-doh kwee'-ah im-pos-sih'-bih-leh, ap-suhr'-duhm, est] *L*—I believe because it is impossible. An expression frequently cited out of its context, where it appears in a series of paradoxes. Tertullian, *On the Body of Christ*, 5.

Credo ut intelligam [kray'-doh uht in-tel'-lih-gahm] *L*—I believe in order that I may understand. A dictum proclaiming the superiority of faith over reason. Anselm.

Credula res amor est [kray'-duh-lah rays ah'-mor est] *L*—Love is a credulous thing. Ovid, *Metamorphoses*, 7; 826.

Crème de la crème [krehm duh lah krehm] *Fr*—The cream of the cream; the very best.

Crescat scientia, vita excolatur [krays'-kaht skih-en'-tih-ah wee'-tah ex-koh-lah'-tuhr] *L*—May knowledge increase and life be ennobled. Motto of the University of Chicago.

Crescit amor nummi, quantum ipsa pecunia crescit [krays'-kit ah'-mor nuhm'-mee kwahn'-tuhm ip'-sah peh-koo'-nih-ah krays'-kit] *L*—The love of money increases as the pile grows. The best texts of the original use *crevit*, the perfect tense, instead of *crescit*, the present. Juvenal, 14; 139.

Crescite et multiplicamini [krays'-kih-teh et muhl-tih-plih-kah'-mih-nee] *L*—Increase and multiply. Motto of Maryland. *Vulgate, Genesis*, 1; 28.

Crescit eundo [krays'-kit eh-uhn'-doh] *L* —It grows as it goes. Motto of New Mexico.

Creta an carbone notandum? [kray'-tah ahn kahr'-boh-neh no-tahn'-duhm] *L*—Is it to be marked with chalk or charcoal? The Romans noted a lucky day with chalk, an unlucky day with charcoal. This is adapted from a passage in which Horace asks if extravagant men should be listed with chalk as sound of mind or with charcoal as mad men. Horace, *Satires*, 2; 3, 246.

Cri du coeur [kree dü kuhr] *Fr*—A heartfelt cry of anguish.

Crise de foie [kreez duh fwah] *Fr*—A liver attack.

Croix de guerre [krwah duh ghehr] *Fr*— A decoration given for exceptional bravery or service in war.

Crúiskín lán [krus' keen lawn] *Ir*—Little jug. Title of a drinking song by Thomas Moore.

Crux ansata [kroox ahn-sah'-tah] *L*—The cross with a hilt. The title of a work by H. G. Wells.

Crux criticorum [kroox krih-tih-koh'-ruhm] *L*—A puzzle for critics.

Crux interpretum [kroox in-tayr'-preh-tuhm] *L*—An especially difficult passage for translators.

Crux mathematicorum [kroox mah-tay-mah-tih-koh'-ruhm] *L*—A puzzle for mathematicians.

C. S. C. Congregatio Sanctae Crucis [kon-greh-gah'-tsih-oh sahnk'-tay kroo'-sis] *L*— Congregation of the Holy Cross.

C. S. Sp. Congregatio Sancti Spiritus [kon-greh-gah'-tsih-oh sahnk'-tee spee'-rih-tuhs] *L*—Congregation of the Holy Spirit.

Cuando a Roma fueres, haz como vieres [kwahn'-doh ah roh'-mah foo-ay'-rehs az koh'-moh bee-ay'-rehs] *Sp*—When in Rome, do as the Romans do. Cervantes, *Don Quixote*, 2; 54.

Cucullus non facit monachum [kuh-kool'-luhs nohn fah'-kit moh'-nah'-kuhm] *L*— The cowl does not make the monk. For a contradictory maxim *see* Vestis virum facit.

Cuéntaselo a tu abuela [kwen'-tah-say-loh ah too ah-bway'-lah] *Sp*—Tell that to your grandmother.

Cui adhaereo praeest [kwee ahd-hay'-reh-oh pray'-est] *L*—The one I support wins out. Henry VIII of England is credited with this statement of the balance of power.

Cui bono? [kwee bo'-noh] *L*—For whose good? It is incorrectly used to mean, What's the use of it? *or* What good end will be served? Cicero, *For Milo*, 12; 32.

¡Cuidado! [kwee-dah'-doh] *Sp*—Watch out; take care.

Cuidado con el tren [kwee-dah'-doh kon el trayn] *Sp*—Watch out for the train.

Cui malo? [kwee mah'-loh] *L*—Who will be harmed?

Cui peccare licet, peccat minus [kwee payk-kah'-reh lih'-ket payk'-kaht mih'-nuhs] *L*—He who is free to sin, sins less. Ovid, *Amores*, 3; 4, 9.

Cujus est regio, illius est religio [koo'-yus est reh'-gih-oh il-lee'-uhs est reh-lih'-gih-oh] *L*—Whoever governs the region controls the religion. The maxim of countries that have a state religion.

Cujus est solum, ejus est usque ad caelum [koo'-yus est soh'-luhm eh'-yus est oos'-kweh ahd kĭ-lum] *L*—Whoever owns land also owns the air above it. Legal maxim.

Cul-de-sac [kül duh sahk] *Fr*—Blind alley; dead end; passage with only one outlet.

Culpa lata [kuhl'-pah lah'-tah] *L*—A fault involving gross negligence.

Culpa levissima [kuhl-pah leh-wis'-sih-mah] *L*—A very slight fault.

Culpam majorum posteri luunt [kuhl'-pahm mah-yoh'-ruhm pos'-teh-ree luh'-uhnt] *L*—Descendants pay for the shortcomings of their ancestors; children pay for the sins of their fathers. Adapted from Q. Curtius Rufus, *The Exploits of Alexander*, 7; 5, 35.

Culpam poena premit comes [kuhl'-pahm poi'-nah preh'-mit koh'-mehs] *L*—Punishment follows at the heels of crime. Horace, *Odes*, 4; 5, 24.

Cum grano salis [kuhm grah'-noh sah'-lis] *L*—With a grain of salt; to be taken with reservations.

Cum inimico nemo in gratiam tuto redit [kuhm in-ih-mee'-koh nay'-moh in grah'-tih-ahm too-toh reh'-dit] *L*—Nobody safely returns into favor with an enemy. Publilius Syrus.

Cumini sectores [kuh-mee'-nee sek-toh'-rayss] *L*—Literally, splitters of a very small seed called cumin; hairsplitters.

Cum laude [kuhm low'-deh] *L*—With praise; a phrase appearing on diplomas indicating better than average scholarship. *Magna cum laude*, with great praise is a grade higher, while *summa cum laude* indicates the highest performance.

Cum licet fugere, ne quaere litem [kuhm lih'-ket fuh'-geh-reh nay kwI'-reh lee'-tem] *L*—When you can get off, do not seek a contest with the law.

Cum onere [kuhm oh'-neh-reh] *L*—Along with the burden or obligation.

Cum privilegio ad imprimendum solum [kuhm prih-wih-lay'-gih-oh ahd im-prih-men'-duhm soh'-luhm] *L*—The privilege of exclusive right to publication.

Cum tacent, clamant [kuhm tah'-kent klah'-mahnt] *L*—When they are silent, they shout. Cicero in denouncing Catiline says that the listening senators show their dis-

approval of their colleague by their silence, whereas if he brought such charges against certain worthy men, the Senate would have laid violent hands upon him. This is an excellent example of the figure of speech called oxymoron. Cicero, *1 Against Catiline*, 8; 21.

Cunctando restituit rem [koonk-tahn'-doh reh-stih'-tuh-it rem] *L*—*See* Unus homo nobis cunctando . . .

Cura animarum [koo'-rah ah-nih-mah'-ruhm] *L*—The care of souls.

Curia advisari vult [koo'-rih-ah ahd-vih-sah'-ree vult] *LL*—The court wishes to be advised; the court needs time to deliberate.

Curia regis [koo'-rih-ah ray'-jiss] *L*—The king's courts.

Curiosa felicitas [koo-rih-oh'-sah fay-lee'-kih-tahs] *L*—A felicity of expression that is the result of careful, studied effort to find the right phrasing. Applied to the style of Horace. Petronius, *Satyricon*, 118; 5.

Currente calamo [koor-ren'-teh kah'-lah-moh] *L*—A free style; a facile pen.

Curriculum vitae [koor-rih'-kuh-luhm wee'-tI] *L*—Biographical data including items of interest to an employer, such as education and experience.

Currus bovem trahit praepostere [koor'-ruhs boh'-wem trah'-it prI-pohs'-teh-ray] *L*—The wagon drags the ox behind it; to put the cart before the horse.

Cursus honorum [koor'-suhs hoh-noh'-ruhm] *L*—Course of honors; a succession of offices held by the public servant in Rome and separated by the proper intervals.

Cushla machree, mavourneen [koosh'-leh mah-kree' mah-voor'-neen] *Ir*—Pulse of my heart, my darling.

Custos Brevium [koos'-tohs breh'-wee-uhm] *L*—Keeper of the Briefs; an officer in the old English Court of Common Pleas in charge of documents.

Custos morum [koos'-tohs moh'-ruhm] *L*—A censor of morals.

Custos Privati Sigilli [koos'-tohs pree-wah'-tee sih-gihl'-lee] *L*—Keeper of the Privy Seal.

Custos Rotulorum [koos'-tohs roh-tuh-loh'-ruhm] *L*—Keeper of the Rolls; in England the principal justice of the peace in a county who was charged with the custody of rolls and records.

Custos Sigilli [koos'-tohs sih-gihl'-lee] *L* —Keeper of the Seal.

c. v. cheval-vapeur [shuh-vahl vah-puhr] *Fr* —Horsepower.

C V P Corporación venezolana del petróleo [kor-po-rah-see-ohn' bay-nay-zoh-lah'-nah del peh-troh'-lay-oh] *Sp*—Venezuelan Petroleum Corporation.

Cymini sectores *L*—*See* Cumini sectores.

D

Dabit deus his quoque finem [dah'-bit
deh'-uhs hees kwoh'-kweh fee'-nehm] *L*—
God will put an end to these troubles, too.
Vergil, *Aeneid*, 1; 199.

Da camera [dah kah'-may-rah] *It*—Referring
to music written for a small room; hence,
chamber music.

Da capo [dah kah'-poh] *It*—In a musical
score, a direction to return to the beginning
and repeat a passage.

Da capo al fine [dah kah'-poh ahl fee'-
nay] *It*—From the beginning to the end;
a direction in a music score.

**Da chi mi fido, mi guardi Iddio: da chi
non mi fido mi guarderò io** [dah kee mee
fee'-doh mee gwahr'-dee ihd-dee'-oh dah kee
nonn mee fee'-doh mee gwahr'-day-roh'
ee'-oh] *It*—From those I trust, may God
protect me; from those I do not trust, I
will protect myself.

Daemon languebat . . . [dI'-mohn lahng-
gay-baht] *L*— *See* Aegrotat daemon…

Daemon meridianus [dI'-mohn meh-ree-
dih-ah'-nuhs] *L*—The mid-day devil, who
reportedly tempted the monks of the desert
when the sun was hottest.

Dail Eireann [doll air'-un] *Ir*—House of
Representatives in the *Oireachtas* [eh'-
rukh-thus], the Irish Parliament.

Dal detto al fatto vi è un gran tratto
[dahl deht'-toh ahl faht'-toh vee eh oon
grahn traht'-toh] *It*—It's a long haul from
words to deeds.

Dalla mano alla bocca si perde la zuppa
[dahl'-lah mah'-noh ahl'-lah bok'-kah see
pair'-day lah tsoop'-pah] *It*—The soup is
lost from the hand to the mouth; there's
many a slip 'twixt cup and lip.

Dalla rapa non si cava sangue [dahl'-
lah rah'-pah nonn see kah'-vah sahn'-gway]
It—You cannot get blood out of a turnip.

Da locum melioribus [dah loh'-kuhm
meh-lih-oh'-rih-buhs] *L*—Give place to
your betters. Terence, *Phormio*, 3; 2, 37.

Dame de compagnie [dahm duh kohN-
pah-nyee] *Fr*—Woman serving as a paid
companion.

Dame d'honneur [dahm duh-nuhr] *Fr*—
Maid of honor; lady-in-waiting.

Dames de la halle [dahm duh lah ahl]
Fr—Market women.

Damnant quod non intelligunt [dahm'-
nahnt kwod nohn in-tel'-lih-guhnt] *L*—
They damn what they do not understand.
Adapted from Quintilian, 10; 1, 26.

Damnosa hereditas [dahm-noh'-sah hay-
ray'-dih-tahs] *L*—An inheritance damaging
because of consequent obligations.

Damnum absque injuria [dahm'-nuhm
ahps'-kweh in-yoo'-rih-ah] *L*—Loss without legal wrong; damage done without
intended wrong.

Damocles. *See* De pilo pendet.

Dance du ventre [dahNs dü vahN-tr] *Fr*—
Belly dance.

Danke schön [dahn'-kuh shöhn] *Ger*—
Thank you.

Danse macabre [dahNss mah-kah-br] *Fr*—
A ghoulish dance, the dance of death. A
popular theme that probably originated in
early 14th-century poetry. In subsequent
painting and literature, Death was often
pictured leading men of various stations
of life to the grave.

Dans l'amour il y a toujours celui qui baise et celui qui tend la joue [dahN lah-moor eel ee ah too-zhoor suh-lwee kee behz ay suh-lwee kee tahN lah zhoo] *Fr*—In love there is always one who gives the kiss and one who extends the cheek. The cynical attitude that in love one person loves and the other merely permits affection.

Dans le doute, abstiens-toi [dahN luh doot ahp-styaN twah] *Fr*—When in doubt, don't.

Dare pondus idonea fumo [dah'-reh pohn'-duhs ih-doh'-neh-ah foo'-moh] *L*—Useful only to give weight to smoke. An expression used in hostile criticism of a book. Persius, 5; 20.

Darne consiglio/Spesso non sa chi vuole,/Spesso non vuol chi sa [dahr'-nay kon-sil'-yoh spes'-soh nonn sah kee vwoh'-lay spes'-soh nonn vwohl kee sah] *It*—Often those who do not know are ready to give counsel, while those who do know are unwilling. Metastasio.

Das bessere ist des Guten Feind [dahs beh'-suhr-uh ist des goo'-tun fInt] *Ger*—The better is the enemy of the good. Let matters take their course.

Das Beste ist gut genug [dahs bes'-tuh ist goot guh-nook'] *Ger*—The best is good enough. In the source this sentence begins with *In der Kunst*, meaning In matters of art. Goethe, *Italian Journey*, Letter 2.

Das Ding an sich [dahs ding ahn zikh] *Ger*—The thing in itself, the metaphysical reality. A term in Kantian philosophy.

Das Erste und Letzte, was vom Genie gefordert wird, ist Wahrheitsliebe [dahs ehr'-stuh unt letts'-tuh vahs fuhm zhay-nee' guh for'-dert virt ist vahr-hIts-lee'-buh] *Ger* —The first and last thing that is asked of genius is the love of truth. Goethe, *Maxims in Prose*, 52.

Das Ewig-Weibliche/zieht uns hinan [dahs ay'-vik-vIp'-li-khuh tseeht uhns hee-nahn'] *Ger*—The eternal feminine/draws us up and on. Goethe, *Faust*, pt. 2; 5, closing lines.

Das fünfte Rad am Wagen [dahs fünf'-tuh raht ahm vah'-gun] *Ger*—The fifth wheel on the wagon; a useless appendage.

Das Gelobte Land [dahs guh-lohp'-tuh lahnt] *Ger*—The promised land.

Das Gesetz nur kann uns Freiheit geben [dahs guh-zetts' noor kahn uhns frI'-hIt gay'-bun] *Ger*—Only the law can give us freedom. Goethe.

Das ist mir Wurst oder Wurscht [dahs ist meer voorst oh'-duhr voorsht] *Ger*—That's all the same to me; I am indifferent. *Wurst* and *Wurscht* are the north and south German pronunciations of the word for sausage.

Das kleine Weib [dahs klI'-nuh vIp] *Ger*—The little woman, a term of endearment Goethe gave his young mistress Christiane Vulpius.

Das kleinste Haar wirft seinen Schatten [dahs klIn'-stuh hahr virft zI'-nun shaht'-tun] *Ger*—The smallest hair casts its own shadow. Goethe includes this in his *Maxims. See also* Etiam capillus unus . . .

Das Weib sieht tief; der Mann sieht weit [dahs vIp zeet teef dayr mahn zeet vIt] *Ger* —Woman sees deep; man sees far.

Das Werk lobt den Meister [dahs vehrk lohpt dayn mIs'-tuhr] *Ger*—The work praises the master.

Data et accepta [dah'-tah et ak-kep'-tah] *L*—Expenses and receipts.

Davus sum, non Oedipus [dah'-wuhs suhm nohn oi'-dih-puhs] *L*—I am Davus, not Oedipus; I am a simple man, not a problem solver. Terence, *Andria*, 2; 24.

D. C. *See* Da capo.

D. C. Democrazia Cristiana [day-moh-krah'-tsee-ah krees-tee-ah'-nah] *It*—Party of Christian Democrats.

d/c. dinero contante [doo nay'-roh kon-tahn'-tay] *Sp*—Cash.

d. C. dopo Cristo [doh'-poh kree'-stoh] *It.* —A.D. (*q.v.*).

DD. dedicavit [day-dih-kah'-wit] *L*—He dedicated.

D. d. deo dedit [deh'-oh deh'-dit] *L*—He gave to God.

D. D. Doctor Divinitatis [dok'-tohr dee-vee-nih-tah'-tis] *L*—Doctor of Divinity.

d. d. dono dedit [doh'-noh deh'-dit] *L*—He gave as a gift.

D. D. D. Dono dat, dedicat [doh'-noh daht day'-dih-kaht] *L*—He gives as a gift and dedicates. Sometimes this is understood in the past tense: *Dono dedit, dedicavit.* D.D.D. is also interpreted as *Dat, dicat, dedicat:* He gives, devotes and dedicates; also *dat, donat, dicat:* He gives, presents and dedicates.

D. D. R. Deutsche Demokratische Republik [doit'-shuh day-moh-krah'-tih-shuh ray-poo-bleek'] *Ger*—German Democratic Republic; East Germany.

Debitor non praesumitur donare [day'-bih-tor nohn prI-soo'-mih-tuhr doh-nah'-reh] *L*—The presumption is that a debtor is not making gifts.

De bon augure [duh boh-noh-gür] *Fr*—Auspicious; an event of good omen.

De bonis propriis [day boh'-nees proh'-prih-ees] *L*—Out of his own goods; payment made from his own funds.

De bonne grâce [duh buhn grahss] *Fr*—With good grace.

De bons propositos está o inferno cheio [dee boNz proo-poh'-zee-toos ish-tah' oo eeN-fair'-noo shay'-yoo] *Port*—Hell is paved with good intentions. *See* Di buona voluntà . . .

Deceptio visus [day-kehp'-tih-oh wee'-suhs] *L*—Optical illusion.

Decessit sine prole [day-kes'-sit sih'-neh proh'-leh] *L*—He died without issue.

Decies repetita placebit [deh'-kih-ays reh-peh-tee'-tah plah-kay'-bit] *L*—In its original context this means that even though a painting is seen ten times, it is still a pleasing picture; by extension, even though a story has been told ten times, it is still a good one. Horace, *Art of Poetry*, 365.

Decipimur specie recti [day-kih'-pih-moor speh'-kih-ay rayk'-tee] *L*—We are deceived by what appears virtuous; crime is often disguised as virtue.

Decipit frons prima multos [day'-kih-pit frohns pree'-mah muhl'-tohs] *L*—The first appearance deceives many; first appearances are often deceptive. Phaedrus, 4; 2, 6.

De Civitate Dei [day kee-wih-tah'-teh deh'-ee] *L*—*On the City of God*, a work written by Augustine of Hippo in answer to those who claimed that the invasions of the barbarians were punishment by the gods for the neglect of the pagan religion.

De Consolatione Philosophiae [day kohn-soh-lah-tih-oh'-neh fih-lo-so-fih'-I] *L*—*The Consolation of Philosophy*, a work by Boethius, who lived during the first quarter of the sixth century.

Decori decus addit avito [deh'-kor-ee deh'-kuhs ahd'-dit ah-vee'-toh] *L*—He adds honor to the honors of his ancestors.

De die in diem [day dih'-ay in dih'-em] *L*—From day to day.

De droit [duh drwah] *Fr*—By right; rightfully.

De duobus malis semper minus malum est eligendum [day duh-oh'-buhs mah'-lees sem'-pehr mih'-nuhs mah'-luhm est ay-lih-gen'-duhm] *L*—Of two evils one ought always to choose the lesser. Thomas à Kempis, *Imitation of Christ*, 3; 12, 2. *See also* Minima ex malis.

De facto [day fahk'-toh] *L*—In fact; actually; as a matter of fact, but not necessarily de jure (*q.v.*).

De fait [duh feh] *Fr*—Truly; in reality. As opposed to *de droit*, in law or by legal right.

Défauts de ses qualités *Fr*—*See* Il a les défauts . . .

Défense de — [day-fahNss duh—] *Fr*—One is forbidden to—. This is followed by an infinitive, e.g., *Défense d'afficher* [dah-fee-shay], Post no bills; *Défense d'entrer* [dahN-tray], Keep out; *Défense de fumer* [duh fü-may], No smoking.

Defensor Fidei [day-fen'-sor fih'-deh-ee] *L*—Defender of the Faith. This title on British coins was conferred by Pope Leo X on Henry VIII for his Latin tract on the Seven Sacraments.

De fide [day fih'-day] *L*—A matter of faith; said of Catholic dogmas that may not be questioned by the faithful.

De fond en comble [duh fohN ahN kohN-bl] *Fr*—From top to bottom.

De fontibus non disputandum [day fohn'-tih-buhs nohn diss-puh-tahn'-duhm] *L*—There is no disputing about sources. This is to be understood in areas where science has no definite knowledge, as, for example, the beginning of human speech.

De gaieté de coeur [duh geh-tay duh kuhr] *Fr*—From cheerfulness of heart; out of sheer gaiety.

D'égal à égal [day-gal ah ay-gal] *Fr*—Equally.

Dégénéré supérieur [day-zhay-nay-ray sü-pay-ryuhr] *Fr*—A person of superior mental ability with degenerate tendencies.

De gran subida, gran caída [day grahn soo-bee'-dah grahn kah-ee'-dah] *Sp*—The greater the height, the longer the fall; the taller they come, the harder they fall.

De gustibus non est disputandum [day guhs'-tih-buhs nohn est diss-puh-tahn'-duhm] *L*—There is no disputing about tastes. Different people have different tastes in matters of food and drink; arguing will not change anyone's taste buds. By extension this saying is often applied to intellectual and esthetic questions.

Dei gusti non se ne disputa [day'-ee gus'-tee nohn say nay dee-spoo'-tah] *It*—See De gustibus non est disputandum.

De haute lutte [duh oht lüt] *Fr*—By force of arms; after a great struggle.

De haut en bas [duh oh ahN bah] *Fr*—Downwards; from top to bottom; disdainfully.

Dei gratia [deh'-ee grah'-tih ah] *L*—By the grace of God.

Dei judicium [deh'-ee yoo-dih'-kih-uhm] *L*—The judgment of God. This was the name given to the ordeal, sometimes of fire or of water; a superstitious method of determining guilt by exposing a person to serious bodily harm or even death. Survival was considered proof of innocence.

De integro [day in'-teh-groh] *L*—Beginning anew.

De internis non judicat praetor [day in-tehr'-nees nohn yoo'-dih-kaht prI'-tor] *L*—The court does not pass judgment on a defendant's intentions. "I didn't mean to do it" is not regarded as an excuse in court.

Dei plena sunt omnia [deh'-ee play'-nah suhnt om'-nih-ah] *L*—All things are filled with divinity.

Déjà vécu [day-zha vay-kü] *Fr*—An impression that something has been experienced previously.

Déjà vu [day-zha vü] *Fr*—Literally, already seen. Sometimes applied to a mental disorder in which a person imagines he has seen certain scenes or events before. Art critics sometimes dismiss a work with this phrase.

De jure [day yoo'-reh] *L*—Rightfully; legally. It often appears in the same context with De facto (*q.v.*).

De la mano a la boca se pierde la sopa [day lah mah'-noh ah lah boh'-kah say pee-ehr'-day lah soh'-pah] *Sp*—See Dalla mano alla bocca . . .

De lana caprina [day lah'-nah kah-pree'-nah] *L*—The subject concerns goat's wool; a discussion on a matter of no importance.

Delator temporis acti [day-lah'-tohr tem'-po-ris ahk'-tee] *L*—An accuser of the past. A pun on Laudator temporis acti (*q.v.*)

De l'audace, encore de l'audace, toujours de l'audace [duh loh-dass ahN-kor duh loh-dass too-zhoor duh loh-dass] *Fr*—Boldness, more boldness, always boldness. Danton.

Del credere [dell kray'-deh-reh] *It*—Of trust. A legal term applied to an agent who, for an extra charge, undertakes to bring about payment for goods which he has sold.

Del dicho al hecho hay gran trecho [del dee'-choh ahl eh'-choh ah'-y grahn treh'-choh] *Sp*—There is a big gap between saying and doing.

Delenda est Carthago [day-len'-dah est kahr-tah'-goh] *L*—Carthage must be destroyed. The final words of speeches given by Cato the Elder in the Roman senate.

Often written: *Ceterum censeo Carthaginem esse delendam,* As for the rest I think Carthage must be destroyed.

Deliberando saepe perit occasio [day-lee-beh-rahn'-doh sI'-peh peh'-rit ok-kah'-sih-oh] *L*—Opportunity is often lost by too long debate. Publilius Syrus.

Deliciae epularum [day-lih'-kih-I eh-puh-lah'-ruhm] *L*—The delight, the pleasurable items of the banquet.

Deliciae generis humani [day-lih'-kih-I geh'-neh-ris hoo-mah'-nee] *L*—The delight of the human race. Suetonius' tribute to the Emperor Titus, who won general esteem because of his talent, personality, and good fortune. Suetonius, *Titus,* 1.

Deliciae meae puellae [day-lih'-kih-I meh'-I puh-el'-lI] *L*—The delight of my girl. From a poem to Lesbia's sparrow. Catullus, 2; 1.

Delirant reges, plectuntur Achivi [day-lee'-rahnt ray'-gays plek-tuhn'-tuhr ah-kee'-wee] *L*—Kings make mistakes, and the Greeks (the people) are punished. Horace, *Epistles,* 1; 2, 14.

Delirium tremens [day-lee'-rih-uhm treh'-mayns] *L*—Mental disorder, characterized by uncontrollable trembling, resulting from excessive consumption of alcohol. Often referred to as the d.t.'s.

De litteris colendis [day liht'-teh-reess ko-len'-deess] *L*—On the cultivation of letters; Charlemagne's ordinance to improve the state of learning in his realm.

Delle ingiurie il remedio è lo scordarsi [del'-lay een-joo'-ree-ay eel ray-may'-dee-oh eh loh skor-dahr'-see] *It*—The remedy for wrongs done you is to forget them.

Del senno di poi n'è piena ogni fossa [del sen'-noh dee poy neh pee-ay'-nah ohn'-yee fohs'-sah] *It*—Every ditch is full of the wisdom that came too late. We speak of twenty-twenty hindsight and Monday morning's quarterback.

De lunatico inquirendo [day loo-nah'-tih-koh in-kwee-ren'-doh] *L*—A commission appointed by a court to determine the mental competence of a person.

50

De luxe [duh lüx] *Fr*—Literally, of luxury; applied to a product that is elegant or sumptuous. *See* Edition de luxe.

De mal en pis [duh mal ahN pee] *Fr*—From bad to worse.

De mémoire de rose, on n'a jamais vu mourir de jardinier [duh may-mwahr duh rohz oh-nah zha-meh vü moo-reer duh zhahr-dee-nyay] *Fr*—You have never seen a gardener die of nostalgia for roses. Stendahl, *Histoire de la Peinture,* vol. 2, ch. 52. Perhaps a contradiction of Pope's "Die of a rose in aromatic pain." *Essay on Man,* 1; 200.

Dementia praecox [day-men'-tih-ah prI'-kox] *L*—Early insanity; mental disorder beginning in adolescence; now commonly called schizophrenia.

Dementia senilis [day-men'-tih-ah seh-nee'-liss] *L*—Insanity of the aged.

De minimis non curat lex [day mih'-nih-mees nohn koo'-raht layx] *L*—The law is not concerned with trifles.

Demi-tasse [duh-mee tahss] *Fr*—Literally, half a cup; a small cup.

De mortuis nil nisi bonum [day mor'-tuh-ees neel nih'-sih boh'-nuhm] *L*—Say nothing but what is good about the dead. Chilo, fl. 600 B.C.

Denarius Dei [day-nah'-ree-uhs deh'-ee] *L*—God's penny; a small sum of money given by the purchaser to make a contract of sale valid. In French it is known as the *Denier à Dieu.*

De nihilo nihil [day nih'-hih-loh nih'-hil] *L*—*See* Ex nihilo nihil fit.

De nobis fabula narrabitur [day noh'-bees fah'-buh-lah nahr-rah'-bih-tuhr] *L*—Of us the tale will be told.

De novo [day noh'-woh] *L*—Anew.

Deo adjuvante, non timendum [deh'-oh ahd-yuh-wahn'-teh nohn tih-men'-duhm] *L*—With God's assistance there is nothing to be feared.

Deo duce, ferro comitante [deh'-oh duh'-keh fehr'-roh ko-mih-tahn'-teh] *L*—With God as our leader and sword in hand.

Deo favente [deh'-oh fah-wen'-teh] *L*— With the favor of God.

Deo gratias [deh'-oh grah'-tih-ahs] *L*— Thanks be to God.

Deo juvante [deh'-oh yuh-wahn'-teh] *L*— With God's assistance.

De omni re scibili et quibusdam aliis rebus [day om'-nee ray skee'-bih-lee et kwih-buhs'-dahm ah'-lih-ees ray'-buhs] *L*—About everything knowable and certain other items. Sometimes used in criticism of an over-ambitious book.

Deo, non fortuna [deh'-oh nohn for-too'-nah] *L*—From God, not from luck.

Deo optimo maximo [deh'-oh op'-tih-moh max'-ih-moh] *L*—To the supreme deity.

Deo volente [deh'-oh wo-len'-teh] *L*—God willing; often abbreviated D.V.

De pied en cap [duh pyay ahN kahp] *Fr*— From head to foot; completely armed. In English *cap-à-pie* is often used, and has the same meaning.

De pilo pendet [day pee'-loh pehn'-det] *L*—It hangs by a hair. Used to indicate that a matter is in a precarious situation, that the slightest mistake might mean disaster. Dionysius, the tyrant of Syracuse, gave Damocles, one of his flatterers, an opportunity to enjoy the pleasures he thought so delightful. While Damocles was being showered with attention by all the court, the tyrant ordered a sword that was suspended from the ceiling by a horse hair to be lowered. If the hair were to break, the sword would strike the courtier's head. The sword of Damocles has thus come to mean an impending danger. The story may be found in Cicero, *Tusculan Disputations*, 5; 21.

Depositum fidei [day-po'-sih-tuhm fih'-deh-ee] *L*—Deposit of the faith; the doctrines which the Church holds as originating directly or indirectly from the apostles.

De proche en proche [duh pruhsh ahN pruhsh] *Fr*—Step by step; nearer and nearer.

De profundis clamavi ad te, Domine [day proh-fuhn'-dees klah-mah'-wee ahd tay do'-mih-neh] *L*—Out of the depths have I cried unto Thee, O Lord. A penitential psalm. *Vulgate, Psalms,* 129; 1.

De proprio motu [day proh'-prih-oh moh'-too] *L*—Of one's own volition.

De race [duh rass] *Fr*—Pure; thoroughbred.

Der Baum fällt nicht vom ersten Streiche [dehr bowm fellt nikht fuhm ehr'-stun shtrI'-kuh] *Ger*—The tree does not fall at the first blow. *See also* Al primo colpo . . .

Der Feind steht im eigenen Lager [dehr fInt shtayt im I'-guh-nun lah'-guhr] *Ger*— The enemy is in one's own camp. *Karl Liebknect,* an opponent of Germany's entry into World War I.

Der Fürst ist der erste Diener seines Staats [dehr fürst ist dehr ehr'-stuh dee'-nuhr zI'-nehs shtahts] *Ger*—The prince is the first servant of his state. An ideal approved by Frederick the Great.

Der gottbetrunkene Mensch [dehr guht-buh-troon'-kuh-nuh mensh] *Ger*—The God-intoxicated man. A description of Spinoza by Novalis.

Der grosse Heide [dehr grohs'-suh hI-duh] *Ger*—The great pagan, a name given Goethe.

De rigueur [duh ree-guhr] *Fr*—Compulsory; obligatory in matters of etiquette.

Der Krieg ist lustig den Unerfahrenen [dehr kreek ist loos'-tick dehn uhn-ehr-fahr'-en-un] *Ger*—War is fine fun for the inexperienced.

Der Krug geht so lange zu Wasser bis er bricht [dehr krook gayt zoh lahn'-guh tsoo vahs' uhr biss ehr brihkht] *Ger*—The pitcher goes to the well so often that it comes home broken at last.

Der Mensch denkt, Gott lenkt [dehr mensh dengkt guht lengkht] *Ger*—Man proposes, God disposes.

Der Mensch ist was er isst [dehr mensh ist vahs ehr isst] *Ger*—Man is what he eats.

Dernier ressort [dehr-nyay ruh-sawr] *Fr*—*See* En dernier ressort.

51

Der Tag [dehr tahk] *Ger*—The day; a toast German officers drank before the First World War to the day when they would defeat their military rivals, notably the British.

Der Zeitgeist [dehr tsIt′-gIst] *Ger*—The spirit of the age.

De sa façon [duh sa fa-sohN] *Fr*—Of one's own making.

D. ès L. Docteur ès Lettres [dok-tuhr ess leh-tr] *Fr*—Doctor of Letters.

D. ès S. Docteur ès Sciences [dok-tuhr ess syahNss] *Fr*—Doctor of Sciences.

Desunt inopiae multa, avaritiae omnia [day′-suhnt ih-noh′-pih-I muhl′-tah ah-wah-rih′-tih-I om′-nih-ah] *L*—Poverty wants many things, but avarice wants everything. Publilius Syrus.

De temps en temps [duh tahN zahN tahN] *Fr*—From time to time; occasionally.

Detinet [day′-tih-net] *L*—He detains; a legal action to regain possession of specific property.

De trop [duh troh] *Fr*—Too much; too many.

Detur digniori [day′-tuhr dig-nih-oh′-ree] *L*—Let it be given to one more worthy.

Detur pulchriori [day′-tuhr puhl-krih-oh′-ree] *L*—Let it be given to the more beautiful one. A translation of words written on a golden apple which Paris awarded Aphrodite in a beauty contest with Hera and Pallas Athene.

Deum cole, regem serva [deh′-uhm ko′-leh ray′-gem sehr′-wah] *L*—Worship God and protect the king.

Deus est in pectore nostro [deh′-uhs est in peck′-to-reh nos′-troh] *L*—There is a divinity in our hearts. Ovid, *Epistles from the Pontus*, 3; 4, 93.

Deus ex machina [deh′-uhs ex mah′-kih-nah] *L*—Literally, a god from the machine. In Greek dramas when the resolution of the plot was difficult by natural means, a god or goddess was lowered on a machine to the stage and exercised supernatural

power in solving the problem. Hence, by extension, any contrived ending to a play or book.

Deus providebit [deh′-uhs proh-wih-day′-bit] *L*—God will provide.

Deus vult [deh′-uhs vuhlt] *L*—God wills it. The battle cry of the First Crusade. *See also* Dieu li volt.

Deutsches Reich [doitsh′-uhs rIkh] *Ger*—The German Empire (1871-1919). This name continued in use under the Republic.

Deutschland, Deutschland über Alles [doitsh′-lahnt doitsh′-lahnt ü-buhr ahl′-luhss] *Ger*—Germany over all. German national anthem, the music for which was taken from Haydn.

Deux s'amusent, trois s'embêtent [duh sa-müz trwah sahN-beht] *Fr*—Two enjoy themselves, three are bored; two is company, three's a crowd.

Devastavit [day-wahs-tah′-wit] *L*—Literally, he wasted. A term indicating an administrator's improper management of an estate.

D. F. *See* Defensor Fidei.

D. F. distrito federal [dee-stree′-toh fay-day-rahl′] *Sp*—Federal District.

D. G. Dei gratia [deh′-ee grah′-tih-ah] *L*—By the grace of God.

Dia duit [dee′-ah dhit] *Ir*—God save you.

Dia linn [dee′-ah lin] *Ir*—God with us. An exclamation after sneezing.

Di bravura [dee brah-voo′-rah] *It*—With brilliance. Musical term.

Di buona volontà sta pieno l'inferno [dee bwoh′-nah voh-lon-tah′ stah pee-ay′-noh leen-fehr′-noh] *It*—Hell is full of good will; hell is paved with good intentions. *See also* De bons propositos ...

Dicere solebat nullum esse librum tam malum ut non aliqua parte prodesset [dee′-keh-reh so-lay′-baht nool′-luhm ess′-seh lih′-bruhm tahm mah′-luhm uht nohn ah′-lih-kwah pahr′-teh pro-des′-set] *L*—[Pliny the Elder] used to say that there was no book so bad that it was not profitable in some particular. Pliny the Younger, *Letters*, 3; 5.

Dichosa la madre que te parió [dee-choh'-sah lah mah'-dray kay tay pah-ree-oh'] *Sp*—Happy the mother who bore you.

Dicho y hecho [dee'-choh ee ay'-choh] *Sp*—No sooner said than done.

Dicique beatus ante obitum nemo supremaque funera debet [dee-kee'-kweh beh-ah'-tuhs ahn'-teh oh'-bih-tuhm nay'-moh suh-pray'-mah-kweh foo'-neh-rah day'-bet] *L*—No man should be accounted happy until after his death. Ovid, *Metamorphoses*, 3; 136.

Dic mihi, si fias ut leo, qualis eris? [deek mih'-hih see fee'-ahs uht leh'-oh kwah'-liss eh'-riss] *L*—Tell me, if you should become a lion, what sort of lion would you be? Martial, 12; 92.

Dictum meum pactum [dihk'-tuhm meh'-uhm pahk'-tuhm] *L*—My word is my bond. Motto of the London Stock Exchange.

Dictum (verbum) sapienti sat est [dihk'-tuhm wehr'-buhm sah-pih-en'-tee saht est] *L*—A word to the wise is sufficient. Terence, *Phormio*, 3; 3.

Die Alten zum Rat, die Jungen zur Tat [dee ahl'-tun tsoom raht dee yoong'-un tsoor taht] *Ger*—Age for counsel, youth for action.

dieb. alt. diebus alternis [dih-ay'-buhs ahl-tehr'-nees] *L*—Every other day. A medical direction.

Die Baukunst ist eine erstarrte Musik [dee bow'-kuhnst ist I'-nuh ehr-star'-tuh moo-zeek'] *Ger*—Architecture is frozen music. Goethe, *Maxims in Prose*, no. 63, where he credits "a noble philosopher" with the metaphor. Schopenhauer substituted the word *gefrorne* (frozen) for *erstarrte*.

Die Götterdämmerung [dee göt'-tuhr dem'-muh-ruhng] *Ger*—The twilight of the gods.

Die kleinen Diebe hängt man, die grossen lässt man laufen [dee klI'-nun dee'-buh hengt mahn dee grohs'-sun lehsst mahn low'-fuhn] *Ger*—Petty thieves are hanged, the big ones go free.

Die Lage ist hoffnungslos aber nicht ernst [dee lah'-guh ist hohf'-nuhngs-lohs ah'-buhr nikht ehrnst] *Ger*—The situation is hopeless but not serious. A humorous German saying from World War I.

Diem perdidi [dih'-em pehr'-dih-dee] *L*—I have lost a day. Words spoken by Titus one day at supper when he reflected that he had performed no kindness that day. Suetonius, *Titus*, 8.

Die non [dih'-ay nohn] *L*—A day on which the court does not sit.

Die Philosophie des Als-ob [dee fee-lo-zuh-fee' dess ahls-ohp] *Ger*—*The Philosophy of As-If*. The title of a work by H. Vaihinger in which he upholds the view that even though certain religious doctrines are not true, they are not to be regarded as valueless.

Die Politik ist keine exakte Wissenschaft [dee po-lee-teek' ist kI'-nuh ehg-zahk'-tuh vis'-sen-shahft] *Ger*—Politics is not an exact science. Bismarck.

Die Probe eines Genusses ist seine Erinnerung [dee proh'-buh I'-nuhs guh-nuhs'-suhs ist zI'-nuh ehr-in'-uh-ruhng] *Ger*—The test of a pleasure is the remembrance of it. Jean Paul Richter.

Die Religion . . . ist das Opium des Volkes [dee ray-lee-ghee-ohn' ist dahs o'-pee-uhm dess fuhlk'-uhs] *Ger*—Religion is the opiate of the masses. Karl Marx, *Introduction to a Critique of the Hegelian Philosophy of Right*.

Dies ater [dih'-ays ah'-tehr] *L*—A dark, unfortunate day.

Dies faustus [dih'-ays fows'-tuhs] *L*—A day of good omens; a favorable day.

Dies infaustus [dih'-ays in-fows'-tuho] *L*—An unlucky day.

Dies Irae [dee'-ays ee'-ray] *L*—Day of wrath. The first words of a 13th-century hymn attributed to Thomas of Celano.

Dies natalis [dih'-ays nah-tah'-liss] *L*—Birthday.

Dies non juridicus [dih'-ays nohn yoo-rih'-dih-kuhs] *L*—A day on which court is not held.

53

Die stille Woche [dee shtihl'-luh wo'-khuh] *Ger*—Passion week.

Dieu avec nous [dyuh avek noo] *Fr*—God with us; God is on our side.

Dieu défend le droit [dyuh day-fahN luh drwah] *Fr*—God defends the right.

Dieu est toujours pour les gros batail-lons [dyuh eh too-zhoor poor lay groh ba-ta-yohN] *Fr*—God is always on the side of the big battalions. Voltaire, *Correspondence*, vol. 74, letter 15143.

Dieu et mon droit [dyuh ay mohN drwah] *Fr*—God and my right. Motto on royal arms of Britain.

Dieu le veuille! [dyuh luh vuh-yuh] *Fr*—Please God! God grant it!

Dieu li volt [dyuh lee volt] *OF*—God wills it. The cry that is said to have swept over the crowd attending the Council of Clermont in 1095 when Pope Urban urged warring European knights to undertake a crusade to free the Holy Sepulcher in Jerusalem.

Dieu mesure le vent (froid) à la brebis tondue [dyuh muh-zür luh vahN, frwah, ah lah bruh-bee tohN-dü] *Fr*—God tempers the wind (the cold) to the shorn lamb.

Dieu vous garde [dyuh voo gahrd] *Fr*—May God keep you.

Die Wacht am Rhein [dee vahkht ahm rIn] *Ger*—"The Watch on the Rhine," German national anthem at the time of the First World War.

Die Wahrheit ist eine Perle; wirf sie nicht vor die Säue! [dee vahr'-hIt ist I'-nuh pehr'-luh vihrf zee nikht fohr dee zoi'-yuh] *Ger*—Truth is a pearl; don't cast it before swine. Adapted from *Matthew*, 7; 6.

Die Weisheit der Gasse [dee vIs'-hIt dayr gahs'-suh] *Ger*—Wisdom of the street. Proverbs are often referred to in this way. The expression is adapted from *The Book of Proverbs*, 1; 20.

Die Weisheit ist nur in der Wahrheit [dee vIs'-hIt ist noor in dayr vahr'-hIt] *Ger*—Wisdom is found only in truth. Goethe, *Maxims in Prose*, 79.

Die Weltgeschichte ist das Weltgericht [dee velt-guh-shikh'-tuh ist dahs velt-guh-rikht'] *Ger*—World history is the world's judgment of the past. Schiller, *Resignation*.

Di faciant, laudis summa sit ista tuae. [dee fah'-kih-ahnt low'-diss suhm'-mah sit is'-tah tuh'-I] *L*—May the gods grant that this will be the peak of your merit. In Shakespeare's *King Henry the Sixth*, Part 3, Act 1, 3. These words are uttered by the innocent young Earl of Rutland as he dies at the hand of Lord Clifford.

Difficile est custodire quod multis placet [dif-fih'-kih-leh est kuhs-toh-dee'-reh kwuhd muhl'-tees plah'-ket] *L*—It is difficult to guard what is pleasing to many. Publilius Syrus.

Difficile est longum subito deponere amorem [dif-fih'-kih-leh est lon-guhm suh'-bih-toh day-poh'-neh-reh ah-mor'-rem] *L*—It is difficult to relinquish in an instant a long-cherished love. Catullus, 77; 13.

Difficile est proprie communia dicere [dif-fih'-kih-leh est proh'-prih-ay kohm-moo'-nih-ah dee'-keh-reh] *L*—It is difficult to give an individual style to common things; it is difficult to avoid clichés when discussing common matters. Horace, *Art of Poetry*, 128.

Difficile est saturam non scribere [dif-fih'-kih-leh est sah'-tuh-rahm nohn skree'-beh-reh] *L*—It is difficult not to write satire. An ethical man sees so much to censure in society. Juvenal, 1; 30.

Difficilia quae pulchra [dif-fih-kih'-lih-ah kwI puhl'-krah] *L*—Beautiful things are difficult.

Difficilis in otio quies [dif-fih'-kih-lis in oh'-tih-oh kwih'-ays] *L*—It is difficult to find peace of mind in leisure.

dig. digeratur [dee-geh-rah'-tuhr] *L*—Let it be digested. A medical direction.

Dignus vindice nodus [dihg'-nuhs win'-dih-keh noh'-duhs] *L*—A complication worthy of its deliverer. In a play the supernatural solution through the **deus ex machina** should not be invoked unless the problem is worthy of such divine interference. Horace, *Art of Poetry*, 191.

54

Di grado in grado [dee grah'-doh een grah'-doh] *It*—From step to step.

Di il vero e affronterai il diavolo [dee eel vay'-roh ay ahf-fron-tay-rah'-ee eel dee-ah'-voh-loh] *It*—Tell the truth and shame the devil.

Di immortales [dee im-mor-tah'-lays] *L*—The immortal gods.

Di indigetes [dee in-dih'-geh-tays] *L*—The native gods.

Di inferi [dee een'-feh-ree] *L*—The gods of the lower world.

Dii penates [dih'-ee pay-nah'-tays] *L*—Household gods among the Romans.

Dilexi justitiam et odi iniquitatem; propterea morior in exilio [dee-lex'-ee yoos-tih'-tih-ahm et oh'-dee in-ee-kwih-tah'-tem prop-teh'-reh-ah mo'-rih-or in ex-ih'-lih-oh] *L*—I have loved justice and hated iniquity; therefore I die in exile. Last words of Pope Gregory VII, who had fled to Salerno to escape the anger of Emperor Henry IV of the Holy Roman Empire. The first part of this quotation is adapted from *Vulgate, Psalms, 44; 7.*

Di manes [dee mah'-nays] *L*—Kindly shades of the deified dead; gods of the lower world.

Dime con quien andas, decirte he quien eres [dee'-may kon kyehn' ahn'-dahs day-seer'-tay ay kyehn' eh'-rays] *Sp*—Tell me who your friends are and I'll tell you what you are. Cervantes, *Don Quixote,* 2; 23. *See also* Dimmi con chi vai . . .

Dimidium facti qui coepit habet [dee-mih'-dih-uhm fahk'-tee kwee koi'-pit hah'-bet] *L*—The man who makes a start has half the work done. Horace, *Epistles,* 1; 2, 40.

Dimmi con chi vai, e ti dirò chi sei [dee'-mee kon kee vah'-ee ay tee dee-roh' kee say'-ee] *It*—Tell me your company, and I'll tell you what you are. *See also* Gleich und gleich . . . *and* Sage mir, mit wem . . .

Di nuovo [dee nwoh'-voh] *It*—Anew; over again.

Dios bendiga nuestro (este) hogar [dyohss' behn-dee'-gah nwehs'-troh, ess'-tay, oh-gahr'] *Sp*—God bless this home.

Dios le da confites a quien no puede roerlos [dyohss' lay dah kon-fee'-tays ah kyehn' noh pweh'-day roh-ehr'-lohs] *Sp*—God gives candies to those who cannot chew them. Alarcón, *The Three-Cornered Hat,* 21, last sentence.

Dio vi benedica [dee'-oh vee bay-nay-dee'-kah] *It*—God bless you.

Dipl.-Ing. Diplom-Ingenieur [dee-plom' in-zhay-nee-uhr'] *Ger*—Fully accredited engineer.

Dirigo [dee'-rih-goh] *L*—I direct. The motto of Maine, the only state holding its elections in September. Politicians keep their eyes on these elections for evidence of a trend. Prior to the New Deal, Republicans claimed, "As Maine goes, so goes the nation."

dir. prop. directione propria [dee-rehk-ti-oh'-neh pro'-prih-ah] *L*—With a proper direction.

Dis aliter visum [dees ah'-lih-tehr wee'-suhm] *L*—The gods decreed otherwise; man proposes and God disposes. Vergil, *Aeneid,* 2; 428.

Di salto [dee sahl'-toh] *It*—By leaps.

Disce ut doceas [diss'-keh uht do'-keh-ahs] *L*—Learn in order to teach. Motto of Alcuin, principal of the cathedral school at York and later leader in the revival of learning at the court of Charlemagne.

Disciplina arcani [dis-kih-plee'-nah ahr-kah'-nee] *L*—Literally, the discipline of the secret. The policy among early Christians of maintaining secrecy about their doctrines and ceremonies.

Disciplina praesidium civitatis [dis-kih-plee'-nah prI-sih'-dih-uhm kee-wee-tah'-tiss] *L*—Training is the safeguard of the state. Motto of the University of Texas.

Di seconda mano [dee say-kon'-dah mah'-noh] *It*—Secondhand.

Disjecti (disjecta) membra poetae [dis-yehk'-tee, dis-yehk'-tah, mem'-brah po-ay'-tI] *L*—Scattered members. Horace speaks of the scattered members of the poet, meaning that his work is subjected to garbled quotation. Horace, *Satires*, 1; 4, 62.

Dis krambe thanatos [dis krahm'-bay thah'-nah-tohs] *Gk*—Warmed-over cabbage is death; repetition is tedious. *See also* Crambe repetita.

Dis manibus [dees mah'-nih-buhs] *L*—To the kindly shades of the departed. Used in dedications to persons dead. Dative case of Di manes (*q.v.*).

Dis-moi ce que tu manges, je te dirais ce que tu es [dee-mwah suh kuh tü mahNzh zhuh tuh dee-reh suh kuh tü eh] *Fr*—Tell me what you eat and I'll tell you what you are. Brillat-Savarin, *Physiology of Taste*, Aphorism 4.

Ditat Deus [dee'-taht deh'-uhs] *L*—God enriches. Motto of Arizona.

Divide et impera [dee'-wih-deh et im'-peh-rah] *L*—Divide and conquer. A political maxim. The technique of playing one party against another to gain ascendancy, or of conquering by piecemeal.

Divide ut regnes [dee'-wih-deh uht rayg'-nays] *L*—Divide the opposition so that you may rule.

Divina natura dedit agros, ars humana aedificavit urbes [dee-wee'-nah nah-too'-rah deh'-dit ah'-grohs ahrs hoo-mah'-nah I-dih-fih-kah'-wit uhr'-bays] *L*—God made the country and man made the town, as William Cowper translated it. Varro, *On Agriculture*, 3; 1.

Divina particula aurae [dee-wee'-nah pahr-tih'-kuh-lah ow'-rI] *L*—A particle of the divine in man.

D. Jur. et Rer. Pol. Doctor Juris et Rerum Politicarum [dok'-tor yoo'-ris et ray'-ruhm poh-lee-tih-kah'-ruhm] *L*—Doctor of Law and Politics.

DM. Deutsche Mark [doitsh'-uh mark] *Ger*—German mark.

D. M. P. Docteur en Médecine de la faculté de Paris [dok-tuhr ahN mayd-seen duh lah fa-kül-tay duh pah-ree] *Fr*—Doctor of Medicine, Paris.

DNB Deutsches Nachrictenbüro [doitsh'-us nahkh-rikh'-tun-bü-roh'] *Ger*—German News Agency.

D. N. P. P. Dominus Noster Papa Pontifex [do'-mih-nuhs nos'-tehr pah'-pah pohn'-tih-fehx] *L*—Our Lord the Supreme Pontiff.

Dobriy den [dah'-bruh-ee dyehn] *Rus*—Good afternoon.

Dobriy vecher [dah-bruh-ee vieh'-cher] *Rus*—Good evening.

Dobroye utro [dah'-bruh-ye oo'-troh] *Rus*—Good morning.

Docendo discimus [do-ken'-doh diss'-kih-muhs] *L*—We learn by teaching.

Docteur ès lettres [dok-tuhr ess leh-tr] *Fr*—Doctor of Literature.

Doctor Angelicus [dok'-tor ahn-jel'-lih-kuhs] *L*—The Angelic Doctor, Thomas Aquinas (1225-1274), the most renowned Scholastic.

Doctor Invincibilis [dok'-tor in-vin-see'-bih-liss] *L*—The Invincible Doctor, William of Occam (1280-1347).

Doctor Irrefragabilis [dok'-tor ir-reh-fra-gah'-bih-liss] *L*—The Irrefragable Doctor, Alexander of Hales (d.1245).

Doctor Legum [dok'-tor lay'-guhm] *L*—Doctor of Laws.

Doctor Mirabilis [dok'-tor mee-rah'-bih-liss] *L*—The Wonderful Doctor, Roger Bacon (1214?-1294).

Doctor Seraphicus [dok'-tor seh-rah'-fih-kuhs] *L*—The Seraphic Doctor, St. Bonaventure (1221-1274).

Doctor Subtilis [dok'-tor suhb'-tih-liss] *L*—The Subtle Doctor, Joannes Duns Scotus (1271-1308) a Franciscan whose system was critical of the school of Thomas Aquinas.

Doctor Universalis [dok'-tor oo-nih-vehr-sah'-liss] *L*—The Universal Doctor, Albertus Magnus (1193-1280).

Dolce far niente [dohl'-chay fahr nee-en'-tay] *It*—It is sweet to do nothing.

Dolce stil nuovo [dohl'-chay steel noo-oh-voh] *It*—The sweet new style. A style of lyric love poetry that had its origins in the songs of the troubadors and reached its finest expression in Dante. Dante, *Purgatory*, 24; 57.

Dolendi modus, timendi non item [dohlen'-dee mo'-duhs tih-men'-dee nohn ih'-tem] *L*—There is an end to sorrow, but none to fear.

Doli capax [doh'-lee kah'-pahx] *L*—Capable of doing wrong. Applied to a person old, sane, and intelligent enough to distinguish between right and wrong.

Dolus an virtus quis in hoste requirat? [doh'-luhs ahn weer'-toos kwiss in hos'-teh reh-kwee-raht] *L*—Who asks whether an enemy won by guile or courage? After slaying some Greeks in a brief encounter, some of the Trojans put on the armor of their victims. It was then that one of the Trojans spoke this sentence, which emphasized the importance of victory without inquiring too carefully into the means by which it was won. Vergil, *Aeneid*, 2; 390.

D. O. M. Deo Optimo Maximo [deh'-oh op'-tih-moh max'-ih-moh] *L*—To the Supreme Deity.

Domine, dirige nos [do'-mih-neh dee'-rih-geh nohs] *L*—Direct us, O Lord. The motto of the City of London.

Domini canes [do'-mih-nee kah'-nays] *L*—Hounds of the Lord. Medieval pun on the order of the Dominicans, noted for their zeal in pursuing heretics.

Dominus illuminatio mea [do'-mih-nuhs il-loo-mih-nah'-tih-oh meh'-ah] *L*—The Lord is my light. Motto of Oxford University. *Vulgate, Psalms*, 26; 1.

Dominus vobiscum [do'-mih-nuhs vohbiss'-kuhm] *L*—The Lord be with you.

Domus aurea [do'-muhs ow'-reh-ah] *L*—The Golden House; an area of ancient Rome on which Nero constructed his palace and gardens.

Domus Procerum [doh'-muhs proh'-seh-ruhm] *L*—The House of Lords.

Donatio mortis causa [do-nah'-tih-oh mor'-tis kow'-sah] *L*—A gift made at a time of illness because of the fear of death.

Donde una puerta se cierra, otra se abre [dohn'-deh oo'-nah pwehr'-tah say see-ay'-rrah oh'-trah say ahb'-ray] *Sp*—Where one door closes, another opens. Cervantes, *Don Quixote*, 1; 21.

Donec eris felix, multos numerabis amicos [doh'-nek eh'-ris fay'-leex muhl'-tohs nuh-meh-rah'-bis ah-mee'-kohs] *L*—While fortune favors you, you'll have many friends. Ovid, *Sorrows*, 1; 9, 5.

Don gratuit [dohN grah-twee] *Fr*—A voluntary donation.

Donner und Blitz! [duhn'-nuhr unt blitz] *Ger*—Thunder and lightning! A mild expletive.

Dos-à-dos [doh sah doh] *Fr*—Back to back. A term applied to seats on which occupants sit back to back, and to a turn in square dancing; a style of binding in which two books are bound so that they can be opened from opposite sides.

Dos linajes solo hay en el mundo . . . que son el tener y el no tener [dohs lee-nah'-hays soh'-loh ah'-ee en el moon'-doh kay sohn el tay-nehr' ee el noh tay-nehr'] *Sp*—There are only two groups in the world: the haves and the havenots. Cervantes, *Don Quixote*, 2; 20.

Dos moi pou sto kai kino ten gen [dos moi poo stoh kI kee-noh' tayn gayn] *Gk*—Give me a place to stand and I will move the earth (the world). Archimedes.

Do svidanya! [duh svee-dah'-nyah] *Rus*—Good-bye; so long.

Double entendre [doo-blahN-tahN-dr] *Fr*—See Double entente.

Double entente [doo-blahN-tahNt] *Fr*—An expression with two meanings, one of which is often risqué.

Douceur et lumière [doo-suhr ay lü-myehr] *Fr*—Sweetness and light.

Do ut des [doh uht days] *L*—I give so that you may give. In civil law a commutative contract in which equality between giving and receiving is emphasized. This designates an agreement partially fulfilled and therefore binding. In addition to *do ut des*, there are three others: *do ut facias* (*q.v.*), I give that you may do; facio ut des (*q.v.*), I do so that you may give; facio ut facias (*q.v.*), I do that you may do.

Do ut facias [doh uht fah'-kih-ahs] *L—See* Do ut des.

D'outre mer [doo-tr mehr] *Fr*—From overseas.

Dove l'oro parla, ogni lingua tace [doh'-vay loh'-roh pahr'-lah ohn'-yee leeng'-gwah tah'-chay] *It*—When gold talks, every tongue is silent.

Dove sono molti cuochi, la minestra sarà troppo salata [doh'-vay soh'-noh mohl'-tee kwoh'-kee lah mee-nehs'-trah sah-rah' trop'-poh sah-lah'-tah] *It*—When there are many cooks, the soup will be too salty; too many cooks spoil the broth.

D. P. Domus Procerum [doh'-muhs proh'-seh-ruhm] *L*—The House of Lords.

Dramatis personae [drah'-mah-tiss pehr-soh'-nI] *L*—A prefatory list of characters in a play; by extension, the term is sometimes used to describe the participants in an actual episode in life.

Drang nach Osten [drahng nahkh os'-tuhn] *Ger*—The push toward the East. The policy of Germany prior to World War I of expanding its influence into Asia.

Droit au travail [drwah oh trah-vI] *Fr*—The right to labor.

Droit d'impression réservé [drwah daN-preh-syohN ray-zehr-vay] *Fr*—Copyright.

Droit du mari [drwah dü mah-ree] *Fr*—The right of a husband.

Droit du Seigneur [drwah dü seh-nyuhr] *Fr—See* Jus primae noctis.

Droit et avant [drwah ay ah-vahN] *Fr*—Right and forward. Inscription on insignia of the Inspector General of United States Army.

DRP Deutsches Reichspatent [doitsh'-us rIkhs-pah-tent'] *Ger*—German patent.

Dr. phil. Doctor philosophiae [dok'-tor fih-lo-so'-fih-I—or, in current usage fih-loh-soh fih'-I] *L*—Ph.D., Doctor of philosophy.

58

D. s. p. *See* Decessit sine prole.

Dubium facti [duh'-bih-uhm fahk'-tee] *L*—Doubt about a fact. *See also* Dubium juris.

Dubium juris [duh'-bih-uhm yoo'-riss] *L*—Doubts as to the application of a law in a particular case, to be distinguished from *Dubium facti*, a doubt about a fact.

Duces tecum [doo'-says tay'-kuhm] *L*—Literally, you shall lead with you. A writ ordering a person to bring certain evidence into court with him.

Ducit amor patriae [doo'-kit ah'-mor pah'-trih-I] *L*—Love for my country is my guide.

Ducunt volentem fata, nolentem trahunt [doo'-kuhnt woh-len'-tem fah'-tah noh-len'-tem trah'-huhnt] *L*—The Fates lead the well disposed; they drag the rebellious. Seneca, *Letters to Lucilius*, 107.

Du, du liegst mir im Herzen [doo doo leegst meer im hehr'-tsen] *Ger*—You lie close to my heart. A song popular for group singing dating from about 1820; author unknown.

Due teste valgono più che una sola [doo'-ay tess'-tay vahl'-goh-noh pee-yoo' kay oo'-nah soh'-lah] *It*—Two heads are better than one.

Du fort au faible [dü fohr oh feh-bl] *Fr*—From the strong to the weak.

Du haut en bas [dü oh ahN bah] *Fr*—From top to bottom; disdainfully. *See also* De haut en bas.

Dulce decus meum [duhl'-keh deh'-kuhs meh'-uhm] *L*—My sweet ornament or glory; my sweet source of fame. Horace's tribute to his literary patron Maecenas. Horace, *Odes*, 1; 1, 2.

Dulce est desipere in loco [duhl'-keh est day-sip'-peh-reh in lo'-koh] *L*—It is pleasant to play the fool at times. Horace, *Odes*, 4; 12, 28.

Dulce et decorum est pro patria mori [duhl'-keh et deh-kohr'-ruhm est proh pah'-trih-ah moh'-ree] *L*—It is sweet and honorable to die for one's country. Horace, *Odes*, 3; 2, 13.

Dum bene se gesserit [duhm beh'-neh say ges'-seh-rit] *L*—As long as he conducts himself properly.

Dum casta [duhm kahs'-tah] *L*—As long as she remains chaste. A limitation on a bequest to a widow.

Dum Deus calculat, fit mundus [duhm deh'-uhs kahl'-kuh-laht fit muhn'-duhs] *L* —While God calculates, the world comes into being. A famous aphorism of Leibnitz.

Dummodo sit dives, barbarus ipse placet [duhm'-mo-doh sit dee'-wehs bahr'-bah-ruhs ip'-seh plah'-ket] *L*—Even a barbarian pleases, if only he is rich. Ovid, *Art of Love*, 2; 276.

Dum spiro spero [duhm spee'-roh spay'-roh] *L*—While I breathe I hope. Motto of South Carolina. For a second motto, *see* Animis opibusque . . .

Dum vita est, spes est [duhm wee'-tah est spays est] *L*—While there is life, there is hope.

Dum vitant stulti vitia in contraria currunt [duhm wee'-tahnt stuhl'-tee wih'-tih-ah in kohn-trah'-rih-ah kuhr'-ruhnt] *L*—While fools avoid one kind of vice they run to the opposite extreme.

Dum vivimus, vivamus [duhm wee'-wih-muhs wee-wah'-muhs] *L*—Let us live while we're living.

Duos qui sequitur lepores neutrum capit [duh'-ohs kwee seh'-kwih-tuhr leh'-poh-rays noi'-truhm kah'-pit] *L*—The man who chases two rabbits catches neither one.

Duoviri sacris faciundis [duh-oh'-wih-ree sah'-krees fah-kih-uhn'-deess] *L*—Two men charged to perform the public sacrifices.

Dura lex sed lex [doo'-rah layx sed layx] *L*—The law is harsh, but it is the law.

Durante absentia [doo-rahn'-teh ahp-sayn'-tih-ah] *L*—During absence.

Durante minore aetate [doo-rahn'-teh mih-noh'-reh I-tah'-teh] *L*—As long as the subject is a minor; until the subject is of age.

Durante viduitate [doo-rahn'-teh wih-duh-ih-tah'-teh] *L*—As long as the subject remains a widow.

Durante vita [doo-rahn'-teh vee'-tah] *L*—During life.

Durchgang verboten [doorkh'-gahng fehr-boh'-tun] *Ger*—Passage through forbidden; no thoroughfare.

Durum et durum non faciunt murum [doo'-ruhm et doo'-ruhm nohn fah'-kih-unt moo'-ruhm] *L*—Stern measures do not build a protecting wall; harsh repressive measures do not ensure security.

Du sublime au ridicule il n'y a qu'un pas [dü sü-bleem oh ree-dee-kül eel nee-ah kuhN pah] *Fr*—It's only a step from the sublime to the ridiculous. An obvious bit of wisdom that is ancient but generally attributed to Napoleon I, who had the retreat from Moscow in mind.

Dux femina facti [duhx fay'-mih-nah fahk'-tee] *L*—A woman (Queen Elizabeth) was leader of the exploit. This motto was put on a medal at the time of the defeat of the Spanish Armada. Vergil, *Aeneid*, 1; 364.

D. V. Deo volente [deh'-oh voh-len'-teh] *L*—God willing.

E

Eadem, sed aliter [eh'-ah-dem sed ah'-lih-tehr] *L*—The same things but in a different way. Schopenhauer proposed this as the motto of history.

Eadem sunt omnia semper [eh'-ah-dem suhnt om'-nih-ah sem'pehr] *L*—All things are always the same. *See also* Plus ça change ...Lucretius, On the Nature of Things, 3; 945.

Eau de vie [oh duh vee] *Fr*—Water of life; brandy.

È cattivo vento che non è buono per qualcheduno [eh kaht-tee'-voh venn'-toh kay nonn eh bwoh'-noh pehr kwal-keh-doo'-noh] *It*—It's an ill wind that blows nobody good.

Ecce convertimur ad gentes [ek'-keh kohn-wehr'-tih-muhr ahd gen'-tays] *L*—Behold, we turn to the Gentiles. The title of an essay by Matthew Arnold.

Ecce homo [ek'-keh ho'-moh] *L*—Behold the man. An attempt on the part of Pilate to arouse sympathy in the mob for Christ after the scourging and crowning with thorns. *Vulgate, John*, 19; 5.

Ecce iterum Crispinus! [ek'-keh ih'-teh-ruhm krihs-pee'-nuhs] *L*—Lo, Crispin again; we're back to the same old subject. Said of a person who is constantly putting in an appearance where least expected. Juvenal, 4; 1.

Ecce signum [ek'-keh sihg'-nuhm] *L*—Behold the proof.

Ecclesia semper reformanda [ek-klay'-sih-ah sem'-pehr reh-for-mahn'-dah] *L*—The Church must always be subjected to reform.

Ecclesia supplet [ek-klay'-sih-ah suhp'-plet] *L*—The Church supplies. In cases

60

where a technicality is not observed or a ministrant unwittingly exceeds his powers, the Church regards the action as valid. A term used in theology.

École des beaux-arts [ay-kul day boh-zahr] *Fr*—School of fine arts.

École maternelle [ay-kul mah-tehr-nell] *Fr*—School for very young children; preschool and kindergarten in the United States.

E consensu gentium [ay kohn-sayn'-soo gen'-tih-uhm] *L*—An argument based on the general agreement of mankind on a subject.

E contra [ay kohn'-trah] *L*—On the other hand.

E contrario [ay kohn-trah'-rih-oh] *L*—On the contrary.

E converso [ay kohn-wehr'-soh] *L*—Conversely.

Écrasez l'infâme! [ay-krah-zay laN-fahm] *Fr*—Crush the vile system! The slogan of Voltaire and other precursors of the French Revolution. Voltaire was accused of referring to Christ as *l'infâme*, but the charge seems unwarranted. His hostility was directed against the bigotry and the injustice of the age in which he lived. *Letter to Jean Le Rond d'Alembert*, Nov. 28, 1762.

Edel ist, der edel tut [ay'-dul ist dehr ay'-dul toot] *Ger*—Handsome is that handsome does.

Édition à tirage restreint [ay-dee-syohN ah tee-razh reh-straN] *Fr*—Limited edition.

Édition classique [ay-dee-syohN klah-seek] *Fr*—A standard recognized edition of a work.

Édition de luxe [ay-dee-syohN duh lüx] *Fr*—An expensive edition of a book, richly bound, printed on special paper, and finely illustrated.

Édition ne varietur [ay-dee-syohN nay vah-rih-ay'-tuhr] *Fr & L*—This edition is not to be altered; a definitive edition.

Editio princeps [ay-dih'-tih-oh preen'-keps] *L*—First edition.

EE. UU. Estados Unidos [es-tah'-dohs oo-nee'-dohs] *Sp*—United States.

Effodiuntur opes, irritamenta malorum [ef-foh-dih-uhn'-tuhr oh'-pays ihr-ree-tah-mehn'-tah mah-loh'-ruhm] *L*—Wealth is dug from the earth, an incentive to evil. Ovid, *Metamorphoses*, 1; 140.

E flamma petere cibum [ay flahm'-mah peh'-teh-reh kih'-buhm] *L*—To snatch food from the flames; to attempt a dangerous exploit. The Romans used to throw food on a burning pyre; those who tried to salvage such food were the poorest of the poor. Terence, *Eunuch*, 3; 2, 38.
e. g. exempli gratia [ex-em'-plee grah'-tih-ah] *L*—For example.

Egli è povero come un topo di chiesa [ehl'-yee eh poh'-vay-roh koh'-meh oon toh'-poh dee kee-ay'-zah] *It*—He is as poor as a church mouse.

Ego et Rex meus [eh'-goh et rayx meh'-uhs] *L*—I and my king. Cardinal Wolsey is using proper Latin when he puts himself before King Henry VIII.

Ego sum rex Romanus (imperator Romanorum) et super grammaticam [eh'-goh suhm rayx roh-mah'-nuhs, im-pehr-rah'-tohr roh-mah-noh'-ruhm, et suh'-pehr grah-mah'-tee-kahm] *L*—I am the king of Rome and above grammar. Words spoken by the Holy Roman Emperor Sigismund at the Council of Constance (1414-18) when a cardinal corrected his Latin.

Eh bien! [ay byaN] *Fr*—Well! Well now! Used as a mild interjection.

Eheu fugaces, Postume, Postume, labuntur anni [eh'-hoi fuh-gah'-kays pohs'-tuh-meh pohs'-tuh-meh lah-buhn'-tuhr ahn'-nee] *L*—Alas, my Postumus, the fleeting years slip by. Horace, *Odes*, 2; 14, 1.

Ehre, dem Ehre gebührt [ay'-ruh daym ay'-ruh guh-bürt'] *Ger*—Honor to whom honor is due.

Ehrlich währt am längsten [ayr'-likh vehrt ahm leng'-stun] *Ger*—Honesty is the best policy.

Eile mit Weile [I'-luh mit vI'-luh] *Ger*—The more hurry, the less speed; make haste slowly.

Eine feste Burg ist unser Gott [I'-nuh fes'-tuh boork ist uhn'-zuhr gott] *Ger*—A mighty fortress is our God. The first line of Luther's greatest hymn.

Eine Hand wäscht die andere [I'-nuh hahnt vehsht dee ahn'-druh] *Ger*—See Manus manum lavat.

Ein eigner Herd, ein braves Weib sind Gold und Perlen wert [In Ig'-nuhr hert In brah'-vuhs vIp zint golt unt pehr'-lun vert] *Ger*—One's own hearth and an honest wife are worth gold and pearls. Mephistopheles is citing a proverb. Goethe, *Faust*, pt. 1, 3155-6.

Eine kleine Wurst is auch eine Wurst [I'-nuh klI'-nuh voorst ist owkh I'-nuh voorst] *Ger*—A little sausage is still a sausage; no matter how thin you slice it, it is still baloney.

Eine Schwalbe macht keinen Sommer [I'-nuh shvahl'-buh mahkt kI'-nun zuhm'-muhr] *Ger*—One swallow does not make a summer. *See also* Mia gar chelidon . . .

Ein fröhliches Neujahr [In fruh'-likh-ess noi'-yahr] *Ger*—A happy new year.

Einkreisungspolitik [In-krI-zoongs-po-lih-teek'] *Ger*—Encirclement policy; one of the reasons Hitler gave for going to war with neighboring countries.

Ein Reich, ein Volk, ein Führer [In rIkh In fohlk In für'-ruhr] *Ger*—One rule, one people, one leader. The Nazi ideal.

Ein Unglück kommt selten allein [In oon'-glükh kuhmmt sel'-tun ahl-lIn'] *Ger*—Bad luck seldom comes alone; "When sorrows come, they come not single spies but in battalions," as Shakespeare put it in *Hamlet*, 4; 5. *See also* Le disgrazie . . .

Ein unnütz Leben ist ein früher Tod
[In oon'-nuts lay'-buhn ist In frü'-uhr toht]
Ger—A useful life is an early death. Goethe, *Iphigenia*, 1; 2, 62.

Eisen und Blut [I'-sun unt bloot] *Ger*—
Usually heard in English as Blood and iron.
Bismarck's philosophy that the great problems of the world can be settled by military force.

Ejusdem farinae [eh-yuhs'-dem fah-ree'-nI] *L*—Literally, of the same flour; of the same temperament or type.

Ejusdem generis [eh-yuhs'-dem geh'-neh-ris] *L*—Of the same kind.

Ejus nulla culpa est, cui parere necesse sit [eh'-juhs nool'-lah kuhl'-pah est kwee pah-ray'-reh neh-kehs'-seh sit] *L*—The man who is forced to obey is not at fault for what he does.

Elapso tempore [ay-lahp'-soh tem'-po-reh] *L*—After a certain amount of time has elapsed.

E la sua volontate è nostra pace [ay lah suh'-ah voh-lonn-tah'-tay eh noss'-trah pah'-chay] *It*—His will is our peace. Matthew Arnold calls this a simple but perfect single line of poetry. Dante, *Paradiso*, 3; 85.

Eli eli, lama sabachthani [ay-lee' ay-lee' lah-mah' sah-bahk-thah-nee'] *Aramaic*—My God, my God, why hast thou forsaken me? *Vulgate, Matthew*, 27; 46.

El ingenioso hidalgo [el een-hay-nyoh'-soh ee-dahl'-goh] *Sp*—The ingenious gentleman, Don Quixote de la Mancha.

Elixir vitae [ay-lix'-ir wee'-tI] *L*—The elixir of life; in alchemy the magic formula for extending human life.

El no y el sí son breves de decir, y piden mucho pensar [el noh ee el see sohn bray'-vays day day-seer' ee pee-dehn moo'-choh pen-sahr'] *Sp*—No and yes are quickly said, but much thought is needed before they are uttered. Baltasar Gracián, *The Oracle*, no. 70.

El sabio muda consejo; el necio, no [el sah'-byoh moo'-dah kon-say'-hoh el nay'-syoh noh] *Sp*—The wise man changes his plans; the foolish man, never.

Embarras de richesses [ahN-bah-rah duh ree-shess] *Fr*—The state of having more good things than one knows what to do with; embarrassment caused by a rich variety of possible choices.

Embarras du choix [ahN-ba-rah dü shwah] *Fr*—Difficulty of choice arising from a number of possible selections.

È meglio aver oggi un uovo che domani una gallina [eh mayl'-yoh ah-vehr' ohd'-jee oon oo-oh'-voh kay doh-mah'-nee oo'-nah gahl-lee'-nah] *It*—Better an egg today than a hen tomorrow; a bird in the hand is worth two in the bush.

È meglio domandar che errare [eh mayl'-yoh doh-mahn-dahr' kay ehr-rahr'] *It*—Better to ask than lose your way.

È meglio esser mendicante che ignorante [eh mayl'-yoh ehs'-sehr men-dee-kahn'-tay kay een-yohr-rahn'-tay] *It*—Better be poor than ignorant.

È meglio il cuor felice che la borsa piena [eh mayl'-yoh eel kwohr fay-lee'-chay kay lah bohr'-sah pee-ay'-nah] *It*—Better a happy heart than a full purse.

È meglio piegare che rompere [eh mayl'-yoh pee-ay-gah'-ray kay rohm'-pay-ray] *It*—It is better to bend than break.

È meglio tardi che mai [eh mayl'-yoh tahr'-dee kay mah'-ee] *It*—Better late than never.

È meglio un uccello in gabbia che cento fuori [eh mayl'-yoh oon uht-chel'-loh een gahb'-bee-ah kay chehn'-toh foo-oh'-ree] *It*—Better a bird in the cage than a hundred outside; a bird in the hand is worth two in the bush.

Éminence grise [ay-mee-nahNss greez] *Fr*—Literally, gray eminence, referring to Père Joseph, a Capuchin, the secretary and agent of Cardinal de Richelieu. The expression has come to mean the power behind the throne.

Empta dolore docet experientia [aymp'-tah do-loh'-reh do'-ket ex-pehr-rih-ehn'-tih-ah] *L*—Experience gained in pain is a good teacher; a burnt child shuns the fire.

Emptoris sit eligere [aymp-toh'-ris sit ay-lih'-geh-reh] *L*—It is the buyer's privilege to make a choice.

En ami [ahn-ah-mee] *Fr*—As a friend.

En arrière [ahn-ah-ryehr] *Fr*—Behind; in arrears.

En attendant [ahn-ah-tahN-dahN] *Fr*—In the meantime.

En avant [ahn-ah-vahN] *Fr*—Forward!

En banc [ahN bahN] *Fr*—In full court; all judges participating.

En bloc [ahN bluhk] *Fr*—As one unit, piece, lump, etc.

En boca cerrada no entran moscas [ehn boh'-kah seh-rrah'-dah noh ehn'-trahn mohs'-kahs] *Sp*—Flies do not enter a shut mouth.

En bonne foi [ahN bun fwah] *Fr*—In good faith.

En brosse [ahN bruhss] *Fr*—Said of hair cut short like a brush; a crew cut.

En cachette [ahN kah-shet] *Fr*—Stealthily, secretly, on the sly.

Encheiresin naturae [en-kheh'-ree-sin nah-too'-rI] *Gr/L*—Literally, an undertaking of nature; the technical classifying of the various parts of beings. Mephistopheles is critical of scientists handling and giving names to the parts of dead animals. Goethe, *Faust*, pt. 1; 1.

En clair [ahN klehr] *Fr*—In the clear; referring to messages that are not sent in code.

En congé [ahN kohN-zhay] *Fr*—On leave.

En courant [ahN koo-rahN] *Fr*—While on the run; on the side.

En cueros [ehn kway'-rohs] *Sp*—Naked.

Ende gut, alles gut [enn'-duh goot ahl'-luss goot] *Ger*—All's well that ends well.

En dernier ressort [ahN dehr-nyay ruh-sohr] *Fr*—As a last resort.

En déshabillé [ahN day-za-bee-yay] *Fr*—Dressed scantily or carelessly, as in a dressing gown.

En deux mots [ahN duh moh] *Fr*—Literally, in two words; in short.

En Dieu est ma fiance [ahN dyuh eh mah fee-ahNss] *Fr*—My trust is in God.

En Dieu est tout [ahN dyuh eh too] *Fr*—In God is everything.

En effet [ahn-eh-feh] *Fr*—In reality; in fact; quite so.

En évidence [ahn-ay-vee-dahNss] *Fr*—In a conspicuous position.

En famille [ahN fah-mee] *Fr*—In the bosom of one's family; at home.

Enfant de famille [ahN-fahN duh fah-mee] *Fr*—A son or daughter of a reputable family.

Enfant de son siècle [ahN-fahN duh sohN syeh-kluh] *Fr*—A child of his age.

Enfant gâté [ahN-fahN gah-tay] *Fr*—Spoiled child.

Enfants perdus [ahN-fahN pehr-dü] *Fr*—Literally, lost children; an abandoned hope. The term is military and is used to designate troops that are in an indefensible position and are considered as good as lost.

Enfant terrible [ahN-fahN teh-ree-bluh] *Fr*—A child hard to manage; a holy terror.

Enfant trouvé [ahN-fahN troo-vay] *Fr*—A foundling.

En grande tenue [ahN grahNd tuh-nü] *Fr*—In full military dress.

En grande toilette [ahN grahNd twah-let] *Fr*—In full dress.

En grand style [ahN grahN steel] *Fr*—On a large scale; in an imposing way.

En le persiflant [ahN luh pehr-see-flahN] *Fr*—In rallying or mocking him.

En Martes ni te cases, ni te embarques, ni de tu casa te apartes [ehn mahr'-tehs nee tay kah'-sehs nee tay ehm-bahr'-kays nee deh too kah'-sah tay ah-pahr'-tays] *Sp*—On Tuesday do not marry, go on a voyage, or leave your home. In Spain and Mexico Tuesday is regarded as an unlucky day.

En masse [ahn mahss] *Fr*—In a crowd; in a heap.

En mauvaise odeur [ahn muh-vehz oh-duhr] *Fr*—In bad odor.

En nukti boule tois sophois gignetai [en nük-tee' boo-lay' tois so-fois' geeg'-neh-tI] *Gk*—In the night counsel comes to the wise; take counsel of your pillow. Menander, *Monostichs*, 150.

En pantoufles [ahN pahN-too-fluh] *Fr*—In slippers; in a free, relaxed style.

En papillotes [ahN pah-pee-yuht] *Fr*—Decorative ends for cutlets; said of hair done up in paper curlers.

En parenthèse [ahN pa-rahN-tehz] *Fr*—In parentheses.

En passant [ahN pa-sahN] *Fr*—In passing.

En petit comité [ahN puh-tee koh-mee-tay] *Fr*—In an informal, select group.

En plein air [ahN plehn air] *Fr*—In the open air.

En plein jour [ahN plaN zhoor] *Fr*—In the full light of day where all may observe.

En principe [ahN praN-seep] *Fr*—Set down as a principle or a rule but recognizing the possibility of exceptions.

En queue [ahN kuh] *Fr*—In a line, as at a box office; behind; in the rear.

En rappport [ahN ra-pohr] *Fr*—In harmonious relation; in agreement.

En règle [ahN reh-gluh] *Fr*—In order; correct.

En revanche [ahN ruh-vahNsh] *Fr*—By way of compensation; to make up for something.

En route! [ahN root] *Fr*—Full speed ahead!

En rústica [ehn roos'-tee-kah] *Sp*—Unbound; in paper cover.

Ense petit placidam sub libertate quietem [ayn'-seh peh'-tit plah'-kih-dahm suhb lee-behr-tah'-teh kwih-ay'-tehm] *L*—By the sword she seeks placid peace under free government. Motto of Massachusetts.

En somme [ahN suhm] *Fr*—In short.

En surtout [ahN sür-too] *Fr*—Literally, above all. Used in heraldry to indicate position of personal arms, for example, at the top of a shield.

En tapinois [ahN ta-pee-nwah] *Fr*—On the sly; stealthily departing.

Entbehre gern was du nicht hast [ent-bay'-ruh gern vahs doo nikht hahst] *Ger*—Gladly do without what you do not have.

Entbehren sollst du! [ent-bay'-run zollst doo] *Ger*—You must refrain, you must renounce pleasure! Faust is complaining that he is too old to devote himself solely to pleasure and too young to crush desire. You must restrain yourself is the only advice he receives. Goethe, *Faust*, pt. 1, 1549.

Entelecheia [en-teh-lekh'-eh-ah] *Gk*—In Aristotle's philosophy a form-giving energy in living things directing an organism to the realization of its perfection.

Entente cordiale [ahN-tahNt kor-dyahl] *Fr*—A cordial understanding, especially between two governments.

Entente demi-cordiale [ahN-tahNt duh-mee kor-dyahl] *Fr*—A half-cordial understanding; a half-hearted reconciliation.

Entia non sunt multiplicanda sine necessitate [ehn'-tih-ah nohn sunt muhl-tih-plih-kahn'-dah sih'-neh neh-kes-sih-tah'-teh] *L*—Beings must not be multiplied without necessity. William of Occam. This is known as Occam's law of parsimony or Occam's razor. He held that the subtle distinctions of Scholastic philosophy, such as that between essence and existence, should be cut away in the interests of simplification.

En tierra de ciegos el tuerto es rey [en tyeh'-rah day syay'-gohs el twayr'-toh es ray'-ee] *Sp*—In the country of the blind the man with one eye is king. See also In terra di ciechi . . .

En titre [ahN tee-tr] *Fr*—Of regular or official status.

En tout cas [ahN too kah] *Fr*—In any case; applied by extension to a combination umbrella and parasol and to an all-weather tennis court.

Entr'acte [ahN-trakt] *Fr*—Interval, intermission.

Entre chien et loup [ahN-truh shyan-ay loo] *Fr*—Literally, between the dog and the wolf; at nightfall.

Entre deux feux [ahN-tr duh fuh] *Fr*—Between two fires.

Entre deux vins [ahN-tr duh vaN] *Fr*—Between two wines; neither drunk nor sober.

Entre nous [ahN-tr noo] *Fr*—Between us; a private understanding.

Entre padres y hermanos no metas tus manos [en'-treh pah'-drays ee ehr-mah'-nohs noh may'-tahs toos mah'-nohs] *Sp*—Don't meddle in the family affairs of others.

En vérité [ahN vay-ree-tay] *Fr*—In truth; indeed.

En voiture! [ahN vwah-tür] *Fr*—All aboard!

Eo ipso [eh'-oh ihp'-soh] *L*—By the very fact.

e. o. o. e. erreur ou omission exceptée [eh-ruhr oo oh-mee-syohN ehk-sehp-tay] *Fr*—With the exception of any error or omission.

Épater les bourgeois [ay-pa-tay lay boor-zhwah] *Fr*—See Pour épater ...

E. P. D. en paz descanse [ehn pahs dehs-kahn'-seh] *Sp*—May he rest in peace.

Epea pteroenta [eh'-peh-ah pte-roh'-en-tah] *Gk*—Winged words. An expression much used by Homer. *See also* Geflügelte Worte.

E pluribus unum [ay ploo'-rih-buhs oo'-nuhm] *L*—One from many. Motto on the great seal of the United States. Adapted from Vergil, *Moretum*, 104.

E' principali fondamenti che abbino tutti li stati ... sono le buone legge e le buone arme ay preen-chee-pah'-lee fon-dah-men'-tee kay ahb'-bee-noh toot'-tee lee stah'-tee soh'-noh lay boo-oh'-nay lay'-djay ay lay boo-oh'-nay ahr'-may] *It*—The principal foundations that all states should have are good laws and good arms. Machiavelli, *The Prince*, 12.

E pur si muove! [ay puhr see mwoh'-vay] *It*—Nevertheless it does move! Fictional remark of Galileo on leaving the trial at which he was forced to renounce his scientific conclusion that the earth moves around the sun.

E (ex) re nata [ay, ex, ray nah'-tah] *L*—Arising from the present circumstances; according to the exigencies of the case.

Erfahrung ist die beste Schule [ehr-fah'-roong ist dee bes'-tuh shoo'-luh] *Ger*—Experience is the best school. *See also* Usus est optimus magister.

Erin go bragh! [eh'-rinn goh brah] *Ir*—Ireland forever!

Eripuit caelo fulmen, mox sceptra tyrannis [ay-rih'-puh-it kI-loh fuhl'-men mox skayp'-trah tih-rahn'-neess] *L*—He snatched lightning from heaven and later the scepter from tyrants. Inscription on a bust of Benjamin Franklin recalling his experiment with electricity and his part in the American Revolution. The words are inspired in part by Manilius, *Astronomica*, 1; 104.

Errare humanum est [ehr-rah'-reh hoo-mah'-nuhm est] *L*—To err is human.

Errata (pl. of **erratum**) [ehr-rah'-tah, ehr-rah'-tuhm] *L*—A list of errors in a book.

Erzb. Erzbischof [ehrts-beesh'-hohf] *Ger*—Archbishop.

ès [ess] *OF*—A contraction of *en les*, in the. It is mostly used in academic degrees, such as bacc. ès. (*q.v.*).

escte. escompte [ehs-kohNt] *Fr*—Discount.

Es de vidrio la mujer [ess day bee'-dryoh lah moo-hehr'] *Sp*—Woman is made of glass. Cervantes, *Don Quixote*, 1; 33.

È sempre l'ora [eh sem'-pray loh'-rah] *It*—The right time is always now.

Ese te quiere bien que te hace llorar [ay'-say tay kee-ay'-reh byehn' kay tay ah'-say yoh-rahr'] *Sp*—The man who makes you weep loves you very much. Cervantes, *Don Quixote*, 1; 20.

Es gibt, sagt man, für den Kammerdiener keinen Helden [ess gihbt zahgt mahn für dayn kahm-muhr-dee'-nur kI'-nun hel'-dun] *Ger*—Literally, there is, they say, no hero for a valet; no man is a hero to his valet. Goethe, *Maxims in Prose*, 164. *See also* Il n'y a pas de grand homme . . .

Es irrt der Mensch, solang er strebt [ess eerrt dehr mensh zolahng ehr shtraypt] *Ger*—Man errs as long as he aspires. Goethe, *Faust, Prologue in Heaven.*

Es ist nicht alles Gold was glänzt [ess ist nihkt ahl'-luss golt vahs glehntst] *Ger*—All that glitters is not gold.

Es ist Schade [ess ist shah'-duh] *Ger*—It is a pity.

Es kann der Frömmste nicht im Frieden bleiben, / Wenn es dem bösen Nachbar nicht gefällt [ess kahn der fruhmm'-shtuh nikht im free'-dun blI'-bun venn ess daym buh'-sun nahk'-bahr nikht guh-fehlt'] *Ger*—The gentlest man cannot live in peace, if it does not please his wicked neighbor. Schiller, *Wilhelm Tell,* 4; 3, 124.

Esprit de corps [eh-spree duh kor] *Fr*—The spirit of internal harmony and common purpose that animates an organization.

Esprit de finesse [eh-spree duh fee-ness] *Fr*—A witty or shrewd mind.

Esprit des lois [eh-spree day lwah] *Fr*—*Spirit of the Laws*, title of a work by Montesquieu.

Esprit fort [eh-spree fohr] *Fr*—A person of strong mind or will; a fearless thinker; a skeptic.

Esprit gaulois [eh-spree gohl-wah] *Fr*—The Gallic spirit; a certain freedom of speech characterized by broad, off-color humor. A sharp contrast to the puritanical spirit.

Esse oportet ut vivas, non vivere ut edas [ays'-seh o-pohr'-tet uht wee'-wahs nohn wee'-weh-reh uht ay'-dahs] *L*—One should eat to live, not live to eat. Cicero, *Herennius*, 4; 28, 39.

Esse quam videri [es'-seh kwahm wih-day'-ree] *L*—To be rather than to seem to be. The motto of North Carolina. According to Sallust, Cato the Younger preferred to be good rather than to seem good. Sallust, *Catiline*, 54.

Esse rei est percipi [es'-seh reh'-ee est pehr'-kih-pee] *L*—The reality of a thing consists in its being perceived. The theory

of being propounded by the empirical philosopher George Berkeley.

Est ars etiam maledicendi [est ahrs eh'-tih-ahm mah-leh-dee-kehn'-dee] *L*—There is even an art to slandering.

Est-ce possible? [ehs po-see-bluh] *Fr*—Is it possible? Last words of Paul Doumer, president of France, shot by a Russian Fascist in 1932.

Est modus in rebus [est mo'-duhs in ray'-buhs] *L*—There is a middle course in everything; there must be moderation in all things. Horace, *Satires*, 1; 1, 106.

Esto perpetua [es'-toh pehr-peh'-tuh-ah] *L*—Live forever. Motto of Idaho.

Esto quod esse videris [es'-toh kwuhd es'-seh wih-day'-riss] *L*—Be what you seem to be.

Est quaedam flere voluptas [est kwI'-dahm flay'-reh wo-luhp'-tahs] *L*—There is a certain pleasure in weeping. Ovid, *Sorrows*, 4; 3, 37.

Estque pati poenas quam meruisse minus [est'-kweh pah'-tee poi'-nahs kwahm meh-ruh-is'-seh mih'-nuhs] *L*—It is better to suffer punishment than to deserve it. Ovid, *Epistles from Pontus*, 1; 1, 62.

Es wird nichts so schön gemacht / Es kommt einer der's veracht! [ess virt nikhts zoh shuhn guh-mahkt' ess kuhmt I'-nuhr dehrs fehr-ahkt'] *Ger*—There is nothing, no matter how beautiful, that is not held in contempt by someone.

ETA Euskadi Ta Askatasuna [oos'-kuh-dee tah ahs'-kuh-tuh-soo'-nuh] *Basque*—Basque separatist organization.

et al. *See* et alibi.

et al. *See* et alii.

Et alibi [et ah'-lih-bee] *L*—And elsewhere.

Et alii, *or* **aliae** [et ah'-lih-ee, ah'-lih-I] *L*—And others.

Et bonum quo antiquius, eo melius [et bo'-nuhm kwoh ahn-tee'-kwih-uhs eh'-oh meh'-lih-uhs] *L*—The more ancient a good, the better.

etc. *See* Et cetera.

Et cetera [et kay'-teh-rah; in general use, et-set'-uhr-ruh] *L*—And so forth.

Éternel devenir [ay-tehr-nehl duh-vuh-neer] *Fr*—Eternal becoming.

Et hoc genus omne *L*—See Hoc genus omne.

Etiam capillus unus habet umbram suam [eh'-tih-ahm kah-pihl'-luhs oo'-nuhs hah'-bet uhm'-brahm suh'-ahm] *L*—Even a single hair has its own shadow; in any investigation the smallest bit of evidence can be valuable. Publilius Syrus.

Et id genus omne [et id geh'-nuhs om'-neh] *L*—See Hoc genus omne.

Et ignotas animum dimittit in artes [et ig-noh'-tahs ah'-nih-muhm dee-mit'-tit in ahr'-tays] *L*—He turns his attention to unknown arts. Quoted by James Joyce on the title page of *A Portrait of the Artist as a Young Man.* Ovid, *Metamorphoses*, 8; 188.

Et in Arcadia ego [et in ahr-kah'-dih-ah eh'-goh] *L*—I, too, lived in Arcadia. This was an area in the Peloponnesus where happy shepherds were pictured as living a blissful life. These words were written on a painting by Bartolomeo Schedone (1570-1615) in which two young shepherds examine a human skull that is imagined as recalling happy days in youth. A second translation is possible when death is represented as saying, "Even in Arcadia I hold sway."

Et qui nolunt occidere quemquam, posse volunt [et kwee noh'-luhnt ok-kee'-deh-reh kwehm'-kwahm pos'-seh wo'-luhnt] *L*—Those who do not wish to kill any man wish they were able. Juvenal, 10; 96.

Et semel emissum volat irrevocabile verbum [et seh'-mehl ay-miss'-suhm wo'-laht ir-reh-wo-kah'-bih-leh wehr'-buhm] *L*—The word once uttered cannot be recalled. Horace, *Epistles*, 1; 18, 71.

et seq. *See* Et sequentes.

Et sequentes *or* **et sequentia** [et seh-kwehn'-tays, et seh-kwen'-tih-ah] *L*—And the following.

Et sic de ceteris [et seek day kay'-teh-reess] *L*—And similarly as to the others.

Et sic deinceps [et seek deh-een'-keps] *L*—And so forth.

Et sic de similibus [et seek day sih-mih'-lih-buhs] *L*—And in the same way about similar matters.

Et sic porro [et seek pohr'-roh] *L*—And so on.

Et spes et ratio studiorum in Caesare tantum [et spays et rah'-tih-oh stuh-dih-oh'-ruhm in kI'-sah-reh tahn'-tuhm] *L*—The future of literature and the inducement to it rest with Caesar alone. Juvenal does not mention which emperor he is addressing; critics feel he may have had Trajan or Hadrian in mind. Juvenal, 7; 1.

Et tu, Brute [et too broo'-teh] *L*—And thou, too, Brutus. In Shakespeare the last words spoken by Caesar. Shakespeare, *Julius Caesar*, 3; 1. *Tu quoque, Brute* is a variation of what Caesar is supposed to have said. *See also* Kai su ei ekeinon . . .

et ux. et uxor [et uhx'-or] *L*—And wife.

Et uxor. *See* Et ux.

Et verbum caro factum est [et vehr'-buhm kah'-roh fahk'-tuhm est] *L*—And the Word was made flesh. *Vulgate, John*, 1; 14.

Et vir [et wihr] *L*—And husband.

E. U. Estados Unidos [es-tah'-dohs oo-nee'-dohs] *Sp*—United States.

É.-U. États-Unis [ay-tahz ü-nee] *Fr*—United States.

Eureka! [hoi'-ray-kah] *Gk*—I have found it! The exclamation of Archimedes who, while bathing, discovered how to determine the gold content of a crown made for King Hiero II of Syracuse. This experiment led to the discovery of the law of specific gravity. Motto of California. Vitruvius Pollio, *On Architecture*, 9; 3 and Plutarch, *Pleasure Not Attainable According to Epicurus*, 2.

Euskadi Ta Askatasuna [oos'-kuh-dee tah ahs-kuh-tuh-soo'-nuh] *Basque*—Basque separatist organization.

E. V. Eccellenza Vostra [et-chel-len'-tsah voss'-trah] *It*—Your Excellency.

Ex abrupto [ex ahb-ruhp'-toh] *L*—Suddenly.

Ex abundantia cordis os loquitur [ex ah-buhn-dahn'-tih-ah kor'-diss ohs lo'-kwih-tuhr] *L*—Out of the abundance of the heart the mouth speaketh. *Vulgate, Matthew,* 12; 34.

Ex aequo [ex I'-kwoh] *L*—Of equal merit.

Ex animo [ex ah'-nih-moh] *L*—With spirit; from the heart.

Ex capite [ex kah'-pih-teh] *L*—Literally, from the head; from memory.

Ex cathedra [ex kah'-theh-drah *or* kah-thay'-drah] *L*—Literally, from the chair. Dogmatic utterances of the Pope on matters of faith and morals. The term is sometimes applied to the arrogant, positive expressions of the uninformed.

Excellentia sanandi causa [ex-kel-len'-tih-ah sah-nahn'-dee kow'-sah] *L*—Excellence in order to cure. A hospital motto.

Excelsior [ex-sel'-sih-or] *L*—Ever upward. Motto of New York State.

Exceptio probat regulam [ex-kep'-tih-oh proh'-baht ray'-guh-lahm] *L*—The exception proves the rule. A Roman legal maxim.

Exceptis excipiendis [ex-kep'-tees ex-kih-pih-en'-deess] *L*—After exceptions have been made.

Ex comitate [ex ko-mih-tah'-teh] *L*—Out of courtesy.

Ex concesso [ex kon-kess'-soh] *L*—From what has already been conceded. An argument based on what has already been granted by an opponent.

Ex contractu [ex kon-trahk'-too] *L*—A legal action arising from a contract.

Ex curia [ex koo'-rih-ah] *L*—Out of court.

Excusatio non petita fit accusatio manifesta [ex-koo-sah'-tih-oh nohn peh-tee'-tah fit ahk-koo-sah'-tih-oh mah-nih-fess'-tah] *L*—An excuse given when unasked betrays clear guilt. *See also* Qui s'excuse . . .

Excussit subjecto Pelion Ossae [ex-kuhs'-sit suhb-yek'-toh pay'-lih-ɵn os'-sI] *L*—(Jove) shook off Pelion from underlying

Ossa. The giants were piling mountain upon mountain—here Pelion upon Ossa—to reach Jove and dethrone him. The story suggests the folly of violence. Ovid, *Metamorphoses,* 1; 155. *See also* Imponere Pelio Ossam.

Ex debito justitiae [ex day'-bih-toh yoos-tih'-tih-I] *L*—By reason of a just debt.

Ex delicto [ex day-leek'-toh] *L*—Literally, out of a wrong; a cause for legal action following a crime or a tort.

Ex desuetudine amittuntur privilegia [ex day-suh-ay-too'-dih-neh ah-mit-tuhn'-tuhr pree-wih-lay'-gih-ah] *L*—Privileges are lost through disuse. Legal maxim.

Ex dono [ex do'-noh] *L*—As a gift.

Exeat [ex'-eh-aht] *L*—Let him leave. Form used in schools when a student is given permission for temporary absence.

Exegi monumentum aere perennius [ex'-ay-ghee mo-nuh-men'-tuhm I'-reh peh-ren'-nih-uhs] *L*—I have built a monument more lasting than bronze. Horace, *Odes,* 3; 30, 1.

Exemplaire d'auteur [ehg-zahN-plehr doh-tuhr] *Fr*—Autographed copy owned by the author.

Exempla sunt odiosa [ex-em'-plah suhnt oh-dih-oh'-sah] *L*—Examples are odious.

Exempli gratia *L—See* e.g.

Ex ephebis [ex ef-fay'-bees] *L*—Out of the ranks of youths; just arrived at manhood.

Exeunt omnes [ex'-eh-uhnt om'-nays] *L*—All leave the stage.

Ex gratia [ex grah'-tih-ah] *L*—By special favor, not because of any legal right.

Ex grege [ex greh'-geh] *L*—From the flock; singled out from a group.

Ex hypothesi [ex hih-poh'-teh-sih] *L*—According to the supposition that is the basis of an inquiry.

Ex imo corde [ex ee'-moh kor'-deh] *L*—From the bottom of the heart.

Exitus acta probat [ex'-ih-tuhs ahk'-tah proh'-baht] *L*—The result justifies the action. George Washington's family motto. Ovid, *Heroides*, 2; 85.

Ex libris [ex lihb'-reess] *L*—A book plate; from the books of — (followed by the name of the owner).

Ex luna scientia [ex loo'-nah skih-en'-tih-ah] *L*—Knowledge from the moon. The motto of the project Apollo moon flights.

Ex malis moribus bonae leges natae sunt [ex mah'-leess moh'-rih-buhs bo'-nI lay'-gays nah'-tI suhnt] *L*—Good laws have come about because of bad customs.

Ex mero motu [ex meh'-roh moh'-too] *L*—Of one's own free will; without compulsion or restraint.

Ex necessitate rei [ex neh-kehs-sih-tah'-teh ray'-ee] *L*—Arising from the urgency of the case.

Ex nihilo nihil fit [ex nih'-hih-loh nih'-hihl fit] *L*—From nothing nothing comes. Xenophanes' axiom, basic to his doctrine of the eternity of matter. This Latin proverb is found with slightly different wording in Lucretius, *The Nature of Things*, 1; 155 and 206.

ex off. *See* Ex officio.

Ex officio [ex of-fee'-sih-oh] *L*—By virtue of holding an office.

Ex opere operantis *L*—*See* Ex opere operato.

Ex opere operato [ex oh'-peh-reh oh-peh-rah'-toh] *L*—A theological phrase indicating that the efficacy of a spiritual act or a sacrament does not depend upon the state of grace of the ministrant, but upon the proper performance of the rite.

Ex ore infantium [ex oh'-reh in-fahn'-tih-uhm] *L*—Out of the mouth of infants. *Vulgate, Psalms*, 8; 2.

Ex Oriente lux; ex Occidente frux [ex oh-rih-en'-teh loox ex ok-kih-den'-teh froox] *L*—From the East light; from the West fruit. The East has given us philosophy; the West practical, productive industries.

Ex parte [ex pahr'-teh] *L*—A statement proceeding from one side only in an argument or investigation and, therefore, likely to be prejudiced.

Ex pede Herculem [ex peh'-deh hehr'-kuh-lem] *L*—Judge the size of Hercules from his foot; from one part you can estimate the whole.

Experientia docet stultos [ex-peh-rih-en'-tih-ah do'-ket stuhl'-tohs] *L*—Experience teaches even fools. The meaning of this proverb is debatable. Even men who have a reputation for wisdom rarely learn the lessons of experience, e.g., that no nation wins a war.

Experimentum crucis [ex-peh-rih-men'-tuhm kruh'-kis] *L*—A crucial test; a decisive experiment.

Experto crede *L*—*See* Experto credite.

Experto credite [ex-pehr'-toh kray'-dih-teh] *L*—Believe the experienced. Generally used in the singular, *Experto crede.* Vergil, *Aeneid*, 11; 283.

Expertus metuit [ex-pehr'-tuhs meh'-tuh-it] *L*—The person with experience is fearful; the burnt child dreads the fire. This originally referred to the cultivation of the friendship of the powerful, which seems so pleasant to the inexperienced but in reality is bitter. Horace, *Epistles*, 1; 18, 87.

Explication de texte [ehk-splee-kah-syohN duh tehkst] *Fr*—The detailed and sometimes painfully slow explanation of a literary text.

Explicit [ex'-plih-kit] *L*—Here ends. This word found at the end of Latin manuscripts is followed by the title of the work, often the name of the scribe, and the place and date of the copying or publication; a colophon.

Ex post facto [ex post fahk'-toh] *L*—After the deed is done; retroactive. Usually applied to legislation.

Expressis verbis [ex-prehs'-sees wehr'-beess] *L*—In express terms; in so many words.

Ex professo [ex proh-fehs'-soh] *L*—Professedly; openly; expertly.

Ex relatione [ex reh-lah-tih-oh'-neh] *L*—A phrase on a legal document indicating a relation to a former proceeding, or designating the person on whose behalf action is being taken.

69

Ex (e) silentio [ex, ay, sih-len′-tih-oh] *L*—From silence; an argument drawn from failure of an opponent to mention a circumstance that might be damaging.

Exstinctus amabitur idem [ex-stink′-tuhs ah-mah′-bih-tuhr ee′-dem] *L*—The same man will be loved when dead. Because of envy a man's talent, virtue, and services are often not recognized when he is alive. Horace, *Epistles*, 2; 1, 14.

Ex tacito [ex tah′-kih-toh] *L*—Tacitly.

Ex tempore [ex tem′-po-reh] *L*—Extemporaneously.

Extra ecclesiam nulla salus [ex′-trah ek-klay′-sih-ahm nool′-lah sah′-loos] *L*—Outside the church there is no salvation. This dictum, attributed to St. Cyprian (210-258), caused much debate among theologians. One explanation that would lessen its rigor is that the Church has a soul and a body; one may be spiritually joined to the Church, but not belong to the visible body of the faithful.

Extra muros [ex′-trah moo′-rohs] *L*—Beyond the walls.

Extra ordinem [ex′-trah or′-dih-nehm] *L*—Outside of its natural order; out of its proper place.

Extra situm [ex′-trah sih′-tuhm] *L*—Away from its natural setting.

Ex umbris et imaginibus in veritatem [ex uhm′-brees et ih-mah-gi′-nih-buhs in way-rih-tah′-tem] *L*—From shadows and imaginings into the truth. The epitaph written by John Henry, Cardinal Newman, for himself.

Ex ungue leonem [ex uhn′-gweh leh-oh′-nem] *L*—One can sketch a lion from its claw. *See also* Ex pede Herculem.

Ex uno disce omnes *L*—*See* Ab uno disce omnes.

Ex vi termini [ex wee tehr′-mih-nee] *L*—From the force of the term; by definition.

Ex vitio alterius sapiens emendat suum [ex wih′-tih-oh ahl-teh-ree′-uhs sah′-pih-ayns ay-men′-daht suh-uhm] *L*—A wise man corrects his faults when seeing another's. Publilius Syrus.

Ex voto [ex voh′-toh] *L*—In fulfillment of a vow or promise. When used as an adjective it applies to an offering made to a shrine or to a philanthropic or pious cause.

F

f. forte [fohr′-tay] *It*—Loudly. *See also* fff.

f. à. b. franco à bord [fraN-koh ah bohr] *Fr*—f.o.b. (free on board).

f. a. b. franco a bordo [frahn′-koh ah bohr′-doh] *It*—Free on board.

Faber quisque fortunae suae [fah′-behr kwis′-kweh for-too′-nI suh′-I] *L*—Every man is the maker of his own fortune. A Roman proverb.

Fabricando fit faber [fah-brih-kahn′-doh fit fah′-behr] *L*—One becomes a craftsman by working at a craft.

Fabula palliata [fah′-buh-lah pahl-lih-ah′-tah] *L*—Roman drama in which the characters wore a Greek garment called a *pallium.* Such Latin plays stressing Greek manners were translated by Plautus and Terence from Greek originals, now extant only in fragments.

Fabula togata [fah′-buh-lah toh-gah′-tah] *L*—Roman drama stressing Roman rather than Greek characters and dress. *See also* Fabula palliata.

Facile est inventis addere [fah′-kih-leh est in-wen′-teess ahd′-deh-reh] *L*—It is easy to add to what has already been invented.

Facile omnes, quom valemus, recta consilia aegrotis damus [fah′-kih-leh om′-nays kwom wah-lay′-muhs rayk′-tah kohn-sih′-lih-ah I-groh′-teess dah′-muhs] *L*—When we are well, we readily give good counsel to the sick. Terence, *Andria,* 3; 1, 9.

Facile princeps [fah′-kih-leh preen′-keps] *L*—Easily the leader.

Facilis descensus Averno [fak′-kih-lis day-skayn′-suhs ah-wehr′-noh] *L*—The descent to hell is easy. Vergil, *Aeneid,* 6; 126.

Facilité de parler, c'est impuissance de se taire [fah-see-lee-tay duh pahr-lay seh taN-pwee-sahNss duh suh tehr] *Fr*—Fluency in speech is an inability to stop talking.

Facio ut des [fah′-kih-oh uht days] *L*—*See* Do ut des.

Facio ut facias [fah′-kih-oh uht fah′-kee-ahs] *L*—*See* Do ut des.

Facit indignatio versum [fah′-kit in-dig-nah′-tih-oh wehr′-suhm] *L*—Indignation gives birth to verses. In a similar vein Quintilian wonders why anger makes the unlearned eloquent. Juvenal, 1; 79.

Façon de parler [fa-soN duh pahr-lay] *Fr*—Manner of speaking.

Facta, non verba [fahk′-tah nohn wehr′-bah] *L*—Deeds, not words; action, not talk.

Faenum habet in cornu [fI′-nuhm hah′-bet in kor′-noo] *L*—He has hay on his horns; he is dangerous. The figure is based upon the practice in ancient Rome of putting hay on the horns of a dangerous bull. Horace, *Satires,* 1; 4, 34.

Faex populi, faeces (*pl*) **populi** [fIks po′-puh-lee fI′-kays po′-puh-lee] *L*—The dregs of society: the mob. A disparaging reference to the lowest classes.

Faire d'une mouche un éléphant [fehr dün moosh uhn ay-lay-fahN] *Fr*—To make an elephant out of a fly; to make a mountain out of a molehill.

Faire les yeux doux [fehr lay zyuh doo] *Fr*—To look with love at someone; to make sheep's eyes.

Fait accompli [feht ah-kohN-plee] *Fr*—An accomplished fact; an action which cannot be undone or revoked.

Fait à peindre [feht ah-paN-druh] *Fr*—Made to be painted; paintable.

Faites votre devoir et laissez faire aux dieux [feht vuh-truh duh-vwahr ay leh-say fehr oh dyuh] *Fr*—Do your duty and leave the rest to the gods. Corneille, *Horace*, 2; 8, line 710.

Fait nouveau [feh noo-voh] *Fr*—A new fact or development.

F. A. L. N. Fuerzas Armadas de Liberación National [fwayr'-sahs ahr-mah'-dahs day lee-bay-rah-syon' nah-see-oh-nahl'] *Sp*—Armed Forces for National Liberation (of Puerto Rico).

Falsa lectio [fahl'-sah layk'-tih-oh] *L*—A false reading; a word erroneously transcribed by an editor or copyist of a manuscript.

Falsus in uno, falsus in omnibus [fahl'-suss in oo'-noh fahl'-suss in om'-nih-buhs] *L*—Faithless in one thing, faithless in all. The entire testimony of a witness who has lied in one particular may be rejected.

Fama clamosa [fah'-mah klah-moh'-sah] *L*—Noisy rumor or scandal.

Fama, malum qua non aliud velocius ullum [fah'-mah mah'-luhm kwah nohn ah'-lih-ud way-loh'-kih-uhs ool'-luhm] *L*—No evil travels faster than scandal. Vergil, *Aeneid*, 4; 174.

Fama nihil est celerius [fah'-mah nih'-hil est keh-leh'-rih-uhs] *L*—Nothing travels faster than scandal. Adapted from Fama, malum qua . . . (*q.v.*).

Fama semper vivat [fah'-mah sem'-pehr wee'-waht] *L*—May his fame live forever.

Fames est optimus coquus [fah'-mays est op'-tih-muhs koh'-kwuss] *L*—Hunger is the best cook.

Far d'una mosca un elefante [fahr doo'-nah mohs'-kah oon ay-lay-fahn'-tay] *It*—To make an elephant out of a fly; to make a mountain out of a molehill. *See also* Faire d'une mouche un éléphant.

Fas est et ab hoste doceri [fahs est et ahb hos'-teh do-kay'-ree] *L*—There is nothing wrong in learning a lesson even from the enemy. Ovid, *Metamorphoses*, 4; 428.

Fata obstant [fah'-tah op'-stahnt] *L*—The Fates oppose.

Fata viam invenient [fah'-tah wih'-ahm in-weh'-nih-ent] *L*—The Fates will find a way. Vergil, *Aeneid*, 3; 395.

Fatti maschii, parole femine [faht'-tee mah'-skee pah-roh'-lay fay'-mee-nay] *It*—Manly deeds, womanly words. Motto of Maryland.

Fausse couche [fohss koosh] *Fr*—Miscarriage.

Faute de mieux [foht duh myuh] *Fr*—For lack of something better.

Faux ami [foh zah-mee] *Fr*—A false friend. Applied to a French word spelled the same as a word in English but having a different meaning, e.g., *sensible*, which in French means "sensitive."

Faux frais [foh freh] *Fr*—False expenses.

Faux pas [foh pah] *Fr*—A false step; a blunder, especially in social conventions.

Fax mentis incendium gloriae [fahks men'-tis in-ken'-dih-uhm gloh'-rih-I] *L*—The passion for glory sets fire to the mind.

Fay ce que vouldras [fay suh kuh vool-drah] *OF*—Do what you will; follow your heart's desires. Rule of Gargantua's Abbey of Thélème. Rabelais, *Gargantua*, 1; 57.

f. c. ferrocarril [fehr'-roh-kahr-reel'] *Sp*—Railroad.

fco franco [fraN-ko] *Fr-It-Sp*—Free of charge; transportation paid.

F. D. *See* Defensor Fidei.

F. de T. Fulano de Tal [foo-lah'-noh day tahl] *Sp*—Mr. So-and-So; equivalent of John Doe.

Fec. *See* Fecit.

Fecit [fay'-kit] *L*—He made it. Found inside violins, on paintings, or on statuary with the name of the maker or artist.

Felice ritorno! [fay-lee'-chay ree-tohr'-noh] *It*—Welcome back!

Felices Pascuas [fay-lee'-sehs pahs'-kwahs] *Sp*—Literally, Happy Easter; also used to mean Merry Christmas, or Happy holiday.

Felicitas multos habet amicos [fay-lee'-kih-tahs muhl'-tohs hah'-bet ah-mee'-kohs] *L*—Prosperity has many friends. The implication is that these are not disinterested friends.

Felix quem faciunt aliena pericula cautum [fay'-leex kwem fah'-kih-uhnt ah-lih-ay'-nah peh-ree'-kuh-lah kow'-tuhm] *L* —Fortunate the man who is made cautious by the perils of others.

Felix qui patitur quae numerare potest [fay'-leex kwee pah'-tih-tuhr kwI nuh-meh-rah'-reh po'-test] *L*—Happy the man who can list all his sufferings. Ovid, *Tristia.*

Felix qui potuit rerum cognoscere causas [fay'-leex kwee po'-tuh-it ray'-ruhm kog-nohs'-keh-reh kow'-sahs] *L*—Happy the man who has been able to discover the causes of things. Vergil, *Georgics*, 2; 490.

Feliz Natal [fay-leez' nah-tahl'] *Port*—Merry Christmas.

Felo de se [feh'-loh deh see] *Anglo-L*—A felon upon himself; a person who kills himself.

Femme couverte [fam koo-vert] *Fr*—A married woman.

Femme de chambre [fam duh shahN-bruh] *Fr*—Chambermaid.

Femme de charge [fam duh shahrzh] *Fr*—Housekeeper.

Femme de trente ans [fam duh trahNt ahN] *Fr*—Literally, a woman aged thirty; one who knows the world. Title of a novel by Balzac.

Femme fatale [fam fa-tahl] *Fr*—Siren; a seductive woman.

Femme savante [fam sa-vahNt] *Fr*—Learned woman. *Les Femmes savantes* (the plural form, here used ironically) is the title of a play by Molière.

Ferae naturae [feh'-rI nah-too'-rI] *L*—Of a wild, ferocious nature. A legal term applied to undomesticated animals and birds.

Feriunt summos fulgura montes [feh'-rih-uhnt suhm'-mohs fuhl'-guh-rah mohn'-tays] *L*—Lightning strikes the mountain tops. Horace, *Odes*, 2; 10, 12.

Ferme acerrima proximorum odia [fehr'-may ah-kehr'-rih-mah prox-ih-moh'-ruhm oh'-dih-ah] *L*—Hatred among close relatives is generally the bitterest. Tacitus, *Histories*, 4; 70.

Ferme générale [fehrm zhay-nay-rahl] *Fr*—A general farming out of taxes. The object of financiers was to reap a generous profit for collecting what they had advanced the government. This system was abolished in France in 1791.

Fermiers généraux [fehr-myay zhay-nay-roh] *Fr*—Farmers general; private financiers who collected taxes for the French government.

Ferrum, dum in igni candet, cudendum est tibi [fehr'-ruhm duhm in ihg'-nee kahn'-det koo-den'-duhm est tih'-bih] *L*—Strike the iron when it is hot. Publilius Syrus. *See also* Man muss das Eisen . . .

Ferrum ferro acuitur [fehr'-ruhm fehr'-roh ah-kuh'-ih-tuhr] *L*—Iron is sharpened by iron.

Festina lente [fes-tee'-nah lehn'-tay] *L*—Hasten slowly.

Fête champêtre [feht shahN-peh-tr] *Fr*—Rural feast with open-air entertainment and rustic sports.

Fête de fleurs [feht duh fluhr] *Fr*—Festival of flowers.

Fête des Fous [feht day foo] *Fr*—A festival of fools. In medieval times, a period of carousing.

Fêtes de nuit [feht duh nwee] *Fr*—Night festivals.

Feu d'artifice [fuh dahr-tee-feess] *Fr*—Fireworks.

Feu de joie [fuh duh zhwah] *Fr*—A firing of guns on a joyous occasion; a bonfire.

Feu d'enfer [fuh dahN-fehr] *Fr*—Hellish fire (from guns).

Feu follet, feux follets (*pl*) [fuh foh-leh] *Fr*—*See* Ignis fatuus.

F. f. Fortsetzung folgt [fort-zet'-tsoong fuhlgt] *Ger*—To be continued.

FF. Frères [frehr] *Fr*—Brothers. Used mostly in company names, as "Bros."

fff. fortississimo [fohr-tiss-siss'-see-moh] *It* —As loudly as possible. A super-superlative. *ff* (fortissimo) is the usual superlative.

FF. SS. Ferrovie dello Stato [fehr-roh-vee'-ay del'-loh stah'-toh] *It*—State Railroads.

F. h. Fiat haustus [fee'-aht how'-stuhs] *L* —Let a potion be made. A medical direction.

fha. fecha [feh'-chah] *Sp*—Date of a document.

Fianna Fail [fee-uh'-nuh foil] *Ir*—Literally, warriors of the land; followers of Eamon de Valera, who organized the Nationalist Party in 1927.

F. I. A. T. Fabbrica italiana automobili Torino [fahb'-bree-kah ee-tah-lee-ah'-nah ow-toh-moh'-bee-lee toh-ree'-noh] *It*—Italian Automobile Factory of Turin.

Fiat experimentum in corpore vili [fee'-aht ex-peh-rih-men'-tuhm in kor'-po-reh wee'-lee] *L*—Let experiments be done on a worthless body; experiment on inexpensive materials.

Fiat justitia pereat mundus [fee'-aht yoo-stih'-tih-ah peh'-reh-at muhn'-duhs] *L*—Let justice be done even though the world perish.

Fiat justitia ruat caelum [fee'-aht yoo-stih'-tih-ah ruh'-aht kI'-luhm] *L*—Let justice prevail even though the heavens fall. The original use of this maxim is not so elevating. Seneca tells that a man being hanged for murder was sent by the executioner to Piso when the supposed victim appeared. Piso would not change the sentence of death, but ordered all three hanged: the supposed criminal because the sentence had been passed, the executioner because he had been derelict in his duty, and the supposed victim because he had been the cause of the death of two innocent men.

Fiat lux [fee'-aht loox] *L*—Let there be light. *Vulgate, Genesis,* 1; 3.

Fiat mixtura [fee'-aht mix-too'-rah] *L*— Let a mixture be made. A medical direction.

Fiat voluntas tua [fee'-aht voh-luhn'-tahs tuh'-ah] *L*—Thy will be done. *Vulgate, Matthew,* 6; 10.

FIDE Fédération Internationale des Échecs [fay-day-rah-syohN aN-tair-na-syoh-nahl day zay-shek] *Fr*—International Chess Federation.

Fide et amore [fih'-day et ah-moh'-reh] *L*—With faith and love.

Fide et fiducia [fih'-day et fih-doo'-kih-ah] *L*—By faith and confidence.

Fide et fortitudine [fih'-day et for-tih-too'-dih-neh] *L*—By faith and fortitude.

Fidei corticula crux [fih'-deh-ee kor-tih'-kuh-lah kroox] *L*—The cross is the test or touchstone of faith.

Fidei Defensor *L*—*See* Defensor Fidei.

Fideli certa merces [fih-day'-lee ker'-tah mehr'-kays] *L*—The man who is faithful is certain of reward.

Fide, non armis [fih'-day nohn ahr'-meess] *L*—By faith, not by arms.

Fide, sed cui vide [fee'-deh sed kwee wih'-day] *L*—Trust, but take care whom you trust.

Fides et justitia [fih'-days et yoo-stih'-tih-ah] *L*—Faith and justice.

Fides Punica [fih'-days poo'-nih-kah] *L*— *See* Punica fides.

Fides quaerens intellectum [fih'-days kwI'-rayns in-tel-lek'-tuhm] *L*—Faith seeking understanding.

Fidite ne pedibus [fee'-dih-teh nay peh'-dih-buhs] *L*—Place no trust in flight. Vergil, *Aeneid,* 10; 372.

Fidus Achates [fee'-duhs ah-kah'-tays] *L*— Faithful Achates, loyal friend of Aeneas, often mentioned in the *Aeneid;* by extension, a loyal friend.

Fidus et audax [fee'-duhs et ow'-dahx] *L*—Faithful and intrepid.

FIEC Fédération Internationale des Associations d'Études Classiques [fay-day-rah-syohN aN-tair-na-syoh-nahl day zah-so-see-ah-syohN day-tüd klah-seek] *Fr*—International Federation of the Associations of Classical Studies.

Fieri facias [fee'-eh-ree fah'-kih-ahs] *L*— Order to be done. A writ to the sheriff ordering the debtor's property to be reduced to money to cover the amount of the judgment.

Figlie e vetri son sempre in pericolo [feel'-yay ay vay'-tree sohn sem'-pray een pay-ree'-koh-loh] *It*—Lasses and glasses are always in danger.

Figurae orationis [fih-goo'-rI oh-rah-tih-oh'-nis] *L*—Figures of speech.

Filioque *L*—See Qui ex patre filioque etc.

Filius nullius [fee'-lih-uhs nool-lee'-uhs] *L*—An illegitimate son.

Filius populi [fee'-lih-uhs po'-puh-lee] *L*—Son of the people; a bastard.

Filius terrae [fee'-lih-uhs tehr'-rI] *L*—A son of the earth; a peasant.

Fille de joie [fee duh zhwah] *Fr*—A woman of pleasure; a prostitute.

Fille d'honneur [fee duh-nuhr] *Fr*—Maid of honor.

Fille d'intrigue [fee daN-treeg] *Fr*—A scheming young woman; an adventuress.

Fils à papa [feess ah pah-pah] *Fr*—Son of an influential father; the fair-haired boy.

Finchè la pianta è tenera, bisogna drizzarla [feen'-kay lah pee-ahn'-tah eh tay'-nay-rah bee-zohn'-yah dreed-tsahr'-lah] *It*—Bend the tree while it is young; as the twig is bent, the tree's inclined.

Fin de siècle [faN duh syeh-kluh] *Fr*—End of the century.

Finesse d'esprit [fee-nehss deh-spree] *Fr* —Shrewdness of mind.

Finis coronat opus [fee'-nis ko-roh'-naht oh'-puss] *L*—It is the end that crowns the work.

Finis litium [fee'-nis lee'-tih-uhm] *L*—An end of lawsuits.

Finis operantis [fee'-nihs o-peh-rahn'-tihs] *L*—The aim of the worker, such as the making of money.

Finis operis [fee'-nihs o'-peh-rihs] *L*—The purpose of a work.

Finis origine pendet [fee'-nis o-ree'-gih-neh pen'-det] *L*—The end depends on the beginning. This motto stresses the importance of getting the right start. Motto of Paul Revere and the seal of Phillips Andover Academy.

fl. *See* Floruit.

Flagellum Dei [flah-gel'-luhm deh'-ee] *L*— The scourge of God, a name given Attila, the leader of the Huns.

Flagrante bello [flah-grahn'-teh bel'-loh] *L*—While the war is raging.

Flagrante delicto [flah-grahn'-teh day-leek'-toh] *L*—In the very act of committing a crime.

Flak Fliegerabwehrkanone [flee-gehr-ahp-vehr-kah-noh'-nuh] *Ger*—Antiaircraft artillery; the exploding shells sent up by these guns.

Flamma fumo est proxima [flahm'-mah foo'-moh est prox'-ih-mah] *L*—Flame is very close to smoke; where there's smoke there's fire. Plautus, *Curculio,* 1; 1, 53.

Flectere si nequeo superos, Acheronta movebo [flehk'-teh-reh see neh'-kweh-oh suh'-peh-rohs, ah-keh-rohn'-tah moh-way'-boh] *L*—If I cannot sway the gods, I will stir up hell. Words of the vengeful Juno. Vergil, *Aeneid,* 7; 312.

Flecti, non frangi [flek'-tee nohn frahn'-gee] *L*—To bend, not to break.

Fleur de lys [fluhr duh lee] *Fr*—Literally, flower or blossom of the lily. Heraldic ornament of French royalty.

Floruit [floh'-ruh-it] *L*—He flourished. Often used when exact dates are unknown.

Flosculi sententiarum [flos'-kuh-lee sen-ten-tih-ah'-ruhm] *L*—Beautiful selections; an anthology of beautiful thoughts.

Flotará sola [floh-tah-rah' soh'-lah] *Sp*—It will float alone. A symbol of the independence party in Puerto Rico; seen on decals with the island's flag.

FLQ Fédération Liberté Québecoise [fay-day-rah-syohN lee-behr-tay kay-beh-kwahz] *Fr*—Federation for the Freedom of Quebec.

F. L. Q. Front de libération de Québec [frohN duh lee-bay-rah-syohN duh kay-bek] *Fr*—Quebec Liberation Front.

Fluctuat nec mergitur [flook'-tuh-aht nek mayr'-gi-tuhr] *L*—She is tossed but does not sink. Motto of the city of Paris.

Flux de bouche [flü duh boosh] *Fr*—Flow of words; talkativeness. *See also* Flux de paroles.

Flux de paroles [flü duh pah-ruhl] *Fr*—Flow of words; garrulity. *See also* Flux de bouche.

Folie de grandeur [fuh-lee duh grahN-duhr] *Fr*—Delusions of grandeur.

Fons et origo [fohns et oh-ree'-goh] *L*—The very fountain and source.

Fons et origo malorum [fohns et oh-ree'-goh mah-loh'-ruhm] *L*—The fountain and source of misery.

Force de frappe [fohrss duh frahp] *Fr*—A striking force of atomic weapons.

Force majeure [fohrss mah-zhuhr] *Fr*—Circumstances beyond one's control. *See also* Vis major.

Forensis strepitus [foh-ren'-sis streh'-pih-tuhs] *L*—The clamor of the forum; the noisy turmoil of the court.

Foris ut moris, intus ut libet [foh'-reess uht moh'-riss in'-tuhss uht lih'-bet] *L*—In public, follow custom; in private, your own sweet will.

Forma bonum fragile [for'-mah bo'-nuhm frah'-gih-leh] *L*—Beauty is a fragile possession. Ovid, *Art of Love*, 2; 113.

Forma flos, fama flatus [for'-mah flohss fah'-mah flah'-tuhss] *L*—Beauty is a flower, fame a breath.

Forsan et haec olim meminisse juvabit [for'-sahn et hIk oh'-lim meh-mih-nihs'-seh yuh-wah'-bit] *L*—Perhaps it will be pleasant to remember these hardships some day. Vergil, *Aeneid*, 1; 203.

Fors Clavigera [fohrs klah-wih'-geh-rah] *L*—Literally, key-bearing or club-bearing; the ambiguous title of a series of volumes by John Ruskin covering a wide range of subjects.

Forte [for'tay] *It*—Loudly. *See also* fff.

Forte scutum, salus ducum [for'-teh skoo'-tuhm sah'-looss duh'-kuhm] *L*—A brave shield is the safety of commanders.

Fortes fortuna adjuvat [for'-tayss for-too'-nah ahd'-yuh-waht] *L*—Fortune aids the brave. Terence, *Phormio*, 2; 2, 25.

Fortes fortuna juvat [for'-tayss for-too'-nah yuh'-waht] *L*—Fortune helps the brave. Pliny the Younger, 6; 16.

Forti et fideli nihil (nil) difficile [for'-tee et fih-day'-lee nih'-hil, neel, dif-fih'-kih-leh] *L*—Nothing is difficult for the brave and loyal.

Fortis cadere, cedere non potest [for'-tiss kah'-deh-reh kay'-deh-reh nohn po'-test] *L*—The brave man may fall but he cannot yield.

Fortiter et recte [for'-tih-tehr et rehk'-tay] *L*—Bravely and righteously.

Fortiter, fideliter, feliciter [for'-tih-tehr fih-day'-lih-tehr fay-lee'-kih-tehr] *L*—Bravely, loyally, successfully.

Fortiter in re *L*—*See* Suaviter in modo . . .

Fortuna belli semper ancipiti in loco est [for-too'-nah bel'-lee sem'-pehr ahn-kih'-pih-tee in loh'-koh est] *L*—The fortunes of war are always in doubt. Seneca, *Phoenician Women*, 629.

Fortunae filius [for-too'-nI fee'-lih-uhs] *L*—A child of fortune. Horace, *Satires*, 2; 6, 49.

Fortuna favet fatuis [for-too'-nah fah'-wet fah'-tuh-eess] *L*—Fortune favors fools.

Fortuna fortibus favet [for-too'-nah for'-tih-buhss fah'-wet] *L*—Fortune favors the brave.

Fortuna meliores sequitur [for-too'-nah meh-lih-oh'-rayss seh'-kwih-tuhr] *L*—Fortune follows the better man; the better man has all the luck. Sallust, *History*, 1; 48, 21.

Fortuna multis dat nimis, satis nulli [for-too'-nah muhl'-teess daht nih'-miss sah'-tiss noo'-lee] *L*—Fortune gives too much to many, enough to nobody. Martial, *Epigrams*, 12; 10, 2.

Fortuna nimium quem fovet, stultum facit [for-too'-nah nih'-mih-uhm kwem foh'-wet stuhl'-tuhm fah'-kit] *L*—Fortune often makes her darling a fool. Publilius Syrus.

Fou qui se tait passe pour sage [foo kee suh teh pahss poor sahzh] *Fr*—The silent fool passes for a sage.

Fou rire [foo reer] *Fr*—Uncontrollable laughter.

Fra Modesto non fu mai priore [frah moh-dess-toh nonn foo mah'-ee pree-oh'-ray] *It*—Brother Modest was never made prior; a modest man does not rise in administration.

Franc-alleu [frahN-kah-luh] *Fr*—Land held absolutely free of feudal obligations.

Franco de Porto [frahn'-ko day pohr'-toh] *Sp*—Postpaid.

Franc-tireur [frahN tee-ruhr] *Fr*—An irregular infantryman in the French army; a sniper.

Frangas, non flectes [frahn'-gahs nohn flek'-tays] *L*—You may break but you cannot bend me. *See also* Flecti, non frangi.

Frappé au froid [frah-pay oh frwah] *Fr*—Literally, stamped when cold; blind-tooled. A term used in bookbinding.

Fraus est celare fraudem [frowss est kay-lah'-reh frow'-dem] *L*—It is a fraud to conceal a fraud.

Frère de lait [frehr duh leh] *Fr*—Foster-brother.

Friede auf Erden [free'-duh owf ayr'-duhn] *Ger*—Peace on earth.

Frisch begonnen, halb gewonnen [frish buh-guhn'-nun hahlp guh-vuhn'-nun] *Ger*—Well begun is half done. *See also* Arche hemisy pantos.

Frl. Fräulein [froi'-lIn] *Ger*—Miss.

Fröhliche Weihnachten [fruh'-likh-kuh vI-nahkh'-tun] *Ger*—Merry Christmas.

Froides mains, chaud amour [frwahd maN shoh dah-moor] *Fr*—A cold hand but a warm heart.

Frontis nulla fides [fron'-tiss nool'-lah fih'-days] *L*—Place no trust in appearances; appearances are deceptive. Juvenal, 2; 8.

Fructu non foliis arborem aestima [fruhk'-too nohn foh'-lih-eess ahr'-boh-rem I'-stih-mah] *L*—Judge a tree by its fruit, not its leaves.

Frustra laborat qui omnibus placere studet [froos'-trah lah-boh'-raht kwee om'-nih-buhss plah-kay'-reh stuh'-det] *L*—He labors in vain who strives to please everybody.

F. S. Faire suivre [fehr swee-vruh] *Fr*—Please forward. A postal term.

¡Fuera los Yankis! [foo-ay'-rah lohs yan'-kees] *Sp*—Out with the Yankees! Yankees, go home. An example of contemporary graffiti.

Fugit irreparabile tempus [fuh'-git ihr-reh-pah-rah'-bih-leh tem'-puhss] *L*—Irrecoverable time flies away. Vergil, *Georgics*, 3; 284.

Fuimus Troes, fuit Ilium [fuh'-ih-muhs troh'-ays fuh'-it ee'-lih-uhm] *L*—We were Trojans, and there was a Troy; our glory is past, our day is over. Vergil, *Aeneid*, 2; 325.

Fuit Ilium [fuh'-it ee'-lih-uhm] *L*—See Fuimus Troes . . .

Functus officio [fuhnk'-tuhs off-fih'-kih-oh] *L*—Having carried out his duties; no longer in office.

Fuori commercio [fwoh'-ree kom-mehr'-choh] *It*—Not available commercially.

Fuori i barbari [fwoh'-ree ee bahr'-bah-ree] *It*—Out with the barbarians. The battle cry of Pope Julius II.

Fuori le mura [fwoh'-ree lay moo'-rah] *It*—Outside the walls (of Rome).

F. U. P. I. Federación Universitaria per Independencia [fay-day-rah-syon' oo-nih-vehr-see-tah'-ree-ah pehr een-day-pehn-dehn'-see-ah] *Sp*—University Federation for Independence (of Puerto Rico).

Für Herren [für hehr'-run] *Ger*—For gentlemen only.

Furia francese [foo'-ree-ah frahn-chay'-say] *It*—French fury. Doubtless modeled on Furor Teutonicus (*q.v.*).

Furor arma ministrat [fuh'-ror ahr'-mah mih-nis'-traht] *L*—Rage supplies weapons. Vergil, *Aeneid*, 1; 150.

Furor loquendi [fuh'-ror loh-kwen'-dee] *L*—An uncontrollable desire to talk.

Furor poeticus [fuh'-ror poh-ay'-tih-kuhss] *L*—The inspired frenzy of the poet.

Furor scribendi [fuh'-ror skree-ben'-dee] *L*—Mania for writing.

Furor Teutonicus [fuh'-ror teh-uh-toh'-nih-kuhss] *L*—Teuton barbarism. A phrase of Lucan used in modern times to describe German conduct in war.

F. u. S. f. Fortsetzung und Schluss folgen [fort-zet'-tsoong unt shloos fuhl'-gun] *Ger*—To be concluded in the next issue.

Fuyez les dangers de loisir [fwee-yay lay dahN-zhay duh lwah-zeer] *Fr*—Flee the dangers of idleness.

f. v. folio verso [foh'-lih-oh wehr'-soh] *L*—On the reverse side of the page.

G

Gage d'amour [gahzh dah-moor] *Fr*—A pledge or token of love.

Gaieté de coeur [gay-tay duh kuhr] *Fr*—Light-hearted gaiety.

gal. général [zhay-nay-rahl] *Fr*—Military general.

Galilaie nenikekas [gah-lih-lI'-eh neh-nih'-kay-kahs] *Gk*—Thou hast conquered, O Galilaean! These supposed last words of Julian the Apostate are first found in the work of the Christian historian Theodoret of the 5th century. The Latin translation, *Vicisti, Galilaee*, is more frequently quoted.

Gallia est omnis divisa in partes tres [gahl'-lih-ah est om'-nis dih-wee'-sah in pahr'-tays trays] *L*—All Gaul is divided into three parts. Caesar, *Gallic War*, 1; 1.

Garde à cheval [gahrd ah shvahl] *Fr*—Mounted guard.

Garde du corps [gahrd dü kor] *Fr*—Body guard.

Gardez la foi [gahr-day lah fwah] *Fr*—Keep the faith.

Gardien de la paix [gahr-dyaN duh lah peh] *Fr*—Guardian of the peace; a policeman.

Gata con guantes no caza ratones [gah'-tah kon gwahn'-tays noh kah'-sah rah-toh'-nays] *Sp*—A cat with gloves on catches no mice.

Gaudeamus, igitur, juvenes dum sumus [gow-deh-ah'-muhs ih'-gih-tuhr yuh'-weh-nays duhm suh'-muhs] *L*—Let us rejoice, therefore, while we are young. The first line of a Latin song once popular in college circles.

Gaudet tentamine virtus [gow'-det ten-tah'-mih-neh wihr'-toos] *L*—Virtue rejoices in trials.

Gaudium certaminis [gow'-dih-uhm kehr-tah'-mih-niss] *L*—Delight in the struggle; joy in the fight.

gaux. généraux [zhay-nay-roh] *Fr*—Military generals.

G. A. Z. *See* Gesamtverzeichnis der ausländischen Zeitschriften.

Geben Sie acht! [gay'-bun zee ahkht] *Ger*—Take care; watch out.

Gebranntes Kind scheut das Feuer [guh-brahn'-tuhs kint shoit dahs foi'-uhr] *Ger*—The burnt child dreads the fire.

Geflügelte Worte [guh-flü'-guhl-tuh vor'-tuh] *Ger*—Winged words. A translation of Epea pteroenta (*q.v.*). It has come to mean an expression that has traveled from one language to another.

Geheime Staatspolizei [guh-hI'-muh shtahts-poh-lee-tsI'] *Ger*—Secret State Police under the Nazis. Generally referred to as Gestapo, a combination of the beginning letters of each of the components.

Geld behält das Feld [gelt buh-helt' dahs felt] *Ger*—Money gains the field; money makes the world go round.

Genius loci [geh'-nih-uhs lo'-kee] *L*—The protecting spirit or deity of a place.

Gens braccata [gayns brah-kah'-tah] *L*—People, such as Gauls and barbarians in general, who wore trousers (breeches), not the toga, as did the Romans.

Gens d'armes [zhahN dahrm] *Fr*—In Middle Ages, men-at-arms; soldiers. The modern term *gendarmes*, policemen, is derived from this phrase.

79

Gens de condition [zhahN duh kohN-dee-syohN] *Fr*—People of rank.

Gens d'église [zhahN day-gleez] *Fr*—Churchmen; ecclesiastics.

Gens de guerre [zhahN duh gehr] *Fr*—The military class.

Gens de la même famille [zhahN duh lah mem fah-mee] *Fr*—People of the same ilk. Usually an un-complimentary remark.

Gens de lettres [zhahN duh leh-truh] *Fr*—The literary world.

Gens de loi [zhahN duh lwah] *Fr*—Lawyers.

Gens de peu [zhahN duh puh] *Fr*—Men of the lower orders, of little influence.

Gens de robe [zhahN duh ruhb] *Fr*—People connected with some aspect of the law: lawyers, judges, magistrates, etc.

Gens du bien [zhahN dü byaN] *Fr*—The people who do good.

Gens du monde [zhahN dü mohNd] *Fr*—People of the world; fashionable people.

Gens togata [gayns toh-gah'-tah] *L*—The toga-clad nation; the Romans; civilians in general, as distinguished from the military class. Vergil, *Aeneid,* 1; 282.

Gente baja [hen'-tay bah'-hah] *Sp*—The lower classes.

Gente fina [hen'-tay fee'-nah] *Sp*—The cultivated, educated class.

Genus homo [geh'-nuhs ho'-moh] *L*—The human race.

Genus irritabile vatum [geh'-nuhs eer-ree-tah'-bih-leh wah'-tuhm] *L*—The wasp-ish race of poets. This suggests the jealousy that exists among versifiers who each resent the others' pretensions. Horace, *Epistles,* 2; 2, 102.

Genus literarium [geh'-nuhs lih-teh-rah'-rih-uhm] *L*—Literary genre.

Georgium sidus [geh-or'-gih-uhm see'-duhs] *L*—Former name of the planet Uranus, so named after George III by its discoverer, William Herschel.

Gerebatur [geh-ray-bah'-tuhr] *L*—It was waged. Used with dates to indicate when a war took place.

Gesagt, getan [guh-zahgt' guh-tahn'] *Ger*—No sooner said than done.

Gesamtverzeichnis der ausländischen Zeitschriften [guh-zahmt-fehr-tsIkh'-nis dehr ows-len'-dish-un tsIt'-shrift-un] *Ger*—Comprehensive Index of Foreign Periodicals; a list of non-German periodicals.

ges. gesch. gesetzlich geschützt [guh-zetts'-likh guh-shüttst'] *Ger*—Legally protected; patented.

Gestapo. *Ger*—*See* Geheime Staatspolizei.

Gesta Romanorum [gehs'-tah roh-mah-noh'-ruhm] *L*—"The Exploits of the Romans," a medieval collection of tales and legends with strong moral lessons.

Gibier de potence [zhee-byay duh puh-tahNss] *Fr*—A gallows bird; jail-bird.

Gigantes autem erant super terram in diebus illis [gih-gahn'-tays ow'-tem eh'-rahnt suh'-pehr ter'-rahm in dih-ay'-buhs il'-leess] *L*—There were giants upon the earth in those days. *Vulgate, Genesis,* 6; 4.

Giovane santo, diavolo vecchio [joh'-vah-nay sahn'-toh dee-ah'-voh-loh veck'-kee-oh] *It*—A young saint, an old devil.

GKW Gesamtkatalog der Wiegendrucke [guh-zahmt-kah-tah-luhk' dehr vee'-gun-druhk'-kuh] *Ger*—Bibliography of incunabula.

Glaucopis Athene [glow-koh'-pis ah-thay'-nay] *Gk*—Owl-eyed, piercing-eyed Athene. An epithet. Homer, *Iliad,* 1; 206 and elsewhere.

Gleich und gleich gesellt sich gern [glIkh unt glIkh guh-sellt' zikh gehrn] *Ger*—Birds of a feather flock together.

Gli assenti hanno torto [lyee ahs-sen'-tee ahn'-noh tor'-toh] *It*—The absent are always wrong. *See also* Les absents . . .

Glissando [glees-sahn'-doh] *It*—Notes played in a sliding, slurring, or gliding manner.

Gli uomini hanno gli anni che sentono, e le donne quelli che mostrano [lyee oo-oh'-mee-nee ahn'-noh lyee ahn'-nee kay sehn'-toh-noh ay lay don'-nay kwel'-lee kay mohs'-trah-noh] *It*—Men are as old as they feel, and women as old as they look.

Gloria in excelsis Deo. Et in terra pax hominibus bonae voluntatis [gloh'-rih-ah in ex-sel'-seess deh'-oh et in tehr'-rah pahx hoh-mih'-nih-buhs boh-nay voh-luhn-tah'-tiss] *L*—Glory to God in the highest and on earth peace to men of good will. Opening words of the Gloria of the Mass. Adapted from *Vulgate, Luke,* 2; 14.

Gloria Patri et Filio et Spiritui Sancto; sicut erat in principio et nunc et semper et in saecula saeculorum. Amen [gloh'-rih-ah pah'-tree et fee'-lih-oh et spih-rih-too'-ee sahnk'-toh; see'-kuht eh'-raht in preen-sih'-pih-oh nuhnk et sem'-pehr et in say'-kuh-lah say-kuh-loh'-ruhm] *L*—Glory be to the Father and to the Son and to the Holy Spirit; as it was in the beginning, is now and ever shall be, world without end. Amen. In Christian churches this is known as the lesser doxology.

Glückliches Neujahr! [glück'-likh-uhs noi'-yahr] *Ger*—Happy New Year!

Glück und Glas wie leicht bricht das [glück unt glahs vee lIkht brikht dahs] *Ger* —Luck and glass, how easily they break.

G. m. b. H. Gesellschaft mit beschränkter Haftung [guh-zell'-shahft mit buh-shrehnk'-tuhr hahf'-toong] *Ger*—Company with limited liability.

Gnothi seauton [gnoh'-thih seh-ow-ton'] *Gk*—Know thyself. A maxim on the walls of Apollo's temple at Delphi, attributed to various Greek philosophers.

Gorge de pigeon [gawrzh duh pee-zhohN] *Fr*—Iridescent throat of the dove; used to describe the variegated colors of shot silk.

Gott behüte! [guht buh-hü'-tuh] *Ger*—God forbid!

Gott macht gesund, und der Doktor bekommt das Geld [guht mahkht guh-zunt' unt dehr dok'-tohr buh-kommt' dahs gelt] *Ger*—God gives us back our health, and the doctor gets the money.

Gott mit uns [guht mit uhns] *Ger*—God with us. A popular slogan of the Germans during the First World War.

Gott sei Dank [guht zI dahnk] *Ger*—Thanks be to God.

Gott soll hüten! [guht zuhl hüt'-tun] *Ger* —God forbid!

Gott strafe dich [guht strah'-fuh dihkh] *Ger*—May God punish you.

Goutte à goutte [goot ah goot] *Fr*—Drop by drop.

G. P. R. genio populi Romani [geh'-nih-oh po'-puh-lee roh-mah'-nee] *L*—To the genius of the Roman people.

G. P. U. *See* O.G.P.U.

G. Q. G. Grand Quartier général [grahN kahr-tyay zhay-nay-rahl] *Fr*—General Headquarters (military).

Grâce à Dieu [grahss ah dyuh] *Fr*—Thanks be to God.

Gracias a Dios [grah'-see-ahs ah dyohss'] *Sp*—Thanks be to God.

Gradu diverso, via una [grah'-doo dee-wehr'-soh wih'-ah oo'-nah] *L*—Following the same route but at a different pace.

Gradus ad Parnassum [grah'-doos ahd pahr-nahss'-suhm] *L*—Steps to Parnassus; title of an English textbook on verse-writing in Latin and of musical works by Fux and by Clementi.

Graecia capta ferum victorem cepit [grI'-kih-ah kahp'-tah feh'-ruhm wihk-toh'-rem kay'-pit] *L*—Captive Greece took its rough victor captive. Though the Romans defeated the Greeks on the battlefield, the conquerors adopted much of the Greek culture. Horace, *Epistles,* 2; 1, 156.

Graeculus esuriens [grI'-kuh-luhs ay-suh'-rih-ayns] *L*—The starving Greek. Represented by Juvenal as a man who would stoop to any skulduggery to make a living. Juvenal, 3; 78.

gral. general [hay-nay-rahl'] *Sp*—Military general.

Grammatici certant et adhuc sub iudice lis est [grahm-mah′-tih-kee kehr′-tahnt et ahd′-hook suhb yoo′-dih-keh leess est] *L*—The grammarians are still quarreling and the matter is still in dispute. Horace, *Art of Poetry*, 78.

Grande dame [grahNd dahm] *Fr*—A woman of queenly bearing; often applied to one who puts on airs.

Grande parure [grahNd pah-rür] *Fr*—Full dress.

Grand seigneur [grahN seh-nyuhr] *Fr*—A great lord; an aristocrat of the higher ranks.

Gratia gratiam parit [grah′-tih-ah grah′-tih-ahm pah′-rit] *L*—Kindness begets kindness.

Gratia placendi [grah′-tih-ah plah-kehn′-dee] *L*—For the sake of pleasing.

Gratias agimus [grah′-tee-ahs ah′-gih-muhs] *L*—We return thanks.

Gratis dictum [grah′-tiss dihk′-tuhm] *L*—A mere assertion unsupported by evidence.

Graviora quaedam sunt remedia periculis [grah-wih-o′-rah kwI′-dahm suhnt reh-meh′-dih-ah peh-ree′-kuh-leess] *L*—Some remedies are worse than the disease. Publilius Syrus.

Grosse Dinge haben kleine Anfänge [groh′-suh dihn′-guh hah′-bun klI-nuh ahn′-fehng-uh] *Ger*—Great things have small beginnings.

Grosse tête, peu de sens [grohss teht puh duh sahNss] *Fr*—Big head but little sense.

Guarda innanzi che tu salti [gwahr′-dah een-nahn′-tsee kay too sahl′-tee] *It*—Look before you leap.

Guarde-vos Deus de amigo reconciliado [gwahr′-dee vooz day′-oosh dee ah-mee′-goo ray-koN-see-lee-ah′-doo] *Port*—God preserve you from a former friend with whom you have become reconciled.

Guerra al cuchillo [gehr′-rah ahl koo-chee′-yoh] *Sp*—War to the knife; deadly conflict.

Guerra cominciata, inferno scatenato [gwehr′-rah koh-meen-chah′-tah een-fehr′-noh skah-tay-nah′-toh] *It*—War begun is hell let loose.

Guerre à mort [gehr ah mohr] *Fr*—War to the death.

Guerre à outrance [gehr ah oo-trahNss] *Fr*—War to the uttermost; a savage war.

Gute Nacht [goo′-tuh nahkht] *Ger*—Good night.

Guten Morgen [goo′-tun mor′-gun] *Ger*—Good morning.

Gute Ware lobt sich selbst [goo′-tuh vah′-ruh lopt sikh zelpst] *Ger*—Good merchandise praises itself; good wine needs no bush.

Gutta cavat lapidem, consumitur annulus usu [guht-tah kah′-waht lah′-pih-dehm kohn-soo′-mih-tuhr ahn′-nuh-luss oo′-soo] *L*—Dripping water hollows the rock; the ring is worn away by use. Ovid, *Epistles from the Pontus*, 4; 10, 5. This inspired the line *Gutta cavat lapidem, non vi sed saepe cadendo:* The drop hollows the stone not by force but frequent falling. An early use is to be found in the seventh sermon of Latimer, given before Edward IV in 1549. *See also* Percussu crebro saxa . . .

H

h. a. hoc anno [hohk ahn'-noh] *L*—In the present year.

Habeas corpus [hah'-beh-ahs kor'-puhs] *L*—You may have the body; a writ of personal freedom exercised when a prisoner posts bail and demands a hearing in court. There are a number of writs that begin with these two words.

Habemus papam [hah-bay'-muhs pah'-pahm] *L*—We have a pope. Words spoken to the waiting crowd in front of St. Peter's in Rome after the cardinals of the Roman Catholic Church have chosen a new pope.

Habendum et tenendum [hah-ben'-duhm et teh-nehn'-duhm] *L*—To have and to hold. An expression found in deeds.

Habent sua fata libelli [hah'-bent suh'-ah fah'-tah lih-bel'-lee] *L*—See Pro captu lectoris . . .

Habet et musca splenem [hah'-bet et muhs'-kah splay'-nem] *L*—Even a fly will show anger.

hab. fac. poss. habere facias possessionem [hah-bay'-reh fah'-kih-ahs pos-sehs-sih-oh'-nem] *L*—Cause a certain person to have possession. A writ of execution in eviction.

Haeret lateri letalis harundo [hI'-ret lah'-tch roo lay-tah'-lis hah-ruhn'-doh] *L*—The deadly arrow sticks in his side; by extension, deep passion or remorse. Vergil, *Aeneid* 4; 73.

Hänge nicht alles auf einen Nagel [hehng'-uh nihkht ahl'-luss owf I'-nehn nah'-gul] *Ger*—Don't hang everything on one nail; don't carry all your eggs in one basket.

Hannibal ad portas [hahn'-nih-bahl ahd por'-tahs] *L*—Hannibal is at the gates. A call for action; a cry of alarm. The Carthaginian general was a terror to the Romans during the Second Punic War (218-201).

Hapax legomenon [hah'-pahx leh-go'-meh-non] *Gk*—Said once; a word or an expression used only once. A term used in classical philology.

Hasta la muerte todo es vida [ahs'-tah lah mu-ehr'-tay toh'-doh ess bee'-dah] *Sp*—All is life up to death; never say die; where there's life there's hope. Cervantes, *Don Quixote*, 2; 59.

Hasta la vista [ahs'-tah lah bees'-tah] *Sp*—Until we meet again.

Hasta luego [ahs'-tah lway'-goh] *Sp*—So long; see you later.

Hasta mañana [ahs'-tah mah-nyah'-nah] *Sp*—Until tomorrow.

Haud facile emergunt quorum virtutibus obstat/res angusta domi [howd fah'-kih-leh ay-mehr'-guhnt kwoh'-ruhm wihr-too'-tih-buhs op'-staht rays ahn-guhs'-tah do'-mee] *L*—Men who are held back by straitened circumstances at home do not easily succeed. Juvenal, 3; 164. Samuel Johnson's version, even more concise than the Latin, is "Slow rises worth by poverty depressed." *London*, 177.

Haud passibus aequis [howd pahs'-sih-buhs I'-kwees] *L*—Adapted from Non passibus aequis (*q.v.*).

Haute bourgeoisie [oht boor-zhwah-zee] *Fr*—The upper middle class, especially the more prosperous.

Haute coiffure [oht kwah-für] *Fr*—Fashionable hairdressing.

Haute couture [oht koo-tür] *Fr*—The acme of feminine fashion; high fashion dress designing by couturiers.

Haute cuisine [oht kwee-zeen] *Fr*—Fine, or gourmet, cooking.

Haut goût [oh goo] *Fr*—High flavor in meat that has been kept so long that many consider it tainted; high seasoning.

Haut ton [oh tohN] *Fr*—High tone; elegance in fashion.

h. c. *See* Honoris causa.

h. d. hora decubitus [hoh'-rah day-kuh'-bih-toos] *L*—At bedtime. A medical direction.

h. e. hoc est [hok est] *L*—This is; used in the same sense as i.e. (*q.v.*).

He dicho [ay dee'-choh] *Sp*—I have spoken; I have said what I had to say. The customary final words of a speech in Spanish.

He glossa omomoch', he de phren anomotos [hay glohs'-sah oh-moh'-mokh hay deh frayn ah-noh'-moh-tos] *Gk*—My tongue has sworn but not my mind; a mental reservation. Euripides, *Hippolytus*, 612.

Heil dir im Siegerkranz [hIl deer im zeeg'-uhr-krahnts] *Ger*—Hail to thee wearing the conqueror's wreath. The national hymn of Prussia.

Helluo librorum [hehl'-luh-oh lih-broh'-ruhm] *L*—A devourer of books; a great reader. Adapted from a passage in Cicero, *Chief Good and Evil*, 3; 2, 7.

Hesterni Quirites [hess-tehr'-nee kwih-ree'-tayss] *L*—Roman citizens only yesterday; recently freed slaves. Persius, *Satires*, 3; 106.

Heu mores [heh'-uh moh'-rays] *L*—Alas for the morals of the day.

Heureux les peuples dont l'histoire est ennuyeux [uh-ruh lay puh-pl dohN lees-twahr eh tahn-wee-yuh] *Fr*—Happy the nation whose history makes dull reading.

Heute Deutschland, morgen die ganze Welt [hoi'-tuh doitsh'-lahnt mor'-gun dee gahn'-tsuh velt] *Ger*—Today Germany, tomorrow the whole world. The Nazi dream.

Heute rot, morgen tot [hoi'-tuh roht mor'-gun toht] *Ger*—Today red, tomorrow dead; here today, gone tomorrow.

Heu, vitam perdidi, operose nihil agendo [heh'-uh wee'-tahm pehr'-dih-dee oh-peh-roh'-say nih'-hil ah-gen'-doh] *L*—Alas, I have wasted my life, industriously doing nothing.

H. I., H. J. Hic iacet *or* jacet [heek yah'-ket] *L*—Here lies.

Hiatus maxime (valde) deflendus [hih-ah'-tuhs mahx'-ih-may, wahl'-day, day-flen'-duhs] *L*—A gap much to be lamented. This phrase may be found in ancient classics where a break in the original text is noted. Also used when a person's performance falls short of expectations.

Hibernicis ipsis Hiberniores [hih-behr'-nih-keess ip'-seess hih-behr-nih-oh'-rays] *L*—More Irish than the Irish themselves. Said of certain English settlers in Ireland.

Hic et nunc [heek et nuhnk] *L*—Here and now.

Hic et ubique [heek et uh-bee'-kweh] *L*—Here and everywhere.

Hic jacet *L*—*See* H. I., H. J.

Hic niger est, hunc tu, Romane, caveto [hihk nih'-gehr est huhnk too roh-mah'-neh kah-way'-toh] *L*—This man is a blackhearted fellow; Roman, avoid him. Horace, *Satires*, 1; 4, 85.

Hic sepultus [heek seh-puhl'-tuhs] *L*—Here lies buried. *See also* H. I. S.

Hier stehe ich! Ich kann nicht anders. Gott helfe mir, Amen [heer shtay'-uh ikh ikh kahn nihkt ahn'-duhrs guht hel'-fuh meer ah-men'] *Ger*—Here I take my stand! I cannot do otherwise. God help me! Supposed statement of Luther when he was invited to recant before the Diet of Worms in 1521.

Hilf dir selbst, so hilft dir Gott [hilf deer zelpst zoh hilft deer guht] *Ger*—God helps those who help themselves.

Hinc illae lacrimae [hink ihl'-lI lahk'-rih-mI] *L*—Hence those tears. Terence, *Andria*, 1; 1, 99.

Hinc lucem et pocula sacra [hink loo'-kem et poh'-kuh-lah sah'-krah] *L*—From here (the university) we receive light and sacred inspiration. The motto of the University of Cambridge and its press.

H. I. S., H. J. S. Hic iacet—*or* jacet—sepultus—*or* situs [heek yah'-ket seh-puhl'-tuhs *or* sih'-tuhs] *L*—Here lies buried.

His ego nec metas rerum nec tempora pono [hees eh'-goh nek may'-tahs ray'-ruhm nek tem'-po-rah poh'-noh] *L*—To these (Romans) I place no bounds in space or time. Vergil, *Aeneid*, 1; 278.

Historia vitae magistra [hiss-toh'-rih-ah wee'-tI mah-gis'-trah] *L*—History is the guide of life.

h. m. hoc mense [hohk mayn'-seh] *L*—This month.

H. M. P. Hoc monumentum posuit [hok mo-nuh-men'-tuhm poh'-suh-it] *L*—This monument was erected by ——.

Hnos. Hermanos [ehr-mah'-nohs] *Sp*—Brothers.

Ho anthropos physei politikon zoon [ho ahn'-thro-poss fü-seh poh-lih-tih-konn' zoh'-on] *Gk*—Man is by nature a political animal. Aristotle, *Politics*, 1; 1, 9.

Ho bios brachys, he de techne makre [hoh bih'-os brah-khüs' hay deh tekh'-nay mah-kray'] *Gk*—Life is short; art is long. Hippocrates. *See also* Ars longa . . .

Hoc age [hok ah'-geh] *L*—Do this. At a Roman sacrifice a command from a priest that the victim should be slain. At this order, all present maintained silence; hence the phrase came to mean: Pay attention to this.

Hoc erat in votis [hok eh'-raht in woh'-lees] *L*—This was something I always wanted. Horace, *Satires*, 2; 6, 1.

Hoc est corpus meum [hok est kor'-puhs meh'-uhm] *L*—This is my body. Words used at the consecration in the Latin version of the Mass. *Vulgate, Mark*, 14; 22 and *Luke*, 22; 19.

Hoc genus omne [hok geh'-nuhs om'-neh] *L*—All persons of that classification. Horace used the phrase to end a list of occupations he held in contempt. It is sometimes quoted as *Et id genus omne*,

Id genus omne, Et hoc genus omne. Horace, *Satires*, 1; 2, 2.

Hoc monumentum posuit [hok mo-nuh-men'-tuhm poh'-suh-it] *L*—He erected this monument.

Hoc opus, hic labor est [hok o'-puhs hihk lah'-bohr est] *L*—This is really work, this is really labor. These words were originally used by Vergil to indicate the difficulty of returning to the world above after the descent to Avernus. Vergil, *Aeneid*, 6; 129.

Hoc volo, sic jubeo, sit pro ratione voluntas [hok wuh'-loh seek yuh'-beh-oh sit proh rah-tih-oh'-neh wuh-luhn'-tahs] *L*—This is my wish, this is my command, and for my reason say that it is my pleasure. From Juvenal's picture of a cruel, quarrelsome wife. The motto of the dictator. Juvenal, 6; 223.

Hodie mihi, cras tibi [hoh'-dih-ay mih'-hih krahs tih'-bih] *L*—Today is mine, tomorrow is yours. An inscription found on tombstones.

Hodos chameliontos [ho'-dos kha-mee-lee-on'-tos; the original Greek reads chamai-leh-on'-tos] *Gk*—The path of the chameleon, noted for changing his coloration. W. B. Yeats uses this phrase as the title of Book 3 of his autobiography.

Hoi polloi [hoi pol-loi'] *Gk*—The many; the mob. Since *hoi* means *the*, it is redundant to say *the hoi polloi.*

Hombre casado, burro domado [ohm'-bray kah-sah'-doh boo'-rroh doh-mah'-doh] *Sp*—A married man is a tamed burro.

Hominem pagina nostra sapit [ho'-mih-nem pah'-gih-nah nohs'-trah sah'-pit] *L*—My works savor of humanity. Martial, 10; 4.

Homines dum docent discunt [ho'-mih-nays duhm do'-kent dis'-kuhnt] *L*—Men learn while they teach. Seneca, *Letters to Lucilius*, 7; 7.

Hommage d'auteur [uh-mahzh doh-tuhr] *Fr*—With the compliments of the author.

Hommage d'éditeur [uh-mahzh day-dee-tuhr] *Fr*—With the compliments of the publisher (not of the editor).

Homme d'affaires [uhm dah-fehr] *Fr—* Businessman; an agent.

Homme de bien [uhm duh byaN] *Fr—*A good man; a righteous man.

Homme de guerre [uhm duh gehr] *Fr—* A man of war; member of the military forces.

Homme de lettres [uhm duh leh-truh] *Fr—*Man of letters; a literary man.

Homme de paille [uhm duh pI] *Fr—*Man of straw; a dummy; referring to a weak man who is set up to be knocked down easily.

Homme d'épée [uhm day-pay] *Fr—*Man of the sword; military man; one interested in fencing.

Homme d'esprit [uhm deh-spree] *Fr—*A wit; a man of unusual mental ability.

Homme d'état [uhm day-tah] *Fr—*States-man.

Homme de théâtre [uhm duh tay-ah-tr] *Fr—*A man professionally interested in the theater.

Homme du monde [uhm dü mohNd] *Fr—* Man of the world; a social lion.

Homme du peuple [uhm dü puh-pl] *Fr—* Man of the people.

Homme moyen sensuel [uhm mwah-yaN saN-sü-el] *Fr—*A man of average sensual desires; a common man.

Homo covivens [hoh'-moh koh-wee'-wayns] *L—*Man living together. The projected successor to *homo sapiens*, living a strong community life, strictly regulating population and environment.

Homo ferus [hoh'-moh feh'-russ] *L—*Wild man. A species of man listed by Linnaeus. He did not realize that these were abandoned children who had survived as animals in a hostile environment.

Homo homini aut deus aut lupus [hoh'-moh hoh'-mih-nee owt deh'-uhs owt luh'-puhs] *L—*Man is either a god or a wolf toward his fellow man.

Homo homini lupus [hoh'-moh hoh'-mih-nee luh'-puhs] *L—*Man is a wolf toward man. Adapted from Plautus.

Homo latinissimus [hoh'-moh lah-tee-nis'-sih-muhs] *L—*A very scholarly man.

Homo ludens [hoh'-moh loo'-dayns] *L—* The playing man; man devoted to recreation. A term inspired by the phrase homo sapiens (*q.v.*).

Homo memorabilis [hoh'-moh meh-mo-rah'-bih-liss] *L—*A man to be remembered.

Homo mensura [hoh'-moh mayn-soo'-rah] *L—*Man is the measure. *See also* Panton metron anthropos estin.

Homo multarum literarum [hoh'-moh muhl-tah'-ruhm lih-teh-rah'-ruhm] *L—*A man of many letters; a very learned person.

Homo neanderthalensis [hoh'-moh nay-ahn-dehr-tah-len'-sis] *NL—*Neanderthal man. Applied to certain paleolithic cavemen. A skeleton of a member of this race was discovered in a valley near Düsseldorf, Germany, in 1856.

Homo proponit, sed Deus disponit [hoh'-moh proh-poh'-nit sed deh'-uhs dis-poh'-nit] *L—*Man proposes but God disposes. Thomas à Kempis, *Imitation of Christ*, 1; 19, 2.

Homo sapiens [hoh'-moh sah'-pih-ayns] *L—*Wise man; scientific name for the human species.

Homo semper aliud, Fortuna aliud cogitat [hoh'-moh sem'-pehr ah'-lih-ud for-too'-nah ah'-lih-ud koh'-gih-taht] *L—*Man always has one thing in mind, Fortune another. Publilius Syrus.

Homo solus aut deus aut daemon [hoh'-moh soh'-luhs owt deh'-uhs owt dI'-mohn] *L—*A man who lives alone is either a god or a devil.

Homo sum: humani nil a me alienum puto [hoh'-moh suhm hoo-mah'-nee neel ah may ah-lih-ay'-nuhm puh'-toh] *L—*I am a man and nothing that touches humanity is foreign to me. Terence, *Self-Tormentor*, 1; 1, 25.

Homo trium literarum [hoh'-moh trih'-uhm lih-teh-rah'-ruhm] *L—*A man of three letters, i.e., *fur*, the Latin word for thief.

Homo unius libri [hoh'-moh oo-nee'-uhs lih'-bree] *L—*A man of one book. *See also* Timeo hominem (virum) . . .

Hon hoi theoi philousin apothneskei neos [hon hoi the-oi' fih-loo'-sin ah-pothnays'-keh ne'-os] *Gk*—He whom the gods love dies young. Menander. *See also* Quem di diligunt . . .

Honi (honni) soit qui mal y pense [ohnee-swah kee mahl ee pahNss] *Fr*—Evil to him who evil thinks. Motto of the Order of the Garter, supposedly based on a remark of Edward III when he put on his leg a garter that was lost by a countess who was dancing with him. The incident is probably a pleasant fiction.

Honnête homme [uh-net uhm] *Fr*—A gentleman; an honorable man.

Honores mutant mores [ho-noh'-rays moo'-tahnt moh'-rays] *L*—Honors change manners. It is not unusual for those who rise in the world to kick down the ladder by which they ascended.

Honoris causa (gratia) [ho-noh'-ris kow'-sah, grah'-tih-ah] *L*—As a recognition of honor due. Used especially when universities grant honorary degrees.

Honos habet onus [ho'-nohs hah'-bet o'-nuhs] *L*—Honors carry the burden of responsibility.

Horas non numero nisi serenas [hoh'-rahs nohn nuh'-meh-roh nih'-sih seh-ray'-nahs] *L*—I number none but sunny hours. An engraving found on sundials.

Horresco referens [hor-rays'-koh reh'-feh-rayns] *L*—I shudder as I repeat the story. Vergil, *Aeneid*, 2; 204.

Horribile dictu [hor-rih'-bih-leh dik'-too] *L*—Horrible to relate.

Horror vacui [hor'-rohr wah'-kuh-ee] *L* Dread of an empty space; said of artists who fear leaving a blank area in their works.

Hors concours [ohr kohN-koor] *Fr*—Outside the competition; in a class by itself.

Hors de combat [ohr duh kohN-bah] *Fr*—Out of the fight; disabled.

Hors de commerce [ohr duh kom-mehrs] *Fr*—Not available commercially.

Hors de propos [ohr duh pruh-poh] *Fr*—Ill-timed; out of place; irrelevant.

Hors de saison [ohr duh seh-zohN] *Fr*—Out of season.

Hors d'oeuvre [ohr duh-vruh] *Fr*—Tasty bits of food served at the beginning of a meal to stimulate the appetite; appetizer; antipasto.

Hors la loi [ohr lah lwah] *Fr*—Outlawed.

Hortus conclusus [hor'-tuhs kohn-kloo'-sus] *L*—An enclosed garden, a private retreat.

Ho sophos en auto peripherei ten ousian [hoh so-fos' en ow-toh' peh-rih-feh'-reh tayn oo-see'-ahn] *Gk*—The wise man carries all his property within himself. Menander, *Monostichs*, 404.

Hostis humani generis [hos'-tis hoo-mah'-nee geh'-neh-ris] *L*—An enemy of the human race.

Hôtel de ville [oh-tel duh veel] *Fr*—Townhall.

Hôtel-Dieu [oh-tel-dyuh] *Fr*—A hospital.

Hôtel garni [oh-tel gahr-nee] *Fr*—Furnished lodgings.

Hôtel meublé [oh-tel muh-blay] *Fr*—Furnished lodgings.

Hr. Herr [hehr] *Ger*—Mr.

—H. R. I. P. hic requiescit in pace [heek reh-kwih-ays'-kit in pah'-keh] *L*—Here rests in peace —.

h. s. hora somni [hoh'-rah som'-nee] *L*—At bedtime. A medical direction.

H. S. S. Historiae Societatis Socius [hihs-toh'-rih I soh-kih-eh-tah'-tiss soh'-kih-uhs] *L*—Fellow of the Historical Society.

h. t. hoc tempore [hohk tem'-po-reh] *L*—At this time.

Hunde, die bellen, beissen nicht [huhn'-duh dee bel'-lun bIs'-sun nikht] *Ger*—Barking dogs don't bite.

Hunger ist der beste Koch [huhn'-guhr ist dehr bes'-tuh kokh] *Ger*—Hunger is the best cook.

87

Hurler avec les loups [ür-lay ah-vek lay loo] *Fr*—Run with the crowd.

Huyendo del toro, cayó en el arroyo [oo-yen'-doh del toh'-roh kah-yoh' en el ah-rroh'-yoh] *Sp*—While running from the bull, he fell into the stream; out of the frying pan into the fire.

Hypotheses non fingo [hih-poh'-teh-sayss nohn fing'-goh] *L*—I do not make hypotheses; I deal with facts and not suppositions. Sir Isaac Newton.

Hysteron proteron [his'-te-ron pro'-te-ron] *Gk*—Literally, the latter first; transposing the logical order of phrases or clauses so that the more striking or important idea is first; putting the cart before the horse. An example: "Let us die and let us rush into the midst of the fight," in Vergil, *Aeneid*, 2, 353.

I

Iatre, therapeuson seauton [ee-ah-treh′ the-rah′-poi-son seh-ow-ton′] *Gk—See* Medice, cura teipsum.

ibid. ibidem [ih-bee′-dem] *L*—In the same place.

Ich bin der Geist der stets verneint! [ikh bin dehr gIst dehr shtayts fehr-nInt′] *Ger*—I am the spirit that always says No. A line spoken by Mephistopheles. Goethe, *Faust,* pt. 1; 1338.

Ich dien [ikh deen] *Ger*—I serve. Motto of the Prince of Wales.

ICHTHYS [ikh-thüs′] The Greek letters *iota, chi, theta, upsilon, sigma,* which spell *fish Gk*—A symbol of identification among early Christians, the letters standing for the initials of *Iesous Christos, Theou Hyios, Soter* [ee-ay-soos′ kris-tos′ theh-oo′ huh-yos′ soh-tayr′] meaning Jesus Christ, Son of God, Savior.

Ici on parle français [ee-see ohN pahrl frahN-seh] *Fr*—French is spoken here.

I. C. N. in Christi nomine [in kris′-tee noh′-mih-neh] *L*—In the name of Christ.

id. idem [ee′-dem] *L*—The same person.

Id al-Fitr [ah′-eed al-fuhtr] *Arabic*—Breaking of the fast; Moslem festival celebrated on the day after the month-long fast of Ramadan.

Idée fixe [ee-day feex] *Fr*—A fixed idea; an obsession.

Idée maîtresse [ee-day meh-tress] *Fr*—The master faculty, the basic explanation of human nature.

Idem non potest simul esse et non esse [ih′-dem nohn po′-test sih′-muhl ess′-seh et nohn ess′-seh] *L*—It is impossible for the same thing to exist and not to exist at the same time. Axiom in scholastic philosophy.

Idem per idem [ih′-dem pehr ih′-dem] *L*—Literally, the same through the same; an explanation that uses the same explanation to clear up a definition.

Idem velle et idem nolle, ea demum firma amicitia est [ih′-dem wel′-leh et ih′-dem nohl′-leh eh′-ah day′-muhm feer′-mah ah-mee-kih′-tih-ah est] *L*—To wish the same things and to reject the same things, that indeed is true friendship. Sallust, *Catiline,* 20.

I denari del comune sono come l'acqua benedetta, ognun ne piglia [ee day-nah′-ree del koh-moo′-nay soh′-noh koh′-may lah′-kwah bay-nay-det′-tah ohn-yoon′ nay peel′-lyah] *It*—Public funds are like holy water, everybody takes some.

Id facere laus est quod decet, non quod licet [id fah′-keh-reh lowss est kwod deh′-ket nohn kwod lih′-ket] *L*—He deserves praise who does what he ought to do, not what he may do. Seneca, *Octavia,* 454.

Id genus omne [id geh′-nuhs om′-neh] *L—See* Hoc genus omne.

I. D. N. in Dei Nomine [in deh′-ee noh′-mih-neh] *L*—In the name of God.

i. e. id est [id est] *L*—That is to say; namely.

I frutti proibiti sono i più dolci [ee froot′-tee proh-ee-bee′-tee soh′-noh ee pee-oo′ dohl′-chee] *It*—Forbidden fruits are sweetest.

Ignis fatuus [ig′-nihs fah′-tuh-uhs] *L*—Misleading light; will-o′-the-wisp.

Ignorantia facti excusat [ig-noh-rahn′-tih-ah fahk′-tee ex-koo′-saht] *L*—Ignorance of the fact excuses; when an honest error is made, criminal intent is lacking.

Ignorantia legis (juris) neminem excusat [ig-noh-rahn′-tih-ah lay′-gis, yoo′-riss, nay′-mih-nem ex-koo′-saht] *L*—Ignorance of the law excuses nobody.

Ignoratio elenchi [ig-noh-rah′-tih-oh eh-layn′-kee] *L*—Ignorance of the point under discussion. The logical fallacy of proving or disproving a point that is not under discussion.

Ignoscito saepe alteri, numquam tibi [ig-nohs′-kih-toh sI′-peh ahl′-teh-ree nuhm′-kwam tih′-bih] *L*—Often pardon others but never yourself.

Ignoti nulla cupido [ig-noh′-tee nool′-lah kuh-pee′-doh] *L*—Nobody desires what he does not know. Ovid, *Art of Love*, 3; 397.

Ignotum per ignotius [ig-noh′-tuhm pehr ig-noh′-tih-uhs] *L*—To explain a matter that is difficult with an illustration or explanation that is still more difficult.

I gran dolori sono muti [ee grahn dohloh′-ree soh′-noh moo′-tee] *It*—Great sorrows have no tongue.

IHS [iota eta sigma] A Christian symbol; three Greek letters, iota, eta, sigma, an abbreviation of the Greek name, Iesous, i.e., Jesus. It does not mean *Iesous, Hyios, Soter* (Jesus, Son, Savior); *Iesus, Hominum Salvator* (Jesus, Savior of Men); or In hoc signo (vinces) (*q.v.*).

i. J. d. W. im Jahre der Welt [im yah′-ruh dehr velt] *Ger*—In the year of the world. A system of dating events from the supposed date of creation.

I. K. H. Ihre königliche Hoheit [eeh′-ruh kuh′-nik-lihk-kuh hoh′-hIt] *Ger*—Her Royal Highness.

Il a la mer à boire [eel ah lah mehr ah bwahr] *Fr*—He must drink up the sea; he has an impossible task to perform.

Il a le diable au corps [eel ah luh dyahbl oh kor] *Fr*—See Il avait le diable au corps.

Il a les défauts de ses qualités [eel ah lay day-foh duh say kah-lee-tay] *Fr*—He has the defects of his qualities. A frugal man may be stingy with his children without realizing it; a man with more than normal devotion to his job may drive his staff too hard.

Il a le vin mauvais [eel ah luh van muhveh] *Fr*—He is quarrelsome when he drinks.

Il avait le diable au corps [eel ah-veh luh dyah-bl oh kor] *Fr*—He had the devil in his body; he was full of the devil. Sainte-Beuve's appraisal of Voltaire.

Il bel sesso [eel bel sess′-soh] *It*—The fair sex.

Il connaît l'univers, et ne se connaît pas [eel kuh-neh lü-nee-vehr ay nuh suh kuh-neh pah] *Fr*—He knows the universe but not himself. La Fontaine, *Fables*, 8; 26.

Il diavolo non è così brutto come si dipinge [eel dee-ah′-voh-loh nonn eh kohsee′ broot′-toh koh′-may see dee-peen′-jay] *It*—The devil is not as bad as he is painted.

Il dit tout ce qu'il veut, mais malheureusement il n'a rien à dire [eel dee too skeel vuh meh mah-luh-ruhz-mahN eel nah ryan-ah-deer] *Fr*—He says everything he wishes to say, but unfortunately he has nothing to say. A critic's tart comment.

Il est bon d'avoir des amis partout [eel eh bohN dah-vwahr day zah-mee pahr-too] *Fr*—It is good to have friends everywhere.

Il est bon de parler, et meilleur de se taire [eel eh bohN duh pahr-lay ay meh-yuhr duh suh tehr] *Fr*—It is good to speak but better to be silent; speech is silver, but silence is golden.

Il faut bonne mémoire après qu'on a menti [eel foh bun may-mwahr ah-preh koh-nah mahN-tee] *Fr*—A man needs a good memory after he has lied. Corneille, *Le Menteur*, 4.

Il faut cultiver notre jardin [eel foh kül-tee-vay nuh-tr zhahr-daN] *Fr*—We must cultivate our garden. Candide maintains that man was not born for idleness but was placed in the garden of Eden to dress it and keep it. After numerous disasters he learns that life becomes endurable only through work. Concluding words of Voltaire's *Candide*.

Il faut laver son linge sale en famille [eel foh lah-vay sohN laNzh sahl ahN fahmee] *Fr*—We should wash our soiled linen in private. Quarrels of a private nature should not be aired in public, for such disputes hurt a cause. Voltaire.

Il faut manger pour vivre, et non pas vivre pour manger [eel foh mahN-zhay poor vee-vr ay nohN pah vee-vr poor mahN-zhay] *Fr*—We should eat to live, not live to eat. Molière, *The Miser*, 3; 5.

Il faut marcher quand le diable est aux trousses [eel foh mahr-shay kahN luh dyahb-bl eh toh trooss] *Fr*—One must move when the devil drives behind.

Il faut que la jeunesse se passe [eel foh kuh lah zhuh-nehss suh pahss] *Fr*—Youth will have its fling; boys will be boys.

Ilias malorum [ee'-lih-ahs mah-loh'-ruhm] *L*—An *Iliad* of ills; an account of a series of misfortunes.

Ille dolet vere qui sine teste dolet [il'-leh doh'-let way'-ray kwee sih'-neh tes'-teh doh'-let] *L*—He truly grieves who grieves alone. Martial, 1; 33, 4.

Ille hic est Raphael [ih'-leh heek'-est rah'-fah-ehl] *L*—The one who is here is Raphael. The epitaph written on the artist's tomb in the Pantheon. Bembo.

Illotis manibus [il-loh'-teess mah'-nih-buhs] *L*—With hands unwashed.

Il lupo cangia il pelo, ma non il vizio [eel loo'-poh kahn'-jee-ah eel pay'-loh mah nonn eel vee'-tsee-oh] *It*—The wolf changes his fur but not his nature.

Il Maestro di color che sanno [eel mah-ay'-stroh dee koh-lohr' kay sahn'-noh] *It*—The master of those who know. The reference is to Aristotle. Dante, *Inferno*, 4; 131.

Il miglior fabbro [eel meel-yohr' fahb'-broh] *It*—The best maker; by extension, the best creator in the literary sense. In the dedication of *The Waste Land*, T. S. Eliot described Ezra Pound in this way.

Il mondo è di chi ha pazienza [eel mon'-doh eh dee kee ah pah-tsee-en'-tsah] *It*—The world belongs to the man who is patient.

Il mondo è di chi se lo piglia [eel mon'-doh eh dee kee say loh peel'-yah] *It*—The world belongs to the go-getter.

Il mondo è un bel libro, ma poco serve a chi non lo sa leggere [eel mon'-doh eh oon bel lee'-broh mah poh'-koh sehr'-vay ah kee nonn loh sah led'-jay-ray] *It*—The world is a beautiful book, but it is of little use to the man who doesn't know how to read it. Goldoni.

Il n'a ni bouche ni éperon [eel nah nee boosh nee ay-prohN] *Fr*—He has neither mouth nor spur, i.e., neither wit nor courage.

Il n'a pas inventé la poudre [eel nah pah zaN-vahN-tay lah poo-dr] *Fr*—Literally, he didn't discover gunpowder; he will not set the world on fire.

Il n'appartient qu'aux grands hommes d'avoir de grands défauts [eel nah-pahr-tyaN koh grahN zuhm dah-vwahr duh grahN day-foh] *Fr*—Only great men are allowed great faults. La Rochefoucauld, *Maxims*, 190.

Il ne faut jamais défier un fou [eel nuh foh zhah-meh day-fee-ay uhN foo] *Fr*—Never challenge a lunatic.

Il ne faut pas disputer des goûts [eel nuh foh pah dee-spü-tay day goo] *Fr*—There is no disputing tastes. *See also* Chacun à son goût. De gustibus non est disputandum.

Il ne faut pas mettre tous ses oeufs dans le même panier [eel nuh foh pah meh-tr too say zuhf dahN luh mem pa-nyay] *Fr*—Don't put all your eggs in one basket.

Il ne manquerait plus que ça [eel nuh mahN-kreh plü kuh sah] *Fr*—That would be the last straw, the crowning offense.

Il n'entend pas raillerie [eel nahN-tahN pah rah-yuh-ree] *Fr*—He can't take a joke.

Il n'est sauce que d'appétit [eel neh sohss kuh dah-pay-tee] *Fr*—Appetite is the best sauce.

Il nous faut de l'audace, et encore de l'audace, et toujours de l'audace [eel noo foh duh loh-dahss ay ahN-kor duh loh-dahss ay too-zhoor duh loh-dahss] *Fr*—We must dare, we must dare again, and always dare. Danton.

Il n'y a de nouveau que ce qui est oublié [eel nyah duh noo-voh kuh skee eh too-blee-ay] *Fr*—There is nothing new but what has been forgotten. Mlle Bertin.

Il n'y a de pire sourd que celui qui ne veut pas entendre [eel nyah duh peer soor kuh slwee kee nuh vuh pah zahN-tahN-dr] *Fr*—There are none so deaf as those who will not hear.

Il n'y a pas de grand homme pour son valet-de-chambre [eel nyah pah duh grahN tuhm poor sohN va-leh duh shahN-br] *Fr*—No man is a hero in the eyes of his valet. Mme de Cornuel. *See also* Es gibt, sagt man ...

Il n'y a pas moins d'éloquence dans le ton de la voix, dans les yeux, et dans l'air de la personne, que dans le choix des paroles [eel nyah pah mwaN day-loh-kahNss dahN luh tohN duh lah vwah dahN lay zyuh ay dahN lehr duh lah pehr-sun kuh dahN luh shwah day pah-ruhl] *Fr*—There is no less eloquence in the tone of the voice, in the eyes, and in the manner of a person than in the choice of his words. La Rochefoucauld, *Maxims*, 249.

Il n'y a plus de Pyrénées [eel nyah plü duh pee-ray-nay] *Fr*—The Pyrenees no longer exist. Louis XIV is reported to have said this to his grandson Philip V when Philip was leaving Paris to occupy the throne of Spain.

Il n'y a point de déguisement qui puisse longtemps cacher l'amour où il est, ni le feindre où il n'est pas [eel nyah pwaN duh day-geez-mahN kee pweess lohN-tahN ka-shay lah-moor oo eel eh nee luh faN-dr oo eel neh pah] *Fr*—There is no disguise that can long conceal love where it exists or feign it where it does not exist. La Rochefoucauld, *Maxims*, 70.

Il n'y a que ceux qui ne font rien, qui ne se trompent pas [eel nyah kuh suh kee nuh fohN ryaN kee nuh suh trohNp pah] *Fr*—Only those who do nothing make no mistakes.

Il n'y a que le premier pas qui coûte [eel nyah kuh luh pruh-myay pah kee koot] *Fr*—It is only the first step that is difficult. When Cardinal Polignac was marveling at the long distance St. Denis, the martyr, traveled with his head in his hands, Madame du Deffand is supposed to have made this remark.

Il n'y a rien de mieux à faire que de s'amuser [eel nyah ryaN duh myuh ah fehr kuh duh sa-mü-zay] *Fr*—There is nothing else to do but enjoy oneself.

Il penseroso [eel penn-seh-roh'-zoh] *It*—The melancholy man. Title of a poem by Milton. A companion piece to *L'allegro* (*q.v.*).

Il rit bien qui rit le dernier [eel ree byaN kee ree luh dehr-nyay] *Fr*—He laughs best who laughs last.

Il s'attache aux pas de ... [eel sa-tahsh oh pah duh] *Fr*—He dogs the footsteps of ...

Il se noierait dans une goutte d'eau [eel suh nwah-yuh-reh dahN zün goot doh] *Fr*—He would drown himself in a drop of water; he makes a mountain out of a molehill.

Il sent le fagot [eel sahN luh fa-goh] *Fr*—He smells of the fagot, i.e., he is suspected of holding heretical views.

Il se recule pour mieux sauter [eel suh ruh-kül poor myuh soh-tay] *Fr*—He draws back to make a better leap forward.

Il se voit par expérience, que les mémoires excellentes se joignent volontiers aux jugements débiles [eel suh vwah pahr ehk-spay-ryahNss kuh lay may-mwahr zehk-seh-lahNt suh zhwaN-yuh vuh-lohN-tyehr oh zhüzh-mahN day-beel] *Fr*—Experience shows that an excellent memory may quite easily be wedded to weak judgment. Montaigne, *Essays*, 1; 9.

Ils ne passeront pas [eel nuh pah-suh-rohn pah] *Fr*—They shall not pass. The rallying cry of the French at Verdun in 1916.

Ils n'ont rien appris, ni rien oublié [eel nohN ryan ah-pree nee ryan oo-blee-ay] *Fr*—They have learned nothing and they have forgotten nothing. Thirty years after the outbreak of the French Revolution, Talleyrand used these words to describe the returned *émigrés*, the Bourbons and their followers.

Il stilo volgare [eel stee'-loh vohl-gah'-ray] *It*—The language of the people. In Dante's day, Italian instead of Latin, the language of the ecclesiastics and scholars.

Il tempo è denaro [eel tem-poh eh deh-nah'-roh] *It*—Time is money.

Il vaut mieux employer notre esprit à supporter les infortunes qui nous arrivent qu'à prévoir celles qui nous peuvent arriver [eel voh myuh ahN-plwah-yay nuh-treh-spree ah sü-por-tay lay zaN-for-tün kee noo zah-reev kah pray-vwahr sehl kee noo puhv ah-ree-vay] *Fr*—It is much better to set our minds to bearing present ills than to foreseeing those that may befall us. La Rochefoucauld, *Maxims,* 174.

Il vaut mieux s'exposer à l'ingratitude que de manquer aux misérables [eel voh myuh sehk-spoh-zay ah laN-grah-tee-tüd kuh duh mahN-kay oh mee-zay-rah-bl] *Fr*—Better run the risk of ingratitude than fail those in need. La Bruyère, *Characters, Of the Heart,* 48 (v), p. 169 in Garapon's edition (Garnier Frères, 1962).

Il veut prendre la lune avec les dents [eel vuh prahN-dr lah lün ah-vek lay dahN] *Fr*—He wants to catch the moon with his teeth. Said of a person who demands the impossible.

Il y a à parier que toute idée publique, toute convention reçue, est une sottise, car elle a convenu au plus grand nombre [eel yah ah pa-ree-ay kuh too tee-day püb-leek toot kohN-vahN-syohN ruh-sü eh tün soh-teez kahr ell ah kohN-vnü oh plü grahN nohN-br] *Fr*—The odds are that every idea commonly held, every accepted custom is stupid, for it has been agreed upon by the majority. Chamfort, *Maximes et Pensées.*

Imitatores, servum pecus [ih-mih-tah-toh'-rays sehr'-wuhm peh'-kuhs] *L*—You imitators, a servile herd. Horace, *Epistles,* 1; 19, 19.

Immedicabile vulnus ense recidendum est ne pars sincera trahatur [im-meh-dih-kah'-bih-leh wuhl'-nuhs ayn'-seh reh-kee-den'-duhm est nay pahrs sihn-kay'-rah trah-hah'-tuhr] *L*—An incurable wound must be cut out lest the healthy part be infected. Ovid, *Metamorphoses,* 1; 190.

Imo pectore [ee'-moh pek'-to-reh] *L*—From the bottom of the heart. Vergil, *Aeneid,* 11; 377.

Imperium cupientibus nihil medium inter summa aut praecipitia [im-peh'-rih-uhm kuh-pih-en'-tih-buhs nih'-hil meh'-dih-uhm in'-ter suhm'-mah owt prI-kih-pih'-tih-ah] *L*—For those seeking power there is no middle course between the depths and the heights, between the top and the bottom. Tacitus, *Histories,* 2; 74.

Imperium et libertas [im-peh'-rih-uhm et lee-behr'-tahs] *L*—Empire and liberty. Lord Beaconsfield.

Imperium in imperio [im-peh'-rih-uhm in im-peh'-rih-oh] *L*—A government within a government.

Imperium Romanum [ihm-peh'-rih-uhm roh-mah'-nuhm] *L*—The Roman Empire, beginning with Augustus.

Imponere Pelio Ossam [im-poh'-neh-reh pay'-lih-oh os'-sahm] *L*—To pile Ossa on Pelion. *See also* Excussit subjecto Pelion Ossae. Vergil, *Georgics,* 1; 281.

Impos animi [im'-pohs ah'-nih-mee] *L*—Weak-minded. *See also* Non compos mentis.

Impossible n'est pas un mot français [ahN-po-see-bl neh pah zuhn moh frahN-seh] *Fr*—*Impossible* is not a word in the French language. Napoléon I.

Impotens sui [im'-po-tayns soo'-ee] *L*—Lacking self-control.

Imprimatur [im-prih-mah'-tuhr] *L*—It may be printed. A term used to indicate that ecclesiastical permission has been granted to print the work in question. *See also* Permissu superiorum.

Imprimi permittitur [im'-prih-mee pehr-mit'-tih-tuhr] *L*—Permission to print is granted. *See also* Permissu superiorum.

Imprimi potest [im'-prih-mee po'-test] *L*—Permission to print is granted. *See also* Permissu superiorum.

Im Wein ist Warheit [im vIn ist vahr'-hIt] *Ger*—*See* In vino veritas.

In absentia [in ap-sen'-tih-ah] *L*—In absence. Used in connection with the conferring of a degree or the condemnation of a criminal beyond the reach of the law.

In actu [in ahk'-too] *L*—A term used by the scholastics to indicate that what was formerly in a state of possibility is now in existence. *See also* In potentia ad actum.

In aeternum [in I-tehr-nuhm] *L*—Forever.

In agello (*or* **angello**) **cum libello sola quies** [in ah-gel'-loh, ahn-gel'-loh, kuhm lih-bel'-loh so'-lah kwih'-ays] *L*—Tranquillity is found only in a corner with a little book.

In animam malevolam sapientia haud intrare potest [in ah'-nih-mahm mah-leh'-woh-lahm sah-pih-en'-tih-ah howd in-trah'-reh po'-test] *L*—Wisdom can hardly enter the soul of an ill-willed man.

In apricum proferet [in ah-pree'-kuhm proh'-feh-ret] *L*—It will bring to light. The seal of the Pontifical Roman Academy of Archaeology.

In articulo mortis [in ahr-tih'-kuh-loh mor'-tiss] *L*—At the moment of death.

I. N. C. in nomine Christi *L*—*See* I. C. N.

In caelo quies [in kI'-loh kwih'-ays] *L*—In heaven there is rest. In England this phrase appeared on a panel called a hatchment, formerly displayed for a time on the house of a deceased person.

In camera [in kah'-meh-rah] *L*—In the judge's chambers; secretly.

In capite [in kah'-pih-teh] *L*—Literally, in chief; in feudal law a tenure by which lands were held of a lord or directly of the crown.

Incidit in Scyllam qui vult vitare Charybdim [in-kee'-dit in skil'-lahm kwee wult wee-tah'-reh kah-rib'-dim] *L*—He who would avoid the whirlpool Charybdis strikes against the rock Scylla; out of the frying pan into the fire. A dactylic hexameter line based on Vergil, *Aeneid*, 3; 420. It is also quoted: *Incidis in Scyllam cupiens vitare Charybdim.*

Incipit [in'-kih-pit] *L*—Here begins. In

94

Latin manuscripts this word is followed by the title of the work and the author.

In commendam [in kom-men'-dahm] *LL*—Held in trust for a period of time, as in the case of an ecclesiastical benefice directed by an assistant for the benefit of an absent principal.

In concreto [in kon-kray'-toh] *L*—Specifically.

In contumaciam [in kon-tuh-mah'-kih-ahm] *L*—Used of a person who is in contempt of a court order.

In custodia legis [in kuhs-toh'-dih-ah lay'-gis] *L*—In custody of the law.

I. N. D. in nomine Dei [in noh'-mih-neh deh'-ee] *L*—In the name of God.

Index expurgatorius [in'-dex ex-puhr-gah-toh'-rih-uhs] *L*—A list of books to be amended to conform to belief and practice, formerly compiled by the Roman Catholic Church.

Index Librorum Prohibitorum [in'-dex lih-broh'-ruhm proh-hih-bih-toh'-ruhm] *L*—Index of Forbidden Books, a publication issued by the Holy Office of the Roman Catholic Church. This is no longer active.

Index locorum [in'-dex lo-koh'-ruhm] *L*—Index of places.

Index nominum [in'-dex noh'-mih-nuhm] *L*—An index of names.

Index rerum [in'-dex ray'-ruhm] *L*—An index of things; a list of references.

Index verborum [in'-dex wehr-boh'-ruhm] *L*—An index of words.

Indignor quandoque bonus dormitat Homerus [in-dig'-nor kwahn-doh'-kweh bo'-nuhs dor-mee'-taht hoh-may'-ruhs] *L*—I am vexed whenever good old Homer nods. Horace, *Art of Poetry*, 359.

In discrimine rerum [in dis-kree'-mih-neh ray'-ruhm] *L*—In the crisis of events.

Indocilis pauperiem pati [in-do'-kih-lis pow-peh'-rih-ehm pah'-tee] *L*—A man who cannot be taught to bear up under poverty. Horace, *Odes*, 1; 1, 18.

Indoctus juga ferre [in-dok'-tuhs yuh'-gah fehr'-reh] *L*—Untrained to bear the yoke. Based on Horace, *Odes*, 2; 6, 2.

In dubio [in duh'-bih-oh] *L*—In doubt.

In esse [in es'-seh] *L*—In existence.

In extenso [in ek-stayn'-soh] *L*—At length; complete treatment.

In extremis [in ex-tray'-mees] *L*—In the last moment of life; in the final illness.

In facie curiae [in fah'-kih-ay koo'-rih-I] *L*—In the presence of the court.

Infandum renovare dolorem [een-fahn'-duhm reh-no-wah'-reh do-loh'-rem] *L*—To revive an unspeakable sorrow. Vergil, *Aeneid*, 2; 3.

In favorem matrimonii [in fah-woh'-rem mah-trih-moh'-nih-ee] *L*—In favor of the validity of the marriage bond.

In fieri [in fih'-eh-ree] *L*—In the state of becoming; in the process of being realized.

In flagrante delicto [in flah-grahn'-teh day-leek'-toh] *L*—Literally, while the offense is blazing; caught in the commission of the crime.

In forma pauperis [in for'-mah pow'-pehr-iss] *L*—As a pauper. A man whose rights are violated but who is unable to pay legal expenses may be admitted by the court to sue without paying the customary fees.

In foro conscientiae [in fo'-roh kohn-skih-en'-tih-I] *L*—In the court of conscience.

In foro externo [in fo'-roh ex-tehr'-noh] *L*—In the public forum as distinguished from the forum of conscience.

In foro interno [in fo'-roh in-tehr'-noh] *L*—In the judgment of conscience.

Infra dignitatem [in'-frah deeg-nih-tah'-tem] *L*—Beneath one's dignity. Sometimes shortened to *infra dig.*

In futuro [in fuh-too'-roh] *L*—In future; henceforth.

Ingenium mala saepe movent [in-geh'-nih-uhm mah'-lah sI'-peh moh'-went] *L*—Bad luck often stirs genius. Ovid, *Art of Love*, 2; 43. *See also* Necessitas rationum inventrix.

Ingenium res adversae nudare solent, celare secundae [in-geh'-nih-uhm rayss ahd-wehr'-sI noo-dah'-reh so'-lent kay-lah'-reh seh-kuhn'-dI] *L*—Adversity reveals genius; prosperity conceals it. Horace, *Satires*, 2; 8, 73.

Ingenui vultus puer ingenuique pudoris [in-geh'-nuh-ee wuhl'-toos puh'-ehr in-geh-nuh-ee'-kweh puh-doh'-riss] *L*—A boy with a noble countenance and inborn modesty.

In globo [in gloh'-boh] *L*—In a mass of people.

Ingratus unus omnibus miseris nocet [in-grah'-tuhs oo'-nuhs om'-nih-buhs mih'-seh-rees nu'-ket] *L*—One ingrate does harm to all men in misery; the wealthy man closes his purse after one bitter experience. Publilius Syrus.

In gremio legis [in greh'-mih-oh lay'-ghis] *L*—In the lap of the law.

In hoc signo vinces [in hohk sihg'-noh wihn'-kays] *L*—With this sign (a cross) thou shalt conquer. Words reportedly seen in the heavens by Constantine at his victory near the Milvian Bridge in 312 A.D.

INI Instituto Nacional de Industria [een-stee-too'-toh nah-syo-nahl' day een-doos'-tree-ah] *Sp*—National Institute of Industry, a state holding company in Spain.

In ictu oculi [in ihk'-too o'-kuh-lee] *L*—In the twinkling of an eye.

In infinitum [in een-fee-nee'-tuhm] *L*—To infinity.

In initio [in ih-nih'-tih-oh] *L*—In the beginning.

Iniquum petas ut aequum feras [ih-nee'-kwuhm peh'-tahs uht I'-kwuhm feh'-rahs] *L*—Ask for what is unreasonable that you may obtain what is just.

In limine [in lee'-mih-neh] *L*—On the threshold; at the outset.

In loco [in lo'-koh] *L*—On the spot; in the place of.

In loco citato [in lo'-koh kih-tah'-toh] *L—See* Loco citato.

In loco parentis [in lo'-koh pah-ren'-tis] *L—*In the place of a parent.

In manus tuas commendo spiritum meum [in mah'-noos tuh'-ahs kom-men'-doh spee'-rih-tuhm meh'-uhm] *L—*Into thy hands I commend my spirit. Last words of Christ on the cross. *Vulgate, Luke,* 23; 46.

In medias res [in meh'-dih-ahs rayss] *L—*Into the midst of things. The epic poet, says Horace, takes the reader into the middle of the action, postponing the account of earlier events until later in the narrative. *See also* Ab ovo. *Art of Poetry,* 148.

In medio stat virtus [in meh'-dih-oh staht wihr'-toos] *L—*Virtue exists in the middle between two extremes. If courage is the virtue considered, its excess is rashness and its defect cowardice. According to Christian teaching this axiom applies to the moral, not the theological virtues. *See also* Aurea mediocritas.

In medio tutissimus ibis [in meh'-dih-oh too-tiss'-sih-muhs ee'-bis] *L—See* Medio tutissimus . . .

In meditatione fugae [in meh-dih-tah-tih oh'-neh fuh'-gI] *L—*Poised for flight.

In memmoriam ad gloriam sed asthoriam non nomoreum [in mem-mor'-ee-am ahd glo'-rih-ahm sed as-tho'-ree-ahm nohn no-mor'-ee-uhm] Garbled Latin, Irish, and English—Probably means To (her) glorious memory but my dear treasure is no more. Sean O'Casey, *Inishfallen, Fare Thee Well* (in the chapter Mrs. Casside Takes a Holiday).

In memoriam [in meh-mo'-rih-ahm] *L—*Unto the memory.

In morte veritas [in mor'-teh way'-rih-tahs] *L—*The truth comes out at death.

In necessariis unitas, in non necessariis libertas, in utrisque caritas [in neh-kes-sah'-rih-ees oo'-nih-tahs in nohn neh-kes-sah'-rih-ees lee-behr'-tahs, in uh-trees'-kweh kah'-rih-tahs] *L—*In essentials, there should be unity, in nonessentials liberty,

in both cases, charity. This maxim is sometimes quoted: *In necessariis unitas, in dubiis libertas, in omnibus caritas:* In essentials, there should be unity; in doubt liberty; in all things charity. This is falsely attributed to St. Augustine. Its origin (ca. 1625) has been traced to an admonition intended to bring peace into the church, given by Rupertus Meldenius to the theologians of the Augustinian confession.

In nihilum nil posse reverti [in nih'-hih-luhm neel pos'-seh reh-wehr'-tee] *L—*There is nothing that can be reduced to nothing; matter is indestructible. Persius, 3; 84.

In nocte consilium [in nok'-teh kohn-sih'-lih-uhm] *L—*The night brings counsel. *See also* En nukti boule.

In nomine [in noh'-mih-neh] *L—*In the name.

In nomine Domini [in noh'-mih-neh do'-mih-nee] *L—*In the name of the Lord.

In nubibus [in noo'-bih-buhs] *L—*In the clouds; confused.

In nuce [in nuh'-keh] *L—*In a nutshell; briefly.

In omnia paratus [in om'-nih-ah pah-rah'-tuhs] *L—*Prepared for all things; ready for any eventuality.

In omnibus glorificetur Deus [in om'-nih-buhs gloh-rih-fih-kay'-tuhr deh'-uhs] *L—*Let God be glorified in all things.

In omni doctrina grammatica praecedit [in om'-nee dok-tree'-nah grah-mah'-tih-kah prI-kay'-dit] *L—*In all learning the study of grammar comes first. An educational principle in the Middle Ages.

Inopem me copia fecit [ih'-no-pem may koh'-pih-ah fay'-kit] *L—*Abundance has made me poor. These words spoken by Narcissus lamented the fact that he possessed the beauty that he had thought was another's; that the lovely creature he saw mirrored in the water was himself. It has been used to indicate the plight of the man with many ideas and a poverty of expression. Ovid, *Metamorphoses,* 3; 466.

Inops, potentem dum vult imitari, perit [ih'-nops po-ten'-tem duhm wuhlt ih-mih-tah'-ree peh'-rit] *L*—A poor man perishes when he tries to imitate a powerful man. Phaedrus, *Fables*, 1; 24, 1.

In ovo [in oh'-woh] *L*—Still in the egg.

In pace [in pah'-keh] *L*—In peace.

In partibus infidelium [in par'-tih-buhs in-fih-day'-lih-uhm] *L*—In the region of infidels; a phrase used in the Roman Catholic Church to indicate a see of a titular bishop. By extension the phrase *in partibus* has been used ironically in reference to government functionaries without power.

In perpetuam rei memoriam [in pehr-peh'-tuh-ahm reh'-ee meh-mo'-rih-ahm] *L*—In everlasting memory of the event.

In perpetuum [in pehr-peh'-tuh-uhm] *L*—In perpetuity.

In perturbato animo sicut in corpore sanitas esse non potest [in pehr-tuhr-bah'-toh ah'-nih-moh see'-kuht in kor'-po-reh sah'-nih-tahs ess'-seh nohn po'-test] *L*—In a disturbed mind, as in a disturbed body, health is impossible. Cicero, *Tusculan Disputations*, 3; 4.

In petto [in pet'-toh] *It*—In the breast; held back for future announcement. Thus, the pope may have in mind certain ecclesiastics who are to be made cardinals, but he has not made his choice public.

In pios usus [in pih'-ohs oo'-soos] *L*—For pious uses; said of property left by will for religious purposes.

In posse [in pos'-seh] *L*—Potentially; within possibility.

In potentia ad actum [in po-ten'-tih-ah ahd ahk'-tuhm] *L*—A term used by the scholastic philosopher to indicate a state of imminence.

In principio [in preen-sih'-pih-oh] *L*—In the beginning.

In propria persona [in pro'-prih-ah pehr-soh'-nah] *L*—In his or her own person; undisguised.

In proverbium cessit, sapientiam vino adumbrari [in proh-wehr'-bih-uhm kes'-sit sah-pih-en'-tih-ahm wee'-noh ah-duhm-brah'-ree] *L*—It has become a proverb that wisdom is clouded by wine. Pliny the Elder, *Natural History*, 23; 1.

In puris naturalibus [in poo'-rees nah-too-rah'-lih-buhs] *L*—Naked.

In re [in ray] *L*—*See* Re.

In rerum natura [in ray'-ruhm nah-too'-rah] *L*—In the nature of things.

I N R I Iesus nazarenus rex iudaeorum [yay'-sus nah-zah-ray'-nus rayx yoo-day-oh'-ruhm] *L*—Jesus of Nazareth, King of the Jews.

In saecula saeculorum [in say'-kuh-lah say-kuh-loh'-ruhm] *L*—Forever and ever.

In situ [in sih'-too] *L*—In its original position or place.

In solidum (solido) [in soh'-lih-duhm, soh'-lih-doh] *L*—A term used to indicate that parties involved are held jointly and severally.

In specie [in speh'-kih-ay] *L*—In the same or similar form.

In spiritualibus [in spee-rih-tuh-ahl'-lih-buhs] *L*—In matters spiritual.

I. N. S. T. in nomine Sanctae Trinitatis [in noh'-mih-neh sahnk'-tay tree-nih-tah'-tiss] *L*—In the name of the Holy Trinity.

In statu pupillari [in stah'-too poo-pil-lah'-ree] *L*—In the position of a ward or orphan.

In statu quo [in stah'-too kwoh] *L*—In its former state or condition.

In statu quo ante bellum [in stah'-too kwoh ahn'-teh bel'-luhm] *L*—In the condition that existed prior to the war.

In tanto discrimine [in tahn'-toh dis-kree'-mih-neh] *L*—In such a moment of grave crisis.

In te, Domine, speravi [in tay do'-mih-neh spay-rah'-vee] *L*—In thee, O Lord, have I placed my trust. *Vulgate, Psalms,* 30; 1.

Integer vitae scelerisque purus/Non eget Mauris/iaculis neque arcu [in'-teh-gehr wee'-tI skeh-leh-riss'-kweh poo'-ruhs nohn eh'-get mow'-rees yah'-kuh-lees neh'-kweh ahr'-koo] *L*—The man whose life is pure and free from crime/needs no Moorish darts or bow for his protection. These opening lines of a humorous poem by Horace are often quoted in all seriousness. Horace, *Odes*, 1; 22, 1.

Intellectus sibi permissus [in-tehl-layk'-tuhs sih'-bih pehr-mihs'-suhs] *L*—The intellect left free to run without guidance.

In tenebris [in teh'-neh-breess] *L*—In darkness.

Inter alia [in'-tehr ah'-lih-ah] *L*—Among other things.

Inter anum et urinam [in'-tehr ah'-nuhm et oo-ree'-nahm] *L*—Between the anus and the urine. An unflattering view of human birth.

Inter arma leges silent [in'-tehr ahr'-mah lay'-gays sih'-lent] *L*—The laws are silent in time of war. Cicero, *For Milo*, 4; 10.

Inter canem et lupum [in'-tehr kah'-nem et luh'-puhm] *L*—Caught between a dog and a wolf; between the devil and the deep blue sea. Used when a person in difficulty has a choice between two evils.

Interdum stultus opportuna loquitur [in-tehr'-duhm stuhl'-tuhs op-pohr-too'-nah lo'-kwih-tuhr] *L*—Sometimes a fool says the right thing.

Interdum volgus rectum videt; est ubi peccat [in-tehr'-duhm wol'-guhs rayk'-tuhm wih'-det est uh'-bih pek'-kaht] *L*—Sometimes the common man sees aright; sometimes he is wrong. Horace, *Epistles*, 2; 1, 63.

Inter esse et non esse non datur medium [in'-tehr ess'-seh et nohn ess'-seh nohn dah'-tuhr meh'-dih-uhm] *L*—Between existence and nonexistence there is no middle point. An axiom of scholastic philosophy based on Aristotle.

Inter faeces et urinam [in'-tehr fI'-kays et oo-ree'-nahm] *L*—Between faeces and urine. *See also* Inter anum et urinam.

Inter folia fructus [in'-tehr fo'-lih-ah frook'-toos] *L*—There is fruit among the leaves. Said of both trees and books.

Inter nos [in'-tehr nohs] *L*—Between ourselves; a matter to be kept secret.

Inter os et offam [in'-tehr ohs et off'-fahm] *L*—Between the cup and the lip. Gellius, *Attic Nights*, 13; 17.

Inter pocula [in'-tehr poh'-kuh-lah] *L*—In one's cups; a time of revelation. A suggestion that someone has had one cup too many.

In terra di ciechi, beato chi ha un occhio [een tehr'-rah dee chay'-kee bay-ah'-toh kee ah oon ok'-kee-oh] *It*—In the country of the blind, blessed is the man with one eye. In the land of the blind the man with one eye is king. *See also* Au royaume des aveugles . . .

In terrorem [in tehr-roh'-rem] *L*—As a warning. A legal term.

In terrorem populi [in tehr-roh'-rem po'-puh-lee] *L*—To produce terror among the people. Thus, public executions may be staged in the hope of maintaining law and order.

Inter se [in'-tehr say] *L*—Between or among themselves.

Inter spem et metum [in'-tehr spem et meh'-tuhm] *L*—Between hope and fear.

Inter vivos [in'-tehr vee'-vohs] *L*—Among the living. Generally used in connection with a living trust whereby an estate passes from one generation to another without probate.

Inter volentes [in'-tehr wo-len'-tays] *L*—Between or among those freely consenting.

In totidem verbis [in toh'-tih-dem wehr'-bees] *L*—In just so many words.

In toto [in toh'-toh] *L*—Completely.

Intra muros [in'-trah moo'-rohs] *L*—Within the walls.

In transitu [in trahn'-sih-too] *L*—In transit.

Intra vires [in'-trah wee'-rays] *L*—Within one's powers.

In un giorno non si fe' Roma [in oon johr'-noh nonn see fay roh'-mah] *It*—Rome was not built in a day.

In usum Delphini [in oo'-suhm del-fee'-nee] *L*—For the use of the Dauphin, the eldest son of Louis XIV. The King had an expurgated series of classics prepared for his son.

In utero [in uh'-teh-roh] *L*—In the womb; not yet born.

In utrumque paratus [in uh-truhm'-kweh pah-rah'-tuhs] *L*—Prepared for either eventuality. Title of a poem by Matthew Arnold. Vergil, *Aeneid*, 2; 61.

Invenit [in-way'-nit] *L*—He invented it.

In ventre [in wehn'-treh] *L*—In the womb.

Inverso ordine [in-wehr'-soh or'-dih-neh] *L*—In inverse order.

Invidia festos dies non agit [in-wih'-dih-ah fays'-tohs dih'-ays nohn ah'-git] *L*—Envy takes no vacation.

In vili veste nemo tractatur honeste [in wee'-lee wehs'-teh nay'-moh trahk-tah'-tuhr ho-nehs'-tay] *L*—No one in shabby clothes is treated fairly.

In vino veritas [in wee'-noh way'-rih-tahs] *L*—There's truth in wine; the truth slips out when people are drinking.

Invita Minerva [in-wee'-tah mih-nehr'-wah] *L*—Literally, when Minerva (the goddess of wisdom) is unwilling; when natural talent is lacking. Horace, *Art of Poetry*, 385.

In vitro [in vit'-roh] *L*—Within glass; observable, as in a test tube.

In vivo [in vee'-voh] *L*—In or upon a living organism. As opposed to In vitro (*q.v.*).

In vota miseros ultimus cogit timor [in woh'-tah mih'-seh-rohs uhl'-tih-muhs koh'-git tih'-mor] *L*—The fear of death drives the miserable to make vows to the gods. Seneca, *Agamemnon*, 510.

I paragoni son odiosi [ee pah-rah-goh'-nee sonn oh-dee-oh'-see] *It*—Comparisons are odious.

I pensieri non pagano dazio [ee penn-see-ay'-ree nonn pah'-gah-noh dah'-tsee-oh] *It*—Thoughts do not pay a duty; thoughts are free.

i. p. i. *See* In partibus infidelium.

Ipsa scientia potestas est [ip'-sah skihen'-tih-ah po-tes'-tahs est] *L*—Knowledge itself is power. Francis Bacon. *Sacred Meditations, On Heresies.*

Ipse dixit [ip'-seh deex'-it] *L*—He himself said so. The appeal to authority, without offering proof; used by the disciples of Pythagoras. *See* Autos epha.

Ipsissima verba [ip-sis'-sih-mah wehr'-bah] *L*—The identical words; a direct quotation.

Ipso facto [ip'-soh fahk'-toh] *L*—By the very fact.

Ipso jure [ip'-soh yoo'-reh] *L*—By the law itself; by the operation of law.

i. R. im Ruhestand [im roo'-uh-shtahnt] *Ger*—Emeritus status; retired.

Ira de irmãos, ira de diabos [ee'-ruh dee eer-mawN-oosh ee'-ruh dee dee-ah'-boosh] *Port*—The anger of brothers is the anger of devils.

Ira furor brevis est; animum rege; qui nisi paret, imperat [ee'-rah foo'-rohr breh'-wiss est ah'-nih-muhm reh'-geh kwee nih'-sih pah'-ret ihm'-peh-raht] *L*—Anger is brief madness; rule your spirit; unless it obeys, it commands. Horace, *Epistles*, 1; 2, 62.

Iratus cum ad se rediit sibi tum irascitur [ee-rah'-tuhs kuhm ahd say reh'-dih-it sih'-bih tuhm ee-rahs'-kih-tuhr] *L*—When an angry man becomes himself again, then he is angry with himself. Publilius Syrus.

Irrtümer vorbehalten [eerr'-tüm-uhr for'-buh-hahl-tun] *Ger*—Errors excepted.

Ita lex scripta est [ih'-tah layx skrihp'-tah est] *L*—This is the way the law reads; such is the wording of the law.

Italia farà da se [ee-tah'-lee-ah fah-rah' dah say] *It*—Italy will make it alone.

Italia irredenta [ee-tah'-lee-ah eer-ray-den'-tah] *It*—Unredeemed Italy. In 1878 an Italian political party was formed with the object of bringing lands formerly belonging to Italy back into the nation.

Ite, missa est [ee'-tah mihs'-sah est] *L*—Go, the Mass is over; you are dismissed. There is some doubt about the correct translation of this expression.

Iustum est bellum, Samnites, quibus necessarium: et pia arma quibus nulla nisi in armis relinquitur spes [yoos'-tuhm est bel'-luhm sahm-nee'-tays kwih'-buhs neh-kehs-sah'-rih-uhm et pih'-ah ahr'-mah kwih'-buhs nool'-lah nih'-sih in ahr'-mees reh-lihn'-kwih-tuhr spays] *L*—War is just, Samnites, for those to whom it is necessary: and arms are conscientiously employed by those to whom no other hope is left. Livy, 9; 1. Loosely quoted by Machiavelli, *The Prince*, ch. 26.

J

J'accuse [zha-küz] *Fr*—"I accuse." Title of an explosive article, published in 1898, by Émile Zola in which he championed the cause of falsely accused Capt. Alfred Dreyfus.

Jacta alea est [yahk'-tah ah'-leh-ah est] *L*—The die is cast. Words uttered by Julius Caesar when he crossed the Rubicon. Suetonius, *Lives of Twelve Caesars, J. Caesar,* 32.

J'ai vécu [zhay vay-kü] *Fr*—I lived through it. Words spoken by Sièyes when he was asked what he had done during the Reign of Terror in France.

Jalousie de métier [zha-loo-zee duh may-tyay] *Fr*—Professional jealousy.

Jam redit et Virgo, redeunt Saturnia regna [yahm reh'-dit et wihr'-goh reh'-deh-uhnt sah-tuhr'-nih-ah rayg'-nah] *L*—Now the Maiden returns, now the Age of Saturn, a mythical golden age of peace, justice and plenty. The maiden referred to is Astraea, the goddess of justice, who left the earth in the iron age because men had become evil. Now she is returning in the Golden Age of Augustus. Vergil, *Eclogues,* 4; 6.

Jam satis vixi [yahm sah'-tiss weex'-ee] *L*—I have lived long enough.

Januis clausis [yah'-nuh-ees klow'-seess] *L*—Behind closed doors.

Jardins à l'anglaise [zhahr-daN ah lahN-glehz] *Fr*—Gardens in the English style.

J. B. Jurum Baccalaureus [yoo'-ruhm bahk-kah-low'-reh-uhs] *L*—Bachelor of Laws.

J. C., I. C. Jesus Christus [yay'-suhs krihs'-tuhs] *L*—Jesus Christ.

J. C. B. Juris Canonici Baccalaureus [yoo'-riss kah-noh'-nih-chee bahk-kah-low'-reh-uhs] *L*—Bachelor of Canon Law.

J. C. B. Juris Civilis Baccalaureus [yoo'-riss kee-wee'-liss bahk-kah-low'-reh-uhs] *L*—Bachelor of Civil Law.

J. C. D. Juris Canonici Doctor [yoo'-riss kah-noh'-nih-chee dok'-tohr] *L*—Doctor of Canon Law.

J. C. D. Juris Civilis Doctor [yoo'-riss kee-wee'-liss dok'-tohr] *L*—Doctor of Civil Law.

J. C. L. Juris Canonici Lector *or* Licentiatus [yoo'-riss kah-noh'-nih-chee lehk'-tohr *or* lih-chen-tsih-ah'-tuhs] *L*—Reader or Licentiate in Canon Law.

J. D. Juris Doctor [yoo'-riss dok'-tohr] *L*—Doctor of Law.

Jeder Esel kann kritisieren [yay'-duhr ay'-zul kahn kree-tee-zee'-run] *Ger*—Any ass can criticize.

Jeder ist Herr in seinem Hause [yay'-duhr ist hehr in zI'-nuhm how'-zuh] *Ger*—Every man is master in his own house; a man's house is his castle.

Jeder ist seines Glückes Schmied [yay'-duhr ist zI'-nus glük'-uss shmeet] *Ger*—Every man is the architect of his own fortune.

Jeder ist sich selbst der Nächste [yay'-duhr ist zikh zelpst dehr nehk'-stuh] *Ger*—Every man is closest to himself; charity begins at home.

Jeder weiss, wo ihn der Schuh drückt [yay'-duhr vIs voh eehn dehr shoo drükht] *Ger*—Every man knows where his own shoe pinches. *See also* Cada uno sabe ...

Je höher der Baum, desto tiefer der Fall [yay huh'-huhr dehr bowm des'-toh tee'-fuhr dehr fahl] *Ger*—The higher the tree, the farther the fall.

Je le pansay, Dieu le guarit [zhuh luh paN-say dyuh luh gwar-ee] *OF*—I dressed his wound; God cured him. Dictum of the French surgeon Ambroise Paré.

Je maintiendrai [zhuh maN-tyaN-dray] *Fr*—I will stand firm. Motto of the Netherlands.

Je maintiendrai le droit [zhuh maN-tyaN-dray luh drwah] *Fr*—I will maintain what is right.

Je me fais pitié à moi-même [zhuh muh feh pee-tyay ah mwah mem] *Fr*—I feel sorry for myself. Words of Minister of Finance de Calonne, apprehensive of the Revolution that was soon to break out in France.

Je me souviens [zhuh muh soo-vyaN] *Fr*—I remember. Motto of Québec.

Je ne sais quoi [zhuh nuh seh kwah] *Fr*—I don't know what. Used when one is unable to find the right word to express an idea.

Je pense, donc je suis [zhuh pahNs doNk zhuh swee] *Fr*—I think, therefore I am. *See* Cogito, ergo sum.

Je prends mon bien où je le trouve [zhuh prahN mohN byaN oo zhuh luh troov] *Fr*—I take my stuff where I find it. This was Molière's reply when he was accused of plagiarism. This is also quoted as *Je reprends*, indicating that others had stolen his material.

Je sème à tout vent [zhuh sehm ah too vahN] *Fr*—My seed rides on every wind. A publisher's motto.

Je t'aime plus qu'hier, moins que demain [zhuh tehm plüs kyehr mwaN kuh duh-maN] *Fr*—I love you more than I did yesterday, and less than I will tomorrow. Words on a popular pendant.

Jeter de la poudre aux yeux [zhuh-tay duh lah poo-druh oh zyuh] *Fr*—To throw powder in someone's eyes; to blind someone to the real issue.

Jeter le manche après la cognée [zhuh-tay luh mahNsh ah-preh lah kuh-nyay] *Fr*—To throw the handle after the hatchet; to despair.

Jets d'eau [zheh doh] *Fr*—Jets of water; a fountain.

Jeu de mots [zhuh duh moh] *Fr*—Play on words.

Jeu d'esprit [zhuh deh-spree] *Fr*—Witticism.

Jeu de théâtre [zhuh duh tay-ah-tr] *Fr*—A stage trick.

Jeunesse dorée [zhuh-ness do-ray] *Fr*—Gilded youth. A name given wealthy, fashionable men, idle and debauched, who roamed the streets of Paris in gangs. Under the leadership of Robespierre they carried out the Reign of Terror. Eventually the phrase came to mean young men of style and means.

Je vais chercher un grand Peut-être! [zhuh veh shehr-shay uhN grahN puh-teh-tr] *Fr*—I go to seek a great May-be! Apocryphal last words of Rabelais. *See also* La farce est jouée.

Je veux que le dimanche chaque paysan ait sa poule au pot [zhuh vuh kuh luh dee-mahNsh shak pay-ee-zahN eh sa pool oh poh] *Fr*—It is my wish that every peasant have a chicken in the pot on Sunday. Henry IV of France.

Je vis d'espoir [zhuh vee deh-spwahr] *Fr*—I live in hope.

Joannes est nomen ejus [yoh-ahn'-nays est noh'-men eh'-yuhs] *L*—John is his name. Words on the seal of Puerto Rico, whose capital is San Juan (Saint John). *Vulgate, Luke*, 1; 63.

Joculatores Dei [yo-kuh-lah-toh'-rays deh'-ee] *L*—Jesters of God. A name that Saint Francis of Assisi gave his followers to indicate the humble spirit of their mission, comparing them to jongleurs.

Johannes fac totum [yoh-hawn'-nehs fahk toh'-tuhm] *L*—Johnny-do-everything. A phrase from Robert Greene's criticism of the young Shakespeare.

Joie de vivre [zhwah duh vee-vr] *Fr*—The joy of living.

Jour gras [zhoor grah] *Fr*—A fat day; a day of feasting.

Jour maigre [zhoor meh-gr] *Fr*—A lean day; a day when a prescribed amount of food or abstinence from meat is enjoined by Church law.

Journée des Barricades [zhoor-nay day ba-ree-kad] *Fr*—Day of Barricades, recalling the times when rioting people of Paris erected barricades in the streets against the government.

Joyeux Noël! [zhwah-yuh noh-el] *Fr*—Merry Christmas!

Jubilate Deo [yoo-bih-lah'-teh deh'-oh] *L*—Rejoice in the Lord.

Jucundi acti labores [yoo-kuhn'-dee ahk'-tee lah-boh'-rays] *L*—The memory of past labors is pleasant. Cicero, *On Ends*, 2; 32, 105.

J. U. D. Juris Utriusque Doctor [yoo'-riss uh-tree-uhs'-kweh dok'-tohr] *L*—Doctor of both civil and canon law.

Judex damnatur ubi nocens absolvitur [yoo'-dex dahm-nah'-tuhr uh'-bih noh'-kayns ahp-sol'-wih-tuhr] *L*—The judge is condemned when a criminal is set free. Publilius Syrus.

Judicium crucis [yoo-dih'-kih-uhm kroo'-kiss] *L*—An ordeal in which contestants vie to see who can hold out his arms longest as if on a cross. The one whose arms fall first loses.

Judicium Dei [yoo-dih'-kih-uhm deh'-ee] *L*—*See* Dei judicium.

Judicium parium aut leges terrae [yoo-dih'-kih-uhm pah'-rih-uhm owt lay'-gays tehr'-rI] *L*—The judgment of one's peers or the laws of the land. It was one of the important concessions granted by King John in the Magna Carta that an Englishman could be condemned only in these two ways.

Juge de paix [zhüzh duh peh] *Fr*—Justice of the peace.

Juge d'instruction [zhüzh d'aN-strük-syohN] *Fr*—Examining magistrate.

Jugement de Dieu [zhüzh-mahN duh dyuh] *Fr*—*See* Dei judicium.

Jugez un homme par ses questions, plutôt que par ses réponses [zhü-zhay uh nuhm pahr say kehs-tyohN plü-toh kuh pahr say ray-pohNss] *Fr*—Judge a man by his questions rather than by his answers.

Juppiter tonans [yuhp'-pih-tehr toh'-nahns] *L*—Thundering Jove. A name sometimes given to the London *Times*.

Jurare in verba magistri [yoo-rah'-reh in wehr'-bah mah-gihs'-tree] *L*—To swear by the words of the teacher; to accept an authority blindly. Horace, *Epistles*, 1; 1, 14.

Jurat [yoo'-raht] *L*—Addition to an affidavit giving details of when, where, and before whom the document was signed.

Juravi lingua, mentem injuratam gero [yoo-rah'-wee ling'-gwah mehn'-tem in-yoo-rah'-tahm geh'-roh] *L*—I have sworn with my tongue but my mind is unsworn. Cicero, *On Duties*, 3; 29. *See also* the Greek original, He glossa omomoch'...

Jure belli [yoo'-reh bel'-lee] *L*—By right or rules of war.

Jure divino [yoo'-reh dee-wee'-noh] *L*—By divine law or right.

Jure humano [yoo'-reh hoo-mah'-noh] *L*—By human law.

Jure uxoris [yoo'-reh uhx-oh'-riss] *L*—By reason of a wife's right.

Juris peritus [yoo'-riss peh-ree'-tuhs] *L*—One learned in the law.

Jus ad rem [yoos ahd rem] *L*—The right to possess a thing.

Jus canonicum [yoos kah-noh'-nih-kuhm] *L*—Canon law; the legal code by which the Catholic Church is governed.

Jus civile [yoos kee-wee'-leh] *L*—Civil law.

Jus civitatis [yoos kee-wih-tah'-tiss] *L*—The right of citizenship.

Jus commercii [yoos kohm-mehr'-sih-ee] *L*—The right to trade.

Jus devolutionis [yoos day-woh-luh-tih-oh'-niss] *L*—Law of transmission by which a possessor's property and rights devolve upon a successor.

Jus et norma loquendi [yoos et nor'-mah lo-kwen'-dee] *L*—The laws and standards of speech.

Jus gentium [yoos gehn'-tih-uhm] *L*—The law of nations. Originally applied to the body of laws common to Rome and her subject states. Later it was identified with natural law, and came to mean international law.

Jus gladii [yoos glah'-dih-ee] *L*—The right of the sword.

Jus hereditatis [yoos hay-ray-dih-tah'-tiss] *L*—The right to inherit.

Jus mariti [yoos mah-ree'-tee] *L*—The right of a husband to a wife's property.

Jus mercatorum [yoos mehr-kah-toh'-ruhm] *L*—The law merchant; mercantile law.

Jus naturae [yoos nah-too'-rI] *L*—Law of nature.

Jus necationis [yoos neh-kah-tih-oh'-nis] *L*—The right to kill.

Jus possessionis [yoos pos-sehs-sih-oh'-niss] *L*—The right of possession.

Jus primae noctis [yoos pree'-mI nok'-tiss] *L*—The right of the first night; the reported claim of the feudal lord to the virginity of the wife of his vassal on the night of her marriage. There is no historically sound evidence for the existence of this practice. The *Droit du Seigneur*, generally translated as the right of the feudal lord, may have been understood as God's right, referring to the religious counsel of practicing continence on the wedding night.

Jus proprietatis [yoos pro-prih-eh-tah'-tiss] *L*—The right of property.

Jus publicum [yoos poo'-blih-kuhm] *L*—Common law.

Jusqu'au bout [zhüs-koh boo] *Fr*—To the very end.

Jus relictae [yoos reh-lihk'-tI] *L*—The widow's right to property of a husband.

Jus sanguinis [yoos sahn'-gwih-niss] *L*—Literally, the right of blood; the right of a child to the citizenship of his parents. The phrase is also used in determining lawful inheritances.

Jus suffragii [yoos suhf-frah'-gih-ee] *L*—The right of suffrage.

Jus summum saepe summa est malitia [yoos suhm'-muhm sI'-peh suhm'-mah est mah-lih'-tih-ah] *L*—Extreme law is often extreme wrong. Terence, *Self-Tormentor*, 4; 5, 48. *See also* Summum jus, summa injuria.

Justitia omnibus [yoos-tih'-tih-ah om'-nih-buhs] *L*—Justice to all. Motto of District of Columbia.

Justitia suum cuique distribuit [yoos-tih'-tih-ah suh'-uhm kwee'-kweh dihs-trih'-buh-it] *L*—Justice gives everyone his due.

Justo titulo [yoos'-toh tih'-tuh-loh] *L*—By legal title; lawfully.

Jus trium liberorum [yoos trih'-uhm lee-beh-roh'-ruhm] *L*—A privilege, mostly political, granted to a Roman father of three children. This was intended to encourage bachelors to marry. Sometimes the privilege was granted to favorites who did not meet the requirements, e.g. Pliny the Younger.

Justum et tenacem propositi virum [yoos'-tuhm et teh-nah'-kem proh-po'-sih-tee wih'-ruhm] *L*—The righteous man in purpose strong. Horace, *Odes*, 3; 3, 1.

Jus ubique docendi [yoos uh-bih'-kwee do-ken'-dee] *L*—The right to teach everywhere, a license conferred by ecclesiastical authorities upon candidates presented by universities in the Middle Ages.

J'y suis, j'y reste [zhee swee zhee rest] *Fr*—Here I am and here I am staying.—General MacMahon. In the Crimean War, after taking the Malakoff fortifications, General MacMahon was advised to withdraw his troops. His victory led to the taking of Sebastopol.

K

Kairon gnothi [kI′-ron gnoh′-thee] *Gk*—Know your opportunity. The advice of Pittacus, one of the seven sages of Greece. It is translated into Latin as *Nosce tempus.*

Kai su ei ekeinon, kai su teknon? [kI sü eh e-keh′-nohn kI sü tek′-non] *Gk*—And thou art one of them, thou, my son? According to Suetonius the last words of Julius Caesar, uttered when he was stabbed by Brutus. Suetonius, *Julius Caesar*, 82. According to Plutarch *(Lives, Marcus Brutus,* 5; 1) Caesar believed that Brutus was his own son by Servilia, a sister of Cato. *See also* Et tu, Brute.

Kai su, teknon *Gk—See* Kai su ei ekeinon . . .

Kak vy pozhyvaete? [kahk vy poh-zhee-vah′-yeh-tyeh] *Rus*—How are you?

Kalendas Graecas [kah-len′-dahs grI′-kahs] *L—See* Ad Kalendas Graecas.

Kalokagathia [kah-loh-kah-gah-thee′-ah] *Gk*—A combination of the beautiful and the good, the ideal qualities of the Athenian gentleman.

Kalte Hände, warme Liebe [kahl′-tuh hehn′-duh vahr′-muh lee′-buh] *Ger*—Cold hands, a warm heart.

Keine Antwort ist auch eine Antwort [kI′-nuh ahnt′-vort ist owkh I′-nuh ahnt′-vort] *Ger*—No answer is also an answer.

Kein Unglück so gross, es ist ein Glück dabei [kIn uhn′-glük zoh grohss ess ist In glük dah-bI′] *Ger*—No misfortune is so great that it does not bring along some good fortune; it's an ill wind that blows nobody good.

KGB Komitet Gosudarstvennoi Bezopasnosti [ka-mee′-tyet guh-soo-darst-ven′-noh-ye byez-uh-pahs′-nost-yeh] *Rus*—Commission for State Security, the Soviet organization in charge of espionage and counter-espionage. *See also* NKVD and OGPU.

Kinder sind Kinder [kind′-uhr zint kind′-uhr] *Ger*—Children are children; you can't put an old head on young shoulders.

Kinder und Narren sprechen die Wahrheit [kind′-uhr unt nahr′-run shprekh′-un dee vahr′-hIt] *Ger*—Children and fools speak the truth.

Kleine Leute grosse Herzen [klI′-nuh loi′-tuh grohs′-suh hehr′-tsun] *Ger*—Sometimes little people have big hearts.

Kommt der Krieg ins Land / Gibt Lügen wie Sand [kuhmt dehr kreek ins lahnt gibt lü′-gun vee zahnt] *Ger*—When war invades a land / Lies are numbered as sand.

Komsomol (*Kommunisticheskii, soiuz, mo*lodezh) [kum-suh-mahl′ —kum-moo-niss-tee-ches′-kee sah-yoos′ mah-lah-doosh] *Rus*—League of Communist Youth (includes young people from nineteen to twenty-three years of age).

Krasnaya zvezda [krahs′-na-ya zvyez-day′] *Rus*—Red star; Soviet military publication.

Ktema es aei [ktay′-mah ess ah-eh′] *Gk*—An eternal possession. In a notable chapter in his *History of the Peloponnesian War*, the author tells of his love for historical truth and his aim to write something for posterity. Thucydides, 1; 22.

Küche, Kirche und Kinder [kü-khuh

keer'-kuh unt kind'-uhr] *Ger*—Kitchen, church and children. An antifeminist, male point of view on the place of woman; an official Nazi policy.

Kürze ist des Witzes Würze [kür'-tsuh ist dess vit'-tsuhss vür'-tsuh] *Ger*—Brevity is the soul of wit.

Kyrie eleison [kü'-rih-eh eh-leh'-ay-son, or kee-rih-ay ay-lay-ee-son] *Gk*—Lord, have mercy. A prayer offered six times immediately after the introit of the Mass in Latin.

L

La barba non fa il filosofo [lah bahr'-bah nohn fah eel fee-loh'-soh-foh] *It*—The beard does not make the philosopher.

La belle dame sans merci [lah bell dahm sahN mehr-see] *Fr*—The beautiful lady without pity. Title of a poem by Keats.

La belle époque [lah bell ay-puhk] *Fr*—The pleasant time; in retrospect the years 1900 to 1914 were happy years.

Labitur et labetur in omne volubilis aevum [lah'-bih-tuhr et lah-bay'-tuhr in om'-neh woh-loo'-bih-liss I'-wuhm] *L*—The river glides on and will glide on forever and ever. The simple-minded peasant waits for it to pass by. Horace, *Epistles*, 1; 2, 43.

La bonne bouche [lah bun boosh] *Fr*—Something good saved for the end; a tidbit.

Laborare est orare [lah-boh-rah'-reh est oh-rah'-reh] *L*—To work is to pray.

Labore et constantia [lah-boh'-reh et kohn-stahn'-tih-ah] *L*—With constant labor. Printer's mark of Christopher Plantin Press, which flourished in Antwerp from 1555 to 1867.

Labor est etiam ipse voluptas [lah'-bor est eh'-tih-ahm ip'-seh wo-luhp'-tahs] *L*—Even work itself is a pleasure. Manilius, *Astronomica*, 4; 155.

Labor improbus [lah'-bor im'-pro-buhs] *L*—Unremitting toil. The complete quotation reads: *Labor omnia vincit improbus.* Vergil, *Georgics*, 1; 145.

Labor ipse voluptas *L*—*See* Labor est etiam ipse voluptas.

Labor omnia vincit [lah'-bor om'-nih-ah win'-kit] *L*—Labor conquers all things.

Motto of Oklahoma. Adapted from Vergil, *Georgics*, 1; 145.

Laborum dulce lenimen [lah-boh'-ruhm duhl'-keh lay-nee'-men] *L*—Sweet solace of my troubled heart. The poet is addressing his lyre. Horace, *Odes*, 1; 32, 14.

La caridad bien entendida empieza por sí mismo [lah kah-ree-dahd' byehn' ehn-tehn-dee'-dah ehm-pee-ay'-sah por see mees'-moh] *Sp*—Charity, properly understood, begins with oneself; charity begins at home.

La codicia rompe el saco [lah koh-dee'-see-yah rohm'-peh el sah'-koh] *Sp*—Avarice breaks the sack. Cervantes, *Don Quixote*, 1; 20.

La Comédie Humaine [lah kuh-may-dee ü-menn] *Fr*—The Human Comedy, the title Balzac gave to his unfinished series of works depicting French society in his day.

La comédie larmoyante [lah kuh-may-dee lahr-mwah-yahNt] *Fr*—Literally, tearful comedy; a tear-jerker. Sentimental domestic theater of 18th-century France.

La commedia è finita [lah kom-may'-dee-ah eh fee-nee'-tah] *It*—The comedy is over; closing line of Leoncavallo's opera *I Pagliacci.*

La condition humaine [lah kohN-dee-syohN ü-menn] *Fr*—The human situation.

La Costa Brava [lah kohs'-tah brah'-vah] *Sp*—Literally, the wild coast; an area in northeastern Spain from the town of Blanes to the French border.

La critique est aisée, et l'art est difficile [lah kree-teek eh teh-zay ay lahr teh dee-fee-seel] *Fr*—Criticizing is easy, but art is difficult. Destouches, *Glorieux*, 2; 5.

106

Lade nicht Alles in ein Schiff [lah'-duh nikht ahl'-luss in In shiff] *Ger*—Don't load everything on one ship; don't carry all your eggs in one basket.

La derrière garde [lah dehr-ryehr gahrd] *Fr*—The rear guard.

La dolce vita [lah dohl'-chay vee'-tah] *It*—The sweet life; life devoted to luxury and pleasure.

La donna è mobile [lah don'-nah eh moh'-bee-lay] *It*—Woman is fickle. The most popular expression of this idea is an aria from Verdi's opera *Rigoletto. See also* Varium et mutabile . . .

La douce France [lah dooss frahNss] *Fr*—Sweet France.

La douceur de vivre [lah doo-suhr duh vee-vr] *Fr*—The sweetness of living.

L'adversité fait l'homme, et le bonheur les monstres [lahd-ver-see-tay feh luhm ay luh buh-nuhr lay mohN-str] *Fr*—Adversity makes men but prosperity makes monsters.

Laesa majestas [ll'-sah mah-yess'-tahs] *L*—Lese majesty; treason. In French, lèse majesté (*q.v.*).

La fame non vuol leggi [lah fah'-may nonn vwohl ledd'-jee] *It*—Hunger knows no law.

La farce est jouée [lah fahrss eh zhoo-ay] *Fr*—The farce is over. Supposed last words of Rabelais. *See also* Je vais chercher un grand Peut-être! *and* Acta est fabula.

La fin couronne les oeuvres [lah faN koo-ruhn lay zuh-vr] *Fr*—It is the end that crowns the work.

La fortuna aiuta i pazzi [lah for-too'-nah ah-yoo'-tah ee pat'-tsee] *It*—Fortune helps fools.

La Forza del destino [lah for'-tsah del dess-tee'-noh] *It*—The power of destiny. The title of an opera by Verdi.

La Garde meurt et ne se rend pas [lah gahrd muhr ay nuh suh rahN pah] *Fr*—The guard dies but it does not surrender. Cambronne, commander of the Old Guard at Waterloo, denied making this statement, embarrassing for him since he was

taken prisoner at Waterloo. However, the words were engraved on his monument. *See also* Le mot de Cambronne.

La génération spontanée est une chimère [lah zhay-nay-rah-syohN spohN-ta-nay eh tün shee-mehr] *Fr*—Spontaneous generation is a chimera, a thing of the imagination. Pasteur.

La génie c'est la patience [lah zhay-nee seh lah pah-syahNss] *Fr*—Genius is patience.

La Grande Voleuse [lah grahNd vuh-luhz] *Fr*—The great robber; a deprecatory assessment of Britain by the French.

La gravité est un mystère du corps inventé pour cacher les défauts de l'esprit [lah gra-vee-tay eh tuhn meess-tehr dü kor aN-vahN-tay poor ka-shay lay day-foh duh leh-spree] *Fr*—The grave manner is a mysterious cloak put on by the body to hide the faults of the soul. La Rochefoucauld, *Maxims*, 257.

La haute politique [lah oht puh-lee-teek] *Fr*—Top-level politics; political affairs in a nation at the summit.

La ilâha illa Allâh [lah eel'-ah-hah eel'-ah ah-lah'] *Arabic*—There is no God but Allah.

Laissez aller [leh-say ah-lay] *Fr*—Allow to go; let things go as they will.

Laissez dire [leh-say deer] *Fr*—Let opinions be permitted.

Laissez faire [leh-say fehr] *Fr*—Let the parties concerned alone. An economic policy of noninterference in business by government. Sometimes written *Laissez nous faire*, Let us alone, or Laissez aller (*q.v.*).

Laissez passer [leh-say pah-say] *Fr*—Literally, allow to pass; a permit.

La Journée des Dupes [lah zhoor-nay day düp] *Fr*—Dupes' Day or Day of Dupes. November 11, 1630. Marie de'Medici won a promise from her son, Louis XIII, to dismiss Cardinal Richelieu, his minister, but the king was influenced by friends of the cardinal to reverse his decision. In the course of a few hours the queen and her followers, awaiting the news of the minister's fall, were exiled from court.

La langue des femmes est leur épée, et elles ne la laissent pas rouiller [lah lahNg day fam eh luhr ay-pay eh el nuh luh lehss pah roo-yay] *Fr*—A woman's tongue is her sword, and she does not let it get rusty. A French proverb.

L'Albion perfide [lahl bee-ohN pehr-feed] *Fr*—Perfidious Albion; treacherous England. A French point of view. The English also have slighting phrases for the French, e.g., *taking French leave. See also* La Grande Voleuse.

La letteratura amena [lah lett-teh-rah-too'-rah ah-may'nah] *It*—Refined, polite literature.

La Ley de fuga [lah lay'-ee day foo'-gah] *Sp*—The law of flight. The captor gives a prisoner hope of escaping and then shoots him as he runs away.

L'allegro [lahl-lay'-groh] *It*—The happy man. Title of a poem by Milton; a companion piece to Il penseroso (*q.v.*).

La mala erba cresce presto [lah mah'-lah ehr'-bah kray'-shay press'-toh] *It*—Bad weeds grow fast.

La mejor salsa del mundo es el hambre [lah may-hohr' sahl'-sah del moon'-doh ess el ahm'-bray] *Sp*—Hunger is the best sauce in the world. Cervantes, *Don Quixote*, 2; 5.

La mémoire est nécessaire à toutes les opérations de l'esprit [lah may-mwahr eh nay-seh-sehr ah toot lay zuh-pay-rah-syohN duh leh-spree] *Fr*—The memory is necessary for all the operations of the mind. Pascal, *Pensées* 6; 369.

La moquerie est souvent indigence d'esprit [lah muhk-ree eh soo-vahN taN-dee-zhahNss deh-spree] *Fr*—Scoffing often betrays a lack of wit. La Bruyère, *Characters, Of Society*, 57 (1), p. 169 in Garapon's edition (Garnier Frères, 1962).

La morgue littéraire [lah mohrg lee-tay-rehr] *Fr*—A file of information or manuscripts that one day may be needed for publication.

L'amour courtois [lah-moor koor-twah] *Fr*—Courtly love of the twelfth and thirteenth centuries characterized by a gentle, chivalric spirit on the part of poets and knights toward aristocratic ladies.

L'amour, . . . de tous les sentiments le plus égoïste, et, par conséquent, lorsqu'il est blessé, le moins généreux [lah-moor duh too lay sahN-tee-mahN luh plüz ay-go-eest ay pahr kohN-say-kahN lors-keel eh bleh-say luh mwaN zhay-nay-ruh] *Fr*—Love is the most selfish of all the emotions and consequently, when wounded, the least generous. Benjamin Constant, *Adolphe*, chap. 6.

L'amour et la fumée ne peuvent se cacher [lah-moor ay lah fü-may nuh puhv suh ka-shay] *Fr*—Love and smoke cannot be hidden.

L'amour-propre est le plus grande de tous les flatteurs [lah-moor pro-pr eh luh plü grahNd duh too lay flah-tuhr] *Fr*—Self-love is the greatest of all flatterers. La Rochefoucauld, *Maxims*, 2.

Langage des halles [lahN-gazh day al] *Fr*—The language of the market place; rough, abusive talk.

L'Angleterre est une nation de boutiquiers [lahN-gluh-tair eh tün nah-syoN duh boo-tee-kyay] *Fr*—England is a nation of shopkeepers. Napoleon Bonaparte.

Langue d'oc [lahNg duhk] *Fr*—The dialects spoken in the south of France, so called because of the use of *oc* for *yes. See also* Langue d'oïl.

Langue d'oïl [lahNg duh-eel] *Fr*—Dialects of Old French spoken in the north of France where the word for *yes* was *oïl*, in modern French, *oui. See also* Langue d'oc.

La noblesse d'épée [lah noh-bless day-pay] *Fr*—The nobility of the sword; a name given the landed gentry in France.

La noblesse de race [lah noh-bless duh rass] *Fr*—The nobility of blood.

La nouvelle cuisine [lah noo-vel kwee-zeen] *Fr*—The new school of cooking.

La novela picaresca [lah noh-vay'-lah pee-kah-res'-kah] *Sp*—Tale of a rogue or rogues who go from one piece of knavery to another.

La novela policiaca [lah noh-vay'-lah poh-lee-see'-ah-kah] *Sp*—Detective story.

La nuit tous les chats sont gris [lah nwee too lay shah sohN gree] *Fr—See* Bei Nacht sind alle Katzen grau.

La paix à tout prix [lah peh ah too pree] *Fr—*Peace at any price.

La paix de Dieu [lah peh duh dyuh] *Fr—*The truce of God. *See also* Treuga Dei.

La parole a été donnée à l'homme pour déguiser sa pensée [lah pah-ruhl ah ay-tay duhn-nay ah luhm poor day-ghee-zay sah pahN-say] *Fr—*Speech was given to man to disguise his thoughts. Talleyrand.

La Pasionaria [lah pah-see-oh-nah'-ree-ah] *Sp—*The Passion Flower, pen name of Dolores Ibarruri Gomez, a powerful voice in the Spanish Civil War; exiled from Spain in 1939.

Lapis philosophorum [la'-pihs fih-lo-so-foh'-ruhm] *L—*The philosophers' stone. An imaginary substance that medieval alchemists believed could change brass metals into gold.

La patience est amère, mais son fruit est doux [lah pa-see-ahNss eh ta-mehr meh sohN frwee eh doo] *Fr—*Patience is bitter, but its fruit is sweet. Rousseau.

La patrie en danger [lah pah-tree ahN dahN-zhay] *Fr—*The fatherland is in danger; the country is in a state of crisis.

La perfide Albion [lah pehr-feed ahl-byohN] *Fr—*Perfidious Albion. A French evaluation of the integrity of the British.

La petite bourgeoisie [lah pteet boor-zhwah-zee] *Fr—*The lower middle class composed for the most part of tradesmen.

La petitesse de l'esprit fait l'opiniâtreté, et nous ne croyons pas aisément ce qui est au delà de ce que nous voyons [lah puh-tee-tess duh leh-spree feh luh-pee-nyah-truh-tay ay noo nuh krwah-yohN pah eh-zay-mahN skee eh toh duh-lah duh skuh noo vwah-yohN] *Fr—*The little mind is opinionated; we do not readily accept what is beyond our understanding. La Rochefoucauld, *Maxims*, 265.

La plaza de toros [lah plah'-sah day toh'-ros] *Sp—*Bull ring.

La plupart des gens ne jugent des hommes que par la vogue qu'ils ont, ou par leur fortune [lah plü-pahr day zhahN nuh zhüzh day zuhm kuh pahr lah vuhg keel zohN oo pahr luhr for-tün] *Fr—*Most men judge their fellows by the popularity or fortune they enjoy. La Rochefoucauld, *Maxims*, 212.

La plupart des hommes emploient la première partie de leur vie à rendre l'autre misérable [lah plü-pahr day zuhm ahN-plwah lah pruh-myehr pahr-tee duh luhr vee ah rahN-dr loh-tr mee-zay-rah-bl] *Fr—*Most men spend the first half of their lives in such a way that they make the second half miserable. La Bruyère, *Characters, On Man*, 102 (1), p. 330 in Garapon's edition (Garnier Frères, 1962).

La politique du pire [lah puh-lee-teek dü peer] *Fr—*Literally, the politics of the worst; the policy of backing the extremists to unseat the moderates.

La politique n'a pas d'entrailles [lah puh-lee-teek nah pah dahN-trah-yuh] *Fr—*Politics has no heart, no mercy.

La pompe des enterrements regarde plus la vanité des vivants que l'honneur des morts [lah pohNp day zahN-tehr-mahN ruh-gahrd plü lah vah-nee-tay day vee-vahN kuh luh-nuhr day mor] *Fr—*Funeral display is more concerned with the vanity of the living than the honor due the dead. La Rochefoucauld, *Maxims*, 612.

La povertà è la madre di tutte le arti [lah poh-vehr-tah' eh lah mah'-dray dee too'-tay lay ahr'-tee] *It—*Poverty is the mother of all the arts. The idea goes back to Theocritus.

L'appétit vient en mangeant [la-pay-tee vyaN ahN mahN-zhahN] *Fr—*Appetite grows with eating.

La pratica val più della grammatica [lah prah'-tee-kah vahl pee-oo' dell'-lah grahm-mah'-tee-kah] *It—*Practice (in speaking) is worth more than grammar.

La prima congettura che si fa del cervello di un signore, è vedere gli uomini che lui ha d'intorno [la pree'-mah kon-jet-too'-rah kay see fah dell chehr-vel'-loh dee oon seen-yoh'-ray eh vay-day'-ray lyee oo-oh'-mee-nee kay loo'-ee ah deen-tor'-noh] *It*—The first impression of a ruler's brains is based on the appearance of his advisers. Machiavelli, *The Prince*, 22.

Lapsus calami [lahp'-suhs kah'-lah-mee] *L*—Slip of the pen.

Lapsus linguae [lahp'-suhs ling'-gwI] *L*—A slip of the tongue.

Lapsus memoriae [lahp'-suhs meh-mo'-rih-I] *L*—A lapse of memory.

La reconnaissance est la mémoire du coeur [lah ruh-kuhn-neh-sahNss eh lah maym-wahr dü kuhr] *Fr*—Gratitude is the heart's memory.

La règle du jeu [lah reh-gl dü zhuh] *Fr*—The rule of the game.

La République n'a pas besoin de savants [lah ray-püb-leek nah pah buh-zwaN duh sa-vahN] *Fr*—The Republic has no need of savants. Words of the prosecutor of Lavoisier, the father of modern chemistry, guillotined in the Reign of Terror.

Lares et penates [lah'-rays et peh-nah'-tays] *L*—Household gods of the Romans protecting the home and fields.

L'art de vivre [lahr duh vee-vr] *Fr*—The art of living; the art of getting the most out of life.

L'Art Nouveau [lahr noo-voh] *Fr*—The New Art. Appeared in the nineties and flourished until World War I. Its style, characterized by sinuous, curving lines, greatly affected the decorative crafts, such as jewelry, ceramics, furniture.

L'art pour l'art [lahr poor lahr] *Fr*—Art for art's sake. Victor Cousin, *Sorbonne Lectures*, 22. *See also* Ars gratia artis.

Lasciate ogni speranza, voi ch'entrate [lahs-shah'-tay ohn'-yee spay-rahn'-tsah voy ken-trah'-tay] *It*—Abandon all hope, you who enter here. The inscription on the entrance to hell. Dante, *Inferno*, 3; 9.

Lasciva est nobis pagina, vita proba est [lahs-kee'-wah est noh'-beess pah'-gih-nah wee'-tah proh'-bah est] *L*—My page is lewd, but my life is pure. Martial, 1; 4.

La senda de la virtud es muy estrecha,

y el camino del vicio, ancho y espacioso [lah sayn'-dah day lah veer-tood' ess moo'-ee ays-tray'-chah ee el kah-mee'-noh del bee'-syoh ahn'-choh y ay-spah-syoh'-soh] *Sp*—The path to virtue is very narrow, the road to evil broad and free. Cervantes, *Don Quixote*, 2; 6.

Lass sie nach Berlin kommen [lahss zee nahkh Behr-leen' kuhm'-mun] *Ger*—Let them come to Berlin. President Kennedy's famous statement on the progress of the city after World War II.

Lateat scintillula forsan [lah'-teh-aht skihn-til'-luh-lah for'-sahn] *L*—Some small spark of life may lie unseen. The motto of the London Royal Humane Society, founded in 1774 by Dr. William Hawes, who believed that artificial means could restore people apparently drowned. The society expanded to include all first aid.

Latet anguis in herba [lah'-tet ahn'-gwiss in hehr'-bah] *L*—A snake lies hidden in the grass. Vergil, *Eclogues*, 3; 93.

Lathe biosas [lah'-theh bee-oh'-sahs] *Gk*—Seek to escape notice in life; try to live in obscurity. Epicurus. *See also* Ama nesciri.

Latino sine flexione [lah-tee'-noh sih'-neh flex-ih-oh'-neh] *L*—Latin without inflections, an artificial language dating from 1903. It has been succeeded by scores of similar attempts to invent an international means of communication.

La tour d'ivoire [lah toor dee-vwahr] *Fr*—The ivory tower.

La troppa familiarità genera disprezzo [lah trop'-pah fah-mee-lee-ah-ree-tah' jay'-nay-rah dee-spret'-tsoh] *It*—Familiarity breeds contempt.

Lauda la moglie e tienti donzello [low'-dah lah mohl'-yay ay tee-en'-tee don-tsel'-loh] *It*—Praise a wife but stay a bachelor.

Laudari a viro laudato [low-dah'-ree ah wih'-roh low-dah'-toh] *L*—To be praised by a man who is himself praised. The full statement: *Laetus sum laudari me abs te, pater, a viro laudato*, I am happy to be praised by you, father, who are yourself praised. A fragment from Naevius, *Hector Proficiscens* (The Departure of Hector); quoted by Cicero, *To Friends*, 15; 6, 1.

Laudator temporis acti [low-dah'-tor tem'-po-riss ahk'-tee] *L*—A praiser of the good old days. Horace, *Art of Poetry*, 173.

Laudum immensa cupido [low'-duhm ihm-mayn'-sah kuh-pee'-doh] *L*—A boundless passion for praise. Vergil, *Aeneid*, 6; 823.

Laus Deo [lowss deh'-oh] *L*—Praise be to God.

Laus perennis [lowss peh-ren'-niss] *L*—Perpetual praise; prayers offered day and night by shifts of monks.

Lá vão os pés onde quer o coração [lah vowN oos pehz oN'-dee kayr oo koo-ruh-sowN'] *Port*—The feet go where the heart wills.

La verità è figlia del tempo [lah vay-ree-tah' eh feel'-yah del tem'-poh] *It*—Truth is the daughter of time; time will eventually bring out the truth. *See also* Veritas temporis filia dicitur.

La vida es sueño [lah bee'-dah ess sway'-nyoh] *Sp*—*Life is a Dream*, title of a play by Calderón regarded as a masterpiece of the Spanish theater.

La vie à trois [lah vee ah trwah] *Fr*—The eternal triangle.

La vie en rose [lah vee ahN rohz] *Fr*—Life in full bloom.

La vieille gloire [lah vyay glwahr] *Fr*—Ancient glory.

Lavoro di commesso [lah-voh'-roh dee kom-mess'-soh] *It*—Italian inlay work.

lb. libra [lee'-brah] *L*—A pound.

l. c., loc. cit. *See* Loco citato.

Leben Sie wohl! [lay'-bun zee vohl] *Ger*—Farewell!

Lebensraum [lay'-benz-rowm] *Ger*—Room in which to live. The Nazi demand.

Le bon Dieu est toujours du côté des gros bataillons [luh bohN dyuh eh too-zhoor dü koh-tay day groh bah-tI-yohN] *Fr*—God is always on the side of the big armies. Attributed to Napoleon I, but the idea has been variously phrased by several writers.

Le bon genre [luh bohN zhahNr] *Fr*—Good form or taste.

Le bon temps viendra [luh bohN tahN vyaN-dra] *Fr*—There's a good time coming.

Le Bourgeois Gentilhomme [luh boor-zhwah zhahN-tee-yum] *Fr*—The commoner turned gentleman; the title of a play by Molière.

Le cabaret est le salon du pauvre [luh kah-bah-reh eh luh sah-lohN dü poh-vr] *Fr*—The pub is the poor man's club. Gambetta.

Le chat qui dort [luh sha kee dohr] *Fr*—*See* Ne réveillez pas . . .

Le cheval volant qui a les narines de feu [luh shvahl vuh-lahN kee ah lay nah-reen duh fuh] *Fr*—The flying horse that breathes fire from its nostrils. A reference to Pegasus, the winged horse.

Le chien retourne à son vomissement, et la truie lavée au bourbier [luh shyaN ruh-toorn ah sohN vuh-mees-mahN ay lah trwee la-vay oh boor-byay] *Fr*—The dog returns to his vomit, and the washed sow to its mire. Said of the fool who repeats his folly. Translation of *Vulgate*, 2 Peter, 2; 22.

Le coeur a ses raisons que la raison ne connaît pas [luh kuhr ah say reh-zohN kuh lah reh-zohN nuh kuhn-neh pah] *Fr*—The heart has its reasons, of which reason knows nothing. The first part of this aphorism served as the title of a book by the Duchess of Windsor. Pascal, *Pensées*, 4; 277.

Le comparazioni sono tutte odiose [lay kom-pah-rah-tsee-oh'-nee soh'-noh too'-tay oh-dee-oh'-say] *It*—All comparisons are odious.

Le courage est souvent un effet de la peur [luh koo-rahzh eh soo-vahN tuhn-ef-feh duh lah puhr] *Fr*—Courage is often born of fear.

Le coût en ôte le goût [luh koo ahn oht luh goo] *Fr*—The cost spoils the flavor.

Lectori benevolo [layk-toh'-ree beh-neh'-wuh-loh] *L*—To the kind reader.

Le demi-monde [luh duh-mee mohNd] *Fr*—A class of women of dubious reputation who live on the fringes of respectability.

111

Le dernier cri [luh dehr-nyay kree] *Fr*— The latest fashion; the last word.

Le dernier mot [luh dehr-nyay moh] *Fr*— The last word.

Le désespoir redouble les forces [luh day-zeh-spwahr ruh-doo-bl lay forss] *Fr*— Despair redoubles one's energies.

Le dessous des cartes [luh duh-soo day kahrt] *Fr*—The underside of the cards.

Le devoir des juges est de rendre justice; leur métier de la différer [luh duh-vwahr day zhüzh eh duh rahN-dr zhüsteess luhr may-tyay duh lah dee-fay-ray] *Fr*—The duty of judges is to render justice; their practice is to defer it. La Bruyère, *Characters, Of Certain Customs,* 43 (1), p. 427 in Garapon's edition (Garnier Frères, 1962).

Le diable au corps [luh dyah-bl oh kor] *Fr*—Possessed by the devil.

Le diable n'est pas si noir qu'on le dit [luh dyah-bl neh pah see nwahr kohN luh dee] *Fr*—The devil is not as black as he is painted.

Le disgrazie non vengon mai sole [lay dees-grah'-tsee-ay nonn venn'-gohn mah'- ee soh'-lay] *It*—Misfortunes never come singly. *See also* Ein Unglück kommt . . .

Le droit des gens [luh drwah day zhahN] *Fr*—International law.

Legalis homo [lay-gah'-liss ho'-moh] *L*—A legal person; a person in the eyes of the law.

Legatus a latere [lay-gah'-tuhs ah lah'- teh-reh] *L*—A specially instructed legate from the side of the pope; a specially commissioned papal envoy.

Leges barbarorum [lay'-gays bahr-bah-roh'-ruhm] *L*—Laws of the barbarians; a code put together by Charlemagne retaining the laws of the German tribes conquered by the Franks.

Leges plurimae, respublica pessima [lay'-gays ploo'-rih-mI rays-puh'-blih-kah pehs'-sih-mah] *L*—The more numerous the laws, the worse the commonwealth.

Legibus solutus [lay'-gih-buhs so-loo'- tuhs] *L*—Freed from obedience to the law; said of a monarch.

Légion étrangère [lay-zhyohN ay-trahN-zhehr] *Fr*—The Foreign Legion, well publicized by the American cinema.

Legio patria nostra [leh'-gih-oh pah'-trih-ah nuhs'-trah] *L*—The legion is our fatherland. Motto of the French Foreign Legion.

Le grand mal [luh grahN mal] *Fr*—Literally, the great illness, as opposed to le petit mal (*q.v.*). The serious attack of epilepsy; the falling sickness.

Le Grand Monarque [luh grahN muh-nahrk] *Fr*—The Great Monarch, Louis XIV.

Le grand monde [luh grahN muhNd] *Fr*— High society.

Le grand prix [luh grahN pree] *Fr*—The first prize.

Le grand siècle [luh grahN syeh-kl] *Fr*— The great century; the age ending with the death of Louis XIV.

Le haut monde [luh oh mohNd] *Fr*—The world of high society.

Leichter ist Vergeben als Vergessen [lIkh'-tuhr ist fehr-gay'-bun ahls fehr-gess'- un] *Ger*—It is easier to forgive than to forget.

Le jeu ne vaut pas la chandelle [luh zhuh nuh voh pah lah shahN-dehl] *Fr*—The game is not worth the candle.

Le jour de l'an [luh zhoor duh lahN] *Fr*—New Year's Day.

Le Juif errant [luh zhweef eh-rahN] *Fr*— The wandering Jew. A medieval legend of a Jew who treated Christ with contempt on his way to Calvary. For that reason he was condemned to wander about the earth until the Second Coming. The title of a novel by Eugène Sue.

Le juste milieu [luh zhüst mee-lyuh] *Fr*—The golden mean; the middle-of-the-road policy. *See also* Aurea mediocritas.

L'élan vital [lay-lahN vee-tahl] *Fr*—The life force. The term is central in the philosophy of Henri Bergson.

Le mal que nous faisons ne nous attire pas tant de persécution et de haine que nos bonnes qualités [luh mal kuh noo feh-zohN nuh noo zah-teer pah tahN duh pehr-say-kü-syohN ay duh ehn kuh noh buhn ka-lee-tay] *Fr*—The evil that we do does not bring upon us as much persecution and hatred as our good qualities. La Rochefoucauld, *Maxims*, 29.

Le méchant n'est jamais comique [luh may-shahN neh zha-meh kuh-meek] *Fr*—A wicked person is never comic. Count Joseph de Maistre.

Le mieux est l'ennemi du bien [luh myuh eh len-mee dü byaN] *Fr*—The best is the enemy of the good; leave well enough alone.

Le moine bourru [luh mwan boo-rü] *Fr*—The churlish monk; a bogeyman invented to frighten misbehaving children.

Le monde est le livre des femmes [luh mohNd eh luh lee-vr day fam] *Fr*—The world is woman's book. The author goes on to say that if she reads it ill, it is her own fault, or else she is blinded by passion. Rousseau, Book 5.

Le monde va de lui même [luh mohNd vah duh lwee mehm] *Fr*—The world goes by itself. An expression of the futile concern of man in the direction of human affairs.

Le mot de Cambronne [luh moh duh kahN-bruhn] *Fr*—When General Cambronne was asked to surrender at Waterloo, he is reported to have said "Merde!" —a mildly indecent expletive. His response was altered by popular accounts to read, La garde meurt . . .*(q. v.)*

Le mot juste [luh moh zhüst] *Fr*—The right word.

Le Moyen Age [luh mwah-yan-ahzh] *Fr*—The Middle Ages.

L'Empire c'est la paix [lahN-peer seh lah peh] *Fr*—The Empire is synonymous with peace.

L'empire des lettres [lahN-peer day leh-tr] *Fr*—The republic of letters.

L. en Dr. Licencié en Droit [lee-sahN-syay ahN drwah] *Fr*—Licentiate in Law.

Le nez de Cléopatre; s'il eût été plus court, toute la face de la terre aurait changé [luh nay duh klay-oh-pah-tr seel üt ay-tay plü koor toot lah fahss duh lah tehr ohr-eh shahN-zhay] *Fr*—If Cleopatra's nose had been shorter, the whole face of the earth would have been changed. Pascal, *Pensées*, 2; 162.

L'enfer des femmes, c'est la vieillesse [lahN-fehr day fam seh lah vyay-ehss] *Fr*—Hell for women is old age. La Rochefoucauld, *Maxims*, 562.

L'ennemi du genre humain [len-mee dü zhahNr ü-maN] *Fr*—Enemy of the human race.

Leonina societas [leh-oh-nee'-nah so-kih'-eh-tahs] *L*—Partnership with a lion; a one-sided arrangement.

Le parole son femmine, i fatti son maschi [lay pah-roh'-lay sonn fehm'-mee-nay ee faht'-tee sonn mah'-skee] *It*—Words are feminine, deeds are masculine. The genders of the nouns suit the proverb. One of the mottoes of Maryland; for the other, *see* Scuto bonae voluntatis . . .

Le pénible fardeau de n'avoir rien à faire [luh pay-nee-bl fahr-doh duh nah-vwahr ry-aN ah fehr] *Fr*—The painful burden of having nothing to do. Boileau, *Epistle 11.*

Le petit caporal [luh ptee ka-po-rahl] *Fr*—The little corporal; Napoleon.

Le petit coin [luh ptee kwaN] *Fr*—Literally, the little corner; the powder room.

Le plus brave des braves [luh plü brahv day brahv] *Fr*—The bravest of the brave.

Le pour et le contre [luh poor ay luh kohN-tr] *Fr*—Pro and con(tra).

Le Proche Orient [luh pruhsh oh-ryahN] *Fr*—The Near East.

Le refus des louanges est un désir d'être loué deux fois [luh ruh-fü day lwahNzh eht uhN day-zeer deh-tr loo-ay duh fwah] *Fr*—We reject praise because we desire to hear it again. La Rochefoucauld, *Maxims*, 149.

Le roi est mort. Vive le roi! [luh rwah eh mohr. Veev luh rwah] *Fr*—The king is

113

dead. Long live the king! Once the courtiers of France heard that the king had died, they immediately saluted his successor.

Le roi le veut [luh rwah luh vuh] *Fr—*The king wills it.

Le roi règne et ne gouverne pas [luh rwah reh-nyuh ay nuh goo-vehrn pah] *Fr—*The king reigns but he does not govern. A translation of Rex regnat . . .*(q. v.)* It appeared in 1830 in *Le National*, which opposed the government of Charles X. L. A. Thiers.

Le roi s'avisera [luh rwah sa-vee-zuh-rah] *Fr—*The king will take the matter under advisement.

Le Roi Soleil [luh rwah suh-lay] *Fr—*The Sun King, a name for Louis XIV, who was represented by a symbol of the sun.

Le roy le veult [luh rwa luh vuhlt] *OF—*The king wills it. This older form of *Le roi (la reine) le veut* is used by the British sovereign when indicating approval of bills in Parliament.

Les absents ont toujours tort [lay zahp-sahN ohN too-zhoor tor] *Fr—*The absent are always in the wrong. The implication is that they are unable to defend themselves.

Les affaires sont les affaires [lay zah-fehr sohN lay zah-fehr] *Fr—*Business is business.

Le sage quelquefois évite le monde de peur d'être ennuyé [luh sahzh kell-kuh-fwah ay-veet luh mohNd duh puhr deh-tr ahn-nwee-yay] *Fr—*The wise man sometimes flees society to escape being bored. La Bruyère, *Characters, Of Society*, 83 (1), p. 179 in Garapon's edition (Garnier Frères, 1962).

Les amis du vin [lay za-mee dü vaN] *Fr—*Friends of wine, an organization interested in winetasting, fine vintages, and wine tours in Europe.

Les beaux esprits se recontrent [lay boh zehs-pree suh rahN-kohN-tr] *Fr—*Great minds think alike.

Les belles actions cachées sont les plus estimables [lay bell zahk-syohN kah-shay sohN lay plü zes-tee-mah-bl] *Fr—*Noble deeds that are kept hidden are the most esteemed.

Les bons comptes font les bons amis [lay bohN kohNt fohN lay bohN zah-mee] *Fr—*Good accounts make good friends.

Les convenances [lay kohN-vuh-nahNss] *Fr—*Accepted rules of behavior; decorum.

Les Diables Bleues [lay dya-bl bluh] *Fr—*The Blue Devils, the name of a noted British polo team.

Les dieux ont soif [lay dyuh ohN swahf] *Fr—The Gods Are Athirst* (for blood). Title of a novel about the French Revolution by Anatole France.

Le secret d'ennuyer est celui de tout dire [luh suh-kreh dahn-nwee-yay eh suh-lwee duh too deer] *Fr—*The secret of being a bore is to tell every detail. Voltaire, *On the Nature of Man*, Discourse 6.

Lèse majesté [lehz ma-zheh-stay] *Fr—*Lese majesty; treason. Derived from laesa majestas.

Les extrêmes se touchent [lay zehk-strehm suh toosh] *Fr—*Extremes meet. Mercier, *Tableau of Paris*, title of chap. 348, vol. 4.

Les femmes peuvent tout, parce qu'elles gouvernent les personnes qui gouvernent tout [lay fam puhv too pahrs kell goo-vehrn lay pehr-suhn kee goo-vehrn too] *Fr—*Women are all-powerful because they govern those who govern everything.

Les fous font les festins et les sages les mangent [lay foo fohN lay feh-staN ay lay sahzh lay mahNzh] *Fr—*Fools prepare the banquet and the smart ones eat it.

Les gens qui hésitent ne réussissent guère [lay zhahN kee ay-zeet nuh ray-ü-seess gehr] *Fr—*Those who hesitate rarely succeed. Napoléon Bonaparte.

Les grands esprits se rencontrent [lay grahN zeh-spree suh rahN-kohN-tr] *See* Les beaux esprits . . .

Les gros bataillons ont toujours raison [lay groh bah-tI-yohN zohN too-zhoor reh-zohN] *Fr—*The big batallions are always right. Tolstoy refutes this maxim in *War and Peace*, stressing the importance of morale in warfare. *See also* Le bon Dieu est toujours . . .

Les hommes rougissent moins de leurs crimes que de leurs faiblesses et de leur vanité [lay zuhm roo-zheess mwaN duh luhr kreem kuh duh luhr feh-bless ay duh luhr vah-nee-tay] *Fr*—Men blush less for their crimes than for their weaknesses and their vanity. La Bruyère, *Characters, Of the Heart*, 74 (5), p. 150 in Garapon's edition (Garnier Frères, 1962).

Les hommes sont cause que les femmes ne s'aiment point [lay zuhm sohN kohz kuh lay fam nuh sehm pwaN] *Fr*—Men are the reason why women do not love one another. La Bruyère, *Characters, Of Women*, 55 (4), p. 128 in Garapon's edition (Garnier Frères, 1962).

Le silence éternel de ces espaces infinis m'effraye [luh see-lahNss ay-tehr-nehl duh say zeh-spahss aN-fee-nee meh-freh] *Fr*—The eternal silence of infinite space frightens me. Pascal, *Pensées*, 3; 206.

L. ès L. Licencié ès Lettres [lee-sahN-syay ess leh-tr] *Fr*—Licentiate in Letters.

Les morts ont toujours tort [lay mohr zohN too-zhoor tor] *Fr*—The dead are always wrong.

Les murailles ont des oreilles [lay mü-rI-yuh zohN day zoh-reh-yuh] *Fr*—The walls have ears.

Les paroles sont faites pour cacher nos pensées [lay pa-ruhl sohN feht poor ka-shay noh pahN-say] *Fr*—Words were invented to disguise our thoughts. A variation of La parole a été donnée à l'homme . . .

Les personnes faibles ne peuvent être sincères [lay pehr-suhn feh-bl nuh puhv eh-tr saN-sehr] *Fr*—The weak cannot be sincere. La Rochefoucauld, *Maxims*, 316.

Les plus sages ne le sont pas toujours [lay plü sahzh nuh luh sohN pah too-zhoor] *Fr*—The wisest men are not always wise.

L'esprit de suite [leh-spree duh sweet] *Fr*—Team spirit; devotion to the cause.

L'esprit est toujours la dupe du coeur [leh-spree eh too-zhoor lah düp dü kuhr] *Fr*—The mind is always deceived by the heart. La Rochefoucauld, *Maxims*, 102.

Les Quarante fauteuils [lay ka-rahNt foh-tuh-yuh] *Fr*—Literally, the forty armchairs; the Académie française, also referred to as the Forty Immortals.

Les querelles ne dureraient pas longtemps si le tort n'était que d'un côté [lay kuh-rehl nuh dü-ruh-reh pah lohNtahN see luh tor nay-teh kuh duhN koh-tay] *Fr*—Quarrels would not last so long if the wrong were only on one side. La Rochefoucauld, *Maxims*, 496.

Les scènes à faire [lay sehn zah fehr] *Fr*—The scenes that must be done. The talented playwright knows what scenes will command interest because of their dramatic content.

Le style c'est l'homme *or* **Le style est l'homme même** [luh steel seh luhm *or* luh steel eh luhm mehm] *Fr*—Literary style is the man himself. Buffon, *Discourse on Style*.

L'état c'est moi [lay-tah seh mwah] *Fr*—The state, I am the state. Young Louis XIV's reply to the president of the French parliament when he made some objections in the interest of the state.

L'état major [lay-tah ma-zhohr] *Fr*—General staff; staff headquarters.

L'étoile du Nord [lay-twahl dü nohr] *Fr*—Star of the North. Motto of Minnesota.

Le tout ensemble [luh too tahN-sahN-bl] *Fr*—The whole or general effect.

Lettre d'avis [leh-tr da-vee] *Fr*—Letter of advice.

Lettre de cachet [leh-tr duh ka-shay] *Fr*—A sealed letter, often containing a warrant for imprisonment without trial.

Lettre de change [leh-tr duh shahNzh] *Fr*—Bill of exchange.

Lettre de créance [leh-tr duh kray-ahNss] *Fr*—Letter of credit.

Le vainqueur du vainqueur de la terre [luh vaN-kuhr dü vaN-kuhr duh lah tehr] *Fr*—The conqueror of the conqueror of the earth. Doctor Samuel Johnson used these words in a stinging letter to Lord Chesterfield when rejecting his tardy offer of patronage.

Levari facias [leh-vah′-ree fah′-kih-ahs] *L*—Cause to be levied. An order to an official to seize a debtor's property.

Levée en masse [luh-vay ahn mahss] *Fr*—A general uprising. Also, general conscription.

Leve fit quod bene fertur onus [leh-weh fit kwod beh′-neh fehr′-tuhr oh′-nuhs] *L*—The load that is cheerfully borne becomes light. Ovid, *Amores*, 1; 2, 10.

Le vin est tiré—il faut le boire [luh vaN eh tee-ray eel foh luh bwahr] *Fr*—The wine is poured and must be drunk; there's no backing out now.

Levius fit patientia quicquid corrigere est nefas [leh′-wih-uhs fit pah-tih-en′-tih-ah kwik′-kwid kor-rih′-ge-reh est neh′-fahs] *L*—Patience makes that more bearable which cannot be changed; what can't be cured must be endured. Horace, *Odes*, 1; 24, 19.

Le vrai honnête homme est celui qui ne se pique de rien [luh vray uh-neht uhm eh suh-lwee kee neh suh peek duh ryaN] *Fr*—The real gentleman prides himself on nothing. La Rochefoucauld, *Maxims*, 203.

Le vrai n'est pas toujours vraisemblable [luh vreh neh pah too-zhoor vreh-sahN-blah-bl] *Fr*—Truth is not always believable.

Le vrai peut quelquefois n'être pas vraisemblable [luh vreh puh kel-kuh-fwah neh-tr pah vreh-sahN-bla-bl] *Fr*—Truth is sometimes stranger than fiction.

Le vrai roi du dix-huitième siècle [luh vray rwah dü deez-wee-tyehm syeh-kl] *Fr*—The true king of the 18th century. Said of Voltaire.

Lex loci [layx loh′-kee] *L*—Law of the place; customs of the region.

Lex loci rei sitae [layx loh′-kee reh′-ee sih′-tI] *L*—The law of the place where the thing is situated.

116

Lex mercatoria (mercatoris) [layx mehr-kah-toh′-rih-ah, mehr-kah-toh′-riss] *L*—Mercantile law; the body of law dealing with commercial traders and their transactions.

Lex non scripta [layx nohn skreep′-tah] *L*—The unwritten law; common law as distinct from statute law.

Lex scripta [layx skreep′-tah] *L*—Written law, statute law.

Lex talionis [layx tah-lih-oh′-niss] *L*—The law of retaliation; an eye for an eye and a tooth for a tooth.

Lex terrae [layx tehr′-rI] *L*—The law of the land.

L'Extrême Orient [lek-strehm oh-ryahN] *Fr*—The Far East.

L'habitude est une seconde nature [lah-bee-tüd eh tün suh-gohNd nah-tür] *Fr*—Habit becomes second nature. *See also* Consuetudo fit altera natura.

L. H. D. Litterarum Humaniorum Doctor [lih-teh-rah′-ruhm hoo-mah-nee-oh′-ruhm dok′-tohr] *L*—Doctor of the Humanities.

L'histoire n'est qu'une fable convenue [lees-twahr neh kün fa-bl kohN-vnü] *Fr*—History is only a fable agreed upon. Variously attributed to Fénelon, Napoléon Bonaparte, and Voltaire.

L'homme absurde est celui qui ne change jamais [luhm ahp-sürd eh suh-lwee kee nuh shahNzh zha-meh] *Fr*—The absurd man is the one who never changes his opinion. A. M. Barthélemy.

L'homme est né libre et il est partout dans les fers [luhm eh nay lee-br ay eel eh par-too dahN lay fehr] *Fr*—Man is born free and is everywhere in chains. Rousseau, *Social Contract*, 1; 1.

L'homme propose et Dieu dispose [luhm pruh-poz eh dyuh dee-spohz] *Fr*—Translation of Homo proponit . . .*(q. v.)*.

L'homme tranquille [luhm trahN-keel] *Fr*—The tranquil man.

L'hôtel des Invalides [loh-tel day zaN-vah-leed] *Fr*—Military Pensioners' Hospital in Paris. Napoleon is buried in this building.

L'hypocrisie est un hommage que le vice rend à la vertu [lee-po-kree-zee eht uhN uhmazh kuh luh vees rahNd ah lah vehr-tü] *Fr*—Hypocrisy is a form of homage that vice renders to virtue. La Rochefoucauld, *Maxims*, 218.

Libera me [lee'-beh-rah may] *L*—Free me.

Libertas est potestas faciendi id quod jure licet [lee-behr'-tahs est po-tes'-tahs fah-kih-en'-dee id kwod yoo'-reh lih'-ket] *L*—Liberty is the freedom of doing what is permitted within the law.

Libertas, quae sera tamen respexit inertem [lee-behr'-tahs kwI seh'-rah tah'-men reh-spex'-it in-ehr'-tem] *L*—Liberty, which tardily looked back upon a sluggish servant. Lamb uses this quotation at the beginning of the essay "The Superannuated Man," in which he sings of the joys of retirement. Vergil, *Eclogues*, 1; 27.

Liberté, égalité, fraternité [lee-behr-tay ay-ga-lee-tay fra-tehr-nee-tay] *Fr*—Liberty, equality, fraternity. The ideals and slogan of the French Revolution.

Liberum veto [lee'-beh-ruhm weh'-toh] *L*—Free veto. In mid-17th-century Poland, respect for the rights of the minority became so exaggerated that a single dissenting deputy could override the will of the majority in the parliament.

Libris clausis [lihb'-reess klow'-sees] *L*—With closed books. A directive used in academic examinations; opposed to an open-book examination.

Licentia vatum [lih-ken'-tih-ah wah'-tuhm] *L*—Poetic license.

Liebe ohne Gegenliebe ist wie eine Frage ohne Antwort [lee'-buh oh'-nuh gay'-gun-lee-buh ist vee I'-nuh frah'-guh oh'-nuh ahnt'-vort] *Ger*—Love without return of love is like a question without an answer.

Lieu de réunion [lyuh duh ray-ü-nyohN] *Fr*—Place of assembly.

Limae labor [lee'-mI lah'-bor] *L*—The labor of the file; the polishing of a literary work. Horace, *Art of Poetry*, 291.

Limbus fatuorum [lim'-buhs fah-tuh-oh'-ruhm] *L*—A paradise for fools.

L'imitazione del male supera sempre l'esempio; come per il contrario, l'imitazione del bene è sempre inferiore [lee-mee-tah-tsee-oh'-nay del mah'-lay soo-pay'-rah sem'-pray lay-sem'-pee-oh koh'-may per eel kon-trah'-ree-oh lee-mee-tah-tsee-oh'-nay del bay'-nay eh sem'-pray een-fay-ree-oh'-ray] *It*—The imitation of evil surpasses the example; on the contrary, the imitation of virtue always falls short. Guicciardini.

Lingua Adamica [ling'-wah ah-dah'-mih-kah] *L*—The language of Adam. Mankind's original language, spoken in the days before the Tower of Babel.

Lingua franca [ling'-gwah frahn'-kah] *L*—Literally, the Frankish tongue. A jargon used for elementary communication by medieval traders and sailors in the Mediterranean, derived for the most part from the Romance languages. In a general sense it describes a mixture of languages used as a means of communication in business. Pidgin English is the lingua franca between Chinese and English speakers.

Lingua toscana in bocca romana [leeng'-gwah toss-kah'-nah een bohk'-kah roh-mah'-nah] *It*—A Tuscan tongue in a Roman mouth. Said to be the ideal Italian pronunciation.

L'injustice à la fin produit l'indépendence [laN-zhü-steess ah lah faN pruh-dwee laN-day-pahN-dahNss] *Fr*—In the end injustice produces independence. Voltaire, *Tancrède*, 3; 2.

Lis litem generat [leess lee'-tem geh'-neh-raht] *L*—Litigation breeds litigation; one quarrel starts another.

Lis pendens [leess pen'-dayns] *L*—Lawsuit pending.

Lis sub judice [leess suhb yoo'-dih-keh] *L*—A suit still in the courts. Horace, *Ars Poetica*, 78.

Lit de justice [lee duh zhüs-tees] *Fr*—Bed of justice. The bed was a cushioned seat on which the kings of France sat in parliament. It also refers to the session itself.

Litem lite resolvere [lee'-tem lee'-teh reh-sol'-weh-reh] *L*—To resolve one dispute by introducing another.

117

Lite pendente [lee'-teh pen-den'-teh] *L*—While litigation is pending.

Literatim, verbatim, punctuatim [lih-teh-rah'-tim wehr-bah'-tim puhnk-tuh-ah'-tim] *L*—Letter for letter, word for word, period for period.

Litt. B. Litterarum Baccalaureus [lih-teh-rah'-ruhm bahk-kah-low'-reh-uhs] *L*—Bachelor of Letters.

Litt. D. Litterarum Doctor [lih-teh-rah'-ruhm dok'-tor] *L*—Doctor of Letters.

Littera canina [liht'-teh-rah kah-nee'-nah] *L*—The dog's letter; the letter *r*, so called by the Romans because it resembled the growl of a dog. Persius, 1; 109.

Litterae humaniores [lit'-tehr-rI hoo-mah-nih-oh'-rays] *L*—Humane letters; the humanities.

Littera enim occidit, spiritus autem vivificat [lit'-teh-rah eh'-nim ohk'-sih-dit spee'-rih-toos ow'-tem vee-vih'-fih-kaht] *L*—The letter kills, the spirit gives life. *Vulgate, Paul, 2 Corinthians, 3; 6.*

Littera scripta manet [lit'-teh-rah skreep'-tah mah'-net] *L*—The written word remains. Used as a caution that what one writes may be used against him.

Livre de chevet [lee-vr duh shuh-veh] *Fr*—A bedside book.

Livre de circonstances [lee-vr duh seer-kohN-stahNss] *Fr*—A book worked up for the occasion.

Livre de poche [lee-vr duh puhsh] *Fr*—A book fitting the pocket; a paperback.

Livres d'heures [lee-vr duhr] *Fr*—Manuscript books of the hours, beautifully ornamented, containing prayers recited at the canonical hours: matins, lauds, prime, tierce, sext, nones, vespers and complin.

LL. B. Legum Baccalaureus [lay'-guhm bahk-kah-low'-reh-us] *L*—Bachelor of Laws.

LL. D. Legum Doctor [lay'-guhm dok'-tor] *L*—Doctor of Laws.

LL. MM. Leurs Majestés [luhr ma-zheh-stay] *Fr*—Their Majesties.

L'occasion fait le larron [luh-kah-zyohN feh luh lah-rohN] *Fr*—The opportunity makes the thief.

Loc. cit. *L*—*See* Loco citato.

Loco citato [loh'-koh sih-tah'-toh] *L*—In the passage cited. Often abbreviated *l.c.* or *loc. cit.*

Locos y niños dicen la verdad [loh'-kohs ee neen'-yohs dee'-sen lah behr-dad] *Sp*—Madmen and children speak the truth.

Locum tenens [loh'-kuhm teh'-nayns] *L*—A substitute. Used, for example, by physicians to designate a temporary practitioner taking care of patients during the absence of the regular doctor.

Locus classicus [loh'-kuhs klahs'-sih-kuhs] *L*—A passage in a classic; more commonly a passage most frequently cited in illustrating some usage in language or proving some point of doctrine.

Locus communis [loh'-kuhs kom-moo'-niss] *L*—A common place, as for the dead; a public place. The plural, *loci communes*, means a listing of arguments; commonplaces. Melanchthon used this as a title of a work in which he explained the doctrines of the Reformation.

Locus criminis [loh'-kuhs krih'-mih-niss] *L*—Scene of the crime.

Locus delicti [loh'-kuhs day-leek'-tee] *L*—The place where the crime took place.

Locus in quo [lok'-kuhs in kwoh] *L*—The place in which, referring to the location of an occurrence or to a passage in a text.

Locus poenitentiae [loh'-kuhs poi-nih-ten'-tih-I] *L*—Literally, chance or opportunity for repentance; chance to withdraw consent before binding oneself to an obligation.

Locus sigilli [loh'-kuhs sih-gihl'-lee] *L*—See l. s.

Locus standi [loh'-kuhs stahn'-dee] *L*—Ground to stand on in a legal sense; a recognized position; the right to have one's case heard.

Lo gran rifiuto [loh grahn reef-yoo'-toh] *It*—The great refusal, referring to the abdication of Pope Celestine V, proclaimed a saint by the church but assigned to hell by Dante. Dante, *Inferno*, 3; 60.

Loin des yeux, loin du coeur [lwaN day zyuh lwaN dü kuhr] *Fr—See* the equivalent Lontan dagli ...

Longo sed proximus intervallo [lon'-goh sed prox'-ih-muhs in-tehr-wahl'-loh] *L*—The next but separated by a long distance; a poor second. Vergil, *Aeneid*, 5; 320.

Longum iter est per praecepta, breve et efficax per exempla [lon'-guhm ih'-tehr est pehr prI-kep'-tah breh'-weh et ef'-fih-kahx pehr ex-em'-plah] *L*—The road to wisdom is long by precept, short and effective by example. Seneca, *Epistles*, 6; 5.

Lontan dagli occhi, lontan dal cuore [lon-tahn' dahl'-yee ohk'-kee lon-tahn' dahl kwoh'-ray] *It*—Literally, far from the eyes, far from the heart; out of sight, out of mind.

Lo peor es siempre cierto [loh pay-ohr' ess see-ehm'-pray see-ehr'-toh] *Sp*—The worst is always certain; the worst is sure to come.

Lo que hoy se pierde se gana mañana [loh kay oy say pih-ehr'-day say gah'-nah mah-nyah'-nah] *Sp*—What a man loses today, he wins back tomorrow. Cervantes, *Don Quixote*, 2; 7.

Loquendum ut vulgus, sentiendum ut docti [lo-kwehn'-duhm uht wuhl'-guhs sehn-tih-ehn'-duhm uht dok'-tee] *L*—We must speak as the crowd does, but think as the learned do. Edward Coke. Another version: *Loquendum est ut plures, sentiendum ut pauci* [lo-kwehn'-duhm est uht ploo'-rays sehn-tih-ehn'-duhm uht pow'-kee] We must speak with the many but think with the few.

Lo que no se puede remediar se ha de aguantar [loh kay noh say pweh'-day ray-may-dee-ahr' say ah day ah-gwahn-tahr'] *Sp*—What can't be cured must be endured.

Lo que se aprende en la cuna siempre dura [loh kay say ah-prehn'-day en lah koo'-nah syem'-pray doo'-rah] *Sp*—What we learn in the cradle always lasts; as the twig is bent, the tree's inclined.

L'Osservatore Romano [los-sehr-vah-toh'-ray roh-mah'-noh] *It*—The Roman Observer, the Vatican newspaper.

Loyauté m'oblige [lwah-yoh-tay muh-bleezh] *Fr*—Loyalty binds me.

L. Q. Lege quaeso [leh'-geh kwI'-soh] *L*—Please read.

l. s. locus sigilli [loh'-kuhs sih-gihl'-lee] *L*—The place where the seal is affixed to a document.

Lucidus ordo [loo'-kih-duhs or'-doh] *L*—A clear, orderly arrangement in a literary composition. Horace, *Art of Poetry*, 41.

Lucus a non lucendo [loo'-kuhs ah nohn loo-ken'-doh] *L*—This is quoted when a ridiculous derivation is given for a word. A grove (*lucus*) is dark because the light cannot penetrate it; therefore, the word for grove is derived from *not shining*.

Lues commentatoria [luh'-ays kom-men-tah-toh'-rih-ah] *L*—The plague of commentators. An abusive term applied to students of a classic who publish interpretations of what they think the author intended to say.

Lügen haben kurze Beine [lü'-gun hah'-bun koorts'-uh bI'-nuh] *Ger*—Lies have short legs, i.e. they are soon overtaken by truth.

L'ultima che se perde è la speranza [lool'-tee-mah kay say pehr'-day eh lah spay-rahnt'-sah] *It*—The last thing we lose is hope.

L'union fait la force [lü-nyohN feh lah forss] *Fr*—In union there is strength. Motto of Belgium.

Lupus est homo homini [loo'-puhs est lü'-moh ho' mih-nee] *L*—Man is a wolf to his fellow man. *See also* Homo homini lupus.

Lupus in sermone (fabula) [loo'-puhs in sehr-moh'-neh, fah'-buh-lah] *L*—The wolf in the fable or the story; talk of the devil and he's sure to appear. Said when a person appears who has been the subject of conversation. Plautus, *Stichus*, 4; 1, 71.

Lupus pilum mutat, non mentem [loo'-puhs pih'-luhm moo'-taht nohn men'-tem]

L—The wolf changes his coat but not his disposition.

Lusus naturae [loo'-suhs nah-too'-rI] *L*— A freak of nature.

Lütte corps à corps [lüt kor ah kor] *Fr*— Literally, a body to body struggle, as in wrestling. The expression may be used to characterize a heated discussion, even among friends.

Lux et veritas [loox et way'-rih-tahs] *L*— Light and truth. Motto of Yale University.

Lux tua vita mihi [loox tuh'-ah wee'-tah mih'-hih] *L*—Your light is my life.

Lympha pudica deum vidit et erubuit [lim'-fah puh'-dih-kah deh'-uhm wee'-dit et ay-ruh'-buh-it] *L*—The modest water saw its lord and blushed. Verse describing the miracle of Cana. Some versions substitute *Nympha* for *lympha*. The translation is unchanged. Crashaw, *Epigrammata Sacra*.

M

M. Monsieur [muh-syuh] *Fr*—Mr.

Ma chérie, ma chère [mah shay-ree, mah shehr] *Fr*—My dear one (*m* and *f*).

Macht geht vor Recht [mahkht gayt for rehkht] *Ger*—Might before right. Bismarck was accused of following this policy.

Macte virtute esto [mahk'-teh wihr-too'-teh es'-toh] *L*—Go forward and prosper. Generally spoken in commendation or encouragement.

Madre divina! [mah'-dray dee-vee'-nah] *Sp-It*—Divine mother (referring to the Virgin Mary). Used as an expletive.

Maestro dei maestri [mah-ay'-stroh day'-ee mah-ay'-stree] *It*—Master of the masters.

Maestro di cappella [mah-ay'-stroh dee kahp-pell'-lah] *It*—A gifted musician in charge of music in an Italian court or a cathedral during the sixteenth century.

Ma foi! [mah fwah] *Fr*—My faith; upon my word!

Maggiore fretta, minore atto [mah-joh'-ray frett'-tah mee-noh'-ray aht'-toh] *It*—More haste, less speed.

Magis illa juvant, quae pluris ementur [mah'-gis ihl'-lah yuh'-wahnt kwI ploo'-ris eh-men'-tuhr] *L*—The greater the cost, the greater the pleasure. This satirical phrase is meant to ridicule those who waste fortunes on delicacies in the belief that the more costly a dish, the more delicious it is. Juvenal, 11; 16.

Magister artis ingenique largitor venter [mah-gis'-tehr ahr'-tis in-geh-nee'-kweh lahr-gee'-tor wen'-tehr] *L*—The stomach is the teacher of art and the giver of genius. Persius, *Prologue to Satires*, 10.

Magister bibendi [mah-gis'-tehr bih-ben'-dee] *L*—*See* Arbiter bibendi.

Magister ceremoniarum [mah-gis'-tehr keh-reh-moh-nih-ah'-ruhm] *L*—Master of ceremonies.

Magister equitum [mah-gis'-tehr eh'-kwih-tuhm] *L*—Master of the horse; chief of the Roman cavalry appointed by a dictator.

Magna Carta [mahg'-nah kahr'-tah] *L*—The Great Charter. A document dating from 1215 in which the English barons stated their right and limited the powers of King John; considered the basis of the parliamentary system.

Magna civitas, magna solitudo [mahg'-nah kee'-wih-tahs mahg'-nah soh-lih-too'-doh] *L*—A great city, a great desert; one can be very lonely in a big city.

Magna cum laude [mahg'-nah kuhm low'-deh] *L*—*See* Cum laude.

Magnae spes altera Romae [mahg'-nI spays ahl'-teh-rah roh'-mI] *L*—The second hope of mighty Rome (Ascanius, the son of Aeneas). This is sometimes applied to a youth of whom much is expected. Vergil, *Aeneid*, 12; 168.

Magna est veritas, et praevalet (not *praevalebit*) [mahg'-nah est vay'-rih-tahs et pray'-vah-let] *L*—Truth is mighty and will prevail. *Vulgate, 3 Esdras*, 4; 41.

Magnas inter opes inops [mahg'-nahs in'-tehr oh'-pays in'-ops] *L*—In poverty amid great riches. Horace, *Odes*, 3; 16, 28.

Magnificat anima mea Dominum [mahg-nih'-fih-kaht ah'-nih-mah meh'-ah do'-mih-nuhm] *L*—My soul doth magnify the Lord. Words spoken by the Virgin Mary to Elizabeth. The hymn, known by the first word, is sung at vespers in the Roman Catholic Church and at evening song in the Church of England. *Vulgate, Luke,* 1; 46-55.

Magni nominis umbra [mahg'-nee noh'-mih-nis uhm'-brah] *L—See* Stat magni nominis . . .

Magno jam conatu magnas nugas [mahg'-noh yahm koh-nah'-too mahg'-nahs noo'-gahs] *L—*To produce tremendous trifles with great labor. Terence, *Self-Tormentor,* 4; 1, 8. *See also* Parturiunt montes . . .

Magnum opus [mahg'-nuhm o'-puhs] *L—*Masterpiece.

Magnum vectigal est parsimonia [mahg'-nuhm wek-tee'-gahl est pahr-sih-moh'-nih-ah] *L—*Economy is a great source of revenue. The complete sentence reads: *O Dii immortales! non intelligunt homines quam magnum vectigal sit parsimonia.* O ye immortal gods, men do not understand what a great source of income economy is. Cicero, *Paradoxa* 6; 3.

M'aidez [meh-day] *Fr—*Help me! The origin of the term *mayday,* an internationally recognized signal of distress.

Maintiens le droit [maN-tyaN luh drwah] *Fr—*Hold to what is right.

Maison de campagne [meh-zohN duh kahN-pah-nyuh] *Fr—*A country house.

Maison de jeu [meh-zohN duh zhuh] *Fr—*Gambling house.

Maison de passe [meh-zohN duh pahss] *Fr—*Disguised brothel.

Maison de santé [meh-zohN duh sahN-tay] *Fr—*Insane asylum; nursing home.

Mais où sont les neiges d'antan? [meh zoo sohN lay nehzh dahN-tahN] *Fr—*But where are the snows of yesteryear? Villon, *The Ballad of Dead Ladies.*

Maître d'armes [meh-tr dahrm] *Fr—*Teacher of fencing.

Maître des hautes oeuvres [meh-tr day hoht uh-vr] *Fr—*Literally, master of lofty works; by a humorous transfer, the hangman.

122

Maître d'hôtel [meh-tr doh-tel] *Fr—*Steward; butler; head waiter; major-domo.

Major domus [mah'-yor doh'-moos] *L—*The Mayor of the Palace; a powerful official in charge of a royal household.

Major e longinquo reverentia [mah'-yor ay lon-gihn'-kwoh reh-weh-ren'-tih-ah] *L—*Respect is greater from a distance. Tiberius had in mind to send his sons to quiet revolts in the Roman armies in Germany and Pannonia, realizing that if he went himself his imperial dignity might suffer. Tacitus, *Annals,* 1; 47.

Maladie du pays [mah-lah-dee dü pay-ee] *Fr—*Homesickness.

Mala fides [mah'-lah fih'-days] *L—*Bad faith.

Mala praxis [mah'-lah prahx'-iss] *L—*Malpractice.

Mal à propos [mal ah pruh-poh] *Fr—*At an inopportune time.

Mal au coeur [mal oh kuhr] *Fr—*Said of one feeling ill.

Mal de mer [mal duh mehr] *Fr—*Seasickness.

Mal du pays [mal dü pay-ee] *Fr—*Homesickness.

Mal (maladie) du siècle [mal, ma-la-dee, dü syeh-kl] *Fr—*The illness of the century, moral decadence.

Male imperando summum imperium amittitur [mah'-leh ihm-peh-rahn'-doh suhm'-muhm im-peh'-rih-uhm ah-mit'-tih-tuhr] *L—*The greatest power can be lost by misrule. Publilius Syrus.

Male parta, male dilabuntur [mah'-leh pahr'-tah mah'-leh dee-lah-buhn'-tuhr] *L—*Ill-got goods are ill-spent. Naevius.

Malgré lui [mal-gray lwee] *Fr—*In spite of himself.

Malheur ne vient jamais seul [mal-uhr nuh vyaN zha-meh suhl] *Fr—*Misfortunes never come in single file.

Mali exempli [mah'-lee ex-ehm'-plee] *L—*In the nature of a bad precedent or example.

Mali principii malus finis [mah'-lee preen-kih'-pih-ee mah'-luhs fee'-niss] *L*—The bad end of a bad beginning.

Malis avibus [mah'-leess ah'-wih-buhs] *L*—Under bad auspices.

Malo modo [mah'-loh moh'-doh] *L*—In an evil manner.

Malo mori quam foedari [mah'-loh moh'-ree kwahm foi-dah'-ree] *L*—I prefer death to disgrace.

Malum est consilium quod mutari non potest [mah'-luhm est kohn-sih'-lih-uhm kwod moo-tah'-ree nohn po'-test] *L*—It is a bad plan that cannot be changed. Publilius Syrus.

Malum in se [mah'-luhm in say] *L*—Evil in itself. *Mala in se* is the plural.

Malum prohibitum [mah'-luhm proh-hih'-bih-tuhm] *L*—An action regarded as criminal because it is prohibited and not because there is anything essentially immoral about the action itself.

Malus pudor [mah'-luhs puh'-dor] *L*—False shame.

Mamma mia! [mahm'-mah mee'-ah] *It*—Literally, my mother. A mild expletive on a level with For goodness' sake!

Mañana es otro día [mah-nyah'-nah ess oh'-troh dee'-ah] *Sp*—Tomorrow is another day.

Manet alta mente repostum [mah'-net ahl'-tah men'-teh reh-pos'-tuhm] *L*—This resentment remains deeply buried in her mind. The reference is to Juno's hatred of the Trojans. Vergil, *Aeneid*, 1; 26.

Mane, thecel, phares [mah'-neh teh'-kel fah-res'] *Aramaic*—The Vulgate reading for Daniel, 5; 25. *See* Mene, mene, tekel, upharsin for the reading in the King James version.

Manger son blé en herbe [mahN-zhay sohN blay ah-nehrb] *Fr*—Literally, to eat one's corn before it is ripe; to spend money before getting it.

Manibus pedibusque [mah'-nih-buhs peh-dih-buhs'-kweh] *L*—With hands and feet; with all one's might.

Man ist was man isst [mahn ist vahs mahn isst] *Ger*—*See* Der Mensch ist was er isst.

Man kann, was man will, wenn man nur will, was man kann [mahn kahn vahs mahn vihl vehn mahn noor vihl vahs mahn kahn] *Ger*—We can do what we will if we only will to do what we can.

Man kennt den Baum an seiner Frucht [mahn kennt dayn bowm ahn zI'-nuhr fruhkht] *Ger*—A tree is known by its fruit.

Man lernt nichts kennen, als was man liebt [mahn lehrnt nikhts kenn'-un ahls vahs mahn leept] *Ger*—One learns to know nothing except what one loves. Goethe, *To F. H. Jacobi*, May 10, 1812.

Man muss das Eisen smieden solang es noch warm ist [mahn muss dahs I'-zun shmee'-dun zoh-lahng' ess nuhkh vahrm ist] *Ger*—One must strike the iron while it is hot. *See also* Ferrum, dum in igni . . .

Mano a mano [mah'-noh ah mah'-noh] *Sp*—Literally, hand to hand; familiarly, alone.

Mano di ferro e guanto di velluto [mah'-noh dee fehr'-roh ay gwahn'-toh dee vel-loo'-toh] *It*—Iron hand in a velvet glove.

Manu forti [mah'-noo for'-tee] *L*—Literally, with a strong hand; forcible entry.

Manu propria [mah'-noo pro'-prih-ah] *L*—By one's own hand.

Manus haec inimica tyrannis [mah'-nuhs hIk ih-nih-mee'-kah tih-rahn'-nees] *L*—This hand is hostile to tyrants.

Manus manum lavat [mah'-nuhs mah'-nuhm lah'-waht] *L*—One hand washes the other. Used to express mutual help or adulation. Petronius, *Satyricon*, 45.

Marchandise qui plaît est à demi vendu [mahr-shahN-deez kee pleh eht ah duh-mee vahN-dü] *Fr*—Goods that please are already half sold; please the eye and pick the purse.

Marcher à pas de loup [mar-shay ah pah duh loo] *Fr*—Walk softly in order to surprise; colloquially, to sneak up on.

Marcher droit [mar-shay drwah] *Fr*—Literally, to walk straight; to behave well.

Mardi gras [mahr-dee grah] *Fr*—Shrove Tuesday, the day before Ash Wednesday, the first day of Lent. Literally, fat Tuesday, a day of feasting before the fast of Lent. Celebration on this day, especially in New Orleans, is known for its revelry.

Mare clausum [mah'-reh klow'-suhm] *L*—A closed sea. A sea where commerce is restricted by reason of the fact that these waters are within the territory of a particular country.

Mare Imbrium [mah'-reh im'-brih-hum] *L*—Sea of Storms, a location on the moon.

Mare liberum [mah'-reh lee'-beh-ruhm] *L*—Open sea.

Mare magnum [mah'-reh mahg'-nuhm] *L*—Literally, a great sea; an extensive collection of monastic privileges.

Mare Nostrum [mah'-reh nos'-truhm] *L*—Our sea; the Roman name for the Mediterranean.

Margaritas ante porcos [mahr-gah-ree'-tahs ahn'-teh por'-kohs] *L*—Pearls before swine. *Vulgate, St. Matthew*, 7; 6.

Mariage de conscience [ma-ry-ahzh duh kohN-syahNss] *Fr*—A marriage performed to satisfy the conscience of one or both parties troubled because of some illegality in a former ceremony.

Mariage de convenance [ma-ry-ahzh duh kohN-vnahNss] *Fr*—A marriage of convenience based on motives other than love.

Mariage de la main gauche [ma-ry-ahzh duh lah maN gohsh] *Fr*—Left-handed marriage; morganatic marriage.

Mariage de politique [ma-ry-ahzh duh puh-lee-teek] *Fr*—A marriage based on political advantage.

Marmoream se relinquere quam latericiam accepisset [mahr-moh'-reh-ahm say reh-lin'-kweh-reh kwahm lah-teh-rih'-kih-ahm ahk-kay-pihs'-set] *L*—Augustus boasted that he had found Rome a city of brick and was leaving it a city of marble. Suetonius, *Augustus*, 29.

Marque de fabrique [mahrk duh fah-breek] *Fr*—Trademark.

Mars gravior sub pace latet [mahrs grah'-wih-or suhb pah'-keh lah'-tet] *L*—A much more serious war lies hidden in the treaty of peace. Claudian, *On the Sixth Consulship of Honorius*, 307.

Mascula sunt maribus [mahs'-kuh-lah suhnt mah'-rih-buhs] *L*—Things masculine are for males.

Más vale maña que fuerza [mahs bah'-lay mah'-nyah kay fwehr'-sah] *Sp*—Cleverness accomplishes more than force.

Más vale muerto que vivo [mahs bah'-lay mwehr'-toh kay bee'-voh] *Sp*—Worth more dead than alive.

Más vale pájaro en mano que buitre volando [mahs bah'-lay pah'-hah-roh en mah'-noh kay bwee'-tray boh-lahn'-doh] *Sp*—A bird in the hand is worth more than a vulture in the air; a bird in the hand is worth two in the bush. Cervantes, *Don Quixote*, 2; 12.

Más vale tarde que nunca [mahs bah'-lay tahr'-day kay noon'-kah] *Sp*—Better late than never.

Mater artium necessitas [mah'-tehr ahr'-tih-uhm neh-kes'-sih-tahs] *L*—Necessity is the mother of the arts.

Mater dolorosa [mah'-tehr doh-loh-roh'-sah] *L*—Mother of Sorrows. Reference to the Virgin Mary.

Mater familias [mah'-tehr fah-mih'-lih-ahs] *L*—Mother of a family.

Materia ex qua [mah-teh'-rih-ah ex kwah] *L*—Material from which something is made.

Materia medica [mah-teh'-rih-ah meh'-dih-kah] *L*—Materials from which remedies are made; a branch of medical science dealing with the nature and property of the materials used in compounding drugs.

Materiam superabat opus [mah-teh'-rih-ahm suh-peh-rah'-baht o'-puss] *L*—The work of art surpassed the priceless material; the masterpiece was superior to the valuable material used. Ovid, *Metamorphoses*, 2; 5.

Materia prima [mah-teh'-rih-ah pree'-mah] *L*—First matter, potentially existing in all things created, but not existing independently. This was the teaching of Aristotle, which was continued by the Scholastics.

Mater Redemptoris [mah′-tehr reh-daymp-toh′-ris] *L*—Mother of the Redeemer.

Mature fieri senem, si diu velis esse senex [mah-too′-ray fih′-eh-ree seh′-nem see dih′-oo weh′-lees ess′-seh seh′-nex] *L*—You must become an old man early if you wish to be an old man long. Cato the Elder quotes this proverb, but he does not agree with it. Cicero, *Old Age*, 10; 32.

Mauvais coucheur [muh-veh koo-shuhr] *Fr*—A bad bedfellow; a touchy, querulous, suspicious person, difficult to get along with.

Mauvaise honte [muh-veh-zohNt] *Fr*—Excessive bashfulness.

Mauvaise plaisanterie [muh-vehz pleh-zahN-tree] *Fr*—Bad taste in jesting; a bad joke.

Mauvais goût [muh-veh goo] *Fr*—Bad taste from an esthetic point of view.

Mauvais quart d'heure [muh-veh kahr duhr] *Fr*—A bad quarter of an hour; an unpleasant experience.

Mauvais sujet [muh-veh sü-zheh] *Fr*—A rogue; in slang, a bad egg.

Maxima bella ex levissimis causis [mahx′-ih-mah bel′-lah ex leh-wis′-sih-meess kow′-seess] *L*—The greatest wars rise from very slight causes.

Maximum remedium est irae mora [mahx′-ih-muhm reh-meh′-dih-uhm est ee′-rI moh′-rah] *L*—The best remedy for anger is delay. Seneca, *On Anger*, 2; 29.

M. B. Medicinae Baccalaureus [meh-dih-kee′-nI bahk-kah-low′-reh-uhs] *L*—Bachelor of Medicine. Also *Musicae Baccalaureus*, Bachelor of Music.

M. B. G. & H. Magna Britannia, Gallia et Hibernia [mahg′-nah brih-tah′-nih-ah gahl′-lih-ah et hee-behr′-nih-ah] *L*—Great Britain, France and Ireland.

M. d. L. Mitglied der Landtags [mit′-gleet dehr lant′-tahks] *Ger*—Member of the Diet, the local or state legislature.

M. d. R. Mitglied der Reichstags [mit′-gleet dehr rIkhs′-tahks] *Ger*—Member of the Reichstag.

Mea culpa [meh′-ah kuhl′-pah] *L*—Through my fault.

M. E. C. Mercato europeo comune [mehr-kah′-toh ay-oo-roh-pay′-oh koh-moo′-nay] *It*—European Common Market.

Médecin, guéris-toi toi-même [mayd-saN gay-ree-twah twah-mehm] *Fr*—Physician, cure thyself. *See also* Medice, cura teipsum.

Medeis ageometretos eisito [may-dess′ ah-geh-oh-meh′-tray-tos es-ee′-toh] *Gk*—Let nobody ignorant of geometry enter. Words reportedly written over the entrance to the Academy of Plato.

Meden agan [may-den′ ah′-gahn] *Gk*—Let nothing be carried to excess. A Greek maxim. *See also* Ne quid nimis.

Medice, cura teipsum [meh′-dih-keh koo′-rah tay-ip′-suhm] *L*—Physician, cure thyself. *Vulgate, Luke*, 4; 23.

Mediocria firma [meh-dih-oh′-krih-ah feer′-mah] *L*—The middle position is the sound one. The doctrine of the mean, so frequently the subject of proverbial wisdom.

Mediocribus esse poetis / non homines, non di, non concessere columnae [meh-dih-oh′-krih-buhs es′-seh poh-ay′-teess nohn ho′-mih-nays nohn dee nohn kon-kehs-seh′-reh ko-luhm′-nI] *L*—Neither men, nor gods, nor publishers have ever agreed that poets may be mediocre. Horace, *Art of Poetry*, 372.

Medio tutissimus ibis [meh′-dih-oh too-tis′-sih-muhs ee′-biss] *L*—You will travel with greatest safety in the middle. Ovid, *Metamorphoses*, 2; 137.

Mega biblion, mega kakon [meh′-gah bih-blee′-on meh′-gah kah-kon′] *Gk*—A big book is a great evil. This is adapted from Callimachus' line *To mega biblion ison, elegen, einai to megalo kako*, A big book is like a great evil, he said. Ancient scrolls could be very cumbersome. This epigram has also been used in criticism of inflated volumes.

125

Meglio tardi che mai [mayl'-yoh tahr'-dee kay mah'-ee] *It*—Better late than never.

Mehr Licht [mehr likht] *Ger*—More light. Supposedly the last words of Goethe.

Meilleurs voeux [meh-yuhr vuh] *Fr*—Best wishes.

Meine Damen und Herren [mI'-nuh dah'-mun unt hehr'-run] *Ger*—Ladies and gentlemen.

Meine Zeit wird shon kommen [mI'-nuh tsIt virt shohn kuhm'-mun] *Ger*—My time will come one of these days. The hope of Mendel, whose theories remained unknown for a long time.

Mein Haus, meine Welt [mIn hows mI'-nuh velt] *Ger*—My house is my world.

Mein Herr [mIn hehr] *Ger*—Sir.

Mein Kampf [mIn kahmpf] *Ger*—My Battle, the title of a book by Adolf Hitler that became the bible of the Nazis. The translated editions have retained the German title.

Mein Name ist Hase; ich weiss von nichts [mIn nah'-muh ist hah'-zuh ikh vIss fuhn nikhts] *Ger*—My name is rabbit; I know nothing about it. Common expression used by a person unwilling to serve as a witness or to answer questions that might get him into trouble.

Mejor morir a pie que vivir en rodillas [may-hohr' moh-reer' ah pyay' kay bee-veer' en roh-dee'-yahs] *Sp*—Better to die standing than to live kneeling. Dolores Ibarruri, known as La Pasionaria, Spanish Communist revolutionary leader (in an address made in Valencia in 1936).

Me judice [may yoo'-dih-keh] *L*—In my opinion.

Mélanges de genre [may-lahNzh duh zhehN-ruh] *Fr*—A mixture of classifications.

Melior est canis vivus leone mortuo [meh'-lih-or est kah'-nis wee'-wuss leh-oh'-neh mor'-tuh-oh] *L*—Better a living dog than a dead lion. *Vulgate, Ecclesiastes*, 9; 4.

Memento, homo, quia pulvis es, et in pulverem reverteris [meh-men'-toh ho'-moh kwih'-ah puhl'-wiss ess et in puhl'-weh-rem reh-wehr-tay'-ris] *L*—Remember, man, thou art but dust and into dust thou shalt return. The service for Ash Wednesday. *Liber Usualis.*

Memento mori [meh-men'-toh mo'-ree] *L*—Remember that you must die.

Memoria in aeterna [meh-mo'-rih-ah in I-tehr'-nah] *L*—In eternal remembrance.

Memoria praeteritorum bonorum [meh-mo'-rih-ah prI-teh-rih-toh'-ruhm bo-noh'-ruhm] *L*—Remembrance of good things past.

Ménage à trois [may-nahzh ah trwah] *Fr*—Literally, a household of three; a marital triangle.

Mendacem memorem esse oportet [mehn-dah'-kehm meh'-mo-rehm es'-seh o-pohr'-tet] *L*—A liar must have a good memory. *Quintilian*, 4; 2, 91. *See also* Il faut bonne mémoire ...

Mendacium jocosum [men-dah'-kih-uhm yoh-koh'-suhm] *L*—A lie told in jest.

Mene, mene, tekel, upharsin [meh'-neh meh'-neh teh'-kel oo-fahr'-sin] *Aramaic*—He has counted, counted, weighed, and they divide. Words that appeared on the wall at Belshazzar's feast and were interpreted by the prophet Daniel to signify that God had judged Belshazzar's kingdom, found it wanting, and would destroy it. *Daniel*, 5; 25.

Mens aequa in arduis [mayns I'-kwah in ahr'-duh-eess] *L*—A calm mind in difficulties. Adapted from Aequam memento rebus in arduis ... (*q.v.*).

Mens agitat molem [mayns ah'-ghi-taht moh'-lem] *L*—Mind stirs the whole mass. In the underworld Anchises explains to Aeneas the doctrine of the *anima mundi*, the soul of the world, which held that an intelligent power infused itself into matter and produced all living beings. In antiquity this doctrine was taught by the Pythagoreans, Platonists, and Stoics. Vergil, *Aeneid*, 6; 727.

Mens et animus et consilium civitatis posita sunt in legibus [maynss et ah'-nih-muhs et kohn-sih'-lih-uhm kee-wih-tah'-tiss po'-sih-tah suhnt in lay'-gih-buhs] *L*—The mind, the spirit and the wisdom of a city reside in the laws. Cicero, *In Defense of Cluentius.*

Mens legis [mayns lay'-gis] *L*—The spirit of the law.

Mensonge magnanime [mahN-sohNzh mah-nyah-neem] *Fr*—High-minded deception.

Mens rea [mayns reh'-ah] *L*—Criminal intent. A legal term.

Mens regnum bona possidet [mayns rayg'-nuhm bo'-nah pos'-sih-det] *L*—A good mind possesses a kingdom. Seneca, *Thyestes,* 380.

Mens sana in corpore sano [mayns sah'-nah in kor'-po-reh sah-noh] *L*—A sound mind in a sound body. Juvenal, 10; 356.

Mens sibi conscia recti [mayns sih'-bih kohn'-skih-ah rayk'-tee] *L*—A mind conscious of its righteousness. Vergil, *Aeneid,* 1; 604.

Menteur à triple étage [mahN-tuhr ah tree-pl ay-tahzh] *Fr*—Literally, a three-storeyed liar; a double-dyed liar.

Menu peuple [muh-nü puh-pl] *Fr*—The lower orders; the common people.

Meo periculo [meh'-oh peh-ree'-kuh-loh] *L*—At my own risk.

Merci beaucoup [mehr-see boh-koo] *Fr*—Thanks very much.

Merum sal [meh'-ruhm sahl] *L*—Pure salt; true wit.

M. ès A. Maître ès Arts [meh-tr eh zahr] *Fr*—Master of Arts.

m. et n. mane et nocte [mah'-neh et nok'-teh] *L*—Morning and night.

Metron ariston [meh'-tron ah'-ris-ton] *Gk*—Moderation is best. A saying of Cleobulus, one of the Seven Wise Men of Greece. *Diogenes Laertius,* 1; 93. The ancients stressed the middle course. *See also* Aurea mediocritas, Est modus in rebus, In medio stat virtus, Meden agan, Medio tutissimus ibis, Ne quid nimis.

Metter il carro innanzi ai buoi [met'-tayr eel kahr'-roh een-nahn'-tsee ah'-ee bwoi'-ee] *It*—To put the wagon before the oxen; to put the cart before the horse.

Mettre de l'eau dans son vin [meh-tr duh loh dahN sohN vaN] *Fr*—To put water in a person's wine; to reduce tensions; to pour oil on troubled waters.

Meubles d'occasion [muh-bl duh-kah-zyohN] *Fr*—Second-hand furniture.

Me vestigia terrent, omnia te adversum spectantia, nulla retrorsum [may wes-tee'-gih-ah tehr'-rent om'-nih-ah tay ahd-wehr'-suhm spek-tahn'-tih-ah nool'-lah reh-trohr'-suhm] *L*—I am terrified that all the footprints lead toward you and none away. This was the excuse offered by the fox for not visiting the sick lion. Horace, *Epistles,* 1; 1, 74. Sometimes *Vestigia nulla retrorsum* is used to mean, Let us take no steps backward.

M. E. Z. Mitteleuropäische Zeit [mit-tel-oy-roh-pay'-ish-uh tsIt] *Ger*—Central European Time.

Mezza voce [med'-tsah voh'-chay] *It*—With moderate volume of the voice.

Mezzo forte [med'-tsoh for'-tay] *It*—Moderately loud.

Mezzo piano [med'-tsoh pee-ah'-noh] *It*—Moderately soft.

Mezzo termine [med'-tsoh tehr'-mee-nay] *It*—Middle course.

mf. *See* Mezzo forte.

Mia gar chelidon ear ou poiei [mee'-ah gahr kheh-lih-dohn' eh'-ar oo poi-eh'] *Gk*—One swallow does not make a summer (literally, a spring). Aristotle, *Nicomachean Ethics,* 1; 7, 16.

Mi-carême [mee-kah-rehm] *Fr*—Mid-Lent.

Mi casa es su casa [mee kah'-sah ess soo kah'-sah] *Sp*—My house is your house.

Mientras se duerme todos son iguales [mee-en'-trahs say dwehr'-may toh'-dohs sohn ee-gwah'-lays] *Sp*—While asleep, all men are equal. Cervantes, *Don Quixote,* 2; 43.

Mieux vaut goujat debout qu'empereur enterré [myuh voh goo-zhah duh-boo kahN-pruhr ahN-teh-ray] *Fr*—It is better to be a live beggar than a dead emperor. La Fontaine, *The Woman of Ephesus,* last line. *See also* Melior est canis ...

Mihi crede [mih'-hih kray'-deh] *L*—Believe me.

Mihi cura futuri [mih'-hih koo'-rah fuh-too'-ree] *L*—I am concerned with the future. Motto of Hunter College.

Miles gloriosus [mee'-lehs gloh-rih-oh'-suhs] *L*—A boastful warrior. A stock dramatic character drawn from a play by Plautus.

Minatur innocentibus qui parcit nocentibus [mih-nah'-tunr in-noh-ken'-tih-buhs kwee pahr'-kit noh-ken'-tih-buhs] *L*—He threatens the innocent who spares the criminal. Sir Edward Coke.

Minima ex malis [mih'-nih-mah ex mah'-leess] *L*—Among evils choose the least. Cicero, *On Duties,* 3; 1. *See also* De duobus malis ...

Mirabile dictu [mee-rah'-bih-leh dikh'-too] *L*—Marvelous to relate.

Mirabile visu [mee-rah'-bih-leh wee'-soo] *L*—Wonderful to see; what a marvelous sight!

Misa del Gallo [mee'-sah del gah'-yoh] *Sp*—Midnight Mass at Christmas, so-called because people return from this service at the hour when the cocks crow.

Mise en page [meez ahN pahzh] *Fr*—Make-up of a printed page.

Mise en scène [meez ahN sehn] *Fr*—Stage setting of a play.

Miserabile dictu [mih-seh-rah'-bih-leh dihk'-too] *L*—A miserable thing to relate.

Miserabile vulgus [mih-seh-rah'-bih-leh wuhl'-guhs] *L*—The miserable herd; the wretched crowd. An aristocratic opinion of the lower classes.

Miserere mei [mih-seh-ray'-reh meh'-ee] *L*—Have mercy on me. *Vulgate, Psalms,* 51 (50); 1.

Missi dominici [miss'-see doh-mih'-nih-kee] *L*—Official inspectors sent out by Charlemagne to check on instruction and observance of discipline in monasteries.

Mit dem Wissen wächst der Zweifel [mit daym viss'-un vehkhst dehr tsvI'-ful] *Ger*—Doubt increases with knowledge. Goethe, *Maxims in Prose,* 76.

Mit der Dummheit kämpfen Götter selbst vergebens [mit dehr duhm'-hIt kempf'-un guht'-tuhr zelpst fehr-gay'-benz] *Ger*—The gods themselves struggle in vain against stupidity. Schiller, *Maid of Orleans,* 3; 6, 28.

Mit grossen Herren ist nicht gut Kirschen essen [mit grohs'-sun hehr'-run ist nikht goot keehr'-shuhn ess'-sun] *Ger*—Literally, it is not good to eat cherries with great lords; he who sups with the devil must have a long spoon.

Mit innigster Ergebenheit in Gott [mit in'-nikh-stuhr ehr-gay'-ben-hIt in guht] *Ger*—With profound devotion to God.

Mitte sectari, rosa quo locorum / Sera moretur [miht'-teh sek-tah'-ree roh'-sah kwoh lo-koh'-ruhm say'-rah mo-ray'-tuhr] *L*—Cease searching for the spot where the last rose lingers. Horace, *Odes,* 1; 38, 3.

Mittimus [mit'-tih-muhs] *L*—We send. A warrant signed by a magistrate for the imprisonment of a criminal.

Mit umgehender Post [mit uhm'-gay-uhn-duhr pohst] *Ger*—By return mail.

Mixtum compositum [mix'-tuhm kompo'-sih-tuhm] *L*—A composite consisting of a number of disparate parts.

Mlle Mademoiselle [mad-mwah-zehl] *Fr*—Miss.

Mme Madame [ma-dahm] *Fr*—Mrs.

Mobile mutatur semper cum principe vulgus [moh'-bih-leh moo-tah'-tuhr sem'-pehr kuhm preen'-kih-peh wuhl'-guhs] *L*—The fickle crowd always changes its allegiance with the prince. Claudian.

Mobile perpetuum [moh'-bih-leh pehr-peh'-tuh-uhm] *L*—Perpetual motion.

Mobile vulgus [moh'-bih-leh wuhl'-guhs] *L*—The unstable, fickle crowd.

Moderato cantabile [moh-day-rah'-toh kahn-tah'-bee-lay] *It*—In a melodious, flowing style at a moderate tempo.

Modeste aisance [muh-dest eh-zahNss] *Fr*—Said of a person living in easy financial circumstances.

Modo et forma [moh'-doh et fohr'-mah] *L*—In manner and form.

Modo praescripto [moh'-doh prI-skrip'-toh] *L*—In the manner prescribed.

Modus operandi [moh'-duhs oh-peh-rahn'-dee] *L*—Method of operation.

Modus vivendi [moh'-duhs wee-wen'-dee] *L*—Literally, a manner of living; a temporary arrangement for coexistence until matters in dispute can be settled.

Mole ruit sua *L—See* Vis consili . . .

Mollia tempora fandi [mol'-lih-ah tehm'-po-rah fahn'-dee] *L*—The proper moment to broach a subject. As in many other Latin quotations, the changed word order more readily conveys the sense of the original. The original is *Mollissima fandi tempora.* Vergil, *Aeneid,* 4; 293.

Molto fumo e poco arrosto [mohl'-toh foo'-moh ay poh'-koh ahr-ross'-toh] *It*—Much smoke and little roast meat; much ado about nothing.

Mon cher [mohN shehr] *Fr*—My dear fellow.

Mon coeur et ton coeur pour la vie [mohN kuhr ay tohN kuhr poor lah vee] *Fr*—My heart and yours together for life. Words on a popular pendant.

Mon Dieu! [mohN dyuh] *Fr*—Literally, my God! This is properly translated as a very mild exclamation, such as, "Dear me!"

Montani semper liberi [mohn-tah'-nee sem'-pehr lee'-beh-ree] *L*—Mountaineers always free. Motto of West Virginia.

Mont-de-piété [mohN duh pee-ay-tay] *Fr*—Literally, mount of piety; a public pawnbroker's agency established to lend money to the needy at low rates.

Monte de piedad [mohn'-tay day pee-ay-dad'] *Sp—See* Mont-de-piété.

Monte di pietà [mon'-tay dee pee-ay-tah'] *It—See* Mont-de-piété.

More humano [moh'-reh hoo-mah'-noh] *L*—As is the custom of mankind.

More majorum [moh'-reh mah-yoh'-ruhm] *L*—According to the customs of our ancestors.

More suo [moh'-reh suh'-oh] *L*—In his own manner.

Morgen, morgen, nur nicht heute, / Sagen alle faulen Leute [mor'-gun mor'-gun noor nikht hoi'-tuh zah'-gun ahl'-luh fow'-lun loi'-tuh] *Ger*—Tomorrow, tomorrow, but not today, / All the lazy people say.

Morgenstund' hat Gold im Mund [mor'-gun-shtuhnd haht gult im muhnt] *Ger*—The morning hour has gold in its power.

Mors acerba, fama perpetua [mohrs ah-kehr'-bah fah'-mah pehr-peh'-tuh-ah] *L*—A bitter death but eternal fame.

Mors communis omnibus [mohrs kom-moo'-niss om'-nih-buhs] *L*—Death is the common fate of all.

Mors janua vitae [mohrs yah'-nuh-ah wee'-tI] *L*—Death is the door to life (everlasting life is meant).

Mort Dieu (Mordieu) [mohr dyuh] *Fr*—Zounds; hang it. An interjection found in Shakespeare.

Mortis causa [mohr'-tiss kow'-sah] *L*—Because of impending death.

Mos majorum [mohs mah-yoh'-ruhm] *L*—The customs of their ancestors, honored by the Romans.

Mos pro lege [mohs proh lay'-geh] *L*—Long-established custom has the force of law.

Mot à mot [moh tah moh] *Fr*—Word for word.

Mot de guet [moh duh geh] *Fr*—Password or watchword.

Mot de l'énigme [moh duh lay-neeg-muh] *Fr*—The word in the puzzle that must be guessed.

129

Mots de terroir [moh duh tehr-rwahr] *Fr*—Regional words or sayings.

Mots d'usage [moh dü-zahzh] *Fr*—Words in common use.

Motu proprio [moh'-too pro'-prih-oh] *L*—On one's own motion. Generally applied to a rescript issued by the pope on matters initiated by himself.

Moulin à paroles [moo-lan ah pah-rohl] *Fr*—Literally, a word mill; a babbler; a windbag.

mp. *See* Mezzo piano.

Mucho más se ha de estimar un diente que un diamante [moo'-choh mahs say ah day ays-tee-mahr' oon dee-ayn'-tay kay oon dee-ah-mahn'-tay] *Sp*—A tooth is worth much more than a diamond. Cervantes, *Don Quixote*, 1; 18.

Muchos van por lana y vuelven trasquilados [moo'-chos bahn por lah'-nah ee bwel'-ven trahs-kee-lah'-dohs] *Sp*—Many go seeking wool and return shorn. Cervantes, *Don Quixote*, 1; 7.

Muet comme un poisson [mü-eh kuhm uhN pwah-sohN] *Fr*—Dumb as a fish.

Mulier cum sola cogitat male cogitat [muh'-lih-ehr kuhm soh'-lah koh'-gih-taht mah'-leh koh'-gih-taht] *L*—When a woman thinks alone she is plotting mischief. A misogynist's idea. Publilius Syrus.

Mulier cupido quod dicit amanti, in vento et rapida scribere oportet aqua [muh'-lih-ehr kuh'-pih-doh kwod dee'-kit ah-mahn'-tee in wehn'-toh et rah'-pih-dah skree'-beh-reh o-por'-tet ah'-kwah] *L*—What a woman says to an eager lover should be written on wind and swift waters. Catullus, 70; 3.

Mulier est hominis confusio [muh'-lier est ho'-mih-nis kohn-foo'-see-oh] *L*—Woman is the ruin of man; a statement frequently found in medieval literature. Chaucer, *Canterbury Tales; Nun's Priest's Tale*, 1; 3164.

Multa cadunt inter calicem supremaque labra [muhl'-tah kah'-duhnt in'-tehr kah'-lih-kem suh-pray'-mah-kweh lah'-brah] *L*—There's many a slip 'twixt the cup and the lip.

130

Multa petentibus desunt multa [muhl'-tah peh-ten'-tih-buhs day'-suhnt muhl'-tah] *L*—Those who desire much are much in need. Horace, *Odes*, 3; 16, 42.

Multis utile bellum [muhl'-teess oo'-tih-leh bel'-luhm] *L*—War is a source of gain to many. Lucan, *Pharsalia*, 1; 182.

Multum in parvo [muhl'-tuhm in pahr'-woh] *L*—Literally, much in little; a marvel of condensation.

Mundi formam omnes fere consentiunt rotundam esse [muhn'-dee for'-mahm om'-nays feh'-ray kohn-sehn'-tih-uhnt roh-tuhn'-duhm ess'-seh] *L*—Almost all men agree that the shape of the world is round. This statement was made in 1481. Pius II (Sylvius Piccolomini).

Mundus vult decipi [muhn'-duhs wuhlt day'-kih-pee] *L*—People want to be deceived.

Munera Pulveris [moo'-neh-rah puhl'-weh-riss] *L*—Gifts of the dust. Used as title of a work by Ruskin. In the passage from which this quotation is taken reference is made to the present of a little dust that would permit the soul of the deceased to cross the Styx. Horace, *Odes*, 1; 28, 3, 4.

Munus Apolline dignum [moo'-nuhs ah-pohl'-lih-neh dihg'-nuhm] *L*—A gift worthy of Apollo. Horace, *Epistles*, 2; 1, 216.

Murus aeneus conscientia sana [moo'-ruhs I'-neh-uhs kohn-skih-en'-tih-ah sah'-nah] *L*—A sound conscience is a wall of brass.

Muscae volitantes [muhs'-kI wo-lih-tahn'-tays] *L*—Literally, flies flitting about; motes moving about in the field of vision.

Muss ist eine harte (bittere) Nuss (ein bitter Kraut) [muss ist I'-nuh hahr'-tuh, bit'-tuhr-uh, nuss, In bit'-tuhr krowt] *Ger*—Necessity is a hard (bitter) nut (a bitter herb); necessity is a hard taskmaster.

Mutatis mutandis [moo-tah'-teess moo-tahn'-deess] *L*—Changing those things that must be changed.

Mutato nomine de te fabula narratur [moo-tah'-toh noh'-mih-neh day tay fah'-buh-lah nahr-rah'-tuhr] *L*—Change only the name and the story might be told of you. Horace, *Satires*, 1; 1, 69.

N

Nach Canossa gehen wir nicht [nahkh kah-nohs'-sah gay'-un veer nikht] *Ger*—We are not going to Canossa. A statement made by Bismarck in 1872 when relations between Germany and the Vatican were strained. He was referring to Henry IV's submission to Pope Gregory VII in 1077.

Nach Christi Geburt [nahkh krees'-tee guh-boort'] *Ger*—After the birth of Christ. *See also* A. D.

Nacheifern ist beneiden [nahkh-I'-fehrn ist buh-nI'-dun] *Ger*—To emulate is to envy; competition implies envy. Lessing, *Die Religion, erster Gesang.*

Nacht und Nebel [nahkht uhnt nay'-buhl] *Ger*—Night and fog. The Nazi expression for death in the gas chambers.

Nager entre deux eaux [nah-zhay ahN-tr duh zoh] *Fr*—To swim between two currents; to waver between two parties, giving the appearance that you are loyal to both.

Nam genus et proavos et quae non fecimus ipsi vix ea nostra voco [nahm geh'-nuhs et proh'-ah-wohs et kwI nohn fay'-kih-muhs ihp'-see wihx eh'-ah nos'-trah wo'-koh] *L*—Race and ancestry and what we ourselves have not accomplished, these I do not consider my own achievements. Ovid, *Metamorphoses*, 13; 140.

Não ha mal que sempre dure, nem bem que nunca se acabe [nowN ah mahl kuh sehN-pree doo'-reh nehN behN kuh nooN'-kuh see uh-kah'-beh] *Port*—There is no ill that lasts forever, nor any boon that never ends.

Narkomvnudel [nahr-kom-vnoo-dyehl] *Rus—See* NKVD.

Nascimur poetae, fimus oratores [nahs'-kih-muhr poh-ay'-tI fee'-muhs o-rah-toh'-rays] *L*—We are born poets, we are trained to be orators.

Natale solum [nah-tah'-leh so'-luhm] *L*—Native soil.

Natura abhorret a vacuo [nah-too'-rah ahb-hor'-ret ah wah'-kuh-oh] *L*—Nature abhors a vacuum. Descartes.

Natura abhorret vacuum [nah-too'-rah ahb-hor'-ret wah'-kuh-uhm] *L*—Nature abhors a vacuum. Rabelais, *Gargantua*, 1; 5.

Natura il fece e poi roppe la stampa [nah-too'-rah eel fay'-chay ay poy rohp'-pay lah stahm'-pah] *It*—Nature made him and then broke the mould. This has often been used to describe a person who, by reason of learning, art, or other achievements, is uniquely distinguished. Ariosto, *Orlando Furioso*, 10; 84.

Natura inest mentibus nostris insatiabilis quaedam cupiditas veri videndi [nah-too'-rah in'-est men'-tih-buhs nos'-treess in-sah-tih-ah'-bih-liss kwI'-dahm kuh-pih'-dih-tahs way'-ree wih-den'-dee] *L*—There is naturally in our minds a certain insatiable desire to know the truth. Cicero, *Tusculan Disputations*, 1; 19.

Natura in operationibus suis non facit saltus [nah-too'-rah in o-peh-rah-tih-oh'-nih-buhs suh'-ees nohn fah'-kit sahl'-toos] *L*—Nature in her operations does not proceed by leaps; evolution in nature is slow and gradual. Attributed to Leibnitz, but this was axiomatic long before his time. *See also* Natura nihil facit . . .

Naturam expelles furca, tamen usque recurret [nah-too'-rahm ex-pel'-lays foor'-kah tah'-men oos'-kweh reh-kuhr'-ret] *L*—Even though you drive out nature with a pitchfork, she will rush right back. Horace, *Epistles*, 1; 10, 24.

Natura naturans [nah-too'-rah nah-too'-rahns] *L*—Nature begetting, a term used by Spinoza. He called the product of this energy *Natura naturata*, nature begotten.

Natura nihil facit per saltum [nah-too'-rah nih'-hil fah'-kit pehr sahl'-tuhm] *L*—Nature does nothing by leaps.

Natura semina nobis scientiae dedit, scientiam non dedit [nah-too'-rah say'-mih-nah noh'-beess skih-en'-tih-I deh'-dit skih-en'-tih-ahm nohn deh'-dit] *L*—Nature has given us the seeds of knowledge but not knowledge itself. Seneca, *Letters to Lucilius*, 120.

Natura simplicitatem amat [nah-too'-rah sihm-plih-kih-tah'-tehm ah'-maht] *L*—Nature loves simplicity. Kepler.

Nazi [nats'-ee] *Ger*—Abbreviation of *Nationalsozialistiche Partei* [nahts-ee-yoh-nahlzohts-yah-lis'-tish-uh pahr-tI'] Hitler's National Socialist German Workers' Party. The pronunciation of the first four letters of the word National in German may have given rise to the shortened form.

N. B. nota bene [no'-tah beh'-neh] *L*—Note well.

n. Br. nördliche Breite [nuhrd'-likh-uh brI'-tuh] *Ger*—North latitude.

n. Chr. G. *Ger*—*See* Nach Christi Geburt.

n/cta. nuestra cuenta [nwehs'-trah kwehn'-tah] *Sp*—Our account.

Ne battre que d'une aile [nuh bah-tr kuh dün ehl] *Fr*—To beat only one wing; when applied to persons, to be on one's last legs.

Nec amor nec tussis celatur [nek ah'-mor nek tuhs'-siss kay-lah'-tuhr] *L*—Neither love nor coughing can be concealed.

Nec deus intersit, nisi dignus vindice nodus [nek deh'-uhs in-tehr'-sit nih'-sih dihg'-nuhs win'-dih-keh noh'-duhs] *L*—A god must not be introduced unless the problem demands divine aid. For similar literary advice, *see also* Dignus vindice nodus.

Ne cede malis *L*—*See* Tu ne cede malis.

Necesse est multos timeat quem multi timent [neh-kes'-seh est muhl'-tohs tih'-

meh-aht kwehm muhl'-tee tih'-ment] *L*—He whom many fear must needs fear many. Publilius Syrus.

Necessitas non habet legem [neh-kehs'-sih-tahs nohn hah'-bet lay'-gem] *L*—Necessity knows no law.

Necessitas rationum inventrix [neh-kehs'-sih-tahs rah-tih-oh'-nuhm in-wehn'-trix] *L*—Necessity is the discoverer of ideas; necessity is the mother of invention.

Nec est quisquam tam malus, ut malus videri velit [nek est kwihs'-kwahm tahm mah'-luhs uht mah'-luhs wih-day'-ree weh'-lit] *L*—No one is so evil that he wishes to be regarded as evil. Quintilian, 3; 8, 2.

Nec judicis ira, nec ignis, nec poterit ferrum, nec edax abolere vetustas [nek yoo'-dih-kiss ee'-rah nek ihg'-niss nek po'-tehr-it fehr'-ruhm nek eh'-dahx ah-bo-lay'-reh weh-tuhs'-tahs] *L*—Neither the anger of a judge, nor fire, nor sword, nor the corrosion of time can destroy my work. Ovid, *Metamorphoses*, 15; 872.

Nec mora nec requies [nek mo'-rah nek reh'-kwih-ays] *L*—Without delay or rest.

Nec pluribus impar [nek ploo'-rih-buhs im'-pahr] *L*—Not unequal to many. The boastful motto of Louis XIV.

Nec prece nec pretio [nek preh'-keh nek preh'-tih-oh] *L*—Neither by entreaty nor bribery; neither by praying nor paying.

Nec quaerere nec spernere honorem [nek kwI'-reh-reh nek spehr'-neh-reh ho-noh'-rem] *L*—Neither to seek nor to spurn honors.

Nec quemquam jam ferre potest Caesarve priorem,/Pompeiusve parem [nek kwem'-kwahm yahm fehr'-reh po'-test kI-sahr'-weh prih-oh'-rem pom-pay-ih-yuhss'-weh pah'-rem] *L*—Caesar cannot tolerate a superior nor Pompey an equal. Lucan, *Pharsalia*, 1; 125.

Nec scire fas est omnia [nek skee'-reh fahs est om'-nih-ah] *L*—We are not permitted to know everything. Horace, *Odes*, 4; 4, 22.

Nec tecum possum vivere, nec sine te [nek tay'-kuhm pos'-suhm wee'-wehr-reh nek sih'-neh tay] *L*—I cannot live with you or without you. Martial, *Epigrams*, 12; 47, 2.

Nec temere nec timide [nek teh'-meh-ray nek tih'-mih-day.] *L*—Neither rashly nor timidly.

Nec verbum verbo curabis reddere fidus interpres [nek wehr'-buhm wehr'-boh koo-rah'-biss red'-deh-reh fee'-duhs in-tehr'-prehs] *L*—As a faithful translator you will not be concerned with making a word-for-word version. Horace, *Art of Poetry*, 133.

Ne exeat provincia [nay ex'-eh-aht proh-win'-kih-ah] *L*—Let him not leave the province of the court. A writ to arrest a debtor absconding from the jurisdiction of the court.

Ne facias per alium quod fieri potest per te [nay fah'-kih-ahs pehr ah'-lih-uhm kwod fih'-eh-ree po'-test pehr tay] *L*—Do not do through another what you can do in person.

Nefasti dies [neh-fahs'-tee dih'-ays] *L*—Unlucky days. No business was conducted on such ill-omened dates.

Ne fronti crede [nay fron'-tee kray'-deh] *L*—Don't be deceived by appearances; don't judge a book by its cover.

Ne Juppiter quidem omnibus placet [nay yuhp'-pih-tehr kwih'-dem om'-nih-buhs plah'-ket] *L*—Not even Jove can please everybody.

nem. con. *L*—*See* Nemine contradicente.

nem. diss. *L*—*See* Nemine dissentiente.

Nemine contradicente [nay'-mih-neh kohn-trah-dee-ken'-teh] *L*—Nobody opposing.

Nemine discrepante [nay'-mih-neh dis-kreh-pahn'-teh] *L*—Nobody dissenting.

Nemine dissentiente [nay'-mih-neh diss-sen-tih-en'-teh] *L*—Without a dissenting vote.

Nemo bis punitur pro eodem delicto [nay'-moh biss poo-nee'-tuhr proh eh-oh'-dem day-leek'-toh] *L*—Nobody is to be punished twice for the same crime. The Fifth Amendment to the Constitution of the United States contains the same provision: "Nor shall any person be subject for the same offence to be twice put in jeopardy of life or limb."

Nemo dat quod non habet [nay'-moh daht kwod nohn hah'-bet] *L*—Nobody can give what he does not possess.

Nemo esse judex in sua causa potest [nay'-moh ehs'-seh yoo'-dex in suh'-ah kow'-sah po'-test] often shortened to: Nemo judex in causa sua *(q. v.)* *L*—Nobody can be a judge in his own case. Publilius Syrus.

Nemo in amore videt [nay'-moh in ah'-moh'-reh wih'-det] *L*—No one in love can see; love is blind. Propertius, 2; 14, 18.

Nemo judex in causa sua [nay'-moh yoo'-dex in kow'-sah suh'-ah] *L*—Nobody is a judge in his own case.

Nemo liber est qui corpori servit [nay'-moh lee'-behr est kwee kor'-po-ree sehr'-wit] *L*—No man is free who is slave to the flesh. Seneca, *Letters to Lucilius*, 92; 31.

Nemo me impune lacessit [nay'-moh may im-poo'-neh lah-kess'-sit] *L*—Nobody harms me with impunity. Motto of the Order of the Thistle and of Scotland.

Nemo mortalium omnibus horis sapit [nay'-moh mor-tah'-lih-uhm om'-nih-buhs hoh'-rees sah'-pit] *L*—No mortal is always wise. Pliny the Elder, *Natural History*, 7; 41 (40), 2.

Nemo propheta acceptus est in patria sua [nay'-moh pro-fay'-tah ahk-kep'-tuhs in pah'-trih-ah suh'-ah] *L*—No prophet is accepted in his own country. *Vulgato, Luko*, 4; 24.

Nemo repente fuit turpissimus [nay'-moh reh-pehn'-teh fuh'-it tuhr-pihs'-sih-muhs] *L*—Nobody ever became a confirmed criminal all at once. Juvenal, 2; 83.

Nemo scit praeter me ubi soccus me pressat [nay'-moh skit prI'-tehr may uh'-bee sohk'-kuhs may press'-aht] *L*—I am the only one who knows where my shoe pinches.

Nemo sine vitiis nascitur [nay'-moh sih'-neh wih'-tih-eess nahs'-kih-tuhr] *L*—No mortal is without faults.

Nemo solus satis sapit [nay'-moh soh'-luhs sah'-tis sah'-pit] *L*—Nobody by himself possesses sufficient wisdom; two heads are better than one. Plautus, *Braggart Warrior*, 3; 3, 12.

Nem um dedo faz mão, nem uma andorinha verão [nehN ooN day'-doo fahz mowN nehN ooN'-mah aN-doo-ree'-nyuh vuh-rowN'] *Port*—One finger doesn't make a hand, nor one swallow a summer. *See also* Mia gar chelidon . . .

Neos d'apollyth' hontin' an phile theos [neh'-os dah-pol'-lüth hon'-tin ahn fih-lay' the-os'] *Gk*—God's favorites die young.

Ne plus ultra [nay ploos uhl'-trah] *L*—The topmost performance or achievement; no farther. The medieval warning that ships could not sail westward beyond Gibraltar.

Ne puero gladium [nay puh'-eh-roh glah'-dih-uhm] *L*—Do not give a sword to a boy.

Ne quid detrimenti respublica capiat [nay kwid day-tree-men'-tee rays-poo'-blih-kah kah'-pih-aht] *L*—So that no harm may come to the republic. The final order of the Roman senate to the consuls when the Republic was in mortal danger. Cicero, *1 Against Catiline*, 1; 3.

Ne quid nimis [nay kwid nih'-miss] *L*—Nothing in excess. Terence, *Andria*, 1; 1, 34. *See also* Meden agan.

Ne réveillez pas le chat qui dort [nuh ray-veh-yay pah luh sha kee dor] *Fr*—Do not waken the sleeping cat; let sleeping dogs lie.

Nervi belli, pecunia infinita [nehr'-wee bel'-lee peh-koo'-nih-ah in-fee-nee'-tah] *L*—The sinews of war are a limitless supply of money. Cicero, *Philippics*, 5; 2, 5.

Nescire autem quid antequam natus sis acciderit, id est semper esse puerum [nehs-kee'-reh ow'-tem kwid ahn'-teh-kwahm nah'-tuhs seess ahk-kih'-deh-rit id est sem'-pehr ess'-seh puh'-eh-ruhm] *L*—To be ignorant of what happened before you were born is always to remain a boy. Cicero, *The Orator*, 34.

134

Nescit plebes ieiuna timere [nehs'-kit play'-bayss yay-yoo'-nah tih-may'-reh] *L*—The starving masses know no fear. Lucan, *Pharsalia*, 3; 58.

Nescit vox missa reverti [nehs'-kit wohx miss'-sah reh-wehr'-tee] *L*—The spoken word cannot be recalled. Horace, *Art of Poetry*, 390.

Nessun maggior dolore, / Che ricordarsi del tempo felice / Nella miseria [ness-soon' mahd-joh'-ray doh-loh'-ray kay ree-kor-dahr'-see dell temm'-poh fay-lee'-chay nel'-lah mee-say'-ree-ah] *It*—There is no greater sorrow than remembering happy days in our misery. Dante, *Inferno*, 5; 121. Tennyson refers to this passage in *Locksley Hall:* "This is truth the poet sings/ That a sorrow's crown of sorrows is remembering happier things."

N'est-ce pas? [ness pah] *Fr*—Is it not so?

Ne stoit blagodarnost' [nyeh stoy'-eht bla-guh-dahr'-nast-yeh] *Rus*—Don't mention it. Used to acknowledge an expression of thanks.

Ne sutor ultra crepidam [nay soo'-tohr uhl'-trah kreh'-pih-dahm] *L*—*See* Sutor ne supra crepidam.

Ne tentes aut perfice [nay ten'-tays owt pehr'-fih-keh] *L*—If you make an attempt, see it through.

Neue Besen kehren gut [noy'-yuh bayz'-uhn kayr'-un goot] *Ger*—New brooms sweep clean. *See also* Una scopa . . .

n. F. neue Folge [noy'-uh fuhl'-guh] *Ger*—New series.

Nicht die Kinder bloss speist man mit Märchen ab [nikht dee kind'-uhr blohss shpIst mahn mit mehr'-khun ap] *Ger*—Children aren't the only ones who are told fairy tales. Lessing, *Nathan the Wise*, 3; 6.

Nicht wahr? [nikht vahr] *Ger*—Not so?

Niente più tosto si secca che lacrime [nee-ehn'-tay pee-oo' toss'-toh see seck'-kah kay lah'-kree-may] *It*—Nothing dries as quickly as tears.

Ni firmes carta que no leas, ni bebas agua que no veas [nee feer'-mays kahr'-tah kay noh lay'-ahs nee bay'-bahs ah'-gwah kay noh bay'-ahs] *Sp*—Do not sign a letter without reading it or drink water without looking at it.

Nihil ad rem [nih'-hil ahd rem] *L*—Nothing to do with the matter; irrelevant.

Nihil dicit [nih'-hil dee'-kit] *L*—He says nothing. A judgment against a defendant who offers no defense.

Nihil enim in speciem fallacius est quam prava religio [nih'-hil eh'-nim in speh'-kih-ehm fahl-lah'-kih-uhs est kwahm prah'-wah reh-lih'-gih-oh] *L*—Nothing is more deceptive in appearance than perverted religion. Livy, 39; 16.

Nihil est ab omni parte beatum [nih'-hil est ahb om'-nee pahr'-teh beh-ah'-tuhm] *L*—Nothing is blessed in every respect. Horace, *Odes*, 2; 16, 27.

Nihil ex omnibus rebus humanis est praeclarius aut praestantius quam de republica bene mereri [nih'-hil ex om'-nih-buhs ray'-buhs hoo-mah'-nees est prI-klah'-rih-uhs kwahm day ray-poo'-blih-kah beh'-neh meh-ray'-ree] *L*—In all human affairs nothing is more honorable or more outstanding than to deserve well of the republic. Cicero, *Letters to Friends*, 10; 5.

Nihil hoc ad edictum praetoris [nih'-hil hokk ahd ay-dihk'-tuhm prI-toh'-riss] *L*—This has nothing to do with the edict of the praetor. A reference to an ancient Roman promulgation of regulations that would hold during a particular praetor's period in office. The reply of Cujas, a 16th-century jurist, when asked during a lecture if he were Protestant or Catholic.

Nihil in intellectu quod non prius in sensibus [nih'-hil in in-tel-lek'-too kwod nohn prih'-uhs in sayn'-sih-buhs] *L*—Nothing is in the intellect that is not first in the senses. An axiom of the scholastic philosophers opposing the doctrine of innate ideas.

Nihil muliebre praeter corpus gerens [nih'-hil muh-lih-eh'-breh prI'-tehr kor'-puhs ge'-rayns] *L*—Having nothing feminine about her except her body. An appraisal of Queen Elizabeth I.

Nihil non commiserunt stupri, saevitiae, impietatis [nih'-hil nohn kom-mee-say'-ruhnt stoo'-pree sI-wih'-tih-I im-pih-eh-tah'-tiss] *L*—There was no kind of lewdness, savagery, or impiety that they did not commit. The reference is to the Roman emperors whose statues stand around the Sheldonian Theatre at Oxford. Max Beerbohm, *Zuleika Dobson*, chap. 1.

Nihil obstat [nih'-hil ohp'-staht] *L*—An official ecclesiastical statement that nothing stands in the way of publication. *See also* Imprimatur.

Nihil quod tetigit non ornavit [nih'-hil kwod teh'-tih-git nohn or-nah'-wit] *L*—*See* Nullum fere scribendi genus . . .

Nihil tam absurde dici potest quod non dicatur ab aliquo philosophorum [nih'-hil tahm ahp-suhr'-day dee'-kee po'-test kwod nohn dee-kah'-tuhr ahb ah'-lih-kwoh fih-lo-so-foh'-ruhm] *L*—There is nothing no matter how absurd that has not been said by some philosopher. Cicero, *Divination*, 2; 58, 119.

Nil actum credens cum quid superesset agendum [neel ahk'-tuhm kray'-dayns kuhm kwid suh-pehr-es'-set ah-gen'-duhm] *L*—Believing nothing done when something remained to be done. Lucan, *Pharsalia*, 2; 657.

Nil admirari [neel ahd-mee-rah'-ree] *L*—The attitude of being astonished at nothing. This is basic in Horace's philosophy, which counseled restraint toward pleasure, money, and fame. *See also* Surtout, point de zèle. Horace, *Epistles*, 1; 6, 1.

Nil conscire sibi, nulla pallescere culpa [neel kohn-skee'-reh sih'-bih nool'-lah pahl-lays'-keh-reh kuhl'-pah] *L*—To have a clear conscience and not pale at any charge. Horace, *Epistles*, 1; 1, 61.

Nil debet [neel day'-bet] *L*—He owes nothing.

Nil desperandum [neel day-spay-rahn'-duhm] *L*—Never despair. A favorite quotation of Mr. Micawber in Dickens' *David Copperfield*. Horace, *Odes*, 1; 7, 27.

Nil dictum quod non dictum prius [neel dihk'-tuhm kwod nohn dihk'-tuhm prih'-uhs] *L*—Nothing has been said that hasn't been said before.

Nil molitur inepte [neel moh-lih'-tuhr ih-nep'-tay] *L*—He makes no show of absurd pretensions in his writing. Horace contrasts with this attitude the bombastic style, which he ridicules in Parturiunt montes ... (*q.v.*). Horace, *Art of Poetry*, 140.

Nil mortalibus ardui est:/Coelum ipsum petimus stultitia [neel mor-tah'-lih-buhs ahr'-duh-ee est koi'-luhm ip'-suhm peh'-tih-muhs stuhl-tih'-tih-ah] *L*—Nothing is too daring for man; we seek to reach heaven itself in our folly. Horace, *Odes*, 1; 3, 37.

Nil nisi cruce [neel nih'-sih kroo'-keh] *L*—No victory without suffering.

Nil sine magno vita labore dedit mortalibus [neel sih'-neh mahg'-noh wee'-tah lah-boh'-reh deh'-dit mohr-tah'-lih-buhs] *L*—Life has given nothing to mortals without much labor. Horace, *Satires*, 1; 9, 60.

Nil sine Numine [neel sih'-neh noo'-mih-neh] *L*—Nothing without Divine Power. Motto of Colorado.

Nil sub sole novum [neel suhb soh'-leh no'-wuhm] *L*—There is nothing new under the sun. *Vulgate, Ecclesiastes*, 1; 10.

Nimium ne crede colori [nih'-mih-uhm nay kray'-deh koh-loh'-ree] *L*—Do not have too much confidence in color; not every blush is a sign of innocence.

N'importe! [naN-pawrt] *Fr*—It makes no difference; forget about it!

Ninguno nace maestro [neen-goo'-noh nah'-say mah-ays'-troh] *Sp*—Nobody is born an expert.

Ni plus, ni moins [nee plü nee mwaN] *Fr*—Neither more nor less.

Nisi Dominus ... frustra [nih'-sih do'-mih-nuhs ... froos'-trah] *L*—Unless the Lord (build the house, they labor) in vain (who build it). *Vulgate, Psalms*, 127; 1. Motto of the city of Edinburgh and also of the Hospital Auxiliary, medically untrained helpers; found on Blue Cross emblem in the United States.

Nisi prius [nih'-sih prih'-uhs] *L*—Literally, unless before; in general usage, a court where cases are tried before a judge and jury.

Nitimur in vetitum semper, cupimusque negata [nee'-tih-muhr in weh'-tih-tuhm sem'-pehr kuh-pih-muhs'-kweh neh-gah'-tah] *L*—We are always striving for what is forbidden, and desiring what is denied us. Ovid, *Amores*, 3; 4, 17.

Nitor in adversum [nee'-tor in ahd-wehr'-suhm] *L*—I struggle against opposition.

NKVD Narkomvnudel [nahr-kom-vnoo-dyehl] *Rus*—People's Commissariat for Internal Affairs. The Russian secret service that succeeded OGPU (*q.v.*) and was itself replaced, in 1946, by MVD and later still by KGB (*q.v.*). The word is made up from the first three letters of each of the Russian words in the name: *Narodni Kommissariat Vnutrennikh Del* [nah-rod'-nee kom-mis-sahr'-ee-aht vnoot'-reh-neekh dyehl]

NN. Nomina [noh'-mih-nah] *L*—The names. Used when proper names are to be inserted.

No adventures mucho tu riqueza / Por consejo de ome que ha pobreza [noh ahd-ben-too'-rays moo'-choh too ree-kay'-sah por kon-say'-hoh day oh'-may kay ah poh-bray'-sah] *Sp*—Don't risk much of your wealth on the advice of a poor man. Juan Manuel, *El Conde Lucanor.*

Nobilitas sola est atque unica virtus [noh-bih'-lih-tahs soh'-lah est aht'-kweh oo'-nih-kah wihr'-toos] *L*—Virtue is the one and only nobility. Juvenal, 8; 20.

Noblesse de robe [noh-bless duh ruhb] *Fr*—Nobility of the robe or gown; applied to judges and lawyers.

Noblesse oblige [noh-bless uh-bleezh] *Fr*—Those who are nobly born must act nobly. This often implies condescension.

Noctes coenaeque deum [nohk'-tayss koi-nI'-kweh deh'-uhm] *L*—Nights and feasts fit for the gods. Horace, *Satires*, 2; 6, 65.

No es oro todo lo que reluce [noh ess oh'-roh toh'-doh loh kay ray-loo'-say] *Sp*—All that glitters is not gold. Cervantes, *Don Quixote*, 2; 33.

No hay cerradura si es de oro la garzúa [noh ah'-ee seh-rrah-doo'-rah see ess day oh'-roh lah gahr-soo'-ah] *Sp*—There is no effective lock if the picklock is made of gold; gold can open any door.

Nolens volens [noh'-layns woh'-layns] *L*—Willy-nilly; whether willing or unwilling.

Noli me tangere [noh'-lee may tahn'-geh-reh] *L*—Do not touch me. *Vulgate, John,* 20; 17.

Noli turbare circulos meos [noh'-lee tuhr-bah'-reh keer'-kuh-lohs meh'-ohs] *L*—Do not disturb my circles. Words spoken by Archimedes, mathematician and physicist, when a Roman soldier stood in the light, blocking the scientist's view of the problem on which he was working. The incident is said to have occurred when the Romans took Syracuse in 212 B.C. Legend has it that Archimedes was killed by a Roman soldier.

Nolle prosequi [nohl'-lay proh'-seh-kwee] *L*—A formal entry on the record that the plaintiff or prosecutor is dropping a case.

Nolo contendere [noh'-loh kohn-ten'-deh-reh] *L*—I do not wish to contest the suit. A plea entered by the defendant which subjects him to a judgment of conviction. Not necessarily an admission of guilt.

Nolo episcopari [noh'-loh eh-pees-koh-pah'-ree] *L*—I do not wish to be a bishop. An expression of humility on the part of a priest being elevated to the episcopate.

nol. pros. *L*—*See* Nolle prosequi.

Nolumus leges Angliae mutari [noh'-luh-muhs lay'-gays ahn'-glih-I moo'-tah-ree] *L*—We object to any change in England's laws.

Nom de guerre [nohN duh gehr] *Fr*—An assumed name; pen name, stage name.

Nom de plume [nohN duh plüm] *Fr*—Pen name.

Nom de théâtre [nohN duh tay-ah-tr] *Fr*—Stage-name.

Nomen conservandum (*pl.* **Nomina conservanda**) [noh'-men kohn-sehr-wahn'-duhm *pl.* noh'-mih-nah kohn-sehr-wahn'-dah] *L*—The name must be kept; in bio-logical sciences, a name that is retained although it is an exception to the rules of scientific classification.

Nomina si nescis perit et cognitio rerum [noh'-mih-nah see neh'-skees peh'-rit et kog-nih'-tih-oh ray'-rum] *L*—If you do not know the names, the knowledge of things is also lost. Linnaeus.

Nomina stultorum parietibus haerent [noh'-mih-nah stuhl-toh'-ruhm pah-rih-eh'-tih-buhs hI'-rent] *L*—The names of fools cling to the walls of buildings; fools' names like fools' faces are always seen in public places.

nom. nud. nomen nudum [noh'-men noo'-duhm] *L*—In biology a mere name used without a scientific description.

Non amo te, Sabidi, nec possum dicere quare; hoc solum scio, non amo te, Sabidi [nohn ah'-moh tay sah-bih'-dee nek pos'-suhm dee'-keh-reh kwah'-ray hokk soh'-luhm skih'-oh nohn ah'-moh tay sah-bih'-dee] *L*—I do not love you, Sabidius, nor can I say why; this only I know, Sabidius, I do not love you. Martial, 1; 32. There is a noted translation of this made by Tom Brown when John Fell, the dean of his college at Oxford University, offered to revoke a suspension against the boy if he could translate this epigram into English verse. He sang out: "I do not love thee, Dr. Fell,/The reason why I cannot tell;/But this I'm sure I know full well,/I do not love thee, Dr. Fell."

Non Angli, sed angeli [nohn ahn'-glee sed ahn'-gel-lee] *L*—Not Englishmen but angels. The substance of a comment Gregory the Great made when told that certain men exposed for sale in a Roman market were Angli. Bede, *Ecclesiastical History,* 2; 1.

Non assumpsi [nohn ahs-suhmp'-see] *L*—A denial by a defendant that any promise was made.

Non compos mentis [nohn kom'-pohs men'-tiss] *L*—Not of sound mind. Legally, incapable of managing one's affairs.

Non concessit [nohn kohn-ses'-sit] *L*—He did not grant. A legal writ.

Non constat [nohn kohn'-stat] *L*—It is not clear; it is not evident from what the court has heard.

Non cuivis homini contingit adire Corinthum [nohn kwee'-wiss ho-mih-nee kohn-tin'-git ah-dee'-reh koh-rin'-tuhm] *L*—It is not every man's good fortune to visit Corinth (a city of luxury in antiquity). Horace, *Epistles,* 1; 17, 36.

Non culpabilis [nohn kuhl-pah'-bih-liss] *L*—Not guilty.

Non deficiente crumena [nohn day-fih-kih-en'-teh kruh-may'-nah] *L*—As long as the money holds out. Horace, *Epistles,* 1; 4, 11.

Non est, crede mihi, sapientis dicere "vivam." Sera nimis vita est crastina; vive hodie [nohn est kray'-deh mih'-hih sah-pih-en'-tiss dee'-keh-reh wee'-wahm say'-rah nih'-miss wee'-tah est krahs'-tih-nah wee'-weh ho'-dih-eh] *L*—It is not, believe me, the mark of a wise man to say, "I shall live." Living tomorrow is too late; live today. Martial, *Epigrams,* 1; 15.

Non est curiosus quin idem sit malevolus [nohn est kuh-rih-oh'-suhs kween ee'-dem sit mah-leh'-wo-luhs] *L*—There is no curious man who does not have ill will to sharpen his curiosity.

Non est inventus [nohn est in-ven'-tuhs] *L*—He has not been found. A sheriff's statement on a summons or subpoena when a person whose presence is demanded has not been found.

Non ex omni ligno, ut Pythagoras dicebat, debet Mercurius exculpi [nohn ex om'-nee lig'-noh uht pee-tah'-go-rahs dee-kay'-baht day'-bet mehr-kuh'-rih-uhs ex-kuhl'-pee] *L*—Mercury ought not to be carved from just any wood, as Pythagoras said; you can't make a silk purse out of a sow's ear. By extension, it means that every mind cannot be trained in scholarship. Apuleius, *Apology,* 43.

Non expedit [nohn ex'-peh-dit] *L*—It is not fitting.

Non fingo hypotheses [nohn fing'-goh hih-poh'-teh-sayss] *L*—I do not form hypotheses. Newton.

138

Non fu mai savio partito fare disperare gli uomini [nonn foo mah'-ee sah'-vih-oh pahr-tee'-toh fah'-ray dee-spay-rah'-ray lyee oo-oh'-mee-nee] *It*—It has never been a wise policy to drive men to desperation. Machiavelli, *Istorie Florentine,* 2; 14.

Non haec in foedera [nohn hIk in foi'-deh-rah] *L*—Not for such alliances as these. This is adapted from Aeneas' excuses to Dido for his flight from her. He says that he did not come as a suitor with any proposal of alliance. Vergil, *Aeneid,* 4; 339.

Non ignara mali, miseris succurere disco [nohn ig-nah'-rah mah'-lee mih'-seh-reess suhk-kuh'-reh-reh dis'-koh] *L*—Having experienced misfortune myself, I have learned to aid the wretched. Vergil, *Aeneid,* 1; 630.

Non inutiles scientiae existimandae sunt, quarum in se nullus est usus, si ingenia acuant et ordinent [nohn in-oo'-tih-lays skih-en'-tih-I ex-ees-tih-mahn'-dI suhnt kwah'-ruhm in say nool'-luhs est oo'-soos see in-geh'-nih-ah ah'-kuh-ahnt et or'-dih-nent] *L*—Sciences which have no practical use in themselves must not be considered useless if they sharpen and order the mind. Francis Bacon.

Non libet [nohn lih'-bet] *L*—It is not pleasing.

Non licet [nohn lih'-ket] *L*—It is not permitted; it is not licit.

Non liquet [nohn lih'-kwet] *L*—It is not clear; a term used by lawyers when a case is not proven.

Non merita nome di creatore, se non Iddio ed il Poeta [nonn may'-ree-tah noh'-may dee kray-ah-toh'-ray say nonn eed-dee'-oh ed eel poh-ay'-tah] *It*—No one merits the name of creator, except God and the Poet.

Non multa sed multum [nohn muhl'-tah sed muhl'-tuhm] *L*—Not quantity but quality.

Non nobis, Domine, non nobis; sed nomini tuo da gloriam [nohn noh'-beess do'-mih-neh nohn noh'-beess sed noh'-mih-nee tuh'-oh dah gloh'-rih-ahm] *L*—Not to us, O Lord, not to us; but to thy name give glory. *Vulgate, Psalms,* 115; 1.

Non nobis solum nati sumus [nohn noh'-beess soh'-luhm nah'-tee suh'-muhs] *L*—We are not born for ourselves alone. Cicero gives credit for this idea to Plato. Cicero, *On Duties*, 1; 7, 22.

Non nostrum inter vos tantas componere lites [nohn nos'-truhm in'-tehr wohs tahn'-tahs kom-poh'-neh-reh lee'-tays] *L*—It is not for us to settle your grave disputes. Originally expressing an unwillingness to decide which of two shepherds was the better poet, it is now used ironically. Vergil, *Eclogues*, 3; 108.

Non obstante veredicto [nohn op-stahn'-teh veh-reh-dick'-toh] *L*—Notwithstanding the verdict. A judgment entered for the plaintiff in spite of a verdict for the defendant.

Non ogni fiore fa buon odore [nonn ohn'-yee fee-oh'-ray fah bwohn oh-doh'-ray] *It*—Not every flower has a sweet odor.

Non ogni giorno è festa [nonn ohn'-yee johr'-noh eh fess'-tah] *It*—Every day is not a holiday.

Non olet [nohn oh'-let] *L*—It does not stink. Said of money acquired by dishonest or disreputable means. When Titus objected to the tax his father Vespasian put on urine used for medical purposes, the latter held under his son's nose a coin derived from this tax, and uttered this cynical expression. Suetonius, *Lives of the Twelve Caesars, Vespasian*, 23.

Non omne licitum honestum [nohn om'-neh lih'-kih-tuhm ho-ness'-tuhm] *L*—Not everything that is permissible is necessarily proper. The law may permit an action that is not respectable.

Non omnia possumus omnes [nohn om'-nih-ah pos'-suh-muss om'-nays] *L*—We cannot all do everything. Vergil, *Eclogues*, 8; 64.

Non omnis moriar [nohn om'-niss moh'-rih-ahr] *L*—I shall not wholly die. Horace prophesied that he would always be remembered, especially for introducing Greek meters into Latin poetry. Horace, *Odes*, 3; 30, 6.

Non passibus aequis [nohn pahs'-sih-buhs I'-kweess] *L*—With unequal steps. Vergil, *Aeneid*, 2; 724.

Non placet [nohn plah'-ket] *L*—It is not pleasing; indicating a negative vote.

Non possumus [nohn pos'-suh-muss] *L*—We cannot. Papal form denying a request.

Non progredi est regredi [nohn proh'-greh-dee est reh'-greh-dee] *L*—Not to progress is to regress; there is no standing still.

non pros. *L*—*See* Non prosequitur.

Non prosequitur [nohn proh-seh'-kwih-tuhr] *L*—A judgment entered for the defendant when the plaintiff fails to prosecute.

Non quis, sed quid [nohn kwis sed kwid] *L*—Not who but what. The matter ought to be considered in itself, without considering who said it.

Non ragioniam di lor, ma guarda e passa [nonn rah-joh-nih-ahm' dee lohr mah gwahr'-dah ay pahs'-sah] *It*—Let us not discuss them; look and pass on. Vergil is describing to Dante the punishment meted out to neutrals who were neither rebellious nor faithful to God: they are in a vestibule of hell, disdained by heaven and hell. Dante, *Inferno*, 3; 51.

Non sanz droict [noN saN drwakt] *OF*—Not without right. Motto on Shakespeare's coat of arms.

Non semper erit aestas [nohn sem'-pehr eh'-rit Is'-tahs] *L*—Summer will not last forever.

Non semper Saturnalia erunt [nohn sem'-pehr sah-tuhr-nah'-lih-ah eh'-ruhnt] *L*—The holidays will not last forever; Christmas comes but once a year. In ancient Rome slaves enjoyed great liberty during the Saturnalia. Seneca, *Apocolocyntosis*, 12; 2.

Non sequitur [nohn seh'-kwih-tuhr] *L*—It does not follow; an illogical reference. This is often used as a noun.

Non sibi sed patriae [nohn sih'-bih sed pah'-trih-I] *L*—Not for himself but for his native land.

139

Non sum qualis eram [nohn suhm kwah'-liss eh'-rahm] *L*—I am not the man I used to be. The sentence in Horace adds: In the reign of kindly Cynara. Ernest Dowson took this as his text for the poem "Cynara." Horace, *Odes*, 4; 1, 3.

Non tanto me dignor honore [nohn tahn'-toh may dihg'-nor ho-nor'-eh] *L*—I do not deem myself worthy of so great an honor. Based on a line in Vergil, *Aeneid*, 1; 335.

Non troppo presto [nonn trop'-poh press'-toh] *It*—Not too fast.

Nonum prematur in annum [noh'-nuhm preh-mah'-tuhr in ahn'-nuhm] *L*—Let your piece of writing be kept unpublished until the ninth year. Horace, *Art of Poetry*, 388.

Non vitae sed scholae discimus [nohn wee'-tI sed skoh'-lI diss'-kih-muhs] *L*—We learn not for life but for school; we devote ourselves to learning, not for the cultivation of the moral life but for a display of cleverness. Seneca, *Letters to Lucilius*, 106; 12.

Non vult contendere [nohn vuhlt kohn-ten'-deh-reh] *L*—He does not wish to contest the suit. *See also* Nolo contendere.

No pasarań [noh pah-sah-rahn'] *Sp*—They shall not pass. Rallying cry of the Loyalists in the Spanish Civil War. *See also* Ils ne passeront pas.

No podemos haber aquello que queremos, queramos aquello que podremos [noh poh-day'-mohs ah-behr' ah-kay'-yoh kay kay-ray'-mohs kay-rah'-mohs ah-kay'-yoh kay poh-dray'-mohs] *Sp*—Since we cannot get what we like, let us like what we can get.

Nosce te ipsum [nohs'-keh tay ihp'-suhm] *L*—Know thyself. *See also* Gnothi seauton.

Nosce tempus [nohs'-keh tem'-puss] *L*—See Kairon gnothi.

Noscitur a sociis [nohs'-kih-tuhr ah soh'-kih-eess] *L*—A man is known by the company he keeps.

No se ganó Zamora en una hora [noh say gah-noh' sah-moh'-rah en oo'-nah oh'-rah] *Sp*—Zamora was not won in an hour; Rome was not built in a day. Cervantes, *Don Quixote*, 2; 71.

Nos morituri te salutamus [nohs moh-rih-too'-ree tay sah-loo-tah'-muhs] *L*—We who are about to die salute thee. Before fighting, gladiators in the arena looked up at the emperor and saluted him with these words. A modification of *Ave imperator, morituri te salutant.* Suetonius, *Claudius*, 21.

Nostalgie de la boue [nuhs-tahl-zhee duh lah boo] *Fr*—Yearning for the gutter, for the low life.

Nota bene [noh'-tah beh'-neh] *L*—See N.B.

Notandum candidissimo calculo [no-tahn'-duhm kahn-dih-dis'-sih-moh kahl'-kuh-loh] *L*—A day to be marked with the whitest stone there is. Pliny the Younger, *Letters*, 6; 11, 3.

Notatu dignum [no-tah'-too dig'-nuhm] *L*—Worthy of note.

Notitiae communes [noh-tih'-tih-I kom-moo'-nays] *L*—Common notions in the world existing always and everywhere.

Not kennt kein Gebot [noht kennt kIn guh-boht'] *Ger*—Necessity knows no law.

Notre Dame [nuh-tr dahm] *Fr*—Our Lady; the Virgin Mary.

Notre défiance justifie la tromperie d'autrui [nuh-tr day-fyahNss zhüs-tee-fee lah trohN-pree doh-trwee] *Fr*—Our distrust of other men justifies them in deceiving us. La Rochefoucauld, *Maxims*, 86.

Notre mérite nous attire l'estime des honnêtes gens, et notre étoile celle du public [nuh-tr may-reet noo zah-teer leh-steem day zuh-net zhahN ay nuh-tr ay-twahl sehl dü püb-leek] *Fr*—Our merit wins the esteem of honest people, our lucky star that of the public. La Rochefoucauld, *Maxims*, 165.

Notre nature est dans le mouvement; le repos entier est la mort [nuh-tr nah-tür eh dahN luh moov-mahN luh ruh-poh ahN-tyay eh lah mor] *Fr*—We are by nature active; complete rest is death. Pascal, *Pensées*, 2; 129.

Nourri dans le sérail, j'en connais les détours [noo-ree dahN luh say-rah-yuh zhahN kuh-neh lay day-toor] *Fr*—I was reared in the harem and know its byways. Said of one who knows the ropes from long experience. Racine, *Bajazet*, 4; 7.

Nous aimons toujours ceux qui nous admirent, et nous n'aimons pas toujours ceux que nous admirons [noo zeh-mohN too-zhoor suh kee noo zahd-meer ay noo neh-mohN pah too-zhoor suh kuh noo zahd-mee-rohN] *Fr*—We always love those who admire us, but we do not always love those whom we admire. La Rochefoucauld, *Maxims*, 294.

Nous avons changé tout cela [noo-zah-vohN shahN-zhay too suh-lah] *Fr*—We've changed all that. Sganarelle answers thus when objection is made to his statement that the heart is on the right side, and the liver on the left. He goes on to say that medicine is now practiced in an entirely different way. The expression is used to satirize those who try to defend their indefensible errors. Molière, *Physician in Spite of Himself*, 2; 4.

Nous avons tous assez de force pour supporter les maux d'autrui [noo zah-vohN toos ass-say duh forss poor sü-por-tay lay moh doh-trwee] *Fr*—We all have enough strength to bear the sufferings of other people. La Rochefoucauld, *Maxims*, 19.

Nous ne trouvons guère de gens de bon sens que ceux qui sont de notre avis [noo nuh troo-vohN gehr duh zhahN duh bohN sahNs kuh suh kee sohN duh nuh-tr ah-vee] *Fr*—We seldom credit people who do not share our views with good sense. La Rochefoucauld, *Maxims*, 347.

Nous pathetikos [noos pah-thay-tih-kos'] *Gk*—The passive intellect.

Nous poietikos [noos poi-ay-tih-kos'] *Gk*—The active, the creative mind.

Nous sommes tous dans le désert! Personne ne comprend personne [noo suhm tooss dahN luh day-zehr pehr-suhnn nuh kohN-prahN pehr-suhnn] *Fr*—We are all in the desert! Nobody understands anybody.

Nous verrons [noo veh-rohN] *Fr*—We shall see.

Nous verrons ce que nous verrons [noo veh-rohN skuh noo veh-rohN] *Fr*—We shall see what we shall see.

Nouveau riche [noo-voh reesh] *Fr*—One who has recently become rich. The implication is that the person is publicizing his new status in a manner offensive to the less fortunate.

Nouvelle série [noo-vel say-ree] *Fr*—New series.

9bre novembre [nuh-vahN-br] *Fr*—November, the ninth month in the early Roman calendar. This deceptive abbreviation is based on *novem* (nine) in Latin.

Novus homo [noh'-wus ho'-moh] *L*—A new man; an upstart. In Roman politics, a newcomer, none of whose ancestors held a high office.

Novus ordo seclorum [noh'-wus or'-doh say-kloh'-ruhm] *L*—*See* Annuit coeptis.

N. P. O. Nihil per os [nih'-hil pehr ohs] *L*—Nothing by way of the mouth. A medical order.

n. s. nouvelle série [noo-vehl say-ree] *Fr*—New series.

n. s. nueva serie [nway'-vah say'-ree-ay] *Sp*—New series.

N. S. I. C. Noster Salvator Iesus Christus [nos'-tehr sahl-vah'-tohr yay'-soos krees'-tuhs] *L*—Our Savior Jesus Christ.

N. U. Nazioni Unite [nah-tsee-oh'-nee oo-nee'-tay] *It*—United Nations.

Nuda veritas [noo'-dah way'-rih-tahs] *L*—The naked truth.

Nudis cruribus [noo'-deess kroo'-rih-buhs] *L*—With naked legs.

Nudis oculis [noo'-deess ok'-uh-leess] *L*—With the naked eye; without a telescope.

Nudis verbis [noo'-deess wehr'-beess] *L*—In plain words.

Nudum pactum [noo'-duhm pahk'-tuhm] *L*—A promise that cannot be enforced legally because of lack of a consideration, such as earnest money. A legal expression.

Nugae canorae [noo'-gI kah-noh'-rI] *L*—Tuneful trifles; songs that have meaningless nonsense syllables.

Nugae literariae [noo'-gI lee-teh-rah'-rih-I] *L*—Literary trifles.

141

Nul bien sans peine [nül byaN sahN pehn] *Fr*—No gain without pain.

Nulla dies sine linea [nool'-lah dih'-ays sih'-neh lee'-neh-ah] *L*—No day without a line. A maxim attributed to the painter Apelles who let no day pass without sketching a little. It is also the motto of industrious writers. Pliny the Elder, *Natural History*, 35; 10.

Nulla fere causa est in qua non femina litem moverit [nool'-lah feh'-ray kow'-sah est in kwah nohn fay'-mih-nah lee'-tem moh'-weh-rit] *L*—There is almost no case of a quarrel that was not started over a woman. Juvenal, 6; 242.

Nulla nuova, buona nuova [nool'-lah nwoh'-vah bwoh'-nah nwoh'-vah] *It*—No news is good news.

Nulla salus bello [nool'-lah sah'-loos bel'-loh] *L*—There is no safety in war. Vergil, *Aeneid*, 11; 399.

Nulla virtute redemptum / A vitiis [nool'-lah wir-too'-teh reh-daymp'-tuhm ah wih'-tih-eess] *L*—A man who is not redeemed from vice by a single virtue. The man censured is Crispinus. *See also* Ecce iterum Crispinus. *Juvenal*, 4; 2.

Nulli sapere casu obtigit [nool'-lee sah'-peh-reh kah'-soo op'-tih-git] *L*—No man ever became wise by chance. Seneca, *Letters to Lucilius*, 76; 4.

Nulli secundus [nool'-lee seh-kuhn'-duhs] *L*—Second to none.

Nullius addictus jurare in verba magistri [nool-lee'-uhs ahd-dik'-tuhs yoo-rah'-reh in wer'-bah mah-gis'-tree] *L*—Not sworn to follow the teaching of any school or professor. Used by those who claim to be independent in their thinking.

Nullius filius [noo-lee'-uss fee'-lih-uss] *L*—Literally, the son of nobody; an illegitimate son.

Nullum est jam dictum quod non sit dictum prius [nool'-luhm est yahm dik'-tuhm kwod nohn sit dik'-tuhm prih'-uhs] *L*—Nothing has been said that hasn't been said before. Terence, *Eunuch, Prologue*, 41.

142

Nullum fere scribendi genus non tetigit, nullum quod tetigit non ornavit [nool'-luhm feh'-ray skree-ben'-dee ge'-nuhs nohn teh'-tih-git nool'-luhm kwod teh'-tih-git nohn or-nah'-wit] *L*—There was almost no literary genre that he did not touch, and he touched nothing that he did not adorn. Samuel Johnson's inscription for Oliver Goldsmith's tomb in Westminster Abbey.

Nullum magnum ingenium sine mixtura dementiae fuit [nool'-luhm mahg'-nuhm in-gen'-nih-uhm sih'-neh mix-too'-rah day-men'-tih-I foo'-it] *L*—There never was great genius without a touch of madness. In *Absalom and Achitophel*, 1; 163 Dryden wrote: "Great wits are sure to madness near allied / And thin partitions do their bounds divide." Seneca, *Tranquillity of Mind*, 15; 16 where he credits Aristotle with this statement.

Nul tiel record [nuhl teel rec-ord] *Anglo-Fr*—No such record.

Numquam aliud natura, aliud sapientia dicit [nuhm'-kwahm ah'-lih-ud nah-too'-rah ah'-lih-ud sah-pih-en'-tih-ah dee'-kit] *L*—Nature never says one thing and wisdom another. A tenet of Stoic philosophy. This is also stated by Marcus Aurelius in his *Meditations*, (7; 2): To the rational animal an act may be in accordance both with nature and reason.

Numquam minus otiosus quam cum otiosus [nuhm'-kwahm mih'-nuhs o-tih-oh'-suhs kwahm kuhm o-tih-oh'-suhs] *L*—Never less at leisure than when at leisure. Cato is quoting P. Scipio Africanus. Cicero, *On Duties*, 3; 1.

Numquam minus solus quam cum solus [nuhm'-kwahm mih'-nuhs soh'-luhs kwahm kuhm soh'-luhs] *L*—Never less alone than when alone. Said of a person who enjoys his own company. Cato wrote that P. Scipio Africanus the Elder frequently used this expression. Cicero, *On Duties*, 3; 1 and *Republic*, 1; 17, 27.

Numquam solus cum sola [nuhm'-kwahm so'-luhs kuhm soh'-lah] *L*—Never be alone with a woman who is alone. Counsel given monks.

Nunc age [nuhnk ah'-geh] *L*—Act now.

Nunc aut nunquam [nuhnk owt nuhn'-kwahm] *L*—Now or never.

Nunc dimittis servum tuum, Domine [nuhnk dee-mit'-tiss sehr'-vuhm tuh'-uhm do'-mih-neh] *L*—Now thou dost dismiss thy servant, O Lord. The first words of the canticle that Simeon uttered when Jesus was presented in the temple. *Nunc dimittis* often means permission to depart. *Vulgate, Luke*, 2; 29.

Nunc est bibendum, nunc pede libero / Pulsanda tellus [nuhnk est bih-ben'-duhm nuhnk peh'-deh lee'-beh-roh puhl-sahn'-dah tel'-loos] *L*—Now is the time for drinking and dancing. Horace, *Odes*, 1; 37, 1.

Nunc pro tunc [nuhnk proh tuhnk] *L*—Now for then. A legal term indicating that action is taken in the present that should have been taken previously.

Nur der verdient sich Freiheit wie das Leben, / Der täglich sie erobern muss [noor dehr fehr-deent' zikh frI'-hIt vee dahs lay'-bun dehr tehg'-likh zee ehr-oh'-buhrn muss] *Ger*—Only he deserves freedom and life who daily wins them anew. Goethe, *Faust*, pt. 2; 5, 11575-6.

Nur wer die Sehnsucht kennt, / weiss, was ich leide! [noor vehr dee zayn'-zuhkht kennt vIss vahs ikh lI'-duh] *Ger*—Literally, only one who knows longing, knows what I suffer. The poem was set to music by Tchaikovsky. Goethe, *Wilhelm Meisters Lehrjahre*, 4; 11.

Nympha pudica deum vidit et erubuit *L*—*See* Lympha pudica . . .

O

Obiit. [oh′-bih-it] *L*—He died.

Obiit sine prole [oh′-bih-it sih′-neh pro′-leh] *L*—He died without issue.

Obiter dictum [oh′-bih-tehr dik′-tuhm] *L*—Said in passing.

Obiter scriptum [oh′-bih-tehr skreep′-tuhm] *L*—Something written by the way or in passing.

Objet d'art [uhb-zheh dahr] *Fr*—An object of artistic value.

Obra de común, obra de ningún [oh′-brah day koh-moon′ oh′-brah day neen-goon′] *Sp*—Everybody's business is nobody's business.

Obscurum per obscurius [op-skoo′-ruhm pehr op-skoo′-rih-uhs] *L*—Explaining the obscure through something still more obscure.

Obsequium amicos, veritas odium parit [op-seh′-kwih-uhm ah-mee′-kohs way′-rih-tahs oh′-dih-uhm pah′-rit]*L*—Compliance breeds friends, truth hatred. Terence, *Andria*, 1; 1, 41.

Obsta principiis [op′-stah preen-kih′-pih-ees] *L*—Resist the opening wedge. A legal maxim.

Obstipui steteruntque comae et vox faucibus haesit [op-stih′-puh-ee steh-tay-ruhnt′-kweh koh′-mI et wohx fow′-kih-buhs hI′-sit] *L*—I was amazed, my hair stood on end, and my voice stuck in my throat. Vergil, *Aeneid*, 2; 774.

Ochen khorosho [oh′-chen khah-rah-shuh′] *Rus*—Very well.

Ochen nemnogo [oh′-chen nyem-nuh′-guh] *Rus*—Very little.

8bre octobre [ok-toh-br] *Fr*—October, the eighth month in the early Roman calendar. *octo* (eight) in Latin.

Oculis subjecta fidelibus [o′-kuh-leess suhb-yek′-tah fih-day′-lih-buhs] *L*—Subjected to competent examination.

Oculus episcopi [o′-kuh-luhs eh-pees′-koh-pee] *L*—The eye of the bishop; said of a clergyman who makes reports to a bishop.

o. d. omni die [om′-nee dih′-ay] *L*—Every day.

Oderint dum metuant [oh′-deh-rint duhm meh′-tuh-ahnt] *L*—Let them hate me so long as they fear me. This is a quotation from the *Atreus* of Accius, who died in 90 B.C. Cicero quotes this in his *On Duties*, 1; 28, 97 and again in *Philippic* 1; 14. It was a favorite remark of the emperor Caligula. Suetonius, *Lives of the Twelve Caesars, Caligula*, 30.

Oderint dum probent [oh′-deh-rint duhm pro′-bent] *L*—Let them hate so long as they approve. Revision by Tiberius of oderint dum metuant (*q.v.*)—Suetonius, *Lives of the Twelve Caesars, Tiberius*, 59.

Odi et amo [oh′-dee et ah′-moh] *L*—I hate and I love. Catullus, 85; 1.

Odi profanum vulgus et arceo [oh′-dee pro-fah′-nuhm wuhl′-guhs et ahr′-keh-oh] *L*—I hate the irreverent mob and I avoid it. Horace, *Odes*, 3; 1, 1.

Odium generis humani [oh′-dih-uhm geh′-neh-riss hoo-mah′-nee] *L*—Hatred of the human race, a crime of which early Christians were accused by Nero. Tacitus, *Annals*, 15; 44.

Odium literarium [oh′-dih-uhm lee-teh-rah'-rih-uhm] *L*—A hostile spirit among authors.

Odium theologicum [oh'-dih-uhm teh-o-loh'-gih-kuhm] *L*—Hatred among theologians over doctrinal differences.

Œil-de-boeuf [uh-yuh duh buhf] *Fr*—Bull's eye, a name given to a circular window seen in architecture of the 17th and 18th centuries.

Œuvre de vulgarisation [uh-vr duh vül-gah-ree-zah-syohN] *Fr*—A book popularizing a subject. Those who fancy themselves profound may sometimes use this phrase to describe a work that has had a wide sale.

Œuvres complètes [uh-vr kohN-pleht] *Fr*—Complete works.

O felix culpa quae talem et tantum meruit habere Redemptorem! [o fay'-lix kuhl'-pah kway tah'-lem et tahn'-tum meh'-ruh-it hah-bay'-reh reh-demp-toh'-rem] *L*—O happy fault (Adam's sin) that merited such a great Redeemer! From the blessing of the paschal candle on Holy Saturday. *Liber Usualis*, p. 655.

O. F. M. Ordo Fratrum Minorum [ohr'-doh frah'-truhm mih-noh'-ruhm] *L*—The Order of Friars Minor.

O fortunatam natam me consule Romam [oh for-too-nah'-tahm nah'-tahm may kohn'-suh-leh roh'-mahm] *L*—How fortunate Rome, born in my consulship! Juvenal, 10; 22. Juvenal was quoting a verse by Cicero, reminding the Romans that he (Cicero) had saved the Republic by crushing the conspiracy of Catiline.

O fortunatos nimium, sua si bona norint! [oh for-too-nah'-tohs nih'-mih-uhm suh'-ah see bo'-nah noh'-rint] *L*—How very happy they would be if they but knew their blessings! This was originally written of farmers, far removed from the field of battle. It has often been quoted as a retort to complainers. Vergil, *Georgics*, 2; 458.

Ogni debole ha sempre il suo tiranno [ohn'-yee day'-boh-lay ah sem'-pray eel soo'-oh tee-rah'-noh] *It*—Every weakling has his tyrant.

Ogni medaglia ha il suo rovescio [ohn'-yee may-dahl'-yah ah eel soo'-oh roh-vess'-choo] *It*—Every medal has its reverse side; there are two sides to every story.

Ogni pazzo vuol dar consiglio [ohn'-yee paht'-tsoh vwohl dahr kon-seel'-yoh] *It*—Every fool is ready to give advice.

OGPU Obiedinionnoe Gosudarstvennoe Politicheskoe Upravlenie [ab-ye-dee-nyon'-nuh-ye guh-soo-dahrst-ven'-no-ye puh-lee-tee-chesh'-kuh-ye oo-prahv-len-ye] *Rus*—Special Government Political Administration. Secret service in Russia until 1935; sometimes referred to as Gay-Pay-Oo (GPU). This organization was replaced by the NKVD (*q.v.*).

Ohne Arbeit kein Gewinn [oh'-nuh ahr'-bIt kIn guh-vinn'] *Ger*—There is no gain without work.

Ohne Hast, ohne Rast [oh'-nuh hahst oh'-nuh rahst] *Ger*—Without hurry but without rest. Goethe's description of the sun. A medal was struck with these words and presented to Goethe by Thomas Carlyle and fourteen other admirers.

OKW Oberkommando Wehrmacht [oh-buhr-koh-mahn'-doh vayr'-mahkht] *Ger*—Hitler's High Command.

o. L. östliche Länge [uhst'-likh-uh lehn'-guh] *Ger*—East longitude.

Olet lucernam [oh'-let luh-kehr'-nahm] *L*—It smells of the lamp, midnight oil. Disparaging reference to a labored literary composition.

Oleum addere camino [oh'-leh-uhm ahd'-deh-reh kah-mee'-noh] *L*—To add oil to the fire. Horace, *Satires*, 2; 3, 321.

O Liberté, O Liberté, que de crimes on commet en ton nom! [oh lee-behr-tay oh lee-behr-tay kuh duh kreem ohN kuh-meh ahN tohn nohN] *Fr*—O Liberty, O Liberty, what crimes are committed in your name! Words spoken by Madame Roland just before her execution when she saw the guillotine set up near a statue of Liberty.

Olla podrida [oh'-yah poh-dree'-dah] *Sp*—A dish of many different foods mixed together; hence, a combination of unlikely elements; a literary hodgepodge.

Omne animal ex ovo [om'-neh ah'-nih-mahl ex oh'-woh] *L*—Every animal comes from an egg. Sir William Harvey's biological axiom.

Omne ignotum pro magnifico est [om'-neh ig-noh'-tuhm proh mahg-nih'-fih-koh est] *L*—Everything unknown is presumed magnificent. Tacitus, *Agricola,* 30.

Omne meum, nihil meum [om'-neh meh'-uhm nih'-hil meh'-uhm] *L*—'Tis all mine, yet none is mine.—Macrobius. The compiler's admission and justification. He takes much from other sources but gives them proper credit. It may be used by a writer who works over the thoughts of other men and creates something that is his own. This was the claim of Robert Burton, the author of *The Anatomy of Melancholy,* who quoted profusely from Latin sources.

Omne ovum ex ovo [om'-neh oh'-wuhm ex oh'-woh] *L*—Every egg comes from an egg.

Omnes artes quae ad humanitatem pertinent habent quoddam commune vinclum [om'-nayss ahr'-tayss kwI ahd hoo-mah-nih-tah'-tem pehr'-tih-nent hah'-bent kwod'-dahm kuhm-moo'-neh wink'-luhm] *L*—All the arts that have to do with culture have a certain common bond. Cicero, *In Defense of the Poet Archias,* 1.

Omne solum forti patria est [om'-neh soh'-luhm for'-tee pah'-trih-ah est] *L*—The whole earth is the fatherland of a brave man. Ovid, *Fasti (Calendar of Roman Festivals),* 1; 493.

Omne tulit punctum, qui miscuit utile dulci [om'-neh tuh'-lit poonk'-tuhm kwee miss'-kuh-it oo'-tih-leh duhl'-kee] *L*—He wins general approval who mingles the useful with the pleasant. Horace, *Art of Poetry,* 343.

Omne vitium in proclivi est [om'-neh wih'-tih-uhm in pro-klee'-wee est] *L*—All the roads of vice are downhill. *See also* Facilis descensus Averno.

Omne vivum ex vivo [om'-neh wee'-wuhm ex wee'-woh] *L*—Life comes from life.

Omnia bona bonis [om'-nih-ah bo'-nah bo'-neess] *L*—To the good all things are good. Good men are sometimes credulous and do not readily believe evil of anyone.

Omnia exeunt in mysterium [om'-nih-ah ex'-eh-unt in mees-tay'-rih-uhm] *L*—Everything ends up in mystery.

Omnia mea mecum porto [om'-nih-ah meh'-ah may'-kuhm por'-toh] *L*—I carry all my possessions with me. The philosopher's scorn of external goods. Bias.

Omnia mors aequat [om'-nih-ah mors I'-kwaht] *L*—Death levels everything. Claudian, *Against Rufinus,* 1; 200.

Omnia mutantur, nihil interit [om'-nih-ah moo-tahn'-tuhr nih'-hil in'-teh-rit] *L*—Everything changes, nothing is destroyed. This is quoted in connection with the doctrine of the transmigration of souls taught by Pythagoras. Ovid, *Metamorphoses,* 15; 165.

Omnia mutantur, nos et mutamur in illis [om'-nih-ah moo-tahn'-tuhr nohs et moo-tah'-muhr in il'-leess] *L*—All things change and we change with them. *See also* Tempora mutantur . . .

Omnia opera [om'-nih-ah oh'-peh-rah] *L*—The complete works.

Omnia orta occidunt et aucta senescunt [om'-nih-ah or'-tah ok'-kih-dunt et owk'-tah seh-nays'-kuhnt] *L*—All things rise only to fall, and flourish to decay. Sallust, *Jugurthine War,* 2.

Omnia vincit Amor et nos cedamus Amori [om'-nih-ah win'-kit ah'-mor et nohs kay-dah'-muhs ah-moh'-ree] *L*—Love conquers everything, and let us yield to Love. Vergil, *Eclogues,* 10; 69.

Omnia vincit veritas [om'-nih-ah win'-kit way'-rih-tahs] *L*—Truth conquers everything.

Omnibus has litteras visuris [om'-nih-buhs hahss lit'-teh-rahs wee-soo'-reess] *L*—To whom it may concern; to all who read this document.

Omnis amans amens [om'-niss ah'-mahns ah'-mayns] *L*—Every lover is out of his mind.

Omnis ars naturae imitatio est [om'-

niss ahrs nah-too'-rI ih-mih-tah'-tih-oh
est] *L*—All art is an imitation of nature.
Seneca, *Letters to Lucilius*, 65; 3.

Omnis cellula e cellula ejusdem generis
[om'-niss kel'-luh-lah ay keh'-luh-lah eh-
yuhs'-dem geh'-neh-riss] *L*—Every cell
comes from a cell of the same kind. A biological axiom.

Omnis cognitio fit a sensibus [om'-niss
kog-nih'-tih-oh fit ah sayn'-sih-buhs] *L*—
All knowledge comes through the senses.
A Scholastic axiom.

Omnis comparatio claudicat [om'-niss
kom-pah-rah'-tih-oh klow'-dih-kaht] *L*—
Every comparison limps.

Omnis definitio periculosa est [om'-
niss day-fee-nee'-tih-oh pehr-cuh-loh'-
sah est] *L*—All definitions are dangerous.

Omnis fama a domesticis emanat
[om'-niss fah'-mah ah do-mess'-tih-keess
ay-mah'-naht] *L*—All fame comes from
domestic servants. Francis Bacon observed
that "discreet followers and servants help
much to reputation."

**Omnium consensu capax imperii, nisi
imperasset** [om'-nih-uhm kohn-sayn'-
soo kah'-pahx im-peh'-rih-ee nih'-sih im-
peh-rahs'-set] *L*—In the opinion of all, a
capable ruler, if only he had not ruled.
The historian's judgment of Galba who was
elected by the army to succeed Nero.
Tacitus, *Histories*, 1; 49.

Omnium gatherum [om'-nih-uhm gath-
uh-ruhm] *L*—The first word is Latin. A
humorous imitation of Latin used to indicate an unlikely collection of items of
a heterogeneous nature.

On connaît l'ami au besoin [ohN kuh-
neh lah-mee oh buh-zwaN] *Fr*—You discover a true friend when in need.

Onde não entra o sol entra o medico
[oN'-dee nowN ehN'-trah oo sol ehN'-trah
oo meh'-dee-koo] *Port*—Where the sun
does not enter, the doctor does.

**On est souvent ferme par faiblesse, et
audacieux par timidité** [oh-neh soo-
vahN fehrm pahr feh-bless ay oh-da-syuh
pahr tee-mee-dee-tay] *Fr*—One is often
firm because of weakness and bold because of timidity. La Rochefoucauld, *Maxims*, 11.

**On n'a jamais bon marché de mauvaise
marchandise** [ohn-nah zha-meh bohn
mahr-shay duh muh-vehz mar-shahN-
deez] *Fr*—One never picks up a bargain
buying bad merchandise; buy cheap, buy
dear.

**On ne donne rien si libéralement que
ses conseils** [ohn nuh duhn ryaN see lee-
bay-ral-mahN kuh say kohN-say] *Fr*—We
are never so generous as when giving advice. La Rochefoucauld, *Maxims*, 110.

**On ne fait pas d'omelette sans casser
des oeufs** [ohn-nuh feh pah duhm-let sahN
ka-say day zuhf] *Fr*—You can't make
an omelet without breaking eggs. *See also*
Chi non rompe l'uova ...

**On ne loue d'ordinaire que pour être
loué** [ohn nuh loo dohr-dee-nehr kuh
poor eh-tr loo-ay] *Fr*—As a rule, we praise
only to be praised. La Rochefoucauld,
Maxims, 146.

On ne se blâme que pour être loué
[ohn nuh suh blahm kuh poor eh-tr loo-
ay] *Fr*—One censures oneself only to be
praised. La Rochefoucauld, *Maxims*, 554.

**On n'est jamais si heureux ni si mal-
heureux qu'on s'imagine** [ohn neh zha-
meh see uh-ruh nee see mal-uh-ruh kohN
see-mah-zheen] *Fr*—One is never as happy
or as unhappy as one imagines. La Rochefoucauld, *Maxims*, 49.

**On n'est jamais si ridicule par les qua-
lités que l'on a que par celles que l'on
affecte d'avoir** [ohn neh zha-meh see
ree-dee-kül pahr lay kah-lee-tay kuh lohn
ah kuh pahr sehl kuh lohn ah-fekt dah-
vwahr] *Fr*—One is never so ridiculous for
the qualities that one has as for those one
feigns to have. La Rochefoucauld, *Maxims*,
134.

**On ne trouve guère d'ingrats tant
qu'on est en état de faire du bien** [ohn
nuh troov gehr daN-grah tahN koh-neh
tah-nay-tah duh fehr dü byaN] *Fr*—One
rarely encounters ingratitude as long as
one is in a position to confer favors. La
Rochefoucauld, *Maxims*, 306.

Onus probandi [oh'-nuhs pro-bahn'-dee]
L—The burden of proof.

O. P. Ordo Praedicatorum *or* **Ordinis Praedicatorum** [or'-doh *or* or'-dih-niss pray-

147

dee-kah-toh'-ruhm] *L*—Order of Preachers (Dominicans); of the Order of Preachers.

O passi graviora, dabit deus his quoque finem [oh pahs'-see grah-wih-oh'-rah dah'-bit deh'-uhs hees kwo'-kweh fee'-nem] *L*—O you who have suffered graver trials, god will put an end to these, too. Vergil, *Aeneid,* 1; 199.

op. cit. opere citato *or* opus citatum [o'-peh-reh kih-tah'-toh *or* o'-puhs kih-tah'-tuhm] *L*—In the work cited.

Ope et consilio [oh'-peh et kohn-sih'-lih-oh] *L*—Literally, with aid and counsel; a term applied to one who is accessory to a crime.

Opera buffa [oh'-pay-rah boof'-fah] *It*—Comic opera.

Operae pretium est [o'-peh-rI preh'-tih-uhm est] *L*—It is worth while.

Opera inedita (*pl.* opere inedite) [oh'-pay-rah een-ay'-dee-tah, een-ay'-dee-tay] *It*—An unpublished work.

Operibus credite, et non verbis [o-peh'-rih-buhs kray'-dih-teh et nohn wehr'-beess] *L*—Trust in deeds and not in words. Cervantes, *Don Quixote,* 2; 50.

Opes irritamenta malorum [oh'-pays ihr-rih-tah-men'-tah mah-loh'-ruhm] *L*—Wealth, the incentive of the wicked. Ovid, *Metamorphoses,* 1; 140.

Opse theon aleousi myloi, aleousi de lepta [op-seh' theh-ohn' ah-leh'-oo-see mü-loi ah-leh'-oo-see day lep-tah'] *Gk*—The mills of the gods grind slowly but they grind exceedingly fine. Sextus Empiricus. *See also* Sero molunt deorum molae.

Optimum est pati quod emendare non possis [op'-tih-muhm est pah'-tee kwod ay-mayn-dah'-reh nohn pos'-seess] *L*—It is best to suffer what you cannot amend; what cannot be cured must be endured. Seneca, *Letters to Lucilius,* 107; 9.

Optimum lege (elige), suave et facile illud faciet consuetudo [op'-tih-muhm lay'-geh, ay-lih'-geh, suh-ah'-weh et fah'-kih-leh ihl'-lud fah'-kih-et kohn-suh-ay-too'doh] *L*—Choose the best; habit will make it pleasant and easy. A precept of the Pythagoreans.

148

Optimus legum interpres consuetudo [op'-tih-muhs lay'-guhm in-tehr'-prehs kohn-suh-ay-too'-doh] *L*—Custom is the best interpreter of the laws.

Opus Dei [o'-puss deh'-ee] *L*—The work of God. An organization of Spanish laymen whose members are pledged to carry out the ideals of Catholic philosophy in public as well as private life.

Opus est interprete [o'-puss est in-tehr'-preh-teh] *L*—There is need of an interpreter.

Opus operatum est [o'-puss o-peh-rah'-tuhm est] *L*—The work is done.

Opus postumum [o'-puss pos'-tuh-muhm] *L*—A work published after the author's death.

O quam cito transit gloria mundi! [oh kwahm kih'-toh trahn'-sit gloh'-rih-ah muhn'-dee] *L*—Oh, how quickly the glory of the world passes! *See also* Sic transit gloria mundi. Thomas à Kempis, *The Imitation of Christ,* 1; 3, 6.

Ora e sempre [oh'-rah ay sem'-pray] *It*—Now and forever.

Ora et labora [oh'-rah et lah-boh'-rah] *L*—Pray and work. The motto of the Benedictines.

Ora pro nobis [oh'-rah pro noh'-beess] *L*—Pray for us.

Orate, fratres [oh-rah'-teh frah'-trays] *L*—Pray, brethren.

Orator fit, poeta nascitur [oh-rah'-tohr fit poh-ay'-tah nahs'-kih-tuhr] *L*—Training and education produce the orator, but the poet is born a poet. *See also* Poeta nascitur, non fit.

Orbis terrarum [or'-bis tehr-rah'-ruhm] *L*—The circle of the earth; the whole world.

Ordines majores [or'-dih-nays mah-yoh'-rays] *L*—Major orders: subdiaconate, diaconate, priesthood, and episcopate.

Ordines minores [or'-dih-nays mih-noh'-rays] *L*—Minor orders: offices of porter, lector, exorcist and acolyte in the Catholic Church.

Oremus [oh-ray'-muhs] *L*—Let us pray.

Ore rotundo [oh'-reh roh-tuhn'-doh] *L—*Polished, well-rounded speech. Horace, *Art of Poetry*, 323.

Oro è che oro vale [oh'-roh eh kay oh'-roh vah'-lay] *It—*That is gold which is worth gold.

Oro y plata [oh'-roh ee plah'-tah] *Sp—*Gold and silver. Motto of Montana.

O rus, quando ego te aspiciam? [oh rooss kwahn'-doh eh'-goh tay ah-spih'-kih-ahm] *L—*O peace of the countryside, when shall I behold thee again? Horace, *Satires*, 2; 6, 60.

O sancta simplicitas! [oh sahnk'-tah sihm-plih'-sih-tahs] *L—*O holy simplicity! Words reportedly uttered by Huss on seeing a pious old woman add a fagot to the fire when he was being burned for heresy.

O. S. B. Ordo Sancti Benedicti [or'-doh sahnk'-tee beh-neh-dik'-tee] *L—*Order of St. Benedict.

Osculum pacis [ohs'-kuh-luhm pah'-kiss] *L—*Kiss of peace, a ceremonial salute formerly restricted to use among the ministers of a High Mass. Currently the faithful exchange greetings. The practice can be traced to the 2nd century.

O. S. F. C. Ordo Sancti Francisci Capuccinorum [or'-doh sahnk'-tee frahn-siss'-see kah-puh-sih-noh'-ruhm]*L—*Order of the Capuchin Franciscans.

O, si sic omnia [oh see seek om'-nih-ah] *L—*Would that he had always acted in this way.

O solitudo, sola beatitudo [oh soh-lih-too'-doh soh'-lah beh-ah-tih-too'-doh] *L—*O solitude, the only happiness. The ideal of the recluse. Saint Bernard.

o. s. p. *See* Obiit sine prole.

Ossa atque pellis totus est [os'-sah aht'-kweh pel'-liss toh'-tuhs est] *L—*He is all skin and bones. Plautus, *The Pot of Gold*, 3; 6, 28.

OTAN Organisation du Traité d'Atlantique Nord [or-gah-nee-zah-syohN dü treh-tay daht-lahN-teek nohr] *Fr—*North Atlantic Treaty Organization, NATO.

O tempora, o mores! [oh tem'-po-rah oh moh'-rays] *L—*Oh, the times, oh the customs! Cicero is denouncing the degeneracy of his day. Cicero, *1 Against Catiline*, 1.

Otia dant vitia [oh'-tih-ah dahnt wih'-tih-ah] *L—*Leisure makes for vice.

Otium cum dignitate [oh'-tih-uhm kuhm dihg-nih-tah'-teh] *L—*Leisure with dignity. Cicero, *For P. Sextius*, 45.

Otium sine dignitate [oh'-tih-uhm sih'-neh dihg-nih-tah'-teh] *L—*Leisure without dignity.

Otium sine litteris mors est [oh'-tih-uhm sih'-neh liht'-teh-reess mors est] *L—*Leisure with nothing to read is death. Seneca, *Letters to Lucilius*, 52; 3.

Ottava rima [ot-tah'-vah ree'-mah] *It—*A stanza of eight iambic lines, the first six rhyming alternately, the last two forming a couplet.

Oublier je ne puis [oo-blee-ay zhuh nuh pwee] *Fr—*I cannot forget.

Où la chèvre est attaché, il faut qu'elle broute [oo lah sheh-vr eh tah-tah-shay eel foh kel broot] *Fr—*The goat must browse where she is tied up; one must make the best of a situation.

Outre mer [oo-tr mehr] *Fr—*Beyond the sea; therefore, foreign lands. Longfellow wrote a book with this title.

Ouvrage de longue haleine [oo-vrahzh duh lohNg ah-lehn] *Fr—*Literally, a work of deep breath; a work involving long labor.

Oxon. Oxoniensis [ox-on-ih-en'-siss] *L—*Noted after degrees granted by Oxford University.

Oyer and terminer [oh-yehr and tehr-mee-nay] *Anglo-Fr—*To hear and settle. Applied to a superior court for the hearing of a criminal trial.

Oyez! [oh-yay, but in court oh-yess] *Anglo-Fr—*Hear ye! A cry used in court to gain attention. It is generally called out three times.

P

p. A. per Adresse [per ah-dres'-suh] *Ger*— In care of.

Pace in terra [pah'-chay een tehr'-rah] *It*—Peace on earth.

Pacem in Maribus [pah'-kehm in mah'-rih-buhs] *L*—Peace on the Seas, an international conference held on Malta in 1970 that attempted to find answers to problems concerning wealth in the world's oceans.

Pace tanti nominis [pah'-keh tahn'-tee noh'-mih-niss] *L*—With due respect for so great a name.

Pace tanti viri [pah'-keh tahn'-tee wih'-ree] *L*—With due respect for so great a man.

Pace tua [pah'-keh tuh'-ah] *L*—By your leave; saving your presence.

Pacta conventa [pahk'-tah kon-ven'-tah] *L*—Conditions agreed upon in a diplomatic arrangement.

Pactum de non petendo [pahk'-tuhm day nohn peh-ten'-doh] *L*—An agreement not to sue.

p. ae., part. aeq., p. e. partes aequales [pahr'-tayss I-kwah'-layss] *L*—In equal parts.

Pagan a veces los justos por los pecadores [pah'-gahn ah vay'-says lohs hoos'-tohs por lohs pay-kah-dohr'-ays] *Sp*—Sometimes the just pay for the wicked.

Pain bénit [paN bay-nee] *Fr*—Blessed, not consecrated, bread, distributed at mass to the faithful who have not received Holy Communion. A regional practice in France.

Paix fourrée [peh foo-ray] *Fr*—Sham, false peace.

Paix sur la terre [peh sür lah tehr] *Fr*—Peace on earth.

Pallida Mors aequo pulsat pede pauperum tabernas regumque turris [pahl'-lih-dah mors I'-kwoh puhl-saht peh'-deh pow'-peh-ruhm tah-behr'-nahs ray-guhm'-kweh tuhr'-reess] *L*—Pale death strikes impartially at the hovels of the poor and the towers of kings. Horace, *Odes*, 1; 4, 13.

Palmam qui meruit ferat [pahl'-mahm kwee meh'-ruh-it feh'-raht] *L*—Let him who won the prize bear it away. Motto of Lord Nelson.

Palmes académiques [pahlm ah-kah-day-meek] *Fr*—Decoration conferred by the French Ministry of Public Instruction for notable service in the field of education.

Panem et circenses [pah'-nehm et kihr-kayn'-sayss] *L*—Bread and the circuses. The cry of the Roman mob for food and entertainment. Juvenal, 10; 81.

Pange, lingua, gloriosi [pahn'-jay ling'-gwah glo-rih-oh'-see] *L*—Sing, O my tongue, the glorious. The first words of two medieval hymns, one generally attributed to Fortunatus (6th century) and the second to Thomas Aquinas (13th century), sung on the feast of Corpus Christi (*q.v.*).

Panis angelicus [pah'-niss ahn-je'-lih-kuhs] *L*—Literally, bread of angels. A short hymn taken from a longer hymn by Thomas Aquinas, sung at matins on the Feast of Corpus Christi.

Panta agan [pahn'-tah ah'-gahn] *Gr*—Everything in excess; adapted from meden agan (*q. v.*) and intended to convey the spirit of youth. Will Durant, *The Pleasures of Philosophy*, p. 399.

Panta rei (rhei) [pahn'-tah reh] *Gk*—Everything is in a state of flux. Heraclitus.

Panton metron anthropos estin [pahn'-tohn met'-ron an'-throh-poss es-tin'] *Gk*—Man is the measure of all things. Quoted by Plato, *Theaetetus*, 178b.

Papier mâché [pah-pyay mah-shay] *Fr*—Paper pulp shaped into various forms which are hardened with glue and other additives.

Par accès [pahr ahk-seh] *Fr*—By fits and starts.

Para mí solo nació Don Quixote, y yo para él [pah'-rah mee soh'-loh nah-syoh' dohn kee-hoh'-tay ee yoh pah'-rah ehl] *Sp*—Don Quixote was born for me alone and I for him. The reason Cervantes gave for taking his hero to the grave. Cervantes, *Don Quixote*, 2; last chap.

Para todo hay remedio si no es para la muerte [pah'-rah toh'-doh ah'-ee ray-may'-dyoh see noh ess pah'-rah lah mwehr'-tay] *Sp*—There's a remedy for everything except death. Cervantes, *Don Quixote*, 2; 43.

Par avance [pahr ah-vahNss] *Fr*—Beforehand; in advance.

par avion [pahr ah-vyohN] *Fr*—By air mail.

Parbleu! [pahr-bluh] *Fr*—Of course! certainly. An expletive derived from *par Dieu*, by God.

Parcere subjectis et debellare superbos [pahr'-keh-reh suhb-yehk'-tees et day-bel-lah'-reh suh-pehr'-bohs] *L*—To spare the lowly and humble the proud. The aim of Roman conquest. Vergil, *Aeneid*, 6; 853.

Par ci, par là [pahr see pahr lah] *Fr*—Here and there.

Par complaisance [pahr kohN-pleh-zahNss] *Fr*—Out of a desire to be pleasant or agreeable.

Par dépit [pahr day-pee] *Fr*—Out of spite.

Pardonnez-moi [par-duh-nay-mwah] *Fr*—Excuse me.

Parens patriae [pah'-rayns pah'-trih-I] *L*—Literally, father of the country; a state official paternally taking care of the interests of persons without parents or guardians or of those incapable of conducting their affairs.

Pares autem cum paribus, vetere proverbio, facillime congregantur [pah'-rays ow'-tem kuhm pah'-rih-buhs weh'-teh-reh pro-wehr'-bih-oh fah-kil'-lih-may kon-greh-gahn'-tuhr] *L*—Persons of like interest very readily get together; birds of a feather flock together. Cicero, *Old Age*, 3; 7.

Pares regni [pah'-rays rayg'-nee] *L*—Peers of the realm.

Par excellence [pahr ehk-seh-lahNss] *Fr*—Preeminently.

Par exemple [pahr ehg-zahN-pl] *Fr*—For example.

Parfum de terroir [pahr-fuhN duh tehr-rwahr] *Fr*—The sweet smell of the soil.

Par hasard [pahr ah-zahr] *Fr*—By chance.

Pari delicto [pah'-ree day-leek'-toh] *L*—In equal guilt.

Pari mûtuel [pah-ree mü-twehl] *Fr*—Literally, mutual wager; a system of betting on horses in which the total amount wagered is given the winners less a percentage for the management.

Pari passu [pah'-ree pahs'-soo] *L*—At an equal step or rate; at a like distance; by similar gradation.

Paris vaut bien une messe [pah-ree voh byaN ün mess] *Fr*—Paris is well worth a mass. Attributed to Henry IV of France, a Protestant, who was accused of becoming a convert to Catholicism for reasons of political expediency.

Paritur pax bello [pah'-rih-tuhr pahx bel'-loh] *L*—Peace is born of war. Cornelius Nepos, *Epaminondas*, 5.

Parler à tort et à travers [pahr-lay ah tor ay ah trah-vehr] *Fr*—To speak confusedly, illogically.

Parliamentum Indoctorum [pahr-lih-ah-men'-tuhm in-dok-toh'-ruhm] *L*—The Unlearned Parliament, a name given to sessions held in 1404 when Henry IV of England forbade lawyers to be present.

151

Par negotiis neque supra [pahr neh-go'-tih-eess neh'-kweh suh'-prah] *L*—Equal to his business and not superior to it; a man well fitted for his occupation. Tacitus, *Annals*, 6; 39.

Parole d'honneur [pah-ruhl duh-nuhr] *Fr*—Word of honor.

Par parenthèse [pahr pa-rahN-tehz] *Fr*—By way of parenthesis.

Par pari refero [pahr pah'-ree reh'-feh-roh] *L*—I give back like for like.

Pars pro toto [pahrs proh toh'-toh] *L*—A part for the whole.

Pars rationabilis [pahrs rah-tih-oh-nah'-bih-liss] *L*—That portion of an estate that a husband must reasonably bequeath to his wife and children.

Pars sanitatis velle sanari fuit [pahrs sah-nih-tah'-tiss wel'-leh sah-nah'-ree fuh'-it] *L*—To be cured one must wish to be cured. Seneca, *Hippolytus*, 249.

Part du lion [pahr dü lyohN] *Fr*—The lion's share. In Aesop's fable the lion takes all of the prey as his share.

Partes infidelium *L*—*See* In partibus infidelium.

Parthis mendacior [pahr'-teess men-dah'-kih-ohr] *L*—More deceitful than the Parthians.

Particeps criminis [pahr'-tih-keps kree'-mih-niss] *L*—An accomplice in a crime.

Participes curarum [pahr-tih'-kih-pays koo-rah'-ruhm] *L*—Sharers in trials and troubles.

Partie carrée [pahr-tee kah-ray] *Fr*—Literally, a square party; a pleasure jaunt composed of two couples; double date.

Parti pris [pahr-tee pree] *Fr*—Preconceived opinion; foregone conclusion; a prejudice.

Partir, c'est mourir un peu [pahr-teer seh moo-reer uhN puh] *Fr*—Parting is like dying a little.

Parturiunt montes, nascetur ridiculus mus [pahr-tuh'-rih-uhnt mon'-tays nahs-kay'-tuhr ree-dih'-kuh-luhs moos] *L*—The

mountains are in labor and a ridiculous mouse will be born. Horace, *Art of Poetry*, 139.

Partus sequitur ventrem [pahr'-tuhs seh'-kwih-tuhr wen'-trem] *L*—The offspring follows the status of the mother. Used in Roman law to determine whether a child was free or slave.

Parva leves capiunt mentes [pahr'-wah leh'-ways kah'-pih-uhnt men'-tays] *L*—Little minds are attracted by trifles.

Parvis componere magna [pahr'-weess kom-poh'-neh-reh mahg'-nah] *L*—To compare great things with small. Vergil, *Eclogues*, 1; 23.

Parvum parva decent [pahr'-wuhm pahr'-wah deh'-kent] *L*—Small things become the humble man. Horace, *Epistles*, 1; 7, 44.

Pas à pas [pah zah pah] *Fr*—Step by step.

Pas à pas on va bien loin [pah zah pah ohN vah byaN lwaN] *Fr*—By taking one step at a time one can go far.

Pas de deux [pah duh duh] *Fr*—Dance for two.

Pas de nouvelles, bonnes nouvelles [pah duh noo-vel bun noo-vel] *Fr*—No news is good news.

Pas de rose sans épines [pah duh roz sahN zay-peen] *Fr*—There is no rose without thorns.

Pas du tout [pah dü too] *Fr*—Not at all.

Paso doble [pah'-soh doh'-blay] *Sp*—Two step; rapid march music heard at bullfights.

Paso fino [pah'-soh fee'-noh] *Sp*—Literally, a dainty step. A small horse bred in Puerto Rico.

Passato il pericolo, gabbato il santo [pahs-sah'-toh eel pay-ree'-koh-loh gah-baht'-toh eel sahn'-toh] *It*—Once the danger is past, the saint is forgotten. A proverb cited by Rabelais, *Pantagruel*, 4; 24. *See also* Aegrotat daemon . . .

Pas seul [pah suhl] *Fr*—A dance performed alone.

Pas si bête [pah see beht] *Fr*—Not so stupid.

Passim [pahs'-sim] *L*—Here and there.

Pâté de foie gras [pah-tay duh fwah grah] *Fr*—Patty or paste of fattened goose liver and truffles.

Pater familias [pah'-tehr fah-mih'-lih-ahs] *L*—The head of a household, not necessarily the father.

Pater noster [pah'-tehr nos'-tehr] *L*—Our Father; the first words of the Lord's prayer. Vulgate, *Matthew*, 6; 9.

Pater patriae [pah'-tehr pah'-trih-I] *L*—Father of his country. A title given several great patriots, e.g. Cicero and Washington.

Patientia fit levior ferendo [pah-tih-en'-tih-ah fit leh'-wih-or feh-ren'-doh] *L*—Suffering becomes lighter when borne patiently.

Patres et conscripti [pah'-trays et kohn-skreep'-tee] *L*—All the members of the ancient Roman senate, whether they held office through inheritance, appointment, or previous election to high office.

Patria cara, carior libertas [pah'-trih-ah kah'-rah kah'-rih-or lee-behr'-tahs] *L*—My country is dear, but liberty is dearer.

Patriae quis exsul se quoque fugit? [pah'-trih-I kwis ex'-suhl say kwoh'-kweh foo'-ghit] *L*—What exile from his fatherland can flee himself? Horace, *Odes*, 2; 16, 19.

Patria est ubicumque vir fortis sedem sibi elegerit [pah'-trih-ah est uh-bih-kuhm'-kweh wihr for'-tiss say'-dem sih'-bih ay-lay'-geh-rit] *L*—A brave man's fatherland is wherever he chooses to settle. Q. Curtius Rufus, *Exploits of Alexander*, 6; 4, 11.

Patria potestas [pah'-trih-ah po-tes'-tahs] *L*—The power of a Roman father over the members of his family. At its peak this power extended to life and limb.

Patte de velours [pat duh vuh-loor] *Fr*—The velvet paw; the velvet glove.

Pattes de mouche [pat duh moosh] *Fr*—Fly tracks; small illegible handwriting.

Pauca sed bona [pow'-kah sed bo'-nah] *L*—A few things but good; not quantity but quality.

Paucas pallabris [pow'-kahs pahl-lah'-brees] *L*—A few words. Shakespeare, *Taming of the Shrew*, 1; 1. Christopher Sly's way of saying *Pocas palabras*. He seems to have crossed the Spanish with the Latin Paucis verbis (*q.v.*).

Pauca verba [pow'-kah wehr'-bah] *L*—A few words.

Paucis verbis [pow'-keess wehr'-beess] *L*—In a few words.

Paulum morati/serius aut citius sedem properamus ad unam [pow'-luhm moh-rah'-tee say'-rih-uhs owt kih'-tih-uhs say'-dem pro-peh-rah'-muhs ahd oo'-nahm] *L*—After a slight delay, sooner or later we hasten to one and the same abode. Ovid, *Metamorphoses*, 10; 32.

Pauvre diable! [poh-vr dyah-bl] *Fr*—Poor fellow!

Pax Britannica [pahx brih-tahn'-nih-kah] *L*—British peace, referring to Great Britain's former extended control over colonies.

Pax ecclesiae (Dei) [pahx ek-klay'-sih-ay deh'-ee] *L*—Peace of the Church (of God). An effort on the part of the medieval church in 11th-century France to protect noncombatants, church property, farm stock, and tools from the ravages of war by excommunicating offenders.

Pax in bello [pahx in bel'-loh] *L*—Peace in war; a war conducted with restraint or incompetence.

Pax orbis terrarum [pahx or'-bis tehr-rah'-ruhm] *L*—The peace of the world. Inscribed on Roman coins.

Pax Romana [pahx roh-mah'-nah] *L*—Roman peace, a peace dictated by strength of Roman arms.

Pax tecum [pahx tay'-kuhm] *L*—Peace be with you. When spoken to more than one person, *Pax vobiscum.*

Pax vobiscum [pahx voh-bis'-kuhm] *L*—Peace be with you.

Paz en la tierra [pahs en lah tyay'-rah] *Sp*—Peace on earth.

P. C. pondus civile [pohn'-duhs kee-wee'-leh] *L*—Avoirdupois.

p. c. post cibum [post kih'-buhm] *L*—After food. A medical direction.

P. C. I. partito comunista italiano [pahr-tee'-toh koh-moo-nees'-tah ee-tah-lee-ah'-noh] *It*—Italian Communist party.

P. D. Privatdozent [pree-vaht-dots-ent'] *Ger*—A teacher in a German university who receives student fees but no salary.

P. D. A. pour dire adieu [poor deer ah-dyuh] *Fr*—To say good-bye. Formerly written on personal cards when one had to leave town without having an opportunity to call on friends.

Peau d'âne [poh dahn] *Fr*—Skin of an ass.

Peau de chagrin [poh duh sha-graN] *Fr*—Shagreen skin. People who sat on this skin were granted their wishes, but the years of their lives were decreased by each wish. The title of a novel by Balzac.

Pecca fortiter [pek'-kah for'-tih-tehr] *L*—Sin bravely. Luther's advice has disturbed many. However, it must be taken in its context, for he goes on to command that one should believe and rejoice in Christ more confidently still.

Peccavi [pek-kah'-wee] *L*—I have sinned. In 1843, when Sir Charles Napier defeated the amirs of Sind in two decisive battles, he sent this punning message to his government.

Pecunia non olet [peh-koo'-nih-ah nohn oh'-let] *L—See* Non olet.

Pede claudo [peh'-deh klow'-doh] *L*—With limping foot. Punishment is represented as traveling slowly behind the criminal but rarely failing to overtake him. Horace, *Odes*, 3; 2, 32.

Pedibus timor addidit alas [peh'-dih-buhs tih'-mor ahd'-dih-dit ah'-lahs] *L*—Fear adds wings to one's feet. Vergil, *Aeneid*, 8; 224.

Peine forte et dure [pehn fort ay dür] *Fr*—Strong, severe punishment inflicted upon criminals who refused to plead. They were pressed under heavy weights until they complied or suffered death. In 1772, England abolished pressing to death.

Pendente lite [pen-den'-teh lee'-teh] *L*—While the litigation is pending.

Penetralia mentis [peh-neh-trah'-lih-ah men'-tiss] *L*—The secret depths or recesses of the mind.

Pensano gl'innamorati che gli altri siano ciechi [pen'-sah-noh leen-nah-moh-rah'-tee kay lyee ahl'-tree see'-ah-noh chay'-kee] *It*—Lovers think that other people are blind.

Pensée fait la grandeur de l'homme [pahN-say feh lah grahN-duhr duh luhm] *Fr*—The greatness of man lies in his power to think.

Per accidens [pehr ahk'-kih-dayns] *L*—Accidentally, not essentially. Opposite of Per se (*q.v.*).

Per ambages [pehr ahm-bah'-gayss] *L*—By circumlocution; beating around the bush.

Per angusta ad augusta [pehr ahn-guhs'-tah ahd ow-guhs'-tah] *L*—Through trials to grandeur.

Per annum [pehr ahn'-nuhm] *L*—By the year.

Per ardua ad astra [pehr ahr'-duh-ah ahd ahs'-trah] *L*—Through hardship to the stars. Motto of the British Royal Air Force.

Per ascensum ab imis [pehr ah-skayn'-suhm ahb ee'-meess] *L*—By ascent from the depths.

Per bacco [pehr bahk-koh] *It*—By Bacchus. A mild oath.

Per capita [pehr ka'-pih-tah] *L*—For each person; share and share alike; by individuals; by the head.

Per consequens [pehr kohn'-seh-kwayns] *L*—Consequently.

Per contante [pehr kon-tahn'-tay] *It*—For cash.

Percontatorem fugito, nam garrulus idem est [pehr-kohn-tah-toh'-rem fuh'-gih-toh nahm gahr'-ruh-luhs ee'-dehm est]

L—Avoid an inquisitive man, for he is certain to be a gossip. Horace, *Epistles*, 1; 18, 69.

Per conto [pehr kon'-toh] *It*—A payment on account.

Per contra [pehr kohn'-trah] *L*—On the contrary; on the other hand.

Per curiam [pehr koo'-rih-ahm] *L*—By the whole court.

Percussu crebro saxa cavantur aquis [pehr-kuhs'-soo kray'-broh sahx'-ah kah-wahn'-tuhr ah'-kweess] *L*—Stones are hollowed out by constant dripping of water. Ovid, *Epistles from Pontus*, 2; 7, 40. *See also* Gutta cavat lapidem . . .

Per diem [pehr dih'-ehm] *L*—By the day.

Pereant qui ante nos nostra dixerunt [peh'-reh-ahnt kwee ahn'-teh nohs nos'-trah deex-ay'-ruhnt] *L*—Damned be those who uttered our ideas before us. A whimsical parallel to the statement that there is nothing new under the sun. Donatus. *See also* Nil dictum quod non dictum prius.

Père de famille [pehr duh fa-mee] *Fr*—Father of a family.

Père du peuple [pehr dü puh-pl] *Fr*—Father of the People, a name given the French King Louis XII by his grateful subjects.

Pereunt et imputantur [pehr'-eh-uhnt et im-puh-tahn'-tuhr] *L*—The hours are lost and are charged against us. An inscription on sundials.

Per fas et (aut) nefas [pehr fahs et, owt, neh'-fahs] *L*—Through right and (or) wrong.

Perfecta aetas [pehr-fehk'-tah I'-tahs] *L*—The age at which a person attains his majority.

Perfervidum ingenium Scotorum [pehr-fehr'-wih-duhm in-geh'-nih-uhm skoh-toh'-ruhm] *L*—The glowing ardor or earnestness of the Scots.

Per gradus [pehr grah'-dooss] *L*—Step by step.

Periculum in mora [peh-ree'-kuh-luhm in moh'-rah] *L*—There is danger in delay.

Peritis in sua arte credendum [peh-ree'-teess in suh'-ah ahr'-teh kray-den'-duhm] *L*—The skilled should be trusted in their own area of competence.

Perjuria ridet amantium Juppiter [pehr-yoo'-rih-ah ree'-det ah-mahn'-tih-uhm yuhp'-pih-tehr] *L*—At lovers' perjuries Jove laughs, to use Shakespeare's translation in *Romeo and Juliet*, 2; 2, 92. *Tibullus*, 3; 6, 49.

Per mare, per terras [pehr mah'-reh pehr ter'-rahs] *L*—By sea and land.

Per mensem [pehr mayn'-sehm] *L*—By the month.

Per mese [pehr may'-say] *It*—By the month.

Per minas [pehr mih'-nahs] *L*—By threats.

Permissu superiorum [pehr-miss'-soo suh-peh-rih-oh'-ruhm] *L*—With the permission of superiors. This or similar expressions are found at the beginning of Catholic books indicating that the doctrine is in conformity with the teachings of the Church. *See also* Imprimatur; Imprimi permittitur; Imprimi potest; Nihil obstat.

Permitte divis cetera [pehr-mit'-teh dee'-weess kay'-teh-rah] *L*—Leave everything else to the gods. Horace, *Odes*, 1; 9, 9.

Per nefas [pehr neh'-fahs] *L*—In error; through a misinterpretation.

Per omnia saecula fama . . . vivam [pehr om'-nih-ah sI'-kuh-lah fah'-mah wee'-wahm] *L*—My fame shall survive through all the ages. Ovid, *Metamorphoses*, 15; 878f.

Per os [pehr ohs] *L*—Through the mouth. A medical direction about the method of administering medication.

Per pares [pehr pah'-rayss] *L*—By one's peers.

Perpetuum mobile [pehr-peh'-tuh-uhm moh'-bih-leh] *L*—Perpetual motion.

Per piacere [pehr pee-ah-chay'-ray] *It*—Please.

Per più strade si va a Roma [pehr pee-oo' strah'-day see vah ah roh'-mah] *It—* You can go to Rome by many roads.

per proc., per pro *L—See* Per procurationem, per procuratorem.

Per procurationem [pehr proh-koo-rah-tih-oh'-nem] *L—*By an agency; by proxy.

Per procuratorem [pehr proh-koo-rah-toh'-rem] *L—*By an agent; by proxy.

Per saltum [pehr sahl'-tuhm] *L—*By a leap; in a sudden advance.

Per se [pehr say] *L—*By, in, or of itself.

Persona grata [pehr-soh'-nah grah'-tah] *L—*In diplomatic usage a person acceptable in the country to which he is assigned.

Persona non grata [pehr-soh'-nah nohn grah'-tah] *L—*An unacceptable person.

Per stirpes [pehr stihr'-payss] *L—*Through a direct line of descent.

Per totam curiam [pehr toh'-tahm koo'-rih-ahm] *L—*By the whole court; a unanimous decision.

Pertusum quicquid infunditur in dolium perit [pehr-too'-suhm kwik'-kwid in-fuhn'-dih-tuhr in doh'-lih-uhm peh'-rit] *L—*All is lost that is put in a riven dish.

Per veritatem vis [pehr way-rih-tah'-tem weess] *L—*Power through truth.

Petit à petit, fait l'oiseau son nid [puh-tee ah puh-tee feh lwah-zoh sohn nee] *Fr—* Little by little the bird builds its nest.

Petit bourgeois [puh-tee boor-zhwah] *Fr—*A French citizen of the lower middle class.

Petit chaudron, grandes oreilles [puh-tee shoh-drohN grahNd oh-reh-yuh] *Fr—* Little pitchers have big ears; little children have keen hearing.

Petite pièce [puh-teet pyess] *Fr—*A minor theatrical production.

Petites gens [puh-teet zhahN] *Fr—*People of small means; people of no importance from the aristocratic point of view.

Petites morales [puh-teet mo-rahl] *Fr—* Small points of politeness and courtesy.

Petitio principii [peh-tee'-tih-oh preen-kih'-pih-ee] *L—*Begging the question.

Petit maître [puh-tee meh-tr] *Fr—*Fop; dandy.

Petit mal [puh-tee mal] *Fr—*A mild epileptic attack; a mild nervous disorder characterized by dizziness or a brief period of unconsciousness.

Petit nom [puh-tee nohN] *Fr—*Pet name, first name.

Petits jeux [puh-tee zhuh] *Fr—*Literally, little games; social games.

Petit souper [puh-tee soo-pay] *Fr—*An informal, light supper for a small number of people after an evening's entertainment.

Peu à peu [puh ah puh] *Fr—*Little by little.

Peu d'hommes ont été admirés par leurs domestiques [puh duhm ohN tay-tay ahd-mee-ray pahr luhr duh-mehs-teek] *Fr—*Few men have been admired by their servants. Montaigne, *Essays*, 3; 2.

P. F. S. A. pour faire ses adieux [poor fehr say zah dyuh] *Fr—*To say good-bye; written on a card to indicate that one is to be absent from the city for a time.

Phi Beta Kappa [fih-loh-so-fee'-ah bee'-oo kü-behr-nay'-tays] *Gk—*Greek letters of the oldest Greek-letter fraternity, signifying *Philosophia biou kubernetes*, philosophy is the guide of life.

Philosophia ancilla theologiae [fih-lo-so'-fih-ah ahn-kil'-lah teh-oh-lo'-gih-I; in practice *philosophia* and *theologia* are accented on the penultimate syllable, following the Greek pronunciation] *L—*Philosophy the handmaid of theology. This assessment of philosophy's role according to the Scholastics has disturbed many philosophers.

Phtheirousin ethe chresth' homiliai kakai [ftheh'-roo-sin ay'-thay khraysth ho-mih-lee'-I kah-kI'] *Gk—*Evil communications corrupt good manners. Menander, *Thais. See also* Corrumpunt bonos mores . . .

Pia fraus [pih'-ah frowss] *L—*A well-intended deception or fraud. Adapted from Ovid, *Metamorphoses*, 9; 711.

Pictoribus atque poetis/quidlibet audendi semper fuit aequa potestas [peektoh'-rih-buhs aht'-kweh po-ay'-teess kwid'-lih-bet ow-den'-dee sem'-pehr fuh'-it I'-kwah po-tes'-tahs] *L*—Painters and poets have always had an equal right to experiment. Horace, *Art of Poetry*, 9.

Pièce à thèse [pyess ah tehz] *Fr*—A play with a thesis, aiming to teach rather than entertain.

Pièce de résistance [pyess duh ray-zees-tahNss] *Fr*—The principal dish of a meal; the principal article on display.

Pièce d'occasion [pyess duh-ka-zyohN] *Fr*—A play written for a special occasion.

Pièces à conviction [pyess zah kohN-veek-syohN] *Fr*—Objects to support conviction; exhibits offered as evidence.

Pied à terre! [pyay tah tehr] *Fr*—Dismount! As a noun, a temporary or small lodging.

Pied-noir *pl.* **pieds-noirs** [pyay-nwahr] *Fr*—Literally, blackfoot. European inhabitants of the former French colony of Algeria, many of whom took up residence in France at the time of Algerian independence.

Pierre qui roule n'amasse pas mousse [py-ehr kee rool nah-mahss pah mooss] *Fr* —A rolling stone gathers no moss.

Pietra mossa non fa muschio [pee-ay'-trah moss'-sah nonn fah moos'-kee-oh] *It* —A rolling stone gathers no moss.

Pinxit [pinx'-it] *L*—He painted it. Noted on paintings with the name of the artist. Sometimes abbreviated by omitting the vowels.

Pis-aller [pee-zah-lay] *Fr*—Last resort.

Pisces natare docere [pihs'-kayss nah-tah'-reh do-kay'-reh] *L*—To teach fish to swim; to carry coals to Newcastle.

Pithecanthropus erectus [pith-ay-kahn'-throh-puss ay-rayk'-tuhs] *NL*—Literally, erect monkey man; the supposed immediate ancestor of homo sapiens (*q.v.*).

Più che il martello dura l'incudine [pee-oo' kay eel mahr-tell'-loh doo'-rah leen-koo'-dee-nay] *It*—The anvil outlasts the hammer.

Più tengono a memoria gli uomini le ingiurie che li beneficii ricevuti [pee-oo' tehn'-goh-noh ah may-moh'-ree-ah lyee woh'-mee-nee lay een-joo'-ree-ay kay lee bay-nay-fee'-chee-ee ree-chay-voo'-tee] *It*—Men are more likely to remember the injuries than the benefits received. Guicciardini.

Piuttosto mendicante che ignorante [pee-oot-toss'-toh men-dee-kahn'-tay kay een-yoh-rahn'-tay] *It*—Better to be a beggar than an ignoramus.

Place aux dames! [plass oh dam] *Fr*—Make way for the ladies; ladies first!

Placebo [plah-kay'-boh; in common usage plah-see'-bo] *L*—Literally, I shall please; in medicine, a prescription given to please a patient who in the physician's opinion needs no medication. The first word in an antiphon sung at Vespers in the Office of the Dead.

Place d'armes [plass dahrm] *Fr*—Parade ground.

Placet [plah'-set] *L*—It is pleasing. An affirmative vote.

Plat du jour [plah dü zhoor] *Fr*—The dish or meal of the day.

Plaza de toros [plah'-sah day toh'-rohs] *Sp*—Stadium where bullfights are held.

Plene administravit [play'-nay ahd-mih-nis-trah'-wit] *L*—He carried out his duties completely. A plea entered when an executor or an administrator has completely accounted for property under his control.

Pleno jure [play'-noh yoo'-reh] *L*—With full right or authority.

P. L. I. partito liberale italiano [pahr-tee'-toh lee-bay-rah'-lay ee-tah-lee-ah'-noh] *It*—Italian Liberal party.

Plus ça change, plus c'est la même chose [plü sah shahNzh plü seh lah mem shohz] *Fr*—The more it is changed, the more it is the same thing.

Plus dolet quam necesse est, qui ante dolet quam necesse est [ploos doh'-let kwahm neh-kes'-seh est kwee ahn'-teh doh'-let kwahm neh-kes'-seh est] *L*—He who grieves before he has cause, grieves more than he need. Seneca, *Letters to Lucilius*, 98; 8.

Plus fait douceur que violence [plü feh doo-suhr kuh vyoh-lahNss] *Fr*—Kindness gains more than violence.

Plus je vois les hommes, plus j'admire les chiens [plü zhuh vwah lay zuhm plü zhahd-meer lay shyaN] *Fr*—The more I see of people, the better I like dogs.

Plus royaliste que le roi [plü rwah-yah-leest kuh luh rwah] *Fr*—More of a royalist than the king himself.

Plus sages que les sages [plü sahzh kuh lay sahzh] *Fr*—Wiser than the wise.

P. M. post meridiem [post meh-ree'-dih-ehm] *L*—Afternoon; from noon to midnight.

Poco a poco [poh'-koh ah poh'-koh] *Sp-It*—Little by little.

Poesía gauchesca [poh-ay-see'-ah gow-chess'-kah] *Sp*—Gaucho poetry of Argentina sung by a cowboy to the accompaniment of the guitar. Regarded as the indigenous literature of Spanish America.

Poeta nascitur, non fit [po-ay'-tah nahs'-kih-tuhr nohn fit] *L*—A poet is born, not made. *See also* Nascimur poetae, fimus or atores.

Point d'appui [pwaN dap-pwee] *Fr*—Point of support; fulcrum; a basis of military operations.

Point d'argent, point de Suisses [pwaN dahr-zhahN pwaN duh swees] *Fr*—No money, no Swiss. The Swiss here referred to were mercenaries who would not serve in a foreign army without pay. Racine, *Les Plaideurs*, 1; 1.

Point de repère [pwaN duh ruh-pehr] *Fr*—Reference or guide mark used in returning to a spot or in rechecking or repeating a process.

Poisson d'avril [pwah-sohN dah-vreel] *Fr*—Literally, fish of April; French equivalent of April fool.

Pollice verso *L*—*See* Verso pollice.

Pomme de terre [puhm duh tehr] *Fr*—Potato.

Pomum Adami [poh'-muhm ah'-dah-mee] *L*—Adam's apple, a thyroid projection in the neck of many men. There is a pretty story to the effect that Eve's apple stuck in Adam's throat.

Pondere non numero [pohn'-deh-reh nohn nuh'-meh-roh] *L*—By weight, not by number.

Pons asinorum [pohnss ah-sih-noh'-ruhm] *L*—Bridge of asses; in Euclid's geometry, the fifth proposition of Book I; generally, a stumbling block for the less talented; a problem that the dull cannot understand.

Pontifex maximus [pon'-tih-fex max'-ih-muhs] *L*—High priest in ancient Rome.

Populus vult decipi [po'-puh-luhs wuhlt day'-kih-pee] *L*—The people want to be deceived. Attributed to a legate of Pope Paul IV who is reported to have said that the people of Paris wished to be deceived. "Let them be deceived and go to the devil," he added.

Por favor [pohr fah-vohr'] *Sp*—Please.

Por mayor [por mah-yor'] *Sp*—Wholesale prices.

Porro unum est necessarium [pohr'-roh oo'-nuhm est neh-ses-sah'-rih-uhm] *L*—Only one thing is necessary. Matthew Arnold used the words of Christ to the complaining Martha as a title for an essay. *Vulgate, Luke* 10; 42.

Posse comitatus [pos'-seh koh-mih-tah'-tooss] *L*—Literally, the power of the county. The power of a sheriff to gather forces to preserve law and order.

Possunt quia posse videntur [pos'-suhnt kwih'-ah pos'-seh wih-den'-tuhr] *L*—They can because they think they can. Vergil, *Aeneid*, 5; 231.

Post bellum auxilium [post bel'-luhm owk-sih'-lih-uhm] *L*—Help after the war; useless aid that comes after the battle is over.

Post cineres gloria sera venit [post kih'-neh-rayss gloh'-rih-ah say'-rah weh'-nit] *L*—Fame comes too late when one is ashes. Martial, 1; 25, 8.

Poste restante [puhst reh-stahNt] *Fr*—The department of a post office where mail is held until called for; general delivery.

Post hoc; ergo propter hoc [post hok ehr'-goh prohp'-ter hok] *L*—Literally, after this; therefore because of it. The fallacy of arguing that something is the effect of a certain cause when there is no certain connection. What is considered an effect may only be a subsequent event.

Post judicium [post yoo-dih'-kih-uhm] *L* —After the judgment; following a decision.

Post litem motam [post lee'-tem moh'-tahm] *L*—After the beginning of litigation.

Post meridiem *L*—*See* p.m.

Post mortem [post mohr'-tem] *L*—After death. An examination of a corpse to determine the cause of death.

post-obit. *See* Post obitum.

Post obitum [post oh'-bih-tuhm] *L*—After death.

Post partum [post pahr'-tuhm] *L*—After birth.

Post proelia praemia [post proi'-lih-ah prI'-mih-ah] *L*—After battles come rewards.

Post tenebras lux [post teh'-neh-brahss loox] *L*—After the darkness the dawn.

Potage au gras [puh-tahzh oh grah] *Fr*—Meat soup.

Potest quis per alium quod potest facere per seipsum [po-test kwis pehr ah'-lih-uhm kwod po'-test fah'-keh-reh pehr say-ip'-suhm] *L*—One can do through another what one can do himself. A legal maxim.

Potior est conditio possidentis [po'-tih-or est kon-dih'-tih-oh pos-sih-den'-tis] *L* —The possessor is in a stronger position; possession is nine points of the the law.

Pour acquit [poor ah-kee] *Fr*—Payment received; paid.

Pour épater les bourgeois [poor ay-pa-tay lay boor-zhwah] *Fr*—To shock the narrow-minded.

Pour faire rire [poor fehr reer] *Fr*—To raise a laugh.

Pour l'amour de Dieu! [poor lah-moor duh dyuh] *Fr*—Literally, for the love of God. For heaven's sake!

Pour le mérite [poor luh may-reet] *Fr*—For merit; the highest decoration in Germany.

Pour passer le temps [poor pass-say luh tahN] *Fr*—To pass away the time.

Pour prendre congé [poor prahN-dr kohN-zhay] *Fr*—To take leave of someone. *See also* P.F.S.A.

Pour rire [poor reer] *Fr*—In jest; as a joke.

Povero come un topo di chiesa [poh'-vay-roh koh'-may oon toh'-poh dee kee-ay'-zah] *It*—Poor as a church mouse.

Pozhaluysta [pah-zhahl'-oo-ees-tah] *Rus*—Please. A shorter form [pah-zhahl'-stah].

p. p. praemissis praemittendis [prI-mihs'-seess prI-mit-ten'-deess] *L*—Omitting preliminaries.

P. P. C. *Fr*—*See* Pour prendre congé.

P. P. S. post post-scriptum [post post-skrip'-tuhm] *L*—An additional postscript.

Praemissis praemittendis [prI-mihs'-sees prI-mit-ten'-dees] *L*—Omitting preliminaries.

Praemonitus, praemunitus [prI-moh'-nih-tuhs prI-moo-nee'-tuhs] *L*—Forewarned, forearmed.

Preguntando se llega a Roma [pray-goon-tahn'-doh say yay'-gah ah roh'-mah] *Sp*—One reaches Rome by asking questions.

Prendre la balle au bond [prahN-dr lah bal oh bohN] *Fr*—To catch the ball on the bounce or the rebound; to seize an opportunity.

Prendre la lune avec les dents [prahN-dr lah lün ah-veck lay dahN] *Fr*—To reach for the moon with one's teeth; to aim at impossible goals.

Prenez garde! [pruh-nay gahrd] *Fr*—Take care; watch out!

Presto e bene, non si conviene [press'-toh ay bay'-nay nonn see kon-vee-ay'-nay] *It*—Haste and quality do not go together.

Presto maturo, presto marcio [press'-toh mah-too'-roh press'-toh mahr'-choh] *It*—The sooner ripe, the sooner rotten.

Pretio parata vincitur pretio fides [preh'-tih-oh pah-rah'-tah win'-kih-tuhr preh'-tih-oh fih'-days] *L*—Fidelity won by bribes is lost by bribes. Seneca, *Agamemnon*, 287.

Pretium affectionis [preh'-tih-uhm ahf-fehk-tih-oh'-nis] *L*—The price set by affection; an excessive value placed on an object for sentimental reasons.

Pretium laborum non vile [preh'-tih-uhm lah-boh'-ruhm nohn wee'-leh] *L*—The cost of toil is not slight.

Preux chevalier [pruh shuh-val-yay] *Fr*—Gallant knight.

PRI partido revolucionario institucional [pahr-tee'-doh ray-voh-loo-tee-oh-nah'-ree-oh een-stee-too-tee-oh-nahl'] *Sp*—Institutional Revolutionary party, the party in power in Mexico since the early 1930s.

Prima donna [pree'-mah don'-nah] *It*—The first lady in an opera. The term is often applied to a temperamental person who demands excessive attention.

Prima facie [pree'-mah fah'-kih-ay] *L*—At first glance or preliminary examination.

Primum mobile [pree'-muhm moh'-bih-leh] *L*—The first moving force. In Aristotle's concept of the heavens, the highest sphere, which, through divine power, carried the other nine with it.

Primum non nocere [pree'-muhm nohn noh-kay'-reh] *L*—First of all, do no harm; i.e., take care that the remedy is not worse than the disease. A medical aphorism.

Primum vivere, deinde philosophari [pree'-muhm wee'-weh-reh deh-ihn'-deh fih-lo-so-fah'-ree] *L*—First live, then philosophize.

Primus in orbe deos fecit timor [pree'-muhs in or'-beh deh'-ohs fay'-kit tih'-mor] *L*—Fear first put gods in the world. Statius, *Thebaid*, 3; 661, a line copied from a fragment by Petronius.

Primus inter pares [pree'-muhs in'-tehr pah'-rays] *L*—The first among equals.

Primus motor [pree'-muhs moh'-tor] *L*—In Aristotelian philosophy the first mover; the cause of all movement which is itself unmoved; the divine power.

Principia, non homines [preen-kih'-pih-ah nohn ho'-mih-nayss] *L*—Principles not men. Men prefer government by law rather than by the whims of rulers.

Principiis obsta: sero medicina curatur [preen-kih'-pih-ees op'-stah say'-roh meh-dih-kee'-nah koo-rah'-tuhr] *L*—Resist beginnings: the cure comes too late when ills have gathered strength by long delay. Ovid, *Remedies for Love*, 91.

Prin d'an teleutese, epischeein mede kaleein ko olbion, all' eutychea [prin dahn teh-loi-tay'-say eh-pis-kheh'-en may-deh' kah-leh'-en koh ol'-bee-on al-loi-tü-kheh'-ah] *Gk*—Before a man dies, do not call him happy but lucky. Herodotus, *The Persian Wars*, 1; 32. *See also* Respice finem.

Prior tempore, prior jure [prih'-or tem'-po-reh prih'-or yoo'-reh] *L*—The one who is first has a prior right; first come, first served.

Prius insolentem serva Briseis niveo colore movit Achillem [prih'-uhs in-so-len'-tem sehr'-wah bree-say'-iss nih'-weh-oh ko-loh'-reh moh'wit ah-kil'-lem] *L*—Long ago the slave girl Briseis with her snow-white skin stirred the haughty Achilles. Horace, *Odes*, 2; 4.

Privatum commodum publico cedit [pree-wah'-tuhm kohm'-moh-duhm poo'-blih-koh kay'-dit] *L*—Private advantage gives way to the public good.

Privilège du roi [pree-vee-lehzh dü rwah] *Fr*—License or special favor granted by the king.

Prix fixe [pree feex] *Fr*—A sign often displayed in stores to indicate that prices are set and not subject to reduction.

p. r. n. pro re nata [proh ray nah'-tah] *L*—Whenever necessary. A medical directive.

Pro aris et focis [proh ah'-rees et fo'-kees] *L*—In defense of one's altars and fires; for hearth and home. Cicero, *The Nature of the Gods*, 3; 40.

Probatum est [proh-bah′-tuhm est] *L*—It has been proved.

Probitas laudatur et alget [proh′bih-tahs low-dah′-tuhr et ahl′-get] *L*—Honesty is praised and turned out into the cold; virtue is often commended and thereafter neglected. Juvenal, 1; 74.

Pro bono publico [proh boh′-noh poo′-blih-koh]*L*—For the common good.

Pro captu lectoris habent sua fata libelli [proh kahp′-too layk-toh′ris hah′-bent su′-ah fah′-tah lih-bel′-lee] *L*—The fate of books depends on the discernment of the reader. Often quoted without the first three words. Terentianus Maurus.

Procès-verbal [pruh-seh vehr-bahl] *Fr*—An official report drawn up for a superior, including minutes of a meeting or a record of an official act.

Prochain ami[proh-shan ah-mee]*Fr*—Next friend; in law, one who acts for a person, not sui juris (*q.v.*).

Pro confesso [proh kohn-fes′-soh] *L*—To take something as granted or conceded.

Procul a Jove, procul a fulmine [pro′-kuhl ah yoh′-weh pro′-kuhl ah fuhl′-mih-neh] *L*—To be far from Jove is to be far from his thunder; being far from the throne has its compensations: one may escape the royal anger.

Procul, O procul este profani [pro′-kuhl oh pro′-kuhl ess′-teh proh-fah′-nee] *L*—Away, far away, you profane intruders. Vergil, *Aeneid*, 6; 258.

Procurator bibliothecarum [proh-koo-rah′-tor bib-lih-oh-tay-kah′-ruhm] *L*—Director of libraries.

Pro Deo et ecclesia [proh deh′-oh et ay klay′-sih-ah] *L*—In defense of God and the church.

Pro Deo et patria [proh deh′-oh et pah′-trih-ah] *L*—For God and country.

Prodesse quam conspici [pro-des′-seh kwahm kohn′-spih-kee] *L*—To be of service rather than to be in the limelight.

Pro domo [proh doh′-moh] *L*—In defense of one's home. One of Cicero's orations is entitled *Pro Domo Sua* (In Defense of His Home). Cicero sought damages for his house, destroyed by his enemies after he went into exile.

Pro Ecclesia et Pontifice [proh ay-klay′-sih-ah et pohn-tih′-fih-cheh] *L*—In defense of the Church and the Pope; a papal medal given outstanding laymen.

Pro et con (pro et contra) [proh et kon, proh et kohn′-trah] *L*—For and against.

Profanum vulgus [proh-fah′-nuhm wuhl′-guhs] *L*—*See* Odi profanum . . .

Profits et pertes [pruh-fee zay pehrt] *Fr*—Profit and loss.

Pro forma [proh for′-mah] *L*—As a matter of form. In commercial use an account drawn up to show market value of certain products. In importing, a *pro forma* invoice must sometimes be presented in advance to arrange for payment or permits; it is understood that this preliminary estimate may not be as exact as the actual invoice to be presented later.

Pro hac vice [proh hahk wih′-keh] *L*—For this occasion.

Proh deum atque hominum fidem [proh deh′-uhm aht′-kweh ho′-mih-nuhm fih′-dem] *L*—By my faith in gods and men.

Pro jure contra legem [proh yoo′-reh kohn′-trah lay′-ghem] *L*—For the right against the law.

Promotor fidei [pro-moh′-tor fih′-deh-ee] *L*—Promoter of the faith, serving as advocatus diaboli (*q.v.*).

Promoveatur ut removeatur [pro-mo-weh-ah′-tuhr uht reh-mo-weh-ah′-tuhr] *L*—Let him be promoted that he may be removed. This is the practice of kicking the incompetent upstairs.

Pro mundi beneficio [proh muhn′-dee beh-neh-fih′-kih-oh] *L*—For the benefit of the world. Motto of Panama.

Pro patria per orbis concordiam [proh pah′-trih-ah pehr or′-bis kohn-kor′-dih-ahm] *L*—For the country through world peace. The motto of the Carnegie Endowment for International Peace.

Proprio motu [pro'-prih-oh moh'-too] L—*See* Motu proprio.

Propter affectum [prop'-ter ahf-fek'-tuhm] L—Because of partiality. A reason for challenging a juror or a jury.

Propter defectum sanguinis [prop'-ter day-fek'-tuhm sahn'-gwih-nis] L—On account of defect of blood. The phrase was used in English feudal law when lands reverted to the lord of the fee when inheritance under the original grant was impossible, for example, because of the death of a tenant leaving no heir.

Propter delictum [prop'-ter day-leek'-tuhm] L—Because of a crime; to take exception to a juror's serving because of past crime.

Propter falsos testes [prop'-ter fahl'-sohs tess'-tayss] L—Because of false witnesses, wrong information.

Propter honoris respectum [prop'-ter ho-noh'-ris reh-spek'-tuhm] L—Because of consideration for rank or honor.

Pro (proh) pudor! [proh puh'-dor] L—For shame!

Pro rata [proh rah'-tah] L—In proportion.

Pro ratione aetatis [proh rah-tih-oh'-neh I-tah'-tis] L—In proportion to age.

Pro rege, lege, grege [proh ray'-geh lay'-geh greh'-geh] L—For the king, the law, and the people.

Pro re nata [proh ray nah'-tah] L—For a special emergency; for the consideration of a sudden development.

Pro salute animae [proh sah-loo'-teh ah'-nih-mI] L—For the good of one's soul.

Pro scientia et religione [proh skih-en'-tih-ah et reh-lih-gi-oh'-neh] L—For science and religion.

Pro se quisque [proh say kwis'-kweh] L—Everybody for himself.

Proshu vashego izvynenya [proh-shoo' vah'-she-voh eez-vee-nyeh'-nee-yah] Rus—I beg your pardon.

Prosit [proh'-sit] L—May it profit you; to your health. A toast frequently heard among Germans.

Prosit Neujahr! [pro'-sit noi'-yahr] Ger—Happy New Year!

¡Próspero año nuevo! [prohs'-pay-roh ahn'-yoh nway'-voh] Sp—Happy (prosperous) New Year!

Prospice [proh'-spih-keh] L—Look forward. Title of a poem by Robert Browning.

Pro tanto [proh tahn'-toh] L—As far as it goes; to a certain extent.

pro tem L—*See* Pro tempore.

Pro tempore [proh tem'-po-reh] L—For the time being. Abbreviated *pro tem.*

prox. proximo [prox'-ih-moh] L—Used in correspondence to indicate a date in the month following the one in which the letter is written.

Proxime accessit [prox'-ih-may ahk-kes'-sit] L—*See* Accessit.

Proximo L—*See* Prox.

Prudens quaestio dimidium scientiae [proo'-dayns kwI'-stih-oh dee-mih'-dih-uhm skih-en'-tih-I] L—A thoughtful question is half of discovery.

P. S. Pferdestärke [pfayr'-duh-shtehr'-kuh] Ger—Horsepower.

P. S. post-scriptum [post skrip'-tuhm] L—Postscript.

P. S. D. I. partito socialista democratico italiano [pahr-tee'-toh soh-chah-lee'-stah day-moh-krah'-tee-koh ee-tah-leè-ah'-noh] It—Italian Socialist Democratic party.

Publici juris [poo'-blih-kee yoo'-ris] L—Reference to the right of all men to what is theirs as common possession, such as light and air.

Publicum bonum privato est praeferendum [poo'-blih-kuhm bo'-nuhm pree-wah'-toh est prI-feh-ren'-duhm] L—The public good is to be preferred to the private advantage. Legal maxim.

Puffistes littéraires [pü-feest lee-tay-rehr] Fr—Boasters who puff up literary works in their advertisements.

Pugnis et calcibus [puhg'-neess et kahl'-kih-buhs] L—With fists and feet; with all one's strength.

Pulchrorum autumnus pulcher [puhl-kroh'-ruhm ow-tuhm'-nuhs puhl'-kehr] *L*—The autumn of beautiful persons is beautiful.

Pulvis et umbra (sumus) [puhl'-wis et uhm'-brah, suh'-muhs] *L*—We are but dust and shadow. Horace, *Odes*, 4; 7, 16. R. L. Stevenson wrote a notable essay with this title.

Punctum saliens [puhnk'-tuhm sah'-lih-ayns] *L*—Salient point. In embryos of higher vertebrates the rudiments of the heart; by extension, a starting point or an important feature.

Punica fides [poo'-nih-kah fih'-days] *L*—Punic duplicity. From the Roman point of view Carthaginian promises were assumed to be treacherous. Sallust, *Jugurthine War*, 108.

Punto de honor [poon'-toh day oh-nohr'] *Sp*—Point of honor, contracted to *pundonor;* an excessive concern among the upper classes with keeping one's honor perfectly clean, a theme in the comedy called *Capa y espada* (*q.v.*).

Purpureus . . . pannus [puhr-puh'-reh-uhs pah'-nuhs] *L*—Purple patch; an excessively ornate literary passage, such as an elaborate description, that is out of place. Horace, *Art of Poetry*, 15.

Pur sang [pür sahN] *Fr*—Full-blooded; thoroughbred.

p. v. t. par voie télégraphique [pahr vwah tay-lay-grah-feek] *Fr*—By telegraph.

Q

Q B F S quibus benedicit filius suus [kwih'-buhs beh-neh-dih'-kit fee'-lih-uhs suh'-uhs] *L*—Their son blesses them. A gravestone inscription.

Q. B. S. M. que besa su mano [kay bay'-sah soo mah'-noh] *Sp*—Who kisses your hand. An expression of courtesy, e.g. in closing personal letters.

Q. B. S. P. que besa sus pies [kay bay'-sah soos pyays] *Sp*—Who kisses your feet. An expression of courtesy.

q. d. quaque die [kwah'-kweh dih'-ay] *L*—Every day.

Q. D. D. G. Que de Dios goce [kay day dyohss' goh'-say] *Sp*—May he rejoice in the Lord.

Q. D. G. Que Dios guarde [kay dyohss' gwahr'-day] *Sp*—May God keep him.

Q. E. D. quod erat demonstrandum [kwod eh'-raht day-mohn-strahn'-duhm] *L*—That which was to be demonstrated. Used at the end of theorems in Euclidean geometry to indicate that the proof is complete.

Q. E. F. quod erat faciendum [kwod eh'-raht fah-kih-en'-duhm] *L*—The thing that was to be done.

Q. E. G. E. Que en gloria esté [kay en gloh'-ree-ah ays-tay'] *Sp*—May he be in glory.

Q. E. P. D. Que en paz descanse [kay en pahs days-kahn'-say] *Sp*—May he rest in peace.

Q. G. A. Quartier général d'armée [kahr-tyay zhay-nay-rahl dahr-may] *Fr*—Army headquarters.

Q. G. C. A. Quartier général de corps d'armée [kahr-tyay zhay-nay-rahl duh kor dahr-may] *Fr*—Army corps headquarters.

164

q. h. quaque hora [kwah'-kweh hoh'-rah] *L*—Every hour. A medical direction.

q. i. d. quater in die [kwah'-tehr in dih'-ay] *L*—Four times a day.

q. l. quantum libet [kwahn'-tuhm lih'-bet] *L*—As much as you please.

q. n. quaque nocte [kwah'-kweh nok'-teh] *L*—Every night.

Q. P. quantum placet [kwahn'-tuhm plah'-set] *L*—As much as one wishes. A medical prescription permitting the patient to take as much of the preparation as desired.

q. q. h. quaque quarta hora [kwah'-kweh kwahr'-tah hoh'-rah] *L*—Every fourth hour.

qq. v. *See* Quae vide.

q. s. quantum satis [kwahn'-tuhm sah'-tiss] *L*—As much as is sufficient.

q. s. quantum sufficit [kwahn'-tuhm suhf'-fih-sit] *L*—As much as suffices. A term used on medical prescriptions to indicate that as much of a certain component should be used as is sufficient, a decision left to the pharmacist.

Qua [kwah] *L*—As; in the character or quality of, e.g. the printer *qua* printer is not concerned with the content of the material being printed.

Qua cursum ventus [kwah kuhr'-suhm wen'-tuhs] *L*—Where the wind called our course. The title of a poem by Arthur Hugh Clough. Vergil, *Aeneid*, 3; 269.

Quadrupedante putrem sonitu quatit ungula campum [kwah-druh-peh-dahn'-teh poo'-trem so'-nih-too kwah'-tit uhn'-guh-lah kahm'-puhm] *L*—The horses beat the dusty plain with galloping hoofs. A famous onomatopoetic line. Vergil, *Aeneid*, 8; 596.

Quae fuerunt vitia mores sunt [kwI fuh-ay′-ruhnt wih′-tih-ah moh′-rayss suhnt] *L*— What once were thought vices are now the usual thing. Seneca, *Letters to Lucilius*, 39, last sentence.

Quae in aliis libertas est, in aliis licentia vocatur [kwI in ah′-lih-eess lee-behr′-tahs est in ah′-lih-eess lih-ken′-tih-ah wo-kah′-tuhr] *L*—What in some men is liberty, in others is called license. Quintilian, 3; 8, 3.

Quae nocent docent [kwI no′-kent do′-kent] *L*—What pains us trains us.

Quae regio in terris nostri non plena laboris [kwI reh′-gih-oh in ter′-reess nos′-tree nohn play′-nah lah-boh′-ris] *L*—What place on earth is not filled with our sufferings? Vergil, *Aeneid*, 1; 460.

Quae vide [kwI wih′-day] *L*—Which *(pl)* see; let the reader look up the items referred to elsewhere in the work. Abbreviated *qq.v.*

Qualis artifex pereo! [kwah′-liss ahr′-tih-fex peh′-reh-oh] *L*—What an artist dies with me! Reported to be the last words of Nero. Suetonius, *Nero*, 49.

Qualis rex, talis grex [kwah′-liss rayx tah′-liss grex] *L*—As the shepherd, so the flock.

Qualis vita, finis ita [kwah′-liss wee′-tah fee′-nis ih′-tah] *L*—As a life has been, so will its end be.

Quam difficile est crimen non prodere vultu! [kwahm dif-fih′-kih-leh est kree′-men nohn proh′-deh-reh wuhl′-too] *L*—How difficult it is for the face not to betray guilt! Ovid, *Metamorphoses*, 2; 447.

Quamdiu se bene gesserit [kwahm-dih′-oo say beh′-neh ges′-seh-rit] *L*—As long as he conducts himself well.

Quam primum [kwahm pree′-muhm] *L*— As soon as possible.

Quand celui à qui l'on parle ne comprend pas et celui qui parle ne se comprend pas, c'est de la métaphysique [kahN suh-lwee ah kee lohN pahrl nuh koN-prahN pah ay suh-lwee kee pahrl nuh suh koN-prahN pah seh duh lah may-tah-fee-seek] *Fr*—When the listener does not

understand and the speaker does not understand, then you have metaphysics. Voltaire.

Quand même [kahN mehm] *Fr*—In spite of everything; notwithstanding.

Quando la gatta non v'è, i sorci ballano [kwahn′-doh lah gaht′-tah nonn veh ee sorr′-chee bahl′-lah-noh] *It*—When the cat's away, the mice will play (literally, the mice dance). *See also* Via il gatto . . .

Quand on parle du loup, on en voit la queue [kahN tohN pahrl dü loo oh nahN vwah lah kuh] *Fr*—Talk of the wolf and you will soon see his tail; talk of the devil and he's sure to appear; talk of the devil and his horns will appear.

Quandoque bonus dormitat Homerus [kwahn-doh′-kweh bo′-nuhs dor-mee′-taht ho-may′-ruhs] *L—See* Indignor quandoque . . .

Quantula sapientia regitur mundus! [kwahn′-tuh-lah sah-pih-en′-tih-ah ray′-gih-tuhr muhn′-duhs] *L*—What little wisdom is shown in the government of the world.

Quantum est quod nescimus! [kwahn′-tuhm est kwod nehs′-kih-muhs] *L*—How much we do not know!

Quantum libet [kwahn′-tuhm lih′-bet] *L*—As much as you please.

Quantum licuit [kwahn′-tuhm lih′-kuh-it] *L*—In so far as permitted.

Quantum meruit [kwahn′-tuhm meh′-ruh-it] *L*—As much as he deserved.

Quantum mutatus ab illo! [kwahn′-tuhm moo-tah′-tuhs ahb ihl′-loh] *L*—How much changed from the man he was! The reference is to Hector's mangled appearance as he appears to Aeneas in a dream. The expression is often used to indicate a startling change. Vergil, *Aeneid*, 2; 274.

Quantum placet [kwahn′-tuhm plah′-set] *L*—As much as you please. Medical direction.

Quantum sufficit [kwahn′-tuhm suf′-fih-sit] *L*—As much as is sufficient.

Quantum valeat [kwahn′-tuhm vah′-leh-aht] *L*—For whatever value there is in it.

165

Quantum valebant [kwahn'-tuhm vah-lay'-bahnt] *L*—As much as they were worth; a reasonable estimate in the absence of an agreement.

Quarante hommes, huit chevaux [kah-rahNt uhm hwee shuh-voh] *Fr*—Forty men or eight horses. In the First World War this was the indicated capacity of box cars on French railroads. Societies were formed with this name.

Quare clausum fregit [kwah'-ray klow'-suhm fray'-git] *L*—Why he broke through the enclosed space; an action brought for trespassing on land.

Quasi per ignem [kwah'-see pehr ihg'-nem] *L*—As if through fire.

Quattrocento [kwaht-troh-chen'-toh] *It*—Literally four hundred; dates beginning with 1400, *i.e.* the fifteenth century.

¡Que aproveche! [kay ah-proh-vay'-chay] *Sp*—May you enjoy it. A greeting to a person who is eating.

Que diable allait-il faire dans cette galère [kuh dyah-bl ahl-leh-teel fehr dahN set ga-lehr] *Fr*—Literally, what the devil was he going to do in that galley? What the deuce was he doing there? Molière, *Fourberies de Scapin*, 2; 7.

¡Qué lástima! [kay lahs'-tee-mah] *Sp*—What a pity!

Quel che pare burla, ben sovent è vero [kwel kay pah'-ray boor'-lah behn soh-vent' eh vay'-roh] *It*—What seems a joke is very often true; many a true word is spoken in jest.

Quel dominio è solo durabile che è volontario [kwel doh-mee'-nee-oh eh soh'-loh doo-rah'-bee-lay kay eh voh-lon-tah'-ree-oh] *It*—The only lasting rules are those that are voluntarily accepted. Machiavelli, *Istorie Fiorentine*, 2; 34.

Quel dommage! [kehl duh-mahzh] *Fr*—What a pity! Too bad!

Quel giorno più non vi leggemmo avante [kwel johr'-noh pee-oo' nonn vee led-jehm'-moh ah-vahn'-tay] *It*—That day we read no further in that book. A line from a celebrated passage in which Francesca da Rimini describes how love took

166

fire when she and her husband's brother were reading together the story of Lancelot. Dante, *Inferno*, 5; 138.

Quelle difese solamente sono buone, sono certe, sono durabili, che dependano da te proprio e dalla virtú tua [kwayl'-lay dee-fay'-say soh-lah-men'-tay soh'-noh bwoh'-nay, soh'-noh chehr'-tay, soh'-noh doo-rah'-bee-lee kay day-pen'-dah-noh dah tay proh'-pree-oh ay dahl'-la veer-too' too'-ah] *It*—Only those defenses are good, are certain, and are lasting which depend upon your own nature and valor. Machiavelli, *The Prince*, 24.

Quelques grands avantages que la nature donne, ce n'est pas elle seule, mais la fortune avec elle qui fait les héros [kel-kuh grahN zah-vahN-tazh kuh lah nah-tür dunn suh neh pah zehl suhl meh lah for-tün ah-vek ehl kee feh lay ay-roh] *Fr*—No matter what great advantages nature confers, without luck she does not produce heroes. La Rochefoucauld, *Maxims*, 53.

Quem di diligunt / adolescens moritur [kwehm dee dee'-lih-guhnt ah-doh-lays'-kayns moh'-rih-tuhr] *L*—He whom the gods love dies young. Translation of Hon hoi theoi . . . (*q.v.*). Plautus, *Bacchides*, 4; 7, 18 (818).

Qu'en dira le monde? [kahN dee-rah luh mohNd] *Fr*—What will the world say?

Que sçais (sais)-je [kuh seh-zhuh] *Fr*—What do I know? Montaigne's motto, indicating self-depreciation and skepticism.

Que será será [kay seh-rah' seh-rah'] *Sp*—What will be will be.

Questo ragazzo ci farà dimenticar tutti [kwess'-toh rah-gaht'-soh chee fah-rah' dee-men-tee-kahr' toot'-tee] *It*—This boy will cause us all to be forgotten. A prophecy uttered by Johann Adolph Hasse, a great contemporary of Mozart, when Mozart was not yet eighteen.

¿Que tal? [kay tahl] *Sp*—How are things? An informal greeting.

Que voulez-vous? [kuh voo-lay-voo] *Fr*—What would you like?

Qui a bu boira [kee ah bü bwah-rah] *Fr*—He who has drunk will drink again; once a drunkard always a drunkard.

Qui bene distinguit bene docet [kwee beh'-neh dihs-tihn'-gwit beh'-neh do'-ket] *L*—He who distinguishes well teaches well. An axiom of the Scholastic philosophers.

Quicquid praecipies esto brevis [kwik'-kwid prI-kih'-pih-ayss ess'-toh breh'-wis] *L*—Whatever your advice be brief. Horace, *Art of Poetry*, 335.

Quid de quoque viro et cui dicas, saepe videto [kwid day kwoh'-kweh wih'-roh et kwee dee'-kahs sI'-peh wih-day'-toh] *L*—Take care of what you say of any man and to whom you say it. Horace, *Epistles*, 1; 18, 68.

Qui de contemnenda gloria libros scribunt, nomen suum inscribunt [kwee day kon-tem-nehn'-dah gloh'-rih-ah lihb'-rohs skree'-buhnt noh'-men suh'-uhm in-skree'-buhnt] *L*—Men who write books in contempt of fame sign their names to their work. Cicero, *For Archias*, 11; 26.

Qui dedit beneficium taceat; narret qui accepit [kwee deh'-dit beh-neh-fih'-kih-uhm tah'-keh-aht nahr'-ret kwee ahk-kay'-pit] *L*—Let the man who performed the kind act keep silent; let the one who received it tell about it. Seneca, *On Benefits*, 2; 11, 2.

Quid enim salvis infamia nummis? [kwid eh'-nim sahl'-wees in-fah'-mih-ah nuhm'-mees] *L*—Why worry about a bad reputation if the plunder is safe? Juvenal, 1; 48.

Quid fiet hominibus qui minima contemnunt, majora non credunt? [kwid fee'-et ho-mih'-nih-buhs kwee mih'-nih-mah kohn-tehm'-nuhnt may-yoh'-rah nohn kray'-duhnt] *L*—What will happen to men who despise matters of least importance but do not believe what is more important? Pascal, *Pensées*, 89.

Qui diligit Deum diligit et fratrem suum [kwee dee'-lih-git deh'-uhm dee'-lih-git et frah-trehm suh'-uhm] *L*—He who loves God loves his brother too.

Quid leges sine moribus vanae proficiunt? [kwid lay'-gayss sih'-neh moh'-rih-buhs wah'-nI proh-fih'-kih-uhnt] *L*—What can idle laws accomplish without morality? Horace, *Odes*, 3; 24, 35.

Quid multa? [kwid muhl'-tah] *L*—Why make a long speech?

Quid non mortalia pectora cogis, auri sacra fames? [kwid nohn mohr-tah'-lih-ah pehk'-toh-rah koh'-gis ow'-ree sah'-krah fah'-mayss] *L*—To what do you not drive the hearts of men, accursed greed for gold? Vergil, *Aeneid*, 3; 56.

Quid nunc? [kwid nuhnk] *L*—What now? The two words have been joined to make an English word, *quidnunc*, meaning a gossip, an over-curious person.

Qui docet discit [kwee do'-ket diss'-kit] *L*—He who teaches learns.

Qui donne tôt, donne deux fois [kee duhn toh duhn duh fwah] *Fr*—He gives twice who gives quickly. *See also* Bis dat qui cito dat.

Quid pro quo [kwid proh kwoh] *L*—Something for something; tit for tat.

Quidquid agas, prudenter agas, et respice finem [kwid'-kwid ah'-gahs proo-dehn'-tehr ah'-gahs et rehs'-pih-keh fee'-nehm] *L*—Whatever you do, act wisely, and consider the end. *Gesta Romanorum*, 103.

Quidquid multis peccatur inultum est [kwid'-kwid muhl'-tees pek-kah'-tuhr in-uhl'-tuhm est] *L*—When many are guilty, the offense goes unavenged. Lucan, *Pharsalia*, 5; 260.

Quid sit futurum cras, fuge quaerere [kwid sit fuh-too'-ruhm krahss fuh'-geh kwI'-reh-reh] *L*—Cease asking what tomorrow will bring. Horace, *Odes*, 1; 9, 13.

Quien calla otorga [kyehn' kah'-yah oh-tohr'-gah] *Sp*—Silence gives consent. *See also* Qui tacet...

Quien canta, sus males espanta [kyehn' kahn'-tah soos mah'-lays ehs-pahn'-tah] *Sp*—The singer scares his woes away. Cervantes, *Don Quixote*, 1; 22.

Quien madruga, Dios le ayuda [kyehn' mah-droo'-gah dyohss' lay ah-yoo'-dah] *Sp*—God helps the man who gets up early; the early bird catches the worm.

Quien mucho abarca (abraza) poco aprieta [kyehn' moo'-choh ah-bahr'-kah, ah-brah'-sah, poh'-koh ah-pryay'-tah] *Sp*—

He who grasps for much lays hold of little; grasp all, lose all.

Quien no ha visto a Sevilla, no ha visto maravilla [kyehn' noh ah bees'-toh ah say-vee'-yah noh ah bees'-toh mah-rah-vee'-yah] *Sp*—He who has not seen Seville has missed a marvel.

Quien padre tiene alcalde, seguro va a juicio [kyehn' pah'-dray tyeh'-nay ahl-kahl'-day say-goo'-roh bah ah hoo-ee'-syoh] *Sp*—The man whose father is mayor goes into court with an easy mind.

¿Quién sabe? [kyehn' sah'-bay] *Sp*—Who knows?

Quien tiene dineros, tiene compañeros [kyehn' tyeh'-nay dee-nay'-rohs tyeh'-nay kom-pah-nyay'-rohs] *Sp*—The man who has money has companions.

Quien todo lo niega, todo lo confiesa [kyehn' toh'-doh loh nyay'-gah toh'-doh loh kon-fyay'-sah] *Sp*—Whoever denies everything, confesses everything.

Qui est près de l'église est souvent loin de Dieu [kee eh preh duh lay-gleez eh soo-vahN lwaN duh dyuh] *Fr*—The person who lives near the church is often far from God.

Quieta non movere [kwih-ay'-tah nohn mo-way'-reh] *L*—Do not disturb what is at peace; let sleeping dogs lie.

Qui ex patre filioque procedit [kwee ex pah'-treh fee-lih-oh'-kweh proh-kay'-dit] *L*—Who proceedeth from the Father and the Son. The words *and the Son* were not included in the original Nicene Creed. The later insertion of these words occasioned the Filioque dispute which is one of the apparently irreconcilable differences between the Latin and Greek Orthodox churches.

Qui facit per alium est perinde ac si facit per seipsum [kwee fah'-kit pehr ah'-lih-uhm est pehr-ihn'-deh ahk see fah'-kit pehr say-ihp'-suhm] *L*—If one does something through another, it is as if he does it personally.

Qui facit per alium facit per se [kwee fah'-kit pehr ah'-lih-uhm fah'-kit pehr say] *L*—What a man does through an agent, he does himself. He must accept respon-

168

sibility when he empowers another to act in his place.

Qui finem quaeris amoris, / cedit amor rebus: res age, tutus eris [kwee fee'-nehm kwI'-riss ah-moh'-riss kay'-dit ah'-mor ray'-buhs rayss ah'-geh too'-tuhs eh'-ris] *L*—You who wish to be rid of love, keep busy, and you will be safe, for love yields to activity. Ovid, *Remedies for Love*, 143.

Qui m'aime, aime mon chien [kee mehm ehm mohN shyaN] *Fr*—Love me, love my dog.

Qui male agit odit lucem [kwee mah'-leh ah'-git oh'-dit loo'-kehm] *L*—The evildoer hates the light.

Qui me amat, amet et canem meum [kwee may ah'-maht ah'-meht et kah'-nem meh'-uhm] *L*—Love me, love my dog. A proverb mentioned by St. Bernard in his *Sermo Primus.*

Qui n'a santé n'a rien [kee na sahN-tay na ryaN] *Fr*—A man has nothing if he doesn't have his health.

Qui nimium probat, nihil probat [kwee nih'-mih-uhm pro'-baht nih'-hil pro'-baht] *L*—The man who tries to prove too much proves nothing.

Qui non discit in pueritia, non docet in senectute [kwee nohn dihs'-kit in puh-eh-rih'-tih-ah nohn do'-ket in seh-nek-too'-teh] *L*—He who does not learn when young will not teach when old. Alcuin, Letter 27.

Qui non proficit deficit [kwee nohn proh'-fih-kit day'-fih-kit] *L*—The man who does not advance slips backward.

Qui plantavit curabit [kwee plahn-tah'-wit koo-rah'-bit] *L*—The one who did the planting will take care of it. Motto over the door of Theodore Roosevelt's home.

Qui pro domina justitia sequitur [kwee proh do'-mih-nah yoos-tih'-tih-ah seh'-kwih-tuhr] *L*—Who follows in defense of Lady Justice. Seal of the United States Department of Justice.

Quis custodiet ipsos custodes? [kwihs kuhs-toh'-dih-eht ihp'-sohs kuhs-toh'-

dayss] *L*—Who will guard the guards? Juvenal, 6; 347.

Quis desiderio sit pudor aut modus tam cari capitis? [kwihs day-see-deh'-rih-oh sit puh'-dor owt moh'-duhs tahm kah'-ree kah'-pih-tiss] *L*—What modesty or measure shall there be to our longing for so dear a friend? Horace, *Odes*, 1; 24, 1.

Qui s'excuse, s'accuse [kee seks-küz sak-küz] *Fr*—He who makes excuses accuses himself. *See also* Excusatio non petita . . .

Quisque iam amavit, cras amet [kwis'-kweh yahm ah-mah'-wit, krahs ah'-met] *L*—Everyone has already loved; let everyone love in future. A variant of Cras amet qui numquam amavit . . . (*q.v.*).

Quis, quid, ubi, quibus auxiliis, cur, quomodo, quando? [kwis kwid koor uh'-bih kwih'-buhs owk'-sih'-lih-eess koor kwoh'-mo-doh kwahn'-doh] *L*—Who, what, where, with whose help, why, how, when? A Latin hexameter prompting the memory to recall the circumstances of an action.

Quis separabit? [kwiss say-pah-rah'-bit] *L*—Who shall separate (us)? Motto of the Order of Saint Patrick, instituted by George III, intended to convey the idea that nobody would separate Great Britain from Ireland. *Vulgate, Paul, Romans*, 8; 35.

Quis talia fando temperet a lacrimis? [kwis tah'-lih-ah fahn'-doh tehm'-peh-reht ah lah'-krih-mees] *L*—Who could refrain from tears while telling this story? Vergil, *Aeneid*, 2; 6.

Qui stat caveat ne cadat [kwee staht kah'-weh-aht nay kah'-daht] *L*—Let him who stands take heed lest he fall. *Vulgate, I Corinthians*, 10; 12.

Quis tulerit Gracchos de seditione querentes? [kwis tuh'-leh-rit grahk'-kohs day say-dih-tih-o'-neh kweh-rehn'-tays] *L*—Who could endure the Gracchi complaining of sedition? The Gracchi brothers headed social reforms favoring the have-nots and were regarded by the conservatives as guilty of sedition. It would be intolerable to hear the Gracchi complain of the uprisings which, according to Juvenal, they promoted. The phrase is applied to those who censure in others the faults of which they are guilty. The pot calls the kettle black. *Juvenal*, 2; 24.

Qui tacet consentire videtur [kwee tah'-ket kohn-sehn-tee'-reh wih-day'-tuhr] *L*—He who is silent seems to give consent. A legal maxim.

Qui timide rogat, docet negare [kwee tih'-mih-day ro'-gaht do'-ket neh-gah'-reh] *L*—He who asks timidly makes denial easy. Seneca, *Hippolytus*, 593.

Qui transtulit sustinet [kwee trahns'-tuh-lit suhs'-tih-net] *L*—He who transplanted us sustains us. Motto of Connecticut.

Qui va là? [kee vah lah] *Fr*—Who goes there?

Qui vive [kee veev] *Fr*—Who goes there? (when used as a question); on the alert.

Quiz seperrabit. A garbling of Quis separabit? (*q.v.*) Who will separate us. Sean O'Casey, *Inishfallen, Fare Thee Well* in the chapter *Into the Civil War*.

Quoad hoc [kwoh'-ahd hokk] *L*—As far as this particular point is concerned.

Quo animo [kwoh ah'-nih-moh] *L*—With what intent. A legal phrase.

Quocumque modo [kwoh-kuhm'-kweh mo'-doh] *L*—In whatever manner.

Quocumque nomine [kwoh-kuhm'-kweh noh'-mih-neh] *L*—Under whatever name.

Quod ali cibus est aliis fuat acre venenum [kwod ah'-lee kih'-buhs est ah'-lih-ees fuh'-aht ahk'-reh weh-nay'-nuhm] *L*—What is food to one man may be rank poison to another; one man's meat is another man's poison. Lucretius, *On the Nature of Things*, 4; 637.

Quod aliquis facit per aliquem, facit per se [kwod ah'-lih-kwis fah'-kit pehr ah'-lih-kwehm fah'-kit pehr say] *L*—What is done through an agent, is done in person. The principle of power of attorney.

Quod avertat Deus! [kwod ah-wehr'-taht deh'-uhs] *L*—God forbid it! Used as a pious parenthetical observation.

Quod bene notandum [kwod beh'-neh no-tahn'-duhm] *L*—Which is to be especially noted.

Quod Deus avertat! [kwod deh'-uhs ah-wehr'-taht] *L*—See Quod avertat Deus!

Quod Deus vult [kwod deh'-uhs wuhlt] *L*—What God ordains.

169

Quod dixi dixi [kwod deex'-ee deex'-ee] *L*—What I have said, I have said. Probably an imitation of Quod scripsi scripsi (*q.v.*).

Quod dubitas ne feceris [kwod duh'-bih-tahs nay fay'-keh-reess] *L*—If you doubt, don't do it. Doctor Johnson's advice to editors of literary texts.

Quod erat demonstrandum. *L*—*See* Q. E. D.

Quod erat faciendum. *L*—*See* Q. E. F.

Quod gratis asseritur, gratis negatur [kwod grah'-tis ahs-seh'-rih-tuhr grah'-tis neh-gah'-tuhr] *L*—What is freely asserted may be freely denied.

Quod hodie non est, cras erit: sic vita truditur [kwod ho'-dih-ay nohn est krahss eh'-rit seek wee'-tah troo'-dih-tuhr] *L*—If things don't work out today, there is always tomorrow: and so life pushes on. Petronius, *Satyricon*, 45.

Quod licet Iovi non licet bovi [kwod lih'-ket yoh'-wee nohn lih'-ket boh'-wee] *L*—What's permitted the divine is not allowed to swine.

Quod non fecerunt barbari fecerunt Barberini [kwod nohn fay-kay'-ruhnt bahr'-bah-ree fay-kay'-ruhnt bahr-bay-ree'-nee] *L*—What escaped the fury of the barbarians, the Barberini destroyed. Pope Urban VIII, a member of the Barberini family, had the bronze pre-Christian objects in the Pantheon cast into cannons.

Quod non opus est, asse carum est [kwod nohn o'-puhs est ahs'-seh kah'-ruhm est] *L*—What is not necessary is dear at a penny. Cato, in Seneca, *Letters to Lucilius*, 94.

Quod scripsi, scripsi [kwod skreep'-see skreep'-see] *L*—What I have written, I have written. Pilate's answer to the chief priest who objected to the title he had put on the cross. *Vulgate, John,* 19; 22.

Quod semper, quod ubique et quod ab omnibus creditum est [kwod sem'-pehr kwod uh-bee'-kweh et kwod ahb om'-nih-buhs kray'-dih-tuhm est] *L*—What all men have always and everywhere believed. A principle or canon for distinguishing heretical from true Christian doctrine. Its in-

terpretation has been the subject of much theological debate. Vincent of Lérins, *Commonitorium*, chap. 2.

Quod sentimus, loquamur, quod loquimur, sentiamus; concordet sermo cum vita [kwod sehn-tee'-muhs lo-kwah'-muhr kwod lo'-kwih-muhr sehn-tih-ah'-muhs kon-kor'-det sehr'-moh kuhm wee'-tah] *L*—Let us say what we feel, feel what we say, and have our words harmonize with our life. Seneca, *Letters*, 75; 4.

Quod vide. *L*—*See* q. v.

Quod volumus, facile credimus [kwod wo'-luh-muhs fah'-kih-lay kray'-dih-muhs] *L*—We readily believe what we want to believe.

Quo fas et gloria ducunt [kwoh fahss et gloh'-rih-ah duh'-kuhnt] *L*—To wherever duty and glory lead.

Quo fata vocant [kwoh fah'-tah wo'-kahnt] *L*—Whither the fates call.

Quo jure? [kwoh yoo'-reh] *L*—By what law?

Quorum pars magna fui [kwoh'-ruhm pahrs mahg'-nah fuh'-ee] *L*—In which I played an important part. Aeneas speaks these words as he begins recounting to Dido and her court the disasters the Trojans suffered. Vergil, *Aeneid,* 2; 6.

Quos Deus vult perdere, prius dementat [kwohs deh'-uhs wuhlt pehr'-deh-reh prih'-uhs day-men'-taht] *L*—Whom God wills to destroy He first makes mad. Translation of a fragment from Euripides.

Quos ego— [kwohs eh'-goh] *L*—Whom I ... Neptune is scolding the winds and suddenly breaks off to quiet the storm that has battered Aeneas and his men. The inference is that he will punish the winds later. This is an excellent example of the rhetorical figure *aposiopesis*, a breaking off with an implied threat. Vergil, *Aeneid,* 1; 135.

Quot homines, tot sententiae [kwot ho'-mih-nayss toht sehn-ten-tih-I] *L*—There are as many opinions as there are men. Terence, *Phormio*, 3; 3, 454.

Quot linguas calles, tot homines vales [kwot ling'-gwahss kahl'-layss toht ho'-mih-nayss wa-layss] *L*—You are as many men as the number of tongues you speak.

Quo vadis? [kwoh vah'-dis] *L*—Where are you going? These words were supposedly uttered by Saint Peter on meeting Christ when the discouraged Apostle was leaving Rome. The title of a novel by Henryk Sienkiewicz on the persecution of the Christians by Nero.

Quo warranto [kwoh wahr-ran'-toh] *Anglo-L*—By what authority; a writ to determine the right or ownership of a franchise or office.

q. v. quantum vis [kwahn'-tuhm weess] *L*—As much as you wish. A medical direction.

q. v. quod vide [kwod wih'-day] *L*—Which see. Often inserted in a text to indicate that the reader unacquainted with some term or fact may find an explanation under the word preceding the *q.v.*

R

R (R) Recipe [reh'-kih-peh] *L*—Take. An abbreviation used at the beginning of a medical prescription.

R. A. República Argentina [ray-poo'-blee-kah ahr-hen-tee'-nah] *Sp*—Argentine Republic.

Radix omnium malorum est cupiditas [rah'-deex om'-nih-uhm mah-loh'-ruhm est kuh-pih'-dih-tahs] *L*—Covetousness is the root of all evil. *Vulgate, I, Timothy,* 6; 10.

Raison de plus [reh-zohN duh plü] *Fr*—One reason more; all the more reason.

Raison d'état [reh-zohN day-tah] *Fr*—A reason given by the government of a state when its laws or standards are violated in the interests of self-preservation.

Raison d'être [reh-zohN deh-tr] *Fr*—Reason for existing.

Rara avis in terra nigroque simillima cycno [rah'-rah ah'-wis in ter'-rah nih-groh'-kweh sih-mihl'-lih-mah cik'-noh] *L*—A rare bird on the earth, very much like a black swan. Juvenal, 6; 165.

Raram facit misturam cum sapientia forma [rah'-rahm fah'-kit mees-too'-rahm kuhm sah-pih-en'-tih-ah for'-mah] *L*—Beauty and wisdom are rarely found together. Petronius, *Satyricon,* 94.

Rast ich, so rost ich [rahst ikh zoh rohst ikh] *Ger*—If I rest, I rust.

Rationes seminales [rah-tih-oh'-nayss say-mih-nah'-layss] *L*—Creative capacities in the mass of created matter from which all things developed. A term used by Saint Augustine in his account of the creation of the world, as told in his twelve books, *De Genesi ad Litteram* (On a Literal Interpretation of Genesis).

Ratio Studiorum [rah'-tih-oh stuh-dih-oh'-ruhm] *L*—A short title for *Ratio atque Institutio Studiorum Societatis Jesu,* The Method and System of Studies of the Society of Jesus (1599).

Ratio vincit [rah'-tih-oh win'-kit] *L*—Reason conquers.

Ratschläge für ausländische Besucher [raht-shlay'-guh für ows'-len'-dish-uh buh-zoo'-kuhr] *Ger*—Advice for foreign visitors.

Re [ray] *L*—In the matter of; with reference to.

Rebus sic stantibus [ray'-buhs seek stahn'-tih-buhs] *L*—As matters stand.

Recoge tu heno mientras que el sol luciere [ray-koh'-hay too ay'-noh mee-en'-trahs kay el sol loo-see-ay'-ray] *Sp*—Make hay while the sun shines.

Recta ratio [rayk'-tah rah'-tih-oh] *L*—The right reason.

Rectus in curia [rayk'-tuhs in koo'-rih-ah] *L*—An honest litigant in court.

Reddite quae sunt Caesaris, Caesari: et quae sunt Dei, Deo [rehd'-dih-teh kwI suhnt kI'-sah-ris kI'-sah-ree et kwI suhnt deh'-ee deh'-oh] *L*—Give to Caesar the things that are Caesar's and to God the things that are God's. *Vulgate, Matthew,* 22; 21.

Reden ist Silber, Schweigen ist Gold [ray'-dun ist zil'-buhr shvI'-gun ist golt] *Ger*—Speech is silver, silence is gold.

Redig. in pulv. redigatur in pulverem [reh-dih-gah'-tuhr in puhl'-veh-rehm] *L*—Let it be reduced to powder.

Redime te captum quam queas minimo [reh'-dih-meh tay kahp'-tuhm kwahm kweh'-ahs mih'-nih-moh] *L*—When taken prisoner, redeem yourself for as little as you can.

Redolet lucerna [reh'-doh-let luh-kehr'-nah] *L*—It smells of the lamp. *See also* Olet lucernam.

Reductio ad absurdum [reh-duhk'-tsih-oh ahd ahb-suhr'-duhm] *L*—Reducing an argument to the absurd. An attempt to show that if the argument in question were followed to its logical conclusion, it would lead to absurdity.

Reductio ad impossibile [reh-duhk'-tsih-oh ahd im-pohs-sih'-bih-leh] *L*—Reducing an argument to the impossible. *See also* Reductio ad absurdum.

Refugium peccatorum [reh-fuh'-gi-uhm pek-kah-toh'-ruhm] *L*—Refuge of sinners.

Regina scientiarum [ray-gee'-nah skih-en-tih-ah'-ruhm] *L*—Queen of the sciences (knowledge). A Scholastic appraisal of philosophy.

Regnabat [rayg-nah'-baht] *L*—He was ruling. Usually associated with a date.

Regnat populus [rayg'-naht po'-puh-luhs] *L*—The people rule. Motto of the state of Arkansas.

Re infecta [ray in-fek'-tah] *L*—Without finishing the business.

Relata refero [reh-lah'-tah reh'-feh-roh] *L*—I tell the story as it was told to me.

Religio Laici [reh-lih'-gih-oh lah'-ih-kee] *L*—*Religion of a Layman*, title of a poem by Dryden.

Religio loci [reh-lih'-gih-oh lo'-kee] *L*—The solemn religious feeling evoked by a particular place. A phrase picked from two lines of Vergil, *Aeneid*, 8; 349.

Religio Medici [reh-lih'-gih-oh meh'-dih-kee] *L*—*Religion of a Physician*, title of a book by Sir Thomas Browne.

Rem acu tetigisti [rem ah'-koo teh-tih-gis'-tee] *L*—You have stated it correctly; you have hit the nail on the head. Plautus, *The Rope*, 5; 2, 19.

Remanet [reh'-mah-net] *L*—It remains. A case left unsettled at the end of a court term.

Rem tene et verba sequentur [rem teh'-nay et wehr'-bah seh-kwehn'-tuhr] *L*—Master the material and the words will follow. The same idea is contained in Horace, *Art of Poetry*, 311: *Verba provisam rem non invita sequentur* [wehr'-bah pro-wee'-sahm rem nohn in-wee'-tah seh-kwehn'-tuhr]. Words will freely follow when the subject is well thought out in advance.

Rentes sur l'État [rahNt sür lay-tah] *Fr*—Government stocks; also the interest therefrom.

Repente liberalis stultis gratus est;/ verum peritis irritos tendit dolos [reh-pen'-teh lee-beh-rah'-liss stuhl'-teess grah'-tuhs est way'-ruhm peh-ree'-teess eer'-rih-tohs ten'-dit doh'-lohs] *L*—A man who is suddenly generous pleases fools, but his tricks make no impression on the experienced. Phaedrus, *Fables*, 1; 23, 1.

Repetatur [reh-peh-tah'-tuhr] *L*—It may be repeated. Used on medical prescriptions.

Repetitio est mater studiorum [reh-peh-tih'-tih-oh est mah'-tehr stuh-dih-or'-uhm] *L*—Repetition is the mother of studies.

Répondez s'il vous plait *See* R. S. V. P.

Répondre en Normand [ray-pohN-dr ahn nor-mahN] *Fr*—To give a noncommittal answer like a Norman; to reply evasively, equivocally.

Requiem aeternam dona eis, domine, et lux perpetua luceat eis [reh'-kwih-em ay-tehr'-nahm doh'-nah eh'-eess do'-mih-neh et loox pehr-peh'-tuh-ah loo'-chay-aht eh'-eess] *L*—Grant them eternal rest, O Lord, and let perpetual light shine round about them.

Requiescat in pace [reh-kwih-ays'-kaht in pah'-seh *or* pah'-chay] *L*—May he rest in peace.

Rerum naturam sola gubernas [ray'-ruhm nah-too'-rahm soh'-lah guh-behr'-nahs] *L*—You (Venus) alone govern the nature of things. Lucretius, *On the Nature of Things*, 1; 21.

Rerum novarum libido [ray'-ruhm no-wah'-ruhm lih-bee'-doh] *L*—Reckless desire for innovations.

Res adjudicata [rays ahd-yoo-dih-kah'-tah] *L*—A case already decided.

173

Res alienae [rays ah-lih-ay'-nI] L—Property of others.

Res angusta domi [rays ahn-guhs'-tah do'-mee] L—Straitened circumstances at home. Juvenal, 3; 165. The entire sentence of which this phrase is a part begins *Haud facile emergunt quorum virtutibus obstat . . . (q.v.).*

Res derelicta [rays day-reh-lik'-tah] L—A thing that is abandoned or thrown away.

Res domesticas noli tangere [rays domess'-tih-kahss noh'-lee tahn'-geh-reh] L—Do not mingle in the domestic affairs of others.

Res gestae [rays gehs'-tI] L—Transactions; things done; exploits.

Res integra [rays in'-teh-grah] L—An entire matter.

Res ipsa loquitur [rays ip'-sah lo'-kwih-tuhr] L—The matter speaks for itself. In a trial involving an accident, the damage is evident; the defendant must prove that the accident was not due to negligence on his part.

Resistendum senectuti [reh-sihs-ten'-duhm seh-nek-too'-tee] L—Old age must be fought. Cicero, *Old Age*, 11; 35.

Res judicata [rays yoo-dih-kah'-tah] L—A matter already settled. *Res Judicatae,* the plural, is the title of a book by Augustine Birrell.

Res non parta labore [rayss nohn pahr'-tah lah-boh'-reh] L—A thing that is not the product of labor.

Res nullius [rays noo-lee'-uhs] L—A thing that has no owner.

Res perit domino [rays peh'-rit do'-mih-noh] L—The thing perishes to the owner; the owner loses possession of a thing when it perishes.

Respice, adspice, prospice [rehs'-pih-keh ahd'-spih-keh prohs'-pih-keh] L—Survey the past, examine the present, look to the future. Motto of the City College of New York.

Respice finem [rehs'-pih-keh fee'-nehm] L—Look to the end of life. Translation of

Solon's warning to Croesus found in Herodotus, 1; 32.

Respicere exemplar vitae morumque jubebo / Doctum imitatorem, et vivas hinc ducere voces [rehs'-pih'-keh exem'-plahr wee'-tI moh-ruhm'-kweh yoobay'-boh dok'-tuhm ih-mih-tah-toh'-rehm et wee'-wahs hink doo'-keh-reh woh'-kays] L—I advise the artist skilled in character description to look for examples in life and customs and draw living words from them. Horace, *Art of Poetry,* 317.

Respondeat superior [rehs-pon'-deh-aht suh-peh'-rih-or] L—Let the superior answer; let the principal reply for his subordinates since he is responsible for their actions.

Responsa prudentium [rehs-pohn'-sah proo-den'-tih-uhm] L—The opinions of eminent jurists on legal questions.

Retro me, Satana! [reh'-troh may sah'-tah-nah] L—Get thee behind me, Satan! *Vulgate, Mark,* 8; 33.

Retro, Satana! [reh'-troh sah'-tah-nah] L—Get thee behind me, Satan!

Revenons à nos moutons [ruhv-nohN zah noh moo-tohN] Fr—Let us get back to our sheep; let us get back to the subject. Anon., *La Farce de Maistre Pathelin.*

Rex bibendi [rayx bih-ben'-dee] L—King of the drinking; master of the revels.

Rex regnat, sed non gubernat [rayx rayg'-naht sed nohn guh-behr'-naht] L—The king reigns but he does not govern. Jan Zamojski.

Rey nuevo, ley neuva [ray'-ee nway'-voh lay'-ee nway'-vah] Sp—New king, new law.

Rez-de-chaussée [ray duh shoh-say] Fr—Ground level; street level; ground floor of a house.

Rhododaktulos eos [rho-doh-dahk'-tü-los ay'-ohs] Gk—The rosy-fingered dawn; frequently found in Homer.

Ridentem dicere verum / quid vetat? [ree-den'-tem dee'-keh-reh way'-ruhm kwid weh'-taht] L—What objection can there be to telling the truth with a smile? Many a true word is spoken in jest. Horace, *Satires,* 1; 1, 24.

Ride si sapis, o puella, ride [ree'-day see sah'-pihs oh puh-el'-lah ree'-day] *L*—Smile, maiden, smile if you are wise. Advice attributed to Ovid by Martial. In this context the poet warns a girl with bad teeth that the advice was not intended for her. Martial, 2; 41, 1.

Rien de plus éloquent que l'argent comptant [ryaN duh plü zay-loh-kahN kuh lahr-zhahN kohN-tahN] *Fr*—Nothing is more eloquent than cash.

Rien ne dure que le provisoire [ryan nuh dür kuh luh pruh-vee-zwahr] *Fr*—Temporary arrangements are the only ones that last.

Rien ne pèse tant qu'un secret [ryan nuh pehz tahN kuhN-suh-kreh] *Fr*—Nothing weighs as much as a secret. La Fontaine, *Fables*, 8; 6.

Rien ne réussit comme le succès [ryan nuh ray-ü-see kuhm luh sük-seh] *Fr*—Nothing succeeds like success.

Rien n'est beau que le vrai [ryan neh boh kuh luh vray] *Fr*—Naught save truth is beautiful. Boileau. *Epistles*, 9, 4, 3.

Rigor mortis [rih'-gor mohr'-tis] *L*—Stiffness occurring after death.

R. I. P. *See* Requiescat in pace.

Rira bien qui rira le dernier [ree-rah byaN kee ree-rah luh dehr-nyay] *Fr*—He laughs best who laughs last.

Rire dans sa barbe [reer dahN sa barb] *Fr*—To laugh in his beard; to laugh up one's sleeve.

Rire et faire rire [reer ay fehr reer] *Fr*—To laugh and make others laugh.

Ris de veau [ree duh voh] *Fr*—Calf's sweetbread.

Risu inepto res ineptior nulla est [ree'-soo in-ep'-toh rayss in-ep'-tih-or noo'-lah est] *L*—Nothing is sillier than silly laughter. Catullus, 39; 16.

Ritardando [ree-tahr-dahn'-doh] *It*—A musical direction indicating that the tempo should gradually become slower.

Rixatur de lana saepe caprina [reex-ah'-tuhr day lah'-nah sI'-peh kah-pree'-nah] *L*—

He often quarrels about goat's wool, i.e. about matters of no consequence. Horace, *Epistles*, 1; 18, 15.

Robe de chambre [ruhb duh shahN-br] *Fr*—Dressing gown.

Rois fainéants [rwah feh-nay-ahN] *Fr*—The Do-Nothing Kings. Weak Frankish rulers of the Merovingian line from 639 to 751 who surrendered their powers to the Major domus (*q.v.*).

Roisin dub [roi'-sin dubh] *Ir*—Little dark rose; allegorical love ballad in which political beliefs are covertly expressed.

Rôle de l'équipage [rohl duh lay-kee-pazh] *Fr*—List of a ship's crew.

Roma locuta, causa finita [roh'-mah lo-koo'-tah kow'-sah fee-nee'-tah] *L*—Rome has spoken, the case is ended. Once papal authority has rendered a decision in a matter, debate among the faithful ceases.

Roman à clef [ruh-mahn ah klay] *Fr*—A novel in which actual persons are introduced under fictitious names.

Roman à thèse [ruh-mahn ah tehz] *Fr*—A novel written to promote a cause or propound an argument.

Roman policier [ruh-mahN puh-lee-syay] *Fr*—Detective story.

Romanus sedendo vincit [roh-mah'-nuhs seh-den'-doh win'-kit] *L*—The Romans achieved their ends through patience.

Rom war nicht in einem Tage gebaut [rom vahr nikht in I'-num tah'-guh guh-bowt'] *Ger*—Rome was not built in a day.

Rosh Hashanah [rosh huh-shah'-nuh] *Heb*—Literally, beginning of the year. Two day holiday at the beginning of the Jewish New Year.

Rota sum: semper, quoquo me verto, stat Virtus [roh'-tah suhm sem'-pehr kwoh'-kwoh may wehr'-toh staht wihr'-toos] *L*—I am a wheel: whithersoever I turn, virtue always stands firm. The motto of Benvenuto Cellini's father; no matter what blows Fortune dealt him, his courage did not fail. Cellini, *Autobiography*, 1; 5.

Rouge-et-noire [roozh ay nwahr] *Fr*—See Trente et quarante.

r. p. réponse payée [ray-pohNss peh-yay] *Fr*—Reply already paid for.

R. S. V. P. Répondez s'il vous plaît [ray-pohN-day seel voo pleh] *Fr*—Please reply.

Rudis indigestaque moles [ruh'-dis in-dee-ges'-tah-kweh moh'-lays] *L*—Unformed disordered mass; a chaotic condition. Ovid, *Metamorphoses,* 1; 7.

Ruse de guerre [rüz duh gehr] *Fr*—A stratagem in war.

Rus in urbe [rooss in uhr'-beh] *L*—City life with the advantages of the country.

Rusticus exspectat dum defluat amnis [roos'-tih-kuhs ek-spehk'-taht duhm day'-fluh-aht ahm'-nis] *L*—The peasant waits until the river will flow past. This might be compared to waiting in a large city until the traffic has passed by. Horace, *Epistles,* 1; 2, 42.

R. V. S. V. P. Répondez vite, s'il vous plaît [ray-pohN-day veet seel voo pleh] *Fr*—Please reply at once.

S

s. a. sine anno [sih'-neh ahn'-noh] *L*—Without date of publication.

S. A. *See* Sociedad anónima.

S. A. Société anonyme [suh-syay-tay ah-noh-neem] *Fr*—A company with limited liability.

S. A. Sudamérica [sood-ah-meh'-ree-kah] *Sp*—South America.

Sacre bleu [sa-kruh bluh] *Fr*—An expletive. A corruption of *sacre Dieu*, i.e. holy God.

Saepe creat molles aspera spina rosas [sI'-peh kreh'-aht mohl'-lays ahs'-peh-rah spee'-nah roh'-sahs] *L*—The sharp thorn often produces soft roses. Ovid, *Epistles from Pontus*, 2; 2, 34.

Saepius locutum, numquam me tacuisse poenitet [sI'-pih-uhs lo-koo'-tuhm nuhm'-kwahm may tah-kuh-iss'-seh poi'-nih-tet] *L*—I have often regretted that I spoke, never that I kept silent. This recalls the remark of Calvin Coolidge: "I have noticed that nothing I never said ever did me any harm."

Sage mir, mit wem du umgehst, so sage ich dir, wer du bist [sah'-guh meer mit vehm doo uhm'-ghayst zoh sah'-guh ikh deer vehr doo bist] *Ger*—Tell me with whom you associate, and I'll tell you what you are. Goethe, *Maxims in Prose*, 141. *See also* Dime con quien andas . . .

S. A. I. Son Altesse Impériale [soh-nahl-tess aN-pay-ryahl] *Fr*—His Imperial Highness.

Salaam aleikum [sah-lahm' ah-lay-koom'] *Arabic*—Peace be on you. A Moslem greeting, spoken with a bow while the right hand is placed on the forehead. *See also* Shalom alekhem.

Sal Atticum [sahl aht'-tih-kuhm] *L*—Literally, Attic salt; witty conversation characteristic of the brilliant society of ancient Athens, the principal city of Attica. The Italians were noted for a sharp, biting wit, *acetum Italum:* literally, Italian vinegar.

Salle à manger [sal ah mahN-zhay] *Fr*—Dining room.

Salle d'attente [sal dah-tahNt] *Fr*—Waiting room.

Salle de jeu [sal duh zhuh] *Fr*—Gambling room.

Salle des pas perdus [sal day pah pehr-dü] *Fr*—Hall of lost footsteps; waiting room outside a court of law or parliament where people walk aimlessly. Specifically the name applies to the large hall in the Palais de Justice in Paris.

Salle du Jeu de Paume [sal dü zhuh duh pohm] *Fr*—Hall of the Tennis Court, scene of the oath taken by the French National Assembly in 1789.

Saludos a todos [sah-loo'-dohs ah toh'-dohs] *Sp*—Greetings to all.

Salus populi suprema lex esto [sah'-loos po'-puh-lee suh-pray'-mah layx es'-toh] *L*—The safety of the people shall be the supreme law. Cicero, *The Laws*, 3; 3, 8. Motto of Missouri.

Saluto il primo Re d'Italia [sah-loo'-toh eel pree'-moh ray dee-tah'-lee-ah] *It*—I greet the first king of Italy. Garibaldi's greeting to Victor Emmanuel, October 26, 1860.

Salva sit reverentia [sahl'-wah sit reh-weh-rayn'-tih-ah] *L*—Let due respect be observed.

Salve [sahl'-way] *L*—Hail; greetings.

177

Salvo jure [sahl'-voh yoo'-reh] *L*—Without prejudice; saving the right of someone, e.g., a king. A clause of exception.

Salvo pudore [sahl'-voh puh-doh'-reh] *L*—Without offense to modesty.

Sanan cuchilladas, mas no malas palabras [sah'-nahn koo-chee-yah'-dahs mahs noh mah'-lahs pah-lah'-brahs] *Sp*—A cut from a knife heals but not one from the tongue.

Sancta simplicitas *L*—*See* O sancta simplicitas!

Sanctum sanctorum [sahnk'-tuhm sahnk-toh'-ruhm] *L*—The holy of holies; a place of quiet where casual visitors are not welcome.

Sang de boeuf [sahN duh böf] *Fr*—Blood of an ox; dark red.

Sang-froid [sahN frwah] *Fr*—Cold blood; coolness in a critical situation; indifference.

Sans appel [sahN za-pehl] *Fr*—A final judgment.

Sans blague? [sahN blahg] *Fr*—No kidding?

Sans cérémonie [sahN say-ray-moh-nee] *Fr*—Without ceremony.

Sans culottes [sahN kü-luht] *Fr*—A man without breeches, an ignominious term given by French aristocrats to republicans who wore pantaloons and not the culottes or breeches worn by the aristocrats.

Sans doute [sahN doot] *Fr*—Without doubt.

Sans façon [sahN fa-sohN] *Fr*—Without style; without ceremony; informally.

Sans gêne [sahN zhen] *Fr*—Without ceremony; free and easy.

Sans pareil [sahN pah-ray] *Fr*—Unparalleled; without equal.

Sans peur et sans reproche [sahN puhr ay sahN ruh-prush] *Fr*—Without fear and without reproach. A title given to a French paragon of chivalry, the Chevalier de Bayard.

178

Sans rime et sans raison [sahN reem ay sahN reh-zohN] *Fr*—Without rhyme or reason.

Sans souci [sahN soo-see] *Fr*—Care-free; easy-going.

Santo Niño [sahn'-toh nee'-nyoh] *Sp*—Image of the Infant Jesus.

Sapere aude [sah'-peh-reh ow'-day] *L*—Dare to think independently. Horace, *Epistles*, 1; 2, 40.

S. A. R. Son Altesse Royale [soh-nahl-tess rwah-yahl] *Fr*—His Royal Highness.

Sartor Resartus [sahr'-tohr reh-sahr'-tuhs] *L*—Literally, the tailor retailored, a work by Thomas Carlyle in which a fictional German philosopher, Teufelsdröckh (devil's dirt), discusses a philosophy of clothes with much humor and wit.

S. A. S. S. Su atento y seguro servidor [soo ah-ten'-toh ee say-goo'-roh sehr-vee-dohr'] *Sp*—Yours very sincerely.

Sat celeriter fieri quidquid fiat satis bene [saht keh-leh'-rih-tehr fih'-eh-ree kwid'-kwid fee'-aht sah'-tiss beh'-neh] *L*—Whatever is done well is done quickly enough. Suetonius, *Life of Augustus*, 25. This was a favorite remark of Augustus, according to Suetonius. It is an adaptation of Sat cito si sat bene (*q.v.*).

Sat cito si sat bene [saht kih'-toh see saht beh'-neh] *L*—Fast enough if good enough. A saying of Cato the Elder. *See also* Sat celeriter fieri . . .; Sat pulchra . . .

Satis eloquentiae, sapientiae parum [sah'-tis ay-lo-kwen'-tih-I sah-pih-ent'-tih-I pah'-ruhm] *L*—Eloquence enough but too little wisdom. Sallust so describes the conspirator Catiline. Sallust, *Catiline*, 5.

Satis et super [sah'-tis et suh'-pehr] *L*—Enough and still more. Sometimes *satis superque*. Catullus, 7; 10.

Sat pulchra si sat bona [saht puhl'-krah see saht bo'-nah] *L*—Beautiful enough if good enough; handsome is as handsome does.

Saturnia tellus [sah-tuhr'-nih-ah tel'-loos] *L*—Land of Saturn. Poetic name for Italy.

Sauve qui peut [sohv kee puh] *Fr*—Let those who are able save themselves; every man for himself!

Savant atomiste [sa-vahN-ta-toh-meest] *Fr*—Nuclear physicist.

Savoir-faire [sah-vwahr-fehr] *Fr*—Tact; cleverness.

Savoir vivre [sah-vwahr vee-vr] *Fr*—Good breeding; polished manners.

s. Br. südliche Breite [süd'-likh-uh brI'-tuh] *Ger*—South latitude.

sc. scilicet [skee'-lih-ket] *L*—Namely; to wit. A contraction of *scire licet* [skee'-reh lih'-ket] As one may learn.

s/c son (sa) compte [sohN, sa, kohNt] *Fr*—His (her) account.

s/c su cuenta [soo kwen'-tah] *Sp*—Your account.

Scala Sancta [skah'-lah sank'-tah] *L*—Holy staircase in Rome, supposedly transferred miraculously from Jerusalem. According to the legend, these stairs were trod by Christ when he was brought to Pilate's palace.

Scandalum magnatum [skahn'-dah-luhm mahg-nah'-tuhm] *LL*—Defamation of the character of a high English official or a person of the upper class. This statute, passed during the reign of Richard II, was repealed in 1887.

Sc. B. Scientiae Baccalaureus [skih-en'-tih-I bahk-kah-low'-reh-uhs] *L*—Bachelor of Science.

Scelere velandum est scelus [skeh'-leh-reh way-lahn'-duhm est skeh'-luhs] *L*—One crime has to be concealed by another. Seneca, *Hippolytus*, 721.

Schlafen Sie wohl! [shlahf'-uhn zee vohl] *Ger*—Sleep well; good night!

Schola cantorum [skoh'-lah kahn-toh'-ruhm] *L*—School of singers of sacred music.

Scientia est veritatis imago [skih-en'-tih-ah est way-rih-tah'-tis ih-mah'-goh] *L*—Science is the image of truth.

Scienti et volenti non fit injuria [skih-en'-tee et wo-len'-tee nohn fit in-yoo'-rih-

ah] *L*—No injustice is done to one who knows and is willing. An axiom of moral theology.

Scilicet. *L*—See sc.

Scire facias [skee'-reh fah'-kih-ahs, *or* sI'-ree fay'-shus] *L*—Cause it to be known; a writ ordering a defendant to show cause why a judgment that is passed should not be carried out.

Scire quid valeant humeri, quid ferre recusent [skee'-reh kwid wah'-leh-ahnt huh'-meh-ree kwid fehr'-reh reh-koo'-sehnt] *L*—To know what one's shoulders can carry and what they refuse to bear; to know one's limitations.

Scribendi recte sapere est et principium et fons [skree-ben'-dee rayk'-tay sah'-peh-reh est et preen-kih'-pih-uhm et fohnss] *L*—Knowledge is the prime source of good writing. Horace, *Art of Poetry*, 309.

Scribimus indocti doctique poemata passim [skree'-bih-muhs in-dok'-tee dok-tee'-kweh po-ay'-mah-tah pahs'-sim] *L*—We all, learned and unlearned alike, write poems at random. Horace, *Epistles*, 2; 1, 117.

Scripta manent, verba volant [skreep'-tah mah'-nehnt wehr'-bah wo'-lahnt] *L*—Written words remain, spoken words fly through the air.

Scriptorum chorus omnis amat nemus et fugit urbem [skreep-toh'-ruhm koh'-ruhs om'-niss ah'-maht neh'-muhs et fuh'-git uhr'-bem] *L*—The whole tribe of writers loves the rural scene and flees the city. Horace, *Epistles*, 2; 2, 77.

Sculpsit [skoolp'-sit] *L*—He engraved or sculptured this work. Written on prints following the artist's name.

Scuto bonae voluntatis tuae coronasti nos [skoo'-toh boh'-nay vol-uhn-tah'-tiss tuh'-ay koh-roh-nahs'-tee nohs] *L*—With the shield of Thy good will Thou hast covered us. *Vulgate, Psalms*, 5; 12. Motto of Maryland. *See also* Le parole son femmine . . .

s. d. sans date [sahN dat] *Fr*—Without date.

Sdegno d'amante poco dura [sdayn'-yoh dah-mahn'-tay poh'-koh doo'-rah] *It*—A lover's indignation does not last long.

S. E. Su Excelencia [soo ex-seh-len'-see-ah] *Sp*—His Excellency.

Seanad Eireann [san'-ahd air'-un] *Ir*—The Senate of the *Oireachtas,* the Irish Parliament.

Secundum artem [seh-kuhn'-duhm ahr'-tehm] *L*—According to the rules of art.

Secundum ipsius naturam [seh-kuhn'-duhm ip-see'-uhs nah-too'-rahm] *L*—According to its very nature.

Secundum legem [seh-kuhn'-duhm lay'-gem] *L*—According to law.

Secundum naturam [seh-kuhn'-duhm nah-too'-rahm] *L*—According to nature.

Secundum ordinem [seh-kuhn'-duhm or'-dih-nem] *L*—According to order.

Secundum quid [seh-kuhn'-duhm kwid] *L*—After a fashion.

Secundum regulam [seh-kuhn'-duhm ray'-guh-lahm] *L*—According to rule.

Secundum usum [seh-kuhn'-duhm oo'-suhm] *L*—According to usage or custom.

Securus judicat orbis terrarum [say-koo'-ruhs yoo'-dih-kaht or'-bis teh-rah'-ruhm] *L*—Calmly, dispassionately, the world makes its judgments. Saint Augustine.

Se defendendo [say day-fen-den'-doh] *L*—In self-defense. The first grave-digger in Hamlet garbles this expression by saying *Se offendendo.*

Sedia gestatoria [say'-dee-ah jess-tah-toh'-ree-ah] *It*—The chair on which the Pope sits when carried aloft in ceremonies.

Seditio civium hostium est occasio [say-dih'-tih-oh kee'-wih-uhm hos'-tih-uhm est ok-kah'-sih-oh] *L*—Civil discord gives the enemy his opportunity.

Sed transeat [sed trahn'-seh-aht] *L*—But let it pass.

Seis meses de invierno y seis meses de infierno [say'-ees may'-says day een-vyehr'-noh ee say'-ees may'-says day een-fyehr'-noh] *Sp*—Six months of winter and six months of hell. A description of Madrid weather.

Selbst ist der Mann [zelpst ist dehr mahn] *Ger*—One must rely on oneself.

Selon les règles [slohN lay reh-gl] *Fr*—According to the rules.

Semel et simul [seh'-mel et sih'-muhl] *L*—Once and all together.

Semel insanivimus omnes [seh'-mel in-sah-nee'-wih-muhs om'-nays] *L*—We have all gone mad at some time or other. Baptista Mantuanus (Battista Spagnuolo), *Eclogues,* 1; 217.

Semel malus, semper praesumitur esse malus [seh'-mel mah'-luhs sem'-pehr prI-suh'-mih-tuhr ess'-seh mah'-luhs] *L*—Those once convicted of wrongdoing are always presumed to be guilty. It is understood that the same kind of wrongdoing is involved, as, for example, perjury. A legal maxim.

Semen est sanguis Christianorum [say'-men est sahn'-gwis krihs-tee-ah-noh'-ruhm] *L*—Blood (persecution) is the seed of Christians. Tertullian, *Apologeticus,* 50.

Semper avarus eget [sem'-pehr ah-wah'-ruhs eh'-get] *L*—The greedy man is always in need; greed is never satisfied. Horace, *Epistles,* 1; 2, 56.

Semper eadem [sem'-pehr eh'-ah-dem] *L*—Always the same. The motto of Queen Elizabeth I of England.

Semper fidelis [sem'-pehr fih-day'-liss] *L*—Always faithful. Motto of the United States Marine Corps.

Semper idem [sem'-pehr ih'-dem] *L*—Always the same.

Semper inops quicumque cupit [sem'-pehr in'-ops kwee-kuhm'-kweh kuh'-pit] *L*—The man who is always wishing for something is poor. Claudian, *Against Rufinus,* 1; 200.

Semper nocuit differre paratis [sehm'-pehr no'-koo-it dif-fehr'-reh pah-rah'-tees] *L*—Delay is always harmful to those who are prepared. Lucan, *Pharsalia,* 1; 281.

Semper paratus [sem'-pehr pah-rah'-tuhs] *L*—Always prepared. Motto of the United States Coast Guard.

Semper timidum scelus [sem'-pehr tih'-mih-duhm skeh'-luss] *L*—Guilt is always fearful; the guilty live in fear.

Semper vivit in armis [sem'-pehr wee'-wit in ahr'-mees] *L*—He is always armed.

Senatus consultum [seh-nah'-toos kohn-suhl'-tuhm] *L*—A decree of the senate in ancient Rome.

S. en C. *See* Sociedad en comandita.

Senectus insanabilis morbus est [seh-nek'-toos in-sah-nah'-bih-liss mor'-buhs est] *L*—Old age is an incurable disease.

Senectus ipsa morbus est [seh-nek'-toos ip-sah mohr'-buhs est] *L*—Old age in itself is a disease. Terence, *Phormio*, 4; 1, 9.

Senex bis puer [seh'-nex biss puh'-ehr] *L*—An old man is a boy again; old age is a second childhood.

Seniores priores [seh-nih-oh'-rayss prih-oh'-rayss] *L*—Older persons first; give place to age.

Se non è vero, è ben trovato [say nonn eh vay'-roh eh bayn troh-vah'-toh] *It*—If it is not the truth, it is a clever invention.

Sens commun [sahNss kuh-muhN] *Fr*—Common sense; also common consent in matters affecting a large section of society.

Sens dessus dessous [sahNss duh-sü duh-soo] *Fr*—Upside down; topsy-turvy.

Sensim sine sensu aetas senescit [sen'-sim sih'-neh sayn'-soo I'-tahs seh-nays'-kit] *L*—Slowly and imperceptibly old age comes on. Cicero, *Old Age*, 11, last sentence.

Sensu bono [sen'-soo bo'-noh] *L*—In a good sense.

Sensu lato [sen'-soo lah'-toh] *L*—In a broad sense.

Sensu malo [sen'-soo mah'-loh] *L*—In a bad sense.

Sensu proprio [sen'-soo pro'-prih-oh] *L*—In its proper and true meaning.

Sensu stricto [sen'-soo strik'-toh] *L*—In a strict sense.

s. e. o. o. sauf erreur ou omission [sohf eh-ruhr oo oh-mee-syohN] *Fr*—Errors or omissions excepted.

7bre septembre [sep-tahN-br] *Fr*—September, the seventh month in the early Roman calendar. This deceptive abbreviation is based on *septem* (seven) in Latin.

seq., seqq., sq., sqq. sequens, *pl*, sequentia [seh'-kwayns, seh-kwehn'-tih-ah] *L*—The following.

Sera nimis vita est crastina: vive hodie [say'-rah nih'-miss wee'-tah est krahs'-tih-nah wee'-weh ho'-dih-ay] *L*—Living tomorrow is too late: live today. *Martial*, 1; 15, 12.

Serit arbores quae alteri saeclo prosint [seh'-rit ahr'-bo-rays kwI ahl'-teh-ree sI'-kloh proh'-sint] *L*—Old men plant trees that benefit a future age. Quoted by Cicero, *On Old Age*, 7; 24 as from a play by Caecilius Statius.

Sermo humi obrepens [sehr'-moh huh'-mee ob-ray'-payns] *L*—Discourse creeping along on the ground.

Sero molunt deorum molae [say'-roh moh'-luhnt dih-oh'-ruhm moh'-ll] *L*—The mills of the gods grind slowly. The implication is that in the end justice will triumph. Erasmus, *Adagia*. The idea has often been expressed by poets. *See also* Opse theon aleousi myloi . . .

Sero sed serio [say'-roh sed say'-rih-oh] *L*—Serious even though late.

Sero venientibus ossa [say'-roh weh-nih-en'-tih-buhs os'-sah] *L*—Those who come late get the bones; first come, first served.

Serpent d'église [sehr-pahN day-gleez] *Fr*—The church serpent, an obsolete musical instrument with a serpentine tube; a reed stop on the organ.

Serta . . . pinus, malus, oliva, apium [ser'-tah, pee'-nuss mah'-luss oh-lee'-wah ah'-pih-uhm] *L*—Crowns . . . pine, apple, olive and parsley. These were awarded the victors respectively at the Olympian,

Pythian, Isthmian and Nemean games of ancient Greece. Ausonius, *Eclogarium de Lustralibus Agonibus.*

Serus in caelum redeas [say'-ruhs in kI'-luhm reh'-deh-ahs] *L*—May it be long before you return to heaven. The poet hopes that Augustus will live a long life. Horace, *Odes,* 1; 2, 45.

Servatur ubique jus Romanum non ratione imperii, sed rationis imperio [sehr-wah'-tuhr uh-bee'-kweh yoos roh-mah'-nuhm nohn rah-tih-on'-eh ihm-peh'-rih-ee sed rah-tih-on'-iss ihm-peh'-rih-oh] *L*—Roman law is observed everywhere not by reason of rule but by the rule of reason.

Servitium forinsecum [sehr-wih'-tih-uhm foh-reen'-seh-kuhm] *L*—Service or labor due a superior lord by a lesser lord, who in turn passed the obligation on to his tenants.

Servus servorum Dei [sehr'-vuhs sehr-voh'-ruhm deh'-ee] *L*—A servant of the servants of God; often applied to the pope.

Sesquipedalia verba [says-kwee-peh-dah'-lih-ah wehr'-bah] *L*—Literally, words a foot and a half long; very long words. Horace, *Art of Poetry,* 97.

Sestertium reliquit trecenties nec unquam philosophum audivit [says-tehr'-tih-uhm reh-lee'-kwiht treh-ken'-tih-ayss nek oon'-kwahm fih-lo'-so-fuhm ow-dee'-wit] *L*—He left an immense fortune and never listened to a philosopher. From the epitaph of C. Pompeius Trimalchio written by himself. Petronius, *Satyricon,* 71.

S. G. D. G. sans garantie du gouvernement [sahN ga-rahN-tee dü goo-vehr-nuh-mahN] *Fr*—A patent issued by the government without necessarily guaranteeing the quality of the product.

S. E. u O. salvo error u omisíon [sahl'-voh eh-rrohr' oo oh-mee-syohn'] *Sp*—Errors or omissions excepted.

S. Excia Sua Excelência [soo'-ah ish-seh-lehN'-see-ah] *Port*—His Excellency.

sf., sfz. sforzando [sfohr-tsahn'-doh] *It*—A note or chord to be accented.

182

Shalom alekhem [shah-lohm' ah-lay'-khem] *Heb*—Peace unto you. A greeting. *See also* Salaam aleikum.

S. H. S. Societatis Historicae Socius [so-kih-eh-tah'-tis his-toh'-rih-kI so'-kih-uhs] *L*—Fellow of the Historical Society.

s. h. v. sub hac voce *or* sub hoc verbo [suhb hahk woh'-keh *or* suhb hohk wehr'-boh] *L*—Under this word.

Sic [seek] *L*—Thus. Often inserted in a quotation when the writer who is quoting wishes to disclaim responsibility for some error in grammar, spelling, or fact.

Sic eunt fata hominum [seek eh'-uhnt fah'-tah ho'-mih-nuhm] *L*—Such is the fate of man.

Sic itur ad astra [seek ee'-tuhr ahd ahs'-trah] *L*—Thus one climbs to the stars; this is the road to renown. Words originally spoken to Ascanius, the son of Aeneas, by Apollo in disguise. Vergil, *Aeneid,* 9; 641.

Sic passim [seek pahs'-sihm] *L*—Thus throughout (this work). Used to indicate that the same sentiment or expression is found in other passages of a book. The translation given in several manuals, "So everywhere," is deceptive.

Sic semper tyrannis [seek sem'-pehr tih-rahn'neess] *L*—May it be ever thus to tyrants. Motto of Virginia. These words were shouted by Booth as he leaped to the stage after shooting President Lincoln.

Sic transit gloria mundi [seek trahn'-sit gloh'-rih-ah muhn'-dee] *L*—Thus passes the glory of the world. During the consecration of a pope, this expression is repeated three times, preceded by *Reverendissime Pater,* Most Reverend Father.

Sicut ante [see'-kuht ahn'-teh] *L*—As before.

Sic utere tuo ut alienum non laedas [seek oo'-teh-reh tuh'-oh uht ah-lih-ay'-nuhm nohn lI'-dahs] *L*—Use what is yours so as not to harm another.

Sicut patribus, sit Deus nobis [see'-kuht pah'-trih-buhs sit deh'-uhs noh'-beess] *L*—May God be with us as he was with our fathers. Motto of Boston, Massachusetts.

Sic vita [seek wee′-tah] L—Such is life.

Sic volo, sic jubeo, stat pro ratione voluntas L—See Hoc volo, sic jubeo . . . for a preferred reading of the original.

Sic vos non vobis [seek wohs nohn woh′-beess] L—Thus you labor but not for yourselves. Vergil wrote of birds that build nests for their young, sheep that grow wool, bees that make honey, and oxen that pull plows, all toiling for others. Vergil felt he was in a similar situation when a contemporary named Bathyllus tried to deprive him of the glory of a line he had written in praise of Augustus.

s. i. d. semel in die [seh′-mehl in dih′-ay] L—Once a day.

Si Deus nobiscum, quis contra nos? [see deh′-uhs noh-bees′-kuhm kwiss kon′-trah nohs] L—If God is with us, who can be against us? In Vulgate, pro nobis instead of nobiscum. Vulgate, Paul, Romans, 8; 31.

Si Dieu n'existait pas, il faudrait l'inventer [see dyuh nehg-zee-steh pah eel foh-dreh laN-vahN-tay] Fr—If God did not exist, it would be necessary to invent him. Supporting this view, Voltaire erected a church at his own expense. Voltaire, Epître à l'Auteur des Trois Imposteurs.

Si Dieu veult [see dyuh vuhlt] OF—If it be God's will.

Si diis placet [see dih′-ees plah′-ket] L—If it is pleasing to the gods.

Si Dios quiere [see dyohss′ kee-ay′-ray] Sp—If it is God's will.

Si discedas, laqueo tenet ambitiosi/ consuetudo mali [see dihs-kay′-dahs lah′-kweh-oh teh′-net ahm-bih-tih-oh′-see kohn-suh-ay-too′-doh mah′-lee] L—If you try to escape, the habits of a clinging evil hold you in its toils. The poet is here lamenting the lot of the literary man who cannot give up writing. Juvenal, 7; 50.

Siècle des ténèbres [syeh-kl day tay-neh-br] Fr—Dark ages.

Siècle d'or [syeh-kl dawr] Fr—Golden age of Louis XIV.

Sieg Heil [zeek hIl] Ger—Hail, Victory. A greeting during the Hitler regime.

Siglo de oro [see′-gloh day or′-oh] Sp—The Golden Age of classical Spanish literature, from the 16th to the middle of the 17th century.

Sig. n. pro. signa nomine proprio [seeg′-nah noh′-mih-neh prop′-rih-oh] L—Label with the proper name.

Si jeunesse savait, si vieillesse pouvait! [see zhuh-nehss sa-veh see vyay-yehss poo-veh] Fr—If youth only knew, if age only could.

Sile et philosophus esto [sih′-lay et fih-lo′-so-fuhs ess′-toh] L—Keep silent and be counted a philosopher.

Silent leges inter arma [sih′-lent lay′-gayss in′-tehr ahr′-mah] L—The laws are silent in time of war. Cicero, For Milo, 4; 10.

S'il vous plaît [seel voo pleh] Fr—If you please. Abbreviated s. v. p.

Simile gaudet simili L—See Similis simili gaudet.

Similia similibus curantur [sih-mih′-lih-ah sih-mih′-lih-buhs koo-rahn′-tuhr] L—Like is cured by like. The principle of homeopathy.

Similis simili gaudet [sih′-mih-liss sih′-mih-lee gow′-det] L—Like likes like; birds of a feather flock together.

Si monumentum requiris, circumspice [see mo-nuh-men′-tuhm reh-kwih′-riss kihr-kuhm′-spih-keh] L—If you seek his monument, look about you. The epitaph, in London's St. Paul's cathedral, of Sir Christopher Wren, the architect of the building.

Simplex munditiis [sim′-plex muhn-dih′-tih-eess] L—Simple in your elegance. Horace, Odes, 1; 5, 5. The poet is addressing Pyrrha, a beautiful flirt.

Simul sorbere ac flare non possum [sih′-muhl sohr-bay′-reh ahk flah′-reh nohn pos′-suhm] L—I cannot exhale and inhale at the same time; it is impossible to move toward two opposite goals at the same time.

Sinanthropus pekinensis [sih-nahn'-throh-puhs peh-kih-nehn'-siss] *NL*—Chinese man of Pekin, considered the oldest species of prehistoric man.

Sine Cerere et Libero friget Venus [sih'-neh keh'-reh-reh et lee'-beh-roh frih'-get weh'-nuhs] *L*—Without bread and wine love grows cold. Terence, *Eunuch,* 4; 5, 6.

Sine cura [sih'-neh koo'-rah] *L*—An office without duties; a sinecure.

Sine die [sih'-neh dih'-ay] *L*—Adjournment without indicating a day for reconvening.

Sine dubio [sih'-neh duh'-bih-oh] *L*—Without doubt.

Sine ictu [sih'-neh ihk'-too] *L*—Without a blow.

Sine invidia [sih'-neh in-wih'-dih-ah] *L*—Without envy.

Sine ira et studio [sih'-neh ee'-rah et stuh'-dih-oh] *L*—Without anger or partiality. Tacitus, *Annals,* 1; 1.

Sine legitima prole [sih'-neh lay-gi'-tih-mah proh'-leh] *L*—Without legitimate issue.

Sine macula et ruga [sih'-neh mah'-kuh-lah et roo'-gah] *L*—Without stain or wrinkle.

Sine mascula prole [sih'-neh mahs'-kuh-lah proh'-leh] *L*—Without male issue.

Sine mora [sih'-neh moh'-rah] *L*—Without delay.

Sine pennis volare haud facile est [sih'-neh pen'-neess wo-lah'-reh howd fah'-kih-leh est] *L*—It is not at all easy to fly without wings; one should not attempt to do something for which he is unprepared. Plautus, *The Carthaginian,* 4; 2, 49.

Sine praejudicio [sih'-neh prI-yoo-dih'-kih-oh] *L*—Without prejudice.

Sine prole superstite [sih'-neh proh'-leh suh-pehr'-stih-teh] *L*—Without surviving offspring.

Sine qua non *L*—*See* Conditio sine qua non.

Sinn Fein [shin fane] *Ir*—Literally, we ourselves; Irish cultural and political movement stressing separation from Great Britain.

Si non caste, saltem caute [see nohn kahs'-tay sahl'-tem kow'-tay] *L*—If not chastely, at least prudently; if you can't be good, be careful.

Si non credideritis, non permanebitis [see nohn kray-dih-deh'-rih-tis nohn pehr-mah-nay'-bih-tis] *L*—If you do not believe, you will not survive. *Isaias,* 7; 9.

Si non val. si non valeat [see nohn vah'-leh-aht] *L*—If it is not effective. A medical directive.

Si non valeat *L*—*See* Si non val.

Si nous n'avions point de défauts, nous ne prendrions pas tant de plaisir à en remarquer dans les autres [see noo nah-vyohN pwaN duh day-foh noo nuh prahN-dryohN pah tahN duh pleh-zeer ah ahN ruh-mahr-kay dahN lay zoh-tr] *Fr*—If we did not have faults ourselves, we would not take so much pleasure in noticing them in others. La Rochefoucauld, *Maxims,* 31.

Sint ut sunt aut non sint [sint uht suhnt owt nohn sint] *L*—Let things stay as they are or not at all.

Si op. sit. Si opus sit [see o'-puhs sit] *L*—If it is necessary.

Si parva licet componere magnis [see pahr'-wah lih'-ket kom-poh'-neh-reh mahg'-nees] *L*—If one dare compare the small with the large. Vergil, *Georgics,* 4; 176. *See also* Parvis componere magna.

Si quaeris peninsulam amoenam circumspice [see kwI'-ris pay-neen'-suh-lahm ah-moi'-nahm kihr-kuhm'-spih-keh] *L*—If you seek a pleasant peninsula, look about you. Motto of Michigan.

Si sic omnes [see seek om'-nays] *L*—If only all people were thus.

Siste, viator [sihs'-teh wih-ah'-tohr] *L*—Tarry, traveler. Often inscribed on Roman tombstones.

Sit tibi terra levis *L*—*See* S. T. T. L.

Si un Allemand peut être bel-esprit?
[see uhn-ahl-mahN puht-eh-tr bel eh-spree]
Fr—Can a German be a real wit? Père
Bonhours.

**Si vis ad summum progredi, ab infimo
ordire** [see weess ahd suhm'-muhm pro'-
greh-dee ahb in'-fih-moh or-dee'-reh] *L*—
If you want to reach the top, start at the
bottom.

**Si vis me flere, dolendum est/primum
ipsi tibi** [see weess may flay'-reh do-len'-
duhm est pree'-muhm ip'-see tih'-bih] *L*—
If you wish me to weep, you must first
show sorrow yourself. Advice given to tra-
gedians. Horace, *Art of Poetry*, 102.

Si vis pacem, para bellum [see wees
pah'-kem pah'rah bel'-luhm] *L*—If you
want peace, prepare for war. *Vegetius*
(Flavius Renatus, 4th century A. D.).

**Si vous lui donnez un pied, il vous en
prendra quatre** [see voo lwee duh-nay
uhN pyay eel voo zahN prahN-dra kah-tr]
Fr—Give him a foot and he'll take a yard.

s. l. a. n. sine loco, anno, vel nomine
[sih'-neh lo'-koh ahn'-noh well noh'-mih-
neh] *L*—Without place, year, or name of
publisher. Said of books not furnishing
this information.

Slan leat [slahn latt] *Ir*—Good-bye.

s. l. n. d. sans lieu ni date [sahN lyuh nee
dat] *Fr*—Without address and date.

s. l. p. *L*—*See* Sine legitima prole.

S. M. Sa Majesté [sah ma-zhehs-tay] *Fr*—
His Majesty.

S. M. E. Sancta Mater Ecclesia [sank'-tah
mah'-tehr ayk-klay'-sih-ah] *L*—Holy
Mother Church.

s. m. p. *See* Sine mascula prole.

s. n. g. sans notre garantie [sahN nuh-tr
gah-rahN-tee] *Fr*—Without our guarantee.

Sobre gustos no hay disputas [soh'-breh
goos'-tohs noh ah'-ee dees-poo'-tahs] *Sp*—
There is no disputing about tastes. *See
also* De gustibus . . .

Sociedad anónima [soh-syay-dahd' ah-
noh'-nee-mah] *Sp*—A company with limited liability.

Sociedad en comandita [soh-say-dahd'
en koh-mahn-dee'-tah]*Sp*—Limited liability company.

Societas leonina [so-see'-eh-tahs leh-oh-
nee'-nah] *L*—A partnership in which one
person takes the lion's share, leaving all
losses and none of the gains to the other.

Société anonyme [suh-syay-tay ah-noh-
neem] *Fr*—Limited liability company.

Société en commandite [suh-syay-tay
ahN kuh-mahN-deet] *Fr*—Limited liability
company; sleeping partnership.

Socorso non viene mai tardi [soh-kohr'-
soh nonn vee-ay'-nay mah'-ee tahr'-dee]
It—Help that comes is never too late.

So geht es in der Welt [zoh gayt ess in
dehr velt] *Ger*—That's the way things go
in this world.

So Gott will [zoh gott vihl] *Ger*—Please
God.

Soi-disant[swah-dee-zahN]*Fr*—Self-styled;
so-called.

Sola nobilitas virtus [soh'-lah noh-bih'-
lih-tahs wihr'-toos] *L*—Virtue is the only
nobility.

**Solem e mundo tollere videntur ei,
qui amicitiam e vita tollunt** [soh'-lem
ay muhn'-doh tol'-leh-reh wih-den'-tuhr
eh'-ee kwee ah-mee-kih'-tih-ahm ay wee'-
tah tol'-luhnt] *L*—They seem to take the
sun from the world who take friendship
from life. Cicero, *On Friendship*, 13; 47.

Soli cantare periti Arcades [soh'-lee
kahn-tah'-reh peh-ree'-tee ahr'-kah-days]
L—Only the Arcadians know how to sing
beautifully. Vergil, *Eclogues*, 10; 32f.

Solitudinem faciunt, pacem vocant
[ooh-lih-tuh'-dih-nem fah'-kih-uhnt pah'-
kem wo'-kahnt] *L*—They make a desert
and call it peace. For the complete expression, *see* Ubi solitudinem faciunt . . .

Soll und Haben [zuhl unt hah'-bun]
Ger—Debit and credit.

Solus contra mundum [soh'-luhs kon'-
trah muhn'-duhm] *L*—Alone against the
world. Words of Athanasius, Bishop of
Alexandria, when he found himself an exile, opposed by civil and religious powers.

Solvitur ambulando [sol'-wih-tuhr ahm-buh-lahn'-doh] *L*—The problem is solved by walking. Zeno held that all things were at rest; Diogenes argued against this doctrine by walking about. The expression is used when a problem in theory is solved by practical experiment.

Son et lumière [soh-nay lü-myehr] *Fr*—Sound and light.

Sophois homilon kautos ekbese sophos [so-fois' hom-ih-lohn' kow-tos' ek-bay'-say sof-os'] *Gr*—If you associate with the wise, you will become wise yourself. Menander, *Monostichs*, 475.

s. op. s. si opus sit [see op'-uhs sit] *L*—If it is necessary.

Sortes bibliorum [sor'-tayss bih-blih-oh'-ruhm] *L*—*See* Sortes sanctorum.

Sortes sanctorum [sor'-tayss sahnk-toh'-ruhm] *L*—Lots of the saints. An attempt to predict the future by opening the Bible at random and taking the verse on which the eye alights as a guide for future action.

Sortes Vergilianae [sor'-tayss wehr-gih-lih-ah'-nI] *L*—A form of augury, surviving into relatively modern times, by which a person placed a finger at random on a verse of the *Aeneid* and applied it to his own life.

So schnell als möglich [zoh shnell ahls muh-klikh] *Ger*—As quickly as possible.

Sot à triple étage [soh tah tree-play-tahzh] *Fr*—A triple-dyed blockhead; a fool of the worst sort.

Sotto voce [sot'-toh voh'-chay] *It*—In a stage whisper; in an undertone.

Souffler le chaud et le froid [soo-flay luh shoh ay luh frwah] *Fr*—To blow both hot and cold; to appear to favor and to oppose the same motion or project. Politicians are often accused of specializing in this art. The idea is found in a fable of Aesop.

Souhaits sincères [soo-eh saN-sehr] *Fr*—Sincere wishes.

Sous tous les rapports [soo too lay ra-pohr] *Fr*—In all respects.

186

Sous toutes réserves [soo toot ray-zehrv] *Fr*—With all proper reservations; without committing oneself.

S. P. A. Service de la poste aux armées [sehr-vees duh lah pohst oh zahr-may] *Fr*—Army Postal Service.

S. P. A. S. Societatis Philosophicae Americanae Socius [so-kih-eh-tah'-tis fih-lo-so'-fih-kI ah-meh-rih-kah'-nI sok'-ih-uhs] *L*—Fellow of the American Philosophical Society.

Speciali gratia [speh-kih-ah'-lee grah'-tih-ah] *L*—By special grace or favor.

Spectemur agendo [spehk-tay'-muhr ah-gehn'-doh] *L*—Let us be known by our deeds. Motto of Stewart Mott's family, adopted as the name of a charitable foundation which he organized.

Sperat infestis, metuit secundis alteram sortem, bene praeparatum pectus [spay'-raht in-fays'-teess meh'-tuh-it seh-kuhn'-deess ahl'-teh-rahm sor'-tem beh'-neh prI-pah-rah'-tuhm pek'-tuhs] *L*—The well-prepared mind hopes in adversity for a change of fortune, and fears it in prosperity. Horace, *Odes*, 2; 10, 13.

Spes anchora vitae [spays an-koh'-rah wee'-tI] *L*—Hope, the anchor of life. Motto of the Social Security Administration.

Spes sibi quisque [spays sih'-bih kwis'-kweh] *L*—Let each person place his hope in himself, in his own resources.

Spes tutissima caelis [spays too-tis'-sih-mah kI'-leess] *L*—Man's surest hope is heaven.

Speude bradeos [spoi'-deh brah-day'-os] *Gk*—Hasten slowly. *See also* Festina lente.

Spicula et faces amoris [spee'-kuh-lah et fah'-kayss ah-moh'-riss] *L*—The arrows and torches of love; love's artillery.

Spirat adhuc amor [spee'-raht ahd'-hook ah'-mor] *L*—Love still lives.

Spiritus frumenti [spee'-rih-tuhs froo-men'-tee] *L*—Whiskey.

Splendide mendax [splen'dih-day men'-dahx] *L*—Nobly deceptive. Originally applied to one of the fifty Danaids who did not kill her husband on their wedding night, thus breaking her promise to her father Danaus. Horace, *Odes*, 3; 11, 35.

Splendor sine occasu [splen'-dor sih'-neh ok-kah'-soo] *L*—Splendor that never fades. Motto of British Columbia.

Spogliar Pietro per vestir Paolo [spoll-yahr' pee-ay'-troh pehr vess-teer' pah'-o-loh] *It*—To strip Peter to dress Paul; to rob Peter to pay Paul.

Spokoynoy nochi [spuh-koy'-noy noh'-chee] *Rus*—Good night.

Spolia opima [spoh'-lih-ah oh-pee'-mah] *L*—Choice spoils; booty taken by a victorious Roman general from the commander of the defeated army.

Sponte sua [spohn'-teh suh'-ah] *L*—Voluntarily; of his own accord.

S. P. Q. R. Senatus Populusque Romanus [seh-nah'-tuhs po-puh-luhs'-kweh roh-mah'-nuhs] *L*—The Senate and the Roman People.

Spretae injuria formae [spray'-tI in-yoo'-rih-ah fohr'-mI] *L*—The injury offered to her spurned beauty. Juno harbored a deep resentment because Paris judged Venus more beautiful than she was. Vergil, *Aeneid*, 1; 27.

Spurlos versenkt [shpoor'-lohs fehr-zengt'] *Ger*—Sunk without a trace.

s/r. su remesa [soo ray-may'-sah] *Sp*—Your remittance.

S. R. C. Santa Romana Chiesa [sahn'-tah roh-mah'-nah kee-ay-zah] *It*—Holy Roman Catholic Church.

S. R. E.. Sancta Romana Ecclesia [sahnk'-tah roh-mah'-nah ayk-klay'-sih-ah] *L*—Holy Roman Church.

S. R. I. Sacro Romano Impero [sah'-kroh roh-mah'-noh eem-pay'-roh] *It*—Holy Roman Empire.

S. R. I. Sacrum Romanum Imperium [sak'-ruhm roh-mah'-nuhm im-peh'-rih-uhm] *L*—The Holy Roman Empire.

S. R. S. Societatis Regiae Socius [so-kih-eh-tah'-tis ray'-gih-I so'-kih-uhs] *L*—Fellow of the Royal Society.

S. S. Santa Sede [sahn'-tah say'-day] *It*—Holy See.

S. S. Sa Sainteté [sa saN-tuh-tay] *Fr*—His Holiness.

S. S. Schutzstaffel [shuts'-shtah-ful] *Ger*—Literally, defense staff; Hitler's guard, a Nazi military unit known as the Black Shirts. They formed a more select body than the Storm Troopers, called the Brown Shirts.

SS. Scilicet [skee'-lih-ket] *L*—A legal abbreviation; a contraction of *scire licet* [skee'-reh lih'-ket] meaning as one may learn.

S. S. Sua Santità [soo'-ah sahn-tee-tah'] *It*—His Holiness.

S. S. S. R. Soyuz Sovetskikh Sotsialisticheskikh Respublik [sah-yoos' soh-viet'-skeekh so-tsee-ahl-ees-tee'-ches-keekh ryes-poob'-leek] *Rus*—Union of Soviet Socialist Republics.

s. s. s. stratum super stratum [strah'-tuhm suh'-pehr strah'-tuhm] *L*—Layer upon layer.

S. S. S. Su seguro servidor [soo say-goo'-roh sehr-vee-dohr] *Sp*—Your faithful servant.

S. S. V. sub signo veneni [suhb seeg'-noh weh-nay'-nee] *L*—Under a label marked "poison."

Stabat Mater [stah'-baht mah'-tehr] *L*—Literally, the mother stood. The first words of a hymn dating from the thirteenth century. Its authorship is disputed but it is generally attributed to Iacopone da Todi.

Stare decisis et non quieta movere [stah'-reh day-kee'-seess et nohn kwih-ay'-tah moh-way'-reh] *L*—To stand by matters that have been decided and not disturb what is tranquil; to uphold precedents and resist change.

Stare super vias antiquas [stah'-reh suh'-pehr wih'-ahss ahn-tee'-kwahss] *L*—To cling to the old ways.

Stat magni nominis umbra [staht mahg'-nee noh'-mih-nis uhm'-brah] *L*—He stands, the mere shadow of a great name. The reference was to Pompey, compared to an oak with dead roots. Said of one who becomes prominent and fails to live up to expectations. Lucan, *Pharsalia*, 1; 135.

Status belli [stah'-tuhs bel'-lee] *L*—A state of war.

Status quaestionis [stah'-tuhs kwIs-tih-oh'niss] *L*—The state of the question; an explanation of terms used in a thesis, together with a review of opinions held on the subject.

Status quo [stah'-tuhs kwoh] *L*—The existing state of affairs.

Status quo ante bellum [stah'-tuhs kwoh ahn'-teh bel'-luhm] *L*—Conditions as they existed before the war.

S. T. B. Sacrae Theologiae Baccalaureus [sah'-kray teh-oh-loh-gih'-ay bahk-kah-low'-reh-uhs] *L*—Bachelor of Sacred Theology.

S. T. D. Sacrae Theologiae Doctor [sah'-kray teh-oh-loh-gih'-ay dok'-tohr] *L*—Doctor of Sacred Theology.

Stemmata quid faciunt? [staym'-mah-tah kwid fah'-kih-uhnt] *L*—Of what value are pedigrees? Juvenal, 8; 1. The poet goes on to say that the only basis of nobility is virtue. *See also* Nobilitas sola est atque unica virtus.

Stet [stett] *L*—Let it stand. Used in proofreading to indicate that something queried or removed from the text should be retained.

Stet processus [stett proh-kehs'-suhs] *L*—Let the process stand; court order suspending further action.

StGB Strafgesetzbuch [shtrahf-guh-zetts'-bookh] *Ger*—Penal code.

S. T. L. Sacrae Theologiae Lector *or* Licentiatus [sah'-kray teh-oh-loh-gih'-ay lek'-tor *or* lih-sen-tsih-ah'-toos] *L*—Reader in Sacred Theology or the Licentiate of Sacred Theology. A degree between the S. T. B. and the S. T. D.

Strictum jus [strick'-tuhm yoos] *L*—Law strictly interpreted according to the letter without consideration of equities.

S. T. T. L. Sit tibi terra levis [sit tib'-bih tehr'-rah leh'-wis] *L*—May the earth rest lightly upon you. Letters found on Roman tombs.

Studium immane loquendi [stuh'-dih-uhm im-mah'-neh lo-kwen'-dee] *L*—A limitless desire to talk. Ovid, *Metamorphoses*, 5; 678.

Stultum facit fortuna quem vult perdere [stuhl'-tuhm fah'-kit for-too'-nah kwem wuhlt pehr'-deh-reh] *L*—Fortune first makes a fool out of the man she wishes to destroy. Publilius Syrus.

Stupor mundi [stuh'-por muhn'-dee] *L*—Wonder of the world. Said of a genius so remarkable that he amazes the world. A notable example was Frederick II, German King and Roman Emperor (1194-1250).

Sturm und Drang [shtoorm uhnt drahng] *Ger*—Storm and stress; a period of late 18th-century German literature characterized by intellectual and emotional upheaval. The name was taken from a play by Klinger.

Sua cuique voluptas [suh'-ah kwee'-kweh wo-luhp'-tahs] *L*—Every man has his own pleasures.

Suadente diabolo [swah-den'-teh dih-ah'-boh-loh] *L*—At the devil's persuasion.

Suave, mari magno turbantibus aequora ventis,/e terra magnum alterius spectare laborem [swah'-weh mah'-ree mahg'-noh tuhr-bahn'-tih-buhs I'-kwoh-rah wehn'-teess ay tehr'-rah mahg'-nuhm ahl-teh-ree'-uhs spek-tah'-reh lah-boh'-rehm] *L*—It is pleasant when safe on the land to watch the great struggle of another out on a swelling sea amid winds churning the deep. Lucretius, *The Nature of Things*, 2; 1.

Suaviter in modo, fortiter in re [swah'-wih-tehr in mo'-doh for'-tih-tehr in ray] *L*—Act gently in manner, vigorously in deed. President Theodore Roosevelt's maxim, Speak softly and carry a big stick.

Sub conditione, *var.* **condicione** [suhb kon-dih-tih-oh'-neh; *or, in legal usage,* suhb kon-dee-shee-oh'-nee] *L*—Upon condition; with a proviso.

Sub dio [suhb dee'-oh] *L*—Under the open sky.

Sub init. sub initio [suhb in-ih'-tih-oh] *L*—At the beginning. Used in citing a literary reference.

Sub judice [suhb yoo'-dih-keh] *L*—Under consideration.

Sublata causa, tollitur effectus [suhb-lah'-tah kow'-sah tol'-lih-tuhr ef-fek'-tuhs] *L*—Once the cause is removed, the effect disappears.

Sub modo [suhb mo'-doh] *L*—In a manner; in a qualified manner.

Sub plumbo [suhb pluhm'-boh] *L*—Literally, under lead; under papal seal, made of lead.

Sub poena [suhb poi'-nah *or in common usage,* sub pee-nah] *L*—Under a penalty; a writ ordering a person to appear in court under pain of punishment.

Sub rosa [suhb ro'-sah] *L*—Secretly; confidentially. The origin is uncertain. In ancient Egypt the rose was an emblem of Horus. The Greeks and Romans wrongly thought him the god of silence. There is also a story that Cupid gave a rose to Harpocrates, the god of silence, to seal his lips about the love affairs of Venus. When a rose was displayed overhead at a party, it was the general understanding that whatever took place was to be kept secret.

Sub sigillo [suhb sih-gihl'-loh] *L*—Under seal (of silence); in confidence, as in confession.

Sub silentio [suhb sih-len'-tih-oh] *L*—In silence. Used when a matter is passed over without formal notice.

Sub specie [suhb speh'-kih-ay] *L*—Under the appearance of.

Sub specie aeternitatis [suhb speh'-kih-ay I-tehr-nih-tah'-tiss] *L*—From the aspect of eternity; the consideration of things in their relation to the perfection of God. Spinoza, *The Ethics*, pt. 5; 29.

Sub verbo [suhb wehr'-boh] *L*—Under the word; a term used in cross reference in dictionaries, etc. *See also* Sub voce.

Sub vi [suhb wee] *L*—Under compulsion. When a man is forced to sign, he may write *s.v.* after his name.

Sub voce [suhb wo'-keh] *L*—Under the word; referring to an entry in an index, vocabulary, etc.

Succès de mouchoir [sük-seh duh mooshwahr] *Fr*—Literally, success of the handkerchief; said of a writer's ability to bring tears to the reader's eyes.

Succès de scandale [sük-seh duh skahN-dal] *Fr*—A success based on scandalous revelations.

Succès d'estime [sük-seh deh-steem] *Fr*—Not a financial success; said of a play appreciated by discerning friends and critics rather than by the general public.

Succès fou [sük-seh foo] *Fr*—Fantastic success.

Sufflaminandus erat [suhf-flah-mih-nahn'-duhs eh'-raht] *L*—He should have been clogged, repressed. In his comments on Shakespeare, *De Shakespeare Nostrati* (On our Fellow-Countryman Shakespeare), Ben Jonson stated that Shakespeare "flowed with that facility that sometimes it was necessary he should be stopped." This expression is based on a remark of Augustus in which he censured Q. Haterius for talking too rapidly.

Sui compos [suh'-ee kom'-pos] *L*—In possession of one's reason.

Sui generis [suh'-ee geh'-neh-riss] *L*—In a class by itself.

Sui juris [suh'-ee yoo'-riss] *L*—Literally, of one's own right; applied to a person in a position to exercise his full rights and not limited by some legal restraint such as being a minor or subject to mental illness.

Summa cum laude *L*—*See* Cum laude.

Summum bonum [suhm'-muhm bo'-nuhm] *L*—The supreme good. Cicero, *On Duties*, 1; 2, 5.

Summum jus, summa injuria [suhm'-muhm yoos suhm'-mah in-yoo'-rih-ah] *L*—Extreme justice is extreme injustice. Cicero, *On Duties*, 1; 10, 33. *See also* Jus summum saepe summa est malitia.

Sumptibus publicis [soomp'-tih-buhs poo'-blih-keess] *L*—At public expense.

Sum quod eris, fui quod sis [suhm kwod eh'-ris fuh'-ee kwod seess] *L*—I am what you will be; I was what you are. A reminder engraved on tombstones.

Sunt lacrimae rerum et mentem mortalia tangunt [suhnt lah'-krih-mI ray'-ruhm et men'-tem mor-tah'-lih-ah tahn'-guhnt] *L*—Human experience is full of sorrow and the lot of man is depressing. Vergil, *Aeneid*, 1; 462.

Suo loco [suh'-oh lo'-koh] *L*—In its proper place.

Suo Marte [suh'-oh mahr'-teh] *L*—By one's own toil, effort, courage. Cicero, *On Duties*, 3; 7. Motto of Wilberforce University, first college owned and operated by Blacks.

Suo nomine [suh'-oh noh'-mih-neh] *L*—By its own name. A physician's direction to a pharmacist that the label on the bottle containing the drug indicate the chemical name of the medicine.

Suo periculo [suh'-oh peh-ree'-kuh-loh] *L*—At one's own risk.

Suo sibi gladio hunc jugulo [suh'-oh sih'-bih glah'-dih-oh huhnk yuh'-guh-loh] *L*—I will cut this man's throat with his own sword; I will turn this man's arguments against himself. Terence, *The Brothers*, 5; 8, 35.

Super visum corporis [suh'-pehr wee'-suhm kor'-poh-ris] *L*—After viewing the body. Term used at a coroner's inquest.

Suppressio veri suggestio falsi [suh-prehs'-sih-oh weh'-ree suhg-gehs'-tih-oh fahl'-see] *L*—Suppressing the truth is a hint of deception.

Surgit amari aliquid quod in ipsis floribus angat [suhr'-git ah-mah'-ree ah'-lih-kwid kwod in ip'-seess floh'-rih-buss ahn'-gaht] *L*—Something bitter always arises to

190

poison our sweetest joys; there is always a fly in the ointment. Lucretius, *The Nature of Things*, 4; 1134 (1135).

Sur le pavé [sür luh pa-vay] *Fr*—On the street; poverty-stricken.

Sur le tapis [sür luh ta-pee] *Fr*—Literally, on the carpet. Formerly tables were covered with carpets; for this reason the expression came to mean that a matter was on the table and, therefore, under consideration.

Sur place [sür plass] *Fr*—On the spot.

Sursum corda [soor'-suhm kor'-dah] *L*—Lift up your hearts.

Surtout, point de zèle [sür-too pwaN duh zehl] *Fr*—Above all, don't be too enthusiastic; don't overdo things; don't lose your poise. Advice of Talleyrand to his subordinates.

Suspendatur per collum [suhs-spen-dah'-tuhr pehr kol'-luhm] *L*—Let him be hanged by the neck; abbreviated *sus. per coll. Suspensus per collum* means that a person was hanged in this manner.

Suspendens omnia naso [suhs-spen'-dayns om'-nih-ah nah'-soh] *L*—Turning up one's nose at everything; ridiculing everything. Horace, *Satires*, 1; 8, 64.

Sus. per coll. *L*—*See* Suspendatur per collum.

Suspiria de Profundis [suhs-pee'-rih-ah day pro-fuhn'deess] *L*—Sighs from the depths; title of a work by Thomas de Quincey.

Sutor ne supra crepidam [soo'-tohr nay suh'-prah kreh'-pih-dahm] *L*—Let the shoemaker stick to his last. According to Pliny the Elder, the Greek painter Apelles accepted the correction of a shoemaker that a shoe in one of his paintings needed another latch. When the shoemaker criticized the painting of the leg, Apelles gave this retort. Pliny the Elder, *Natural History*, 35; 10.

Suum cuique [suh'-uhm kwee'-kweh] *L*—His own to everyone; to each his own.

Suus cuique mos [suh'-uhs kwee'-kweh mohss] *L*—Each person has his own moral point of view.

s. v. spiritus vini [spee'-rih-tuhs vee'-nee] *L*—Alcoholic spirit.

s. v. *See* Sub verbo, Sub vi, Sub voce.

s. v. p. *Fr*—*See* S'il vous plaît.

s. v. r. spiritus vini rectificatus [spee'-rih-tuhs vee'-nee rayk-tih-fih-kah'-tuhs] *L*—Rectified spirit of wine.

s. v. t. spiritus vini tenuis [spee'-rih-tuhs vee'-nee teh'-nuh-ihs] *L*—Proof spirit.

T

t. a. testantibus actis [tes-tahn'-tih-buhs ahk'-teess] *L*—As the records show.

Table d'hôte [tah-bl doht] *Fr*—The table of the host; a meal served to patrons at a fixed price.

Tabula rasa [tah'-buh-lah rah'-sah] *L*—An erased tablet; a clean slate. Locke's image of the mind at birth.

Tace [tah'-kay] *L*—Be silent.

Tacent, satis laudant [tah'-kent sah'-tis low'-dahnt] *L*—They are silent; that's praise enough. Terence, *Eunuch*, 3; 2, 23.

Tâche sans tache [tahsh sahN tash] *Fr*—A work without a stain.

Tacitae magis et occultae inimicitiae timendae sunt quam indictae atque apertae [tah'-kih-tI mah'-gis et ok-kuhl'-tI ih-nih-mih-kee'-tih-I tih-men'-dI suhnt kwahm in-dik'-tI aht'-kweh ah-pehr'-tI] *L*—Silent, hidden enmities are more to be feared than those that are openly declared. Cicero, *Against Verres*, 2; 5, 71.

Taedium vitae [tI'-dih-uhm wee'-tI] *L*—Weariness of living; the feeling that life is not worth living.

Ta gueule [tah guhl] *Fr*—Shut up!

Tal cual [tahl kwahl] *Sp*—So, so.

Tal padrone, tal servitore [tahl pah-droh'-nay tahl sehr-vee-toh'-ray] *It*—Like master, like man.

Tangere ulcus [tahn'-geh-reh ool'-kuhs] *L*—To touch a sore spot.

Tantaene animis caelestibus irae? [tahn-tI'-neh ah'-nih-mees kI-les'-tih-buhs ee'-rI] *L*—Can such great anger dwell in heavenly breasts? Vergil, *Aeneid*, 1; 11.

192

Tant bien que mal [tahN byaN kuh mal] *Fr*—As well as possible.

Tant mieux [tahN myuh] *Fr*—So much the better.

Tanto buono che val niente [tahn'-toh bwoh'-noh kay vahl nee-en'-tay] *It*—So good that it is good for nothing.

Tanto nomini nullum par elogium [tahn'-toh noh'-mih-nee nool'-luhm pahr ay-loh'-gih-uhm] *L*—No eulogy can do justice to so great a name. A tribute to Michelangelo.

Tant pis [tahN pee] *Fr*—So much the worse.

Tant soit peu [tahN swah puh] *Fr*—Ever so little.

Tantum ergo [tahn'-tuhm ehr'-goh] *L*—So great (a Sacrament) therefore. The title and first words of a hymn to the Eucharist by Thomas Aquinas sung at Benediction when Catholic ritual was in Latin. The two stanzas end the hymn *Pange, lingua, gloriosi* (*q.v.*).

Tantum pellis et ossa fuit [tahn'-tuhm pel'-lis et os'-sah fuh'-it] *L*—*See* Ossa atque pellis totus est.

Tantum possumus quantum scimus [tahn'-tuhm pos'-suh-muhs kwahn'-tuhm skee'-muhs] *L*—We are effective in proportion to our knowledge. Francis Bacon.

Tantum religio potuit suadere malorum! [tahn'-tuhm reh-lih'-gih-oh po'-tuh-it swah-day'-reh mah-loh'-ruhm] *L*—For how many evils has religion been responsible! This line was prompted by the sacrifice of Iphigeneia at Aulis. Lucretius, *The Nature of Things*, 1; 101.

Te Deum (laudamus) [tay deh'-uhm low-dah'-muhs] *L*—We praise thee, O Lord. A hymn sung at certain Christian services, especially on occasions of general thanksgiving.

Te judice [tay yoo'-dih-keh] *L*—With you acting as judge; in your judgment.

Tel est notre bon plaisir [tehl eh nuh-tr bohN pleh-zeer] *Fr*—Such is our good pleasure. With these words French kings approved a new law.

Tel font les parents, tel feront les enfants [tel fohN lay pah-rahN tel feh-rohN lay zahN-fahN] *Fr*—As the parents act, so will the children.

Tel maître, tel valet [tehl meh-tr tehl va-leh] *Fr*—Like master, like valet.

Tel père, tel fils [tel pehr tel fees] *Fr*—Like father, like son.

Tel quel [tehl kehl] *Fr*—Just as it is. A business term.

Telum imbelle sine ictu [tay'-luhm im-bel'-leh sih'-neh ik'-too] *L*—A weapon feebly thrown without effect. The poet's description of the spear thrown by the aged Priam at Pyrrhus, the son of Achilles. Used to describe a feeble argument. Vergil, *Aeneid*, 2; 544.

Tempora mutantur, nos et mutamur in illis [tem'-po-rah moo-tahn'-tuhr nohs et moo-tah'-muhr in il'-leess] *L*—Times change and we are changed in them. John Owen, *Epigrams*, 8; 58.

Tempore felici multi numerantur amici [tem'-po-reh fay-lee'-kee muhl'-tee nuh-meh-rahn'-tuhr ah-mee'-kee] *L*—We number many friends when we are prosperous.

Tempori parendum [tem'-po-ree pah-rehn'-duhm] *L*—We must move with the times.

Tempus edax rerum [tem'-puss eh'-dahx ray'-ruhm] *L*—Time that devours all things. Ovid, *Metamorphoses*, 15; 234.

Tempus fugit [tem'-puss fuh'-git] *L*—Time flies.

Tempus omnia revelat [tem'-puss om'-nih-ah reh-weh'-laht] *L*—Time reveals everything.

Teres atque rotundus *L*—*See* Totus teres atque rotundus.

Terminus ad quem [tehr'-mih-nuhs ahd kwehm] *L*—A goal or end toward which an effort is directed.

Terminus ante quem [tehr'-mih-nuhs ahn'-teh kwem] *L*—Literally, the end before which; for example, the date before which an event must have taken place.

Terminus a quo [tehr'-mih-nuhs ah kwoh] *L*—The end from which; the point of departure.

Terrae filius *L*—*See* Filius terrae.

Terra firma [tehr'-rah feer'-mah] *L*—Solid earth. To Venetians it means the dry earth, the mainland.

Terra incognita [tehr'-rah in-kog'-nih-tah] *L*—An unexplored land. It is often used in referring to matters about which one is uninformed.

Terra irredenta [tehr'-rah eer-ray-den'-tah] *It*—Unredeemed land; a territory inhabited for the most part by nationals of one's country but ruled by another that won it by arms.

Terra marique [tehr'-rah mah-ree'-kweh] *L*—By land and sea.

Terre promise [tehr pruh-meez] *Fr*—The Promised Land.

Tertium quid [tehr'-tih-uhm kwid] *L*—A third something, produced by the meeting of two opposing forces.

Terza rima [tehr'-tsah ree'-mah] *It*—Three iambic verses, the first and the third rhyming and the second furnishing the rhyme for the first and third lines of each following triplet; the rhyme scheme of Dante's *Divine Comedy*.

Tête-à-tête [teht ah teht] *Fr*—Literally, head to head; confidential conversation.

Tête de veau [teht duh voh] *Fr*—Calf's-head.

Teterrima causa belli [tay-tehr'-rih-mah kow'-sah bel'-lee] *L*—Most shameful, horrid cause of war.

Textus receptus [tex′-tuhs reh-kep′-tuhs] *L*—The text approved by authorities in a particular academic discipline.

Thalassa, thalassa [thah′-lah-sah thah′-lah-sah] *Gk*—*See* Thalatta, thalatta.

Thalatta, thalatta! [thah′-lah-tah thah′-lah-tah] *Gk*—The sea, the sea! The cry of Greek mercenaries when they sighted the Black Sea on their retreat after the battle of Cunaxa. Xenophon, *Anabasis*, 4; 7.

Theo (i) mono (i) doxa [theh-oh′ moh′-noh dox′-ah. The *i*, or *iota*, is subscript and not pronounced] *Gk*—Glory to the one and only God.

Theos ek mechanes [theh-os′ ek may-khah-nays′] *Gk*—*See* Deus ex machina.

Thesaurus Americae Septentrionis Sigillum [tay-sow′-ruhs ah-may′-rih-kI septen-trih-oh′-niss sih-gihl′-luhm] *L*—Literally, Seal of the Treasury of North America, i.e., the United States.

Tic douloureux [teek doo-loo-ruh] *Fr*—A painful tic; facial neuralgia.

t. i. d. ter in die [tehr in dih′-ay] *L*—Three times a day. A medical direction.

Tiens à la vérité [tyaN ah lah vay-ree-tay] *Fr*—Hold to the truth.

Tiers état [tyehr zay-tah] *Fr*—The third estate, the common people in France in pre-Revolutionary times. A division of society comprising all except the clergy and the nobility.

Timeo Danaos et dona ferentes [tih′-meh-oh dah′-nah-ohs et doh′-nah feh-ren′ tays] *L*—I fear the Greeks even though they bring gifts. Vergil, *Aeneid*, 2; 49.

Timeo hominem (virum) unius libri [tih′-meh-oh ho′-mih-nem, wih′-ruhm, oo-nee′-uhs lih′-bree] *L*—I fear the man of one book. This may be interpreted in two ways: I fear the man who knows one book thoroughly because he will be a strong opponent in an argument, or I have my doubts about the knowledge of a man who knows only one book. In the Middle Ages the first meaning was intended.

Tirage au sort [tee-rahzh oh sawr] *Fr*—

Drawing of lots as for military conscription or impaneling a jury.

Tiré à quatre épingles [tee-ray ah kah-tr ay-paN-gl] *Fr*—Dapper, elegant, neat.

Toga candida [toh′-gah kahn′-dih-dah] *L*—White toga worn by Roman candidates for office.

Toga praetexta [toh′-gah prI-tex′-tah] *L*—Roman garment with purple border worn by magistrates, priests, and children.

Toga virilis [toh′-gah wih-ree′-liss] *L*—Toga worn by Roman males from the age of fifteen.

Toison d'or [twah-zohN dawr] *Fr*—Golden fleece.

To kalon [toh kah-lon′] *Gk*—The beautiful.

Tolle, lege; tolle, lege [tol′-leh leh′-geh tol′-leh leh′-geh] *L*—Take it and read, take it and read. These were a child's words which prompted Augustine to take up the epistles of Saint Paul and read what first struck his eye, a passage from the Epistle to the Romans. Augustine, *Confessions*, 8; 12, 29.

Tombé des nues [tohN-bay day nü] *Fr*—Fallen from the clouds; unexpected arrival.

To me on [toh may onn] *Gk*—Non-being.

Tonnerre de Dieu! [tuhn-nehr duh dyuh] *Fr*—An interjection. Literally, the thunder of God; by thunder!

Totidem verbis [toh′-tih-dem wehr′-beess] *L*—In just so many words.

Toties quoties [toh′-tih-ays kwoh′-tih-ays] *L*—As often as; as often, so often. If a man is fined a certain sum and is similarly fined for each subsequent offense, he is said to be fined *toties quoties*. An indulgence granted *toties quoties* is one that applies each and every time that the conditions for it are fulfilled.

Totis viribus [toh′-tees wee′-rih-buhs] *L*—With all one's strength.

Toto caelo [toh′-toh kI′-loh] *L*—By the whole heavens; to be poles apart. Generally used to express a world of difference.

Totus mundus agit histrionem [toh′-tuhs muhn′-duhs ah′-git his-trih-oh′-nem]

L—All the world plays the actor. As Shakespeare put it in *As You Like It*, 2; 7, 137, "All the world's a stage, and all the men and women merely players."

Totus teres atque rotundus [toh'-tuhs teh'-rehs aht'-kweh roh-tuhn'-duhs] *L*—Complete, smooth, and rounded; the wise man, according to the Stoics, who rolls through the world as smoothly as a sphere. Horace, *Satires*, 2; 7, 86.

Toujours en vedette [too-zhoor ahN vuh-deht] *Fr*—Always on guard. Motto of Frederick the Great.

Toujours l'amour [too-zhoor lah-moor] *Fr*—Love, always love.

Toujours perdrix [too-zhoor pehr-dree] *Fr*—Always partridge; the same old story. The expression of the spiritual adviser of Henri IV when the French King had partridge served at every course of a meal as a jest.

Toujours prêt [too-zhoor preh] *Fr*—Always ready.

Tour de force [toor duh forss] *Fr*—Feat of exceptional strength or cleverness.

Tour d'horizon [toor duh-ree-zohN] *Fr*—A general survey of a situation.

Tous droits réservés [too drwah ray-zehr-vay] *Fr*—All rights reserved.

Tous frais faits [too freh feh] *Fr*—All expenses paid.

Tous mes effets [too may zeh-feh] *Fr*—All my effects and property.

Tout à fait [too tah feh] *Fr*—Entirely; quite; wholly.

Tout à l'heure [too tah luhr] *Fr*—Instantly.

Tout au contraire [too toh kohN-trehr] *Fr*—Quite the contrary.

Tout bien ou rien [too byan oo ryaN] *Fr*—Everything done well or not at all.

Tout chemin mène (va) à Rome [too shuh-man mehn, vah, ah rohm] *Fr*—All roads lead to Rome; there are many ways of reaching one's goal. According to this proverb, the end, not the means, is important.

Tout comprendre c'est tout pardonner [too kohN-prahN-dr seh too par-doh-nay] *Fr*—To understand everything is to pardon everything.

Tout court [too koor] *Fr*—And nothing more, simply, only.

Tout de suite [toot sweet] *Fr*—Immediately; at once.

Tout d'un coup [too duhN koo] *Fr*—All of a sudden.

Toute la dignité de l'homme consiste en la pensée [toot lah dee-nyee-tay duh luhm kohN-seest ahN lah pahN-say] *Fr*—All the dignity of man lies in thought. Pascal, *Pensées*, 365.

Toute(s) proportion(s) gardée(s) [toot pruh-por-syohN gar-day] *Fr*—With due regard for proper proportions; proportionately speaking.

Tout est bien qui finit bien [too teh byaN kee fee-nee byaN] *Fr*—All's well that ends well.

Tout est perdu fors l'honneur [too teh pehr-dü fawr luhn-nuhr] *Fr*—Everything is lost save honor. Not the exact words but the sense of a letter written by the French King Francis I after the defeat at Pavia.

Tout le monde [too luh mohNd] *Fr*—Literally, all the world; everybody.

Tout le monde se plaint de sa mémoire, et personne ne se plaint de son jugement [too luh mohNd suh plaN duh sah may-mwahr ay pehr-suhn nuh suh plaN duh sohN zhuzh-mahN] *Fr*—All complain about their memories, but nobody complains about their judgment. La Rochefoucauld, *Maxims*, 89.

Tout lui rit (sourit) [too lwee ree, soo-ree] *Fr*—Everything smiles upon him; he is always lucky.

Tout s'en va, tout passe, l'eau coule, et le coeur oublie [too sahN vah too pass loh kool ay luh kuhr oo-blee] *Fr*—Everything vanishes, everything passes, water runs away, and the heart forgets. Flaubert.

t/q tale quale [tah'-leh kwah'-leh] *L*—As they come; run of mine; run of the mill. *See also* Tel quel.

Traduttore, traditore [trah-doo-toh'-ray trah-dee-toh'-ray] *It*—The translator is a traitor. He turns out a translation that is better or worse than the original. No translator can possibly convey the full meaning of the original.

Trahimur omnes studio laudis, et optimus quisque maxime gloria ducitur [trah'-hih-muhr om'-nays stuh'-dih-oh low'-dis et op'-tih-muhs kwis'-kweh mahx'-ih-may gloh'-rih-ah doo'-kih-tuhr] *L*—We are all moved by a desire for praise, and the nobler a man is, the more he is influenced by glory. Cicero, *For Archias*, 10; 26.

Trahit sua quemque voluptas [trah'-hit suh'-ah kwehm'-kweh wo-luhp'-tahs] *L*—Everyone is attracted by his own special pleasure. Vergil, *Eclogues*, 2; 65.

Tranche de vie [trahNsh duh vee] *Fr*—Slice of life; a careful, objective description of life as it is, portrayed by naturalistic writers such as Zola, Maupassant, Balzac, and Hardy.

Transeat in exemplum [trahn'-seh-aht in ex-em'-pluhm] *L*—Let it be recorded as a precedent.

Translatio imperii [trahns-lah'-tih-oh im-peh'-rih-ee] *L*—Transfer of the Empire; theory of Innocent III (d. 1216) on the political power of the Papacy.

Travaux forcés [tra-voh fawr-say] *Fr*—Forced labor; penal servitude.

Trente-et-quarante [trahNt ay kah-rahNt] *Fr*—Gambling game with cards in which the players bet on one of two colors, red and black (*rouge et noire*).

Tre ore [tray oh'-ray] *It*—Three hours, referring to the three hours of devotion on Good Friday, from noon to three o'clock.

Très bien [treh byaN] *Fr*—Very well; all right.

Treuga Dei [treh'-uh-gah deh'-ee] *L*—Truce of God. The attempt on the part of the Church beginning in the 11th century to limit by means of excommunication the number of days in the week on which soldiers might fight. The Truce began at noon on Saturday (later on Wednesday evening) and lasted until Monday morning. It also

extended in some places to Advent, Lent, and numerous religious feasts.

Treva Dei [tray'-vah deh'-ee] *L*—Truce of God. *See also* Treuga Dei.

Trêve de Dieu [trehv duh dyuh] *Fr*—Truce of God. *See also* Treuga Dei.

Tria juncta in uno [trih'-ah yoonk'-tah in oo'-noh] *L*—Three joined in one. Motto of the Order of the Bath, Great Britain. The three classes of the Order established in 1725 were combined in 1815 "to commemorate the auspicious termination of the long and arduous contest in which the Empire has been engaged."

Trompe-l'oeil [troNp luh-yuh] *Fr*—Optical illusion; in painting, a still-life deception.

Trop de hâte gâte tout [troh duh aht gaht too] *Fr*—Too much hurry spoils everything; more haste, less speed; haste makes waste.

Tros Tyriusque mihi nullo discrimine agetur [trohs tih-rih-uhs'-kweh mih'-hih nool'-loh dihs-kree'-mih-neh ah-gay'-tuhr] *L*—Whether Trojan or Tyrian, I shall treat them impartially. Queen Dido's promise to the shipwrecked Trojans. Vergil, *Aeneid*, 1; 574.

Truditur dies die [troo'-dih-tuhr dih'-ays dih'-ay] *L*—One day follows on the heels of another. Horace, *Odes*, 2; 18, 15.

T. S. V. P. Tournez s'il vous plaît [toornay seel voo pleh] *Fr*—Please turn the page.

Tua res agitur, paries cum proximus ardet [tuh'-ah rays ah'-gih-tuhr pa'-rih-ays kuhm prox'-ih-muhs ahr'-det] *L*—Your property is at stake when your neighbor's house is on fire. Horace, *Epistles*, 1; 18, 84.

Tu, enim, Caesar, civitatem dare potes hominibus, verbis non potes [too eh'-nim kI'-sahr kee-wih-tah'-tehm dah'-reh po'-tays ho-mih'-nih-buhs wehr'-beess nohn po'-tays] *L*—Caesar, you can give men citizenship but you cannot make rules for language. When Tiberius made a grammatical error in a speech, a court favorite said that the error would be accepted because it was the emperor who made it.

The grammarian M. Pomponius Marcellus objected with these words. Suetonius, *Eminent Grammarians*, 22.

Tuer le veau gras [tü-ay luh voh grah] *Fr*—To kill the fatted calf; to celebrate.

Tu ne cede malis sed contra audentior ito [too nay kay'-deh mah'-leess sed kon'-trah ow-den'-tih-or ee'-toh] *L*—Do not yield to misfortune but oppose it with greater boldness. Vergil, *Aeneid*, 6; 95.

Tu quoque [too kwoh'-kweh] *L*—You, too. A retort charging an opponent with doing the same thing, or having the same fault that he criticizes in another.

Tutte le strade conducono a Roma [too'-tay lay strah'-day kon-doo'-koh-noh ah roh'-mah] *It*—All roads lead to Rome. *See also* Tout chemin mène à Rome.

Tutti i gusti son gusti [too'-tee ee goo'-stee sonn goo'-stee] *It*—All tastes are tastes. *See also* De gustibus . . .

U

u. a. m. und anderes mehr [uhnt ahn′duhr-uhs mayr] *Ger*—And so forth.

U. A. w. g. Um Antwort wird gebeten [uhm ahnt′-vohrt veert guh-bay′-tun] *Ger*—An answer is requested.

Uberrima fides [oo-behr′-rih-mah fih′-dayss] *L*—Absolute confidence; implicit faith.

Ubi bene, ibi patria [uh′-bih beh′-neh ih′-bih pah′-trih-ah] *L*—Wherever I prosper, there is my fatherland.

Ubi est thesaurus tuus, ibi est et cor tuum [uh′-bih est tay-sow′-ruhs tuh′-uhs ih′-bih est et kor tuh′-uhm] *L*—Where your treasure is, there is your heart also. *Vulgate, Matthew, 6; 21.*

Ubi jus, ibi officium [uh′-bih yoos ih′-bih of-fih′-kih-uhm] *L*—Where there is a right, there is also a duty.

Ubi jus, ibi remedium [uh′-bih yoos ih′-bih reh-meh′-dih-uhm] *L*—Where law prevails, there is a remedy; every violation of right has its remedy.

Ubi jus incertum, ibi jus nullum [uh′-bih yoos in-kehr′-tuhm ih′-bih yoos nool′-luhm] *L*—Where one's right is uncertain, no right exists.

Ubi libertas, ibi patria [uh′-bih lee-behr′-tahs ih′-bih pah′-trih-ah] *L*—Wherever there is freedom, there is my fatherland.

Ubi mel, ibi apes [uh′-bih mehl ih′-bih ah′-payss] *L*—Where the honey is, there the bees are.

Ubi nunc fidelis ossa Fabricii manent [uh′-bih nuhnk fih-day′-liss os′-sah fah-bree′-kih-ee mah′-nent] *L*—Where are the bones of faithful Fabricius now? A famous

198

line by Boethius, the inspiration of later writers, e.g., Chaucer. Boethius, *Consolation of Philosophy*, 2; 7, 15.

Ubi panis, ibi patria [uh′-bih pah′-nis ih′-bih pah′-trih-ah] *L*—Wherever there is bread, there is my fatherland. Maxim of the displaced person who is ready to emigrate.

Ubi solitudinem faciunt, pacem appellant [uh′-bih soh-lih-too′-dih-nem fah′-kih-uhnt pah′-kem ap-pel′-lahnt] *L*—Where they make a desert, they call it peace. Used when a conquering nation destroys all opposition. Tacitus, *Agricola*, 30.

Ubi sunt qui ante nos fuerunt [uh′-bih suhnt kwee ahn′-teh nohs fuh-ay′-ruhnt] *L*—Where are those who lived before us? Title of a medieval lyric.

Ubi tu Gaius, ego Gaia [uh′-bih too gah′-yuhs eh′-go gah′-yah] *L*—Wherever you are, Gaius, there I, Gaia, am. Formula used in Roman marriage.

Übung macht den Meister [ühb′-uhng mah′-kht dayn mIs′-tuhr] *Ger*—Practice makes the master; practice makes perfect.

u. dgl. und dergleichen [uhnt dayr-glI′-khun] *Ger*—And so forth.

U. I. O. G. D. Ut in omnibus glorificetur Deus [uht in om′-nih-buhs gloh-rih-fih-chay′-tuhr deh′-uhs] *L*—That God may be glorified in all things.

Uisge beatha [ish′-geh bah′-huh] *Ir*—The water of life; whiskey.

ult. ultimo [uhl′-tih-moh] *L*—Last month.

Ultima ratio mundi [uhl′-tih-ma rah′-tih-oh muhn′-dee] *L*—The world's strongest argument, i.e. that success is virtue. Balzac, *Père Goriot.*

Ultima ratio regum [uhl'-tih-mah rah'-tih-oh ray'-guhm] *L*—The final argument of kings, the resort to force of arms. Engraved on the cannons of Louis XIV.

Ultima Thule [uhl'-tih-mah too'-lay] *L*—The name that the ancients gave the most northern land of which they had knowledge, probably one of the Shetland Islands; figuratively, any distant frontier or remote goal. Vergil, *Georgics*, 1; 30.

Ultimum vale [uhl'-tih-muhm wah'-lay] *L*—The last farewell.

Ultimus regum [uhl'-tih-muhs ray'-guhm] *L*—The last of the kings. A reference to the seventh and last king of Rome, Tarquin the Proud, exiled 510 B.C.

Ultimus Romanorum [uhl'-tih-muhs roh-mah-noh'-ruhm] *L*—The last of the Romans, a title given to a number of historical personages and literary men, e.g., Marcus Junius Brutus, Stilicho, Congreve, Dr. Johnson.

Ultra vires [uhl'-trah wee'-rays] *L*—Beyond (its) powers. Used in connection with acts of a corporation exceeding the authority of its charter.

ü. M. über dem Meeresspiegel [ü'-buhr daym mayr'-uhs-shpee'-gul] *Ger*—Above sea level.

Um Christi willen [uhm khrees'-tee vihl'-luhn] *Ger*—For the sake of Christ.

Una dolo divum si femina victa duorum est [oo'-nah doh'-loh dee'-wuhm see fay'-mih-nah wick'-tah duh-oh'-ruhm est] *L*—(A great feat) if one sole woman is vanquished by the craftiness of two gods. Vergil, *Aeneid*, 4; 95.

Una golondrina no hace verano [oo'-nah goh-lohn-dree'-nah noh ah'-say bay-rah'-noh] *Sp*—One swallow does not make a summer. Cervantes, *Don Quixote*, 1; 13.

Una rondine non fa l'estate [oo'-nah ronn'-dee-nay nonn fah leh-stah'-tay] *It*—One swallow does not make a summer.

Una rondine non fa primavera [oo'-nah ronn'-dee-nay nonn fah pree-mah-vay'-rah] *It*—One swallow does not make a spring.

Una salus victis nullam sperare salutem [oo'-nah sah'-loos wik'-tees nool'-lahm spay-rah'-reh sah-loo'-tem] *L*—The only safety for the conquered lies in hoping for no safety. Vergil, *Aeneid*, 2; 354.

Una scopa nuova spazza bene [oo'-nah skoh'-pah noo-oh'-vah spaht'-sah bay'-nay] *It*—A new broom sweeps clean. *See also* Neue Besen . . .

Un barbier rait l'autre [uhN bar-bee-yay reh loh-tr] *Fr*—One barber shaves the other.

Un bel pezzo di carne [oon bel pet'-tsoh dee kahr'-nay] *It*—A beautiful piece of flesh. A description of a pretty girl.

Un bienfait n'est jamais perdu [uhN byaN-feh neh zha-meh pehr-dü] *Fr*—An act of kindness is never lost.

Undank ist der Welt (en) Lohn [uhn'-dahngk ist dehr velt (un) lohn] *Ger*—Ingratitude is the world's reward.

Und so weiter [uhnt zoh vI'-tuhr] *Ger*—And so forth.

Une bonne race [ün buhn rahss] *Fr*—A good breed.

Une fable convenue [ün fah-bl kohN-vnü] *Fr*—A fable agreed upon. *See also* L'histoire n'est qu'une fable convenue.

Une femme grosse [ün fam grohss] *Fr*—A pregnant woman. To avoid misunderstanding, *see* Une grosse femme.

Une grosse femme [ün grohss fam] *Fr*—A stout woman.

Une hirondelle ne fait pas le printemps [ün ee-rohN-dehl nuh feh pah luh praN-tahN] *Fr*—One swallow does not make a spring.

Une nation boutiquière [ün nah-syoN boo-tee-kyehr] *Fr*—A nation of shopkeepers. Napoleon's disparaging assessment of the English.

Une poire pour la soif [ün pwahr poor lah swahf] *Fr*—Literally, a pear for the thirst; something for a rainy day.

Unguibus et rostro [uhn'-gwi-buhs et rohs'-troh] *L*—With claws and beak; with tooth and nail.

Universitas, societas magistrorum discipulorumque [oo-nih-wehr'-sih-tahs so-kih'-eh-tahs mah-gis-troh'-ruhm diss-kih-puh-loh-ruhm'-kweh] *L*—The university, an association of teachers and students. This was the medieval concept of a university, which was built of men.

Un lever de rideau [uhN luh-vay duh ree-doh] *Fr*—A curtain-raiser, a one-act play preceding the main performance.

Un matto sa più domandare che sette savi rispondere [oon maht'-toh sah pee-oo' doh-mahn-dah'-ray kay set'-tay sah'-vee ree-spohn'-day-ray] *It*—A fool can ask more questions than seven wise men can answer.

Un peu passé [uhN puh pah-say] *Fr*—A little behind the times.

Un roi, une loi, une foi [uhN rwah ün lwah ün fwah] *Fr*—One king, one law, one faith. Motto of Bossuet.

Un "tiens" vaut mieux que deux "tu l'auras" [uhN tyaN voh myuh kuh duh tü loh-rah] *Fr*—One "take it" is worth two "I shall give it to you"; a bird in the hand is worth two in the bush.

Unum post aliud [oo'-nuhm post ah'-lih-uhd] *L*—One thing at a time.

Unus homo nobis cunctando restituit rem [oo'-nuhs ho'-moh noh'-beess koonk-tahn'-doh reh-stih'-tuh-it rem] *L*—One man by delaying restored the state. The reference is to Fabius Maximus the Delayer, a Roman general who fought against Hannibal. Ennius. Cf. Vergil, *Aeneid,* 6; 846.

Uomo universale [oo-oh'-moh oo-nee-vehr-sah'-lay] *It*—The universal man, the Renaissance ideal of well-rounded competence in humane and practical arts.

Urbem venalem et mature perituram, si emptorem invenerit [uhr'-bem way-nah'-lem et mah-too'-ray peh-rih-too'-rahm see aymp-toh'-rem in-way'-neh-rit] *L*—(Jugurtha said that Rome was) a venal city, soon to perish, if it could find a buyer. Sallust, *Jugurthine War,* 35. Cf. Livy, *Epitome of Book 64.*

Urbi et orbi [uhr'-bee et or'-bee] *L*—To the city (of Rome) and the world. A papal phrase.

Urbs in horto [uhrps in hor'-toh] *L*—A city in a garden. Motto of Chicago.

Ursa Major [uhr'-sah mah'-yohr] *L*—Literally, the bigger bear; a constellation known as the Great Bear or the Big Dipper.

u. s. ubi supra [uh'-bih suh'-prah] *L*—Where cited above.

Usque ad nauseam [oos'-kweh ahd now'-seh-ahm] *L*—To the point of creating disgust.

Usus est optimus magister [oo'-suhs est op'-tih-muhs mah-gis'-tehr] *L*—Experience is the best teacher.

Usus loquendi [oo'-suhs lo-kwen'-dee] *L*—Usage of speech.

u. s. w. *or* **usw.** *Ger*—*See* Und so weiter.

Ut ameris, amabilis esto [uht ah-may'-ris ah-mah'-bih-liss es'-toh] *L*—If you want to be loved, be lovable. Ovid, *Art of Love,* 2; 107.

Utcumque placuerit Deo [uht-kuhm'-kweh plah-koo'-eh-rit deh'-oh] *L*—In whatever way it shall please God.

Ut fragilis glacies, interit ira mora [uht frah'-gih-liss glah'-kih-ays ihn'-teh-rit ee'-rah moh'-rah] *L*—Like fragile ice, anger passes if held back for a time. Ovid, *Art of Love,* 1; 374.

Ut fulvum spectatur in ignibus aurum tempore sic in duro est inspicienda fides [uht ful'-wuhn spek-tah'-tuhr in ihg'-nih-buhs ow'-ruhm tem'-poh-reh seek in doo'-roh est in-spih-kih-en'-dah fih'-dayss] *L*—As yellow gold is tried in fire so faithfulness must be tested in times of trouble. Ovid, *Sorrows,* 1; 5, 25.

Utinam noster esset! [uh'-tih-nahm nos'-tehr es'-set] *L*—Would he were one of us; would he were on our side!

Ut infra [uht een'-frah] *L*—As cited below.

Uti possidetis [uh'-tee pos-sih-day'-tiss] *L*—Literally, as you now possess. The diplomatic phrase used when two opposing powers agree to retain what they have won in a conflict.

Ut lapsu graviore ruant [uht lahp'-soo grah-wih-oh'-reh ruh'-ahnt] *L*—That they may be destroyed in a more disastrous fall. Said of Fortune, which lifts men to the heights so that their fall may be greater.

Ut omnes unum sint [uht om'-nays oo'-nuhm sint] *L*—That all may be one. The title of a theology course given by the Daughters of St. Paul.

Ut pignus amicitiae [uht pig'-nuhs ah-mee-kih'-tih-I] *L*—In token of friendship.

Ut quocumque paratus [uht kwoh-kuhm'-kweh pah-rah'-tuhs] *L*—Prepared for any emergency whatever.

Ut sementem feceris, ita metes [uht say-men'-tem fay'-keh-ris ih'-tah meh'-tayss] *L*—As you sow, so shall you reap. Cicero, *On the Orator*, 2; 65.

ut sup. *See* ut supra.

Ut supra [uht suh'-prah] *L*—As cited above.

Ut tamquam scopulum sic fugias insolens verbum [uht tahm'-kwahm skoh'-puh-luhm seek fuh'-gih-ahs in'-so-layns wehr'-buhm] *L*—Avoid the unusual word as if it were a cliff. Advice Caesar gave Roman orators.

V

V. Vide [wih'-day] *L*—See, consult.

v. a. vixit annos [weex'-it ahn'-nohs] *L*—He lived _____ years.

Vade in pace [vah'-deh in pah'-cheh] *L*—Go in peace.

Vade mecum [vah'-deh may'-kuhm] *L*—Literally, go with me; a handy portable volume for ready reference.

Vae victis! [wI wick'-teess] *L*—Woe to the conquered! Livy, *History*, 5; 48.

Vale [wah'-lay] *L*—Farewell, goodbye.

Valeat ancora virtus [wah'-leh-aht ahn'-kor-ah wihr'-toos] *L*—May the anchor of virtue hold.

Valeat quantum valere potest [wah'-leh-aht kwahn'-tuhm wah-lay'-reh po'-test] *L*—Let it stand for as much as it is worth. Used in argument.

Valete [wah-lay'-teh] *L*—Farewell. Plural of *vale*; used when addressing more than one person.

Vanitas vanitatum, et omnia vanitas [wah'-nih-tahs wah-nih-tah'-tuhm et om'-nih-ah wah'-nih-tahs] *L*—Vanity of vanities, and all is vanity. *Vulgate, Ecclesiastes*, 1; 2.

Vare, legiones redde [wah'-reh leh-gih-oh'-nayss red'-deh] *L*—Varus, give me back my legions. In 9 A.D. three Roman legions commanded by Quintilius Varus were trapped in the Teutoberg forest and wiped out. This was the worst military disaster suffered by Roman arms during the principate of Augustus. He was deeply affected by this defeat and would sometimes knock his head against the doorposts and cry out: "Quintilius Varus, give me back my legions." Suetonius, *Caesar Augustus*, 24.

Varia lectio [wah'-rih-ah lek'-tih-oh] *L*—A variant reading. The plural is *variae lectiones*.

Varietas delectat cor hominis [wah-rih'-eh-tahs day-lek'-taht kor ho'-mih-nis] *L*—Variety delights the human heart.

Variorum notae [wah-rih-oh'-ruhm no'-tI] *L*—The notes of several commentators.

Varium et mutabile semper femina [wah'-rih-uhm et moo-tah'-bih-lay sem'-pehr fay'-mih-nah] *L*—Woman is a changeable and fickle thing. Vergil, *Aeneid*, 4; 569.

var. lec. *See* varia lectio.

Vaso vuoto suona meglio [vah'-zoh voo-oh'-toh soo-oh'-nah mayl'-yoh] *It*—An empty vessel gives the loudest sound.

Va-t'en! [va tahN] *Fr*—Go away!

Vaya con Dios [bah'-yah kon dyohss'] *Sp*—Go with God; goodbye.

v/c vuelta de correo [bwehl'-tah day kohr-ray'-oh] *Sp*—Return mail.

v. Chr. G. vor Christi Geburt [for khrees'-tee guh-boort'] *Ger*—Before the birth of Christ.

Vedi Napoli e poi mori [vay'-dee nah'-poh-lee ay poy moh'-ree] *It*—See Naples and then die. Everything else will be an anticlimax.

Velis et remis [way'-leess et ray'-meess] *L*—With sails and oars; with all possible speed.

Veluti in speculum [weh'-luh-tee in speh'-kuh-luhm] *L*—As if in a mirror. Used when reference is made to one's faults.

Venalis populus, venalis curia patrum [way-nah'-liss po'-puh-luss way-nah'-liss koo'-rih-ah pah'-truhm] *L*—The people are venal, and so is the Senate.

Vender il miele a chi ha le api [ven'-dehr eel mee-ay'-lay ah kee ah lay ah'-pee] *It*—To sell honey to a man who keeps bees; to carry coals to Newcastle.

Vendidit hic auro patriam [wayn'-dih-dit hik ow'-roh pah'-trih-ahm] *L*—This man sold his country for gold. Vergil, *Aeneid,* 6; 621.

Venenum in auro bibitur [way-nay'-nuhm in ow'-roh bih'-bih-tuhr] *L*—Poison is drunk from a golden cup. The poor, who drink from cups of clay, are not likely to be poisoned. Seneca, *Thyestes,* 453.

Veniam petimusque damusque vicissim [weh'-nih-ahm peh-tih-muhs'-kweh dah-muhs'-kweh wih-kiss'-sihm] *L*—We beg pardon and give it in return.

Venia necessitati datur [weh'-nih-ah neh-keh-sih-tah'-tee dah'-tuhr] *L*—Pardon is granted to necessity; necessity knows no law.

Veni, Creator, Spiritus [vay'-nee kreh-ah'-tor spee'-rih-tuhs] *L*—"Come, Holy Ghost, Creator blest," a 9th-century hymn.

Venienti occurrite morbo [weh-nih-ehn'-tee ok-kuhr'-rih-teh mor'-boh] *L*—Forestall the oncoming disease; treat disease before it develops; an ounce of prevention is worth a pound of cure. Persius, 3; 64.

Venire *L—See* Venire facias juratores.

Venire facias juratores [veh-nee'-reh fah'-sih-ahs yoo-rah-toh'-rays] *L*—Literally, cause jurors to come; shortened to *venire.* A writ directing a sheriff to summon jurors.

Veni, vidi, vici [way'-nee wee'-dee wee'-kee] *L*—I came, I saw, I conquered. Julius Caesar's summary of his swift victory at Zela in 47 B.C. over Pharnaces in the Pontic campaign. Suetonius, *Julius Caesar,* 37.

Venter non habet aures [wehn'-tehr nohn hah'-bet ow'-rayss] *L*—The belly has no ears; a starving man will not listen to a sermon.

Ventis secundis [wehn'-teess seh-kuhn'-deess] *L*—With favorable winds.

Ventre à terre [vahN-tr ah tehr] *Fr*—Literally, with belly to the ground, an expression originally applied to a running horse; at top speed.

Vera incessu patuit dea [way'-rah in-kess'-soo pah'-tuh-it deh'-ah] *L*—She walked with the dignity of a goddess. Vergil, *Aeneid,* 1; 405.

Verba adulatoria [ver'-bah ah-doo-lah-toh'-rih-ah] *L*—Flattering words.

Verba docent, exempla trahunt [wehr'-bah do'-kent ex-em'-plah trah'-huhnt] *L*—Words teach, examples attract.

Verba volant, scripta manent [wehr'-bah wo'-lahnt skrip'-tah mah'-nent] *L*—Spoken words fly through the air, but written words endure.

Verbum sat sapienti [wehr'-buhm saht sah-pih-en'-tee] *L*—A word to the wise is sufficient. *See also* Dictum (*or* verbum) sapienti sat est.

Verdammte Bedürfnislosigkeit [fehr-dahm'-tuh buh-dürf'-nis-loh'-sik-kIt] *Ger*—Damned wantlessness; a charge brought by Marxists against the passive poor.

Vere scire est per causas scire [way'-ray skee'-reh est pehr kow'-sahs skee'-reh] *L*—Real knowledge lies in knowing causes.

Veritas numquam perit [way'-rih-tahs nuhm'-kwahm peh'-rit] *L*—Truth never dies.

Veritas odium parit [way'-rih-tahs oh'-dih-uhm pah'-rit] *L*—The truth breeds hatred. *See also* Obsequium amicos ...

Veritas temporis filia [way' rih taho tem' po-ris fee'-lih-ah] *L*—Truth is the daughter of time; truth will out. Motto of Queen Mary I. Aulus Gellius, 12; 11, 7.

Veritas temporis filia dicitur [way'-rih-tahs tem'-por-is fee'-lih-ah dee'-kih-tuhr] *L*—Truth is called the daughter of time; eventually the truth becomes known. Aulus Gellius, *Attic Nights,* 12; 11, 7. Aulus Gellius wrote that he had forgotten the source of this aphorism.

Veritas vos liberabit [way'-rih-tahs wohs lee-beh-rah'-bit] *L*—The truth shall make you free. *Vulgate, John,* 8; 32. Motto of Johns Hopkins University.

Veritatis simplex oratio est [way-rih-tah'-tiss sim'-plex oh-rah'-tih-oh est] *L*—The language of truth is simple.

Vérité sans peur [vay-ree-tay sahN puhr] *Fr*—Literally, truth without fear; speak the truth and don't be afraid.

Ver perpetuum [wayr pehr-peh'-tuh-uhm] *L*—Perpetual spring.

Vers de société [vehr duh suh-syay-tay] *Fr*—Light, polished verse written to please a sophisticated audience.

Vers libre [vehr lee-br] *Fr*—Free verse.

Verso pollice [wehr'-soh pol'-lih-keh] *L* —Popularly interpreted, thumbs down. The gesture used at gladiatorial combats in Rome when the spectators demanded that the victor slay his opponent. Actually the Romans pointed the thumb upward toward the chest when they wanted the vanquished slain, and down when they wanted the victor to spare his opponent. The incorrect interpretation may have developed from an ancient relief on which the spectators were represented with thumbs turned upward. The inscription showed that the conquered were spared. *Juvenal,* 3; 36.

Verso sciolto [ver'-soh shol'-toh] *It*—Blank verse.

Ver. St. Vereinigte Staaten [fehr-In'-ihg-tuh shtah'-tun] *Ger*—The United States of America.

Verstand kommt mit den Jahren [fehr-shtahnt' kuhmt mit dayn yah'-run] *Ger*—Wisdom comes with the years.

Ver. St. v. A. Vereinigte Staaten von Amerika [fehr-In'-ihg-tuh shtah'-tun fun ah-may'-ree-kah] *Ger*—The United States of America.

Vertumnis, quotquot sunt, natus iniquis [wayr-toom'-nees kwot'-kwot suhnt nah'-tuhs in-ee'-kwees] *L*—Born under the displeasure of as many gods as there are; said of one who changes opinions frequently.

Vertumnus was a Roman god of many shapes. Horace, *Satires,* 2; 7, 14.

Verweile doch! du bist so schön! [fehr-vI'-luh duhkh doo bist zoh shuhn] *Ger*—Linger a while, you are so fair! Faust is speaking with Mephistopheles with whom he is making a pact that if the moment ever comes when he will ask that some wordly pleasure last a little longer, he will freely hand himself over to the powers of hell. Goethe, *Faust,* 1; 1700.

Vestigia nulla retrorsum *L*—*See* Me vestigia terrent . . .

Vestis talaris [wes'-tihs tah-lah'-riss] *L*—Garment reaching to the feet.

Vestis virum facit [wes'-tihs wih'-ruhm fah'-kit] *L*—Clothes make the man. Erasmus, *Adagia.* Cf. Cucullus non facit monachum.

Vetulam suam praetulit immortalitati [weh'-tuh-lahm suh'-ahm prI'-tuh-lit im-mor-tahl-lih-tah'-tee] *L*—He preferred his aged wife to immortality. Said of Ulysses.

Vexata quaestio [wex-ah'-tah kwI'-stih-oh] *L*—A disputed question.

Vexilla Regis prodeunt [wayx-ihl'-lah ray'-gis proh'-deh-uhnt] *L*—The standards of the King appear. A 6th-century hymn by Fortunatus.

v. g. verbi gratia [vehr'-bee grah'-tsih-ah] *L* —As for example.

Via [vee'-ah] *L*—By way of.

Via il gatto ballano i sorci [vee'-ah eel gaht'-toh bahl'-lah-noh ee sohr'-chee] *It*—When the cat's away, the mice will play.

Via lactea [vee'-ah lahk'-teh-ah] *L*—Milky Way.

Via media [vee'-ah meh'-dih-ah] *L*—The middle path or middle way. An expression much heard during the Oxford Movement. Those who argue for the *via media* believe that the Anglican Church is midway between Protestantism and Catholicism.

Via trita, via tutissima [wih'-ah tree'-tah wih'-ah too-tis'-sih-mah] *L*—The beaten path is the safest.

Vice versa [wih'-keh wehr'-sah, but in common usage vI'-suh ver'-suh] *L*—Reversing the relationship of terms; conversely.

Vicisti, Galilaee [wee-kis'-tee gah-lih-lI'-eh] *L*—*See* Galilaie nenikekas.

Victoire ou la mort [veek-twahr oo lah mawr] *Fr*—Victory or death.

Victrix causa deis placuit sed victa Catoni [wik'-trix kow'-sah deh'-ees plah'-kuh-it sed wick'-tah kah-toh'-nee] *L*—The victorious cause pleased the gods, but the losing cause pleased Cato. Cato the Younger killed himself after the defeat of the senatorial forces by Julius Caesar at Utica in 46 B.C. Lucan, *Pharsalia*, 1; 128.

Vida sin amigos muerte sin testigos [bee'-dah seen ah-mee'-gohs mwehr'-tay seen tehs-tee'-gohs] *Sp*—A friendless life, a lonely death.

Videant consules ne quid res publica detrimenti capiat [wih'-deh-ahnt kohn'-suh-lays nay kwid rays-poo'-blih-kah day-tree-men'-tee kah'-pih-aht] *L*—Let the consuls see to it that the republic suffer no harm. This was the wording of the *consultum ultimum*, the final decree of the Senate by which, according to Cicero's interpretation of the law, conspirators might be put to death without trial.

Video et taceo [wih'-deh-oh et tah'-keh-oh] *L*—I see and I remain silent. Motto of Queen Elizabeth I.

Video meliora proboque, deteriora sequor [wih'-deh-oh meh-lih-oh'-rah pro-boh'-kweh day-teh-rih-oh'-rah seh'-kwor] *L*—I see the better course and I approve it, but I follow the lower path. Ovid, *Metamorphoses*, 7; 20.

Vide supra [wih'-day suh'-prah] *L*—Literally, see above; see previous reference.

Viele Händ' machen bald ein End' [fee'-luh hehnd mahkh'-un bahlt In end] *Ger*—Many hands make light work.

Viele Köche verderben den Brei [fee'-luh kuh'-khuh fehr-dehr'-buhn dayn brI] *Ger*—Too many cooks spoil the broth.

Vi et armis [wee et ahr'-mees] *L*—By force of arms.

Vigueur de dessus [vee-guhr duh duh-süh] *Fr*—Strength from on high.

Vilius argentum est auro, virtutibus aurum [wee'-lih-uhs ahr-gehn'-tuhm est ow'-roh wihr-too'-tih-buhs ow'-ruhm] *L*—Silver is less valuable than gold, and gold than virtue. Horace, *Epistles*, 1; 1, 52.

Vincet amor patriae [wihn'-ket ah'-mor pah'-trih-I] *L*—Love of country will win in the end. Vergil, *Aeneid*, 6; 823.

Vincit omnia veritas [win'-kit om'-nih-ah way'-rih-tahs] *L*—Truth conquers everything.

Vincit qui patitur [win'-kit kwee pah'-tih-tuhr] *L*—The patient man conquers.

Vincit qui se vincit [win'-kit kwee say win'-kit] *L*—He wins control who controls himself.

Vin d'honneur [vaN duh-nuhr] *Fr*—A toast drunk in welcome to a guest.

Vin du pays [vaN dü pay-ee] *Fr*—Wine of the region.

Vino vendibili hedera non opus est [wee'-noh wehn-dih'-bih-lee heh'-deh-rah nohn o'-puhs est] *L*—A popular wine needs no ivy; a good product needs no advertising. The ivy was sacred to Bacchus, and its bush was displayed as a sign outside taverns.

Vinum daemonum [wee'-nuhm dI'-moh-nuhm] *L*—The wine of devils. A hostile view of poetry.

Viola da braccio [vee-oh'-lah dah braht'-choh] *It*—An arm viol, the ancestor of the violin.

Viola da gamba [vee-oh'-lah dah gahm'-bah] *It*—A leg viol, ancestor of the cello.

Violenta non durant [wih-oh-len'-tah nohn doo'-rahnt] *L*—Violence does not last.

Violon d'Ingres [vyuh-lohN daN-gruh] *Fr*—The violin of Ingres, a French painter, who in his early life enjoyed success as a musician; a hobby more interesting to the one who rides it than his regular occupation; a second means of making a living.

Vir bonus dicendi peritus [wihr bo'-nuhs dee-ken'-dee peh-ree'-tuhs] *L*—A good man skilled in public speaking. According to the Roman definition, an orator was supposed to be a virtuous man. Quintilian, 12; 1, 1.

Vires adquirit eundo [wee'-rays ahd-kwee'-rit eh-uhn'-doh] *L*—She acquires strength as she travels on. This describes Fama (Rumor or Gossip) which increases as it spreads. Vergil, *Aeneid*, 4; 175.

Vir, fortis et strenuus [wihr for'-tis et stray'-nuh-uhs] *L*—A man, brave and energetic. According to Cato the Elder, bravery and energy were the qualities that made up the ideal Roman character.

Virginibus puerisque [wihr-gih'-nih-buhs puh-eh-reess'-kweh] *L*—For girls and boys. Horace, *Odes*, 3; 1, 4. The title of a book by Robert Louis Stevenson.

Virgo intacta [wihr'-goh in-tahk'-tah] *L*—An untouched, pure virgin.

Viribus totis [wee'-rih-buhs toh'-teess] *L*—With all one's strength.

Vir sapit qui pauca loquitur [wihr sah'-pit kwee pow'-kah lo'-kwih-tuhr] *L*—He is a wise man who speaks but little.

Virtus ariete fortior [wihr'-toos ah-rih'-eh-teh for'-tih-or] *L*—Virtue is stronger than a battering ram.

Virtus dormitiva [wihr'-toos dor-mih-tee'-wah] *L*—Power to induce sleep, as in the case of opium; by extension, dull writing that induces sleep. Molière, *Malade Imaginaire*, third interlude.

Virtus in actione consistit [wihr'-toos in ahk-tih-oh'-neh kohn-sis'-tit] *L*—Virtue lies in action.

Virtus in arduis [wihr'-toos in ahr'-duh-ees] *L*—Courage in difficulties.

Virtus sola nobilitat [wihr'-toos soh'-lah noh-bih'-lih-taht] *L*—Only virtue ennobles.

Virtute et armis [wihr-too'-teh et ahr'-mees] *L*—By courage and arms. Motto of Mississippi.

Virtute et fide [wihr-too'-teh et fih'-day] *L*—By courage and faith.

206

Virtute et labore [wihr-too'-teh et lah-boh'-reh] *L*—By courage and toil.

Virtute non astutia [wihr-too'-teh nohn ahs-too'-tih-ah] *L*—By virtue, not by cleverness.

Virtute officii [wihr-too'-teh of-fih'-kih-ee] *L*—By virtue of one's office.

Virtutis fortuna comes [wihr-too'-tis for-too'-nah ko'-mays] *L*—Good fortune is the companion of courage.

Vis a fronte [wees ah fron'-teh] *L*—A frontal assault.

Vis a tergo [wees ah tehr'-goh] *L*—Force from behind.

Vis-à-vis [vee-zah-vee] *Fr*—Opposite; face to face.

Vis comica [wees ko'-mih-kah] *L*—Comic force. Caesar used the expression in some lines of poetry about Terence in which he praised his poetic gifts but lamented his lack of comic power. Suetonius, *Lives of the Poets, Terence* (at the end).

Vis conservatrix naturae [wees kohn-sehr-wah'-trix nah-too'-rI] *L*—The protective, defensive power in nature.

Vis consili expers mole ruit sua [wees kohn-sih'-lee ex'-pehrs moh'-leh ruh'-it suh'-ah] *L*—Strength lacking counsel falls by its own weight. Horace, *Odes*, 3; 4, 65.

Vis inertiae [wees in-ehr'-tih-I] *L*—In physics, the force of inertia. By extension this may be applied to resistance in matters of social progress or change.

Vis major [wees mah'-yohr] *L*—Superior force, a legal term covering more than an act of God; circumstances beyond one's control.

Vis medicatrix naturae [wees meh-dih-kah'-trix nah-too'-rI] *L*—The restorative, healing power of nature.

Vis nova [wees no'-wah] *L*—New power, new energy.

Vis unita fortior [wees oo-nee'-tah for'-tih-or] *L*—United strength is stronger; in unity there is strength.

Vis vitae [wees wee'-tI] *L*—The life force. *See also* L'élan vital.

Vis vitalis [wees wee-tah′-liss] *L*—See Vis vitae.

Vita brevis, longa ars [wee′-tah breh′-wis long′-gah ahrs] *L*—Life is short and art is long. *See also* Ho bios brachys . . ., of which the Latin is a translation. It is often quoted as Ars longa, vita brevis (*q.v.*). Adapted from Seneca, *The Shortness of Life*, 1.

Vitam impendere vero [wee′-tahm im-pen′-deh-reh way′-roh] *L*—To risk one's life for the truth.

Vita sine litteris mors est [wee′-tah sih′-neh lit′-teh-rees mors est] *L*—Life without learning (education) is death.

Vitiis nemo sine nascitur [wih′-tih-ees nay′-moh sih′-neh nahs′-kih-tuhr] *L*—Nobody is born without faults. Horace, *Satires*, 1; 3, 68.

Viva il papa [vee′-vah eel pah′-pah] *It*—Long live the pope.

Vivamus, mea Lesbia, atque amemus [wee-wah′-muhs meh′-ah less′-bih-ah aht′-kweh ah-may′-muhs] *L*—Let us live and love, my Lesbia. Catullus, 5; 1.

Vivat regina [wee′-waht ray-gee′-nah] *L*—Long live the queen.

Vivat rex [wee′-waht rayx] *L*—Long live the king.

Viva voce [wee′-wah vuh′-cheh] *L*—Expression by the living voice; orally, as in voting or an oral examination.

Vivebat [wee-way′-baht] *L*—He was living. Given with a date.

Vive la bagatelle! [veev lah ba-gah-tel] *Fr*—Long live trifles! Long live nonsense!

Vive la différence! [veev lah dee-fay-rahNoo] *Fr*—Three cheers for the difference! Used by those who are happy about the differences that exist between men and women.

Vive l'empereur! [veev lahN-peh-ruhr] *Fr*—Long live the Emperor!

Vive le roi! [veev luh rwah] *Fr*—Long live the king!

Vivent les Gueux [veev lay guh] *Fr*—Long live the Beggars, the battle cry of the

opponents of Philip II of Spain who revolted against his enforcement of the Inquisition in the Netherlands.

Vivere sat vincere [wee′-weh-reh saht wihn′-keh-reh] *L*—To live is conquest enough.

Vivida vis animi [wee′-wih-dah wees ah′-nih-mee] *L*—The living vigor of the mind. Lucretius, *On the Nature of Things*, 1; 72.

Vivit post funera virtus [wee′-wit post foo′-neh-rah wihr′-toos] *L*—Virtue survives the grave.

Vivre libre, ou mourir [vee-vr lee-br oo moo-reer] *Fr*—To live free or die; freedom or death. Slogan of the French Commune, which ruled in Paris for sixty-two days in 1871.

Vix ea nostra voco [wix eh′-ah nos′-trah woh′-koh] *L*—I can scarcely call these things my own. This is a reference to one's ancestry for which a modest person takes no credit. *See also* Nam genus et proavos . . .

Vixere fortes ante Agamemnona [weex-ay′-reh for′-tays ahn′-teh ah-gah-mem′-noh-nah] *L*—There were brave men before Agamemnon. Horace, *Odes*, 4; 9, 25.

viz. videlicet [vih-day′-lih-ket] *L*—Namely.

Voce di testa [voh′-chay dee tess′-tah] *It*—Head voice; falsetto.

Vogue la galère! [vuhg lah ga-lehr] *Fr*—Row the galley on! Let's take our chances.

Voilà! [vwah-lah] *Fr*—See there! There you are!

Voilà une autre chose [vwah-lah ün oh-tr shohz] *Fr*—That's an entirely different matter.

Voilà un homme! [vwah-lah uhn uhm] *Fr*—There goes a man. Reportedly said by Napoleon when Goethe left his presence.

Voire dire [vwar deer] *OF*—Literally, to tell the truth; a preliminary examination given a prospective witness or juror to determine his competence to give objective testimony; also the oath administered at such an inquiry.

Voir le dessous des cartes [vwahr luh duh-soo day kahrt] *Fr*—To see the face of the turned-down card; to be in on the trick or secret.

Vol-au-vent [vuhl-oh-vahN] *Fr*—Puff-pie filled with delicacies, usually meat.

Volenti non fit injuria [wo-len'-tee nohn fit in-yoo'-rih-ah] *L*—No injury is done a willing participant. Legal maxim.

Volo, non valeo [wo'-loh nohn wah'-leh-oh] *L*—I am willing but unable.

Volte-face [vuhlt-fass] *Fr*—A right-about-face; complete reversal of one's opinion.

Volto sciolto e pensieri stretti [vohl'-toh sholl'-toh ay pehn-see-ay'-ree stret'-tee] *It*—An open countenance and secret thoughts.

Vomunt ut edant, edunt ut vomant [woh'-muhnt uht eh'-dahnt eh'-duhnt uht woh'-mahnt] *L*—They vomit to eat, they eat to vomit. Seneca, *To Helvia On Consolation*, Dialogue 12, chap. 10, 3. Gluttons at banquets in Rome were accused of this practice.

Vorwärts mit Gott! [for'-wehrts mit guht] *Ger*—Forward with God!

Vos exemplaria Graeca nocturna versate manu, versate diurna [wohs ex-em-plah'-rih-ah grI'-kah nok-tuhr'-nah wehr-sah'-teh mah'-noo wehr-sah'-teh dih-oor'-nah] *L*—Page through the Greek classics by day and by night. The poet is advised to study his predecessors. Horace, *Art of Poetry*, 268.

Vouloir c'est pouvoir [vool-wahr seh poo-vwar] *Fr*—Power is in the will. Where there's a will there's a way.

Vouloir rompre l'anguille au genou [vool-wahr rohN-pr lahN-ghee-yuh oh zhuh-noo] *Fr*—To attempt to break an eel on one's knee; to attempt the impossible.

Vous êtes orfèvre, Monsieur Josse [voo-zeht awr-feh-vr muh-syuh zhohss] *Fr*—Literally, you are a goldsmith, Mr. Josse; you are giving advice that looks to your own interests. Josse urges a father to buy jewels to cure his daughter's melancholy. Molière, *L'Amour Médecin*, 1; 1.

Vous y perdrez vos pas [voo zee pehr-dray voh pah] *Fr*—You will waste your time doing that.

Vox audita perit, littera scripta manet [wohx ow-dee'-tah peh'-rit lit'-teh-rah skreep'-tah mah'-net] *L*—The word that is spoken dies in the air; the written word remains.

Vox clamantis in deserto [wohx klah-mahn'-tiss in day-sehr'-toh] *L*—The voice of one crying in the wilderness. *Vulgate, Matthew*, 3; 3.

Vox et praeterea nihil [wohx et prI-tehr'-eh-ah nih'-hil] *L*—A voice and nothing more. A derogatory expression used to describe speakers whose discourse is without substance.

Vox faucibus haesit [wohx fow'-kih-buhs hI'-sit] *L*—His voice stuck in his throat. *See also* Obstipui steteruntque comae ...

Vox humana [wohx hoo-mah'-nah] *L*—The human voice; an organ stop simulating the human voice.

Vox populi, vox Dei [wohx po'-puh-lee wohx deh'-ee] *L*—The voice of the people is the voice of God.

vs. versus [vehr'-suhs] *L*—Against.

V. T. Vetus Testamentum [weh'-tuhs tes-tah-men'-tuhm] *L*—Old Testament.

Vue d'oiseau [vü dwah-zoh] *Fr*—Bird's-eye view.

Vulgata editio [vuhl-gah'-tah ay-dih-tsyoh] *L*—The Bible in Latin, a translation from the Hebrew and Greek, largely the work of Saint Jerome (340?-420). The name, from the Latin *vulgus* meaning the multitude, indicated that the translation was in the vernacular and could be read by the people.

Vulgus ad deteriora promptum [wuhl'-guhs ahd day-teh-rih-oh'-rah prohmp'-tuhm] *L*—The public, disposed to believe the worst. Tacitus, *Annals*, 15; 64.

Vulgus fingendi avidum [wuhl'-guhs fihn-gen'-dee ah'-wih-duhm] *L*—The public, eager to invent rumors. Tacitus, *History*, 2; 1.

Vulgus ignobile [wuhl'-guhs ihg-noh'-bih-leh] *L*—The low-born crowd.

Vulgus veritatis pessimus interpres [wuhl'-guhs way-rih-tah'-tis pehs'-sih-muhs in-tehr'-prehs] *L*—The public, the worst possible expounder of the truth. Seneca, *Of a Happy Life*, 2.

Vultus est index animi [wuhl'-tuhs est in'-dex ah'-nih-mee] *L*—The face is a guide to the soul.

Vultus nimium lubricus aspici [wuhl'-tuhs nih'-mih-uhm loo'-brih-kuhs ahs'-pih-kee] *L*—A face too seductive to be looked upon. Horace, *Odes*, 1; 19, 8.

W

Wagons-lits [vah-gohN-lee] *Fr*—Sleeping cars.

Wahrheit und Dichtung [vahr'-hIt uhnt dikh'-tuhng] *Ger*—Truth and poetry.

Was ich nicht weiss, macht mich nicht heiss [vahs ikh nikht vIs mahkht mikh nikht hIs] *Ger*—I do not get excited over what I do not know.

Was ihn nicht umbringt, macht ihn stärker [vahs een nikht uhm'-brihngt mahkht een shtehr'-kuhr] *Ger*—What does not kill him makes him stronger. With a change of *him* to *you*, this became the Nazi motto of a training center for young leaders of the Hitler youth movement. Nietzsche, *Ecce Homo*, para. 2.

Was ist los? [vahs ist lohs] *Ger*—What is the matter; what is going on?

Was man nicht kann meiden, muss man willig leiden [vahs mahn nikht kahn mId'-uhn muhs mahn vihl'-lik lId'-uhn] *Ger*—What one cannot avoid must be borne without complaint; what can't be cured must be endured.

Wein auf Bier, das rat ich dir; Bier auf Wein, lass das sein [vIn owf beer dahs raht ikh deer beer owf vIn lahs dahs zIn] *Ger*—Wine on beer, that's my rule; beer on wine, that's for the fool.

Wein, Weib, und Gesang [vIn vIp uhnt guh-zang'] *Ger*—Wine, women, and song.

Welche Regierung die beste sei? Diejenige die uns lehrt uns selbst zu regieren [vehl'-khuh ray-gee'-ruhng dee bes'-tuh zI dee-yay'-nee-guh dee uhns layhrt uhns zehlpst tsoo ray-geer'-uhn] *Ger*—What form of government is the best? The one that teaches us to rule ourselves. Goethe, *Maxims in Prose*, 163.

Weltanschauung [velt-ahn-shau'-uhng] *Ger*—A general, philosophical view of the world.

Weltmacht oder Niedergang [velt'-mahkht oh'-duhr nee'-duhr-gahng] *Ger*—World power or ruin. Hitler's program.

Wenige wissen, wieviel man wissen muss, um zu wissen, wie wenig man weiss [vay'-nih-guh viss'-uhn vee-feel' mahn viss'-uhn muhs uhm tsoo viss'-uhn vee vay'-nik mahn vIs] *Ger*—Few know how much a man must know in order to know how little he knows.

Wenn die Katze nicht zu Hause ist, tanzen die Mäuse auf Tisch und Bänken [venn dee kaht'-suh nikht tsoo how'-zuh ist tahn'-tsuhn dee moi'-suh owf tihsh uhnt behnk'-uhn] *Ger*—When the cat is not home, the mice dance on the table and benches; when the cat's away, the mice will play. *See also* Quando la gatta no v'è ...

Wenn schon, denn schon [vehn shohn denn shohn] *Ger*—If it must be, then let it be.

Wer dem Pöbel dient, hat einen schlechten Herrn [wayr daym puh'-buhl deent haht I'-nun shlekt'-un hehrn] *Ger*—The man who serves the people has a bad taskmaster.

Wer fremde Sprachen nicht kennt, weiss nichts von seiner eigenen [vayr frehm'-duh shprah'-khun nikht kehnt vIs nikhts fun zI'-nuhr I'-guh-nuhn] *Ger*—The man who does not know foreign tongues knows nothing of his own. Goethe, *Maxims in Prose*, 55.

Wer gar zu viel bedenkt, wird wenig leisten [vayr gahr tsoo feel buh-dengkt' virt vay'-nikh lIs'-tun] *Ger*—The man who considers too long accomplishes little. Schiller, *William Tell*, 3; 1, 72.

Wer liebt nicht Weib, Wein und Gesang/Der bleibt ein Narr sein Leben lang [vayr leept nikht vIp vIn uhnt guh-zang' dayr blIpt In nahr zIn lay'-buhn lahng] *Ger*—Who loves not woman, wine and song/Remains a fool his whole life long. Attributed to J. H. Voss.

Wer nicht will, der hat schon [vayr nikht vill dayr haht shohn] *Ger*—He who does not want any more has enough.

Wer verachtet, der will kaufen [vayr fehr-ahkh'-teht dayr vill kow'-fuhn] *Ger*—The man who points out defects wants to buy.

Wer zuletzt lacht, lacht am besten [vayr tsoo-letst' lahkht lahkht ahm bess'-tuhn] *Ger*—He who laughs last laughs best.

Wie der Herr, so der Knecht [vee dayr hehr zoh dayr knekht] *Ger*—Like master, like servant.

Wie geht's? [vee gayts] *Ger*—How are you; how are things going?

Wie gewonnen, so zerronen [vee guh-vuhn'-nuhn zoh tsehr-ruh'-nuhn] *Ger*—Easy come, easy go.

Wir Deutschen fürchten Gott, sonst aber Nichts in der Welt [veer doit'-shun fürkh'-tuhn guht zuhnst ah'-buhr nikhts in dayr velt] *Ger*—We Germans fear God, but nothing else in the world. Bismarck.

Wir lieben unsern Führer [veer lee'-buhn uhn'-zuhrn füh'-ruhr] *Ger*—We love our leader. Shout of German crowds for Hitler.

Wollt ihr immer leben? [vuhlt eehr im'-muhr lay'-buhn] *Ger*—Do you want to live forever? Frederick the Great's question to soldiers who faltered in the face of danger.

Y and Z

Yom Kippur [yohm kip'-uhr] *Heb*—Day of Atonement, an annual Jewish fast day.

Zartem Ohre, halbes Wort [tsahr'-tuhm oh'-ruh hahl'-buhs vort] *Ger*—Half a word is enough for a sharp ear. *See also* Verbum sat sapienti.

Za vashe zdorove [zah vah'-sheh zdoh-roh'-vyeh] *Rus*—To your health!

z. B. zum Beispiel [tsuhm bI'-shpeel] *Ger*—For example.

Zdravstvuityeh [zdrahv'-stvoo-ee-tyeh] *Rus*—How do you do; hello. Popular Russian greeting, often shortened to *zdrah'-styeh*.

Zeit ist teuer [tsIt ist toy'-uhr] *Ger*—Time is precious.

Zoe mou, sas agapo [zoh-ee' moo sahs ah-gah-poh'] *Modern Gk*—My life, I love thee. Byron, *Maid of Athens*.

Zoon dipoun apteron [zoh'-on dee'-poon ahp'-teh-ron] *Gr*—A two-footed animal without feathers; Plato's definition of man successfully ridiculed by Diogenes the Cynic when he brought a plucked cock into the school. Diogenes Laertius, *Diogenes*, 6. *See also* Animal bipes implume.

Zum Donnerwetter! [tsuhm duhn-nuhr-veht'-tuhr] *Ger*—Hang it all!

Zwei Hälften machen zwar ein Ganzes, aber merk': Aus halb und halb getan entsteht kein ganzes Werk [tsvI hehlf'-tuhn mah'-khuhn tsvahr In gahn'-tsuhs ah'-buhr mehrk ows hahlp uhnt hahlp guh-tahn' ent-shtayt kIn gahn'-tsuhs vehrk] *Ger*—It is true that two halves make a whole, but take note: no complete work results from work half done. Rückert.

Zwei Seelen und ein Gedanke, zwei Herzen und ein Schlag [tsvI zay'-luhn uhnt In guh-dahng'-kuh tsvI hehr'-tsuhn uhnt In shlahk] *Ger*—Two souls with but one thought; two hearts that beat together.

Zwei Seelen wohnen, ach! in meiner Brust [tsvI zay'-lun voh'-nuhn ahkh in mI'-nuhr broost] *Ger*—Alas! two souls dwell in my breast. Goethe, *Faust*, pt. 1; 1112.

LIST OF PHRASES
ARRANGED BY LANGUAGE

Arabic

Allahu akbar
Id al-Fitr
La ilāha illa Allāh
Salaam aleikum

Aramaic

Eli eli, lama sabachthani

Mane, thecel, phares
Mene, mene, tekel, upharsin

Basque

Euskadi Ta Askatasuna

Chinookan

Al-ki

French

À barbe de fou, on apprend à raire
À bas
À bâtons rompus
À beau jeu, beau retour
À beau mentir qui vient de loin
À bientôt
À bis ou (et) à blanc
À bon appétit il ne faut point de sauce
À bon chat, bon rat
À bon cheval point d'éperon
À bon chien il ne vient jamais un bon os
À bon commencement bonne fin
À bon compte
Abondance de bien(s) ne nuit pas
À bon droit
À bon marché
À bon vin point d'enseigne
À bras ouverts
Absence d'esprit
Absent le chat, les souris dansent
Accordez vos flûtes
À chacun son fardeau pèse
À chaque fou plaît sa marotte

À chaque oiseau son nid est beau
À chaque saint sa chandelle (cierge)
À cheval
À coeur ouvert
À compte
À confesseurs, médecins, avocats, la verité ne cèle de ton cas
À contre coeur
À corps perdu
À coups de bâton
À coup sûr
À couvert
Acte d'accusation
Acte gratuit
À demi
À dessein
À deux
Adieu, canaux, canards, canaille!
Adieu la voiture, adieu la boutique
À discrétion
À droite
Affaire d'amour
Affaire d'honneur
Affaire du coeur
À fond
À forfait
À fripon fripon et demi
À gauche
À genoux!
Agent provocateur
À grands frais
À haute voix
À huis clos
Aide-de-camp
Aide mémoire
Aide-toi, le ciel t'aidera
Aîné (m), aînée (f)
Ainsi de suite
Ainsi soit-il
À la
À la belle étoile
À la bonne heure
À la bourgeoise
À l'abri

213

French—*Continued*

À la campagne
À la carte
À la dérobée
À la diable
À la française
À la grècque
À la lanterne
À la lettre
À la mode
À la mort
À la napolitaine
À la page
À la presse vont les fous
À la sourdine
À l'extérieur
À l'huile
À l'immortalité
À l'impromptu
À l'improviste
Allez-vous-en!
Allons, enfants de la patrie!
À loisir
À main armée
Âme damnée
Âme de boue
Amende honorable
Âme perdue
À merveille
Ami (amie) de coeur
Ami de cour
Ami du peuple
À moitié
À mon avis
Amour fait beaucoup mais l'argent fait tout
Amour propre
Ancienne noblesse
Ancien régime
À nouvelles affaires, nouveaux conseils
À outrance
À pas de géant
À perte de vue
À peu de frais
A pied
À point
Appartement meublé
Après dommage chacun est sage
Après la mort, le médecin
Après moi le déluge
À propos
À propos de
À propos de bottes
À propos de rien

À quoi bon
À raconter ses maux souvent on les soulage
À reculons
Argent comptant
Arrière-garde
Arrière pensée
À tâtons
À tort et à travers
À tort ou à raison
À tout prix
Au bout de son latin
Au bout du compte
Au contraire
Au courant
Aucun chemin de fleurs ne conduit à la gloire
Au désespoir
Au fait
Au fond
Au grand sérieux
Au gratin
Aujourd'hui roi, demain rien
Au jus
Au lecteur
Au naturel
Au pair
Au pied de la lettre
Au pis aller
Au point
Au reste
Au revoir
Au royaume des aveugles les borgnes sont rois
Au secours!
Au sérieux
Au soleil
Aussitôt dit, ausitôt fait
Autant d'hommes, autant d'avis
Autrefois acquit
Autres temps, autres moeurs
Au voleur!
Aux aguets
Aux armes!
Avant-coureur
Avant-garde
Avant la lettre
Avant propos
Avant que de désirer fortement une chose, il faut examiner quel est le bonheur de celui qui la possède
Avant tout un bon dîner
À volonté
À votre santé

À vue d'oeil

Ballon d'essai
Bas bleu
Bas relief
Bataille rangée
Bâtie en hommes
Beaucoup de bruit, peu de fruit
Beau garçon
Beau geste
Beau idéal
Beau monde
Beau sabreur
Beauté du diable
Beauté insolente
Beaux arts
Beaux esprits
Bel esprit (*pl.* beaux esprits)
Belle indifférence
Belles dames du temps jadis
Belles lettres
Bête noire
Bibliophile de la vieille roche
Bibliothèque bleue
Bien entendu
Billet doux
Bon avocat, mauvais voisin
Bon chien chasse de race
Bon goût
Bon gré, mal gré
Bonjour
Bon marché
Bon mot
Bonne amie
Bonne année
Bonne à tout faire
Bonne chance!
Bonne foi
Bonne humeur
Bonne nuit
Bonne renommée vaut mieux que ceinture dorée
Bonne santé
Bonnet rouge
Bon soir
Bon ton
Bon vivant
Bon voyage!
Bottes de sept lieues

Cabinet d'aisance
Café au lait
Ça-ira
Cap-à-pie
Cape et épée
Carte blanche

Carte de visite
Catalogue raisonné
Cause célèbre
Cela va sans dire
Celui qui a trouvé un bon gendre, a gagné un fils; mais celui que en a rencontré un mauvais a perdu une fille
Cent jours
Ce qui fait que les amants et les maîtresses ne s'ennuient point d'être ensemble, c'est qu'ils parlent toujours d'eux-mêmes
Ce qui n'est pas clair, n'est pas français
C'est à dire
C'est ça
C'est dommage
C'est double plaisir de tromper le trompeur
C'est égal
C'est la guerre
C'est la profonde ignorance qui inspire le ton dogmatique
C'est la vie
C'est le dernier pas qui coûte
C'est magnifique, mais ce n'est pas la guerre
C'est presque toujours la faute de celui qui aime de ne pas connaître quand on cesse de l'aimer
C'est trop fort
C'est une grande habilité que de savoir cacher son habilité
C'est une tempête dans un verre d'eau
Ceux qui s'appliquent trop aux petites choses deviennent ordinairement incapables des grandes
Chacun à sa marotte
Chacun à son goût
Chacun pour soi, et Dieu pour tous
Chacun sait le mieux où le soulier le blesse
Chacun selon ses facultés, à chacun selon ses besoins
Chacun tire de son côté
Chaise longue
Chambres meublées
Champs Elysées
Chanson de geste
Chanson sans paroles
Chansons de toile
Chant du cygne
Chapeau melon
Chapeau rouge de cardinal
Chapeaux bas!
Chapelle ardente

215

French—_Continued_

Chaque heure je vous aime de plus en plus
Char-à-bancs
Chargé d'affaires
Chasseurs à cheval
Châteaux en Espagne
Chat échaudé craint l'eau froide

Chef de cuisine
Chef d'oeuvre
Chef-lieu
Chercher midi à quatorze heures
Cherchez la femme
Chère amie
Cher maître
Cheval de bataille
Cheval-de-frise (_pl._ chevaux)
Chevalier d'industrie
Chez nous
Chose jugée
Chronique scandaleuse
Ci-devant
Ci-gît
Comédie de moeurs
Comme ci, comme ça
Comme deux gouttes d'eau
Comme il faut
Comment ça va?
Comment prétendons-nous qu'un autre garde notre secret, si nous ne pouvons le garder nous-mêmes?
Comme on fait son lit, on se couche
Comme vous-y-allez
Commis voyageur
Compagnon de voyage
Compte rendu
Congé d'élire
Conseil de famille
Conseil d'état
Conseils aux visiteurs étrangers
Conte de fées
Cordon bleu
Cordon sanitaire
Corps de ballet
Corps de bâtiment
Corps de logis
Corps diplomatique
Coup de bourse
Coup d'éclat
Coup de foudre
Coup de grâce
Coup de main

Coup de maître
Coup d'épée
Coup de pied de l'âne
Coup de plume
Coup de soleil
Coup d'essai
Coup d'état
Coup de tête
Coup de théâtre
Coup d'oeil
Courage sans peur
Cour des comptes
Cour du roi
Coureur de bois
Coûte que coûte
Crème de la crème
Cri du coeur
Crise de foie
Croix de guerre
Cul-de-sac

Dame de compagnie
Dame d'honneur
Dames de la halle
Danse du ventre
Danse macabre
Dans l'amour il y a toujours celui qui baise et celui qui tend la joue
Dans le doute, abstiens-toi
De bon augure
De bonne grâce
De droit
De fait
Défauts de ses qualités
Défense de —
De fond en comble
De gaieté de coeur
D'égal à égal
Dégénéré supérieur
De haute lutte
De haut en bas
Déjà vécu
Déjà vu
De l'audace, encore de l'audace, toujours de l'audace
De luxe
De mal en pis
De mémoire de rose, on n'a jamais vu mourir de jardinier
Demi-tasse
De pied en cap
De proche en proche
De race
De rigueur
Dernier ressort

De sa façon
De temps en temps
De trop
Deux s'amusent, trois s'embêtent
Dieu avec nous
Dieu défend le droit
Dieu est toujours pours les gros bataillons
Dieu et mon droit
Dieu le veuille!
Dieu mesure le vent (froid) à la brebis
    tondue
Dieu vous garde
Dis-moi ce que tu manges, je te dirais ce
    que tu es
Docteur ès lettres
Don gratuit
Dos-à-dos
Double entendre
Double entente
Douceur et lumière
Droit au travail
Droit d'impression réservé
Droit du mari
Droit du Seigneur
Droit et avant
Du fort au faible
Du haut en bas
Du sublime au ridicule il n'y a qu'un
    pas

Eau de vie
École des beaux-arts
École maternelle
Écrasez l'infâme!
Édition à tirage restreint
Édition classique
Édition de luxe
Eh bien!
Embarras de richesses
Embarras du choix
Éminence grise
En ami
En arrière
En attendant
En avant
En banc
En bloc
En bonne foi
En brosse
En cachette
En clair
En congé
En courant
En dernier ressort

En déshabillé
En deux mots
En Dieu est ma fiance
En Dieu est tout
En effet
En évidence
En famille
Enfant de famille
Enfant de son siècle
Enfant gâté
Enfants perdus
Enfant terrible
Enfant trouvé
En grande tenue
En grande toilette
En grand style
En le persiflant
En masse
En mauvaise odeur
En pantoufles
En papillotes
En parenthèse
En passant
En petit comité
En plein air
En plein jour
En principe
En queue
En rapport
En règle
En revanche
En route!
En somme
En surtout
En tapinois
Entente cordiale
Entente demi-cordiale
En titre
En tout cas
Entr'acte
Entre chien et loup
Entre deux feux
Entre deux vins
Entre nous
En vérité
En voiture!
Épater les bourgeois
Esprit de corps
Esprit de finesse
Esprit des lois
Esprit fort
Esprit gaulois
Est-ce possible?
Éternel devenir
Exemplaire d'auteur

French—*Continued*

Explication de texte

Facilité de parler, c'est impuissance de
   se taire
Façon de parler
Faire d'une mouche un éléphant
Faire les yeux doux
Fait accompli
Fait à peindre
Faites votre devoir et laissez faire aux
   dieux
Fait nouveau
Fausse couche
Faute de mieux
Faux ami
Faux frais
Faux pas
Femme couverte
Femme de chambre
Femme de charge
Femme de trente ans
Femme fatale
Femme savante
Ferme générale
Fermiers généraux
Fête champêtre
Fête de fleurs
Fête des Fous
Fêtes de nuit
Feu d'artifice
Feu de joie
Feu d'enfer
Feu follet, feux follets
Fille de joie
Fille d'honneur
Fille d'intrigue
Fils à papa
Fin de siècle
Finesse d'esprit
Fleur de lys
Flux de bouche
Flux de paroles
Folie de grandeur
Force de frappe
Force majeure
Fou qui se tait passe pour sage
Fou rire
Franc-alleu
Franc-tireur
Frappé au froid
Frère de lait
Froides mains, chaud amour
Fuyez les dangers de loisir

Gage d'amour
Gaieté de coeur
Garde à cheval
Garde du corps
Gardez la foi
Gardien de la paix
Gens d'armes
Gens de condition
Gens d'église
Gens de guerre
Gens de la même famille
Gens de lettres
Gens de loi
Gens de peu
Gens de robe
Gens du bien
Gens du monde
Gibier de potence
Gorge de pigeon
Goutte à goutte
Grâce à Dieu
Grande dame
Grande parure
Grand seigneur
Grosse tête, peu de sens
Guerre à mort
Guerre à outrance

Haute bourgeoisie
Haute coiffure
Haute couture
Haute cuisine
Haut goût
Haut ton
Heureux les peuples dont l'histoire est
   ennuyeux
Hommage d'auteur
Hommage d'éditeur
Homme d'affaires
Homme de bien
Homme de guerre
Homme de lettres
Homme de paille
Homme d'épée
Homme d'esprit
Homme d'état
Homme de théâtre
Homme du monde
Homme du peuple
Homme moyen sensuel
Honi (honni) soit qui mal y pense
Honnête homme
Hors concours
Hors de combat
Hors de commerce

Hors de propos
Hors de saison
Hors d'oeuvre
Hors la loi
Hôtel de ville
Hôtel-Dieu
Hôtel garni
Hôtel meublé
Hurler avec les loups

Ici on parle français
Idée fixe
Idée maîtresse
Il a la mer à boire
Il a le diable au corps
Il a les défauts de ses qualités
Il a le vin mauvais
Il avait le diable au corps
Il connaît l'univers, et ne se connaît pas
Il dit tout ce qu'il veut, mais malheureusement il n'a rien à dire
Il est bon d'avoir des amis partout
Il est bon de parler, et meilleur de se taire
Il faut bonne mémoire après qu'on a menti
Il faut cultiver notre jardin
Il faut laver son linge sale en famille
Il faut manger pour vivre, et non pas vivre pour manger
Il faut marcher quand le diable est aux trousses
Il faut que la jeunesse se passe
Il n'a ni bouche ni éperon
Il n'a pas inventé la poudre
Il n'appartient qu'aux grands hommes d'avoir de grands défauts
Il ne faut jamais défier un fou
Il ne faut pas disputer des goûts
Il ne faut pas mettre tous ses oeufs dans le même panier
Il ne manquerait plus que ça
Il n'entend pas raillerie
Il n'est sauce que d'appétit
Il nous faut de l'audace, et encore de l'audace, et toujours de l'audace
Il n'y a de nouveau que ce qui est oublié
Il n'y a de pire sourd que celui qui ne veut pas entendre
Il n'y a pas de grand homme pour son valet-de-chambre
Il n'y a pas moins d'éloquence dans le ton de la voix, dans les yeux, et dans l'air de la personne, que dans le choix des paroles

Il n'y a plus de Pyrénées
Il n'y a point de déguisement qui puisse longtemps cacher l'amour où il est, ni le feindre où il n'est pas
Il n'y a que ceux qui ne font rien, qui ne se trompent pas
Il n'y a que le premier pas qui coûte
Il n'y a rien de mieux à faire que de s'amuser
Il rit bien qui rit le dernier
Il s'attache aux pas de . . .
Il se noierait dans une goutte d'eau
Il sent le fagot
Il se recule pour mieux sauter
Il se voit par expérience, que les mémoires excellentes se joignent volontiers aux jugements débiles
Ils ne passeront pas
Ils n'ont rien appris, ni rien oublié
Il vaut mieux employer notre esprit à supporter les infortunes qui nous arrivent qu'à prévoir celles qui nous peuvent arriver
Il vaut mieux s'exposer à l'ingratitude que de manquer aux misérables
Il veut prendre la lune avec les dents
Il y a à parier que toute idée publique, toute convention reçue, est une sottise, car elle a convenu au plus grand nombre
Impossible n'est pas un mot français

J'accuse
J'ai vécu
Jalousie de métier
Jardins à l'anglaise
Je maintiendrai
Je maintiendrai le droit
Je me fais pitié à moi-même
Je me souviens
Je ne sais quoi
Je pense, donc je suis
Je prends mon bien où je le trouve
Je sème à tout vent
Je t'aime plus qu'hier, moins que demain
Jeter de la poudre aux yeux
Jeter le manche après la cognée
Jets d'eau
Jeu de mots
Jeu d'esprit
Jeu de théâtre
Jeunesse dorée
Je vais chercher un grand Peut-être
Je veux que le dimanche chaque paysan ait sa poule au pot

French—*Continued*

Je vis d'espoir
Joie de vivre
Jour gras
Jour maigre
Journée des Barricades
Joyeux Noël!
Juge de paix
Juge d'instruction
Jugement de Dieu
Jugez un homme par ses questions, plutôt que par ses réponses
Jusqu'au bout
J'y suis, j'y reste

La belle dame sans merci
La bonne bouche
La Comédie Humaine
La comédie larmoyante
La condition humaine
La critique est aisée,
    et l'art est difficile
La Derrière Garde
La douce France
La douceur de vivre
L'adversité fait l'homme,
    et le bonheur les monstres
La farce est jouée
La fin couronne les oeuvres
La Garde meurt et ne se rend pas
La génération spontanée est une
    chimère
La génie c'est la patience
La Grande Voleuse
La gravité est un mystère du corps
    inventé pour cacher les défauts
    de l'esprit
La haute politique
Laissez aller
Laissez dire
Laissez faire
Laissez passer
La Journée des Dupes
La langue des femmes est leur épée,
    et elles ne la laissent pas rouiller
L'Albion perfide
La mémoire est nécessaire à toutes
    les opérations de l'esprit
La moquerie est souvent indigence
    d'esprit
La morgue littéraire
L'amour courtois
L'amour, . . . de tous les sentiments

le plus égoïste, et, par conséquent,
    lorsqu'il est blessé, le moins gé-
    néreux
L'amour et la fumée ne peuvent
    se cacher
L'amour-propre est le plus grande
    de tous les flatteurs
Langage des halles
L'Angleterre est une nation
    de boutiquiers
Langue d'oc
Langue d'oïl
La noblesse d'épée
La noblesse de race
La nouvelle cuisine
La nuit tous les chats sont gris
La paix à tout prix
La paix de Dieu
La parole a été donnée à l'homme
    pour déguiser sa pensée
La patience est amère, mais son
    fruit est doux
La patrie en danger
La perfide Albion
La petite bourgeoisie
La petitesse de l'esprit fait
    l'opiniâtreté, et nous ne
    croyons pas aisément ce qui au
    delà de ce que nous voyons
La plupart des gens ne jugent des
    hommes que par la vogue qu'ils ont,
    ou par leur fortune
La plupart des hommes emploient
    la première partie de leur vie à
    rendre l'autre misérable
La politique du pire
La politique n'a pas d'entrailles
La pompe des enterrements regarde
    plus la vanité des vivants que
    l'honneur des morts
L'appétit vient en mangeant
La reconnaissance est la
    mémoire du coeur
La règle du jeu
La République n'a pas besoin
    de savants
L'art de vivre
L'Art Nouveau
L'art pour l'art
La tour d'ivoire
La vie à trois
La vie en rose
La vieille gloire
Le bon Dieu est toujours du côté
    des gros bataillons.

Le bon genre
Le bon temps viendra
Le Bourgeois Gentilhomme
Le cabaret est le salon du pauvre
Le chat qui dort
Le cheval volant qui a les narines
    de feu
Le chien retourne à son vomissement,
    et la truie lavée au bourbier
Le coeur a ses raisons que la
    raison ne connaît pas
Le courage est souvent un effet
    de la peur
Le coût en ôte le goût
Le demi-monde
Le dernier cri
Le dernier mot
Le désespoir redouble les forces
Le dessous des cartes
Le devoir des juges est de rendre
    justice; leur métier de la différer
Le diable au corps
Le droit des gens
Légion étrangère
Le grand mal
Le Grand Monarque
Le grand monde
Le grand prix
Le grand siècle
Le haut monde
Le jeu ne vaut pas la chandelle
Le jour de l'an
Le Juif errant
Le juste milieu
L'élan vital
Le mal que nous faisons ne nous
    attire pas tant de persécution et
    de haine que nos bonnes qualités
Le méchant n'est jamais comique
Le mieux est l'ennemi du bien
Le moine bourru
Le monde est le livre des femmes
Le monde va de lui-même
Le mot de Cambronne
Le mot juste
Le Moyen Age
L'Empire c'est la paix
L'empire des lettres
Le nez de Cléopatre; s'il eût été plus
    court, toute la face de la terre
    aurait changé
L'enfer des femmes, c'est la vieillesse
L'ennemi du genre humain
Le pénible fardeau de n'avoir rien à faire

Le petit caporal
Le petit coin
Le plus brave des braves
Le pour et le contre
Le Proche Orient
Le refus des louanges est un désir
    d'être loué deux fois
Le roi est mort. Vive le roi!
Le roi le veut
Le roi règne et ne gouverne pas
Le roi s'avisera
Le Roi Soleil
Les absents ont toujours tort
Les affaires sont les affaires
Le sage quelquefois évite le monde
    de peur d'être ennuyé
Les amis du vin
Les beaux esprits se rencontrent
Les belles actions cachées sont les
    plus estimables
Les bons comptes font les bons amis
Les convenances
Les Diables Bleues
Les dieux ont soif
Le secret d'ennuyer est celui
    de tout dire
Lèse majesté
Les extrêmes se touchent
Les femmes peuvent tout, parce
    qu'elles gouvernent les personnes
    qui gouvernent tout
Les fous font les festins et les sages
    les mangent
Les gens qui hésitent ne reussissent
    guère
Les grands esprits se rencontrent
Les gros bataillons ont toujours raison
Les hommes rougissent moins de
    leurs crimes que de leurs faiblesses
    et de leur vanité
Les hommes sont cause que les
    femmes ne s'aiment point
Le silence éternel de ces espaces
    infinis m'effraye
Les morts ont toujours tort
Les murailles ont des oreilles
Les paroles sont faites pour cacher
    nos pensées
Les personnes faibles ne peuvent
    être sincères
Les plus sages ne le sont pas toujours
L'esprit de suite
L'esprit est toujours la dupe du coeur
Les Quarante fauteuils
Les querelles ne dureraient pas

221

French—*Continued*

longtemps si le tort n'était que
d'un côté
Les scènes à faire
Le style c'est l'homme *or*
Le style est l'homme même
L'état c'est moi
L'état major
L'étoile du Nord
Le tout ensemble
Lettre d'avis
Lettre de cachet
Lettre de change
Lettre de créance
Le vainqueur du vainqueur
de la terre
Levée en masse
Le vin est tiré—il faut le boire
Le vrai honnête homme est celui
qui ne se pique de rien
Le vrai n'est pas toujours
vraisemblable
Le vrai peut quelquefois n'être pas
vraisemblable
Le vrai roi du dix-huitième siècle
L'Extrême Orient
L'habitude est une seconde nature
L'histoire n'est qu'une fable convenue
L'homme absurde est celui
qui ne change jamais
L'homme est né libre et il est
partout dans les fers
L'homme propose et Dieu dispose
L'homme tranquille
L'hôtel des Invalides
L'hypocrisie est un hommage que
le vice rend à la vertu
Liberté, égalité, fraternité
Lieu de réunion
L'injustice à la fin produit
l'indépendence
Lit de justice
Livre de chevet
Livre de circonstances
Livre de poche
Livres d'heures
L'occasion fait le larron
Loin des yeux, loin du coeur
Loyauté m'oblige
L'union fait la force
Lütte corps à corps

Ma chérie, ma chère
Ma foi!

M'aidez
Maintiens le droit
Maison de campagne
Maison de jeu
Maison de passe
Maison de santé
Mais où sont les neiges d'antan?
Maître d'armes
Maître des hautes oeuvres
Maître d'hôtel
Maladie du pays
Mal à propos
Mal au coeur
Mal de mer
Mal du pays
Mal (maladie) du siècle
Malgré lui
Malheur ne vient jamais seul
Manger son blé en herbe
Marchandise qui plaît est
à demi vendu
Marcher à pas de loup
Marcher droit
Mardi gras
Mariage de conscience
Mariage de convenance
Mariage de la main gauche
Mariage de politique
Marque de fabrique
Mauvais coucheur
Mauvaise honte
Mauvaise plaisanterie
Mauvais goût
Mauvais quart d'heure
Mauvais sujet
Médecin, guéris-toi toi même
Meilleurs voeux
Mélanges de genre
Ménage à trois
Mensonge magnanime
Menteur à triple étage
Menu peuple
Merci beaucoup
Mettre de l'eau dans son vin
Meubles d'occasion
Mi-carême
Mieux vaut goujat debout
qu'empereur enterré
Mise en page
Mise en scène
Modeste aisance
Mon cher
Mon coeur et ton coeur pour la vie
Mon Dieu!
Mont-de-piété

Mort Dieu (Mordieu)
Mot à mot
Mot de guet
Mot de l'énigme
Mots de terroir
Mots d'usage
Moulin à paroles
Muet comme un poisson

Nager entre deux eaux
Ne battre que d'une aile
Ne réveillez pas le chat qui dort
N'est-ce pas?
N'importe!
Ni plus, ni moins
Noblesse de robe
Noblesse oblige
Nom de guerre
Nom de plume
Nom de théâtre
Nostalgie de la boue
Notre Dame
Notre défiance justifie la
    tromperie d'autrui
Notre mérite nous attire l'estime
    des honnêtes gens, et notre
    étoile celle du public
Notre nature est dans le
    mouvement; le repos entier
    est la mort
Nourri dans le sérail, j'en connais
    les détours
Nous aimons toujours ceux qui nous
    admirent, et nous n'aimons pas
    toujours ceux que nous admirons
Nous avons changé tout cela
Nous avons tous assez de force
    pour supporter les maux d'autrui
Nous ne trouvons guère de gens
    de bon sens que ceux qui sont
    de notre avis
Nous sommes tous dans le désert!
    Personne ne comprend personne
Nous verrons
Nous verrons ce que nous verrons
Nouveau riche
Nouvelle série
Nul bien sans peine

Objet d'art
Oeil-de-boeuf
Oeuvre de vulgarisation
Oeuvres complètes
O Liberté, O Liberté, que de crimes
    on commet en ton nom!

On connaît l'ami au besoin
On est souvent ferme par faiblesse,
    et audacieux par timidité
On n'a jamais bon marché de
    mauvaise marchandise
On ne donne rien si libéralement
    que ses conseils
On ne fait pas d'omelette sans
    casser des oeufs
On ne loue d'ordinaire que pour
    être loué
On ne saurait faire une omelette
    sans casser des oeufs
On ne se blâme que pour être loué
On n'est jamais si heureux ni si
    malheureux qu'on s'imagine
On n'est jamais si ridicule par les
    qualités que l'on a que par celles
    que l'on affecte d'avoir
On ne trouve guère d'ingrats tant
    qu'on est en état de faire du bien
Oublier je ne puis
Où la chèvre est attaché,
    il faut qu'elle broute
Outre mer
Ouvrage de longue haleine

Pain bénit
Paix fourrée
Paix sur la terre
Palmes académiques
Papier mâché
Par accès
Par avance
Par avion
Parbleu!
Par ci, par là
Par complaisance
Par dépit
Pardonnez-moi
Par excellence
Par exemple
Parfum de terroir
Par hasard
Pari mûtuel
Paris vaut bien une messe
Parler à tort et à travers
Parole d'honneur
Par parenthèse
Part du lion
Partie carrée
Parti pris
Partir, c'est mourir un peu
Pas à pas
Pas à pas on va bien loin

French—*Continued*

Pas de deux
Pas de nouvelles, bonnes nouvelles
Pas de rose sans épines
Pas du tout
Pas seul
Pas si bête
Pâté de foie gras
Patte de velours
Pattes de mouche
Pauvre diable!
Peau d'âne
Peau de chagrin
Peine forte et dure
Pensée fait la grandeur de l'homme
Père de famille
Père du peuple
Petit à petit, fait l'oiseau son nid
Petit bourgeois
Petit chaudron, grandes oreilles

Petite pièce
Petites gens
Petite morales
Petit maître
Petit mal
Petit nom
Petits jeux
Petit souper
Peu à peu
Peu d'hommes ont été admirés par
    leurs domestiques
Pièce à thèse
Pièce de résistance
Pièce d' occasion
Pièces à conviction
Pied à terre!
Pied-noir, *pl.* pieds-noirs
Pierre qui roule n'amasse pas mousse
Pis-aller
Place aux dames!
Place d'armes
Plat du jour
Plus ça change, plus c'est la
    même chose
Plus fait douceur que violence
Plus je vois les hommes,
    plus j'admire les chiens
Plus royaliste que le roi
Plus sages que les sages
Point d'appui
Point d'argent, point de Suisses
Point de repère
Poisson d'avril

Pomme de terre
Poste restante
Potage au gras
Pour acquit
Pour épater les bourgeois
Pour faire rire
Pour l'amour de Dieu!
Pour le mérite
Pour passer le temps
Pour prendre congé
Pour rire
Prendre la balle au bond
Prendre la lune avec les dents
Prenez garde!
Preux chevalier
Privilège du roi
Prix fixe
Procès-verbal
Prochain ami
Profits et pertes
Puffistes littéraires
Pur sang

Quand celui à qui l'on parle ne
    comprend pas et celui qui parle
    ne se comprend pas, c'est de la
    métaphysique
Quand même
Quand on parle du loup,
    on en voit la queue
Quarante hommes, huit chevaux
Que diable allait-il faire dans
    cette galère
Quel dommage!
Quelques grands avantages que la
    nature donne, ce n'est pas elle
    seule, mais la fortune avec elle
    qui fait les héros
Qu'en dira le monde?
Que sçais (sais)-je?
Que voulez-vous?
Qui a bu boira
Qui donne tôt, donne deux fois
Qui est près de l'église est souvent
    loin de Dieu
Qui m'aime, aime mon chien
Qui n'a santé n'a rien
Qui s'excuse, s'accuse
Qui va là?
Qui vive

Raison de plus
Raison d'état
Raison d'être
Rentes sur l'État
Répondez s'il vous plaît

Répondre en Normand
Revenons à nos moutons
Rez-de-chaussée
Rien de plus éloquent que l'argent
  comptant
Rien ne dure que le provisoire
Rien ne pèse tant qu'un secret
Rien ne réussit comme le succès
Rien n'est beau que le vrai
Rira bien qui rira le dernier
Rire dans sa barbe
Rire et faire rire
Ris de veau
Robe de chambre
Rois fainéants
Rôle de l'équipage
Roman à clef
Roman à thèse
Roman policier
Rouge-et-noire
Ruse de guerre

Sacre bleu
Salle à manger
Salle d'attente
Salle de jeu
Salle des pas perdus
Salle du Jeu de Paume
Sang de boeuf
Sang-froid
Sans appel
Sans blague?
Sans cérémonie
Sans culottes
Sans doute
Sans façon
Sans gêne
Sans pareil
Sans peur et sans reproche
Sans rime et sans raison
Sans souci
Sauve qui peut
Savant atomiste
Savoir-faire
Savoir vivre
Selon les règles
Sens commun
Sens dessus dessous
Serpent d'église
Si Dieu n'existait pas, il faudrait
  l'inventer
Siècle des ténèbres
Siècle d'or
Si jeunesse savait,
  si vieillesse pouvait!

S'il vous plaît
Si nous n'avions point de défauts,
  nous ne prendrions pas tant de
  plaisir à en remarquer dans les
  autres
Si un Allemand peut être bel-esprit?
Si vous lui donnez un pied,
  il vous en prendra quatre
Société anonyme
Société en commandite
Soi-disant
Son et lumière
Sot à triple étage
Souffler le chaud et le froid
Souhaits sincères
Sous tous les rapports
Sous toutes réserves
Succès de mouchoir
Succès de scandale
Succès d'estime
Succès fou
Sur le pavé
Sur le tapis
Sur place
Surtout, point de zèle

Table d'hôte
Tâche sans tache
Ta gueule!
Tant bien que mal
Tant mieux
Tant pis
Tant soit peu
Tel est notre bon plaisir
Tel font les parents, tel feront
  les enfants
Tel maître, tel valet
Tel père, tel fils
Tel quel
Terre promise
Tête-à-tête
Tête de veau
Tic douloureux
Tiens à la vérité
Tiers état
Tirage au sort
Tiré à quatre épingles
Toison d'or
Tombé des nues
Tonnerre de Dieu
Toujours en vedette
Toujours l'amour
Toujours perdrix
Toujours prêt
Tour de force

225

French—*Continued*

Tour d'horizon
Tous droits réservés
Tous frais faits
Tous mes effets
Tout à fait
Tout à l'heure
Tout au contraire
Tout bien ou rien
Tout chemin mêne (va) à Rome
Tout comprendre c'est tout
    pardonner
Tout court
Tout de suite
Tout d'un coup
Toute la dignité de l'homme
    consiste en la pensée
Toute(s) proportion(s) gardée(s)
Tout est bien qui finit bien
Tout est perdu fors l'honneur
Tout le monde
Tout le monde se plaint de sa
    mémoire, et personne ne se
    plaint de son jugement
Tout lui ri (sourit)
Tout s'en va, tout passe, l'eau coule,
    et le coeur oublie
Tranche de vie
Travaux forcés
Trente-et-quarante
Très bien
Trêve de Dieu
Trompe-l'oeil
Trop de hâte gâte tout
Tuer le veau gras

Un barbier rait l'autre
Un bienfait n'est jamais perdu
Une bonne race
Une fable convenue
Une femme grosse
Une grosse femme
Une hirondelle ne fait pas
    le printemps
Une nation boutiquière
Une poire pour la soif
Un lever de rideau
Un peu passé
Un roi, une loi, une foi
Un "tiens" vaut mieux que deux
    "tu l'auras"

Va-t'en!
Ventre à terre
Vérité sans peur

Vers de société
Vers libre
Victoire ou la mort
Vigueur de dessus
Vin d'honneur
Vin du pays
Violon d'Ingres
Vis-à-vis
Vive la bagatelle!
Vive la différence!
Vive l'empereur!
Vive le roi!
Vivent les Gueux!
Vivre libre, ou mourir
Vogue la galère!
Voilà!
Voilà une autre chose
Voilà un homme!
Voir le dessous des cartes
Vol-au-vent
Volte-face
Vouloir c'est pouvoir
Vouloir rompre l'anguille au genou
Vous êtes orfèvre, Monsieur Josse
Vous y perdrez vos pas
Vue d'oiseau

Wagons-lits

Anglo-French

Cestui que (qui) trust
Cestui que use
Cestui que vie

Nul tiel record

Oyer and terminer
Oyez!

Old French

Dieu li volt

ès

Fay ce que vouldras

Je le pansay, Dieu le guarit

Le roy le veult

Non sanz droict

Si Dieu veult

Voire dire

German

Abends wird der Faule fleissig
Adel sitzt im Gemüte, nicht im
  Geblüte
Adler brüten keine Tauben
Alle Länder gute Menschen tragen
Alle Menschen sind Lügner
Aller Anfang ist schwer
Aller guten Dinge sind drei
Allmacht des Gedankens
Amt ohne Geld macht Diebe
Am Werke erkennt man den Meister
An armer Leute Bart lernt der Junge
  scheren
Armut ist keine Schande
Artz, hilf dir selbst
Auch ein Haar hat seinen Schatten
Auch ich war in Arkadien geboren
Auf Wiedersehen
Aus den Augen, aus dem Sinn
Aus der Hand in den Mund
Aus Kindern werden Leute

Bei Nacht sind alle Katzen grau
Bellende Hunde beissen nicht
Besser spät als nie
Blitzkrieg
Blut und Eisen
Borgen macht Sorgen
Böse Beispiele verderben gute Sitten

Danke schön
Das bessere ist des Guten Feind
Das Beste ist gut genug
Das Ding an sich
Das Erste und Letzte, was vom Genie
  gefordert wird, ist Wahrheitsliebe
Das Ewig-Weibliche/zieht uns hinan
Das fünfte Rad am Wagen
Das Gelobte Land
Das Gesetz nur kann uns Freiheit geben
Das ist mir Wurst oder Wurscht
Das kleine Weib
Das kleinste Haar wirft seinen Schatten
Das Weib sieht tief; der Mann sieht weit
Das Werk lobt den Meister
Der Baum fällt nicht vom ersten Streiche
Der Feind steht im eigenen Lager
Der Fürst is der erste Diener seines Staats
Der gottbetrunkene Mensch
Der grosse Heide
Der Krieg ist lustig den Unerfahrenen
Der Krug geht so lange zu Wasser bis er
  bricht
Der Mensch denkt, Gott lenkt

Der Mensch ist was er isst
Der Tag
Der Zeitgeist
Deutsches Reich
Deutschland, Deutschland über Alles
Die Alten zum Rat, die Jungen zur Tat
Die Architektur ist die erstarrte Musik
Die Baukunst ist eine erstarrte Musik
Die Götterdämmerung
Die kleinen Diebe hängt man, die grossen
  lässt man laufen
Die Lage ist hoffnungslos aber nicht ernst
Die Philosophie des Als-ob
Die Politik ist keine exakte Wissenschaft
Die Probe eines Genusses ist seine Erin-
  nerung
Die Religion . . . ist das Opium des Volkes
Die stille Woche
Die Wacht am Rhein
Die Wahrheit ist eine Perle; wirf sie nicht
  vor die Säue
Die Weisheit der Gasse
Die Weisheit ist nur in der Wahrheit
Donner und Blitz!
Die Weltgeschichte ist das Weltgericht
Drang nach Osten
Du, du liegst mir im Herzen
Durchgang verboten

Edel ist, der edel tut
Ehrlich währt am längsten
Ehre, dem Ehre gebührt
Eile mit Weile
Eine feste Burg ist unser Gott
Eine Hand wäscht die andere
Ein eigner Herd, ein braves Weib sind
  Gold und Perlen wert
Eine kleine Wurst ist auch eine Wurst
Eine Schwalbe macht keinen Sommer
Ein fröhliches Neujahr
Einkreisungspolitik
Ein Reich, ein Volk, ein Führer
Ein Unglück kommt selten allein
Ein unnütz Leben ist ein früher Tod
Eisen und Blut
Ende gut, alles gut
Entbehre gern was du nicht hast
Entbehren sollst du!
Erfahrung ist die beste Schule
Es gibt, sagt man, für den Kammerdiener
  keinen Helden
Es irrt der Mensch, solang er strebt
Es ist nicht alles Gold was glänzt
Es ist Schade
Es kann der Frömmste nicht im Frieden

227

German—*Continued*

Es kann der Frömmste nicht im Frieden bleiben,/Wenn es dem bösen Nachbar nicht gefällt
Es wird nichts so schön gemacht/ Es kommt einer der's veracht!

Flak (Fliegerabwehrkanone)
Friede auf Erden
Frisch begonnen, halb gewonnen
Fröhliche Weihnachten
Für Herren

Geben Sie acht!
Gebranntes Kind scheut das Feuer
Geflügelte Worte
Geheime Staatspolizei
Geld behält das Feld
Gesagt, getan
Gesamtverzeichnis der ausländischen Zeitschriften
Gestapo
Gleich und gleich gesellt sich gern
Glückliches Neujahr!
Glück und Glas wie leicht bricht das
Gott behüte!
Gott macht gesund, und der Doktor bekommt das Geld
Gott mit uns
Gott sei Dank
Gott soll hüten!
Gott strafe dich
Grosse Dinge haben kleine Anfänge
Gute Nacht
Guten Morgen
Gute Ware lobt sich selbst

Hänge nicht alles auf einen Nagel
Heil dir im Siegerkranz
Heute Deutschland, morgen die ganze Welt
Heute rot, morgen tot
Hier stehe ich! Ich kann nicht anders. Gott helfe mir, Amen
Hilf dir selbst, so hilft dir Gott
Hunde, die bellen, beissen nicht
Hunger ist der beste Koch

Ich bin der Geist der stets verneint!
Ich dien
Im Wein ist Warheit
Irrtümer vorbehalten

Jeder Esel kann kritisieren
Jeder ist Herr in seinem Hause
Jeder ist seines Glückes Schmied

Jeder ist sich selbst der Nächste
Jeder weiss, wo ihn der Schuh drückt
Je höher der Baum, desto tiefer der Fall

Kalte Hände, warme Liebe
Keine Antwort ist auch eine Antwort
Kein Unglück so gross, es ist ein Glück dabei
Kinder sind Kinder
Kinder und Narren sprechen die Wahrheit
Kleine Leute grosse Herzen
Kommt der Krieg ins Land/Gibt Lügen wie Sand
Küche, Kirche und Kinder
Kürze ist des Witzes Würze

Lade nicht Alles in ein Schiff
Lass sie nach Berlin kommen
Leben Sie wohl!
Lebensraum
Leichter ist Vergeben als Vergessen
Liebe ohne Gegenliebe ist wie eine Frage ohne Antwort
Lügen haben kurze Beine

Macht geht vor Recht
Man ist was man isst
Man kann, was man will, wenn man nur will, was man kann
Man kennt den Baum an seiner Frucht
Man lernt nichts kennen, als was man liebt
Man muss das Eisen schmieden solang es noch warm ist
Mehr Licht
Meine Damen und Herren
Meine Zeit wird schon kommen
Mein Haus, meine Welt
Mein Herr
Mein Kampf
Mein Name ist Hase; ich weiss von nichts
Mit dem Wissen wächst der Zweifel
Mit der Dummheit kämpfen Götter selbst vergebens
Mit grossen Herren ist nicht gut Kirschen essen
Mit innigster Ergebenheit in Gott
Mit umgehender Post
Morgen, morgen, nur nicht heute,/Sagen alle faulen Leute
Morgenstund' hat Gold im Mund
Muss ist eine harte (bittere) Nuss (ein bitter Kraut)

Nach Canossa gehen wir nicht
Nach Christi Geburt

Nacheifern ist beneiden
Nacht und Nebel
Nazi
Neue Besen kehren gut
Nicht die Kinder bloss speist man mit
  Märchen ab
Nicht wahr?
Not kennt kein Gebot
Nur der verdient sich Freiheit wie das
  Leben,/Der täglich sie erobern muss
Nur wer die Sehnsucht kennt,/weiss, was
  ich leide!

Ohne Arbeit kein Gewinn
Ohne Hast, ohne Rast

Prosit Neujahr!

Rast ich, so rost ich
Ratschläge für ausländische Besucher
Reden ist Silber, Schweigen ist Gold
Rom war nicht in einem Tage gebaut

Sage mir, mit wem du umgehst, so sage
  ich dir, wer du bist
Schlafen Sie wohl!
Selbst ist der Mann
Sieg Heil
So geht es in der Welt
So Gott will
Soll und Haben
So schnell als möglich
Spurlos versenkt
Schutzstaffel
Sturm und Drang

Übung macht den Meister
Um Christi willen
Undank ist der Welt (en) Lohn
Und so weiter

Verdammte Bedürfnislosigkeit
Verstand kommt mit den Jahren
Verweile doch! du bist so schön
Viele Händ' machen bald ein End'
Viele Köche verderben den Brei
Vorwärts mit Gott!

Wahrheit und Dichtung
Was ich nicht weiss, macht mich nicht
  heiss
Was ihn nicht umbringt, macht ihn stärker
Was ist los?
Was man nicht kann meiden, muss man
  willig leiden
Wein auf Bier, das rat ich dir; Bier auf
  Wein, lass das sein
Wein, Weib, und Gesang

Welche Regierung die beste sei? Diejenige
  die uns lehrt uns selbst zu regieren
Weltanschauung
Weltmacht oder Niedergang
Wenige wissen, wieviel man wissen muss,
  um zu wissen, wie wenig man weiss
Wenn die Katze nicht zu Hause ist, tan-
  zen die Mäuse auf Tisch und Bänken
Wenn schon, denn schon
Wer dem Pöbel dient, hat einen
  schlechten Herrn
Wer fremde Sprachen nicht kennt, weiss
  nichts von seiner eigenen
Wer gar zu viel bedenkt, wird wenig
  leisten
Wer liebt nicht Weib, Wein und Gesang/
  Der bleibt ein Narr sein Leben lang
Wer nicht will, der hat schon
Wer verachtet, der will kaufen
Wer zuletzt lacht, lacht am besten
Wie der Herr, so der Knecht
Wie geht's?
Wie gewonnen, so zerronnen
Wir Deutschen fürchten Gott, sonst aber
  Nichts in der Welt
Wir lieben unsern Führer
Wollt ihr immer leben?

Zartem Ohre, halbes Wort
Zeit ist teuer
Zum Donnerwetter!
Zwei Hälften machen zwar ein Ganzes,
  aber merk': Aus halb und halb getan
  ensteht kein ganzes Werk
Zwei Seelen und ein Gedanke, zwei
  Herzen und ein Schlag
Zwei Seelen wohnen, ach! in meiner Brust

Greek

Aei gar eu piptousin hoi Dios kyboi
Agapa ton plesion
Anagke oude theoi machontai
Anax andron
Andra moi ennepe, Mousa, polytropon
Aner ho pheugon kai palin machesetai
Anthropos physei politikon zoon
Arche hemisy pantos
Ariston metron
Asbestos gelos
Autos epha

Biblia a-biblia

Chaire

Dis krambe thanatos

Greek—*Continued*

Dos moi pou sto kai kino ten gen

En nukti boule tois sophois gignetai

Entelecheia

Epea pteroenta

Eureka!

Galilaie nenikekas

Glaucopis Athene

Gnothi seauton

Hapax legomenon

He glossa omomoch', he de phren anomotos

Ho anthropos physei politikon zoon

Ho bios brachys, he de techne makre

Hodos chameliontos

Hoi polloi

Hon hoi theoi philousin apothneskei neos

Ho sophos en auto peripherei ten ousian

Hysteron proteron

Iatre, therapeuson seauton

Kairon gnothi

Kai su ei ekeinon, kai su teknon?

Kai su, teknon

Kalokagathia

Ktema es aei

Kyrie eleison

Lathe biosas

Medeis ageometretos eisito

Meden agan

Mega biblion, mega kakon

Metron ariston

Mia gar chelidon ear ou poiei

Neos d'appolyth' hontin' an phile theos

Nous pathetikos

Nous poietikos

Opse theon aleousi myloi, aleousi de lepta

Panta agan

Panta rei (rhei)

Panton metron anthropos estin

Phi Beta Kappa

Phtheirousin ethe chresth' homiliai kakai

Prin d'an teleutese, epischein mede kaleein ko olbion, all' eutychea

Rhododaktulos eos

Sophois homilon kautos ekbese sophos

Speude bradeos

Thalassa, thalassa!

Thalatta, thalatta!

Theo(i) mono(i) doxa

Theos ek mechanes

To kalon

To me on

Zoon dipoun apteran

Modern Greek

Zoe mou, sas agapo

Hebrew

Bar Mizvah (mitzvah, mitzwah)

B'nai B'rith

Rosh Hashanah

Shalom alekhem

Yom Kippur

Irish

A cushla agus asthore machree

A-suilish mahuil agus machree!

Avic machree

Beannacht libh

Cailín bán

Céad míle fáilte!

Colleen bawn

Crúiskín lán

Cushla machree, mavourneen

Dail Eireann

Dia duit

Dia linn

Erin go brah!

Fianna Fail

Roisin dub

Seanad Eireann

Sinn Fein

Slan leat

Uisge beatha

Italian

A beneplacito

A buon vino non bisogna frasca

A cader va chi troppo alto sale

A cane scottato l'acqua fredda pare calda

A cappella

A cavallo donato non si guarda in bocca

Accelerando

A chi consiglia non duole il capo

A chi dici il tuo segreto, doni la tua
   libertà
A chi fa male, mai mancano scuse
A chi ha testa, non manca cappello
A chi vuole, non mancano modi
Adagio ma non troppo
Ad ogni uccello suo nido è bello
Ad un colpo non cade a terra l'albero
Ai mali estremi, estremi rimedi
Aiutati che Dio t'aiuta
Al bisogno si conosce un amico
Al bugiardo non si crede la verità
Al confessor, medico, ed avvocato, non si
   de' tener il vero celato
Al dente
Al fine
Al fresco
Alla barba dei pazzi, il barbier impara a
   radere
Alla cappella
Alla vostra salute
Allegro moderato
All' ottava
Al nemico che fugge, fa un ponte d'oro
Al primo colpo, non cade l'albero
Alta vendetta d'alto silenzio è figlia
Alto rilievo
Ama l'amico tuo col vizio suo
Amato non sarai, se a te solo penserai
Amico d'ognuno, amico di nessuno
Amore è cieco
Anch' io son' pittore
Andante
Apertura a destra
A piacere
Appetito non vuol salsa
A prima vista
A rivederci (usually spelled arrivederci)
Articolo di fondo
A tuo beneplacito
A vostra salute
Avvocato del diavolo

Bacio di bocca spesso cuor non tocca
Basso buffo
Basso rilievo
Batti il ferro mentre è caldo
Bel canto
Berretta in mano non fece mai danno
Bisogna andare quando il diavolo è nella
   coda
Bisogna battere il ferro mentre è caldo
Bona roba
Buona mano
Buona notte

Buon capo d'anno
Buon capo del anno!
Buon giorno
Buon Natale
Buon viaggio

Cane scottato ha paura dell'acqua fredda
Cara sposa
Caro sposo
Casa il figlio quando vuoi, e la figlia
   quando puoi
Castello che dà orecchio si vuol rendere
Cavalier(e) errante
Cavalier(e) servente
Che peccato!
Che sarà sarà
Chi ama, crede
Chi ama me, ama il mio cane
Chi ascolta alla porta, ode il suo danno
Chiave d'oro apre ogni porta
Chi ben vive, ben predica
Chi compra il magistrato, forza è che
   venda la giustizia
Chi dice i fatti suoi, mal tacerà quelli
   d'altrui
Chi dorme coi cani, si sveglia colle pulci
Chiesa libera in libero stato
Chi fa il conto senza l'oste, gli convien
   farlo (lo fa) due volte
Chi ha denti, non ha pane; e chi ha pane,
   non ha denti
Chi la dura la vince
Chi lo sa?
Chi molte cose comincia, poche ne finisce
Chi niente sa, di niente dubita
Chi non ama il vino, la donna, e il canto/
   Un pazzo egli sarà e mai un santo
Chi non fa, non falla
Chi non ha danari in borsa, abbie miel
   in bocca
Chi non rompe l'uova, non fa la frittata
Chi non sa adulare, non sa regnare
Chi si scusa senz' esser accusato, fa chiaro
   il suo peccato
Chi tace acconsente
Chi tace confessa
Chi t'ha offeso non ti perdona mai
Chi troppo abbraccia, poco stringe
Chi va al mulino, s'infarina
Chi va piano, va sano e va lontano
Chi vuol il lavoro mal fatto, paghi innanzi
   tratto
Come sopra
Commedia dell' arte
Con amore

Italian—*Continued*

Concerto grosso
Con diligenza
Con dolore
Con molta passione
Consiglio europeo per le ricerche nucleari
Con svantaggio grande si fa la guerra con chi non ha che perdere
Conti chiari, amici cari
Corpo di Bacco!
Cosa nostra
Cosa rara
Così così
Così fan tutte
Così fan tutti

Da camera
Da capo
Da capo al fine
Da chi mi fido, mi guardi Iddio: da chi non mi fido mi guarderò io
Dal detto al fatto vi è un gran tratto
Dalla mano alla bocca si perde la zuppa
Dalla rapa non si cava sangue
Darne consiglio/Spesso non sa chi vuole,/ Spesso non vuol chi sa
Dei gusti non se ne disputa
Del credere
Delle ingiurie il remedio è lo scordarsi
Del senno di poi n'è piena ogni fossa
Di bravura
Di buona volontà sta pieno l'inferno
Di grado in grado
Di il vero ed affronterai il diavolo
Dimmi con chi vai, e ti dirò chi sei
Di nuovo
Dio vi benedica
Di salto
Di seconda mano
Dolce far niente
Dolce stil nuovo
Dove l'oro parla, ogni lingua tace
Dove sono molti cuochi, la minestra sarà troppo salata
Due teste valgono più che una sola

È cattivo vento che non è buono per qualcheduno
Egli è povero come un topo di chiesa
E la sua volontate è nostra pace
È meglio aver oggi un uovo che domani una gallina
È meglio domandar che errare
È meglio esser mendicante che ignorante
È meglio il cuor felice che la borsa piena

È meglio piegare che rompere
È meglio tardi che mai
È meglio un uccello in gabbia che cento fuori
E' principali fondamenti che abbino tutti li stati . . . sono le buone legge e le buone arme
E pur si muove!
È sempre l'ora

Far d'una mosca un elefante
Fatti maschii, parole femine
Felice ritorno!
Figlie e vetri son sempre in pericolo
Finchè la pianta è tenera, bisogna drizzarla
Forte
Fra Modesto non fu mai priore
Fuori commercio
Fuori i barbari
Fuori le mura
Furia francese

Giovane santo, diavolo vecchio
Gli assenti hanno torto
Glissando
Gli uomini hanno gli anni che sentono, e le donne quelli che mostrano
Guarda innanzi che tu salti
Guerra cominciata, inferno scatenato

I denari del comune sono come l'acqua benedetta, ognun ne piglia
I frutti proibiti sono i più dolci
I gran dolori sono muti
Il bel sesso
Il diavolo non è così brutto come si dipinge
Il mondo è di chi ha pazienza
Il mondo è di chi se lo piglia
Il mondo è un bel libro, ma poco serve a chi non lo sa leggere
Il lupo cangia il pelo, ma non il vizio
Il Maestro di color che sanno
Il miglior fabbro
Il penseroso
Il stilo volgare
Il tempo è denaro
In un giorno non si fe' Roma
I paragoni son odiosi
I pensieri non pagano dazio
Italia farà da se
Italia irredenta

La barba non fa il filosofo
La commedia è finita
La dolce vita

La donna è mobile
La fame non vuol leggi
La fortuna aiuta i pazzi
La Forza del destino
La letteratura amena
L'allegro
La mala erba cresce presto
La povertà è la madre di tutte le arti
La pratica val più della grammatica
Lasciate ogni speranza, voi ch'entrate
La troppa familiarità genera disprezzo
Lauda la moglie e tienti donzello
La verità è figlia del tempo
Lavoro di commesso
Le comparazioni sono tutte odiose
Le disgrazie non vengon mai sole
Le parole son femmine, i fatti son maschi
L'imitazione del male supera sempre l'esempio; come per il contrario, l'imitazione del bene è sempre inferiore
Lingua toscana in bocca romana
Lo gran rifiuto
Lontan dagli occhi, lontan dal cuore
L'Osservatore Romano
L'ultima che se perde è la speranza

Maestro dei maestri
Maestro di cappella
Maggiore fretta, minore atto
Mamma mia!
Mano di ferro e guanto di velluto
Meglio tardi che mai
Metter il carro innanzi ai buoi
Mezza voce
Mezzo forte
Mezzo piano
Mezzo termine
Moderato cantabile
Molto fumo e poco arrosto
Monte di pietà

Natura il fece e poi roppe la stampa
Nessun maggior dolore,/Che ricordarsi del tempo felice/Nella miseria
Niente più tosto si secca che lacrime
Non fu mai partito savio condurre il nemico alla disperazione
Non fu mai savio partito fare disperare gli uomini
Non merita nome di creatore, se non Iddio ed il Poeta
Non ogni fiore fa buon odore
Non ogni giorno è festa
Non ragioniam di lor, ma guarda e passa
Non troppo presto
Nulla nuova, buona nuova

Ogni debole ha sempre il suo tiranno
Ogni medaglia ha il suo rovescio
Ogni pazzo vuol dar consiglio
Opera buffa
Opera inedita (pl. opere inedite)
Ora e sempre
Oro è che oro vale
Ottava rima

Pace in terra
Passato il pericolo, gabbato il santo
Pensano gl'innamorati che gli altri siano ciechi
Per bacco
Per contante
Per conto
Per mese
Per piacere
Per più strade si va a Roma
Pietra mossa non fa muschio
Più che il martello dura l'incudine
Più tengono a memoria gli uomini le ingiurie che li beneficii ricevuti
Piuttosto mendicante che ignorante
Povero come un topo di chiesa
Presto e bene, non si conviene
Presto maturo, presto marcio
Prima donna

Quando la gatta non v'è, i sorci ballano
Quattrocento
Quel che pare burla, ben sovent è vero
Quel dominio è solo durabile che è volontario
Quel giorno più non vi leggemmo avante
Quelle difese solamente sono buone, sono certe, sono durabili, che dependano da te proprio e dalla virtú tua
Questo ragazzo ci farà dimenticar tutti

Ritardando

Saluto il primo Re d'Italia
Sdegno d'amante poco dura
Sedia gestatoria
Se non è vero, è ben trovato
Socorso non viene mai tardi
Sotto voce
Spogliar l'Pietro per vestir Paolo

Tal padrone, tal servitore
Tanto buono che val niente
Terra irredenta
Terza rima
Traduttore, traditore
Tre ore
Tutte le strade conducono a Roma
Tutti i gusti son gusti

Italian—*Continued*

Una rondine non fa l'estate
Una rondine non fa primavera
Una scopa nuova spazza bene
Un bel pezzo di carne
Un matto sa più domandare che sette savi
   rispondere
Uomo universale

Vaso vuoto suona meglio
Vedi Napoli e poi mori
Vender il miele a chi ha le api
Verso sciolto
Via il gatto ballano i sorci
Viola da braccio
Viola da gamba
Viva il papa
Voce di testa
Volto sciolto e pensieri stretti

Latin

Ab abusu ad usum non valet consequentia
Ab asino lanam
Abeunt studia in mores
Ab extra
Ab extrinseco
Ab hoc et ab hac et ab illa
Abiit ad majores
Abiit ad plures
Abiit, excessit, evasit, erupit
Ab imo pectore
Ab incunabulis
Ab initio
Ab initio temporis
Ab intestato
Ab intra
Ab invito
Ab irato
Abnormis sapiens crassaque Minerva
Ab origine
A bove majore discit arare minor
Ab ovo
Ab ovo usque ad mala
Abscissio infiniti
Absens haeres non erit
Absente reo
Absit invidia
Absit omen
Absque argento omnia vana
Absque ulla conditione
Absurdum quippe est ut alios regat qui
   seipsum regere nescit
Ab uno disce omnes

Ab urbe condita
Abusus non tollit usum
A capite ad calcem
Accedas ad curiam
Accessit
Accusare nemo se debet
Acerbarum facetiarum apud praepotentes
   in longum memoria est
Acetum Italum
A cruce salus
Acta est fabula
Actum ne agas
Actus Dei nemini facit injuriam
Actus me invito factus, non est meus actus
Actus non facit reum nisi mens est rea
Actus purus
Ad amussim
Ad arbitrium
Ad astra per aspera
Ad captandam benevolentiam
Ad captandum vulgus
Ad cautelam
Adde parvum parvo, magnus acervus erit
A Deo et Rege
Adeste, Fideles
Ad extremum
Adgnosco veteris vestigia flammae
Ad gustum
Ad hoc
Ad hominem
Adhuc neminem cognovi poetam qui sibi
   non optimus videretur
A die datus
Ad impossibile nemo tenetur
Ad infinitum
Ad interim
Ad internecionem
Ad judicium
Ad Kalendas Graecas
Ad libitum
Ad limina Apostolorum
Ad litem
Ad literam
Ad locum
Ad majorem Dei gloriam
Ad manum
Ad multos annos
Ad nauseam
Ad oculos
Ad patres
Ad perpetuam rei memoriam
Ad rem
Adscriptus glebae *or* glaebae
Adsum
Ad summum

Ad unguem
Ad unum omnes
Ad usum
Ad utrumque paratus
Ad valorem
Adversis etenim frangi non esse virorum
Ad vitam aut culpam
Advocatus diaboli
Advocatus juventutis
Aegrescit medendo
Aegrotat daemon, monachus tunc esse
  volebat:/Daemon convaluit, daemon ut
  ante fuit
Aegroto dum anima est, spes esse dicitur
Aemulatio aemulationem parit
Aemulatio vicini
Aequam memento rebus in arduis servare
  mentem
Aequo animo
Aerarium sanctius
Aere perennius
Aes in praesenti
Aes triplex
Aetas parentum, peior avis, tulit/nos
  nequiores, mox daturos/progeniem
  vitiosiorem
Aetatis suae
Aeternum servans sub pectore vulnus
Affirmanti incumbit probatio
Afflavit Deus et dissipantur
A fortiori
Agenti incumbit probatio
Age quod agis
Ager publicus
Aggregatio mentium
Agnus Dei
Aio te, Aeacida, Romanos vincere posse
Alas sustineo
A latere
Albo lapide notatae
Alcinoo poma dare
Alea jacta est
Aliena vitia in oculis habemus; a tergo
  nostra sunt
Alieni appetens, sui profusus
Alieni juris
Aliquando bonus dormitat Homerus
Aliquis in omnibus, nullus in singulis
Alis volat propriis
Alitur vitium vivitque tegendo
Aliud corde premunt, aliud ore promunt
Alium silere quod voles, primus sile
Alma mater
Alma mater studiorum
Alma Redemptoris Mater

Alter ego
Alter idem
Alter ipse amicus
Altissima flumina minimo sono labuntur
Ama nesciri
Amantes, amentes
Amantium irae amoris integratio est
Ama si vis amari
A maximis ad minima
Ambigendi locus
Ambiguitas latens
Ambiguitas patens
A mensa et toro
Amicus certus in re incerta cernitur
Amicus curiae
Amicus humani generis
Amicus Plato, sed magis amica veritas
Amicus usque ad aras
Amittit merito proprium qui alienum
  appetit
Amoenitates studiorum
Amor dei intellectualis
Amor fati
Amor gignit amorem
Amor nummi
Amor omnibus idem
Amor patriae
Amor tussisque non celantur
Amor vincit omnia
Anathema sit!
Ancilla theologiae
Angeli, non Angli
Anguis in herba
Animae dimidium meae
Animal bipes implume
Anima naturaliter Christiana
Animis opibusque parati
Animo et fide
Animus furandi
Animus testandi
An nescis longas regibus esse manus?
Anno aetatis suae
Anno ante Christum
Anno Domini
Anno humanae salutis
Anno mundi
Anno urbis conditae
Annuit coeptis
Annus luctus
Annus magnus *or* Platonicus
Annus mirabilis
Ante bellum
Ante lucem
Ante tubam trepidat
Ante victoriam ne canas triumphum

Latin—*Continued*

Anulatus aut doctus aut fatuus
Apologia pro vita sua
A posse ad esse
A posteriori
Apparatus belli
Apparatus criticus
Apparent rari nantes in gurgite vasto
Appetitus rationi oboediant
A primo ad ultimum
A priori
Aqua ardens
Aqua fortis
Aqua regia
Aqua vitae
Aquila non captat muscas
Ara pacis
Arbiter bibendi
Arbiter elegantiae (elegantiarum)
Arbiter literarum
Arbores serit diligens agricola, quarum
   adspiciet bacam ipse numquam
Arcades ambo
Arcana imperii
Arcani disciplina
Ardentia verba
Argumenti gratia
Argumentum ad crumenam
Argumentum ad hominem
Argumentum ad ignorantiam
Argumentum ad invidiam
Argumentum ad judicium
Argumentum ad misericordiam
Argumentum ad populum
Argumentum ad rem
Argumentum ad verecundiam
Argumentum baculinum *or* ad baculum
Arma virumque cano
Ars artium omnium conservatrix
Ars (artis) est celare artem
Ars gratia artis
Ars longa, vita brevis
Ars omnibus communis
Ars Poetica
Ars prima regni est posse invidiam pati
Artes perditae
Artis sola domina necessitas
Asinus ad lyram
Asinus asino et sus sui pulcher
Aspice, viator
Astraea Redux
Asylum ignorantiae
A tergo

Athanasius contra mundum
At spes non fracta
Audemus jura nostra defendere
Audendo magnus tegitur timor
Audentes deus ipse juvat
Audentes fortuna juvat
Aude sapere
Audi alteram partem
Aura epileptica
Aura popularis
Aurea mediocritas
Aurea ne credas quaecunque nitescere
   cernis
Auribus teneo lupum
Auri sacra fames
Aurora borealis
Aurum potabile
Aut amat aut odit mulier, nihil est tertium
Aut Caesar aut nullus (aut nihil)
Aut disce, aut discede: manet sors tertia
   caedi
Aut doce aut disce aut discede
Aut vincere aut mori
Avaritiam si tollere vultis, mater eius est
   tollenda, luxuries
Avarus nisi cum moritur nil recte facit
Ave atque vale
Ave Maria
A verbis ad verbera
A vinculo matrimonii

Basis virtutum constantia
Beatae memoriae
Beata solitudo
Beata tranquillitas
Beati pacifici
Beati possidentes
Beati qui lugent
Beatus ille qui procul negotiis
Bella matribus detestata
Bellum ita suscipiatur ut nihil aliud nisi
   pax quaesita videatur
Bellum omnium contra omnes
Benedicite Domino!
Beneficium accipere libertatem est
   vendere
Beneficium clericale
Beneficium egenti bis dat, qui dat
   celeriter
Benemerentium praemium
Bene qui conjiciet, vatem hunc perhibebo
   optimum
Bene qui latuit, bene vixit
Berenicem statim ab urbe dimisit invitus
   invitam

Biblia pauperum
Bis dat qui cito dat
Bis peccare in bello non licet
Bis pueri senes
Bona fide
Bona rerum secundarum optabilia, adversarum mirabilia
Bona vacantia
Boni mores
Boni pastoris est tondere pecus, non deglubere
Bonis avibus
Bonis nocet quisquis pepercerit malis
Bonum commune
Bonum ex integra causa, malum ex quocumque defectu
Brevi manu
Brevis esse laboro, obscurus fio
Brutum fulmen (*pl.* bruta fulmina)

Cacoethes carpendi
Cacoethes loquendi
Cacoethes scribendi
Cadit quaestio
Caelum, non animum mutant, qui trans mare currunt
Calceus major subvertet
Callida junctura
Calvo turpius est nihil comato
Canimus surdis
Canis in praesepi
Canis major
Canis minor
Canis timidus vehementius latrat quam mordet
Cantabit vacuus coram latrone viator
Cantus planus
Capias
Capias ad satisfaciendum
Caput gerat lupinum
Caput mortuum
Caput mundi
Carpe diem, quam minimum credula postero
Carthago. *See* Delenda est Carthago
Cassis tutissima virtus
Casta est, quam nemo rogavit
Castella in Hispania
Castigat ridendo mores
Castigo te non quod odio habeam, sed quod amem
Casus belli
Casus conscientiae
Casus foederis
Casus fortuitus

Causa finalis
Causa mortis
Cave ab homine unius libri
Caveat emptor
Caveat venditor
Cave canem
Cavendo tutus
Cave quid dicis, quando et cui
Cedant arma togae
Celsae graviore casu decidunt turres
Censor deputatus
Cepi corpus
Certiorari
Cetera desunt
Ceteris paribus
Ceterum censeo. . . . *See* Delenda est Carthago
Chimaera bombitans in vacuo
Christianos ad leonem, *sic*
Cineri gloria sera venit
Circuitus verborum
Circulus in probando
Circulus vitiosus
Citius venit periculum cum contemnitur
Civilitas successit barbarum
Civiliter mortuus
Civis Romanus sum
Civitas Dei
Civitas optimo jure
Civitas sine suffragio
Civitates foederatae
Civitates liberae et immunes
Civium in moribus rei publicae salus
Clarum et venerabile nomen
Clausula rebus sic stantibus
Cloaca maxima
Coelestia canimus
Coeptis ingentibus adsis
Cogito, ergo sum
Cognovit actionem
Coma Berenices
Comes facundus in via pro vehiculo est
Comitas inter gentes
Comitia centuriata
Communibus annis
Communi consensu
Comoedia finita est
Compelle intrare
Conatus sese praeservandi
Concordia discors
Conditio sine qua non
Congregatio de Propaganda Fide
Conjunctis viribus
Conscia mens recti famae mendacia risit
Consensus facit legem

237

Latin—*Continued*

Consilio melius vinces (vincas) quam iracundia
Consilium abeundi
Consuetudo fit altera natura
Consuetudo pro lege servatur
Consultum ultimum
Consummatum est
Conticuere omnes, intentique ora tenebant
Contra bonos mores
Contra mundum
Copia verborum
Coram judice
Coram nobis
Coram non judice
Coram populo
Coram publico
Cormach MacCarthy fortis me fieri facit, A.D. 1446
Cor ne edito
Corpus Christi
Corpus delicti
Corpus Juris Canonici
Corpus Juris Civilis
Corpus juris clausum
Corrigenda
Corrumpunt bonos mores colloquia mala
Corruptio optimi pessima
Corruptissima in republica plurimae leges
Corva sinistra
Crambe repetita
Cras amet qui numquam amavit, quique amavit cras amet
Crassa negligentia
Credat qui vult
Credebant hoc grande nefas et morte piandum,/Si juvenis vetulo non assurrexerat
Crede experto
Crede ut intelligas
Credo quia impossibile (absurdum) est
Credo ut intelligam
Credula res amor est
Crescat scientia, vita excolatur
Crescit amor nummi, quantum ipsa pecunia crescit
Crescite et multiplicamini
Crescit eundo
Creta an carbone notandum?
Crux ansata
Crux criticorum
Crux interpretum
Crux mathematicorum
Cucullus non facit monachum

Cui adhaereo praeest
Cui bono?
Cui malo?
Cui peccare licet, peccat minus
Cujus est regio, illius est religio
Cujus est solum, ejus est usque ad caelum
Culpa lata
Culpa levissima
Culpam majorum posteri luunt
Culpam poena premit comes
Cum grano salis
Cum inimico nemo in gratiam tuto redit
Cumini sectores
Cum laude
Cum licet fugere, ne quaere litem
Cum onere
Cum privilegio ad imprimendum solum
Cum tacent, clamant
Cunctando restituit rem
Cura animarum
Curia regis
Curiosa felicitas
Currente calamo
Curriculum vitae
Currus bovem trahit praepostere
Cursus honorum
Custos Brevium
Custos morum
Custos Privati Sigilli
Custos Rotulorum
Custos Sigilli
Cymini (cumini) sectores

Dabit deus his quoque finem
Daemon languebat. . . . See Aegrotat daemon . . .
Daemon meridianus
Da locum melioribus
Damnant quod non intelligunt
Damnosa hereditas
Damnum absque injuria
Damocles. See De pilo pendet
Dare pondus idonea fumo
Data et accepta
Davus sum, non Oedipus
Debitor non praesumitur donare
De bonis propriis
Deceptio visus
Decessit sine prole
Decies repetita placebit
Decipimur specie recti
Decipit frons prima multos
De Civitate Dei
De Consolatione Philosophiae
Decori decus addit avito

De die in diem
De duobus malis semper minus malum est
   eligendum
De facto
Defensor Fidei
De fide
De fontibus non disputandum
De gustibus non est disputandum
Dei gratia
Dei judicium
De integro
De internis non judicat praetor
Dei plena sunt omnia
De jure
De lana caprina
Delator temporis acti
Delenda est Carthago
Deliberando saepe perit occasio
Deliciae epularum
Deliciae generis humani
Deliciae meae puellae
Delirant reges, plectuntur Achivi
Delirium tremens
De litteris colendis
De lunatico inquirendo
Dementia praecox
Dementia senilis
De minimis non curat lex
De mortuis nil nisi bonum
Denarius Dei
De nihilo nihil
De nobis fabula narrabitur
De novo
Deo adjuvante, non timendum
Deo duce, ferro comitante
Deo favente
Deo gratias
Deo juvante
De omni re scibili et quibusdam aliis
   rebus
Deo, non fortuna
Deo optimo maximo
Deo volente
De pilo pendet
Depositum fidei
De profundis clamavi ad te, Domine
De proprio motu
Desunt inopiae multa, avaritiae omnia
Detinet
Detur digniori
Detur pulchriori
Deum cole, regem serva
Deus est in pectore nostro
Deus ex machina
Deus providebit

Deus vult
Devastavit
Dicere solebat nullum esse librum tam
   malum ut non aliqua parte prodesset
Dicique beatus ante obitum nemo supre-
   maque funera debet
Dic mihi, si fias ut leo, qualis eris?
Dictum meum pactum
Dictum (verbum) sapienti sat est
Diem perdidi
Die non
Dies ater
Dies faustus
Dies infaustus
Dies Irae
Dies natalis
Dies non juridicus
Di faciant, laudis summa sit ista tuae
Difficile est custodire quod multis placet
Difficile est longum subito deponere
   amorem
Difficile est proprie communia dicere
Difficile est saturam non scribere
Difficilia quae pulchra
Difficilis in otio quies
Dignus vindice nodus
Di immortales
Di indigetes
Di inferi
Dii penates
Dilexi justitiam et odi iniquitatem; prop-
   terea morior in exilio
Di manes
Dimidium facti qui coepit habet
Dirigo
Dis aliter visum
Disce ut doceas
Disciplina arcani
Disciplina praesidium civitatis
Disjecti (disjecta) membra poetae
Dis manibus
Ditat Deus
Divide et impera
Divide ut regnes
Divina natura dedit agros, ars humana
   aedificavit urbes
Divina particula aurae
Docendo discimus
Doctor Angelicus
Doctor Invincibilis
Doctor Irrefragabilis
Doctor Legum
Doctor Mirabilis
Doctor Seraphicus
Doctor Subtilis

Latin—_Continued_

Doctor Universalis
Dolendi modus, timendi non item
Doli capax
Dolus an virtus quis in hoste requirat?
Domine, dirige nos
Domini canes
Dominus illuminatio mea
Dominus vobiscum
Domus aurea
Domus Procerum
Donatio mortis causa
Donec eris felix, multos numerabis amicos
Do ut des
Do ut facias
Dramatis personae
Dubium facti
Dubium juris
Duces tecum
Ducit amor patriae
Ducunt volentem fata, nolentem trahunt
Dulce decus meum
Dulce est desipere in loco
Dulce et decorum est pro patria mori
Dum bene se gesserit
Dum casta
Dum Deus calculat, fit mundus
Dummodo sit dives, barbarus ipse placet
Dum spiro spero
Dum vita est, spes est
Dum vitant stulti vitia in contraria currunt
Dum vivimus, vivamus
Duos qui sequitur lepores neutrum capit
Duoviri sacris faciundis
Dura lex sed lex
Durante absentia
Durante minore aetate
Durante viduitate
Durante vita
Durum et durum non faciunt murum
Dux femina facti

Eadem, sed aliter
Eadem sunt omnia semper
Ecce convertimur ad gentes
Ecce homo
Ecce iterum Crispinus!
Ecce signum
Ecclesia semper reformanda
Ecclesia supplet
E consensu gentium
E contra
E contrario
E converso

Editio princeps
Effodiuntur opes, irritamenta malorum
E flamma petere cibum
Ego et Rex meus
Ego sum rex Romanus (imperator Romanorum) et super grammaticam
Eheu fugaces, Postume, Postume, labuntur anni
Ejusdem farinae
Ejusdem generis
Ejus nulla culpa est, cui parere necesse sit
Elapso tempore
Elixir vitae
Empta dolore docet experientia
Emptoris sit eligere
Encheiresin naturae
Ense petit placidam sub libertate quietem
Entia non sunt multiplicanda sine necessitate
Eo ipso
E pluribus unum
E (ex) re nata
Eripuit caelo flumen, mox sceptra tyrannis
Errare humanum est
Errata (_pl. of_ erratum)
Esse oportet ut vivas, non vivere ut edas
Esse quam videri
Esse rei est percipi
Est ars etiam maledicendi
Est modus in rebus
Esto perpetua
Esto quod esse videris
Est quaedam flere voluptas
Estque pati poenas quam meruisse minus
Et alibi
Et alii, aliae
Et bonum quo antiquius, eo melius
Et cetera
Et hoc genus omne
Etiam capillus unus habet umbram suam
Et id genus omne
Et ignotas animum dimittit in artes
Et in Arcadia ego
Et qui nolunt occidere quemquam, posse volunt
Et semel emissum volat irrevocabile verbum
Et sequentes _or_ et sequentia
Et sic de ceteris
Et sic deinceps
Et sic de similibus
Et sic porro
Et spes et ratio studiorum in Caesare tantum
Et tu, Brute

Et uxor. *See* Et ux.
Et verbum caro factum est
Et vir
Ex abrupto
Ex abundantia cordis os loquitur
Ex aequo
Ex animo
Ex capite
Ex cathedra
Excellentia sanandi causa
Excelsior
Exceptio probat regulam
Exceptis excipiendis
Ex comitate
Ex concesso
Ex contractu
Ex curia
Excusatio non petita fit accusatio manifesta
Excussit subjecto Pelion Ossae
Ex debito justitiae
Ex delicto
Ex desuetudine amittuntur privilegia
Ex dono
Exeat
Exegi monumentum aere perennius
Exempla sunt odiosa
Exempli gratia. *See* e.g.
Ex ephebis
Exeunt omnes
Ex gratia
Ex grege
Ex hypothesi
Ex imo corde
Exitus acta probat
Ex libris
Ex luna scientia
Ex malis moribus bonae leges natae sunt
Ex mero motu
Ex necessitate rei
Ex nihilo nihil fit
Ex officio
Ex opere operantis
Ex opere operato
Ex ore infantium
Ex Oriente lux; ex Occidente frux
Ex parte
Ex pede Herculem
Experientia docet stultos
Experimentum crucis
Experto crede
Experto credite
Expertus metuit
Explicit
Ex post facto

Expressis verbis
Ex professo
Ex relatione
Ex (e) silentio
Exstinctus amabitur idem
Ex tacito
Ex tempore
Extra ecclesiam nulla salus
Extra muros
Extra ordinem
Extra situm
Ex umbris et imaginibus in veritatem
Ex ungue leonem
Ex uno disce omnes
Ex vi termini
Ex vitio alterius sapiens emendat suum
Ex voto

Faber quisque fortunae suae
Fabricando fit faber
Fabula palliata
Fabula togata
Facile est inventis addere
Facile omnes, quom valemus, recta consilia aegrotis damus
Facile princeps
Facilis descensus Averno
Facio ut des
Facio ut facias
Facit indignatio versum
Facta, non verba
Faenum habet in cornu
Faex populi, faeces *(pl)* populi
Falsa lectio
Falsus in uno, falsus in omnibus
Fama clamosa
Fama, malum qua non aliud velocius ullum
Fama nihil est celerius
Fama semper vivat
Fames est optimus coquus
Fas est et ab hoste doceri
Fata obstant
Fata viam invenient
Fax mentis incendium gloriae
Fecit
Felicitas multos habet amicos
Felix quem faciunt aliena pericula cautum
Felix qui patitur quae numerare potest
Felix qui potuit rerum cognoscere causas
Ferae naturae
Feriunt summos fulgura montes
Ferme acerrima proximorum odia
Ferrum, dum in igni candet, cudendum

Latin—*Continued*

est tibi
Ferrum ferro acuitur
Festina lente
Fiat experimentum in corpore vili
Fiat justitia pereat mundus
Fiat justitia ruat caelum
Fiat lux
Fiat mixtura
Fiat voluntas tua
Fide et amore
Fide et fiducia
Fide et fortitudine
Fidei corticula crux
Fidei Defensor
Fideli certa merces
Fide, non armis
Fide, sed cui vide
Fides et justitia
Fides Punica
Fides quaerens intellectum
Fidite ne pedibus
Fidus Achates
Fidus et audax
Fieri facias
Figurae orationis
Filioque. *See* Qui ex patre filoque ...
Filius nullius
Filius populi
Filius terrae
Finis coronat opus
Finis litium
Finis operantis
Finis operis
Finis origine pendet
Flagellum Dei
Flagrante bello
Flagrante delicto
Flamma fumo est proxima
Flectere si nequeo superos,
   Acheronta movebo
Flecti, non frangi
Floruit
Flosculi sententiarum
Fluctuat nec mergitur
Fons et origo
Fons et origo malorum
Forensis strepitus
Foris ut moris, intus ut libet
Forma bonum fragile
Forma flos, fama flatus
Forsan et haec olim meminisse juvabit
Fors Clavigera
Forte scutum, salus ducum

Fortes fortuna adjuvat
Fortes fortuna juvat
Forti et fideli nihil (nil) difficile
Fortis cadere, cedere non potest
Fortiter et recte
Fortiter, fideliter, feliciter
Fortiter in re
Fortuna belli semper ancipiti in loco est
Fortunae filius
Fortuna favet fatuis
Fortuna fortibus favet
Fortuna meliores sequitur
Fortuna multis dat nimis, satis nulli
Fortuna nimium quem fovet, stultum facit
Frangas, non flectes
Fraus est celare fraudem
Frontis nulla fides
Fructu non foliis arborem aestima
Frustra laborat qui omnibus placere studet
Fugit irreparabile tempus
Fuimus Troes, fuit Ilium
Fuit Ilium
Functus officio
Furor arma ministrat
Furor loquendi
Furor poeticus
Furor scribendi
Furor Teutonicus

Gallia est omnis divisa in partes tres
Gaudeamus, igitur, juvenes dum sumus
Gaudet tentamine virtus
Gaudium certaminis
Genius loci
Gens braccata
Gens togata
Genus homo
Genus irritabile vatum
Genus literarium
Georgium sidus
Gerebatur
Gesta Romanorum
Gigantes autem erant super terram in
   diebus illis
Gloria in excelsis Deo. Et in terra pax
   hominibus bonae voluntatis
Gloria Patri et Filio et Spiritui Sancto;
   sicut erat in principio et nunc et
   semper et in saecula saeculorum.
   Amen
Gradu diverso, via una
Gradus ad Parnassum
Graecia capta ferum victorem cepit
Graeculus esuriens
Grammatici certant et adhuc sub

iudice lis est
Gratia gratiam parit
Gratia placendi
Gratias agimus
Gratis dictum
Graviora quaedam sunt remedia periculis
Gutta cavat lapidem, consumitur annulus
    usu

Habeas corpus
Habemus papam
Habendum et tenendum
Habent sua fata libelli
Habet et musca splenem
Haeret lateri letalis harundo
Hannibal ad portas
Haud facile emergunt quorum virtutibus
    obstat/res angusta domi
Haud passibus aequis
Helluo librorum
Hesterni Quirites
Heu mores
Heu, vitam perdidi, operose nihil agendo
Hiatus maxime (valde) deflendus
Hibernicis ipsis Hiberniores
Hic et nunc
Hic et ubique
Hic jacet
Hic niger est, hunc tu, Romane, caveto
Hic sepultus
Hinc illae lacrimae
Hinc lucem et pocula sacra
His ego nec metas rerum nec tempora pono
Historia vitae magistra
Hoc age
Hoc erat in votis
Hoc est corpus meum
Hoc genus omne
Hoc monumentum posuit
Hoc opus, hic labor est
Hoc volo, sic jubeo, sit pro ratione
    voluntas
Hodie mihi, cras tibi
Hominem pagina nostra sapit
Homines dum docent discunt
Homo covivens
Homo ferus
Homo homini aut deus aut lupus
Homo homini lupus
Homo latinissimus
Homo ludens
Homo memorabilis
Homo mensura
Homo multarum literarum
Homo neanderthalensis

Homo proponit, sed Deus disponit
Homo sapiens
Homo semper aliud, Fortuna aliud cogitat
Homo solus aut deus aut daemon
Homo sum: humani nil a me alienum puto
Homo trium literarum
Homo unius libri
Honores mutant mores
Honoris causa (gratia)
Honos habet onus
Horas non numero nisi serenas
Horresco referens
Horribile dictu
Horror vacui
Hortus conclusus
Hostis humani generis
Hypotheses non fingo

Idem non potest simul esse et non esse
Idem per idem
Idem velle et idem nolle, ea demum firma
    amicitia est
Id facere laus est quod decet, non quod licet
Id genus omne
Ignis fatuus
Ignorantia facti excusat
Ignorantia legis (juris) neminem excusat
Ignoratio elenchi
Ignoscito saepe alteri, numquam tibi
Ignoti nulla cupido
Ignotum per ignotius
Ilias malorum
Ille dolet vere qui sine teste dolet
Ille hic est Raphael
Illotis manibus
Imitatores, servum pecus
Immedicabile vulnus ense recidendum
    est ne pars sincera trahatur
Imo pectore
Imperium cupientibus nihil medium
    inter summa aut praecipitia
Imperium et libertas
Imperium in imperio
Imperium Romanum
Imponere Pelio Ossam
Impos animi
Impotens sui
Imprimatur
Imprimi permittitur
Imprimi potest
In absentia
In actu
In aeternum
In agello (*var.* angello) cum libello sola
    quies

Latin—_Continued_

In animam malevolam sapientia haud
   intrare potest
In apricum proferet
In articulo mortis
In caelo quies
In camera
In capite
Incidit in Scyllam qui vult vitare
   Charybdim
Incipit
In concreto
In contumaciam
In custodia legis
Index expurgatorius
Index Librorum Prohibitorum
Index locorum
Index nominum
Index rerum
Index verborum
Indignor quandoque bonus dormitat
   Homerus
In discrimine rerum
Indocilis pauperiem pati
Indoctus juga ferre
In dubio
In esse
In extenso
In extremis
In facie curiae
Infandum renovare dolorem
In favorem matrimonii
In fieri
In flagrante delicto
In forma pauperis
In foro conscientiae
In foro externo
In foro interno
Infra dignitatem
In futuro
Ingenium mala saepe movent
Ingenium res adversae nudare solent,
   celare secundae
Ingenui vultus puer ingenuique pudoris
In globo
Ingratus unus omnibus miseris nocet
In gremio legis
In hoc signo vinces
In ictu oculi
In infinitum
In initio
Iniquum petas ut aequum feras
In limine
In loco

In loco citato
In loco parentis
In manus tuas commendo spiritum meum
In medias res
In medio stat virtus
In medio tutissimus ibis
In meditatione fugae
In memoriam
In morte veritas
In necessariis unitas, in non necessariis
   libertas, in utrisque caritas
In nihilum nil posse reverti
In nocte consilium
In nomine
In nomine Domini
In nubibus
In nuce
In omnia paratus
In omnibus glorificetur Deus
In omni doctrina grammatica praecedit
Inopem me copia fecit
Inops, potentem dum vult imitari,
   perit
In ovo
In pace
In partibus infidelium
In perpetuam rei memoriam
In perpetuum
In perturbato animo sicut in corpore
   sanitas esse non potest
In pios usus
In posse
In potentia ad actum
In principio
In propria persona
In proverbium cessit, sapientiam vino
   adumbrari
In puris naturalibus
In re
In rerum natura
In saecula saeculorum
In situ
In solidum (solido)
In specie
In spiritualibus
In statu pupillari
In statu quo
In statu quo ante bellum
In tanto discrimine
In te, Domine, speravi
Integer vitae scelerisque purus/Non eget
   Mauris/iaculis neque arcu
Intellectus sibi permissus
In tenebris
Inter alia

Inter anum et urinam
Inter arma leges silent
Inter canem et lupum
Interdum stultus opportuna loquitur
Interdum volgus rectum videt; est ubi
    peccat
Inter esse et non esse non datur medium
Inter faeces et urinam
Inter folia fructus
Inter nos
Inter os et offam
Inter pocula
In terrorem
In terrorem populi
Inter se
Inter spem et metum
Inter vivos
Inter volentes
In totidem verbis
In toto
Intra muros
In transitu
Intra vires
In usum Delphini
In utero
In utrumque paratus
Invenit
In ventre
Inverso ordine
Invidia festos dies non agit
In vili veste nemo tractatur honeste
In vino veritas
Invita Minerva
In vitro
In vivo
In vota miseros ultimus cogit timor
Ipsa scientia potestas est
Ipse dixit
Ipsissima verba
Ipso facto
Ipso jure
Ira furor brevis est; animum rege;
    qui nisi paret, imperat
Iratus cum ad se rediit sibi tum irascitur
Ita lex scripta est
Ite, missa est
Iustum est bellum, Samnites, quibus neces-
    sarium: et pia arma quibus nulla nisi in
    armis relinquitur spes

Jacta alea est
Jam redit et Virgo, redeunt Saturnia regna
Jam satis vixi
Januis clausis
Joannes est nomen ejus

Joculatores Dei
Johannes fac totum
Jubilate Deo
Jucundi acti labores
Judex damnatur ubi nocens absolvitur
Judicium crucis
Judicium Dei
Judicium parium aut leges terrae
Juppiter tonans
Jurare in verba magistri
Jurat
Juravi lingua, mentem injuratam gero
Jure belli
Jure divino
Jure humano
Jure uxoris
Juris peritus
Jus ad rem
Jus canonicum
Jus civile
Jus civitatis
Jus commercii
Jus devolutionis
Jus et norma loquendi
Jus gentium
Jus gladii
Jus hereditatis
Jus mariti
Jus mercatorum
Jus naturae
Jus necationis
Jus possessionis
Jus primae noctis
Jus proprietatis
Jus publicum
Jus relictae
Jus sanguinis
Jus suffragii
Jus summum saepe summa est malitia
Justitia omnibus
Justitia suum cuique distribuit
Justo titulo
Jus trium liberorum
Justum et tenacem propositi virum
Jus ubique docendi

Kalendas Graecas

Labitur et labetur in omne volubilis aevum
Laborare est orare
Labore et constantia
Labor est etiam ipse voluptas
Labor improbus
Labor ipse voluptas
Labor omnia vincit
Laborum dulce lenimen

Latin—*Continued*

Lapsus memoriae
Lares et penates
Lasciva est nobis pagina, vita proba est
Lateat scintillula forsan
Latet anguis in herba
Laudari a viro laudato
Laudator temporis acti
Laudum immensa cupido
Laus Deo
Laus perennis
Lectori benevolo
Legalis homo
Legatus a latere
Leges barbarorum
Leges plurimae, respublica pessima
Legibus solutus
Legio patria nostra
Leonina societas
Levari facias
Leve fit quod bene fertur onus
Levius fit patientia quicquid corrigere
    est nefas
Lex loci
Lex loci rei sitae
Lex mercatoria (mercatoris)
Lex non scripta
Lex scripta
Lex talionis
Lex terrae
Libera me
Libertas est potestas faciendi id quod jure
    licet
Libertas, quae sera tamen
    respexit inertem
Liberum veto
Libris clausis
Licentia vatum
Limae labor
Limbus fatuorum
Lingua Adamica
Lingua franca
Lis litem generat
Lis pendens
Lis sub judice
Litem lite resolvere
Lite pendente
Literatim, verbatim, punctuatim
Littera canina
Litterae humaniores
Littera enim occidit, spiritus autem
    vivificat
Littera scripta manet
Loco citato

Locum tenens
Locus classicus
Locus communis
Locus criminis
Locus delicti
Locus in quo
Locus poenitentiae
Locus sigilli
Locus standi
Longo sed proximus intervallo
Longum iter est per praecepta, breve et
    efficax per exempla
Loquendum ut vulgus, sentiendum
    ut docti
Lucidus ordo
Lucus a non lucendo
Lues commentatoria
Lupus est homo homini
Lupus in sermone (fabula)
Lupus pilum mutat, non mentem
Lusus naturae
Lux et veritas
Lux tua vita mihi
Lympha pudica deum vidit et erubuit

Macte virtute esto
Magis illa juvant, quae pluris ementur
Magister artis ingenique largitor venter
Magister bibendi
Magister ceremoniarum
Magister equitum
Magna Carta
Magna civitas, magna solitudo
Magna cum laude
Magnae spes altera Romae
Magna est veritas, et praevalet
    (*not* praevalebit)
Magnas inter opes inops
Magnificat anima mea Dominum
Magni nominis umbra
Magno jam conatu magnas nugas
Magnum opus
Magnum vectigal est parsimonia
Major domus
Major e longinquo reverentia
Mala fides
Mala praxis
Male imperando summum imperium
    amittitur
Male parta, male dilabuntur
Mali exempli
Mali principii malus finis
Malis avibus
Malo modo
Malo mori quam foedari

Malum est consilium quod mutari
   non potest
Malum in se
Malum prohibitum
Malus pudor
Manet alta mente repostum
Manibus pedibusque
Manu forti
Manu propria
Manus haec inimica tyrannis
Manus manum lavat
Mare clausum
Mare Imbrium
Mare liberum
Mare magnum
Mare Nostrum
Margaritas ante porcos
Marmoream se relinquere quam latericiam
   accepisset
Mars gravior sub pace latet
Mascula sunt maribus
Mater artium necessitas
Mater dolorosa
Mater familias
Materia ex qua
Materia medica
Materiam superabat opus
Materia prima
Mater mea sus est mala
Mater Redemptoris
Mature fieri senem, si diu velis esse senex
Maxima bella ex levissimis causis
Maximum remedium est irae mora
Mea culpa
Medice, cura teipsum
Mediocria firma
Mediocribus esse poetis/non homines,
   non di, non concessere columnae
Medio tutissimus ibis
Me judice
Melior est canis vivus leone mortuo
Memento, homo, quia pulvis es, et in
   pulverem reverteris
Memento mori
Memoria in aeterna
Memoria praeteritorum bonorum
Mendacem memorem esse oportet
Mendacium jocosum
Mens aequa in arduis
Mens agitat molem
Mens et animus et consilium civitatis
   posita sunt in legibus
Mens legis
Mens rea
Mens regnum bona possidet

Mens sana in corpore sano
Mens sibi conscia recti
Meo periculo
Merum sal
Me vestigia terrent, omnia te adversum
   spectantia, nulla retrorsum
Mihi crede
Mihi cura futuri
Miles gloriosus
Minatur innocentibus qui parcit nocentibus
Minima ex malis
Mirabile dictu
Mirabile visu
Miserabile dictu
Miserabile vulgus
Miserere mei
Missi dominici
Mitte sectari, rosa quo locorum/Sera
   moretur
Mittimus
Mixtum compositum
Mobile mutatur semper cum principe
   vulgus
Mobile perpetuum
Mobile vulgus
Modo et forma
Modo praescripto
Modus operandi
Modus vivendi
Mole ruit sua. *See* Via consili . . .
Mollia tempora fandi
Montani semper liberi
More humano
More majorum
More suo
Mors acerba, fama perpetua
Mors communis omnibus
Mors janua vitae
Mortis causa
Mos majorum
Mos pro lege
Motu proprio
Mulier cum sola cogitat male cogitat
Mulier cupido quod dicit amanti, in vento
   et rapida scribere oportet aqua
Mulier est hominis confusio
Multa cadunt inter calicem supremaque
   labra
Multa petentibus desunt multa
Multis utile bellum
Multum in parvo
Mundi formam omnes fere consentiunt
   rotundam esse
Mundus vult decipi
Munera Pulveris

Latin—*Continued*

Munus Apolline dignum
Murus aeneus conscientia sana
Muscae volitantes
Mutatis mutandis
Mutato nomine de te fabula narratur

Nam genus et proavos et quae non fecimus
  ipsi vix ea nostra voco
Nascimur poetae, fimus oratores
Natale solum
Natura abhorret a vacuo
Natura abhorret vacuum
Natura inest mentibus nostris insatiabilis
  quaedam cupiditas veri videndi
Natura in operationibus suis non facit
  saltus
Naturam expelles furca, tamen usque
  recurret
Natura naturans
Natura nihil facit per saltum
Natura semina nobis scientiae dedit, scien-
  tiam non dedit
Natura simplicitatem amat
Nec amor nec tussis celatur
Nec deus intersit, nisi dignus vindice nodus
Ne cede malis
Necesse est multos timeat quem multi
  timent
Necessitas non habet legem
Necessitas rationum inventrix
Nec est quisquam tam malus,
  ut malus videri velit
Nec judicis ira, nec ignis, nec poterit fer-
  rum, nec edax abolere vetustas
Nec mora nec requies
Nec pluribus impar
Nec prece nec pretio
Nec quaerere nec spernere honorem
Nec quemquam jam ferre potest Caesarve
  priorem,/Pompeiusve parem
Nec scire fas est omnia
Nec tecum possum vivere, nec sine te
Nec temere nec timide
Nec verbum verbo curabis reddere fidus
  interpres
Ne exeat provincia
Ne facias per alium quod fieri potest per te
Nefasti dies
Ne fronti crede
Ne Juppiter quidem omnibus placet
Ne, mater, et suam
Nemine contradicente
Nemine discrepante

Nemine dissentiente
Nemo bis punitur pro eodem delicto
Nemo dat quod non habet
Nemo esse judex in sua causa potest
Nemo in amore videt
Nemo judex in causa sua
Nemo liber est qui corpori servit
Nemo me impune lacessit
Nemo mortalium omnibus horis sapit
Nemo propheta acceptus est in patria sua
Nemo repente fuit turpissimus
Nemo scit praeter me ubi soccus me pressat
Nemo sine vitiis nascitur
Nemo solus satis sapit
Ne plus ultra
Ne puero gladium
Ne quid detrimenti respublica capiat
Ne quid nimis
Nervi belli, pecunia infinita
Nescire autem quid antequam natus sis
  acciderit, id est semper esse puerum
Nescit plebes ieiuna timere
Nescit vox missa reverti
Ne sutor ultra crepidam
Ne tentes aut perfice
Nihil ad rem
Nihil dicit
Nihil enim in speciem fallacius est quam
  prava religio
Nihil est ab omni parte beatum
Nihil ex omnibus rebus humanis est
  praeclarius aut praestantius quam
  de republica bene mereri
Nihil hoc ad edictum praetoris
Nihil in intellectu quod non prius in
  sensibus
Nihil muliebre praeter corpus gerens
Nihil non commiserunt stupri, saevitiae,
  impietatis
Nihil obstat
Nihil quod tetigit non ornavit
Nihil tam absurde dici potest quod non
  dicatur ab aliquo philosophorum
Nil actum credens cum quid superesset
  agendum
Nil admirari
Nil conscire sibi, nulla pallescere culpa
Nil debet
Nil desperandum
Nil dictum quod non dictum prius
Nil molitur inepte
Nil mortalibus ardui est:/Coelum ipsum
  petimus stultitia
Nil nisi cruce
Nil sine magno vita labore

dedit mortalibus
Nil sine Numine
Nil sub sole novum
Nimium ne crede colori
Nisi Dominus . . . frustra
Nisi prius
Nitimur in vetitum semper, cupimusque
    negata
Nitor in adversum
Nobilitas sola est atque unica virtus
Noctes coenaeque deum
Nolens volens
Noli me tangere
Noli turbare circulos meos
Nolle prosequi
Nolo contendere
Nolo episcopari
Nolumus leges Angliae mutari
Nomen conservandum (*pl.* Nomina
    conservanda)
Nomina si nescis perit et cognitio rerum
Nomina stultorum parietibus haerent
Non amo te, Sabidi, nec possum dicere
    quare; hoc solum scio, non amo te,
    Sabidi
Non Angli, sed angeli
Non assumpsi
Non compos mentis
Non concessit
Non constat
Non cuivis homini contingit adire
    Corinthum
Non culpabilis
Non deficiente crumena
Non ex omni ligno, ut Pythagoras dicebat,
    debet Mercurius exculpi
Non expedit
Non fingo hypotheses
Non haec in foedera
Non ignara mali, miseris succurere disco
Non inutiles scientiae existimandae sunt,
    quarum in se nullus est usus, si ingenia
    acuant et ordinent
Non libet
Non licet
Non liquet
Non multa sed multum
Non nobis, Domine, non nobis; sed nomini
    tuo da gloriam
Non nobis solum nati sumus
Non nostrum inter vos tantas
    componere lites
Non obstante veredicto
Non olet
Non omne licitum honestum

Non omnia possumus omnes
Non omnis moriar
Non passibus aequis
Non placet
Non possumus
Non progredi est regredi
Non prosequitur
Non quis, sed quid
Non semper erit aestas
Non semper Saturnalia erunt
Non sequitur
Non sibi sed patriae
Non sum qualis eram
Non tanto me dignor honore
Nonum prematur in annum
Non vitae sed scholae discimus
Non vult contendere
Nosce te ipsum
Nosce tempus
Noscitur a sociis
Nos morituri te salutamus
Nota bene
Notandum candidissimo calculo
Notatu dignum
Notitiae communes
Novus homo
Novus ordo seclorum
Nuda veritas
Nudis cruribus
Nudis oculis
Nudis verbis
Nudum pactum
Nugae canorae
Nugae literariae
Nulla dies sine linea
Nulla fere causa est in qua non femina
    litem moverit
Nulla salus bello
Nulla virtute redemptum/A vitiis
Nulli sapere casu obtigit
Nulli secundus
Nullius addictus jurare in verba magistri
Nullius filius
Nullum est jam dictum quod non sit
    dictum prius
Nullum fere scribendi genus non tetigit,
    nullum quod tetigit non ornavit
Nullum magnum ingenium sine mixtura
    dementiae fuit
Numquam aliud natura, aliud
    sapientia dicit
Numquam minus otiosus quam cum otiosus
Numquam minus solus quam cum solus
Numquam solus cum sola
Nunc age

Latin—*Continued*

Nunc aut nunquam
Nunc dimittis servum tuum, Domine
Nunc est bibendum, nunc pede libero/
  Pulsanda tellus
Nunc pro tunc
Nympha pudica deum vidit et erubuit

Obiit
Obiit sine prole
Obiter dictum
Obiter scriptum
Obscurum per obscurius
Obsequium amicos, veritas odium parit
Obsta principiis
Obstipui steteruntque comae et vox fauci-
  bus haesit
Oculis subjecta fidelibus
Oculus episcopi
Oderint dum metuant
Oderint dum probent
Odi et amo
Odi profanum vulgus et arceo
Odium generis humani
Odium literarium
Odium theologicum
O felix culpa quae talem et tantum
  meruit habere Redemptorem
O fortunatam natam me consule Romam
O fortunatos nimium, sua si bona norint!
Olet lucernam
Oleum addere camino
Omne animal ex ovo
Omne ignotum pro magnifico est
Omne meum, nihil meum
Omne ovum ex ovo
Omnes artes quae ad humanitatem perti-
  nent habent quoddam commune vin-
  clum
Omne solum forti patria est
Omne tulit punctum, qui miscuit utile
  dulci
Omne vitium in proclivi est
Omne vivum ex vivo
Omnia bona bonis
Omnia exeunt in mysterium
Omnia mea mecum porto
Omnia mors aequat
Omnia mutantur, nihil interit
Omnia mutantur, nos et mutamur in illis
Omnia opera
Omnia orta occidunt et aucta senescunt
Omnia vincit Amor et nos cedamus Amori
Omnia vincit veritas

Omnibus has litteras visuris
Omnis amans amens
Omnis ars naturae imitatio est
Omnis cellula e cellula ejusdem generis
Omnis cognitio fit a sensibus
Omnis comparatio claudicat
Omnis definitio periculosa est
Omnis fama a domesticis emanat
Omnium consensu capax imperii, nisi im-
  perasset
Onus probandi
O passi graviora, dabit deus his quoque
  finem
Ope et consilio
Operae pretium est
Operibus credite, et non verbis
Opes irritamenta malorum
Optimum est pati quod emendare non
  possis
Optimum lege (elige), suave et facile il-
  lud faciet consuetudo
Optimus legum interpres consuetudo
Opus Dei
Opus est interprete
Opus operatum est
Opus postumum
O quam cito transit gloria mundi!
Ora et labora
Ora pro nobis
Orate, fratres
Orator fit, poeta nascitur
Orbis terrarum
Ordines majores
Ordines minores
Ordo Fratrum Minorum. *See* O.F.M.
Oremus
Ore rotundo
O rus, quando ego te aspiciam?
O sancta simplicitas!
Osculum pacis
O, si sic omnia
O solitudo, sola beatitudo
Ossa atque pellis totus est
O tempora, o mores!
Otia dant vitia
Otium cum dignitate
Otium sine dignitate
Otium sine litteris mors est

Pacem in Maribus
Pace tanti nominis
Pace tanti viri
Pace tua
Pacta conventa
Pactum de non petendo

Pallida Mors aequo pulsat pede pauperum tabernas regumque turris
Palmam qui meruit ferat
Panem et circenses
Pange, lingua, glóriosi
Panis angelicus
Parcere subjectis et debellare superbos
Parens patriae
Pares autem cum paribus, vetere proverbio, facillime congregantur
Pares regni
Pari delicto
Pari passu
Paritur pax bello
Parliamentum Indoctorum
Par negotiis neque supra
Par pari refero
Pars pro toto
Pars rationabilis
Pars sanitatis velle sanari fuit
Partes infidelium
Parthis mendacior
Particeps criminis
Participes curarum
Parturiunt montes, nascetur ridiculus mus
Partus sequitur ventrem
Parva leves capiunt mentes
Parvis componere magna
Parvum parva decent
Passim
Pater familias
Pater noster
Pater patriae
Patientia fit levior ferendo
Patres et conscripti
Patria cara, carior libertas
Patriae quis exsul se quoque fugit?
Patria est ubicumque vir fortis sedem sibi elegerit
Patria potestas
Pauca sed bona
Pauca verba
Paucis verbis
Paulum morati/serius aut citius sedem properamus ad unam
Pax Britannica
Pax ecclesiae (Dei)
Pax in bello
Pax orbis terrarum
Pax Romana
Pax tecum
Pax vobiscum
Pecca fortiter
Peccavi
Pecunia non olet

Pede claudo
Pedibus timor addidit alas
Pendente lite
Penetralia mentis
Per accidens
Per ambages
Per angusta ad augusta
Per annum
Per ardua ad astra
Per ascensum ab imis
Per capita
Per consequens
Percontatorem fugito, nam garrulus idem est
Per contra
Per curiam
Percussu crebro saxa cavantur aquis
Per diem
Pereant qui ante nos nostra dixerunt
Pereunt et imputantur
Per fas et (aut) nefas
Perfecta aetas
Perfervidum ingenium Scotorum
Per gradus
Periculum in mora
Peritis in sua arte credendum
Perjuria ridet amantium Juppiter
Per mare, per terras
Per mensem
Per minas
Permissu superiorum
Permitte divis cetera
Per nefas
Per omnia saecula fama . . . vivam
Per os
Per pares
Perpetuum mobile
Per procurationem
Per procuratorem
Per saltum
Per se
Persona grata
Persona non grata
Per stirpes
Per totam curiam
Pertusum quicquid infunditur in dolium perit
Per veritatem vis
Petitio principii
Philosophia ancilla theologiae
Pia fraus
Pictoribus atque poetis/quidlibet audendi semper fuit aequa potestas
Pisces natare docere

Latin—*Continued*

Placebo
Placet
Plene administravit
Pleno jure
Plus dolet quam necesse est, qui ante dolet quam necesse est
Poeta nascitur, non fit
Pollice verso
Pomum Adami
Pondere non numero
Pons asinorum
Pontifex maximus
Populus vult decipi
Porro unum est necessarium
Posse comitatus
Possunt quia posse videntur
Post bellum auxilium
Post cineres gloria sera venit
Post hoc; ergo propter hoc
Post judicium
Post litem motam
Post meridiem *See* p.m.
Post mortem
Post obitum
Post partum
Post proelia praemia
Post tenebras lux
Potest quis per alium quod potest facere per seipsum
Potior est conditio possidentis
Praemissis praemittendis
Praemonitus, praemunitus
Pretio parata vincitur pretio fides
Pretium affectionis
Pretium laborum non vile
Prima facie
Primum mobile
Primum non nocere
Primum vivere, deinde philosophari
Primus in orbe deos fecit timor
Primus inter pares
Primus motor
Principia, non homines
Principiis obsta: sero medicina curatur
Prior tempore, prior jure
Prius insolentem serva Briseis niveo colore movit Achillem
Privatum commodum publico cedit
Pro aris et focis
Probatum est
Probitas laudatur et alget
Pro bono publico
Pro captu lectoris habent sua fata libelli

Pro confesso
Procul a Jove, procul a fulmine
Procul, O procul este profani
Procurator bibliothecarum
Pro Deo et ecclesia
Pro Deo et patria
Prodesse quam conspici
Pro domo
Pro Ecclesia et Pontifice
Pro et con (pro et contra)
Profanum vulgus
Pro forma
Pro hac vice
Proh deum atque hominum fidem
Pro jure contra legem
Promotor fidei
Promoveatur ut removeatur
Pro mundi beneficio
Pro patria per orbis concordiam
Proprio motu
Propter affectum
Propter defectum sanguinis
Propter delictum
Propter falsos testes
Propter honoris respectum
Pro (proh) pudor!
Pro rata
Pro ratione aetatis
Pro rege, lege, grege
Pro re nata
Pro salute animae
Pro scientia et religione
Pro se quisque
Prosit
Prospice
Pro tanto
Pro tempore
Proxime accessit
Proximo. *See* prox.
Prudens quaestio dimidium scientiae
Publici juris
Publicum bonum privato est praeferendum
Pugnis et calcibus
Pulchrorum autumnus pulcher
Pulvis et umbra (sumus)
Punctum saliens
Punica fides
Purpureus . . . pannus

Qua
Qua cursum ventus
Quadrupedante putrem sonitu quatit ungula campum
Quae fuerunt vitia mores sunt
Quae in aliis libertas est, in aliis licentia

vocatur
Quae nocent docent
Quae regio in terris nostri non plena laboris
Quae vide
Qualis artifex pereo!
Qualis rex, talis grex
Qualis vita, finis ita
Quam difficile est crimen non prodere vultu!
Quamdiu se bene gesserit
Quam primum
Quandoque bonus dormitat Homerus
Quantula sapientia regitur mundus!
Quantum est quod nescimus!
Quantum libet
Quantum licuit
Quantum meruit
Quantum mutatus ab illo!
Quantum placet
Quantum sufficit
Quantum valeat
Quantum valebant
Quare clausum fregit
Quasi per ignem
Quem di diligunt/adolescens moritur
Qui bene distinguit bene docet
Quicquid praecipies esto brevis
Quid de quoque viro et cui dicas, saepe videto
Qui de contemnenda gloria libros scribunt, nomen suum inscribunt
Qui dedit beneficium taceat; narret qui accepit
Qui diligit Deum diligit et fratrem suum
Quid fiet hominibus qui minima contemnunt, majora non credunt?
Quid leges sine moribus vanae proficiunt?
Quid multa?
Quid non mortalia pectora cogis, auri sacra fames?
Quid nunc?
Qui docet discit
Quid enim salvis infamia nummis?
Quid pro quo
Quidquid agas, prudenter agas, et respice finem
Quidquid multis peccatur inultum eot
Quid sit futurum cras, fuge quaerere
Quieta non movere
Qui ex patre filioque procedit
Qui facit per alium est perinde ac si facit per seipsum
Qui facit per alium facit per se
Qui finem quaeris amoris,/cedit amor re-

bus: res age, tutus eris
Qui male agit odit lucem
Qui me amat, amet et canem meum
Qui nimium probat, nihil probat
Qui non discit in pueritia, non docet in senectute
Qui non proficit deficit
Qui plantavit curabit
Qui pro domina justitia sequitur
Quis custodiet ipsos custodes?
Quis desiderio sit pudor aut modus tam cari capitis?
Quisque iam amavit, cras amet
Quis, quid, ubi, quibus auxiliis, cur, quomodo, quando?
Quis separabit?
Quis talia fando temperet a lacrimis?
Qui stat caveat ne cadat
Quis tulerit Gracchos de seditione querentes?
Qui tacet consentire videtur
Qui timide rogat, docet negare
Qui transtulit sustinet
Quoad hoc
Quo animo
Quocumque modo
Quocumque nomine
Quod ali cibus est aliis fuat acre venenum
Quod aliquis facit per aliquem, facit per se
Quod avertat Deus!
Quod bene notandum
Quod Deus avertat!
Quod Deus vult
Quod dixi dixi
Quod dubitas ne feceris
Quod erat demonstrandum. See Q.E.D.
Quod erat faciendum. See Q.E.F.
Quod gratis asseritur, gratis negatur
Quod hodie non est, cras erit: sic vita truditur
Quod licet Iovi non licet bovi
Quod non fecerunt barbari fecerunt Barberini
Quod non opus est, asse carum est
Quod scripsi, scripsi
Quod semper, quod ubique et quod ab omnibus creditum est
Quod sentimus, loquamur, quod loquimur, sentiamus; concordet sermo cum vita
Quod vide. See q.v.
Quod volumus, facile credimus
Quo fas et gloria ducunt
Quo fata vocant
Quo jure?

253

Quorum pars magna fui
Quos Deus vult perdere, prius dementat
Quos ego
Quot homines, tot sententiae
Quot linguas calles, tot homines vales
Quo vadis?

Radix omnium malorum est cupiditas
Rara avis in terra nigroque simillima
  cycno
Raram facit misturam cum sapientia forma
Rationes seminales
Ratio Studiorum
Ratio vincit
Re
Rebus sic stantibus
Recta ratio
Rectus in curia
Reddite quae sunt Caesaris, Caesari: et
  quae sunt Dei, Deo
Redime te captum quam queas minimo
Redolet lucerna
Reductio ad absurdum
Reductio ad impossibile
Refugium peccatorum
Regina scientiarum
Regnabat
Regnat populus
Re infecta
Relata refero
Religio Laici
Religio loci
Religio Medici
Rem acu tetigisti
Remanet
Rem tene et verba sequentur
Repente liberalis stultis gratus est;/verum
  peritis irritos tendit dolos
Repetatur
Repetitio est mater studiorum
Requiem aeternam dona eis, domine, et
  lux perpetua luceat eis
Requiescat in pace
Rerum naturam sola gubernas
Rerum novarum libido
Res adjudicata
Res alienae
Res angusta domi
Res derelicta
Res domesticas noli tangere
Res gestae
Res integra
Res ipsa loquitur
Resistendum senectuti
Res judicata

Res non parta labore
Res nullius
Res perit domino
Respice, adspice, prospice
Respice finem
Respicere exemplar vitae morumque
  jubebo/Doctum imitatorem, et vivas
  hinc ducere voces
Respondeat superior
Responsa prudentium
Retro me, Satana!
Retro, Satana!
Rex bibendi
Rex regnat, sed non gubernat
Ridentem dicere verum/quid vetat?
Ride si sapis, o puella, ride
Rigor mortis
Risu inepto res ineptior nulla est
Rixatur de lana saepe caprina
Roma locuta, causa finita
Romanus sedendo vincit
Rota sum: semper, quoquo me verto,
  stat Virtus
Rudis indigestaque moles
Rus in urbe
Rusticus exspectat dum defluat amnis

Saepe creat molles aspera spina rosas
Saepius locutum, numquam me
  tacuisse poenitet
Sal Atticum
Salus populi suprema lex esto
Salva sit reverentia
Salve
Salvo jure
Salvo pudore
Sancta simplicitas
Sanctum sanctorum
Sapere aude
Sartor Resartus
Sat celeriter fieri quidquid fiat satis bene
Sat cito si sat bene
Satis eloquentiae, sapientiae parum
Satis et super
Sat pulchra si sat bona
Saturnia tellus
Scala Sancta
Scelere velandum est scelus
Schola cantorum
Scientia est veritatis imago
Scienti et volenti non fit injuria
Scilicet. *See* sc.
Scire facias
Scire quid valeant humeri, quid ferre re-
  cusent

Scribendi recte sapere est et principium et fons
Scribimus indocti doctique poemata passim
Scripta manent, verba volant
Scriptorum chorus omnis amat nemus et fugit urbem
Sculpsit
Scuto bonae voluntatis tuae coronasti nos
Secundum artem
Secundum ipsius naturam
Secundum legem
Secundum naturam
Secundum ordinem
Secundum quid
Secundum regulam
Secundum usum
Securus judicat orbis terrarum
Se defendendo
Seditio civium hostium est occasio
Sed transeat
Semel et simul
Semel insanivimus omnes
Semel malus, semper praesumitur esse malus
Semen est sanguis Christianorum
Semper avarus eget
Semper eadem
Semper fidelis
Semper idem
Semper inops quicumque cupit
Semper nocuit differre paratis
Semper paratus
Semper timidum scelus
Semper vivit in armis
Senatus consultum
Senectus insanabilis morbus est
Senectus ipsa morbus est
Senex bis puer
Seniores priores
Sensim sine sensu aetas senescit
Sensu bono
Sensu lato
Sensu malo
Sensu proprio
Sensu stricto
Sera nimis vita est crastina: vive hodie
Serit arbores quae alteri saeclo prosint
Sermo humi obrepens
Sero molunt deorum molae
Sero sed serio
Sero venientibus ossa
Serta . . . pinus, malus, oliva, apium
Serus in caelum redeas
Servatur ubique jus Romanum non ratione

imperii, sed rationis imperio
Servitium forinsecum
Servus servorum Dei
Sesquipedalia verba
Sestertium reliquit trecenties nec unquam philosophum audivit
Sic
Sic eunt fata hominum
Sic itur ad astra
Sic passim
Sic semper tyrannis
Sic transit gloria mundi
Sicut ante
Sic utere tuo ut alienum non laedas
Sicut patribus, sit Deus nobis
Sic vita
Sic volo, sic jubeo, stat pro ratione voluntas
Sic vos non vobis
Si Deus nobiscum, quis contra nos?
Si diis placet
Si discedas, laqueo tenet ambitiosi/consuetudo mali
Sile et philosophus esto
Silent leges inter arma
Simile gaudet simili
Similia similibus curantur
Similis simili gaudet
Si monumentum requiris, circumspice
Simplex munditiis
Simul sorbere ac flare non possum
Sine Cerere et Libero friget Venus
Sine cura
Sine die
Sine dubio
Sine ictu
Sine invidia
Sine ira et studio
Sine legitima prole
Sine macula et ruga
Sine mascula prole
Sine mora
Sine pennis volare haud facile est
Sine praejudicio
Sine prole superstite
Sine qua non
Si non caste, saltem caute
Si non credideritis, non permanebitis
Si non valeat
Sint ut sunt aut non sint
Si parva licet componere magnis
Si quaeris peninsulam amoenam circumspice
Si sic omnes
Siste, viator

Latin—*Continued*

Sit tibi terra levis. *See* S.T.T.L.
Si vis ad summum progredi, ab infimo
　ordire
Si vis me flere, dolendum est/primum
　ipsi tibi
Si vis pacem, para bellum
Societas leonina
Sola nobilitas virtus
Solem e mundo tollere videntur ei, qui
　amicitiam e vita tollunt
Soli cantare periti Arcades
Solitudinem faciunt, pacem vocant
Solus contra mundum
Solvitur ambulando
Sortes bibliorum
Sortes sanctorum
Sortes Vergilianae
Speciali gratia
Spectemur agendo
Sperat infestis, metuit secundis alteram
　sortem, bene praeparatum pectus
Spes anchora vitae
Spes sibi quisque
Spes tutissima caelis
Spicula et faces amoris
Spirat adhuc amor
Spiritus frumenti
Splendide mendax
Splendor sine occasu
Spolia opima
Sponte sua
Spretae injuria formae
Stabat Mater
Stare decisis et non quieta movere
Stare super vias antiquas
Stat magni nominis umbra
Status belli
Status quaestionis
Status quo
Status quo ante bellum
Stemmata quid faciunt?
Stet
Stet processus
Strictum jus
Studium immane loquendi
Stultum facit fortuna quem vult perdere
Stupor mundi
Sua cuique voluptas
Suadente diabolo
Suave, mari magno turbantibus aequora
　ventis,/e terra magnum alterius spectare
　laborem
Suaviter in modo, fortiter in re

Sub conditione, *var.* condicione
Sub dio
Sub judice
Sublata causa, tollitur effectus
Sub modo
Sub plumbo
Sub poena
Sub rosa
Sub sigillo
Sub silentio
Sub specie
Sub specie aeternitatis
Sub verbo
Sub vi
Sub voce
Sufflaminandus erat
Sui compos
Sui generis
Sui juris
Summa cum laude
Summum bonum
Summum jus, summa injuria
Sumptibus publicis
Sum quod eris, fui quod sis
Sunt lacrimae rerum et mentem mortalia
　tangunt
Suo loco
Suo Marte
Suo nomine
Suo periculo
Suo sibi gladio hunc jugulo
Super visum corporis
Suppressio veri, suggestio falsi
Surgit amari aliquid quod in ipsis floribus
　angat
Sursum corda
Suspendatur per collum
Suspendens omnia naso
Suspiria de Profundis
Sutor ne supra crepidam
Suum cuique
Suus cuique mos

Tabula rasa
Tace
Tacent, satis laudant
Tacitae magis et occultae inimicitiae
　timendae sunt quam indictae atque
　apertae
Taedium vitae
Tangere ulcus
Tantaene animis caelestibus irae?
Tanto nomini nullum par elogium
Tantum ergo
Tantum pellis et ossa fuit

Tantum possumus quantum scimus
Tantum religio potuit suadere malorum!
Te Deum (laudamus)
Te judice
Telum imbelle sine ictu
Tempora mutantur, nos et mutamur in
    illis
Tempore felici multi numerantur amici
Tempori parendum
Tempus edax rerum
Tempus fugit
Tempus omnia revelat
Teres atque rotundus
Terminus ad quem
Terminus ante quem
Terminus a quo
Terrae filius
Terra firma
Terra incognita
Terra marique
Tertium quid
Teterrima causa belli
Textus receptus
Thesaurus Americae Septentrionis
    Sigillum
Timeo Danaos et dona ferentes
Timeo hominem (virum) unius libri
Toga candida
Toga praetexta
Toga virilis
Tolle, lege; tolle, lege
Totidem verbis
Toties quoties
Totis viribus
Toto caelo
Totus mundus agit histrionem
Totus teres atque rotundus
Trahimur omnes studio laudis, et optimus
    quisque maxime gloria ducitur
Trahit sua quemque voluptas
Transeat in exemplum
Translatio imperii
Treuga Dei
Treva Dei
Tria juncta in uno
Tros Tyriusque mihi nullo discrimine
    agetur
Truditur dies die
Tua res agitur, paries cum proximus ardet
Tu, enim, Caesar, civitatem dare potes
    hominibus, verbis non potes
Tu ne cede malis sed contra audentior ito
Tu quoque

Uberrima fides

Ubi bene, ibi patria
Ubi est thesaurus tuus, ibi est et cor tuum
Ubi jus, ibi officium
Ubi jus, ibi remedium
Ubi jus incertum, ibi jus nullum
Ubi libertas, ibi patria
Ubi mel, ibi apes
Ubi nunc fidelis ossa Fabricii manent
Ubi panis, ibi patria
Ubi solitudinem faciunt, pacem appellant
Ubi sunt qui ante nos fuerunt
Ubi tu Gaius, ego Gaia
Ultima ratio mundi
Ultima ratio regum
Ultima Thule
Ultimum vale
Ultimus regum
Ultimus Romanorum
Ultra vires
Una dolo divum si femina victa duorum
    est
Una salus victis nullam sperare salutem
Unguibus et rostro
Universitas, societas magistrorum disci-
    pulorumque
Unum post aliud
Unus homo nobis cunctando restituit rem
Urbem venalem et mature perituram, si
    emptorem invenerit
Urbi et orbi
Urbs in horto
Ursa Major
Usque ad nauseam
Usus est optimus magister
Usus loquendi
Ut ameris, amabilis esto
Utcumque placuerit Deo
Ut fragilis glacies, interit ira mora
Ut fulvum spectatur in ignibus aurum tem-
    pore sic in duro est inspicienda fides
Utinam noster esset!
Ut infra
Uti possidetis
Ut lapsu graviore ruant
Ut omnes unum sint
Ut pignus amicitiae
Ut quocumque paratus
Ut sementem feceris, ita metes
Ut supra
Ut tamquam scopulum sic fugias insolens
    verbum
Vade in pace
Vade mecum
Vae victis!
Vale

Latin—*Continued*

Valeat ancora virtus
Valeat quantum valere potest
Valete
Vanitas vanitatum, et omnia vanitas
Vare, legiones redde
Varia lectio
Varietas delectat cor hominis
Variorum notae
Varium et mutabile semper femina
Velis et remis
Veluti in speculum
Venalis populus, venalis curia patrum
Vendidit hic auro patriam
Venenum in auro bibitur
Veniam petimusque damusque vicissim
Venia necessitati datur
Veni, Creator, Spiritus
Venienti occurrite morbo
Venire
Venire facias juratores
Veni, vidi, vici
Venter non habet aures
Ventis secundis
Vera incessu patuit dea
Verba adulatoria
Verba docent, exempla trahunt
Verba volant, scripta manent
Verbum sat sapienti
Vere scire est per causas scire
Veritas numquam perit
Veritas odium parit
Veritas temporis filia
Veritas temporis filia dicitur
Veritas vos liberabit
Veritatis simplex oratio est
Ver perpetuum
Verso pollice
Vertumnis, quotquot sunt, natus iniquis
Vestis talaris
Vestis virum facit
Vetulam suam praetulit immortalitati
Vexata quaestio
Vexilla Regis prodeunt
Via
Via lactea
Via media
Via trita, via tutissima
Vice versa
Vicisti, Galilaee
Victrix causa deis placuit sed victa Catoni
Videant consules ne quid res publica detrimenti capiat
Video et taceo

Video meliora proboque, deteriora sequor
Vide supra
Vi et armis
Vilius argentum est auro, virtutibus aurum
Vincet amor patriae
Vincit omnia veritas
Vincit qui patitur
Vincit qui se vincit
Vino vendibili hedera non opus est
Vinum daemonum
Violenta non durant
Vir bonus dicendi peritus
Vires adquirit eundo
Vir, fortis et strenuus
Virginibus puerisque
Virgo intacta
Viribus totis
Vir sapit qui pauca loquitur
Virtus ariete fortior
Virtus dormitiva
Virtus in actione consistit
Virtus in arduis
Virtus sola nobilitat
Virtute et armis
Virtute et fide
Virtute et labore
Virtute non astutia
Virtute officii
Virtutis fortuna comes
Vis a fronte
Vis a tergo
Vis comica
Vis conservatrix naturae
Vis consili expers mole ruit sua
Vis inertiae
Vis major
Vis medicatrix naturae
Vis nova
Vis unita fortior
Vis vitae
Vis vitalis
Vita brevis, longa ars
Vitam impendere vero
Vita sine litteris mors est
Vitiis nemo sine nascitur
Vivamus, mea Lesbia, atque amemus
Vivat regina
Vivat rex
Viva voce
Vivebat
Vivere sat vincere
Vivida vis animi
Vivit post funera virtus
Vix ea nostra voco
Vixere fortes ante Agamemnona

Volenti non fit injuria
Volo, non valeo
Vomunt ut edant, edunt ut vomant
Vos exemplaria Graeca nocturna versate
    manu, versate diurna
Vox audita perit, littera scripta manet
Vox clamantis in deserto
Vox et praeterea nihil
Vox faucibus haesit
Vox humana
Vox populi, vox Dei
Vulgata editio
Vulgus ad deteriora promptum
Vulgus fingendi avidum
Vulgus ignobile
Vulgus veritatis pessimus interpres
Vultus est index animi
Vultus nimium lubricus aspici

Anglo-Latin

Felo de se

Quo warranto

Late Latin

Banco regis

Curia advisari vult

In commendam

Scandalum magnatum

New Latin

Pithecanthropus erectus

Sinanthropus pekinensis

Portuguese

A caridade começa por casa
Amor com amor se paga
Amor e carinho tudo vendem
Ao medico, ao advogado, e ao abade fa-
    lar verdade
Até amanhã
Até logo
Auto-da-fé
Azeite, vinho e amigo, o mais antigo

Boa noite
Boa tarde
Boca de mel, coração de fel
Bom dia
Bons dias

Cada cabelo faz sua sombra na terra

Com fogo não se brinca

De bons propósitos está o inferno cheio

Feliz Natal

Guarde-vos Deus de amigo reconciliado

Ira de irmãos, ira de diabos

Lá vão os pés onde quer o coração

Não ha mal que sempre dure, nem bem
    que nunca se acabe

Nem um dedo faz mão, nem uma ando-
    rinha verão

Onde não entra o sol entra o medico

Russian

Akademiya Nauk

Blagodaryu vas
Bozhe moy

Cheka

Dobriy den
Dobriy vecher
Dobroye utro
Do svidanya!

Kak poshivayetye?
Kak vy pozhyvaete?
Komsomol (Kommunisticheskii, soiuz,
    molodezh)
Krasnaya zvezda

Narkomvnudel. See NKVD
Ne stoit blagodarnost'

Ochen khorosho
Ochen nemnogo

Pozhaluysta
Proshu vashego izvynenya

Spokoynoy nochi

Za vashe zdorove
Zdravstvuityeh

Spanish

A buen entendedor, pocas palabras
A caballo
A cara o cruz
A casar y a ir a guerra no se aconseja
A cavallo regalado no hay que mirarle el
    diente
A cuenta
A falta de hombres buenos, le hacen a
    mi padre alcalde

Spanish—*Continued*

A idos de mi casa, y qué queréis con mi
    mujer, no hay responder
A la rústica
Al contado
Allá van leyes do quieren reyes
Amar y saber no puede ser
Amigo de todos y de ninguno, todo es uno
A mucho hablar, mucho errar
A muertos y a idos, pocos amigos
A paso de buey
A plazo
A precio fijo
Aquí se habla español
A Roma por todo
Arroz con pollo
A sus órdenes
A toda prisa
Aunque la mona se vista de seda, mona
    se queda
Auto de fe
Auto sacramental
A vuelta de correo
A vuestra salud
¡Ay, bendito!

Barba a barba
Bien predica quien bien vive
Buena fama hurto encubre
Buena ganga
Buenas noches
Buenas tardes
¡Buena suerte!
Buenos días
Buey viejo surco derecho
Buon principio, la mitad es hecha

Caballero andante
Cada cabello hace su sombra en el suelo
Cada maestro tiene su librito
Cada uno es hijo de sus obras
Cada uno sabe donde le aprieta el zapato
Camino de Santiago
Camino real
Capa y espada
Con furia
Consejo a los visitantes extranjeros
Contra fortuna no vale arte ninguna
Corrida de toros
Cuando a Roma fueres, haz como vieres
Cuéntaselo a tu abuela
¡Cuidado!
Cuidado con el tren

De gran subida, gran caída

De la mano a la boca se pierde la sopa
Del dicho al hecho hay gran trecho
Dichosa la madre que te parió
Dicho y hecho
Dime con quien andas, decirte he quien
    eres
Dios bendiga nuestro (este) hogar
Dios le da confites a quien no puede
    roerlos
Donde una puerta se cierra, otra se abre
Dos linajes solo hay en el mundo . . . que
    son el tener y el no tener

El ingenioso hidalgo
El no y el sí son breves de decir, y piden
    mucho pensar
El sabio muda consejo; el necio, no
En boca cerrada no entran moscas
En cueros
En Martes ni te cases, ni te embarques,
    ni de tu casa te apartes
En rústica
En tierra de ciegos el tuerto es rey
Entre padres y hermanos no metas tus
    manos
Es de vidrio la mujer
Ese te quiere bien que te hace llorar

Felices Pascuas
Flotará sola
Franco de Porto
¡Fuera los Yankis!

Gata con guantes no caza ratones
Gente baja
Gente fina
Gracias a Dios
Guerra al cuchillo

Hasta la muerte todo es vida
Hasta la vista
Hasta luego
Hasta mañana
He dicho
Hombre casado, burro domado
Huyendo del toro, cayó en el arroyo

La caridad bien entendida empieza por sí
    mismo
La codicia rompe el saco
La Costa Brava
La Ley de fuga
La mejor salsa del mundo es el hambre
La novela picaresca
La novela policiaca
La Pasionaria
La plaza de toros

La senda de la virtud es muy estrecha, y
   el camino del vicio, ancho y espacioso
La vida es sueño
Locos y niños dicen la verdad
Lo peor es siempre cierto
Lo que hoy se pierde se gana mañana
Lo que no se puede remediar se ha de
   aguantar
Lo que se aprende en la cuna siempre
   dura

Madre divina!
Mañana es otro día
Mano a mano
Más vale maña que fuerza
Más vale muerto que vivo
Más vale pájaro en mano que buitre
   volando
Más vale tarde que nunca
Mejor morir a pie que vivir en rodillas
Mi casa es su casa
Mientras se duerme todos son iguales
Misa del Gallo
Monte de piedad
Mucho más se ha de estimar un diente
   que un diamante
Muchos van por lana y vuelven
   trasquilados

Ni firmes carta que no leas, ni bebas agua
   que no veas
Ninguno nace maestro
No adventures mucho tu riqueza/Por con-
   sejo de ome que ha pobreza
No es oro todo lo que reluce
No hay cerradura si es de oro la garzúa
No pasarán
No podemos haber aquello que queremos,
   queramos aquello que podremos
No se ganó Zamora en una hora

Obra de común, obra de ningún
Olla podrida
Oro y plata

Pagan a veces los justos por los pecadores
Para mí solo nació Don Quixote, y yo
   para él
Para todo hay remedio si no es para la
   muerte
Paso doble
Paso fino
Paucas pallabris
Paz en la tierra

Plaza de toros
Poco a poco
Poesía gauchesca
Por favor
Por mayor
Preguntando se llega a Roma
¡Próspero año nuevo!
Punto de honor

¡Que aproveche!
¡Qué lástima!
Que será será
¿Que tal?
Quien canta, sus males espanta
Quien madruga, Dios le ayuda
Quien mucho abarca (abraza) poco aprieta
Quien no ha visto a Sevilla, no ha visto
   maravilla
Quien padre tiene alcalde, seguro va a
   juicio
¿Quién sabe?
Quien tiene dineros, tiene compañeros
Quien todo lo niega, todo lo confiesa

Recoge tu heno mientras que el so luciere
Rey nuevo, ley nueva

Saludos a todos
Sanan cuchilladas, mas no malas palabras
Santo Niño
Seis meses de invierno y seis meses de
   infierno
Si Dios quiere
Siglo de oro
Sobre gustos no hay disputas
Sociedad anónima
Sociedad en comandita

Tal cual

Una golondrina no hace verano

Vaya con Dios
Vida sin amigos muerte sin testigos

Mixed Languages

Édition ne varietur
Encheiresin naturae

In memmoriam ad gloriam sed asthoriam
   non nomoreum

Latino sine flexione

Omnium gatherum

Quiz seperrabit